Terror in the Heart of Freedom

Terror
in the Heart of
Freedom

CITIZENSHIP, SEXUAL VIOLENCE,
AND THE MEANING OF RACE IN
THE POSTEMANCIPATION SOUTH

Hannah Rosen

The University of North Carolina Press

Chapel Hill

Designed by Heidi Perov
Set in Arno Pro
by Keystone Typesetting, Inc.
Manufactured in the United States of America

The paper in this book meets the guidelines for permanence and
durability of the Committee on Production Guidelines for
Book Longevity of the Council on Library Resources.

The University of North Carolina Press has been a member
of the Green Press Initiative since 2003.

Library of Congress Cataloging-in-Publication Data
Rosen, Hannah.
   Terror in the heart of freedom : citizenship, sexual violence, and the
meaning of race in the postemancipation South / by Hannah Rosen.
      p. cm. — (Gender and American culture)
   Includes bibliographical references and index.
ISBN 978-0-8078-3202-8 (cloth: alk. paper)
ISBN 978-0-8078-5882-0 (pbk.: alk. paper)
   1. African Americans—Civil rights—Southern States—History—
19th century. 2. African American women—Crimes against—
Southern States—History—19th century. 3. Rape—Southern States—
History—19th century. 4. Rape—Political aspects—Southern States—
History—19th century. 5. Slaves—Emancipation—Social aspects—
Southern States. 6. Citizenship—Social aspects—Southern States—
History—19th century. 7. Sex role—Southern States—History—19th
century. 8. Racism—Southern States—History—19th century.
9. Southern States—Race relations—History—19th century.
10. Southern States—History—1865–1877. I. Title.
E185.2.R75   2008
323.1196′073075—dc22
2008029870

cloth   13 12 11 10 09   5 4 3 2 1
paper   13 12 11 10 09   5 4 3 2 1

for Richard

CONTENTS

ILLUSTRATIONS

Terror in the Heart of Freedom

Introduction

"Have you been a slave?" This question was put to many of the African Americans who, in the early summer of 1866, testified before a congressional committee holding hearings in the Gayoso House hotel in downtown Memphis, Tennessee. These witnesses had come to testify about a murderous riot that occurred in Memphis a few weeks before and a little over a year after the end of the Civil War. Many offered a response similar to that of Mary Wardlaw, a thirty-seven-year-old woman who, along with her husband, Matthew, had been a victim of the riot. "I have been but am free now," Wardlaw replied. She thereby acknowledged her past enslavement while in the same breath affirming her recent acquisition of freedom, despite the fact that her current status could not have been otherwise following the ratification of the Thirteenth Amendment abolishing slavery throughout the United States five months before.[1] Her husband, Matthew Wardlaw, responded in similar fashion. "Yes sir," he said, "but I have been free for four years." A neighbor to the Wardlaws, Ann Patrick Ayr, told the committee, "I was a slave to Mr. Patrick for seventeen years. I am now free." And James E. Donahue answered, "Yes, sir; but [I] became free 31st July, 1863. It was said the proclamation of Mr. Lincoln freed us." While some credited the late president Abraham Lincoln, others highlighted their own role in gaining their freedom. "I belonged to J. B. Griffin & Co., of this city, until two or three years ago," Albert Harris testified, "when I got tired of living that way, and quit." And Cynthia Townsend explained that she had been able to acquire funds with which to purchase her freedom or, as she put it, to purchase her "self," ironically only moments before the wartime Union Army occupation of Memphis in June 1862 began the process of general abolition in the city: "Yes; but I worked and bought myself. I finished paying for myself a few days before they took this place."[2]

These unsolicited affirmations of a present status of freedom may have been the witnesses' way of critiquing their interrogator's gratuitous reminder of their pasts. This reminder singled them out among the pool of witnesses, the majority of whom were white, as former slaves. Through their replies, the witnesses were, it seems, refusing such a distinction and insisting that their prior condition as slaves had been definitively superseded by their current status as citizens.

In the years immediately following the end of the Civil War in the United States, those who had been enslaved in the U.S. South were taking part in the great emancipatory project of the nineteenth century, the abolition of slavery and the creation of liberal republics based on universal manhood suffrage and promising universal civil rights. Systems of slavery, which had grown to unprecedented proportions across much of the Americas in the eighteenth century, were steadily dismantled in the nineteenth, abolished in one part of the Americas after another between 1793, in Saint Domingue, and 1888, in Brazil.[3] These transformations took place in, and helped to define and radicalize, an era of ascendant liberalism, when following on the heels of a spate of revolutions throwing off colonial powers in the Americas and establishing republics in the Americas and Europe, discourses of universal liberty and equality were widely broadcast and mobilized. Thus those who gained their freedom in this period believed that to be free was not only not to be enslaved but also to be a citizen, that is, to be an equal member of a political community represented by a state that bestowed the same rights and obligations upon all its (adult male) members.[4] The African Americans who testified about the violence they suffered during the Memphis Riot were among many escaping slavery in this era who anticipated, and sought to realize, a freedom buttressed by state recognition as universal citizens.[5]

The man who posed the question "Have you been a slave?" was himself a participant in the liberal discourses of the era. Congressman Elihu Washburne, a Republican from Illinois, the chair of the congressional committee investigating the riot and a close associate of the recently assassinated president Abraham Lincoln, had throughout his political career opposed slavery and endorsed measures called for in the name of advancing the civil and political rights of all men.[6] What Washburne intended by his question is unclear. He may simply have meant to distinguish those African Americans who had been free people before the Civil War from those who were enslaved. More likely, though, Washburne asked the question seeking to highlight for the record that it was former slaves who had been brutalized by white southerners in this riot, and thus to demonstrate that federal force continued to be necessary to assure that they receive even a modicum of the liberties appropriate to citizens. Indeed, Washburne was among Washington's strongest advocates of federal legislation intervening into civil and political matters—matters that until this time had been the purview of state governments—in order to establish and protect the rights of freedpeople (as former slaves were then called).[7] Whatever his conscious intention, by suggesting a distinction among citizens—those who had once been slaves and those who had always been free—Washburne's query seems to have communicated to those asked a continuing assertion of difference and a dangerous denial of universal status. These witnesses resisted the implication of second-class citizenship, and the idea that previous condition of servitude should have any relevance to one's rights or to one's testimony, by hinting that his question was irrelevant; they were, were they not, now free?

Affirming their new status as free and equal citizens may also have seemed important given that they were present at this hearing in order to claim one of that status's prerogatives, namely, the right to live free of violence. African American witnesses at this hearing spoke of being free in the context of testifying to terror. Specifically, they spoke of how the violence of the Memphis Riot and its consequences had made being free in this time and place a terrifying experience. Witnesses recalled their alarm at the enormous crowds of white men involved in a riot targeted at those newly emerged from slavery: "I never saw so many together," Cynthia Townsend explained; "they gathered from every direction."[8] They described hearing these men curse them and their neighbors and watching the men set fire to their houses, churches, and schools; shoot pistols at occupants as they fled the burning structures; and ignore others' pleas that the rioters cease shooting to allow their children to escape the flames. Witnesses also told of seeing neighbors as well as strangers shot at point-blank range in the streets with no seeming provocation and then watching them "kicking and struggling in death."[9] Along with describing such horrific scenes, witnesses recounted losing all of their possessions in the houses destroyed by fire. And they described how men broke into their homes and held guns to their heads while making demands, how the intruders injured family members, and how they stole their cash. Witnesses also stressed how they had been cut off from family, as those working in the countryside dared not return until, as Townsend said, "all this fuss was over."[10] Finally, witnesses reported that several women had been raped by rioters. Townsend told the committee that a group of rioters had "had connexion" with a freedwoman living near her, and to assure that the congressmen understood that what she was describing was an act of force, she added, "They drew their pistols before her and made her submit."[11] Townsend found it difficult to speak about such things, telling the committee, "I do not believe that I could express what I saw." She nonetheless felt it was her duty and so found the means to do so, adding, "I am telling you the truth and I know I have to give an account of it."[12] Townsend and others seem to have believed that finding the words to narrate and record the violence of the riot and its resulting loss, dislocation, and fear, though difficult and painful to do, was a crucial step in establishing the kind of freedom they sought and in protecting the status as citizens they had just claimed.

In fact, the testimony of victims of the Memphis Riot did have powerful effect. Their words were used in Congress and the northern press to build support for federal measures enfranchising African American men in the South. And yet, the kind of violence freedpeople hoped to end through their testimony not only continued but expanded in subsequent months and years. Indeed, in the United States, the project of emancipation and the creation of a liberal republic based on the ideal of equal citizenship was shot through with racist terror. This terror ultimately brought forth the potential for exclusion inherent within a political rhetoric construing those escaping slavery as "former slaves" and thus allowing African Americans to be represented as less than, or as a lesser form of, citizens.[13] Thus the men and women gathered in the Gayoso House in 1866 testified about the very sort of violence that would soon exclude them from full membership in the post–Civil War nation. And Washburne's illiberal and impertinent question, asked at the beginning of a brief era in the United States of an imperfect but nonetheless far more inclusive political community and nation, presaged a time a few decades later when those who had been slaves or whose ancestors had been slaves, and who were associated with a racial group with a past of slavery, would have their rights compromised, their testimony distrusted, and their powers and privileges as citizens denied.

TERROR IN THE HEART OF FREEDOM tells a story of the simultaneity of enormous hope and disillusioning terror, of extraordinary possibility and overwhelming constraint, of radical openings and violent closures. It tells the story of the hope and anticipation of a meaningful freedom that brought Mary Wardlaw, Cynthia Townsend, and others to the Gayoso House to testify, and that brought former slaves from throughout the South to federal officials to speak out against violence, and of the terror of which they spoke. Both hope and terror characterized the lives of southern African Americans in the years following emancipation and the Civil War, the period of U.S. history known as Reconstruction (roughly 1861 to 1877),[14] when former slaves looked ahead to the opportunities and experiences made possible by their new status as free persons while many white southerners resisted those possibilities by targeting freedpeople with violence.[15]

At stake both in the violence of the period and in testimony about it after the fact were meanings for race, meanings that are crucial to understanding how a liberal republic that had abolished slavery and declared legal racial equality nonetheless ultimately excluded African Americans from full citizenship for nearly a century afterward.[16] Those living in the immediate post-emancipation years could not at first be certain that race would continue to carry the significance it had in antebellum society. The end of slavery, the massive social and economic disruption caused by war, the exacerbated class tensions among southern whites that resulted from that disruption, and the profound political changes ushered in by the legal delineation of national citizenship guaranteeing for the first time membership to all those born in the United States and suffrage to all men meant that race had come unfixed. No longer could racial meanings be anchored in the exclusivity of both slavery (black) and full citizenship (white, as well as male). Nor was it inevitable that distinctions based on European versus (any) African descent would continue to structure the postemancipation polity—its public life, family patterns, personal identity, and constructs of community and nation.[17]

This book illuminates contests over the unstable significance of race at this critical juncture in U.S. history by exploring in particular how such battles were routinely fought on the terrain of gender.[18] Both the hopeful visions of former slaves and the terror that ultimately dashed their hopes were frequently expressed through discourses and practices of manhood and womanhood. We will see this in incidents of sexual violence that African American women suffered at the hands of white men during episodes of political violence—rapes similar to the one described by Cynthia Townsend in her testimony about the Memphis Riot.[19] And we will see this in a flood of racist rhetoric circulated in these same years that cast African American women and men as lacking what were considered to be honorable gender norms, sexualities, and family relationships. I argue that this gendered rhetoric of race was both reflected in and reproduced through the acts of cross-racial sexual violence that occurred during this period, and I show how sexual violence and racist rhetoric worked together to produce a climate of terror in which black men and women were forced to maneuver as they sought to claim their rights as citizens.

That maneuvering began immediately following emancipation, when former slaves in the southern states, both men and women, dramatically entered public life, public spaces, and official politics. The chapters that follow trace this movement into and through public and political spaces in the post–Civil War South and explore how, through this mobility, African Americans claimed membership in a national political community that had previously excluded them from the rights and identities accorded to "citizens."[20] In so doing, they challenged the erstwhile meanings and significance of whiteness and blackness as social and political identities in southern society.[21]

Many white southerners fervently resisted the entry into formerly white domains by African Americans, and one of the first ways they did so was by describing the new black presence as socially, sexually, and politically dangerous. Such descriptions appeared in the news stories and editorials of the conservative southern press,[22] in the speeches of white southern politicians demanding constitutional prohibitions on interracial marriage, and in both vigilante and police discourses alleging widespread criminal conduct among former slaves. In these discursive spaces, black women were accused of lewd public behavior, openly promiscuous sexual relations, a supposedly incurable tendency toward prostitution, and, implicitly, a refusal to be subordinated to patriarchal control within families. Complementing these representations were reports about the vagrancy and criminality that supposedly characterized African American men and their alleged neglect of the obligation to support their wives and children through honest labor. Black men, in some moments depicted as unwilling to meet their domestic obligations, in others were portrayed as seeking romantic and domestic relations that violated customs segregating social life, that is, of seeking "social equality," a pejorative term that at the time denoted racial integration in personal relationships as well as public space.[23] This imagery suggested that public power in the hands of black men threatened not only white political dominance but also the patriarchal, and thus private, power of white men.[24]

Such imagery did not originate in the period following emancipation. It reflected long-standing racist discourses as well as an antebellum political culture that had conflated white men's right to exclusive political authority with their roles as putatively honorable patriarchs in contrast to others.[25] In previous decades, and even centuries, the articulation of dishonorable and dependent genders had rationalized the exclusion of people of color, as well as all women and many white men, from public power.[26] In a postemancipation context, and applied to freedwomen and freedmen, these recurrent representations took on new and particular meaning. The liberal ideology embraced by most abolitionists and those guiding emancipation policy in the United States privileged self-control and voluntary submission to contractual obligations of both labor and marriage as the essence of modern freedom and the basis of a virtuous citizenry necessary to sustain a virtuous republic.[27] Portrayals of freedpeople as incapable of such voluntary submission to the obligations as well as norms, customs, and legal codes of a liberal society—that is, as incapable of sustaining respectable marriages and of fulfilling their responsibility to be law-abiding, self-supporting wage laborers—powerfully connoted people incapable of, and unworthy of, freedom.[28] This discourse contained a critique not only of freedpeople but also of northern lawmakers and the federal government—on their own terms—for the illegitimate empowerment in public life of men and women devoid of private and thus public "virtue."[29]

The ideological conflation of private and public power during the antebellum era had helped to unite white southerners across class lines, offering all white men regardless of wealth membership in a select group exclusively entitled to political voice.[30] Their supposed unique worthiness for public influence rested in their status as "freemen," that is, men imagined to be independent because they supposedly answered to no master and instead were the masters of the numerous dependents among whom they lived and worked—their wives, their children, and for some, their slaves.[31] After emancipation, representations of African Americans as the opposite of independent and masterful men were invoked by white political leaders and other influential figures, such as the editors of the region's conservative newspapers, to call war-weary and disaffected white men back into alliance with the region's elites under a banner of "white supremacy" and in opposition to black political power.

The gendered imagery that recurred throughout this conservative political discourse also functioned as what historian Mary Renda might call a "cultural vehicle" for the perpetuation of violence, facilitating and excusing individual acts of white-on-black rape.[32] Indeed, such imagery can be found in the utterances and gestures of assailants leading up to sexual attacks. The pages that follow explore rapes that occurred in the midst of political violence, namely, during the Memphis Riot in 1866 and night rides of vigilante gangs known as "regulators" and the Ku Klux Klan and other Klan-like groups between 1866 and 1871.[33] Victims and other witnesses recounted these attacks to federal officials, detailing what were often wrenching and prolonged scenes surrounding sexual assault. Through this testimony, we will see how the language assailants used and the roles they imposed during these attacks scripted events that represented as normative and unexceptional white men soliciting black women in their own homes for sex, that repudiated the possibility of black women in chaste and respectable marriage relations, that portrayed all black women as sexually available and subservient to all white men, that erased or denied the coercion and violence necessary on the part of assailants to enact sex in various forms, and that portrayed black men as uninterested in preventing their wives' and daughters' denigration. White-on-black rape in this context simultaneously embodied and dramatized a larger gendered discourse of race. White men forcing black women to engage in sex and creating circumstances under which black fathers and husbands could not prevent the violence against their family members enacted white fantasies of racial difference and inferiority. Black men and women were forced to perform gendered roles revealing a putative unsuitability for citizenship. This book thus highlights the discursive dimensions of violence—the power of violence to articulate (racist) meanings—as well as the material, even violent, effects of discourse—that is, how discursive technologies enable acts of (racist) violence.[34] Rape emerges not as the product of unrestrained sexual impulses or simply as the conscious pursuit of power but, rather, as a performance of social and political inequality whose very possibility is conditioned upon a broader discourse investing gendered identities and sexual practices with other, and in this case racist, meanings, and whose effect is not only physical pain and emotional suffering but also a rearticulation and reproduction of the very gendered discourse of race that made it possible.[35]

Throughout this book, I investigate not only the climate of terror that emerged from physical violence and racist rhetoric but also African Americans' resistance to it. That resistance is evident in the lengths to which freedwomen and freedmen went to document to federal officials the sexual violence they and their communities suffered. Their efforts created a unique historical record of black women speaking about their experiences of rape in the records of congressional investigating committees and the Bureau of

Refugees, Freedmen, and Abandoned Lands.[36] Testimony found in these sources offers a window both onto the details of actual white-on-black rape attacks and onto how former slaves claimed citizenship by demanding protection from violence and affirming their rights and identities as individuals with the same bodily integrity and "honor" as others. Indeed, freedwomen seized the opportunity granted to them by federal forums not only to testify about postemancipation rape but also to document coerced sexual relationships with white men prior to the end of slavery. Their testimony reveals how new rights to refuse the demands of white men for sex, and thus to control their bodies and sexual relationships, were for African American women a central part of the meaning of freedom. Freedwomen's testimony also showed their readiness to confront sexist as well as racist constructs of womanhood in dominant understandings of rape. Disregarding the fact that their sexual histories and their responses to sexual assault often did not fit within patriarchal definitions of who was a legitimate victim of rape (i.e., a woman whose "virtue" had been demonstrated by prior chaste behavior as well as a willingness to risk even death to prevent coerced sex), freedwomen called on federal authorities to recognize them as willful subjects capable of refusal or consent and as honorable women worthy of state protection from sexual abuse. Thus as they testified about rape and claimed the right to be protected by the state against sexual assault, they both demanded equality without regard to race and offered a progressive vision of a woman's citizenship. This book, then, brings together histories of rape and histories of citizenship, seeking to tell the story of the rise and fall of Reconstruction—and of the possibility of a genuine, legal racial equality being established after the Civil War—by demonstrating how race and racism were resisted, reformulated, and ultimately reconsolidated through gendered discourses and violence.

Rape, Race, and the Law

To understand the history of rape during Reconstruction, and specifically how profound it was for black women to protest in official state arenas rape that they had suffered at the hands of white men, it is necessary to consider the particular history of white men's sexual exploitation of enslaved women that followed both white and black southerners into the postwar era. This history involved widespread coerced sex between white men and enslaved women and the exclusion of this form of coerced sex from legal understandings of the term "rape."[37] Antebellum southern state law depicted enslaved women as both incapable of consent—because, as slaves, they had no will or honor of their own—and simultaneously as always consenting to sex; in other words, the law represented enslaved women as lacking the will and honor to refuse consent.[38] This image was supported by allegations of black women's lascivious character as well as by the refusal of the state to acknowledge marital relations, and thus domestic identities, of slaves.[39] In the 1859 Mississippi state supreme court decision in *George (a Slave) v. the State*, a conviction of an enslaved man for rape upon an enslaved child was overturned, the court accepting the argument of the defense that "our laws recognize no marital rights as between slaves; their sexual intercourse is left to be regulated by their owners. The regulations of law, as to the white race, on the subject of sexual intercourse, do not and cannot, for obvious reasons, apply to slaves; their intercourse is promiscuous, and the violation of a female slave by a male slave would be mere assault and battery."[40] Thus, within this legal logic, state-sanctioned marriage was necessary to constitute the specifically sexual injury indicated by the term "rape," as opposed to simple battery, rape being understood to be the violation of another man's "marriage bed" (as it was termed by a defense attorney in another state supreme court case involving an enslaved couple and sexual violence).[41] By "recognizing no marital rights as between slaves," then, the state effectively placed slaves outside the community of citizens who, in theory at least, shared equally in protection under the law. Thus white men's ability to coerce black women under their control into sex and either to represent these relations as consensual or to simply sidestep the question of consent in both social and legal contexts served not only as a demonstration of white male mastery or only as a means of instilling terror in slave communities or even of reproducing an enslaved labor force. It also served to exclude enslaved women from legal personhood and to subject them to the public identity and position of will-less subject, of noncitizen to whom the protective powers of the state did not apply, and simultaneously to the position of a woman who was unchaste (by definition, since she could not be legally married) and thus undeserving of state protection against sexual abuse. These subject positions imposed through the operation of the law legitimated the violence all black women suffered and reinforced hierarchical racial distinctions.[42]

In this legal context, it was exceedingly difficult to represent in an official judicial or other government arena the sexual coercion that black women suffered under slavery. And it was exceedingly difficult for black women to speak of this coercion outside their own communities and families.[43] Further hindering the representation of this violence was the requirement in nineteenth-century law that utmost physical resistance on the part of a woman was necessary to prove that an act of intercourse was rape. The rape that enslaved women suffered may have involved their utmost physical resistance. But perhaps more often it involved a kind of forced submission, or a negotiated or calculated submission under enormous constraints, in exchange for benefits or protection for self and loved ones. Historian Sharon Block, studying numerous cases of sexual abuse in early America, has described how a slaveowner rarely had to resort to pure physical force in order to have sexual intercourse with his slaves but, rather, was able "to use his position to create opportunities for sexual coercion, backing a woman into a corner where capitulation was her best option."[44] Many enslaved women were forced into a calculated submission based on an assessment of relative harm, often leading to experiences of long-term sexual exploitation by the same white man that were difficult within dominant legal discourses to represent as "rape."[45]

Freedom promised African American women options other than submission and also limited white men's opportunities to back them into that corner. It offered other means of securing subsistence and security. And it offered access to the protective power of the federal state, however limited that power ultimately may have been. These new resources allowed black women to realize a construction of self and its embodied experience that had been denied to them under slavery. We will see that for black women one important aspect of being free and becoming persons recognized under the law as possessing rights—that is, of being citizens—was to assert their will and bodily integrity before white men.

Reconstruction's Politics of Citizenship and Suffrage

Freedwomen testifying in official state forums that they had been raped offer striking examples of how African American women who had once been slaves now acted and identified as citizens.[46] By doing so, they became participants in the broad revolution in American citizenship that defined the period of Reconstruction. As its name suggests, this was an era of rebuilding and redefinition. Specifically, this was an era in which African Americans and their sometimes reluctant white allies—primarily from the North but also some southerners—engineered profound transformations in the boundaries of American citizenship and the contours of the American nation.[47] These transformations included the first federal legislation defining national citizenship (the law had been silent on this subject, even though such citizenship was presumed to exist), laws guaranteeing civil rights to all persons born in the United States (with the major exception of Native Americans) and, eventually, suffrage to all adult male citizens. This expansion of the right to vote represented what historian Eric Foner has termed "a massive experiment in interracial democracy,"[48] in which white and black communities shared for the first time a common relationship to the state along with the spaces and practices of public life. This formed a potential foundation for white and black Americans to develop a shared identity as members of the same nation, as a single "people," in contrast to their profoundly different and unequal experiences prior to this time in relationship to the law.

Such shared nationhood was indeed inconceivable before Reconstruction, when citizenship distinguished not only the condition of "freemen" from that of slaves but also in many ways that of white from black people.[49] Citizenship as legal status had been clearly intertwined with matters of race since the early moments of U.S. history, as in 1790 when federal legislation permitted only "free white persons" to become naturalized citizens.[50] The citizenship of native-born free African Americans had also been explicitly limited and was increasingly so into the antebellum period. In the early decades of the nineteenth century, free African Americans in many northern states, and even in some slave states of the Upper South, had been recognized by state law as "citizens."[51] And in these states, black men meeting the same property requirements imposed on white men for suffrage were eligible to vote.[52] However, the "democratizing" trend of the Jacksonian era that expanded and consolidated white male suffrage by lifting erstwhile property requirements for voting in the 1820s and 1830s was accompanied by growing restrictions on the franchise for black men, often imposed in the same constitutional or legislative act.[53] For instance, black men with property who had had the right to vote in Tennessee and North Carolina lost those rights in 1834 and 1835, respectively, in new state constitutions that simultaneously extended the franchise to all white men.[54] By midcentury, most southern state courts concurred in the necessity of actively excluding free black men and women from the status of citizen altogether.[55] And in 1857 the majority opinion of the U.S. Supreme Court in the case of *Dred Scott v. Sandford* stated explicitly that no African Americans were, or ever had been, citizens of the United States.[56] On the eve of the Civil War, citizenship had become increasingly the domain, privilege, and identity of white men.

Yet, the decision in the *Dred Scott* case did not represent legal consensus or clarity. It inspired a strong dissent by Justice Benjamin R. Curtis and was opposed and criticized by the new Republican Party that emerged in the 1850s.[57] The divide over this ruling reflected, in fact, continued disagreement and confusion over the definition of U.S. citizenship. Such was suggested by Attorney General Edward Bates, serving under Republican president Abraham Lincoln, when in 1862 he rejected the legal basis of Justice Roger Taney's decision. Bates, who responded to a query from the secretary of the treasury as to "whether or not colored men can be citizens of the United States" by searching for definitions of citizenship in the nation's legal history, concluded that, in fact, nothing precluded men of color from citizenship. But he also found that what rights exactly accompanied their or anyone else's status as "citizen" was unclear. Citizenship, he wrote, was "now as little understood in its details and elements, and the question as open to argument and speculative criticism as it was at the beginning of the Government. Eighty years of practical enjoyment of citizenship, under the constitution, have not sufficed to teach us either the exact meaning of the word, or the constituent elements of the thing we prize so highly."[58]

White Republican politicians formulating Reconstruction policy in Washington attempted to specify those elements for the first time. Their initial effort, the Civil Rights Act of 1866, passed on April 9 of that year, recognized those born in the United States as "citizens" of the nation and granted to citizens the right to enter contracts, to sue and to testify, to inherit and in all other ways exchange property, and to enjoy "full and equal benefit of all laws and proceedings for the security of person and property." Though the wording of the statute appeared to make basic civil rights universal among those born within U.S. territory, it was in actuality far more limited. The act explicitly excluded Native Americans and others "subject to any foreign power." And although it clearly stipulated otherwise, lawmakers agreed in Congress that the act would not undermine existing restrictions on women's rights (for instance, to sign contracts).[59] Furthermore, this statute laid out the terms of a new American citizenship without including the right to vote. Both this act and the Fourteenth Amendment, proposed later that month and approved in its final form by Congress in June 1866, reflected a consensus at the center of the Republican Party that citizenship entailed certain civil protections but it did not guarantee political rights. The division between civil and political rights that defined the latter as a privilege was expressed by Attorney General Bates in his opinion on citizenship from 1862. Bates wrote that "as to voting and holding office, as that privilege is not essential to citizenship, so the deprivation of it by law is not a deprivation of citizenship. No more so in the case of a negro than in the case of a white woman or child."[60]

This position contradicted the expectations and demands of many black leaders of the period who sought in addition to basic civil rights the right of suffrage for at least all black men, what a gathering of prominent black men in Arkansas in 1865 termed a *"bona fide"* citizenship.[61] Many African American political figures argued for the need also to enfranchise women, while women's right to suffrage remained a matter of lively debate among other African Americans in this period.[62] Freedwomen and freedmen themselves rarely envisaged suffrage as the right or possession of an individual man but, rather, as an opportunity for a community to express its political consensus, a consensus that was shaped by and reflected the voices of women as well as men.[63] However, the demands of black leaders and former slaves for political equality —either for suffrage rights for individual black men or for broad community representation through suffrage—as a necessary component of a universal citizenship and as the only means of protecting their newly won freedom were not yet embraced by white Republican leaders.[64] Suffrage was not, it appeared, to be guaranteed by citizenship.

However, several dramatic violent incidents in these immediate postemancipation years—one of which was the Memphis Riot—contributed to a new openness among white northern lawmakers to heeding the warnings of black leaders that without suffrage for black men there would be no protection of life and property for former slaves in the South. This riot and another murderous attack on African Americans in New Orleans three months later seemed to many northerners to be clear evidence of the unwillingness of former Confederates to accept the terms of their military defeat and the even limited forms of citizenship proposed by Republican leaders for former slaves. This pushed many of those leaders into supporting a broader vision of citizenship and its attendant rights and into backing what were then perceived as radical measures, including suffrage for former slaves.[65]

Coming on the heels of the widely publicized riots, refusal by ten former Confederate state legislatures to ratify the Fourteenth Amendment in 1866 and 1867 was the final straw that prompted an angry Republican majority in Congress to shift course and pass the Reconstruction Acts. These acts permitted seceded states to regain their rights in the Union only after enfranchising African American men. The first act, passed March 2, 1867, imposed military control over former Confederate state governments and predicated their readmittance into the Union on new state constitutions granting the right to vote to all of "the male citizens of said State, twenty-one years old and upward, of whatever race, color, or previous condition, . . . except such as may be disfranchised for participation in the rebellion or for felony at common law." A supplement to the Reconstruction Act, passed on March 23, 1867, authorized military commanders to administer voter registration for the election of delegates to conventions to design these new state constitutions, thereby creating the first official opportunity for African American men, since the early antebellum years, to participate as voters in an election in the South.[66] Freed communities reacted quickly, mobilizing throughout the region both for initial referenda on whether or not to call constitutional conventions and elections of delegates to those conventions and for subsequent elections to ratify the new constitutions and to fill elective offices within the new state governments.

It was in the period of Reconstruction, then, that citizenship became the right of all persons born in the United States other than Native Americans and that suffrage was deemed an inherent feature of citizenship for all men. The Civil War and the radical opening that followed in its wake made these reforms possible. Yet in this promising revolutionary moment the seeds of potential failure were already present in the specifically gendered patterns of racism that developed during Reconstruction. These gendered forms of racism would be echoed over the next several decades and beyond and would play a key role in the creation and evolution of Jim Crow–era segregation and disfranchisement.[67] Indeed, historian Jane Dailey has argued that gendered logics would become "the cornerstone of racist politics in the New South."[68] The highly gendered character of southern racist discourse and practice into the twentieth century was in many ways first consolidated during Reconstruction.

Yet the conservative forces that produced this form of racism did not succeed in their primary aim—the exclusion of African Americans from the rights of citizenship—during Reconstruction. Their triumph was kept at bay by the alliance between African Americans and northern white political leaders that had made the period's rapid and dramatic changes possible. This biracial and cross-regional coalition would, though, prove fragile and would begin to unravel already by the mid-1870s.[69] Without strong federal backing for the full inclusion of African Americans in the postemancipation polity, conservative political movements that variously participated in and condoned racist rhetoric and terror were eventually able to triumph, drawing most southern white male voters together in opposition to black citizenship and in support of "white supremacy." The legal scaffolding for a biracial democracy would remain in place, but it could no longer be sustained in practice. After Reconstruction's ephemeral moment of incorporation, southern whites would use violence, intimidation, and manipulation of new property and literacy requirements for voting to exclude once again African Americans from the "*bona fide*" citizenship they sought after emancipation.[70] Despite continuing political mobilization and struggle on the part of southern African Americans over the next several generations, the promise of universal suffrage and legal equality without regard to race would lay dormant for another hundred years.

THIS BOOK MOVES through increasingly broad geographic frames in order to explore the critical role of gender and sexuality in the tragedy of Reconstruction. Part I (Chapters 1 and 2) examines the city of Memphis. A key Union Army base during and after the war, Memphis was also the site of a major "race riot" in the immediate postwar years. This riot, moreover, was instrumental to congressional approval of the Reconstruction Acts making male suffrage without regard to race a requirement for Confederate states' readmission to the Union. The extension of voting rights had to be implemented through the writing of new state constitutions, a process that is at the heart of Part II (Chapters 3 and 4). This section of the book takes the story across the Mississippi River to Arkansas to explore that state's heated debates both before and during its constitutional convention over extending the franchise to African American men and over issues rhetorically linked to the extension of suffrage, such as interracial marriage and "social equality." These debates led ultimately to acceptance of a new constitution that established universal male suffrage, as did similar contests in nine other former Confederate states. But as African Americans gained political power in the South, many white southerners responded with violence. Part III (Chapters 5 and 6) analyzes this white-on-black terror in the South at large. Thus, as the book moves forward in time it also broadens in scope—from city to state to region—as histories of smaller areas were folded into larger ones after the events and dynamics in the former helped trigger those in the latter. In this progression, the book combines narrative detail at the local level with a broader picture of the particular ways sex and gender were mobilized—both in discourse and in action—in battles over the meaning of race and citizenship during Reconstruction.

The shifting sites of the book's narrative—the city of Memphis, the state of Arkansas, and then various states and counties across the South—were selected because they lend themselves particularly well to research of the book's central themes and questions. The story commences in Memphis both because of the historical importance of the Memphis Riot and because of the wealth of sources that riot produced, above all testimony recorded by the congressional committee investigating it. This testimony sheds much light on the bloody local conflicts that followed emancipation, including on the forms of sexual assault within those conflicts. The narrative then moves to the state of Arkansas both because there the battles in and around the constitutional convention that ultimately enfranchised black men were particularly dramatic and because they left a rich historical record. These struggles, and specifically arguments over whether black male suffrage would lead to what some white delegates posited as undesirable "social equality" that demanded new prohibitions on interracial marriage, are evident in the editorials of the state's conservative press, but above all in the exceptionally detailed transcription of the 1868 constitutional convention. Few other state conventions kept, as Arkansas did, a verbatim record of their debates.[71]

Part III ranges across the southern region as a whole in order to gather material sufficient and broad enough to allow us to discern patterns in the triggers and contours of vigilante violence involving sexual assault. By examining these patterns, I hope to reveal larger forces at work than simply the aberrant actions of "a few bad men" in each locale. So here, again, the narrative travels to where ample sources could be found. Although the era of Reconstruction was extraordinary for the degree to which black women secured the means to overcome long-standing obstacles to their publicly denouncing rape by white men, such testimony still remained limited, inhibited no doubt by the difficulty of speaking about rape in public forums of often unsympathetic white officials. However, in contexts where federal bodies interviewed hundreds of witnesses—as did the joint congressional committee charged with investigating "the Condition of Affairs of the Late Insurrectionary States"—a surprising and relatively ample number of African American women were willing to come forward to denounce acts of rape by white men. Some of the material documenting sexual violence in Part III comes from the Freedmen's Bureau records in Tennessee. Most, though, derives from the testimony taken by this joint congressional investigation, which concentrated on the Carolinas, Georgia, Alabama, Mississippi, and Florida (it held no hearings in Tennessee and Arkansas). Impelled by the need for a substantial body of evidence, then, I have followed the sources across state lines and to increasingly wider domains.

As the book moves geographically, it also takes us through diverse spaces in the immediate, still tense and violent, postwar and postemancipation South— spaces urban and rural, public and private, official and criminal, white and black, revolutionary and reactionary. We pass through city neighborhoods, streets, and shanties; small farms and large plantations; freedpeople's cabins; and state convention halls. We witness informal political gatherings and a constitutional convention and the violence of a "race riot" and night rides of the Ku Klux Klan. As we move across each of these spaces, we will hear a cacophony of opposing voices drawing on sex and gender to debate—or to impose by force—the deeply contested meaning of race in a postemancipation world.

White southern women appear only infrequently in this book. The sources I have pursued to illuminate the histories I am telling rarely contain information about their ideas and actions. Certainly, the social and economic upheaval caused by the Civil War and emancipation disrupted relations between white women and men as well as between blacks and whites. For instance, white women often took on novel roles and responsibilities with the wartime death or disability of white men and new economic hardships. But, as far as we know from the existing literature, for the most part these disruptions did not lead to a divide between white women and men on matters of race.[72] It appears likely that white southern women generally joined with the men of their families, and the overall politics of their class, in either opposing or, in rarer instances, supporting the exercise of citizenship and suffrage by African Americans.[73] Where I have found evidence of white women as agents in the frequent everyday and often violent battles between white and black southerners in this period, I have included it. But I have found no evidence of white women's participation in, for instance, the violence of night riders. I presume, nonetheless, that they often supported at least the goals of vigilante actions. (This is suggested perhaps by the fact that men disguised as "Ku Klux" often wore robes sewn by their wives or sisters or even wore their wives' dresses as robes.)[74] I hope that scholars focused on white women's history of this period will investigate these questions in the future. The specific roles of white women in the racist terror of the Reconstruction period, though, within the confines of this study at least, remain a matter of speculation.

THIRTY YEARS AFTER the destruction of slavery in the wake of the American Civil War, rapidly expanding realms of legal racial segregation would be enshrined into law in *Plessy v. Ferguson*, African American men would be effectively disfranchised across the southern states, and former slaves and their descendants would confront violence, economic exploitation, and systematic exclusion from public space and dominant public spheres. All of this might appear as merely an uninterrupted line of racial domination across the divide of slavery and freedom, what cultural critic Saidiya Hartman has called "the tragic continuities in antebellum and postbellum conditions of blackness."[75] Yet the articulation of such continuity elides what was for those who lived through emancipation a very real and dramatic rupture in the certainties of white supremacy and black subjection after the Civil War.[76] At this time, the future meaning of race in a society without slavery seemed far from obvious or inevitable to both those resisting and those reasserting racial hierarchy— hence, the terror as well as the hope and excitement of the period. As African Americans crafted new visions for American citizenship in the immediate postemancipation years, and as former slaves visibly entered public life, public spaces, and official politics, the rigid and legally enforced racial segregation and political disfranchisement that would ultimately be consolidated in southern society at the end of the nineteenth century might indeed have seemed unimaginable to many, even probably most, white and black southerners.[77] Through an exploration of both violence and rhetoric, and of the rhetorical power of violence and the violent power of rhetoric, *Terror in the Heart of Freedom* seeks to illuminate the uncertainty and volatility surrounding race during the immediate postemancipation years, the hopes and visions of citizenship developed by former slaves, the violent contests over these visions between former slaves and white southerners, and, most of all, the central role of gender and sexuality in the contestation and reconstitution of racial difference and inequality in the postemancipation United States.

PART ONE

A City of Refuge

Emancipation in Memphis, 1862–1866

CHAPTER ONE

City Streets and Other Public Spaces

In the midst of the Civil War, Louis Hughes told his wife, Matilda, "in low tones" about his intention "to try to get to Memphis." The Hugheses were being held as slaves by Edmund McGee in Panola County, Mississippi. They knew that "others, here and there, all through the neighborhood, were going," fleeing to the city that was now under Union Army control. Louis later wrote of how Matilda was overcome with fear at hearing his news. They both understood that "there was a law or regulation of the rebel government . . . authorizing the hanging of any slave caught running away." Having a few years earlier suffered the death of their infant twins, losing her husband as well was perhaps more than Matilda could bear to contemplate. But Louis was convinced that he would be among those who would succeed at an escape and, "bent on freedom," planned a journey back to the city where they had lived with McGee before the war. He set out on his first attempt without Matilda, promising to return for her once he found his way to the city. He returned much sooner, though, having been captured by Confederate "bushwhackers" and spared execution only because one of his captors recognized him as a slave of the McGee family. Two months later, he and Matilda attempted to flee with two other slaves. But this group, too, was captured, tracked down by bloodhounds and returned to their owner to face severe beatings. Finally, on a third attempt, Louis's determination was rewarded. He and another enslaved man reached Memphis in June 1865. By this point, the Confederacy had been defeated. Knowing "it was our right to be free, for the [emancipation] proclamation had long been issued," Louis quickly enlisted the aid of two Union soldiers, returned to Mississippi, and, under the protection of Union arms, left the plantation for the last time in the company of Matilda, their newborn baby, and other family and friends. Many among them traveling without hats or shoes, this "tired, dirty and rest-broken" group concluded their long journey and arrived at freedom in Memphis on July 4, 1865.[1]

Louis later described the remarkable scene he discovered on first reaching Memphis: "The city was filled with [former] slaves, from all over the south, who cheered and gave us a welcome." He also noted that on his return to the city with his family, "aside from the citizens of Memphis, hundreds of colored refugees thronged the streets. Everywhere you looked you could see soldiers. Such a day I don't believe Memphis will ever see again—when so large and so motley a crowd will come together."[2] The spectacle of racially integrated city streets and of large numbers of African Americans filling public spaces in celebratory fashion was dramatically different from any of Louis's memories of the city from a few years before. He later recalled, "I could scarcely recognize Memphis, things were so changed."[3]

The changes that Louis found so striking were the product of the mass exodus from slavery—of which he and Matilda were a part—that commenced with the first Union Army presence in Confederate territory during the Civil War. People fleeing slavery, most of whom likely encountered obstacles and risks similar to those of the Hugheses, sought out Union Army lines, the "contraband camps" eventually established by Union Army officials, and especially cities captured by Union forces.[4] These cities became oases of freedom for slaves from plantations in the surrounding countryside. "Thousands . . . in search of the freedom of which they had so long dreamed" flocked to Memphis, Louis Hughes later wrote, transforming this strategic river port into a "city of refuge."[5]

Once in this refuge, former slaves acted in anticipation of new rights and freedoms. They took their place as active citizens in the markets, saloons, streets, and other visible centers of public life; in civil institutions such as schools, churches, and benevolent societies; at sites of state authority, such as the courts, police stations, and the Freedmen's Bureau; and at speaking events and parades. Their actions redrew the racial boundaries that all Memphians experienced in everyday public life, integrating spaces and sharing activities and roles—as workers, students, soldiers, worshipers, participants in public festivals, or litigants in court—with whites in ways unheard of before the war. New visions of race and citizenship were being forged in the city's public spaces.[6]

Some whites living in Memphis took these changes in stride—especially many recent white migrants to the city who themselves had been devastated by a costly civil war—and others actively promoted and embraced them, such as the numerous northern missionaries, teachers, and businessmen who came to Memphis during or after the war.[7] But other white Memphians responded with hostility in a variety of ways. The city's conservative newspapers, in both editorial commentary and news reports, condemned the new African American presence in the city, characterizing it as "disorderly," "lewd," and "criminal."[8] These reports helped to legitimate the misconduct of many police, who frequently arrested freedpeople under false charges of theft, vagrancy, and prostitution. These arrests were often preceded by or carried out with excessive force.[9] Police violence was only magnified as officers continually ran up against not only freedpeople's resistance but also federal authorities who often intervened on freedpeople's behalf. During the war, the commander of the occupying Union forces ordered police to cease arresting and punishing under antebellum slave codes refugees arriving in the city. Continuing objections to the conduct of the city police led the army eventually to disband the entire civilian government for "disloyalty" and "incompetence."[10] After the war, local officials and police returned to power but were further limited in their authority over freedpeople by the continued Union military presence, made up largely of black Union soldiers assigned to patrol the city's streets, and the judicial powers granted to the provost marshal of freedmen and the Freedmen's Bureau Court. During the years of the war and Reconstruction in Memphis, the freed population, empowered by the federal government, embraced new roles in public life, and many white Memphians responded with resistance to both federal power and the emerging forms of equality, universal citizenship, and inclusion of African Americans in the nation embodied in what they observed around them.

Memphis would receive national attention when resultant tensions culminated in a murderous attack against freedpeople living in the city. This attack, which became known as the Memphis Riot, was in fact a massacre of black Union soldiers and other African Americans by city police and white civilians. Although depicted in the city's conservative press as the suppression of an uprising of black Union soldiers and as an appropriate response to "negro domination," the violence appeared to many white northerners as evidence of an unregenerate and unsubdued Confederate South. Northern outrage at events in Memphis contributed to growing support for further action on the part of the federal government to create and protect the civil and political

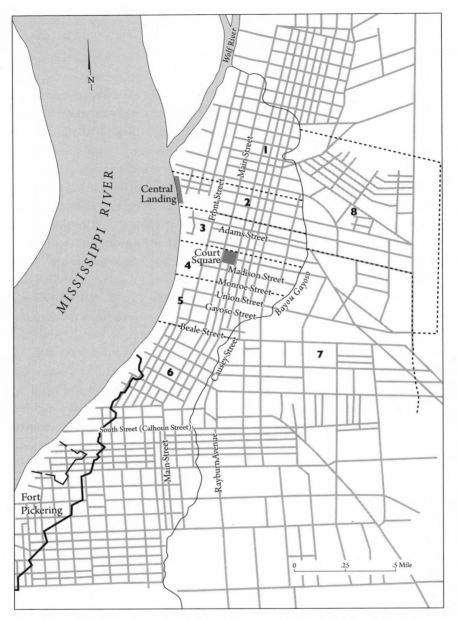

Map of Memphis, Tennessee, 1860s. Wards 6 and 7 composed the neighborhood of South Memphis.

liberties of former slaves. This support led ultimately to the Reconstruction Acts, the first legislative step toward establishing suffrage as a universal right of male citizens of the United States.[11] The process of enfranchising black men, then, began, at least in part, in conflicts over public space and race in Memphis.

These conflicts also offer a window onto the central role that gender played in battles over the future meaning and significance of race in a society without slavery. Representations in both the conservative press and police discourses justifying action against freedpeople enlisted constructions of gender, specifically representations of emancipation as the illegitimate empowerment of depraved women and violent men. Similarly gendered representations of African Americans as people who should play only subordinated and marginal roles in public life were voiced in acts of sexual violence suffered by African American women during the Memphis Riot (discussed in Chapter 2). Through both rhetoric and violence, white southern men articulated gendered meanings for race that reaffirmed racial hierarchy, a hierarchy that was being challenged daily by the immediate and profound sign of equality enacted on the stage of the city's public space.

Urban Spaces, Racial Meanings, and Contests over Rule

Memphis had grown from a small town to a major port city in the decades before the Civil War. Its growth was fueled by an economy deeply rooted in slavery. Sitting high on a cliff overlooking the Mississippi River and, by the 1850s, at the intersection of four railroad lines, Memphis became the main center for trade in the products and needs of a fast-expanding agricultural economy in surrounding Tennessee, Mississippi, and Arkansas.[12] That economy's primary product was cotton—in the 1850s Memphis was often called the "Biggest Inland Cotton Market in the World"[13]—and its primary need was labor. As a result, the offices of cotton brokers and factors, cotton warehouses, and wagons carrying bales to and from the levee shared space in the city's commercial district with traders of slaves. More than a dozen such businesses regularly ran advertisements in the city's newspapers announcing "Negroes for Sale" at their markets on the district's main thoroughfares, including Main, Adams, Monroe, Union, and Madison Streets and Court Square. Visitors to the city arriving by river were greeted on the steamboat landing by the sign BOLTON, DICKENS & CO., SLAVE TRADERS. Two "slave markets" identified their establishments with large signs hung across from each other on a nearby commercial street.[14] The largest slave trader in the city, Nathan Bedford Forrest, bought and sold more than 1,000 slaves annually from his downtown slave market on Adams Street during the 1850s.[15]

The prominence of slave trading in the city contributed to a visual landscape that, for whites at least, virtually equated blackness with enslavement. Following long-standing patterns, slave dealers often advertised that they were selling "negroes" rather than "slaves." "Negroes for Sale," one advertisement read: "A. DELAP & CO. have just received a large stock of South Carolina and Virginia Negroes at their Mart on Adams street, and expect to receive fresh supplies every two to three weeks." "ACCLIMATED COTTON NEGROES FOR SALE!" ran another, "from the state of Georgia, consisting of men, women, boys and girls. Among them are some very likely families."[16] The language employed in such advertisements moved back and forth between "negroes" and "families" and "sale," "stock," and "supplies," oddly juxtaposing human and commercial terms and ultimately reducing black people to commodities available for purchase by whites.

Also contributing to a conflation of blackness and slavery for whites was the unusually small size of the free population of color and the slavelike constraints under which most free blacks lived in antebellum Memphis. The city's overall black population was small relative to both the surrounding countryside and other southern cities, comprising 3,882 people, or 17 percent of the city's inhabitants, in 1860.[17] And 95 percent of this population was enslaved, leaving only 198 free black people—less than 1 percent of the overall city population.[18] The public conduct of free people of color was strictly regulated by city ordinance.[19] Along with slaves, free blacks were prohibited from congregating for political or social activities without permission from the mayor, as well as from public drinking and "loitering in or around the market-house." Their ability to gather for religious worship, also along with slaves, was limited to observing services at white churches from the balconies or holding prayer meetings in those churches' basements with a white person present. Indeed, free people of color in Memphis and in Tennessee more generally were increasingly subject to regulations and legal treatment similar to that of slaves.[20] In the 1850s, all free black persons were required to register with the city government and to document their employment by a white person (if they intended to remain in Memphis for more than forty-eight hours). They could be stopped and required to show their papers by police at any time. Any person of color found in the city without such papers was presumed to be a slave and, unless he or she could identify an owner living within the city, would be arrested as a runaway.[21]

Some additional restrictions were imposed only on slaves: city ordinances allowed slaves to move about the city only with passes from their owners, prohibited their "lounging about the streets, drinking or gambling shops," and forbade them from being outdoors after 9:00 P.M. Slaves were forbidden to live in quarters not owned by their masters and to hire out their own time and labor. Police were instructed to use "corporeal punishment" against slaves found violating these ordinances.[22] Such laws could never be fully enforced, especially those requiring slaves to have a pass to move through the city's streets. An 1858 station register from the Memphis police, for instance, shows large numbers of slaves arrested for being outdoors without a pass.[23] This suggests both that enslaved African Americans were able at times to circumvent the constraints imposed by city ordinances and that police were not hesitant to use the power bestowed upon them by the city government to interfere. It does seem that laws against slaves living on their own, as they often did in other cities, were more effective. In Memphis slaves generally lived in close proximity to owners, not among the small free black population, just less than half of whom in 1860 lived in the city's seventh ward and the rest of whom lived dispersed throughout the city. Ward 7, though, was a majority-white area.[24] There were no "black neighborhoods" in Memphis; black residents were integrated into the city in hierarchical and isolating ways. City and state laws regulating the movement and gathering of black people, both free and slave, meant that there were no public spaces with a significant or visible black presence; black institutions and community life were forced largely underground.[25]

The Civil War permanently altered the racial landscape in Memphis, as public space was suddenly transformed by both the new, free status and dramatic increase in the number of African Americans in the city. The Union Army's occupation of Memphis in June 1862 almost immediately ushered in thousands of African American migrants. In 1863 the army designated Memphis as the recruiting and administrative center for black troops in the upper Mississippi Valley region, drawing thousands of slaves-turned-soldiers through the city's streets.[26] Seven regiments of black Union soldiers, ultimately comprising 10,000 troops, were stationed at the Union Army's Fort Pickering, located at the southern edge of the city.[27] Following these troops came their family members and other fugitive slaves seeking the protection of the Union forces. Most of these refugees settled near the fort in the neighborhood of

South Memphis. According to an 1865 city census, these migrants together with African Americans already living in Memphis comprised 40 percent of the city's total population, just under 11,000 people and almost three times the antebellum black population. Another census taken by the Freedmen's Bureau a few months later found 16,509 freedpeople in Memphis and its environs (including growing neighborhoods just outside the city limits and people living on President's Island, the nearby location of a federal camp for refugees).[28] The significance of this migration for social relations and public life in Memphis lay not only in its size. In the past, African Americans had been brought to Memphis by force, to be sold in slave markets and to labor as slaves in white-owned businesses and homes. After the Union Army occupation, they entered Memphis as a "city of refuge" in which they would be free and, they hoped, equal citizens.

Although General William Tecumseh Sherman, who took over command of the Union forces in Memphis in July 1862, reportedly claimed, "I do not think it is to our interest to set loose negroes too fast," the process of emancipation had already begun and would continue beyond his and the army's control.[29] African Americans migrating to the city in search of freedom had the backing of federal law, namely the Second Confiscation Act passed by Congress on July 17, 1862, which confirmed that those fleeing "disloyal" slaveowners in Confederate states would be free once they came within areas under federal military command.[30] Sherman himself was soon forced to loosen the hold of slavery. He forbade the enforcement of city and state slave codes and insisted instead that all African Americans in the city be presumed to be free unless and until federal authorities could assess the legitimacy of claims to the contrary (in other words, claims that they had run away from owners loyal to the United States).[31] Finally in 1865 an amendment to the Tennessee constitution abolished slavery in the state and finalized the process of emancipation that had begun de facto for most several years before.[32]

Despite this official end of slavery, the legal status of African Americans in Memphis remained uncertain. They were no longer slaves, yet they had no formal political rights. According to law, neither former slaves nor those who had been free before the war could vote or hold office, nor could they testify in civil or criminal courts. Until the Civil Rights Act was passed in April 1866, African Americans lacked even nominal legal recognition as citizens.[33] Indeed, former slaves were subject to various coercive efforts first of the army and then of the Freedmen's Bureau to remove many of them from the city. For the most part, freedpeople successfully resisted these efforts—black Union soldiers, for instance, refused to comply with orders that their wives and children living near the fort in South Memphis relocate to President's Island. And numerous Freedmen's Bureau attempts to force unemployed freedpeople to move to the countryside to find work on plantations met with similar failure.[34] Through such resistance, freedpeople made clear that they believed it was their right to choose where, how, and with whom they now lived and worked. Although they had not yet been granted political or civil rights under the law, freedpeople expected to live as citizens in the city.

In order to remain in the city, freedpeople had to find work or other means of support. Although destitution was never far, many labored and established family economies in ways that allowed them to sustain themselves in the city. Most freedpeople had been field hands before the war.[35] Now many labored for wages for the first time. Some women possessed the skills to work as seamstresses and cooks. Others found employment as laundresses and maids.[36] Men worked as barbers, draymen, carpenters, plasterers, painters, blacksmiths, dock hands, and often as soldiers for the Union Army.[37] A few freed families ran small groceries and saloons.[38] For a number of freedwomen, the earnings of family members were sufficient for them to devote themselves to domestic chores and raising children.[39] A portion of these earnings came from family members working on plantations outside Memphis.[40] Some single, wage-earning women pooled their resources and shared homes.[41] Other freedpeople lived in multigenerational families.[42] A substantial number lived with their spouses. Some married people they had met in Memphis, others reunited with lovers from whom they had been separated under slavery, and still others married under the law those whom they had considered their spouses for years.[43] Some freedwomen left husbands from an earlier time and took up with new partners in the city.[44] At times men proved unreliable, leading a few women to press charges through the Freedmen's Bureau against their lovers for "breach of promise to marry" and child support.[45] Through various collective strategies for material support and through new family relationships, freedwomen and freedmen exercised choice and experienced forms of independence that had long been available to citizens but denied to them as slaves.

Freedpeople in Memphis also enjoyed basic forms of public and community life that had previously been reserved for whites. In South Memphis, for instance, where African Americans were most concentrated, they fashioned social lives that centered around lively grocery-saloons and street corners. Businesses "all up and down South street" selling food and liquor, a few run by blacks but most by whites, served as gathering places for black men and women.[46] When military regulations prohibited soldiers from purchasing alcohol, women filled canteens at these saloons and joined soldiers for parties in the streets.[47] Dance halls, such as one on Grady's Hill run by Mary Grady, a white woman, were also favored locations for entertainment into the morning hours and became evidence of a marked increase in the racial integration of the city's nightlife.[48]

At the same time, churches were becoming increasingly separate, even as black worshipers and their church-sponsored activities became more visible to others than they had been in antebellum years. Leaving the slave galleries or basements of white-run churches where African Americans had worshiped before the war, many former slave preachers and their congregants began to construct their own church buildings.[49] Here the practices observed in contraband camps during the war, where one white missionary reported that "we may hear praying and singing . . . at all hours of the night," moved to city churches. Freedpeople gathered around the clock first in open lots and then in new churches to give thanks for freedom.[50] Neither the churches nor their members would have survived without the fund-raising activities of members, who sponsored public fairs and picnics to collect money for church construction and also organized benevolent associations to assist each other in times of need.[51] White missionaries also built numerous churches in Reconstruction-era Memphis hoping to serve the freed population. Collins Chapel, established by the white Methodist Episcopal Church, South, for black members in 1859, housed in the basement of the white-run Wesley Chapel, and named after the white minister hired as its preacher, reached out to former slaves. But the most popular churches were the black-run African Methodist Episcopal Church and the numerous Baptist chapters in the city.[52] Ewing O. Tade, then a missionary with the U.S. Christian Commission, reported in 1865 that white ministers in Memphis were "very ready to complain because the colored people prefer to hear their own preachers."[53]

Freedpeople also sought out instruction from "their own" teachers. Excluded by law from the nascent public school system, freedpeople founded a small number of their own schools that employed black instructors, some sponsored by churches and others based on tuition paid by pupils. Resources of these independent schools were too limited, though, to meet demand, and many freedpeople attended schools run by northern missionary societies and staffed by white teachers that were operated with Freedmen's Bureau sanction and support. Schools met in government barracks, abandoned houses, churches, and one private school building owned by the AME Church and run by Rev. H. N. Rankin. Both the independent schools and those sponsored by the bureau survived on shoestring budgets and under enormously difficult circumstances. Nonetheless, a total of twelve schools managed to teach some 1,200 students in 1866, offering day and night classes in order to accommodate both adults and children eager to learn.[54] Children attending these schools occasionally publicized their accomplishments by performing for their families and friends in theaters and other public places. The children's performances, often "sneered at" and "hissed in the theatres" by angry whites and "abused in the public press," according to a Freedmen's Bureau superintendent, included patriotic tunes manifesting devotion to the Union, such as when children sang the songs "Red, White, and Blue" and "Rally 'round the Flag." At other times, schoolchildren were overheard invoking the triumph of abolitionism by singing "John Brown's Body," a Union Army marching tune that, when sung by former slaves, became a tribute to a fallen hero—John Brown, the white abolitionist who led the 1859 raid on Harpers Ferry—for taking up arms against slavery ("John Brown died that the slaves might be free," went a line in at least one version).[55]

A small professional and entrepreneurial African American elite, many of whom were free people before the war, also emerged in early Reconstruction-era Memphis. This group attempted to distinguish themselves from the former slaves making up the bulk of African Americans living in South Memphis by, for instance, choosing Congregational or Presbyterian over Baptist or Methodist churches and even at one point requesting that the Freedmen's Bureau take action to limit the number of "vagrant" freedpeople in the city.[56] Thus it is not surprising that freedpeople did not turn to this elite to lead their churches, schools, and benevolent societies but, rather, chose former slave preachers and others they imagined to be more like themselves.[57] Better-off black Memphians nonetheless financed activities and institutions that enriched the public life of freedpeople, from picnics where "there is to be a fine string and brass band in attendance" sponsored by saloon and restaurant owner Robert Church to the Young Men's Literary Society founded by, among others, Joseph Caldwell.[58] Caldwell owned Caldwell Hall, the meeting place for the society's Monday evening debates and lectures such as "The Rudiments of Public Speaking."[59] It is noteworthy that women were excluded from this elite-sponsored opportunity to develop skills useful for active political participation and leadership, as is clear not only from the society's name but also from the recollection of a white missionary that he had "sometimes spoken in their literary societies to young men."[60] Nonetheless, another meeting also held at Caldwell Hall, on April 10, 1866, to "discuss and promote . . . interest in the Freedmen's Savings Bank," the announcement for which stated that "all are invited to attend," was most likely of great interest to women and popular among African Americans of all classes in the city.[61] Many African American women and men in South Memphis, including unskilled laborers and people with little income, opened accounts in this bank, a branch of the Freedmen's Savings and Trust Company chartered by Congress especially for freedpeople in 1865. (Funds in these accounts were tragically lost when the bank failed in 1874.)[62]

Also popular among freedpeople were parades, frequent precursors to picnics and large meetings, sponsored by African American benevolent societies and conducted in the downtown areas of the city. Parades and demonstrations were held to celebrate January 1, or Emancipation Day, and June 6, the day Union forces captured Memphis. Parading in itself proudly called attention to African Americans' new status as free people able to move without restriction through the city's streets. But parades were also forums for broadcasting demands for legal and political equality. One parade in the spring of 1865 included banners that read, "Liberty Two Years Old—We Are Marching On," "General Superintendent of Freedmen—Our Rights Protected," and "Liberty, Education, and The Right of Free Sufferage." Another banner reading "Willing to Work" identified participants as responsible members of a laboring class.[63]

Finally, African Americans acted as citizens of Memphis and formed parts of larger imagined communities in the city by reading and being read about in local newspapers. There was no newspaper published by African Americans in Memphis during Reconstruction, but the Republican newspaper, the *Memphis Daily Post*, reported on the civic activities and social life of freedpeople. This paper began publication in January 1866 under the editorial guidance of John Eaton, former general superintendent for freedmen for the Union Army. It argued for political rights for African Americans, for instance by supporting the proposal of Tennessee's Republican governor in April 1866 that some black men be allowed to vote. And the paper offered constant editorial criticism of the positions on local and national politics taken by the city's conservative papers.[64] Already by 1864, before starting up the *Post*, Eaton wrote to the secretary of the American Missionary Association that "the Freedmen are becoming newspaper subscribers. They often want to know what is the best paper for them to take."[65] It seems possible, then, that despite limited literacy, black Memphians' thirst for a medium through which to share knowledge of their local community as well as perspectives on the national political debates of the day that were critical to their future may have helped give rise to a new voice in Memphis's public sphere.[66] Due to the fact that the majority of its subscribers were former slaves with limited resources and that it received little advertising revenue from city businesses hostile to its views, the *Post* faced constant financial woes. Yet it nonetheless managed to continue to publish daily for four years.[67]

Life was enormously difficult for most freedpeople in Memphis. Steady work and sufficient income and food were hard to find. After suffering the hardships of war and risking life and limb to get to Memphis either during or just after the conflict, many also found the city's streets inhospitable and unsafe. Reports of assault and murder of former slaves were common.[68] Memphis did not prove in many ways to be a "city of refuge." The challenges freedpeople faced, though, make even more extraordinary the communities and institutions that they managed to build in Memphis. These challenges make even more extraordinary the degree to which freedpeople transformed the city's public life in a few short years. African Americans' novel participation in leisure, family, religious, and community activities left indelible marks on Memphis's public, changing the city materially and breaking down racial boundaries around citizenship and freedom. Almost overnight, a world divided between white citizens and black slaves had vanished. The significance and power of race in this world, constituted through this division between free and slave, had been manifest on a daily basis through the visible contrast between black people's containment within slave markets and white citizens' enjoyment of the freedom to move through and to congregate—for work, politics, and pleasure—in urban spaces, what historian Mary Ryan has called "the customary rights of the street."[69] But now what was obvious to whites living throughout Memphis was the development of vibrant public life among African Americans and the emergence of a citizenry no longer limited to whites.

The dynamics of this new world were particularly palpable in South Memphis, the neighborhood where freedpeople were concentrated and where the majority of the violence enacted during the Memphis Riot would occur. This neighborhood consisted of two city wards that had been added to Memphis's southern limits in the 1850s (Wards 6 and 7, consisting of the former towns known as South Memphis and Fort Pickering) to make room for an expanding white population. Native-born whites composed the majority of residents of the neighborhood. Close to half of the city's free black population made up another tiny portion. But the growth in numbers of residents during the decade preceding the war came from white immigrant groups (Irish, Germans, and Italians) settling in the area.[70] Antebellum Memphis was a city of immigrants—"the proportion of the foreign-born to the native white population in Memphis [one in three] was far greater in 1860 than it ever was before or since," according to historian Sterling Tracy—and Irish immigrants made up the largest and fastest-growing foreign-born group.[71] Many of these people settled in Memphis after having come to the region as laborers building new railway lines. But this was not the neighborhood where impoverished and unskilled Irish workers lived (they predominated in the city's first ward).[72] Residents of South Memphis, diverse in terms of ethnicity and immigrant status, nonetheless shared an intermediate economic station. An 1865 city census reported that 75 percent of white men residing in South Memphis held occupations as skilled workers, artisans, and small businessmen. In addition, numerous city police officers and members of volunteer fire companies lived in the neighborhood.[73] Historian Altina Waller has studied in detail a subsection of neighborhood residents, those identified as participating in violence against freedpeople during the Memphis Riot, and found that few of at least this group appeared in the 1850 census. This along with their reported occupations suggests that they, and probably many of the other immigrants in the neighborhood, had arrived with others from Ireland or elsewhere during the 1850s but were among the few who had achieved a degree of class mobility by 1865.[74] It was among this community of petty bourgeois and skilled and "respectable" working-class[75] whites that freedpeople coming to Memphis found space to live, at times renting adjoining houses or taking rooms in the same home.[76] These homes were on and near the main thoroughfares of the neighborhood, particularly South Street but also Causey, Main, Gayoso, and Beale Streets, and were interspersed with groceries and saloons where black Union soldiers and other freedpeople intermingled with their white neighbors.[77] The owners and operators of these groceries and saloons, which served as important gathering places, were particularly prominent neighborhood residents. These included, for instance, John Pendergrast, who ran a South Memphis grocery and saloon with his wife and two sons and was described by one freedwoman from the area as "such a notable man I could not help but know him."[78]

At the time that African Americans began settling in South Memphis, Civil

War conditions had recently given the white immigrants residing there a new degree of leverage in city politics and governance. During the war most male members of the antebellum commercial and political elite had left the city, either to serve in the Confederate Army or to flee the Union forces of occupation.[79] Under this occupation, men who had shown disloyalty to the federal government were disfranchised. A new class of leaders took control of city government who, according to historian Kathleen Berkeley, "were a group of upwardly mobile small business and professional men, yet to make their fortunes or leave their mark on society."[80] These Civil War and Reconstruction-era political figures depended on the votes of white men like many of those living in South Memphis, the primarily foreign-born who may have supported secession but did not hold the Confederacy in such high esteem that they were unwilling to take the oath of allegiance to the federal government necessary to vote.[81] And elected officials, such as the Civil War–era mayor John Park, rewarded these voters with city government positions, such as jobs on the police force. Indeed, Park and the police committee of the city's Board of Mayor and Aldermen ran the police as a virtual patronage fiefdom. Even Park's own chief of police complained of his lack of authority over the hiring and firing of officers, reporting that the board frequently returned to the force men whom he had tried to dismiss for misconduct.[82] The patronage potential of the police force grew further when Union commanders pressed the city government to increase its size and promised to collect new taxes to pay for the increase, in the interest of preserving order in the city.[83] That these patronage spots often went to recent immigrants is suggested by reports that at times more than 90 percent of the police force had surnames common among people of Irish descent.[84]

One arena in which Memphis's new governing group asserted its authority was the city's streets. Police officers frequently harassed African Americans engaged in work or leisure in public places, threatening them with arrest and often extorting fines from them in lieu of forcing them to come to the police station.[85] Policing everyday conduct was also the domain of a popular elected official, John C. Creighton, the recorder of the police court, who presided over hearings and determined punishment for those charged with violating city ordinances. These responsibilities gave Creighton significant control over the public activities of average people, both white and black. Born in Ireland and a skilled laborer before becoming recorder, Creighton exercised his new authority (apparently at times corruptly—he was at one point charged with pocketing fines collected in court) by working closely with city police.[86] These officers were prominent figures in South Memphis and were frequently observed socializing with the owners of the area's grocery stores and saloons.[87]

However, the authority of the group governing Memphis, and that of their official representatives policing the city's streets, was insecure, being constantly challenged and easily curtailed by the federal army occupying the city. Although Union commanders at first promised city officials they would be free to continue municipal government without interference, this proved untenable, as the city became a center for contraband trade with Confederate forces and matters of sanitation and crime seemingly ignored by municipal officials consumed the army's time. Federal commanders frequently overturned municipal ordinances and imposed their own rules and fines. When Mayor Park was reelected in the last year of the war, then-commander of the city General Cadwallader Colden Washburn dismissed the entire city government for "inefficiency," "want of sympathy" for the Union, and "indisposition to cooperate with Military authorities."[88] He fired all policemen in the city's employ and established both a provisional council and a new police force to supervise city affairs. Significantly, after the war's end, when power was returned to civilian hands, including a reelected Mayor Park and Recorder Creighton, one of the first acts of the returning Board of Mayor and Aldermen was to fire the provisional government's police force and hire back many officers who had lost their jobs while the city was under military control.[89] In 1865, city officials were again reined in by federal forces. Because under state law African Americans were still not permitted to testify in Tennessee's courts, the new Freedmen's Bureau established its own Freedmen's Court. Presided over by the provost marshal of freedmen, this court held legal jurisdiction "in all cases involving the rights of Colored people" and used Union soldiers, many of whom were black, when necessary to carry out its decisions.[90] The bureau thus curtailed the city police force's power to control and interfere with the activities of freedpeople in the city. Police were still able to arrest African Americans; but soldiers were also authorized to patrol and make arrests, and all charges were supposed to be brought before and heard by the bureau. Its offices, located in South Memphis, were often filled with freedpeople answering charges and filing complaints; some reported long lines and waits of up to two hours before being heard.[91]

This new system was deeply resented by the police and often circumvented, leading to frequent conflicts over police practices between civilian and military authorities. For instance, on learning that Recorder Creighton was holding a freedman on charges for which he had already been tried in the Freedmen's Court, Provost Marshal Michael Walsh wrote, "I respectfully request that you have the man be released [sic] and save further trouble in the matter. I dislike very much having the military and civil authorities conflicting with one another and hope that it may not occur again." Two days later Walsh wrote to Creighton a second time, as the freedman still had not been released from the city jail.[92] Two months earlier another provost marshal, S. S. Garrett, had complained when the police arrested and fined Private James H. Reynolds, an African American soldier; Garrett stated, "I am inclined to believe that Private Reynolds is innocent, at any rate the city authorities have no power to fine him."[93] That same month Garrett had also objected that "Wm Reagan Policeman has this day charged Albert Hill, a colored man, $2.50 for going with him from the Police Station to the house of the colored man to procure the money to pay fine imposed by me. . . . If such proceedings are not stopped I shall execute the mittimus in each case myself."[94] Apparently even when under the jurisdiction of the Freedmen's Court, police attempted to reclaim some of the privileges of their former position.

White residents of South Memphis were well aware of these conflicts. If they themselves were not involved or did not know intimately people who were, they nonetheless observed frequent clashes between soldiers and policemen in the streets of their neighborhood. And they read renditions of these clashes in the city's newspapers, sold and often read by patrons in the neighborhood's groceries and saloons.[95] Articles in the conservative newspapers presented daily evidence of an ongoing power struggle between, on one hand, the city government and police and, on the other, the federal army, the Freedmen's Bureau, and freedpeople.[96] Residents of South Memphis encountered these conflicts in the context of battles raging in Washington, D.C., over Reconstruction and the rights of African Americans, also reported in the press. The Civil Rights Act of 1866, for instance, first went through a contentious veto battle with President Andrew Johnson that filled the pages of city papers.[97] This act recognized all African Americans as "citizens" of the nation and, at least on paper, provided "full and equal benefit of all laws and proceedings for the security of person and property."[98] Although this nominal citizenship came with no guarantee of political rights, it was nonetheless believed by many whites in Memphis to be a revolutionary measure that threatened, and lessened, their own rights as "citizens." On April 28, 1866, one of the city's conservative papers, the *Argus*, commented, "The Civil Rights bill, recently passed . . . over the President's veto may be well described as a bill to destroy the civil rights of white men in the States, and to exalt the negro to superior immunities and privileges."[99]

This account, and many others like it, represented basic liberal equality as "negro domination." Conservative press reports similarly cast freedpeople in the streets of South Memphis and the city more generally as unjustly diminishing the power and freedom of white people. Local news reporting and commentary depicted freedpeople as a domineering presence that threatened white people's previously "safe" space, and thus as a social problem requiring regulation. The police both acted on and contributed to this imagery through their treatment of former slaves in the city. It is in this imagery that one finds not only notions of racial inequality but ones that were highly gendered, specifically ones that relied on concepts of black versus white "manhood" and "womanhood" to convey the allegedly oppressive and ominous outcome of emancipation for whites and for the nation.

"Riot of Crime in Our Midst"

Press accounts of freedpeople in Memphis were interwoven with an ongoing public conversation about the general disorder, danger, and "moral decay" allegedly afflicting the city after the Civil War.[100] Prominent in this conversation were expressions of concern over a putative growth of prostitution and the number of "lewd women" in the city and of the vices with which they were assumed to be associated, crime and vagrancy. The tone and content of an article titled "The Riot of Crime in Our Midst" from November 1865 were common:

> Perhaps nowhere within the broad area of this country, is there another city . . . that supports and harbors a larger number of disreputable women, and their twin companions—gamblers and thieves—than this one of ours. In almost every portion of the city . . . will be found abodes made infamous by the calling and character of their inmates—lewd women—lost to all shame and virtue. . . . These creatures congregate here from all parts, . . . and find in Memphis an unbridled license to their calling, where crime and prostitution runs riot and laughs scorn at the impotency of the laws.[101]

White citizens frequently complained of, and the city government and military authorities made gestures toward controlling, the visible and institutional aspects of the sex trade. Exchanging sex for money was not in itself penalized, but "public women" were prohibited from moving freely through the streets at night or soliciting in public. Keeping or being an "inmate" of a "house of ill-fame" or allowing property one owned "to be kept for the purposes of prostitution" was also illegal.[102] By January 1866, related "evils" thought to be "rapidly on the increase" were "concert saloons" or "Free and Easys." With names such as "The Climax" (a concert saloon located on Beale Street), these drinking and entertainment establishments were known for minstrel shows, drunken brawls, "vulgar and obscene dancing," and "waiter girls" who were allegedly the saloons' "principal attraction."[103] Descriptions of these establishments and their staff and patrons sat side by side with the crime reporting that crowded the city pages of the Memphis daily papers, where readers were told through numerous reports of robberies, assaults, and murders that "the property and lives of our citizens remains in imminent danger."[104] Concerns about crime and prostitution and condemnations of dangerous and illicit nightlife, staples of nineteenth-century urban discourse, were not solely about African Americans; they often focused on white "fallen women" and frequently complained of "lawless characters, white and black" or "dissolute whites and negroes."[105] In fact, the racially integrated character of Memphis's illicit nightlife may have been what particularly disturbed white conservatives. Nonetheless, the side-by-side placement of these depictions of a crime- and prostitution-ridden city with portrayals of freedpeople in the newspaper columns of the conservative press implied to whites that freedom for African Americans brought disorder and danger.

The conservative papers often attributed the alleged growing danger and crime in the city to what they depicted as a burgeoning social problem of vagrancy. A "vagrant" was defined in the city's laws as an individual guilty of "being an able-bodied person and having no apparent means of subsistence, and neglecting to apply one's self to an honest calling, or being found habitually loitering about street corners, tippling houses, or bawdy houses."[106] Applauding the actions of the city's police chief to enforce the vagrancy ordinance late in 1865, one Memphis daily wrote of the need "to promote the public good, and relieve our citizens of the disquietude and uneasiness incident to the presence of so large a number of scoundrels, thieves and their hangers-on, who at present infest the city in all quarters."[107]

The conservative press conflated the supposed post–Civil War problem of "vagrancy" with the increased presence of African Americans in the public spaces of the city. For instance, the editors of the *Memphis Daily Argus* asserted that freedom for African Americans, unlike whites, led to idleness: "There are but few white men in the South who are 'not willing to labor for their own support.' In the whole circle of our acquaintance, we do not know a single one. But for the last two or three years, wherever in the South the negroes have felt themselves practically free, they have for the most part ceased to work."[108] Whites often interpreted the decision of freedpeople to come to the city to live, rather than respond to the demand for workers on plantations in the surrounding countryside, as evidence of an unwillingness to labor and a preference for idleness. "The difficulty was not that laborers were scarce," wrote a would-be cotton planter about his unsuccessful efforts to recruit laborers in Memphis, "for in and around Memphis it is estimated that there are from ten thousand to fifteen thousand colored people, . . . and the large majority of these are apparently unemployed. The streets are filled with them, and at every corner are seen knots of them playing, idling, and sleeping in the sun."[109] The violence and fraud freedpeople faced in the countryside at the hands of former slaveowners and employers was a primary motivation for reluctance to leave the city.[110] This, however, was not countenanced by white commentators. Rather, they explained freedpeople's judgment on where they chose to live and work as reflecting "the false ideas entertained by them of freedom," a weakness for "the attractions and fascinations of city life," and a predilection for criminal activity.[111] In April 1866, the *Memphis Daily Argus* declared, "There are several hundred [freedpeople] in and around Memphis . . . who have no visible means of support, who could make corn and cotton plenty to support themselves, if they would; instead, though, of working, they band together to rob and steal."[112]

Newspaper editors' concern that the very urban "amusements" reported on so widely in the press were a powerful draw for freedpeople to the city was shared by the Freedmen's Bureau. This is not surprising given the bureau's overall commitment to establishing an effective system of free wage labor in the South. This required a predictable and stable labor force, something achieved at times through blatant coercion of freedpeople and alliances with planters.[113] At one point in 1865, a bureau official forbade ferrymen from transporting freedpeople across the Mississippi River from Arkansas into Memphis unless the prospective passengers carried a note from their employer authorizing their travels. He justified this restriction of freedpeople's mobility and this blatant distinction between the rights of "freedmen" and those of "freemen" by arguing that "a constant leaving of their labors and visiting the cities and large towns for amusement" was not in keeping with the labor contracts all freedpeople should have signed.[114] The Freedmen's Bureau participated in attacks on freedpeople for "vagrancy" in more direct ways as well. In August 1865, the bureau in Memphis established patrols for the purpose of "remov[ing] that portion of the freed people about this city, who have no legitimate means of support and distribute them in the country where they will have a better opportunity of leading useful and happy lives."[115] These policies were encouraged by prominent white residents. A Freedmen's Bureau official noted that "I am daily urged by influential persons in the city" to force freedpeople to labor on plantations.[116] But the patrols were eventually disbanded, as freedpeople resisted their coercion and members of the city's black elite—who had once endorsed such policies—formally complained to the bureau of "indiscriminate arresting of persons of color" that had at times included the arresting of "school children with books in their hands."[117] Nonetheless, as late as April 1866, Brigadier General Benjamin Runkle, superintendent of the Freedmen's Bureau in Memphis, warned that freedpeople "crowding into the city" would be arrested as vagrants.[118]

The majority of black "vagrants" may well have been the dependents of soldiers and other employed freedpeople who were successfully doing exactly what was demanded of them by the antivagrancy discourse, supporting their families. When P. D. Beecher, a doctor with the Freedmen's Bureau, commented, "I am satisfied . . . great numbers [of freedpeople] lead a life of prostitution, . . . idleness or depending as means of support upon those who are more industrious," he may well have been observing African American women liberated from the necessity of plantation labor by the wages of soldiers in the Union Army or other employed family or community members. These women may have thus been freed to engage in other labor that was irregular or unpaid and often invisible to an outsider.[119] A Freedmen's Bureau superintendent complained in September 1865 that freedpeople "who have no visible means of support . . . are, however, in a great measure induced to remain about the city by the employed colored people."[120] Perhaps it was not so much that they were induced as enabled to remain by the wages of family and friends.

This, however, was not the perspective of most white observers. When convenient, the conservative press depicted even the Freedmen's Bureau itself and Republican policy in general as what was "inducing" freedpeople into idleness. Newspaper editors at times represented freedpeople as innocent victims of an imposed vagrancy caused by actions of the federal government, as in this editorial: "The insane fanaticism of the North has plunged the negro into the deepest distress. It has taken him from his comfortable home where he was surrounded with all the comforts of life, and made him a vagrant upon society."[121] Regardless of where a given editorial placed blame, the association of African Americans with vagrancy by white conservatives and even by freedpeople's supposed allies in the Freedmen's Bureau was pervasive. This emerging "truth" circulating in public discourse about race and vagrancy, and about the social and moral conditions in the city in general, joined with certain normative understandings of gender to shape white responses to the presence of freedpeople in Memphis.

African American Men in the Army of Occupation

Black soldiers among the federal troops occupying Memphis became key figures in the city's freed community. They patrolled parts of the city for the Freedmen's Bureau as a provost guard, paraded in ceremonial processions through the city's streets, and played in bands in the downtown's main square.[122] Off-duty or discharged soldiers were the most commonly noted black patrons of the groceries, saloons, and dance halls of South Memphis. They often gathered in groups in the neighborhood's streets, drinking, socializing, and even racing horses down Main Street.[123] These men were often armed, many of them surreptitiously purchasing pistols of their own—contrary to army policy—in addition to the muskets issued by the Union Army.[124] The presence of armed black soldiers in the city's public arenas emboldened other freedpeople, providing a sense of protection and a show of force that supported former slaves in their daily activities and in challenges to exploitation and abuse.[125]

White Memphians bitterly resented the presence of black soldiers among the federal troops occupying the city. As former slaves armed and in uniform commanded power and pleasure in the streets of Memphis, they represented in no uncertain terms the overthrow of the Confederate order and the revolution in racial meanings and racial hierarchy that this defeat promised.[126] Black soldiers were also a daily reminder to whites that Memphis was an occupied territory where they were not in control of local affairs. An editorial in the *Memphis Daily Avalanche* concluded that black troops were used "only for the purpose of humiliation of the people of the South."[127] In petitions to federal officials and in editorials and letters in the press, many whites demanded that black Union soldiers be withdrawn from the city.[128] Most notably, the objections of many white Memphians to black Union soldiers were framed as opposition to the domination of the city by violent and criminal men.

White middle-class concepts of "manliness" in the nineteenth century encompassed both a fear and a glorification of what was imagined to be the passionate and aggressive "nature" of all men. Self-restraint of inner drives, or what historian Gail Bederman has referred to as the "willful control of sin," was the centerpiece of "manliness," the hallmark of civilization, and the demonstration of a man's character and strength. Furthermore, the ability to impose such restraint when appropriate and to release it when necessary to preserve honor or social order was both the measure and justification of a man's right to rule.[129] These notions of masculine nature and civilized manhood were invoked by whites in Memphis in response to the presence and powers of African American Union soldiers. In particular, the conservative press's reporting and the actions of city police depicted the visible presence of black Union soldiers in Memphis and the challenges these men posed to the authority of white men in the city as the irresponsible empowerment of a dangerous, because consistently and inappropriately unrestrained, black masculinity.

As black Union soldiers patrolled and socialized in the streets of Memphis, they came in constant conflict with the city's civilian police force. The two groups repeatedly collided with and resisted each other's authority. As one Shelby County official observed, "[The police] seem to assume to themselves an authority which has come in continual conflict with that of the colored guards. There has seemed to be a competition which should excel in authority. The policemen did not want to give up to them, and the colored guards did not want to give up to the police. . . . One was not disposed to submit to the other."[130] This contest of authority between police and soldiers in daily interaction often took the form of challenges over courage and strength. When their paths crossed in the streets, police and soldiers often taunted each other and, as one observer noted, used "very hard language . . . , daring each other to fight." In this particular instance, the witness, a white woman who had recently moved to Memphis from Illinois, recalled that a soldier who was hit in the head with a pistol by a police officer, on getting up "dared the policeman to fight—to 'come on'—that he was ready for him. Of course the policeman said come on, but there was no more fighting between them."[131] Although one doctor who had served in the Union Army recalled seeing black soldiers "shout[ing] at police, their language sometimes being abominable,"[132] other white men from the North denied the frequency with which this happened. Many, in fact, believed that the police were generally the instigators, insulting, shoving, and threatening black men in uniform and often arresting soldiers and other freedpeople these soldiers sought to protect under unspecified or fabricated charges and beating those taken into custody.[133] The superintendent of the Freedmen's Bureau in Memphis, Benjamin Runkle, observed that "a policeman could not arrest a negro without knocking him in the head before he carried him to the station-house. . . . Many negroes were arrested and taken up when they had done nothing; they were abused a great deal."[134] James Donahue, a former slave working in Memphis as a carpenter, reported that "sometimes the police would arrest a colored soldier when he had no right to. . . . Whenever a policeman arrested a colored man, the first thing he did was to strike him. . . . I have seen, perhaps, as many as a hundred colored people arrested here, and I do not remember ten who were not struck by policemen."[135]

Nonetheless, conservative press reports repeatedly depicted conflicts between soldiers and police as a result of the soldiers' illegitimate aggression and lack of self-restraint. They also revealed ongoing battles over manhood between black soldiers and white men in general. The following article described such a conflict subsequent to one soldier's attempt to avoid the rain by squeezing into an already-crowded stage coach: "[The soldier] was told there was no room, still he persisted in making his way inside, till at last a gentleman was compelled to eject him rather rudely. The negro commenced in the presence of the ladies to swear and threaten vengeance against the party inside, saying he would kill him, etc. The presence of the ladies of course saved him a severe drubbing, and possibly something more." Both men acted aggressively, and the white "gentleman" was the one who used physical force. Yet the soldier was portrayed as impulsive, inappropriate, and irrational, in contrast to the "gentleman's" calm demeanor and reasoned restraint from violence given the presence of "ladies." In the company of men alone, the article's author implied, the "gentleman" giving the soldier a "severe drubbing" would have been a legitimate response to his supposed insubordination. The author then used the image of illegitimate and undisciplined black male aggression to question the claim of all black soldiers to membership in a community of honorable men. The article, titled simply "Negro Soldiers," concluded, "For the good of this class of soldiers, we would say, by way of advice, that freedom does not license them to disobey the laws of the land. That if they expect to live in the community they must conduct themselves as law-abiding and peaceable citizens."[136] By instructing soldiers in what they should be, this article told its readers what black men were not, men who could control their aggressive impulses and who thus deserved the privileges and powers of a male citizenship equivalent to that of white men.

Freedom as a license for lawlessness continued as a theme in the press's portrayal of black Union soldiers as, at best, disorderly and, at worst, violent criminals who had overtaken South Memphis. Soldiers engaging in the activities of "freemen" were repeatedly depicted as endangering public safety, while their sense of entitlement to these liberties was conveyed as a perilous misconception of the meaning of freedom. Objections to the presence of off-duty or discharged soldiers in South Memphis's groceries, saloons, dance halls, and streets often focused on public drinking. In October 1865, the clerk of the chief of police complained to the Freedmen's Bureau of having "very frequently seen the colored soldiers . . . very much intoxicated and very insulting and abusive to citizens."[137] Many living near and among black soldiers, in fact, observed that they were no more drunk and disorderly than were white soldiers or white men in general.[138] Nonetheless, images of a particular predilection for drunken conduct among black soldiers that posed a new and pressing danger to the "citizens" of South Memphis were pervasive in press accounts. Military orders prohibited the selling of liquor to enlisted men, but this regulation was difficult if not impossible to enforce, leading to editorial comments such as the following describing South Memphis: "Here whiskey . . . is retailed to negro soldiers and negro civilians, without the slightest molestation from any authority, either civil or military. It is a trait indisputable in the composition of the negro . . . that when under the influence of liquor, every fiendish and brutal passion is aroused, and revenge sought for the fancied wrongs perpetrated on him, or the imaginary rights that is his due—instilled into his ignorant brain by the words or action of fanatical demagogues." Black Union soldiers' challenge to white men's exclusive enjoyment of leisure in public was cast as the dangerous release of black men's "fiendish and brutal" natures. This in conjunction with Republican policy supporting freedpeople's rights and privileges as citizens was imagined to pose a threat of violent retribution to white Memphians. In theory, this danger could be removed by excluding soldiers from the enjoyment of a social activity accepted and widely practiced as a white man's right, public and social drinking.[139] The editorial concluded by conflating the alleged problem of black soldiers and the public consumption of alcohol with the general crime and disorder purported to have followed emancipation in Memphis: "The source of all our troubles here . . . is unquestionably attributable to the sale of liquor to negroes."[140]

Also eliciting critical commentary from the city's conservative papers was African American soldiers' access to weapons. It seems that soldiers were in the habit of firing pistols into the air, perhaps as a form of celebration or a reminder to white men that they were armed. When asked if many soldiers owned their own guns, one army captain responded, "I know there were some who had pistols, because as they would go along they would fire them in the air."[141] Another captain reported "having noticed considerable pistol firing near Fort Pickering, . . . I went about through that locality, and discovered the cause to be drunken negro soldiers who attended a dance-house . . . [in] South Memphis. These soldiers . . . coming and going from this house, were in the habit of firing their pistols promiscuously."[142] As one would expect, the conservative newspapers objected to this demonstration of black men's control over means of violence. The *Appeal* reported, "There is a great deal of complaint from the citizens residing in the southeastern portion of the city in regard to the practice the negro soldiers have of firing off their pieces at all hours of the night, to the annoyance and fears of safety of the whole neighborhood." The objection, though, was not merely to the noise or possibility of an accident resulting from this "dangerous sport."[143] White concern about soldiers with guns was directly connected to fears of crime in the constant news reports of supposed "outrages" committed by black troops. Almost daily accounts alleged that armed African American Union soldiers were responsible for muggings, burglaries, and murders.[144] "Scarcely a day passes, without depredations of some sort being committed . . . by negro soldiers," wrote the *Memphis Daily Appeal*.[145] "How much longer are our people to be the witnesses and victims of such lawless brutality?" the *Avalanche* asked after reporting that a white man had been shot and killed by a black man in federal uniform.[146] Many crimes reported in the papers, typically in short entries appearing in the local news columns, involved far less serious offenses. For instance, it is unlikely that the burglary of Mr. and Mrs. Finney's grocery by soldiers allegedly looking for whiskey but who had to settle for "four dressed turkeys and a black hat" was reported because of the value of the goods stolen. Recounting that the intruders had threatened Mrs. Finney with a gun seemed to be the point of the brief news story.[147]

It is probable that theft of clothing and food was common in South Memphis by white and black people dislocated and impoverished by the war.[148]

Nonetheless, reports of crimes committed by black soldiers were often inaccurate. One press account alleged that fifteen soldiers broke into a store, firing indiscriminately and killing the establishment's owner, J. W. Hanks. However, the only possible witness to these events was Hanks himself, and he reportedly did not live long enough to tell the tale.[149] Even the *Appeal* admitted the tendency of newspapers to print rumors or falsehoods. "Mr. Wm. Ryan is a living refutation of the report of his murder by negro soldiers on Monday night last, published yesterday morning in several of our enterprising contemporaries."[150] Two of the *Appeal*'s "contemporaries" had earlier reported that police officer Richard Clark murdered an African American soldier after catching the soldier in the act of stealing vegetables from a garden. They also reported that City Recorder John C. Creighton was called to oversee an inquest at the sight of the murder, and that there he determined that Clark had acted in self-defense. However, when the Freedmen's Bureau conducted its own investigation, it found that the victim was actually a young man of sixteen years, unarmed and not a soldier, carrying an empty sack on his way to collect vegetables from a garden cultivated by his family.[151]

The visible and audible presence of black soldiers in public endowed with the trappings of manhood—guns, alcohol, leisure time, and power over others—challenged whites' sense of privilege as the only urban residents who were "citizens" and white men's sense of privilege as the only ones who were "men." White critics responded rhetorically by associating black soldiers' presence with danger and the men themselves with illegitimate and uncontrolled violence, relying on understandings of gender to restore meanings of racial difference to the world they observed around them. White conservative newspaper editors in Memphis told their audience that black men were not sufficiently in control of the inner nature—the violence understood to be lurking inside all men but mastered by those men who were "civilized"—to be worthy of power and authority in public.

Freedwomen in Public

African American women were also central actors in the process of claiming a new urban citizenship in ways that dramatically transformed public life in Memphis. Women constituted a sizable proportion of those former slaves who made their way to Memphis both during and after the Civil War.[152] White Memphians quickly experienced the reality of emancipation and aspects of a new multiracial citizenship through these women's movement through public space and their use of public authority in the form of the Freedmen's Bureau Court and police protection of the Union Army. Some whites responded by attempting to cast black women's new public presence in a disparaging light. Both white police officers and newspaper editors from the city's conservative press, in their conduct toward and representation of freedwomen, enlisted gendered constructions of race, specifically a discourse representing all black women as without virtue, as "bad women," and often as prostitutes, and thereby depicted black women as unworthy of citizenship.[153]

It was specifically to realize their freedom that African American women migrated to Memphis after the end of the Civil War. Freedwomen fled conditions reminiscent of slavery in the countryside—physical violence, work with no pay, forced separation from family—and undertook the difficult journey to the city hoping to seek the assistance and protection made possible by the growing African American community, and particularly by the power of armed African American Union soldiers and the federal authority of the bureau. A freedwoman named Lizzie Howard explained to the provost marshal of freedmen that she had fled to the city from the home of her former owner, Robert Bond, in Raleigh, Tennessee, to escape from slavelike treatment. Howard had agreed to continue to work for Bond for wages after the war. However, once she received a severe beating from him and his son, she "left the plantation and came to Memphis, as I could not be satisfied with such abuse."[154] Eliza Jane House similarly refused to remain on the plantation of James R. House after he tied her up and beat her with a branch.[155] Other women were forced off plantations, such as Ellen Clifton, whose employer beat her and "did drive me away, refusing to let me have my children."[156] In search of means to resist such blatant violations of their freedom, women often came to the bureau to enlist the aid of Union soldiers.[157] The record does not indicate how often the provost marshal actually provided guards to accompany freedwomen back to plantations to demand from angry owners the children and possessions the women had been forced to leave behind. However, when soldiers did arrive at an abusive employer's place, they doubtless created an indelible image of black women enlisting the power of the state, in the form of armed black men, to assert new rights as free people—as parents, as property owners, and as citizens demanding to live free of violence.[158]

In addition to protection from violence, African American women sought assistance from federal authorities in Memphis to secure compensation for past labor. During the summer of 1865, freedpeople arriving in the city after being driven from plantations without pay by former owners or current employers crowded the offices of the Freedmen's Bureau in order to lodge their complaints.[159] Many freedwomen sued these employers in the Freedmen's Court for wages that had been promised but never paid to them or their children after emancipation. For instance, Hannah Biby came to Memphis to file a complaint against William Trice, for whom she had been working ten miles outside the city "under the impression that I should get good wages since January 1st 1864. And on the 2d day of August, 1865, the said William Trice told me he could not keep me any longer but did not offer to pay me."[160] Some planters, such as James Robinson from Panola County, Mississippi, offered no wages and refused to acknowledge emancipation altogether. His former slave Betsy Robinson escaped to Memphis, where she filed this complaint with the Freedmen's Bureau: "I have been kept out at work very hard for him also three of my children. he fed and clothed us very badly. he never gave me any information in regard to my being free, but kept me very close at work for him. I left him because myself and children were suffering for food and clothing."[161] The provost marshal of freedmen apparently did not believe Betsy Robinson and assumed instead that James Robinson had intended to pay her once his crop was harvested. She was penalized for leaving the plantation, the court determining that "plaintiff . . . left defendant in busy season without cause. It is considered that she has no claim for wages."[162] Amy Covington's similar charges of painful abuse led to a happier outcome. Covington came to Memphis after being driven from the plantation where she and her four children lived "in a miserable destitute condition with hardly enough clothing to cover my nakedness." She requested that the bureau assist her in securing the release of her children from her former owner, who had since hired them out to parts unknown and was receiving compensation for their services. Her children were eventually returned to her along with the wages they had earned.[163]

Presumably, many women also came to the city knowing of the presence of kin (blood relations or people with whom they had lived under the ownership of the same slaveholder before the war) living in Memphis to whom they could turn for help. As was often the case, Ellen Clifton's statement to the bureau was witnessed by individuals sharing her last name, suggesting that she migrated to the city at least in part to find these people who accompanied her to the offices of the Freedmen's Bureau to lodge her complaint.[164] Seeking out family members in the city could also cause a dispute with an employer. A former slave named Mary Ann was driven from her home when her employer became enraged that she had come to Memphis to visit her daughter.[165] Others came to the city to join and seek protection from male family members now in the Union Army. For instance, Lucy Williams joined Randall Williams of the 59th Colored Infantry in Memphis after being beaten and driven from the plantation of her employer and presumably former owner, Joseph Williams. This planter was enraged on learning that Lucy had attended a speech by General Tillson of the Freedmen's Bureau in Grand Junction, Tennessee. The planter "commenced kicking and kicked so bad that I could not speak for several minutes. . . . He then told me to get off of his premises and never return." In Memphis Lucy reunited with three other Williamses who witnessed her affidavit concerning this abuse.[166]

Freedwomen in Memphis became particularly prominent actors in the freed community's religious life. They constituted the backbone of the city's black churches, forming the committees that raised the funds necessary to create permanent institutions and organizing the mutual aid societies on which its members depended. For instance, the women of the First Baptist Church in Memphis organized a fair in 1865 that raised $406.50, enough to make a down payment for a lot on Beale Street on which, in 1869, the congregation began construction of a brick church building.[167] These women's organizational activities continued with the Baptist Sewing Society, founded to raise more funds to cover the church's debts.[168] By September 1865, destitute freedpeople could no longer receive financial assistance from the Freedmen's Bureau.[169] In their churches, black women took up responsibility for caring for the community's poorest and sick. According to historian Kathleen Berkeley, a "ladies aid society" developed in affiliation with almost every black church in the city to tend to cases of need, supported by numerous fund-raising picnics, balls, and fairs.[170] The leadership of these organizations came largely from the ranks of unskilled, working-class black women living in South Memphis.[171]

Women were also prominent among those freedpeople in Memphis who used the power of the federal government to secure their personal safety and livelihood in the city. Acting as citizens, freedwomen pressed charges against white Memphians in the Freedmen's Bureau Court to claim unpaid wages and protest violent assaults. For instance, after John Montgomery attacked Catherine Martin in South Memphis, "assault[ing] and knock[ing] me down with a brick, hurting me badly," she reported him to the provost marshal of freedmen.[172] The Freedmen's Court heard a case of "Assault and Battery" against H. B. C. Miles brought by freedwoman Susan Hill and a complaint of attempted rape against Gustavis Fisher brought by Salena Jones.[173] The impact of legal action at times spilled over from the courts into the streets, when whites resisted verdicts and clashed with soldiers making arrests, collecting fines, and confiscating property. The provost marshal of freedmen revealed his reliance on the coercion of Union soldiers to enforce his judgments when he wrote to Ira Moore, "Judgement having been rendered against you in favor of Mary Moore (col'd) for the sum of Ninety eight ($98) dollars which should have been paid some time since, I respectfully request that you come forward and settle the same according to agreement, and save me the trouble and necessity of sending a guard for you to the matter."[174] In February 1866, an assistant provost marshal was sent to the railroad depot to intercept Stephen M'Ginness, who was attempting to leave town before paying Belle Holland and Minnie Brown the $23 he owed them.[175] After William Noland refused to comply with the Freedmen's Court's judgment that he owed Betty Maywell $50 in overdue wages, the provost marshal ordered that his property be seized and sold at public auction. Hoping to avoid the loss and public humiliation from the seizure of his personal belongings by Union soldiers, Noland quickly paid Maywell what he owed her.[176]

Even when cases did not lead to convictions, freedwomen's actions brought charges of white abuse against blacks into the public eye. One case that became particularly notorious also reveals the conflictual and political nature of even the most intimate social relations between black and white people in Memphis. Early in February 1866, freedwoman Elizabeth Burns accused Archy Fuller, a white man, of killing Sam, a discharged black Union soldier. Elizabeth had been the roommate of another freedwoman, Amanda Fuller, in a house in South Memphis. Archy Fuller often stayed in this house as well, because Amanda, presumably the former slave of Archy or of his family, was now "kept" by Archy as his mistress. Most likely through this connection, Archy hired Elizabeth and her friend Sam to work for him on a farm that he had rented outside town. A few days after Elizabeth and Sam arrived at the farm, Archy demanded that Sam hand over his pistol, saying he would not allow armed black men on his land. Instead of forfeiting his weapon, Sam departed, refusing to work under those conditions. A little while later, Elizabeth heard gunfire and saw Archy and his companions walk away from an area where she soon found Sam lying slain in the woods. Archy held Sam's pistol in his hand. Horrified by her employer's actions, Elizabeth immediately returned to Memphis, to Amanda Fuller's Beale Street home.[177]

Archy also soon came to Amanda's home. Perhaps fearing Archy's retaliation, Elizabeth remained quiet about the murder for a few days. However when Sam's wife came to the house inquiring about her husband's whereabouts, Elizabeth recounted what she had seen. Hearing this, Amanda broke her own silence, telling the other women that Archy had admitted to her that he had committed the murder. "She (Manda) then commenced crying saying that she could not help it, that Mr. Fuller brought it on himself." With this evidence, Elizabeth brought the charge of murder against Archy on February 9, 1866, before the provost marshal of freedmen, who then sent a guard composed of twenty black soldiers and one white officer to arrest Fuller and his companions.[178] Due to Burns's actions, what began as a claim by Archy Fuller to the class and racial privilege of an exclusively white masculine power—only white men, and employers, would carry guns—ended with armed black men arresting Archy Fuller and bringing him back to the city under their control.

This case reveals the multiple and layered publics that were affected by freedwomen's actions in Memphis. There was the cross-racial local public composed of people who knew one another well—Elizabeth, Archy, Amanda, and Sam. And there was a neighborhood and even citywide public composed of those people who read and discussed the city's newspapers and those who observed public spectacles in the city's streets. As people watched Archy Fuller and the other white men under arrest marched through the city and into the station house under guard of twenty black soldiers, or as they read about it in the newspaper, these arrests displayed for residents of Memphis new meanings for race. The images of black men arresting white men and white men charged with murder because of the testimony of black women challenged previous associations of whiteness with dominance and of blackness with subordination, of whiteness with voice and citizenship and of blackness with voicelessness and servitude. However, when it was learned that one of the white men arrested, J. M. Warr, was injured when kicked by a soldier's horse, white conservatives circulated within their public discourse a new interpretation of this case. They used Warr's complaint of callous and life-threatening treatment as an opportunity to represent black people, not white, as threats to public order. Conservative papers used his charge to argue that empowering black Union soldiers menaced public safety, given black men's inability to control their alleged violent tendencies. Warr's complaint and the publicity it received contributed to the Freedmen's Bureau's decision to acquit the accused on all charges.[179]

This acquittal was also made possible by Amanda Fuller's retraction of her testimony and by the many white witnesses willing to testify that there had never been a man named Sam on Archy Fuller's place.[180] One can easily speculate about what pressures led Amanda Fuller to change her story. Did she fear violent retaliation from Archy or the loss of the financial support he provided for her? Given Elizabeth's close relationship with Amanda and Amanda's relationship with Archy, both women likely faced tensions and even danger after Archy Fuller was acquitted. Freedwomen took great risks in seeking the authority of the Freedmen's Bureau on their side in conflicts with whites. Their access to state power in no way broadly protected them in Memphis in 1865 and 1866.

The events put in motion by Elizabeth Burns's charges against Archy Fuller were turned around by reporting in the city's conservative newspapers. When the presence of freedwomen in Memphis in general was noted by the conservative press of the city, it was never in reference to victims or opponents of exploitation and abuse. Nor were black women represented as "respectable" churchwomen or "ladies" participating in the civic life of their community.[181] Rather, the rhetoric of newspaper editors and the focus of most reporting suggest efforts to denigrate the public activities of freedwomen in the city by insinuating connections between their presence and the alleged increase in crime and disorder, specifically of "lewd women" or prostitutes, supposedly threatening white Memphians in the city's streets and alleys. Onto the real activities of women in public, in all their variety and unpredictability, was imposed a bifurcated concept of "womanhood." As was common in nineteenth-century depictions of urban life in the United States, women were represented as inhabiting one of two opposing realities: the delicate, chaste, and virtuous "lady" or the vicious, rude, "public woman," or prostitute. The former was the woman whom society must protect; the latter, by whom society was threatened.[182] In postemancipation Memphis, this binary imagery operated along racial lines. Representations of African American women in the conservative press implied their essential relation to the latter category. Depictions were not at all uniform. The negative characteristics associated with freedwomen were presented at times as menacing and at others as comical—at times threatening real violence and at times merely demonstrating a childlike or foolish nature. Together, though, these images of freedwomen appearing throughout commentary on local affairs elaborated the racial power and privilege of whites in Memphis by gendering black women as "bad" women, as inappropriately aggressive and thus as unfeminine, often as sexually indiscriminate, and as operating outside the confines of proper patriarchal domestic relations. Newspaper reports labeled black women's presence in the public space of the city as illegitimate and thus challenged their claim to identities as citizens.

The newspaper report of a confrontation between Neely Hunt, a freedwoman, and the Rutters, a white family, shows the distinctions made between white and black women in the rhetoric of the conservative press. Hunt and several other freedwomen arrived at the home of Mrs. Rutter and demanded the return of Hunt's child, whom Hunt believed was being held unwillingly in the Rutters' home. When Mrs. Rutter denied any knowledge of the child, Hunt enlisted the aid of a squad of black Union soldiers with whom she forcibly entered and searched the house. For her action, Hunt was vilified in the city's conservative newspapers. The *Memphis Daily Appeal* described Hunt as a "negress" who was "enraged," "raving," "threatening," and "us[ing] very abusive and insulting language" in contrast to "the ladies of the house," whose delicate constitutions were unsettled by this confrontation. The *Appeal* labeled Hunt a liar, given that the Rutters insisted "positively that no negro child of the description was ever on the place." The paper suggested that Hunt's deceitful and disreputable character could be generalized to all freedwomen, by reminding readers of the recent accusation of murder made against Archy Fuller "at the instance of another negress [Elizabeth Burns], who swore to seeing the dead body of a negro that never had existed."[183]

Ultimately, Hunt paid dearly for the pursuit of her child. The son of the woman she confronted was the president of the Tennessee National Bank. Although Hunt did find her child (though the record does not indicate where), the bank president filed a complaint against her with the Freedmen's Bureau, claiming that the child had never been in his home. Accepting the bank president's version of events, the provost marshal of freedmen had Hunt arrested and fined $10 and costs. Unable to pay, Hunt was at once hired out to labor for a planter for the amount of her fines. (The record does not reveal what happened to Hunt's child while she labored in the country to work off her fine.) This exploitation of Hunt as convict labor was justified by the bureau through the same kind of language by which Hunt had been described in the press. The provost marshal imagined her exile to the countryside to be for the public good. Referring to the planter who bought Hunt's labor, the provost marshal wrote to the bank president, "I trust he may be able to keep her there for the good of this community. I am satisfied that she is a bad woman."[184]

When the press identified Neely Hunt, Elizabeth Burns, and other assertive black women with terms such as "negress," they avoided describing them as women. Such terminology distanced black women from images of respectable womanhood and associated them with marginality and disrepute. Newspaper editors often combined this term with other insulting labels, such as when the *Appeal* reported the charge of theft of a pistol made against "an ugly looking negress."[185] Another report titled "Sharp Wench" described a black woman charged with drunk and disorderly conduct.[186] ("Wench" was a term indicating "young female" that also had implications of servitude and sexual wantonness and, in the nineteenth century, implied blackness as well.)[187] Another article reported the arrest of five "female roughs of African descent" and speculated about the origins of black women's alleged misbehavior: "Freedom seems to have an intoxicating effect on colored females."[188] Other accounts that depicted black women as outside the realm of "respectable womanhood" focused on dress, describing some freedwomen's alleged finery as signifying questionable character and respectability. A report of a robbery by three black soldiers who supposedly stole a number of hoopskirts editorialized that the skirts were intended as gifts for "some of their dark paramours."[189] Through an assertion of both theft and illicit sexual relations, this report questioned the legitimacy and honor of freedwomen appearing in public in fine clothes.

Images associating black women in Memphis with disrepute, aggression, and sexual promiscuity circulating in the city's conservative press were reinforced by police action against freedwomen, such as frequent arrests for "lewdness," "vagrancy," and "drunk and disorderly conduct." The frequency with which city police arrested black women is suggested by the city prison keeper's complaint to the city council that nearly half the freedpeople in jail were female.[190] These arrests, at times under false charges and amounting to harassment of black women by police, were then highlighted and exaggerated in newspaper accounts. Some reports implied that a specific incident indicated an epidemic of black prostitution. For instance, note the use of the word "more" in the following news item: "Six more negro prostitutes were yesterday arrested and brought before the officers of the Freedmen's Bureau, who sent them out to work on different farms in the country."[191] Others simply labeled as prostitutes black women arrested on charges that may or may not have been associated with prostitution: "Three colored prostitutes were arrested, charged with vagrancy, and were hired out to contractors to go into the country and work," and "Viney Springer, Mary Jane Springer, and Sarah Parker, colored nymphs *du pave*, were arrested for disorderly conduct and incarcerated."[192] These reports make clear the high price that freedwomen paid for these arrests; they were either imprisoned in the city jail or forced to leave the city and labor on plantations. Although some black women may well have been engaged in prostitution or criminal activity, there is evidence that many of these arrests were fraudulent and abusive. A "prominent citizen" reported one such case to the city's Republican newspaper. He had witnessed a white man "kicking a colored woman, who was calling loudly for a 'watch' [night watchman or police]. Soon a well known officer came running to the rescue, and without asking her for explanations, seized the woman, threw her down, slapped her in the face, dragged her on the ground and finally took her to the station-house and locked her up for disorderly conduct."[193] Other officers similarly as "well known" as the policeman described here made a practice of harassing, insulting, and abusing freedwomen. In fact, some of these same officers would be recognized by freedpeople among the men instigating the Memphis Riot, the murderous attack on the freed community that began on May 1, 1866.

One such policeman named Carrol appears to have been attempting to extort money from Amanda Olden, a freedwoman living in South Memphis, when he charged her with running a brothel just days before the Memphis Riot. Olden was not intimidated and complained of his harassment to the Freedmen's Bureau:

> On Sunday evening, April 29 [1866], one Carol or Carrol, a city police-man, came to my house, and compelled me to give him twenty-two dollars ($22) at the same time falsely charging me with keeping a house of ill-fame, and stating that it was not necessary for me to appear before the Re-corder of the City for trial, as he would attend to that matter himself, and pay any fine out of the money he thus took from me, which amount would just pay it. On Monday morning I appeared before the Recorder, ready for an investigation of these false charges, but this policeman did not ap-pear, nor had he made any report of this action in my case to his proper officer.[194]

Another police officer, John Egan, engaged in a similar extortion scheme, taking $50 from freedwoman Mollie Davis. Davis also reported Egan to the Freedmen's Bureau, recounting that he had insisted that she give him the cash as "forfeit money" after he arrested her.[195] It seems that through false charges against African American women, city police not only contributed to the representation of freedwomen as "lewd" in Memphis's public. They also at-tempted to use those representations to exploit individual freedwomen in ways that could be hidden from the public under the cloak of that same imagery. In these two cases, it appears that they were not successful. The provost marshal of freedmen assisted Olden in seeking redress, requesting of the city's mayor "that you have the Policeman Carrol refund the money or be dismissed from the Police Force."[196] Whether or not the mayor complied with his request in Carrol's case is unknown, but in the case of Egan, the bureau's actions led to his suspension from the police force in April 1866 and to the refunding of Davis's money.[197]

The actions of Officers Sweatt and Welch offer further evidence of police using arrests to denigrate the activities of black women in Memphis's public space rather than to punish real offenders. According to a complaint filed with the Freedmen's Bureau by three elite black men, Robert Church, C. C. Swears, and John Gains, who had attended a "negro ball," the two officers intruded into the party and "proceeded to arrest some two or three of the ladies" in attendance. The black men, familiar with this form of extortion, offered "to put up a forfeit" to prevent the arrests. In this case the police refused the money and insisted instead on placing the women in custody, actions that equally imputed a disreputable character to black women enjoying the privileges of "ladies" in public. Men from the party physically intervened and prevented the police from taking the women away. Unwilling to concede, Welch and Sweatt retreated to a nearby engine house seeking reinforcements. They soon returned with a group of armed white firemen, who "cocking their weapons demanded a surrender" and "behaved in a very rough and boisterous manner, crying 'shoot the damned niggers.' "[198] That the men and women attending this ball were apparently members of the city's small African American elite seems to have prevented violent incident and allowed the African Americans involved to reassert respectable gender identities as ladies and gentlemen. They received an apology from the firemen, who explained that Welch and Sweatt "had misrepresented the affair," and from the mayor, who responded to the provost marshal's complaint that such incidents were "becoming so frequent as to demand attention."[199]

After these conflicts with freedwomen and the Freedmen's Bureau, Officers Egan, Sweatt, and probably Carrol were identified as being among the white men who participated in the Memphis Riot.[200] These men's involvement in the riot suggests a connection between the everyday micro-struggles that freedwomen engaged in with police and the extensive, collective, and murderous hostility that city police and other white Memphians demonstrated toward freedpeople—and toward the changes in racial meanings and local governing power that their presence in the city's public indicated—during the riot. As freedwomen pursued their rights to enjoy free movement, work, and leisure in Memphis and as their pursuit was supported by the Freedmen's Bureau and by the presence and authority of black Union soldiers, they ran up against resistance from many whites. Certain white Memphians, such as police, city officials, and newspaper editors, sought instead to reassert their own control over the city's public and over the meanings for race signified by a free black presence in public. This white resistance to the rights of citizenship claimed by African Americans in various public arenas of Memphis would culminate in three days of deadly violence.

WHEN LOUIS HUGHES at last reached Memphis from the plantation in Mississippi where he was held as a slave during the war, he did not recognize the city. The presence of so many free black people, including black soldiers, in the city's streets represented, in an immediate and unmistakable fashion, how much and how rapidly the city's visible economy of race and citizenship had changed as a result of the Civil War. Many white Memphians did not recognize the city either. They no longer recognized themselves and their prewar privileges as white people in the organization of the city's public life. They saw instead African Americans taking on the rights and identities of "citizens," an appellation and social position that white Memphians had used to distinguish themselves from African Americans and from slaves. Most whites responded with hostility to the effacement of racial difference contained in what they observed around them. Their hostility toward freedpeople in the city mirrored national political battles over African American citizenship, as well as local conflicts between civilian and military authorities over control of the city. And their hostility was manifested in the violence and harassment with which white city police officers treated freedpeople, and in the images of unvirtuous black womanhood and manhood circulated by the city's conservative newspapers. In both police action and the conservative discourse of the press, white aggression against African Americans took gendered form. We will see in the next chapter how gendered representations of racial difference would be echoed in the words and actions of the men who violently attacked the freed community in Memphis during the three-day riot in 1866, and particularly in their actions surrounding the rape of black women.

CHAPTER TWO

A Riot and Massacre

On June 1, 1866, a former slave named Frances Thompson sat in a room in Memphis's Gayoso House hotel facing three U.S. congressmen and a stenographer. The congressmen formed a congressional investigating committee before whom Thompson had come to testify, and the stenographer was there to write down her words. Among the testimony he recorded was Thompson's recounting of how several weeks earlier, some time after 1:00 in the morning, seven white men broke into the house that she shared with another African American woman, Lucy Smith, and demanded "some woman to sleep with." "I said that we were not that sort of women, and they must go," Thompson testified. Yet her assertion was not heeded by the intruders. "All seven of the men violated us two," Thompson told the committee, describing how both she and Lucy Smith were raped.[1]

The assault on these two women in their home in the middle of the night was one of hundreds of incidents of collective violence against recently emancipated slaves that together became known as the Memphis Riot. The attacks commenced in the late afternoon of May 1, 1866, and persisted for three days. They took place primarily in the neighborhood of South Memphis,[2] and the assailants were mostly city policemen and the owners of small businesses such as grocery-saloons. Many of the attackers lived in South Memphis along with their victims.[3] The violence was the culmination of escalating tensions between a growing freed community and white Memphians, and above all between African American Union soldiers stationed at the federal army's Fort Pickering in South Memphis and white city police officers.

It is possible that many victims of the violence did not have the opportunity, as did Thompson, to record their experiences by testifying before the congressional committee or other federal officials. Those who were killed were, of course, unable to speak, and many others fled the city.[4] And some simply may not have come forward. But those who did testify presented evidence that the perpetrators of the riot killed at least 48 African Americans and wounded between 70 and 80 more.[5] They set fire to 91 houses and cabins, 4 African American churches, and all 12 schools that served African Americans in the city. They also burned down Caldwell Hall and threatened to burn the offices of the Freedmen's Bureau and of the *Memphis Daily Post*. They robbed at least 100 freedpeople and destroyed the food, clothing, furnishings, and other belongings of many more.[6] And the assailants in the attack also raped at least 5 freedwomen.[7]

Scholars have repudiated simple understandings of "riots" as spontaneous eruptions of violence among the "lower sorts" and instead have demonstrated across various locales and time periods how "riots" were often planned in advance and even at times were led or sponsored by local elites.[8] To understand the motivations and significance of "riots" to their perpetrators, historians have also mined the patterns and targets of violence, arguing, as Suzanne Desan has written, that for participants, "certain ritual patterns . . . fit their violence within a coherent symbolic context and endowed their actions with legitimacy and meaning."[9] Most recent accounts of the Memphis Riot concur, finding convincing evidence that the riot was a well-orchestrated attack. They have also found, through close examinations of the actions of rioters and how they targeted their attacks, evidence of clear political expression—arguing variously that the riot was an expression of white opposition to the power exercised by black Union soldiers in Memphis, of the resentment of upwardly mobile white immigrant residents of South Memphis toward the influx into their neighborhood of poor and unskilled former slaves, and of the efforts of Irish immigrants to "become white" through violence against black people.[10] But in these various efforts to interpret the political expression contained in the "ritual patterns" of this violence, the particular contours of sexual assault suffered by African American women remain largely unexplored.[11]

When historians of the riot do point to the occurrence of rape, it is usually for the purpose of highlighting the atrocities and terror that freedpeople suffered over those tumultuous three days.[12] Yet the sexual violence that occurred in the midst of this riot embodied more than extreme brutality. What follows is an attempt to read closely these incidents of coerced sex focusing on what they suggest about the "coherent symbolic context" of the Memphis Riot and specifically the nexus of racial and gendered meanings within which the perpetrators and to some extent the communities from which they sprang were immersed. This nexus of signification simultaneously provided the setting for sexual assault and was performed and rearticulated through it. And it shaped a perilous terrain upon which freedwomen would have to struggle to render freedom meaningful for themselves and their communities. For some, that struggle included testifying in a legal forum to the fact that they had been raped.

The Gendered Meanings of a "Race Riot"

The violence known as the Memphis Riot began as a clash between African American Union soldiers and city police. Since the initial occupation of Memphis by the federal army, these two groups had been on the front lines in the ongoing battle between civilian and military authorities over governance of the city. Soldiers had become increasingly incensed at the harassment and violence they suffered at the hands of police. In the last days of April, two cases of severe beatings of soldiers by police led to calls from the former for revenge if such practices were repeated.[13] "There was considerable excitement among [the soldiers] at the time," a surgeon with the Freedmen's Bureau observed. "They were talking on the corners pretty loud, . . . denouncing these things."[14] Given the escalating tensions, it would seem not to be a coincidence that several policemen waited until Tuesday, May 1, 1866, to provoke another major conflict with soldiers. This was the day after most black soldiers had been mustered out of service and forced to turn in their army weapons. This event was common knowledge in Memphis; plans to discharge all black soldiers still in the U.S. Army, and specifically to muster out the Third U.S. Colored Heavy Artillery in Memphis, had been announced ahead of time in the city's newspapers.[15] The police thus knew that on this day they would have the upper hand.

The violence began as a clash over a festive gathering of African Americans on South Street, a main thoroughfare of South Memphis and where much of the attacks over the next three days occurred. On Tuesday afternoon, several police officers interrupted an impromptu street party that had gathered outside several saloons near the intersection of South and Causey Streets. Here a large group comprised of black soldiers and freedwomen and children were "laughing and shouting and making considerable noise."[16] "Some of them [were] hallooing 'Hurrah for Abe Lincoln,' and so on," recalled Tony Cherry, a discharged soldier and participant in the celebration.[17] Under orders from Recorder John C. Creighton, who sat in a buggy nearby, and while watched by white civilians who were also present, most likely because they knew what was about to happen, the policemen stepped in.[18] "A policeman came along and told them to hush, and not to be hallooing in that way, and another policeman said, 'Your old father, Abe Lincoln, is dead and damned,'" Cherry remembered.[19] This policeman's insult of Lincoln, and by extension emancipation, led to a scuffle between police and soldiers, and the police quickly took two soldiers into custody. As the police began to retreat with these soldiers across the South Street Bridge, other soldiers fired pistols in the air or perhaps at the police.[20] On hearing these gunshots and seeing one police officer fall—his foot apparently slipped down between two planks on the bridge, causing him to shoot himself in the leg with his own gun—the police turned and, along with the other white men present, began shooting indiscriminately into the crowd.[21] Soldiers attempted to defend themselves, but only a few had weapons. "They were doing the best they could," noted Cherry, who himself did not have a gun, "but they had hardly anything to fight with; a good many of them who had pistols had no ammunition."[22] That the soldiers were indeed outgunned is evident in the fact that they neither injured nor killed any white men. Two white men did die in this first clash (the only two white men to be killed in the riot), but neither was shot by soldiers. The policeman who accidentally shot himself in the leg died from his wound. The other white man who was killed was shot by John Pendergrast, whose grocery sat on South Street near where the fighting began. Pendergrast was heard saying later, "We have killed one of our own men; I thought it was a damned yellow nigger."[23]

After an initial scattering following this first exchange of bullets, the police and white civilians from the neighborhood returned to South Street and commenced what was termed by a former Union Army doctor drawn to the scene by the sound of gunfire "an indiscriminate slaughter" of all black men in federal uniform.[24] Other African Americans were also attacked. One policeman was heard calling out, "Kill every nigger, no matter who, men or women."[25] Rumors that there was an uprising of African American soldiers in South Memphis quickly spread through the city, bringing other white men from surrounding areas into the neighborhood, armed and ready for a fight. Recorder Creighton was observed, now on horseback, encouraging participants in the crowd.[26] Well-known figures in the neighborhood, such as John Pendergrast and policeman David Roach, also appeared to be acting as ringleaders.[27] The shooting went on for several hours. By nightfall, Union Army officers from Fort Pickering arrived to quell the disturbance, forcibly dispersing any crowds they encountered and marshaling most black soldiers back into the fort. The army leadership calculated that keeping soldiers out of the city's streets would prevent further atrocities.[28] Thus most soldiers were held in the fort over the next few days against their will and despite the efforts of many to leave, rendered powerless to protect their families from the violence that ensued.[29]

Around ten o'clock that night, large numbers of white civilians together with police spread throughout South Memphis. They set fire to the buildings, cabins, and shanties where freedpeople lived and to the places where they gathered for leisure, study, and worship. Under the pretense of searching for weapons to preempt any further violence on the part of black soldiers who, they alleged, had instigated the initial fighting, these men also intruded into freedpeople's homes, brutalizing residents and beginning the looting, assault, murder, and rape that would continue until Thursday evening. Suggesting the complicity of many of these men's wives, sisters, and daughters in the attack on the freed community, witnesses noted two incidents where white women participated in stealing the belongings of freedpeople. These thefts occurred during daylight hours.[30] The bulk of the violence, though, was carried out at night and was the business of men.

The kind of brutality that occurred over the next seventy-two hours in Memphis defies explanation. Terms customarily used to attribute causes to historical events seem inadequate to the task of capturing the excesses and cruelty of the violence. Yet, there does appear to have been a logic to the attacks, one that cannot be reduced to their cause but which may nonetheless help to illuminate the nature of the political conflicts in which these events were embedded and the ideologies guiding perpetrators' actions. That logic was captured in the riot's opening scene: police responding with hostility toward a large, audible, and visible gathering of black men still wearing their federal uniforms celebrating with the women and children in their community that they were now free. The social revolution represented by this scene seems indeed to have been understood by at least one of the city's conservative papers to be the motive underlying the attacks. The primary lesson of the riot, according to the *Appeal*, was "the fact of the 'irrepressible conflict' that exists, deeply ingrained in human nature, whenever anything approaching to social equality of the black and white races is sought to be established. A political equality before the law . . . may be, and is accorded to the black man; but when the enfranchisement goes beyond this, and it is sought to establish a personal, social equality between the inferior and the superior races, the inextinguishable instincts . . . of the white race are awakened in their resistance to the innovation."[31] The Civil Rights Act passed by Congress just a few weeks earlier, which granted legal civil equality to African Americans, did not amount to "political equality before the law" as claimed here. But the relative freedom with which African Americans now moved throughout Memphis, the integration evident in the city's markets and saloons, the visibility of numerous schools in which former slaves were learning to read, and their proud celebrations of emancipation in the city's main squares did challenge white Memphians on a daily basis through social encounters that were not structured by racial inequality. These encounters, rather, displayed a form of "social equality" and an initial realization of the everyday meanings of universal citizenship. The legitimating ideology evident throughout the violence of the riot was indeed "resistance to the innovation" of equality in everyday public life. City police and the local city government and community they represented were, it seems, engaged in a major offensive in their ongoing battle with military authorities over rule in and of the city, and specifically over meanings for race signified by activity in the city's streets and other public spaces.

This offensive was framed, in part, through gendered language and imagery. This can be seen not only in that black Union soldiers—symbols of an empowered masculinity that, at least in public space, had previously been reserved for whites—were consistent targets of violence, but also in how men participating in the violence represented their actions. Calls to "drive all the Yankees out of town" and to "kill every damned nigger" were accompanied by claims that it was black men who were shooting and that white men acted only to restore order.[32] Rumors that the violence was a defensive reaction to an uprising of criminal, out-of-control black men made their way into the conservative press. Reports in newspapers printed as the violence was ongoing depicted black Union soldiers as the aggressors in a "negro riot" and justified all outrages committed by whites as a legitimate response to the "lawless aggression on the part of the vicious negroes infesting South Memphis" and to "the disorderly and overbearing conduct of some of the negro soldiers who have recently been mustered out of service."[33] When the dust

"Scenes in Memphis, Tennessee, during the Riot." Sketch by Alfred R. Waud, *Harper's Weekly*, May 26, 1866, 321. Courtesy of the Library of Congress.

settled and the responsibility of white men for much of the violence was inescapable, the press then depicted what had occurred as a necessary re-action by white city residents to the overall domination of Memphis by black Union soldiers, whom they continued to represent as ignorant and brutish men. "The late riots in our city have satisfied all of one thing, that the *southern man* will not be ruled by *the negro*," wrote the editor of the *Memphis Daily Avalanche*, claiming manhood and southern citizenship for white men only. This editorial, printed the day after the violence had stopped, attributed the source of the "trouble" to the "insolence" of "negro troops," "brutes" who mistakenly believed that they could "manage things their own way." This language contrasted with that used for white men, who were referred to as "citizens" and "our people," those who sought "order, confidence, and the good will of old days," and "a restoration of the old order of things." In this way rioters themselves played the role of defenders of the city and acted out a courageous white manhood in juxtaposition to the allegedly unrestrained and criminal masculinity of black soldiers. This editorial concluded, "Thank Heaven, the white race are once more rulers of Memphis."[34]

The logic justifying violent actions by white men against black men during the riot—that this violence represented necessary resistance to an illegitimate federal occupation of the city and the supposed domination of black Union soldiers—also appears to have been at work justifying, and shaping, violence against women. Ann Freeman later recounted to a Freedmen's Bureau agent that a party of white men broke into her home and declared that "they were going to kill all the women they caught with soldiers or with soldiers' things."[35] Directing violence against black women who were connected to black soldiers was made particularly evident in the case of rape. Four of the survivors of rape during the riot were connected to soldiers in ways that figured prominently in the women's recollections of what they had suffered.

One of these women was Lucy Tibbs. Tibbs was not sure of her age but believed that she had been about twenty-one years old when she came to Memphis from Arkansas soon after the Civil War broke out.[36] She came to the city with her husband, who by 1866 had found work on a steamboat and was away from home much of the time. She lived on Rayburn Avenue close to the corner of South Street with her two small children—ages two and five—and was nearly five months pregnant with her third. She was out on South Street around 6:00 in the evening when she heard the first shootings over on the South Street Bridge. "They broke and run in every direction, boys and men, with pistols, firing at every black man and boy they could see," she later testified.[37] About 100 yards from where she stood, she could see grocery owner Pendergrast and other white men shooting unarmed black soldiers as they attempted to flee. " 'Look here,' " she remembered crying out, " 'see John Pendergrast shooting down innocent men in that way.' " As these same men began "going from house to house" to search, she presumed, for other black soldiers, she urged Bob Taylor, her older brother who had been a member of the 59th U.S. Colored Infantry stationed in Memphis, to flee. He tried to run but was found dead the next morning near the bayou in back of Tibbs's house. Later that night, "a crowd of men" broke into her one-room home and stole $300 that had belonged to Taylor. One of these men raped her while "the other men were plundering the house." She later speculated that she had not been randomly chosen for attack: "I think they were folks who knew all about me, who knew that my brother had not long been out of the army and had money."[38]

Harriet Armour came to Memphis as a slave before the Civil War began. After the war, she married an African American Union soldier; he was among those held in Fort Pickering during the three days of violence. She lived on South Street, around the corner from Lucy Tibbs, and she, too, watched the initial clashes and killings of Tuesday evening. Early Wednesday morning, two armed men came to her door; one was a young man named Dunn who ran a grocery store on South Street near the South Street Bridge.[39] Molly Hayes, a white widow who had recently moved to Memphis from Georgia and lived in an adjacent room, overheard these men confronting Armour: "There were two men who came there and asked her where her husband was. She said he was in the fort. They said, 'Is he a soldier?' She said, 'Yes.' . . . The last word I heard him say was, 'Shut the door.' "[40] Armour testified that after they barred her door shut, they both raped her: "Mr. Dunn had to do with me twice and the other man once, which was the same as three."[41]

Sixteen-year-old Lucy Smith had been raised in slavery in Memphis. Frances Thompson, who was ten years older, had been a slave in Maryland. At the time of the riot, Smith and Thompson shared a South Memphis home on Gayoso Street and supported themselves by taking in sewing, washing, and ironing. Between 1:00 and 2:00 in the morning on Wednesday, Smith and Thompson awoke when seven white men, two of whom were police officers, forced their way into their house. Over the course of the next four hours ("it was near getting day when they left"), these men threatened, assaulted, and robbed them. The assailants took all of their money ($100 that Thompson had saved and another $200 she was holding for a friend) and clothes ("They took three silk dresses of mine and a right nice one of Lucy's," Thompson reported) and dumped their food into the bayou outside their house. Smith testified that one of these men also choked and then raped her, and that another began to rape her but stopped before he had. Thompson recounted being beaten by one of the rioters and raped by four. Thompson and Smith also both remembered that the rioters noticed quilts they had been sewing using red, white, and blue fabric. "You niggers have a mighty liking for the damned Yankees," Smith recalled one of the intruders saying, apparently unsettled by these women displaying patriotic symbols of the national government. The men demanded to know for whom the quilts were being made, and, Thompson later testified, "When we told them we made them for the soldiers they swore at us, and said the soldiers would never have them on their beds, and they took them away with the rest of the things." The men had also noticed pictures of white Union Army officers in the room (one was of General Joseph Hooker, commander of the Army of the Potomac, perhaps belonging to Thompson, who came from this region). Smith later remembered, "They said they would not have hurt us so bad if it had not been for these pictures."[42]

Some of the perpetrators of sexual assault, then, explicitly articulated their actions as springing from resentment toward Union military authorities and black Union soldiers—soldiers who had defeated them and now occupied their city. Yet it was not only because of their relationship to soldiers that freedwomen were attacked. Incidents of sexual violence during these gruesome days in Memphis also suggest ways in which perpetrators sought to enact particular relations with freedwomen themselves. These relations seemed to conjure up the perpetrators' image of the status quo ante—an antebellum era very much at odds with postemancipation developments where, as we have seen, black women dramatically entered public space as active citizens rather than being cast as marginal women who were available sexual objects for white men.

The sexual assaults described by witnesses were far from abrupt acts of sexual aggression. Instead they often involved elaborate scenes that simulated the appearance, at least at first, of normal solicitations for illicit sex—that is, normative exploitation rather than violent acts of domination. Many perpetrators began these scenes with casual, even seemingly perfunctory requests for sex, as if the women they confronted were likely to have been amenable or even indifferent to anonymous sex with white men.[43] For instance, Lucy Smith recalled that the men who broke into her and Frances Thompson's home in the middle of the night at first demanded that they be served supper: "They told us to get up and get some supper for them. We got up, and made a fire and got them supper."[44] Thompson similarly recounted the rioters saying "they must have some eggs, and ham, and biscuit. I made them some biscuit and strong coffee, and they all sat down and ate."[45] When they were finished eating, the intruders announced that "they wanted some woman to sleep with." Thompson recounted that it was when she insisted that she and Smith "were not that sort of women" that the men physically attacked her and asserted that Thompson's attempt to claim her own identity—that she was a free woman with the capacity to refuse sex, not a sexual servant, as the perpetrators identified her—"didn't make a damned bit of difference."[46] Smith also refused the rioters' demand and the identity they imputed to her. She testified that when "they tried to take advantage of me, . . . I told them that I did not do such things, and would not." In response, one of the men "said he would make me."[47] It was then that these men "drew their pistols and said they would shoot us and fire the house if we did not let them have their way with us."[48] First placing an order for food, then one for sex, the intruders' initial demeanor suggested almost nonchalance, as if the women would have no reason to refuse. They acted as if Thompson and Smith were "waiter girls" in a concert saloon or prostitutes in a brothel. When the women refused to participate in their fantasy by refusing to have sex, the intruders imposed it through threats and physical violence.

A freedwoman named Elvira Walker was alone, she told the congressional committee, on the night of May 2 when "some men came and knocked at my door." The men first stated that they were searching for weapons, presuming, it seems, that Walker might have been the wife of a soldier or veteran. Then "one of them put his hands into my bosom. I tried to stop him, and he knocked down my hands with his pistol, and did it again. He may have been searching for money. He then said there was $5 forfeit money, and that [otherwise] I must come to the station-house with him."[49] This demand for cash (strikingly similar to Officer Carrol's attempted extortion of Amanda Olden a few days earlier)[50] suggests that this man was a member of the police force. Were robbery his only object, he would presumably have simply demanded Walker's money and not asked for a certain amount and deemed it a "forfeit." Instead, he staged a scene in which Walker was accused of being a prostitute who, now caught, had to pay a fine—a bribe really—or go to jail. Whether or not Walker's home was a place of prostitution—and there was no evidence of that—the intruder insisted that it was. That was the role of free black women, it seems, in the Memphis he envisaged.

These same intruders then entered the room adjoining Walker's, where Peter and Rebecca Ann Bloom had been sleeping, and continued to insist that this was a house of prostitution. They forced Peter into Walker's room and then demanded that he go out and obtain the $5 needed to avoid Walker's arrest.[51] One intruder remained behind. As Rebecca Ann Bloom recounted, "He wanted to know if I had anything to do with white men. I said no. He held a knife in his hand, and said that he would kill me if I did not let him do as he wanted to. I refused. He said, 'By God, you must,' and then he got into bed with me, and violated my person, him still holding the knife."[52] The man who raped Bloom, like those who attacked Thompson and Smith, first solicited her for sex and then employed force when his request was rejected. "To do with," a phrase also used by Harriet Armour and Frances Thompson in their testimony, was a common colloquial term for intercourse.[53] By asking Bloom if she had sex with "white men," the assailant indicated his presumption that Bloom was a prostitute used to being visited by "white men." The question at the very least implied that Bloom was an unscrupulous woman, especially given that she was married, her husband having just been dragged from the bed in which she still lay and being at one point close enough to have "heard them trying to ravish my wife."[54] There was no basis for the assailant's projections that Bloom was accustomed to having sex with white men other than her blackness. When Bloom refused to play the role of a woman available for illicit sex with an anonymous white man, she was forced to under the threat of deadly violence.

The narratives framing these sexual assaults were not ones of hurting un-willing women—which may have been more central to sexual assaults within other contexts such as war[55]—but, rather, of engaging in illicit or casual sex with women likely to be amenable to solicitation by white men and who would have had no reason to resist. By speaking and acting with a seemingly non-chalant or normative discourse of sexual exploitation toward the women they assaulted, the assailants cast the victims as prostitutes or "loose" women or, instead, simply as women in such a low and vulnerable position in the social hierarchy that they were used to having to acquiesce to demands for sex from more powerful men, whether in the hope of material benefit or from fear of retribution or, as in the case of slaves, because they simply lacked the power to refuse.[56] Most of the women assaulted made clear they were no longer under any such obligation, if they ever had been. Yet the assailants acted as if all black women were, as if the world had not been fundamentally altered with eman-cipation and the empowered black presence now evident throughout the public spaces of the city. The assailants thereby asserted, through their words and gestures, that emancipation was of no significance and that black women continued to be different from white women—at least those deemed "honor-able"—who were (in principle and to some degree reality) protected from sexual exploitation by patriarchal family structures and the rights of citizens.[57]

Not only did women's words, and at times physical resistance, interrupt the attackers' violent fantasies, but so did their tears. Harriet Armour remem-bered one of the men who raped her objecting to her crying. This man, whose name was Dunn, tried to force her into having oral sex. "Then Mr. Dunn tried to make me suck him. I cried. He asked what I was crying about, and tried to make me suck it."[58] Crying would not be appropriate if this kind of sex were normal for Armour; nor was crying, it seems, a desirable end for Dunn (as it might have been in certain acts of rape foregrounding harm and humiliation of resistant women).[59] In a seemingly similar effort to envisage normative sexual exploitation rather than violence, one of the men who broke into the home of Lucy Tibbs, who was pregnant, objected to the conduct of another man when he began to rape her. Tibbs remembered him saying, " 'Let that woman alone'—that she was not in any situation to be doing that." Although he seemed to object to rape, his words also implied that had Tibbs not been pregnant, it would have been acceptable for her to have sex with a stranger in front of other strange men. As well, his choice of the active voice to describe Tibbs in this moment—"*she* was not in any situation to be *doing* that"—seemed to belie her lack of consent to sexual intercourse.[60]

However acceptable and normal sexual exploitation of black women was supposed to be in the assailants' imaginations, this did not prevent the attackers from threatening and inflicting horrific violence when their racist terms were resisted. "One of them . . . choked me by the neck," Lucy Smith remembered. "My neck was swollen up next day, and for two weeks I could not talk to anyone. After the first man had connexion with me, another got hold of me and tried to violate me, but I was so bad he did not. He gave me a lick with his fist and said I was so damned near dead he would not have anything to do with me. . . . I bled from what the first man had done to me. I was injured right smart. . . . They were in the house a good while after they hurt me, but I lay down on the bed, for I thought they had killed me. . . . I was in bed two weeks after."[61] The women surviving rape experienced prolonged physical pain and terror. Each rape was ultimately carried out through violence or threats of death that belied the casual and matter-of-fact discourse of normative exploitation that the perpetrators articulated.

Placing this sexual violence in the context of postemancipation struggles over the meaning of race and freedom, including the conflicts over public space in Memphis leading to the riot, further suggests the impetus, conscious or otherwise, for envisaging free black women as free only to occupy the marginal spaces that had been granted to people of color under slavery, not to secure a more meaningful freedom as that promised by legal equality. The discourse of rape was in this sense parallel to that of the conservative white press prior to the riot that had identified virtually all black women as "loose," "lewd," or prostitutes and that implied that they were the "sort of women" who had no role in a legitimate public as active citizens. This discourse drawing on gendered constructions of racial difference was already deeply embedded in the world of white opponents of Reconstruction in Memphis, including those who participated in the violence. The white men who raped freedwomen during the Memphis Riot enacted a fantasy of social subordination that echoed an existing gendered discourse of racial inequality, one that had already politicized gender identities in contests over the meaning of race and citizenship in the context of legally imposed equality.

Opposition to racial integration in the context of equality was evident in other incidents of violence during the riot. For instance, on the first night of the attack, a group of men broke into Grady's Dance Hall, the grocery and saloon in South Memphis run by Mary Grady and popular among freedpeople as well as white Union soldiers and other residents of the area. Both white and black soldiers also often rented rooms from Grady and her husband. Earlier in the evening, Mary Grady had intervened to stop a white man from shooting a black man who was one of her renters. When a group of men returned to her establishment later that night, they verbally abused Grady, emptied her cash box, and threatened to kill her. They justified this violence by calling her establishment a "nigger resort" and a "nigger ball-room." Rioters apparently identified Grady, though a white woman, as an enemy of their community, someone who defied and confused racial hierarchies through her business relations ("there were a great many colored people who thought a heap of us, and they would come here often") and her political beliefs ("I have never been secesh in my life and never intend to be"). These same men also attempted to molest both Grady's ten-year-old daughter and a black woman who was sleeping alongside her in a back room. The men were prevented from getting into bed with the woman and child by the approach of several discharged white Union soldiers who had been sleeping in another room. Apparently even white children were not protected from sexual assault in contexts that embraced "social equality."[62]

Another white woman whose relations with black people suggested racial integration on equal terms—she had married Henry Bankett, a black Union soldier—also suffered violence from rioters. A white man named Charles Lloyd, seeing a group of white men heading toward the Banketts' house, asked them "what was up now." One of them replied that "there was a white woman down there living with a negro."[63] These men invaded the Banketts' home, destroyed their furniture, and set their house on fire. When Mrs. Bankett attempted to go into the burning house to save some of her possessions, the men threatened to set her ablaze.[64] The symbol of legitimate interracial relations and family, the Banketts' home, went up in flames.

The possibility of a "respectable" sexual relationship between whites and blacks also appears to have been the object of violence when a crowd of men threatened David T. Egbert, a white man from Illinois who kept a saloon in South Memphis. Egbert lived in the saloon with "a yellow woman" (a light-skinned woman of mixed African and European descent) who, according to his landlord, A. N. Edmunds, "was there all the time." That Egbert's relationship with this woman was more than a passing affair seemed to disturb Edmunds, who said repeatedly to the committee that Egbert was "sleeping in her room with her, staying all the while," and "sleeping with this yellow woman every night." On the first night of the riot, Egbert was surrounded on the street by men who called him "a damned abolition son-of-a-bitch" and threatened him with a pistol. Other men threatened to burn down his saloon. Edmunds reported to the investigating committee that "the common talk" among those participating in the violence had been that "a man who lived there with negroes would not be safe." Needless to say, a white man having sexual intercourse with a black woman did not, in and of itself, disturb Edmunds or the men who attacked Egbert. Rather, their objection stemmed from the legitimate—as opposed to exploitative and illicit—appearance of this relationship. In this postemancipation moment, when the potential meanings of race and of the citizenship granted to former slaves were so uncertain, so variously promising and threatening, the combination of Egbert's northern origins and his regular, live-in relationship with this woman, one that appeared as a marriage and accorded her a certain status and identity as "respectable" and thereby suggested a postemancipation world in which racial hierarchies might be undermined rather than reinscribed, earned him the rioters' wrath.[65]

Freedwomen who had used the law to challenge white men were also at risk during the riot. Recall policeman John Egan's attempt to extort money from Mollie Davis and Davis's successful action against him.[66] Davis told the congressional investigating committee that "[Egan] is mad with me because I had him arrested. Egan arrested me, and I had to put up fifty dollars forfeit money. Egan had to pay me back the fifty dollars forfeit, and he had to pay twenty dollars costs, and he was turned off [from the police force] for getting money under false pretenses. This is what he was mad about." Davis guessed that the riot offered an opportunity for Egan to take revenge. "During the riot, I kept close, for I knew John Egan would kill me if he saw me."[67] Egan did indeed seek Davis out. He came to her house on the first night of the violence and banged on the door, demanding that Davis open it. Seeing it was Egan through a window, Davis's roommate Ellen Brown refused. He threatened to burn the house down but left without incident; his partner policeman Clark told a neighbor that "they were coming down the next night to burn us out." The house and all of Davis's and Brown's belongings were consumed in flames twenty-four hours later.[68]

Freedwomen Testify

The Memphis Riot finally ended on Thursday, May 3, when federal troops spread throughout the city.[69] By that time the murderous events of the past three days had drawn national attention. Radical Republicans in Washington, D.C., took particular note. On May 14, 1866, Congressman Thaddeus

Stevens, a leader of this group opposing President Andrew Johnson's conservative Reconstruction measures, proposed to Congress that a congressional committee go to Memphis "to make an investigation into all matters connected with the recent bloody riots in that city."[70] This proposal came in the midst of contentious political debates in Washington about the future of Reconstruction policy. Only weeks before the riot, Congress had passed the civil rights bill over Johnson's veto, and, just after, the House had opened debate on the Fourteenth Amendment.[71] Radical Republicans looked to this investigation to provide support for their position that stronger federal intervention into the affairs of southern states was needed in order to protect the rights and lives of freedpeople.

Stevens's plan was adopted. A House select committee composed of Elihu B. Washburne of Illinois and John M. Broomall of Pennsylvania, both Republicans, and George S. Shanklin of Kentucky, a Democrat, arrived in Memphis on May 22.[72] Once there, the committee found that both the Freedmen's Bureau and a military commission under the charge of General George Stoneman, Union Army commander in Memphis at the time, had already collected testimony from freedpeople and others who observed or were injured in the rioting.[73] Two days after he arrived, Washburne wrote to Thaddeus Stevens, "We have got to work, and it is plain to see we have a long job before us. We are aided, however, very much by the examinations already made by General Stoneman and the Freedmen's Bureau."[74] The committee used names taken from the findings of these previous inquiries to call some of these and additional witnesses before its own hearings; many other witnesses volunteered to testify.[75] Over thirteen days, the committee heard from 164 individuals, 66 of whom were black and 98 of whom were white.[76] It is not possible to know exactly how many freedpeople had already spoken to the other investigating bodies, but in addition to those who also appeared before the congressional committee, there were approximately 22 before the military commission and 178 before the Freedmen's Bureau.[77]

The more than 250 African Americans who came before these bodies to testify exercised a key right of citizenship still denied them in city and state courts.[78] Their version of events, moreover, refuted the images that had been emerging from the front and editorial pages of the city's conservative papers for weeks of a riot caused by the overbearing and violent behavior of unruly black Union soldiers. Particularly for the freedwomen who testified about sexual violence, the federal government offered forums of unprecedented state power in which to articulate new public identities as citizens and to counter racist constructions of black womanhood.[79] African American women testifying that they had been raped was a radical act within the context of southern state law and tradition that had negated the possibility that black women could be raped. Postemancipation imagery of freedwomen as devoid of feminine "virtue" drew upon this prewar exclusion of black women from the category of "women" who could be raped. When black women represented their experience of coerced sexual intercourse with white men as a violation of their will, they asserted a claim to the status of "woman" and "citizen." In the process, they would also counter conventional perspectives on the proper response of a virtuous woman to sexual assault.

Freedwomen employed language of violation and harm that identified assailants' actions as rape. Rebecca Ann Bloom maintained before the Freedmen's Bureau that the man who got into bed with her had "violated my person, by having connexion with me."[80] Before the congressional committee, Frances Thompson affirmed that she and Lucy Smith were "violated" by the men who intruded into their home.[81] Lucy Smith chose similar words to describe rioters' actions: they "tried to violate me . . . [and] they hurt me."[82] When asked by Congressman Washburne whether the men who plundered her home had hurt her, Lucy Tibbs responded, "They done a very bad act," and confirmed Washburne's assumption that by this she meant that they had "ravish[ed]" her.[83] Freedwomen also recounted their fear. Harriet Armour recalled how she cried but was too terrified to call for help.[84] Lucy Smith believed that there were seven men who came into her house on the night she was raped, but "I was so scared I could not be certain."[85] Lucy Tibbs recounted that "I was so scared I could not tell whether they were policemen or not" and described begging her assailants to leave her and her children in peace.[86] This testimony resisted the meanings that assailants had attempted to stage during the riot. It also inverted the conservative discourse of unruly black soldiers by showing white men, not black, acting in inappropriately aggressive and criminal fashion.[87]

Some of the women who testified had to defend their honor in the face of hostile and insinuating questioning from members of the committee. After answering in the affirmative Washburne's question, "Did they ravish you?" Lucy Tibbs still had to contend with the committee's apparent doubt. Washburne continued, "Did they violate your person against your consent?" to which Tibbs again insisted, "Yes Sir. I had just to give up to them. They said they would kill me if I did not." Washburne again suggested the possibility that the attack was somehow a product of Tibbs's own conduct: "Were you dressed or undressed when these men came to you?" She stated that she was dressed. "Did you make any resistance?" the chair then asked. Tibbs responded by sharing with him the information she had used to calculate her safest course of action. "No sir; the house was full of men. I thought they would kill me; they had stabbed a woman near by the night before." Tibbs had heard others report that this same woman had also been raped.[88] Believing that resistance might result in her own death, Tibbs surrendered to the assailant physically. But in the committee's hearing room she resisted both the rioters' and the congressmen's insinuations that what happened in some way reflected her consent and therefore cast shame on herself.

Harriet Armour also underwent challenging questioning by the committee. She recounted that she had seen no possibility of escape from the men who attacked her, because one of these men had barred her door shut. Washburne then asked, "What did he do with the window?" Armour explained that she could not have fled through the window because two slats were nailed across it. "And you made no resistance?" he asked. "No," she answered, repeating that "they had barred the door. I could not get out, and I could not help myself." Yet the suspicions persisted. "Did I understand you that you did not try to prevent them from doing these things to you?" Congressman Broomall asked in disbelief. "Could not the people outside have come to help you?" Armour tried again to explain her strategy to survive the attack: "No, sir; I did not know what to do. I was there alone, was weak and sick, and thought I would rather let them do it than to be hurt or punished. . . . I should have been afraid to call [for help]. . . . I thought I had just better give up freely; I did not like to do it, but I thought it would be best for me."[89] Both Armour and Tibbs had yielded to the rioters' demands in order to prevent further violence and, in the case of Tibbs, perhaps to protect her children.[90] Yet their judgment of what to do in such a situation did not conform to the patriarchal framework within which the elite white men on the committee appear to have imagined rape. The congressmen's questioning implied that even under the threat of potentially deadly force, anything but ceaseless resistance to sexual violation raised questions about a woman's "virtue."

Washburne and Broomall may have sincerely doubted Armour's and Tibbs's testimony that they had been raped, because it seemed to these men that the women had not resisted enough.[91] It is also possible that the Republican congressmen's questions were intended to elicit further details so as to shape the testimony in ways that would best represent the women's claims before a national audience. This is suggested by the fact that the hostile questioning came from the two Republican members of the committee, while Shanklin, the committee's minority Democrat who showed frequent support for white southerners during his questioning of witnesses, did not ask any questions about rape. In either case, when faced with the congressmen's apparent uneasiness about their testimony, Armour and Tibbs defended their actions. They made clear that, as much as they had suffered from the rapes they experienced, they did not share the assumption that rape would damage them in ways worth risking death to prevent. Nor did they accept the implications of the rioters, that their submission implied that they were marginal and powerless women with no virtue and thus no capacity or reason to resist illicit sex. Armour and Tibbs both firmly maintained that despite physical acquiescence, the sex occurred against their will. To defend their honor and represent the events as violation, the women struggled to make intelligible to the committee a perspective that grew out of their experiences during the riot, and perhaps out of their experiences as slaves. They had recently lived under a system of slavery in which many women faced a grim choice between submitting to coerced sexual intercourse with white men or risking other physical harm to themselves and their loved ones. By inserting black women's experiences of and perspectives on sexual violence into public discourse, they challenged the prevailing discourse of rape and also of honorable womanhood. To them, in this context, honor depended more on surviving a horrific experience of violence and violation and protesting its injustice than on privileging and protecting a patriarchal notion of women's sexual "virtue."

Perhaps Armour's persistence in demonstrating, under hostile insinuation, that her strategy for survival in no way reflected her own dishonor stemmed from the fact that she had already suffered from another's sense that she was less valuable as a woman as a result of the attack. Cynthia Townsend, a freedwoman and neighbor of Armour's, testified that "when [Armour's husband] came out of the fort, and found what had been done, he said he would not have anything to do with her any more." Other freedpeople were more sympathetic. Townsend herself described what the rioters did to Armour as "very bad acts" and offered her opinion to the committee that Armour had no culpability for what had happened. Nonetheless, it was clear that Armour suffered enormously from her husband's rejection. "She has sometimes been a little deranged since then," Townsend explained.[92] In her testimony, Armour moved from subject to subject quickly, suggesting that recounting these stories was particularly difficult for her, more difficult than it appeared to be for the other women who testified about rape. She segued directly from her description of Dunn's efforts to force her to perform fellatio to "I have not got well since my husband went away," thus connecting the attack with her husband's departure.[93]

Armour was the only woman testifying to indicate any ostracism by a member of their community as a result of rape.[94] It is possible that Armour's experience was exacerbated by the fact that she was attacked in daylight and thus suspected that others were aware of what was being done to her. Referring to her white neighbors, Armour told the committee, "They knew about as much about it as I did. Molly Hayes knew it was going on. . . . It was an open shanty, and they could see right in."[95] The fact of oral penetration was also known and talked about in the neighborhood. When Henry Porter, a black barber and grocery keeper living nearby was asked by the investigating committee if he knew of any "acts of violence committed on women," he answered, "I did not know it to see it, but it was done close by our house. . . . Harriet, I believe is her name. Some three or four or five men had to do with her, and afterwards made her suck them."[96] Washburne then asked, "Was it understood that this was going on with Harriet on the outside?" Porter answered, "Yes, sir. I learned of it from a colored man. He told me they were in there with the colored woman."[97] The fact that Armour understood her ordeal to have been a public spectacle of sorts may have been a factor in her devastation; it may have alienated her from her community and contributed to her husband's rejection.

What is so striking, then, is the courage that Armour showed coming forward to tell this story again in another public setting, the congressional hearing. There was no practical need for Armour or other women to discuss sexual assaults in order to condemn the rioters. When Armour, Lucy Tibbs, Lucy Smith, and Frances Thompson testified before this committee, they all reported theft and battery in addition to rape. That they chose to recount having suffered sexual violence, despite the risks involved, suggests that this testimony served ends important to them: the public condemnation of and protest against these acts as violation and the implicit affirmation of their identities as free women with the will to choose or refuse sexual relations and with the right to be protected by law. In light of the police harassment of black women in Memphis and of the conservative pre-riot discourse that imputed dishonorable gendered identities to African American women, both of which discounted black women's rights to citizenship, these women's public assertions of honor and demands for legal protection appear as important political acts in the struggle of African Americans to realize their freedom.[98]

Freedwomen's courage shown in making their suffering public received the support of the Republican majority of the congressional investigating committee. Despite the committee's hostile questioning, freedwomen's narratives served Republican interests in representing southern white men as "unreconstructed" and thus unworthy of self-rule. The committee majority's final report highlighted the rape of African American women to depict the white rioters as uncivilized and dishonorable men. Eleven thousand copies of the report were printed, and it was excerpted in newspapers across the country.[99] Describing the riot as "an organized and bloody massacre of the colored people of Memphis," this report read, "The crowning acts of atrocity and diabolism committed during these terrible nights were the ravishing of five different colored women by these fiends in human shape. . . . It is a singular fact, that while this mob was breathing vengeance against the negroes and shooting them down like dogs, yet when they found unprotected colored women they at once 'conquered their prejudices,' and proceeded to violate them under circumstances of the most licentious brutality."[100] To bolster this representation of the rape of black women as the ultimate atrocity of the riot, the authors described the victims as "defenceless and terror-stricken women."[101] They also assured readers that Lucy Smith was "a girl of modest demeanor and highly respectable in appearance." They described Lucy Tibbs as "intelligent and well-appearing" and noted that both Harriet Armour and Tibbs were married—and thus legitimate—women, and that Tibbs had two young children and was pregnant with her third.[102] Through these images of female respectability, the committee's majority sought to preempt doubts about these women's legitimacy as victims of sexual assault.[103] Once freedwomen's narratives concerning rape entered the arena of national politics, their words were forced into a discourse of womanhood and "virtue" not of their own choosing.[104]

After the congressional investigation, no rioters were arrested or charged with any crimes. General Stoneman explained to Washburne that he had been instructed to "take no further steps until orders are rec'd from Washington." When those orders were not forthcoming, he lamented, "No heavy hand has yet fallen upon the murderers. I greatly fear they will escape all punishment."[105] Less surprisingly, local authorities also failed to move against the rioters. Instead, the city's Board of Mayor and Aldermen approved compensation for some police officers who claimed they had been injured "endeavoring to suppress the Riot then going on between the whites and the blacks."[106] Thus, neither federal nor local officials acted on behalf of freedpeople beyond documenting the events.

Nonetheless, freedwomen's testimony had a profound effect on local and national politics. The conservative press in Memphis was silenced by the overwhelming evidence of violence enacted by white men presented by the committee's report. The conservative *Appeal*, earlier full of condemnations of black women as deceitful, disreputable, and depraved, offered no immediate critique of the freedwomen who testified that they had been raped.[107] Furthermore, freedwomen's testimony helped to promote several state and national measures that extended greater protection and political power to African Americans during Reconstruction. The riot provided the final piece of evidence marshaled to help pass the metropolitan police bill in the Tennessee state legislature. This act, placing control of the city police in the hands of a commission appointed by the governor, led to the dismissal of the entire force, whose members had spearheaded the riot, and to the end of the career of Recorder of the Police Court John C. Creighton, who had been a thorn in the side of all African Americans in Memphis as well as a leading force in the violence.[108] More broadly still, the congressional committee's report on the Memphis Riot, along with other reports of widespread racial violence in the South, helped undermine support for President Johnson's conservative approach to the former Confederate states and to the passage instead of the far more radical Reconstruction Acts in Congress.[109]

African American women in Memphis had publicly asserted their rights and identities as citizens. And their testimony about having been raped during the riot had, at least temporarily, changed public discourse. Their words had circulated narratives of decent and patriotic black women and men not responsible for the disorder plaguing the city or for the riot but, rather, protecting themselves against the depraved violence and seemingly backward-looking racist imagination of criminally violent white men. Undaunted by the setting of a congressional hearing, or by challenging questions from their interrogators, freedwomen had also secured official recognition of the fact that black women —regardless of past condition of enslavement, of poverty, of having chosen to save their lives rather than resist violation—could be and had been raped.

TWO WEEKS AFTER the end of the riot, a Meeting of the Colored Citizens of Helena met in that city in Arkansas. William Henry Grey, a prominent black leader in Helena, served as the meeting's secretary. This gathering had been called for the purpose of conferring with the general superintendent of freedmen's schools, but the participants took the opportunity to express their outrage over the recent violence in Memphis and their support for its victims.

The meeting passed a resolution stating, "That we enter our solemn protest against the wholesale murder of helpless and unarmed men, women and children in Memphis and call upon all good men everywhere to denounce [it]." This meeting occurred before the congressional committee had begun taking testimony in Memphis, and thus before the rape of five black women during the riot was widespread knowledge. If they had not yet heard of this aspect of the riot, doubtless Grey and his companions would learn of it soon, when the committee majority's report was published on the front pages of the *Memphis Daily Post*. The gathering in Helena also passed a resolution promising to "patronize . . . and aid in [the *Post's*] widest circulation."[110]

This meeting in Helena suggests that the freedwomen and freedmen who testified about the violence they suffered during the Memphis Riot were not engaged in a singular conversation with congressmen or representatives of the Freedmen's Bureau. They were participating in a regionwide effort and protest against the violence freedpeople were suffering after the Civil War. The representations of black women raped by white men and of black women's "virtue," too, were not limited to the committee's hearing room in Memphis. William Henry Grey himself would speak publicly against this kind of violence as part of his effort to secure a meaningful citizenship for former slaves. The next chapter turns to these efforts on the part of Grey and his colleagues in Arkansas, and more generally to the process of enfranchising black men during congressional Reconstruction that followed from northern outrage over white southern violence such as that during the Memphis Riot. Thus in addition to moving our story to a new locale, the next chapter will also move from contests over race and citizenship in urban public space to another realm of public rights, that of the multiple public spheres of political discourse and action operating around electoral politics. Here, too, struggles over who would practice citizenship and how, and over what such practices would indicate about the meaning of race in the postemancipation South, were fought on the ground of gender.

PART TWO

A State of Mobilization

Politics in Arkansas, 1865–1868

CHAPTER THREE

The Capitol and Other Public Spheres

By nine o'clock in the morning of April 2, 1867, large numbers of African Americans were already moving through the streets of Little Rock. An air of anticipation was noted by a reporter for the *Arkansas Gazette*: "The crowds which thronged the streets of our city . . . gave indications that more than usual daily events were about to transpire."[1] People were heading toward the state's capitol building, the State House, intending to listen to the proceedings of a political convention meeting to shape a "Union" platform for the reorganization of Arkansas's state government. But the convention was not to begin until noon. Those collecting on the grounds of the capitol came early hoping to learn whether or not three black men would be seated with Pulaski County's white-elected delegation to this convention. A few days earlier, Little Rock's black community had gathered in Bethel AME Church to elect their own representatives to this political event. They were responding to the recent passage of the federal Reconstruction Acts, which authorized the participation of black men as voters in the state's reorganization. Whether or not the existing Pulaski County delegation would agree to include the six new delegates selected at Bethel Church, especially the three who were black, was being decided in a meeting in the State House.[2] Word was soon issued from the meeting that indeed the three black men would be seated with the other Pulaski delegates. After the news that their representatives would be included in the forthcoming official political event, the former slaves in Little Rock that morning decided to use the time remaining before the convention to construct a political theater of their own.

What they had in mind was a speaking event. Someone among the group of perhaps 500 freedmen, freedwomen, and children placed a large box underneath the portico of the capitol building to serve as a platform for political speeches. Others soon pressed in close to hear. Over the next hour or so, local Republican leaders, both white and black, also at the capitol for the soon-to-begin convention, addressed the audience from this makeshift platform. But it was the audience members themselves, "waving shawls, bandannas, etc.," who orchestrated the proceedings, calling for and cheering on those speakers from whom they desired to hear and "show[ing] signs of weariness" to hurry along those who did not please.[3] On this day, freedpeople claimed the grounds of the state capitol for themselves, as a space in which to create a public sphere for the discussion and expression of political opinion and for the exercise of their citizenship.

Throughout the South in this early stage of congressional Reconstruction, people who had once been slaves were demanding a voice in public affairs. Following emancipation, African Americans formed multiple public spheres for political discussion outside white-dominated political discourse and, when the opportunity arose, seized the right both to speak and to vote in existing white-controlled public arenas.[4] Their actions posed a formidable challenge to antebellum constructions of citizenship, which had presupposed that those speaking and voting in public would be white men.

Freedpeople's ability to challenge what it meant to be a citizen in southern society was greatly facilitated by actions of the federal government (which was, in turn, responding to the protests and demands of African Americans in the South). Most important among these actions was the enfranchisement of African American men in the former Confederate states through the Reconstruction Act of March 2, 1867. The supplement to the Reconstruction Act of March 23, organizing voter registrations and elections of delegates to state constitutional conventions, produced the first official opportunity for African American men to enter the debate and record their voices in Arkansas's electoral politics. And, as happened on this April morning in Little Rock, when black men entered this public sphere, black women entered as well.

The actions of African Americans in Arkansas in April 1867 were echoed throughout the southern region, where former slaves responded to congressional Reconstruction policy by mobilizing for political conventions, voter registration, and elections.[5] Both urban leaders and rural masses embraced liberal political rights as a signifier of freedom and as a tool in economic and social struggles.[6] Their activities reveal an emerging political culture that envisaged an open and inclusive political community as the basis of a republic organized on the principle of equality. The enactment of radically inclusive notions of citizenship by African Americans disrupted the racial hierarchy, and even to some extent the gender inequality, previously signified by and secured through antebellum political practices.[7]

In Arkansas, whites faced this challenge to antebellum constructions of citizenship in what was already a fractured political world. The Civil War had destroyed the state's economy and exacerbated class differences among whites.[8] Increasing class tension disrupted old political alliances and identities, and new ones were still taking shape. In this context, former Democratic leaders, calling themselves "conservatives," sought to regain political control of the state by reuniting the divided political community of white male voters in opposition to black male suffrage. In the pages of Arkansas's main conservative newspaper, the *Gazette*, writers and editors vilified black men participating in electoral politics as lacking a "virtuous manhood"—in both their political and domestic lives—that would make them worthy of political power and equal participation in the public sphere. They further presented the empowerment of such men as a threat to white southern manhood and to white men's ability to fulfill their own domestic responsibilities—to provide for and protect their families—making these the matters at stake in black political enfranchisement. Using this gendered imagery and argumentation in the *Gazette*, conservatives initiated a campaign for the formation of a "White Man's Party" to protect the republic and white men's homes from the putative threats posed by black political empowerment. They thereby sought to reinvigorate a splintered white male electorate under the political banner of "White Men," presenting race and gender as the only significant aspects of white men's political identities and reasserting a racialized notion of who could fully embody the rights, powers, and identity of citizens.[9]

The Boundaries of Political Community in Antebellum Arkansas

To understand contests over the meaning of citizenship in postemancipation Arkansas, it is necessary first to ask what citizenship and political participation meant to the white men of this state in the antebellum years. Arkansas was a relatively young state at the outbreak of the Civil War, having joined the

Union in 1836. It came into existence amidst the trend in the United States in the 1830s toward removing property qualifications for voting while imposing racial restrictions. This trend was accompanied by shifting definitions of what constituted the "independence" required among the citizenry. Perhaps the most important ideological justification of white men's exclusive political authority had long been the notion that the defining feature of a virtuous citizenry was the independence of those who were enfranchised. Dependence of either an economic or intellectual character in theory invited manipulation and corruption of the political process, and thus threatened political liberty.[10] In the decades after the American Revolution, ownership of property had been the primary demonstration of independence, signifying an independent means of support (and thereby avoidance of subordination to another in a wage labor relationship), thus independence from the economic control and manipulation of others, and thus the independence necessary to be a respon- sible voter.[11] This principle led to the incorporation of property-holding black men into the franchise in some states and, in New Jersey, to the inclusion of women property holders for a short time. Overall, though, owning property did not justify black men's and women's or white women's political empower- ment. Although free women could under certain circumstances own property, the principles of coverture treated women as a group as dependents.[12] African Americans were also generally represented as dependent regardless of their economic self-sufficiency, their exclusion from public life itself serving at times as supposed evidence of a dependent condition.[13]

Meanings shifted in the early nineteenth century when increased industri- alization and wage labor led to a smaller proportion of white men being independent property holders. Correspondingly, the importance of property as a signifier of independence became less dominant and wage labor less a sign of politically disabling dependence.[14] The dependence of others, namely women and children, always an important marker of men's independence, increasingly became sufficient evidence in and of itself of the possession of the independence necessary to be worthy of political authority.[15] At the time that Arkansas formed as a state in the 1830s, then, U.S. citizenship was sym- bolically, and in large part materially, equivalent with being a white male head of household. Political and domestic authority merged in the figure of a white citizen/patriarch.[16]

The valorization of white male independence and its relationship to citi- zenship in nineteenth-century political culture were reflected in the process by which Arkansas became a state. In the mid-1830s a movement for statehood in Arkansas Territory was gaining among white settlers. Although seeking statehood primarily to increase economic opportunities in Arkansas by attracting both more settlers and federal funds for internal improvements and border defense (Arkansas sat on the southern frontier and bordered lands held by Native Americans), the territory's leaders posed their quest as one for "independence."[17] Those pursuing statehood frequently represented remaining a territory as being in a "dependent condition."[18] And a report of a joint committee of the territorial legislature addressing concerns that the territory could not legally call a constitutional convention prior to federal legislation authorizing such a move objected that this position "would make them not only dependents in name, but vassals in fact," and added, "even a slave has the right to stipulate with his master for his freedom." This same document, though, quickly rejected its own analogy between territorial status and slavery. It was not necessary to await congressional authorization to pursue their liberty, the committee argued, because "such a being as a *freed-man* cannot exist where there are no slaves. The citizens of Arkansas are *free men*, and most of them descendants of those, who sixty years since battled for freedom against the assumed 'divine right' of sovereignty in kings."[19] The American Revolution's overthrow of monarchical power thus justified white men's claim to liberty, a claim contrasted to the supposedly equally legitimate denial of that liberty to those excluded from the American revolutionary tradition, those most dependent, slaves.

Articulating political representation as both the necessary condition for and the due of independent "freemen" resonated with the aspirations of many of the white men who had settled in this frontier region. These settlers had traveled to Arkansas from other parts of the South beginning in the early nineteenth century in search of the material and everyday independence that accompanied economic self-sufficiency and prosperity.[20] They thus came seeking the independence that had eluded them in their previous homes in other southern states. At the time that settlers in Arkansas sought statehood and for years thereafter, land prices in Arkansas were low and cotton prices were high, conditions allowing white men to perceive that opportunity abounded. Describing Arkansas in 1842, a white migrant from South Carolina wrote, "Many of our citizens have been of the unfortunate & came here to get homes and repair their conditions."[21] One white man settling in Arkansas in the late 1840s wrote home, "I feel certain I can make a living here & lie [*sic*] as well as my neighbours & be independent."[22]

These aspirations were apparent on January 4, 1836, when delegates from

Arkansas Territory came together in convention to design a state constitution, a document that they would then present to Congress in hopes of being admitted as an equal member to the United States.[23] The document produced by this convention rejected what were perceived as aristocratic pretensions and entrenched hierarchies characterizing southern society on the eastern seaboard.[24] It evinced instead the goal of establishing a political system that would secure the greatest degree of opportunity for white men to become independent regardless of family or class origins, and the greatest degree possible of equality among white men. Most importantly, the constitution imposed no property requirements for electors or for office holding.[25] Slavery was institutionalized in the document (it was never in dispute), but no representational benefits accrued to the regions with greater numbers of slaves, and thus to wealthier whites. The basis of apportionment for seats in the legislature was the only contentious issue at the convention. This issue divided delegates from the lowland districts in the southeastern portions of the state, or the Delta, where the economy was dominated by cotton production and slave labor and where blacks outnumbered whites in several counties, and those from the northern and western highlands, or Hill country, where there were fewer slaves, larger white populations, and more diversity in agricultural output. This contest was settled through a compromise that favored those in the north and west: representation would be based not on total population but, rather, on only "the free white male inhabitants of the State."[26]

This system of apportionment excluded not only those who were enslaved but also white women (who presumably were considered citizens in some senses, though state citizenship was not defined in the document), and free African Americans. In fact, most rights associated with citizenship were explicitly limited to "free white men" by the constitution. A voter was to be a "free white male citizen . . . of the United States" over the age of twenty-one who met residency requirements in Arkansas.[27] Only a free white male citizen would be eligible to serve as a representative in the new government. And only free white men were guaranteed "a right to keep and to bear arms for their common defense."[28] The constant refrain of "free white male citizen" in Arkansas's first constitution is suggestive. Two years earlier in neighboring Tennessee, a delegate to a constitutional convention there had to defend that state's proposal to deny all black men the franchise, including those whose property holdings had until then allowed them to vote, arguing that by " 'We the people of the United States,' [the authors of the U.S. Constitution] meant we the *free white* people."[29] By including "white" in their constitution, Arkansas's founders both echoed this argument about national citizenship and precluded any future ambiguity about who was originally intended as members of Arkansas's political community. Notably, after identifying that political community as white, presumably the word "free" was no longer necessary, as there were no unfree white men in Arkansas at the time (unless the authors intended to exclude prisoners). Nonetheless, all three words were repeatedly used to describe the politically empowered, its authors apparently seeking to highlight all three axes—status (slave/free), race, and gender—along which they identified themselves as different from those who did not have public power, who were not independent and thus not worthy of political citizenship. The compact that formed the state of Arkansas for the purpose of protecting the independence of white men did so by actively excluding from key means and indications of independence—political representation and even armed self-defense—all others. The dependence of free African Americans and white women, which justified their exclusion from political rights, was itself produced and reinforced through the legal document creating those rights for white men.

The importance to the founders of this new republic that the political community be an exclusive one, that access to the rights commonly associated with citizenship be limited, was revealed in the crafting of one of its first sections. Article II, the Declaration of Rights, began, "That the great and essential principles of liberty and free government may be recognized and unalterably established, we declare . . . that all freemen, when they form a social compact, are equal and have certain inherent and indefeasible rights."[30] This language was offered as a substitute for what had been originally proposed for the Declaration of Rights. The committee drafting this section had first written, "that all men are born equally free and independent, and have certain inherent and indefeasible rights."[31] The convention rejected language that identified a natural and pre-social origin of freedom, equality, and independence, and thus that raised the possibility that these were the possession of all "men," which might be interpreted as including free blacks, white women, or even slaves. Instead, they choose words that rested equality and rights on the political action of "freemen" forming a contract. They thus explicitly recognized this document and the rights it conferred as instruments for distinguishing those within the political community from those without, in other words for distinguishing freemen from slaves, white from black, and men from women. The rights to which "free white men" had access that differentiated them from all others were "enjoying and defending life and liberty; of acquiring, possessing and protecting property and reputation; and of pursuing their own happiness."[32] The founders of the state of Arkansas consciously constructed a white man's republic.

The social groups excluded from citizenship in this white man's republic represented many of those who labored within the households of free white male citizens and under their control. The organization of political authority in Arkansas under its new constitution thus mirrored the organization of domestic authority in what was the central economic unit of this overwhelmingly rural society, the household.[33] Whether a small subsistence farm in the north or western highlands, a cotton plantation run with a large enslaved labor force in the Arkansas Delta, or something in between, the household was the basic unit of economic production in Arkansas. The household was also the "domestic" or "private" realm in which white women, children, and slaves were subordinated to, and perceived to be dependent upon, white men; it thus was the source of white men's shared "public" identities as independent freemen and citizens.[34] Both economic independence and identities as independent freemen were thus made possible through white men's unequal relations within their households with those people excluded from political power.[35]

Most white men in antebellum Arkansas owned at least some land.[36] Surveying eight Arkansas counties from various regions of the state, historian Carl Moneyhon has found that the percentage of propertyless white men in 1860 ranged from 4.8 to 24.4 percent, with the percentage in all but two counties falling below 10. And these percentages included sons of propertied men who had yet to inherit their families' assets.[37] Although the vast majority of white men owned property, few were wealthy enough to run plantations. Cotton was the product of choice among the state's farmers; some cotton was produced for market by even small farmers throughout the state. But it was not until the cotton boom of the 1850s, fueled by high cotton prices and favorable weather conditions, that an economy based on large plantation production began to take hold in the eastern and southern Delta regions. During the 1850s, large plantation units increased in number, expanded in size, gained a larger share of the slave labor force, and spread geographically.[38] Yet, even in this decade, the population in northern and western parts of the state, where the mountainous terrain and lack of river transport kept large-scale agriculture to a minimum, continued to be dominated by small farmers.[39] As late as 1860, only 3.5 percent of the state's 39,004 farms were plantations with twenty or more slaves.[40]

In this society where white men ran primarily small farms on which both cash crops and food, clothing, and supplies for daily subsistence were produced, the labor of wives was crucial. In her research on women's labor in the Arkansas Delta, Elizabeth Anne Payne concludes that, in addition to making cloth and soap, tending animals and vegetable gardens, birthing babies and caring for the sick, both black and white women provided essential labor in the fields.[41] John Meek, a white migrant to Arkansas from South Carolina in the 1840s, appeared to recognize this when he commented on the prosperity of another man, perhaps his brother or cousin, in a letter written in 1842: "James Meek will make a bale of 500 lb cotton to each acre & has noble corn, oats, wheat. . . . He has got open 102 acres of land in fine improvement, good buildings, you would be surprised to see his place. Such good buildings, fine fences & fruit trees & a first rate wife, well educated and healthy, industrious."[42] John's noting that James's wife was "healthy" and "industrious," especially in conjunction with a description of James's property and the productivity of his farm, suggests that white men understood that marital relations could be key factors in their economic well-being.

Production and the promise of individual economic growth for white men in antebellum Arkansas also depended on the institution of slavery. Most whites in Arkansas did not own slaves. Historian Orville Taylor has estimated that by 1860 one white person in six in Arkansas either owned slaves or was a member of a slaveholding family.[43] This was far less than the South's average of close to one in three, and Arkansas's slave population was small relative to that of other southern states.[44] Nonetheless, for most white men slavery made possible the reality, or at least the dream, of economic expansion. For a small farmer to improve his economic station, he needed to buy more land and increase production, which in turn depended on an increase in his labor force. Buying or renting one or more slaves represented the most expeditious route to such expansion. This route seems to have been taken by a growing number of small farmers during the antebellum years in Arkansas, especially during the economic growth of the 1850s.[45] By 1860, there were 111,115 slaves in the state (representing 25 percent of the state's overall population) held by 11,481 owners, nearly doubling the 5,999 owners holding 47,100 slaves in 1850.[46] A few wealthy planters owned large numbers of slaves: 7 owned 200 or more, 66 owned 100 or more, and 345 owned 50 or more. However, the largest category of slaveholders in 1860 owned 1 slave each, and more than 50 percent of owners owned fewer than 4 slaves. There were 5,806 small slaveholders in 1860, up from 3,334 just a decade earlier.[47] Throughout the antebellum years slaveholding was spreading and was increasingly being used by small farmers to expand cash crop production. In fact, as wealth grew in the 1850s for all classes, small farmers showed the highest rates of social mobility in the state.[48] If a white man did not use enslaved labor on his farm, he knew another white man who did and most likely aspired to slaveholding himself as a means of expanding his own wealth in similar fashion.

The unprecedented economic growth of the last decade of the antebellum era pushed up prices for slaves and land, leading to increasingly apparent class differences among white men in Arkansas.[49] These differences would be brought fully to the surface by divergent experiences and interests during and after the Civil War. However, before the war inexpensive land remained in the highlands. Even in Phillips County, a center of cotton plantations in the Delta, small farmers still outnumbered cotton planters in 1860.[50] Throughout the 1850s most white men in Arkansas continued to believe that economic independence via landownership and small-scale agricultural production was accessible to, if not yet in hand for, all white men.[51] And growing class divisions did not produce deep political divisions. Party disputes within the state tended to revolve around divisions within the elite over differing geographic and local interests, not serious differences in perceived interests, ideology, or political identity.[52]

One place in Arkansas where a white working class developed was Little Rock. When diverging interests between this class and the city's elite threatened a serious political showdown, the conflict was settled through an attack on free African Americans. Skilled white workers organized in Little Rock in the late 1850s against labor competition from skilled slaves. In 1858, their union appealed to all white mechanics to oppose candidates for office who owned skilled slaves and to boycott projects that employed them. Elites heard in their campaign a general attack on slavery. In the charged atmosphere of sectional disputes over antislavery activism, the labor organization could not afford to be perceived as abolitionist and so retreated. Workers resolved their disputes with elites by joining forces on a different but related objective, a proposal that all free blacks be expelled from the state or enslaved for one year (after which the earnings from their labor would be used to pay for their relocation). Similar proposals had been debated in Arkansas for as long as the state had been in existence but were usually defeated for fear that such action would prove unconstitutional. However, the U.S. Supreme Court removed constitutional concerns with its decision in the Dred Scott case in 1857. Whites uniting across class lines in Little Rock took the lead in the expulsion movement in 1858, and the proposal became state law in 1859. Thus class conflict among whites was diverted through a racist political effort, an effort that, by eliminating a free black population, tied freedom and citizenship even more tightly to race. Free African Americans fled Arkansas for other states. In 1860, of an estimated 700 free black people who had resided in the state, there remained a mere 144, and these were mostly the elderly and others without the financial or physical resources necessary to relocate.[53]

Apparently, in antebellum Arkansas a cross-class community of white men was able to unite over a shared commitment to preserving independence and economic opportunity for themselves, through slavery, racism, and white male dominance over (the labor of) the other members of their households. Almost all white men in Arkansas shared, or anticipated sharing, the experience and identity of being a head of household, or in historian Stephanie McCurry's phrase, the master of at least a small world.[54] This common experience shaped the meaning of white men's citizenship. Only those who were masters at home came together to exercise the powers and participate in the rituals of political citizenship. The political vocabulary that justified white men's exclusive public roles through their "independence" and "virtue" invoked those gender and race relations of dependency in households as the basis of white men's citizenship. Whiteness, manhood, and domestic authority constituted what it meant to be a citizen in antebellum Arkansas, and exclusive citizenship as well as domestic authority constituted what it meant to be a white man.

This political world was fractured by the Civil War and emancipation. The war divided the political community of white men along class lines, and emancipation undermined the material and symbolic basis of the white manhood this community had shared. The transformation of slaves into citizens removed the racial dimension of white men's domestic authority, and the extension of suffrage to black men disrupted white men's exclusive claim to powers in public. The significance of this for meanings of race and citizenship was manifested daily after the Civil War through African Americans' political mobilization. Former slaves came together in public forums throughout Arkansas to claim their rights and to construct a new kind of citizenship for a postemancipation republic.

Laying Claim to Citizenship: African Americans
in the Public Sphere in Postemancipation Arkansas

Even before the federal government's official extension of juridical citizenship and then suffrage to former slaves, black men and women throughout the southern states seized the right to participate in political debate and decision making. Explicitly through political demands and implicitly by acting as citizens—participating in political meetings, marching in demonstrations, listening to and giving speeches, and attending conventions and elections—they intervened in contests over the form and meaning of citizenship in postemancipation society.[55] Their actions also created new political rituals that reflected a vision for political community very different from that of southern white men. An emerging black political culture promoted widespread participation in citizenship and involved collective political rituals aimed at demonstrating and enforcing African American political solidarity.[56] With the passage of the Reconstruction Acts, this form of political activity moved onto center stage of official politics, an arena that had previously been the primary setting of the white man's republic. Black rights and political action undermined citizenship's role as a mark of racial privilege and also undermined a key component of constructions of white manhood, namely exclusive control over the public sphere.

Organized political protest urging an inclusive and nonracial citizenship in Arkansas appeared first among the state's emerging black political leadership. This group consisted primarily of city and town dwellers who had risen to local prominence as key figures in either urban slave communities or wartime institutions. On November 30, 1865, members of this local political elite gathered in Little Rock for the "first colored convention ever held in the State of Arkansas" in order "to confer with each other as to the best means of completing the Emancipation, Enfranchisement, and elevation of our race."[57]

The two participants in this event to go on to statewide political prominence were free-born men who came to Arkansas only after the Civil War broke out. The first, William Henry Grey, had received an early education in formal politics working as a servant and clerk to Henry A. Wise of Virginia while Wise served as that state's congressman and then governor. The special attention Wise paid to Grey from the time Grey was a boy; the fact that Grey's mother appears to have been a slave of Wise's who was granted her freedom before she moved to Washington, D.C., where Grey was born; and Grey's middle name suggest that Grey was most likely Wise's son.[58] He did not remain close to Wise, however, as a grown man. Before 1860, Grey migrated with his wife and children to St. Louis, Missouri, where he worked on a steamboat. Sometime before 1863 he moved to Helena, Arkansas, presumably hoping to take advantage of new opportunities for black political leadership opened up by Union occupation of that city. In Helena, Grey was identified as a minister. He was not wealthy, owning no real estate in 1870 (though he had personal property valued at $500), but he would be a constant presence in politics during Reconstruction. He would be a common speaker at events in Helena and prominent in organizing protests in that city against the violence of the Ku Klux Klan. He would also be elected as a delegate to the 1868 constitutional convention and subsequently as a representative to the Arkansas house of representatives. And he would later be appointed an assistant U.S. assessor.[59] James T. White, the second most prominent delegate at the convention, was a Baptist minister from Indiana who came to Helena with a unit of African American Union soldiers during the war. He was wealthier than Grey, owning $9,200 in real estate and personal property worth $300 in 1870. He would also serve as a delegate to the 1868 constitutional convention and would later be elected to both the Arkansas house of representatives and senate and as a delegate to the constitutional convention of 1874.[60]

Because Arkansas's free African American population had always been small, and after the eviction law of 1859 was practically eliminated, it seems likely that other than Grey and White, most of the twenty African American men who gathered for the Colored Citizens Convention had once been slaves.[61] Two ex-slave delegates had nonetheless been leaders of black churches in antebellum Little Rock. Wilson Brown was an ordained preacher and the pastor of a forty-two-member black Baptist church permanently established in 1858.[62] William Wallace Andrews founded Mt. Warren Chapel in 1848, which grew under his leadership to 200 members by 1851 and after emancipation became the Bethel AME Church.[63] Another delegate born a slave, Nathan Warren, had purchased his freedom at least two decades before the Civil War. He had left the state with his family in 1856 under increasing threats that the legislature would expel all free black people and returned sometime after 1862 to participate in the state's reconstruction. Warren, the only member of the convention to appear in Arkansas's 1850 census as a free man, was an aspiring minister (he was ordained in the 1880s) who supported himself and his family first as a carriage driver and then as a confectioner popular with wealthy white clients in Little Rock.[64] Together these men filled the leadership positions at the convention. White was named president and Andrews was vice president, while Grey gave the only long and recorded address to the convention, "The Present Condition and Future Prospects of the Colored People of the South." Grey also chaired the important Committee on Resolutions and Memorials and presented the product of this committee's work to the convention. Andrews and Brown sat on this Resolutions Committee and also worked with Grey on the Finance Committee. And both Warren and White led the convention in prayer.[65]

That the other delegates to the convention were less educated than this leading group is suggested by the first day of the gathering's proceedings, when a white man present not as a delegate but as an observer, J. W. Demby, was temporarily appointed secretary. Demby was promptly replaced on the second day of the convention by Richard E. Wall, a delegate from Phillips County who arrived at the convention one day late along with William Henry Grey. Grey's first motion to the convention was for Wall's appointment as secretary, because "his efficiency in chirography peculiarly fitted him for the position." Apparently, none of the other delegates at the convention before Grey and Wall's arrival who had not yet been appointed to an office had past experiences or training that equally suited them for the role of scribe.[66] It was thus a group consisting largely of former slaves with at most rudimentary literacy led by well-educated ministers and other professional and skilled men, men privileged relative to the masses of freedpeople in the state, who initiated formal political organization among African Americans in Arkansas.

The assembling of this group, even its more privileged leadership core, was not a simple feat. "Many of us have braved many difficulties to be present at this Convention," remarked Grey, who spent six days traveling to Little Rock from Phillips County and made the last part of that journey on foot.[67] Not only was travel physically difficult, but traveling for the explicit purpose of participating in political protest and organization was dangerous for black men at this time. During this first year following the end of the Civil War, African Americans were largely unprotected from widespread violence of returning Confederates and former slaveowners, many of whom bitterly opposed black political participation and sought to reimpose conditions of slavery.[68] James H. Harris, a black leader from North Carolina later described black men coming to similar conventions in other southern states: "Some bring credentials, . . . others had as much as they could do to bring themselves, having to escape from their homes stealthily at night."[69]

Although all delegates' home counties were not identified, it is clear that only a small number—at least five and at most eleven—of Arkansas's fifty-five counties were represented at the convention.[70] Delegates from four of the five identified counties came from areas with large black populations—Phillips (68.3 percent), Chicot (74.7 percent), Pulaski (42.7 percent), and Dallas (30.7 percent)—which were in the southeastern portion or plantation region of the state.[71] And like Grey, many of the delegates who were able to attend came from areas of the state that had been occupied early in the war by Union forces. This federal presence brought freedom sooner and facilitated political organization among the growing communities of refugees from slavery who sought protection in these locations.[72] This is reflected in a mass meeting of "the Colored Citizens of Helena" held in that city's Brick Church in late October to select their representatives who would attend the convention.[73] It it is not known, though, how each of the men attending from other locales came to be appointed as a delegate. It is apparent that nothing approaching proportional representation was achieved. Seven of the twenty delegates represented Pulaski County alone, where Little Rock was the county seat. This points to an urban bias among the state's black leaders as well as to obstacles to communication, planning, and travel across the state that made it impossible for many from farther away to attend. It also suggests that the convention was more a meeting of a community of men already in leadership roles and engaged in political discussions with one another than a body representing the varied interests of black Arkansans.[74] Nonetheless, despite the danger, the difficulties in communication and travel, and the problematic nature of the "representation" that was at this point possible, the need for "conferring with each other" was apparently too urgent to delay.[75]

Such a conference was urgent because the form of republic that would be created to replace the dismantled "slave republic" was being debated in the official and white-dominated public arenas of Arkansas and the nation at the time,[76] and arguments against black enfranchisement were being made close to home. Just weeks earlier, at a meeting in Little Rock of "National Union Men," white Unionist candidate for Congress George H. Kyle had endorsed a platform recognizing the rights of African Americans to personal security, liberty, and private property. However, on the issue of suffrage he stated, "Let the future determine the *status* of the negro in this respect."[77] Thus even white leaders in Arkansas who ostensibly endorsed black civil liberties were proposing, at least for now, a citizenship for African Americans that did not include a voice in the political system. Conservative white politicians, who offered more definitive objections to enfranchising African American men—arguing that they were "utterly unfit for" suffrage—had fared well in the Arkansas congressional election in early October.[78] And at the time of the Convention of Colored Citizens, the *Arkansas Gazette* quoted President Andrew Johnson doubting that freedpeople would be able to join "our system of government" as citizens.[79] The Convention of Colored Citizens rejected the notion that a disfranchised citizenship for African Americans would be just and instead petitioned the Arkansas state legislature and Congress to "clothe us with the power of self-protection, by giving us our equality before the law and the right of suffrage, so we may become *bona fide* citizens of the State in which we live."[80]

The key component of what the convention termed a *"bona fide"* citizenship was political voice. In a speech made to the convention, William Henry Grey portrayed taking on the power to speak as a critical moment in the transformation from the condition of slavery to the status of citizenship: "[Slaveholders] had always been accustomed to hear their advice received respectfully, in short monosyllables—yes, sir, massa; or no, sir, massa. They never once dreamed that under this seeming respect there was a human soul, with a will and a purpose of its own. We have now thrown off the mask, hereafter to do our own talking, and to use all legitimate means to get and to enjoy our political privileges."[81] Grey equated autonomous speech, doing "our own talking," with freedom and opposed it to the enforced silence and deference of slavery. Autonomous speech, a voice in the public sphere, was itself prized and was also the agency by which "political privileges," the tools for enacting former slaves' "will" and "purpose," would be secured. Rejecting the notion that a continued "dependent" condition could legitimately replace slavery and justify the continued disfranchisement of former slaves, Grey continued that "we don't want anybody to swear for us or to vote for us; we want to exercise those privileges for ourselves."[82] And the delegates to the convention resolved that "for the first time in our existence we can answer for ourselves."[83]

Political voice was depicted in both Grey's speech before the convention and the "Memorials and Resolutions" approved by the entire body as particularly necessary for a social group under siege from hostile enemies. "Equality before the law" and "our oath, before the Civil Courts, and the right of suffrage," were represented as the means of "self-protection" that constituted a meaningful citizenship. Grey and his colleagues imagined liberal political rights as an equalizing factor, a means to aid African Americans in the unequal battles in which they were engaged with those far more powerful— landowners and employers, local judges and sheriffs, even night riders and thieves. Before Congress implemented its plan for Reconstruction, southern states had unabashedly sought to control former slaves and their labor through vagrancy and fencing laws, professional and poll taxes, and local law enforcement that harassed freedpeople seeking independent means of subsistence while refusing to punish whites for coercive violence.[84] Although Arkansas, unlike many other southern states, did not impose new restrictive laws under a "Black Code," the legislature instead simply left in effect the state's codes affecting "slaves and free negroes" until February 1867.[85] Thus some influence over and through the state via political representation and a voice in the courts, the convention believed, were necessary for African Americans to protect themselves. "Emancipation as it now stands," the convention's "Memorials and Resolutions" read, "[is] without the protection of law or guarantee of its future existence in fact; therefore, we, . . . as an earnest of our future liberties, pray that the Legislature grant us equality before the law."[86] In effect, the convention argued that political power was necessary to counter the economic and social control wielded by former slaveholders throughout the state. These rights would assure the conditions under which African Americans could achieve independence, rather than independence, as an indicator of "virtue," being necessary to demonstrate African Americans' worthiness for a voice in political and civil affairs.

In this sense, the gathering challenged widespread conservative assertions that African Americans were "unfit" for membership in the political community.[87] Grey explicitly dismissed this idea: "There is no use in arguing the abstract question of our fitness to exercise these duties of the citizen—that is simply begging the question. Establish the principle irrevocably and universally, and then reduce us to the restrictions imposed on others." Grey thus rejected a construction of citizenship as the privilege of political authority granted to only those who were imagined to be "worthy." He replaced this construction with one based on the notion of inherent and natural rights to which "all men" were equally entitled and found authority for his position in the founding texts of American democracy: "We are not asking that the people should try any new experiment in this matter; we do not ask them to go outside the great charter of American liberty—the Constitution and the Declaration of Independence—but rather that they should strictly conform to the letter and spirit of those time-honored documents." Grey offered the enfranchisement of African American men as the path toward finally building the republic intended by the nation's founders, in place of that formed by "the haughty, self-willed people [who] declared, in the face of an enlightened world, that slavery was divine, and accepted it as the corner-stone of a bastard republic."[88]

The most immediate refutation of charges that black men were not fit for citizenship was the fact itself of black men conferring with one another. In addition to the concrete demands made by the convention, the gathering also served as a public performance of African Americans' claims on the status of citizen. Through speeches, debates, committee meetings, and resolutions, the convention was an exercise in political voice and specifically in black men's entry into the dominant public sphere.[89] This performance was addressed explicitly to the state legislature, Congress, and Republican leaders to whom the convention turned for support and implicitly to the observing public. On one hand, it was a conciliatory performance, one of black men's political moderation and humility, directed at the powerful white men, such as then Arkansas governor Isaac Murphy, who were invited to observe the proceedings and address the convention.[90] The convention's resolutions gave thanks for freedom and expressed "our confidence in the eventual justice of the American people" toward "a down-trodden and helpless race."[91] Grey also seems to have worked to appear unthreatening, pairing his dramatic description of former slaves "throwing off the mask" with the promise to use only "legitimate means" to secure their rights.[92] Finally, the convention avoided taking a position on the contentious issue of land confiscation and redistribution, a primary concern and aspiration of the masses of freedpeople in rural areas of the state at the time.[93] Rather than demanding land and an independent means of subsistence for freedpeople, the convention's "Memorials and Resolutions" asked that they be treated fairly as workers, thus reassuring plantation owners that freedpeople intended to continue in this capacity: "Believing, as we do, that we are destined in the future, as in the past, to cultivate your cotton fields, we claim for Arkansas the first to deal justly and equitably for her laborers."[94]

Yet, a double message was apparent throughout. In Grey's speech, he declared that the convention was asking for political rights "calmly, dispassionately, and respectfully," while in the same sentence he insisted, somewhat more threateningly, that the "peace and quiet" of the state depended on their obtaining these rights.[95] Also, the convention appealed as "humble petitioners" to the Arkansas state legislature and Congress, asking that African Americans be granted the rights of a "*bona fide*" citizenship. Yet the convention made clear that they were not, in fact, asking for but, rather, seizing these rights. Suffrage and citizenship were confidently asserted as the "inalienable right" of

African Americans and thus justly already theirs, even if not yet recognized by white political authority in the state or nation at the time.[96] The convention claimed the label "citizen" without waiting for permission from the state, by calling the convention one of "the Colored Citizens of Arkansas," addressing each other as "Fellow Citizens," and directing their resolutions to "Fellow Citizens of the United States of America."[97] Though attempting both to assure their audience of their constituents' unthreatening intentions (and thus misrepresenting most freedpeople's aspirations) and to impress their audience with their intelligence and capacity to participate in the public sphere, the convention was not only a performance for whites. It was simultaneously the practice of political protest and citizenship, an engagement with one another, a forum in which to begin experimenting with different political rhetorics and strategies, and the expression of these men's own militancy.

Grey concluded his speech before the convention by claiming not only membership in the political community but also membership in the American nation for African Americans, explicitly rejecting arguments that former slaves should migrate to Africa and implicitly promoting the concept new in U.S. politics at the time of national, as opposed to state, citizenship: "Our future is sure. God has marked it out with his own finger; here we have lived, suffered, fought, bled, and many have died. We will not leave the graves of our fathers, but here we will rear our children; here we will educate them to a higher destiny; here, where we have been degraded, will we be exalted—AMERICANS IN AMERICA, ONE AND INDIVISIBLE."[98] And yet, though they claimed membership in an American nation and demanded a race-neutral political system, the convention's delegates were not advocating a society without racial groups or identity. Both Grey's and White's comments and the convention's resolutions repeatedly invoked a communal identity for African Americans distinct from that of whites. The first-person plural—"we," "us," "our," and "ourselves" —was used almost exclusively to refer to African Americans, and rights were demanded for this collective, not for an abstract, individual "citizen." And despite the conciliatory, diplomatic nature of some of the convention's discourse, and the relatively privileged status of some of its delegates, the group identity expressed at the convention crossed differences of class, color, and previous condition. The masses of freedpeople in Arkansas's rural communities may not have elected these men as their representatives, and they may well have represented themselves differently from how Grey represented them. Nonetheless, when Grey explained that "we were scarcely awakened in our prison-house of slavery" when the Civil War began, or that "when escaping from rebel masters, we were worked upon Union fortifications," he identified himself with the plight of former slaves.[99]

In these ways, this first recorded black political event in Arkansas echoes what historian Elsa Barkley Brown has argued was the case in Virginia and other southern states, that an overall "ethos of mutuality" and sense of "community responsibility" that characterized the worldview of former slaves during Reconstruction was reflected in African American political practices and conceptualizations of suffrage. Barkley Brown has found that African Americans "understood the vote as a collective, not an individual possession," that each individual who voted did so for the community as a whole. She further argues that black women were welcomed as participants in political decision making internal to black communities as well as in activities in the external public sphere.[100] Did a citizenship constructed in relation to community as opposed to individual men have a similar effect in Arkansas?

The Convention of Colored Citizens is suggestive on this question. When members of the convention depicted citizenship, even suffrage, as a communal right sought for "us," the convention made no appeals to patriarchal identities and duty to "protect" hearth and family. Not one reference to "manhood" was recorded during the convention's proceedings. The only reference to family relations was an appeal for education for "our children."[101] And yet, the convention's delegates had available to them a long rhetorical tradition among black men fighting slavery and discrimination of referring to citizenship as "manhood rights." This tradition itself drew on the gendered political rhetoric of the Jacksonian era. And it was part of a larger black protest tradition in which William Henry Grey had demonstrated that he was well versed.[102] Historians have debated the extent to which African American political leaders in general pursued racial equality through patriarchal political discourse. Many have noted the rhetoric of manhood rights, and some have argued that this rhetoric indicated that upon emancipation, black men believed that they should monopolize public roles or that freedmen and freedwomen believed that a patriarchal social organization was one of the gains of freedom.[103] It is striking, though, that in Arkansas at this early point in Reconstruction politics, one does not find an embrace of patriarchy for political purposes, even among fairly privileged black men. An available political rhetoric of citizenship and "manhood" was not employed by the convention's leaders. This suggests at least the possibility that these African American men imagined, or attempted to speak for constituents who imagined, citizenship in terms far more inclusive and less gendered than had been the norm among

whites in antebellum Arkansas. Patriarchal rhetoric would increasingly become a part of these leaders' politics as they confronted white conservative
efforts to exclude them based on race. Still, ordinary freedpeople would not
necessarily embrace a gendered construct of citizenship. And at this early
stage in Arkansas's postemancipation politics, even leaders demanded political voice for a community, not for male patriarchs or heads of households.

The absence of gendered rhetoric in the proceedings of the Convention of
Colored Citizens, though, does not mean that the delegates did not draw on
gender difference or practice gender exclusion. They of course did, most
obviously in the fact that only men participated as official delegates. Also, the
question of women's right to suffrage, a topic being discussed in various
arenas of the state and nation at the time, was not raised.[104] And finally,
military service was invoked as the means by which black men had "earned"
their citizenship. William Grey asserted, "We have won [suffrage] fairly, honestly, and righteously; . . . it was the negro thrown into the scale on the side of
the nation that broke the back of the rebellion and saved the nation. . . . The
Government of the United States is pledged to secure our rights; we wrote the
contract in blood, when her own children were about to destroy her."[105] Grey
was echoing the sentiments already expressed by the convention's president,
James T. White. White had opened the proceedings declaring that "we have
earned [equality before the law and suffrage] and, therefore, we deserve it
[sic]; we have bought it with our blood."[106] Still, though, these words did
not clearly invoke the masculine "citizen-soldier" ideal so common in republican rhetoric (an ideal that was often called on by black leaders in other
parts of the South as well as the North to argue for black men's political
rights).[107] In fact, the convention never explicitly valorized the role of men
on the battlefield. Rather, it depicted African American communities, because
of their allegiance to the Union, paying dearly to support the war effort with
"our blood."

Thus even rhetoric concerning African Americans' roles in the Civil War
did not uniformly promote masculine constructs of citizenship. Rather, a
variety of meanings were evident in emerging African American political
discourses on citizenship and gender immediately following the end of slavery. As Elsa Barkley Brown has concluded, it seems that in these early years of
freedom African Americans were more open to a gender-inclusive construct
of citizenship than in subsequent decades. "Black women's vision of . . .
democracy," Barkley Brown writes, "like that of black people as a whole, may
never have been that expansive again."[108] The lack of much experimentation

with an explicit rhetoric of manhood rights in Arkansas in these early years reflects the possibility, perhaps, that, because Arkansas's free population of color was almost entirely expelled just before the Civil War, recently enslaved men and women had an unusual degree of influence over the discourse in Arkansas's black public sphere. In any case, it seems that while the African American men leading the state's first official political event in an emerging black public sphere recognized gender difference in politics, they did not approach citizenship from the same commitment to or experience of gender hierarchy as did white men.

Glimpses of the political activities of ordinary freedwomen that appear in descriptions of political events in Arkansas leave a similar impression. These glimpses come largely from the observations of white critics, such as newspaper reporters and Freedmen's Bureau agents, who were disturbed by the novel forms of political expression they observed around them. Although their portrayals were distorted by racism, one can discern between the lines of white criticism important aspects of an emerging African American political culture, in which various forms of gender inclusion were part of an overall expansive vision of citizenship.

This political culture was made visible to its critics when federal action brought freedpeople, men and women, into the official political arenas of Arkansas. The first Reconstruction Act effectively unseated the state's current government—dominated by members of the antebellum elite who had been victorious in state elections held in August 1866—by declaring it provisional and placing it under military command.[109] The supplement to this act put in place the process for replacing it. Five days later, "the colored population" of Little Rock held a meeting in the Bethel AME Church. It was here that delegates were elected for the Union State Convention already planned for April 2, just a few days later. This convention was basically the initiation of a Republican Party organization in the state, titled "Union" in an attempt to attract the support of white unionists unwilling to identify themselves with the Republican Party.[110] Now that black men were legalized voters, Little Rock's black community intended to be represented in shaping the party's upcoming campaign. The Bethel Church meeting named three African American men, A. L. Richmond, George J. Rutherford, and John Peyton, and three white men, Dr. Granger, James Hinds, and George W. McDiarmid, to join an existing Pulaski County delegation to the convention.[111] The meeting also adopted resolutions endorsing the Reconstruction Acts as "magnanimous and just," pledging their support only to those "men and measures . . . recogniz[ing] the absolute equality of all men before the law," and favoring legislation using state property to fund public schools for all of the state's children.[112]

This gathering showed notable continuity with the political concerns, and some of the political figures, of the earlier Convention of Colored Citizens. Two of the delegates chosen for the Union State Convention had participated in the earlier gathering: A. L. Richmond had been a delegate and Dr. Granger was among a group thanked "for their kind sympathies and gentlemanly courtesies toward us" in the "Memorials and Resolutions" approved by the convention. And the church where the meeting was held had been the congregation of Rev. William Wallace Andrews, who had died in 1866, also a delegate to the Convention of Colored Citizens.[113] Through the existing structure of an important community institution, the largest black church in Little Rock, and drawing on past efforts at political protest, Little Rock's black community mobilized immediately to assure their voice was heard in the important political events of the months to come.[114] White Arkansans took notice: the *Arkansas Gazette* referred to the gathering at the Bethel Church as "a forcible reminder of the severe changes which the past six years have wrought."[115]

Those who convened the meeting at Bethel Church reportedly "invited friends from abroad to come among them to discuss the questions of the day."[116] It seems that many heeded this call for expanding participation in an emerging black public sphere. The crowd observed moving through the streets toward the State House in Little Rock on the morning of April 2 when the Union State Convention was to open, according to a *Gazette* reporter, "was composed of the main of negroes, who from distant plantations had flocked into town." He noted that freedpeople were "dressed in every conceivable style, bedizened with tinsel and decked out in assorted colors."[117] Clothing of different colored fabrics has been identified by historian Julie Saville as a means of distinguishing contingents of freedpeople traveling from different locales to come together for large political demonstrations.[118] This suggests that what the reporter read as mere decorative costume among "a promiscuous crowd" may in fact have been an indication of the grassroots organization that had spread the call to come to Little Rock and that had facilitated freedpeople's travel from surrounding rural areas. "Tinsel," cloth decorated with metallic thread, may well have served to mark leaders, such as local Union League members or perhaps former Union soldiers, now marshaling their neighbors from their respective plantations into town.[119] Freedpeople might also have dressed in brightly colored and shiny fabrics in celebration of the

State House, Little Rock, Arkansas. Photograph taken between 1869 and 1878 (the metal fence had not yet been constructed in 1868). Courtesy of the Butler Center for Arkansas Studies, Central Arkansas Library System.

inauguration of their political citizenship. In either case, it seems that freed-people coming into the city to "discuss the questions of the day" were engaged in a conscious and coordinated form of political expression.

Both women and men came to Little Rock to participate in this discussion on the day of the convention. Women were present, though somewhat on the sidelines, at this early experience of citizenship.[120] The *Gazette* reporter noted that while the Pulaski County delegation deliberated inside the capitol build-ing, freedpeople collected outside. "The steps of the building opposite [the capitol] could be seen occupied by a large crowd of negro women," the reporter observed, "and the capitol grounds were filled with negro men." That freedpeople divided themselves spatially in this way may indicate that the men felt they alone should prepare a forceful protest if those meeting inside re-jected the black delegates. The reporter believed, however, that the women did not intend to forgo a role in the day's planned events. He noted that "all [were] evidently expecting something to come off in which they were to take part."[121]

Once the Pulaski delegation announced its decision to include the black delegates, men, women, and children moved together toward the State House steps. Here the reporter described the crowd, estimated at over 500 people, as including "negroes of all sizes and conditions, from infants just large enough to walk to the decrepit old men, [and] both sexes." Despite his pejorative tone, the reporter's description reveals the widespread community involvement that was achieved for this event. It was this diverse group that set up a platform for political speeches that morning outside the capitol building and directed the proceedings with their cheers for or dismissals of those who rose to speak. Addressed first by three white Republicans, the crowd called for John Peyton, a prominent preacher in post–Civil War Little Rock who had first come to the city as a slave in 1832 and one of the black delegates elected in Bethel Church a few days before. When Peyton appeared, he warned his audience that the legitimacy of white Republicans should depend upon the degree to which they included African American voices in the political process: "When they went electioneering, they must take a colored man along with them, or they would not be believed." Peyton also admonished the crowd to refuse to allow others to think or to speak for them, cautioning them to receive with skepticism the words of white men seeking their votes and to "prepare themselves to rightly use [their] freedom." The *Gazette* reporter noted that Peyton "was listened to with profound attention, and loudly cheered by the assemblage."[122]

Many among the crowd took Peyton's advice and rejected a passive role in the actual convention. Once the formal meeting began, freedpeople followed their delegates into the hall to listen to its proceedings. The *Gazette* reporter observed freedpeople "jammed" in the gallery, "congregated" in the lobby, and "loitered in the nooks of the stairwell" as the convention commenced. He also noted that still others remained outside, some "gathered in groups," others engaged in "foot-racing and wrestling" (suggesting again the presence of children).[123] Whether following the convention's debates, engaging in political discussion among themselves, or enjoying moments of sport, African Americans in Arkansas made the day their own. They occupied the literal spaces of politics—the state's capitol building and its grounds—and organized a public sphere for debate during the first official political gathering following their acquisition of formal political rights.

Freedpeople's pursuit of information about and discussion of political issues evinced in Little Rock during the Union State Convention had counterparts in the more remote rural areas of the state. Freedmen's Bureau agents recorded freedpeople's "great interest to become posted on their duty about registration and voting" and their willingness to travel across one and even two counties to find a Freedmen's Bureau office offering accurate information about registration.[124] An agent in Columbia County contrasted how well informed freedpeople in towns were with those working on plantations: "Usually the negroes on the plantations had but a confused knowledge of affairs transpiring at present, but always anxious to gain all the information possible."[125] The difficulty of obtaining accurate information and communicating it across and into the rural regions of the state were some of the obstacles freedpeople faced in efforts to mobilize their communities' votes. Political speeches, which freedpeople sought out eagerly, were one means of securing news that could then be circulated by word of mouth. The bureau agent for Lafayette County reported that "the freedmen are very easily excited on political topics" and that the slightest rumor of a potential political speech in nearby Lewisville would lead many "to walk ten or fifteen miles only to be disappointed."[126]

Information gathered by men and women attending political speeches was shared with others in the neighborhood through local political organizations. The Lafayette County agent concerned about freedpeople traveling long distances on news of a political speech also found freedpeople organizing Republican clubs on individual plantations. Though for a primarily illiterate population speeches and meetings were the most effective way of learning about the political positions of candidates in upcoming elections, there were other innovative means of securing needed information.[127] In August 1867 the agent at Camden described the effort made by freedpeople in his area to gain information for themselves: "The freedmen have organized a reading club at this place, have subscribed for several prominent northern newspapers, and have gained much knowledge politically and socially. I have secured a suitable person . . . to read their papers to them at least once a week."[128] Male and female, young and old, were attending meetings frequently. By the summer of 1867, freedpeople in the district around Little Rock (Pulaski and Saline Counties) were holding political meetings as often as three times per week. After numerous complaints from whites, the Freedmen's Bureau agent there convinced them to meet only on Saturdays.[129]

Black Arkansans organizing to spread details about registration, voting, and the upcoming election had to contend with conservative whites' complaints that politics were distracting freedpeople from their labor. The *Gazette* objected that the freedpeople attending the Union State Convention had "left their work at a time, when, by reason of the late season, they were most needed in the fields."[130] The agent at Lafayette County reported that the formation of Republican clubs by freedpeople in his area "causes their employers to make a great many frivolous complaints to me."[131] Many white Republicans who accepted the principle of black enfranchisement too would have preferred less democratic participation and fewer opportunities to "speak." One Freedmen's Bureau agent reported that "many have . . . joined the Union League or the Grand Army of the Republic; they are becoming quite enthusiastic and are getting rather over zealous in attending barbecues and other political meetings . . . to the detriment of their crops."[132] And most likely responding to the large crowd attending the Union State Convention on April 2, the bureau's assistant commissioner for Arkansas issued a circular on April 8 that stated, "Freedmen . . . must realize that the highest privileges of a freeman do not absolve them from labor; that even the right and privilege of voting will not provide them with food, raiment, and shelter, without which no one can be truly free, but that these are the products of industry alone."[133]

Some white opposition to black political activity went farther than complaints. Reports of interference with voter registration through the intentional dissemination of misinformation were common. For instance, many freedpeople were told by white neighbors that registration was for the purposes of taxation or military service.[134] Freedpeople who lived farthest from towns where alternative sources of information were abundant were most vulnerable to these misinformation campaigns. To address the challenge of reaching everyone with accurate information and sufficient encouragement regarding registration, one Freedmen's Bureau agent reported that "the freedmen organized societies, and sent out committees to the remote precincts."[135]

Similar efforts were at times successful in organizing freedpeople even where whites threatened violence against African Americans registering to vote. These threats were most common, and freedpeople were most vulnerable to them, in counties with large white conservative and small black and white unionist populations. Agent William A. Inman of Craighead County, where black residents constituted only 5.5 percent of the population, discovered that "in one precinct the Freedmen appeared to be under some fears—being intimidated by threats that had been made by white men." Inman's efforts to persuade freedmen in this county to register were unsuccessful. Yet, after sending "some intelligent and trusty Freedmen" to discuss the situation with those who were afraid, Inman reported that most had come to the county registration site and added their names to the rolls. In other areas, though, efforts to overcome fear either failed or never reached those who needed support. Inman also found that in Greene and Poinsett Counties, with black populations of 2 and 13.1 percent, respectively, freedmen had been told by local whites either that they were too young to vote or that they would be allowed to vote without registering. Inman concluded, "As there are not fifteen Union men in the counties of Greene and Poinsett consequently the Freedmen are under the influence of the disloyal element and feel it unsafe to Register, as a general thing." In these counties, freedpeople or bureau agents were unable to convince voters that they would be protected; only nine freedmen from Greene County registered to vote. "From Greene County I understand that the Freedmen were afraid to present themselves"[136]

Despite cases such as this, freedpeople's efforts to disseminate information and to encourage registration were on the whole remarkably successful. In July 1867, Circular No. 13 ordered all bureau agents to visit every plantation in their districts to ensure that freedpeople understood the reason for registration and that they faced no interference with their efforts to register.[137] The next month, agents' reports of their findings flowed into the assistant adjutant general's offices. Though some reported conditions such as those noted by Agent Inman, overall most agents found that freedpeople were, as one agent reported, "universally well informed" on "their duty in registering." This same agent found that "the effects of my visits only tended to confirm them in their previous notions."[138] Agents also reported strategies for registering safely and without interference. J. H. Carhart, agent from Columbia County, learned that many freedmen had delayed registering until the last week and then did so only by traveling into the county seat, Magnolia, even though they might have registered earlier and with less effort at other precincts closer to home. It seems that freedmen felt safer becoming voters in town, surrounded by other freedpeople and away from their employers.[139] Acting under Circular No. 13, most agents found that the vast majority of, if not all, black men in their districts were already registered to vote despite the resistance and danger they faced.[140]

Widespread registration and voter preparation was achieved not by individual men coming to registration sites but, rather, through a collective effort by members of freed communities overall to gather and share information and to assist one another in laying the groundwork for voting on election day. The motivation for such effective grassroots organization, one that perhaps sustained freedpeople in the face of the enormous risks involved, is suggested by the desperate economic conditions and growing class conflict described in these same Freedmen's Bureau agents' reports. Throughout the state, weather problems brought insufficient crop yields in 1866 and 1867, leading to widespread hunger as well as conflicts over unpaid wages and deepening debt for laborers, sharecroppers, and landowners alike.[141] In several counties, local bureau agents reported employers' efforts to defraud freedpeople working on shares when the time came to divide up crops and settle debts.[142] In others, landowners and laborers argued over pay for work done on plantations after crops were "laid by."[143] In addition to poverty and labor conflict, in many areas freedpeople were terrorized by the violence of white "lawless characters" given free rein by local law enforcement officials, still in place in practice even if now subordinate to federal military authority.[144] Under these circumstances, freedpeople sought an effective voice in governmental affairs to free themselves from the crush of landlords' control, to address economic exploitation, and to protect their communities from violence.

Political mobilization had, of course, a clear and practical end. The aim of organizing was to achieve a vote sufficient to secure black male suffrage and oust conservative regimes. Freedpeople acted collectively because alone they were more vulnerable to violence and intimidation. There was also, though, significance simply in the act of mobilizing itself. To organize politically was also to realize freedom in a tangible way. Indeed, political participation, "speaking for ourselves," was the embodiment of being free in a liberal system. The act of voting was both an experience and a display of equality. Regardless of a voter's social status and economic resources, on election day one vote was equal to every other. To attend a political speech, join a Republican club, debate election strategy at a meeting, or participate in casting ballots was to be a citizen. To do those things collectively was to empower entire communities and realize a vision for an inclusive public sphere. That political participation produced sensations of equality and empowerment among African Americans was suggested in a letter written by John Stayton, a white man living in Jacksonport, Arkansas, to his brother. Stayton conflated participation in public life with new forms of self-assertion, noting that "the negroes in this County . . . of late have shown signs of trouble by being a little too impudent and by public meetings and other demonstrations."[145] A bureau agent reporting on registration in the same town in August 1867 also objected to manifestations of equality accompanying political citizenship: "The excitement consequent among the Freedmen as to registering, placing them in a new status of society, has in some cases gave [sic] them an undue and exalted idea of their importance causing them in some instances to act with unnecessary impudence, the result of which invariably leads to difficulty." In his next line, he marveled at the gender dynamics of this "excitement" over freedpeople's new political status: "Strange as it may appear however, this seems to be confined to the females." Although his frustrating lack of details leaves few clues as to how this "impudence" was manifested, it suggests again the participation of freedwomen in the experience of citizenship and their place in the political community formed by freedpeople in Arkansas.[146]

The successful mobilization of freedpeople in the summer and fall of 1867 contributed to the vote in November approving the call for a constitutional convention.[147] Freedpeople demonstrated loyalty to the local branches of the Republican Party by supporting most of the candidates the party nominated as convention delegates.[148] "My candid impression is that most if not all of [the negroes] will vote with the radicals," speculated R. S. Gantt of Prairie County, one of few conservative delegates elected to the convention, to his colleague Jesse Turner, adding, "While many of them fully admit that the Southern man is their best friend in the ordinary affairs of life they manifest an unwillingness to trust us politically."[149] Yet, freedpeople did not fully trust white Republicans either. The freed community in Fort Smith, for instance, apparently opposed the candidacy of Moses Bell, the white southerner nominated by Republicans for the convention from Sebastian County. On election day many black voters tore Bell's name off their ballots before submitting their "yes" votes for the convention.[150] This presumably required coordination among freedmen going to the polls, given that most of them were unable to read.

African American and white Republican voters succeeded in approving a convention and electing to it a majority of Republican delegates, including eight African American men. William Henry Grey and James T. White were among the delegation from Phillips County. The other six black men were former slaves without prior political prominence, five of whom were long-term residents of Arkansas and four of whom identified as "farmers."[151] Thus this group selected through a formal election represented, to some extent at least, the experiences and interests of the state's rural masses.[152] And once the convention began, freedpeople themselves closely watched its proceedings. "The attendance of negroes in the lobby and gallery has been very fair every day of the session," the *Gazette* reported about the convention.[153] Those attending observed firsthand several dramatic moments in which the voices of African Americans challenged those of white southern elites. William Murphy, a black delegate and farmer from Jefferson County, told opponents of black male suffrage at the convention, "The colored man has not only the right to liberty, but to every privilege of an American citizen. . . . I would never have spoken here, but to say this to the men that have been our masters, men whom we have brought to the very condition they are in and have not only fed them, but have clothed them, have tied their shoes, and finally have fought until they were obliged to surrender. Yet, now that they have surrendered, they say we have no rights!"[154] Thomas Johnson, a minister representing Pulaski County, responded to one conservative delegate repeating the cliche that white southern men were the "best friends" of freedpeople by telling the convention, "My God! I hope he will put his hand over his mouth, and never speak that word again. We are very much inclined to believe that the men who are trying to secure equal rights for us, are our best friends."[155] On the night of the convention's final vote on the constitution, even though the debates had continued past midnight, freedpeople remained in the galleries until the end. When the president of the convention announced, "The Ayes have it," freedpeople demonstrated their support for a document that enfranchised all male citizens of the state willing to swear to the "civil and political equality of all men": "The announcement of the result of the vote was received with . . . vehement and prolonged expressions of approbation from the spectators in the lobbies and galleries."[156] The convention had been a success. Freedpeople in the galleries and the black delegates on the floor had joined together to secure the basis for a "*bona fide*" citizenship by "speaking for themselves." As Murphy told the convention, having to listen to attacks on the "fitness" of African Americans for citizenship "is enough to fill any man with the inspiration to rise and express the sentiments of his mind."[157]

"The ex-slave voted like fire directly after the war," Moses Jeffries, a freedman from Arkansas, recounted decades later.[158] Perhaps he was describing the scene in Little Rock when the new constitution was submitted to the voters for ratification. In an election that began on March 13, 1868, and lasted for two weeks, freedpeople coordinated a massive voting effort that involved collective political rituals derived from earlier celebrations. During prior commemorations of emancipation in Little Rock, worshipers at different black churches had formed processions that converged at a prearranged site and then marched through the city's main streets.[159] This pattern was repeated now for the purposes of facilitating votes for the constitution. On the morning that the election commenced, freedpeople collected in Little Rock churches for prayer before forming a procession that marched down Markham Street toward the State House, where many cast their ballots.[160] That freedpeople who felt threatened in their home districts traveled to the city and gathered at precincts where they could vote in large groups was suggested by the *Gazette*'s report that in Little Rock, "many planters who happened to be in the city" claimed to recognize "their negro employees in the various processions which paraded the streets."[161] This effort was complimented by the *Little Rock Evening Republican*, which noted that "hundreds of . . . humble but courageous colored men walked and rode miles to where they could vote freely and fairly."[162] One large contingent traveled from three counties away to cast their ballots in the relative safety of Little Rock; they slept on the outskirts of the city at night and marched in formation to the polls the next morning. This parade of over 200 people, "with martial music," guided voters in large groups to various polling places throughout the city. The proceedings were led by black men "carrying clubs and wearing red sashes," insignias identifying them as marshals of this polling effort.[163] As Julie Saville has argued concerning South Carolina, such election-day parades to polling places "lent dignity to Republican partisans who generally walked to polls that the opposition reached on horseback."[164]

Conservatives in Arkansas appealed to local party organizations to "watch" the polls for fraud, an effort that historian Carl Moneyhon suggests was a scarcely veiled call for intimidation.[165] Under these circumstances, freedpeople gathered at polling places to protect others coming to cast ballots.[166] When a white man in Little Rock challenged the ballot of a black man whom he accused of having already cast his vote elsewhere, the black man was defended by a crowd of freedpeople who reportedly "swore that no white man should interfere with their voting."[167] Freedpeople demonstrated solidarity on other matters as well. When Lee Morrison, a freedman, came to the polls in Helena to cast his vote, the sheriff attempted to arrest him on apparently pending murder charges. Morrison escaped with the aid of freedpeople surrounding the polls. In particular, black women were accused by an angry newspaper correspondent of intentionally creating a diversion, calling out that another freedman had shot someone at the other side of the gathering, and thereby distracting officials' attentions while Morrison fled. "These . . . women, knowing the numerical strength of the blacks, endeavored to precipitate a riot, by running among the negro men and commanding them to form a line of battle, as the shooting had commenced."[168] Though likely exaggerated, this report suggests that women were present at the polls to assist in protecting voters. Freedpeople traveling from town to town to oversee and defend the vote for the constitution reinforced a communal understanding and experience of citizenship among African Americans and displayed partisan solidarity never before seen in Arkansas.[169] Novel voting practices suggested that election day was no longer the ritual enactment of the powers of white manhood that it had been before emancipation.

Outraged at the events and the spectacle of the election, the *Gazette* ranted that former slaves had "paraded the streets and . . . took complete possession of any place that suited them."[170] For a brief time, freedmen and freedwomen in Arkansas had indeed made the public places of politics their own and had inserted their voices into the public sphere and the public space of the city as citizens. Although William Henry Grey had told his audience at the Convention of Colored Citizens, "We are not asking that the people should try any new experiment in this matter," what was being demanded and then practiced by freedpeople in Arkansas was, in fact, a new kind of citizenship.[171]

The Gendered Language of Conservative Politics

The "new experiment" in citizenship undertaken by African Americans in Arkansas during Reconstruction challenged an antebellum political community of free white men that had been split apart by war. Wartime policies of conscription that exempted large slaveholders, confiscation that left many ordinary civilians destitute, and martial law that violently suppressed dissent had brought new importance to class differences. The death and destruction left in the wake of one and sometimes two armies further exacerbated tensions. The losses suffered by yeoman and poorer whites were smaller but far more devastating than the losses of the wealthy, and the former's enthusiasm for a war fought to defend the slave property of their rich neighbors quickly waned.[172] After the war, many whites saw in cooperation with Reconstruction an opportunity to seize political power from the antebellum elites who had led them down the destructive path of secession. Antebellum political leaders recognized that reclaiming their political dominance would depend on diverting attention from class divisions and reuniting white southern men against Reconstruction.

Faced with a dual challenge to their erstwhile political dominance—from black male voters and from non-elite white men—Arkansas's conservatives desperately sought to foreground race as the determining factor in political alliances. Political identifications as, and divisions among, Whigs, Democrats, Unionists, and Secessionists had lost their prewar significance, and new alliances were taking shape. White conservative leaders struggled to replace old labels and counter new ones with the political designation of simply "White Men." Drawing on the gender ideologies and identities of antebellum white southern society, they strove to convince disaffected white men that the cost of uniting with Republicans in support of black male suffrage would be their own manhood. Specifically, conservatives represented the political participation of former slaves as the illegitimate empowerment of men who lacked the masculine "virtue" that would make them worthy of political authority. And conservatives further represented the presence of such men in the community of citizens as an affront to white manhood and as a threat to the domestic sources of white men's power, their patriarchal control over their families and property. Conservative rhetoric thus employed gendered meanings to redraw racial boundaries around the political community of "virtuous" citizens.[173]

The gendered terms within which white conservatives framed what was at stake in black men's enfranchisement is revealed by revisiting the events of congressional Reconstruction in Arkansas from the perspective of the conservative press, and specifically from the state's leading conservative paper, the *Arkansas Gazette*.[174] The *Gazette* was a primary medium for circulation of highly partisan conservative discourse in the state, and the actors behind its rhetoric were male members of Arkansas's antebellum political and economic elites.[175] William E. Woodruff Jr., the son of an outspoken white supremacist and slaveholder who founded the *Gazette*, ran the paper together with W. D. Blocher, co-owner, and John W. Wright, associate editor.[176] Woodruff in particular corresponded and associated with the elite planters and lawyers of the state, a group that David Walker, president of Arkansas's 1861 secession convention, would refer to in a letter to Woodruff as "those firmly united in a common cause, and who are inevitably bound in a common destiny" despite their occasional differences over tactics.[177] The editorial opinion expressed in the *Gazette*, then, offers a window onto how the state's leading conservative men understood and sought to frame the profound political changes of their era.

The newspaper run by Woodruff and his colleagues and expressing the opinions and objectives of elite conservatives of the state frequently employed gender and sexual imagery in bitter partisan attacks on the Reconstruction Acts and the extension of suffrage to African American men. The first Reconstruction Act represented "unwarrantable innovations upon our rights as free citizens," a *Gazette* editorial argued, and indicated that "republicanism is swallowed up in despotism."[178] The threat congressional Recon-struction posed to a republican form of government was specified over the next several months when the editors of the *Gazette*, in their editorials and news reports, produced gendered imagery of a republic endangered by the inclusion of black men in its political community.

"Upon the intelligence and virtue of the masses of the people depends the perpetuity of our republican form of government," wrote the *Gazette*'s edi-tors.[179] Repeatedly they would insist, however, that black men were inca-pable of this "intelligence and virtue" and that their political empowerment threatened to corrupt the political process. Demonstrations of black civic participation—black men and women acting in politically informed and en-gaged fashion as citizens—were derided by the press as manifestations of an incapacity for the independent reason, integrity, and self-control crucial to a strong citizenry and a strong republic. Black political activity was portrayed as the product of the agency of white radicals, and black men and women were depicted as naive, childlike pawns easily manipulated and excited by false promises of free land and irresponsible pronouncements on "equality."[180] These portrayals were reinforced by news reports of freedpeople's participa-tion in politics allegedly resulting in lawlessness and violence, leading to editorial comment such as "The facility with which the negroes here have been incited to mob violence by evilly disposed men must influence many to oppose giving them suffrage."[181] Black men were also represented as too ignorant to exercise citizenship responsibly when, for instance, at voter regis-tration they did not know their full names or exact ages, or when after registering they allegedly sold their registration certificates to others.[182] Fi-nally, these derogatory portrayals were elaborated with class imagery. One report portrayed black men's lower-class status as diminishing the aura of privilege and dominance around the practice of casting ballots, claiming that "no decent, respectable, intelligent white man will care to possess the privilege of the ballot" if his "vote would be neutralized by that of an ignorant corn-field negro and held of only equal weight with that of his illiterate negro boot-black."[183] After months of such attacks against black men and Reconstruction policies in the press, a Pulaski County Democratic convention met in Little Rock and summed up the argument formed by the *Gazette*: "We are unalter-ably opposed to conferring the elective franchise upon the negro. Having just emerged from a condition of servitude and subordination to the white race, he has shown in every instance where he has been permitted to vote, that he was not possessed of the intelligence and virtue which should be pre-requisite to the exercise of this privilege, and that he is but the tool of designing and interested white men."[184]

Not only did the *Gazette* represent black men as lacking the civic virtue necessary to be responsible citizens; the paper's editors also depicted black men as incapable of domestic virtue, of fulfilling the role of patriarchs who responsibly rule over households and provide for their families. The struggle over Reconstruction was represented in the *Gazette* as "the contest . . . between substantial, intelligent and well-disposed white citizens, fathers of families and property owners who have a real interest in the state's welfare, and the unlettered hordes of landless negroes duped and misled by white allies."[185] Regardless of the fact that black men were also "fathers of families," in this juxtaposition the *Gazette* did not allow them the place of proper patriarchs.

The newspaper's editors often mirrored the Freedmen's Bureau's rhetoric promoting free wage labor as the essence of "freedom" for former slaves.[186] For instance, when the commander of the fourth military district, which included Arkansas, issued an order stating, "The most important duty devolving upon freedmen in their new condition, is that of providing, by their own labor, for the support of themselves and families. . . . Freedmen are therefore urged not to neglect their business to engage in political discussions," the *Gazette* reprinted it and advocated that all planters read it to the freedpeople in their employ.[187] Motivated perhaps to promote planter interests in more work and less politics on the part of laborers, the *Gazette* also seems to have embraced the opportunity that repeating Freedmen's Bureau policy presented to produce and circulate images of black men as refusing to labor and thus failing as providers. And this failure was frequently tied to politics. This connection was at times made explicit, as in the editorial comment, "Since these loyal leagues have been organized among [freedmen], their efficiency as plantation laborers has been almost utterly destroyed"; at other times the connection was presented in more seemingly neutral but no less effective terms: "Twenty-six colored persons were arrested in New Orleans as vagrants one day last week. They were all registered voters."[188]

In actuality, freedpeople's capacity to support themselves through labor for others was becoming increasingly difficult as economic conditions worsened in the fall and winter of 1867. Floods and low cotton prices on top of two consecutive seasons of crop failures led to widespread destitution. Planters were unable or unwilling to pay freedpeople, and many abandoned plantations seeking other means of subsistence, namely, through hunting and poaching in the woods. Not surprisingly, the conservative press began to complain of theft of planters' animals: "In the rural districts where the negroes are numerous, the planters have been compelled to abandon the profitable business of stock raising . . . for the reason that the freedmen are continually scouring the woods with fire arms shooting down cattle and hogs even within sight of the owners' houses." The press was alarmed at more than the theft of pigs and cows: "When remonstrated with, [the freedmen] are insolent and insulting, and not unfrequently they claim the right to do so as they have worked for and have an interest in everything in the whole country."[189] The possibility that such radical reformulation of understandings of "property" might be justified was, of course, not considered. Instead, disputes over open-range livestock were represented as a battle between responsible patriarchs and irresponsible and uncivilized men. The *Gazette* printed a petition from "citizens, grand jurors, judges and other officials of the county of Chicot," asking that the military authorities provide for impoverished freedpeople there. This provision was made necessary by "the failure of the freedmen to make provisions to feed them and their families." As a result, the petition asserted, "the freedmen, as a general thing, throughout the county, are already depredating upon our stock . . . and by the first of February we believe they will nearly have consumed all of our stock, unless some means can be devised for supplying their wants." And yet the primary appeal of this petition was not for food for starving freedpeople but, rather, for troops to be sent to Chicot "for the protection of our families and property" from what was feared to be an inevitable "collision between the races."[190]

In the same weekly edition, the *Gazette* also protested a military order reminding local governments of their responsibility to provide for paupers in their communities. This editorial insisted that "idle negroes" were not paupers but, rather, vagrants, defined, in part, as "able-bodied person[s] who shall be found loitering or rambling about, . . . and who quit their houses, and leave their wives and children without the means of subsistence."[191] A subsequent editorial contended that the state's economic destitution was the result of Republican policies that had disrupted harmonious relationships between "the employer and the employed," and thus "the barbarous, brutish race just emerged from slavery . . . has been deprived of the opportunity of working for subsistence and turned loose, a hungry naked horde, to beg, or plunder for a living. An impoverished, industrious people must provide for them or see them perish from want, or perhaps, what is worse, defend themselves and families against their murderous raids."[192] Not only had black men's inability to establish families and labor for their support left idle, undomesticated "naked hordes" of freedpeople to wander the countryside and threaten violence, the *Gazette* argued. The paper also alleged that the failure of black men as patriarchs put at risk the ability of white men to provide for and protect their own families. An imperiled white manhood rooted in property ownership and the power to provide for and protect their dependents was contrasted with images of an unpropertied, undomesticated, and dangerous black masculinity.

Interpretations of the impact of Reconstruction policy emerging from the pages of the *Gazette* both denigrated black manhood and represented all white men as honorable and worthy of citizenship. In return for opposition to Reconstruction, then, the paper offered all of its white male readers, regardless of economic condition, the role of virtuous men acting to protect their state and their hearth and home. On the other hand, for white men to choose not to fight this battle, to allow the corruption of the republic by men depicted as incapable of exercising both public and private power responsibly, was portrayed by the *Gazette*'s editors as not to be men themselves. This was implied in the form of the paper's discourse, specifically in its frequent recourse to sexual metaphors. Editorials employed gendered and sexual imagery of domination and subordination, activity and passivity, raping and being raped, to implicate manliness or its undoing in political events.[193]

To drive home the image of white masculine honor at stake in the political battle over black male suffrage, conservative discourse cast political dominance in sexual terms. When Alabama held the first constitutional convention to meet under the Reconstruction Acts, the *Gazette* graphically described it as "the offspring of a political rape committed by the rump congress upon a sovereign state held down by the military power of the government."[194] A few weeks later, the editors termed Mississippi's convention "an illegitimate twin sister of a political rape."[195] The *Gazette* recalled this image repeatedly in references to Arkansas's and other states' constitutional conventions as "bastard conventions," the illegitimate product of illegitimate power imposed on the southern states.[196] In these images, federal power in the form of military governments and the Reconstruction Acts was figured as rapist, and southern states and the "free white male citizens" whose political will was overpowered were depicted as being raped. In other instances, federal authority was conflated with the local empowerment of black men allowed by that authority through the ubiquitous use of vague terms such as "negro domination."[197] A letter reprinted in the *Gazette* depicted southern whites as struggling to "shake off the incubus of negro rule."[198] The author may have intended no more by "incubus" than a figurative term for nightmare, but it also suggested the mythical demons imagined to descend on and rape women in their sleep. The *Gazette* told its readers that Arkansas was indeed in the position of a woman threatened with violation by both black men and white Republicans when it called for the organization of "the white people of the state who would save her fair fame and rescue her from the control of negroes and their more unscrupulous allies." White men dare not, this editorial warned, "fail their state in her hour of peril."[199] This rhetoric was metaphorical; it did not represent explicit and consistent charges that sexually predatory black men threatened white women with rape, as would become common by the end of the nineteenth century.[200] What was consistent was "negro domination" being portrayed metaphorically as rape, the loss of political power being represented as sexual subordination and violation, and political action being depicted in sexual terms. Whether white men reading the *Gazette* were to fear seeing themselves in the position of men who fail to protect their women/state from violation or in the position of the raped woman (or man) was left unclear.[201] To be in either position destroyed the most intimate foundations of white men's sense of themselves as men, their dominance in sexual acts and their control over access to the sexuality of "their" women.

In addition to images of sexually predatory men, rhetoric in the *Gazette* employed the figure of a sexually unvirtuous woman to depict the imperiled manhood of white southern men. The paper's editors likened the proposed compromise of accepting universal male suffrage along with universal amnesty to "a case . . . where an innocent young man was prosecuted at the instance of a degraded mother, as being a close relative of her illegitimate child, and he was abject enough to *compromise* the matter by marrying the woman."[202] The *Gazette* editors' abhorrence at being forced to share political power with black men was conveyed by likening such a prospect to union with an unchaste woman. Only men in an abject, submissive position, it was alleged, would accept such an impure arrangement. White Republicans' supposed lack of political integrity and their promotion of black male suffrage for their own political gain was also figured in terms of female sexual purity: "The fall of the republican party from virtue has been rapid, and it must needs prostitute itself now to provide the means of prolonging its existence. It has embraced the negro, and must be damned forever with all white men."[203] Thus the slippage between politics and sex, and the representation of a political contest in sexual terms, worked in various ways. Images of prostitution, rape, abjection, disrepute, and illegitimacy came together to represent the challenge to white men's exclusive political control over southern society in terms of pending sexual subordination and powerlessness, suggesting that Republican rule and black enfranchisement threatened the intimate sources of white men's identities as men.

Although the specific strategy that the *Gazette* advocated in response to federal Reconstruction policy changed over time, its metaphors remained the same. The paper's editors had initially encouraged readers to show themselves "men" by refusing to cooperate in any way with the Reconstruction Acts.[204] After having rejected the Fourteenth Amendment "as derogating from our rights as States, and our honor as men," would white men now "bow our heads, and accept . . . not only the constitutional amendment we so proudly declined but the humiliation of negro suffrage also and the disfranchisement of our leading men?" The *Gazette* argued no, calling for resistance based on the "high moral courage, and heroic civic fortitude, which faces danger unappalled . . . [and] is alone becoming men who proved their courage in arms."[205] The *Gazette* described white southerners advocating cooperation with the Reconstruction Acts as giving in to "unmanly despair and fear of future ills"[206] and praised those meeting to oppose the Reconstruction Acts as demonstrating "that the honor and manhood of the southern people were left."[207] However, as it became increasingly clear to Woodruff and his colleagues that a convention and a new constitution were unavoidable, they began to seek ways to try to influence the process and lay the groundwork for regaining control in the future. Thus, soon after accusing white men supporting cooperation with congressional Reconstruction of being "unmanly," the paper reversed its position and depicted its own previously advised course as passive submission to federal power. Now the *Gazette*'s editors called on every conservative white man eligible to register and vote to do so.[208] Participating in the elections and convention was represented as the means of retrieving southern white manhood through action.

Introducing their new strategy, the *Gazette*'s editors announced, "While we deny the constitutionality of the reconstruction acts, we have no other alternative but to quietly submit to their enforcement, and to take such steps as suggest themselves to a prudent man to save himself from harm."[209] The editors labored to ensure, however, that quiet submission not be mistaken for inaction. On April 23, 1867, the *Gazette* reprinted excerpts from a letter written by William Hicks, then state senator from Jackson and White Counties, to the *White County Record* advising all conservative white men to try to register and vote. Hicks called on his audience to "come forward now and show yourselves men, in cloud as well as in sunshine." Drawing on gendered imagery of activity and passivity and invoking the image of a woman failing to resist rape, he countered those who opposed his strategy: "Listen not to those who say, lie still, do nothing, let the radicals have it their own way, etc. This is no time to lie still. . . . Suppose you lie still and a radical convention shall adopt a constitution disfranchising forever all who did not register. You will then be permitted to lie still for all time to come."[210] Continuing the debate the next week over whether manliness was lost in "submission" or "inactivity," the *Gazette* rejected the position of the governor of Georgia that "a patient, manly endurance of military government" was preferable to "acquiescence," promoting instead the need for "active means to ward off the greater evils which threaten to fall with crushing weight upon us."[211] Now *not* to act under the congressional plan was figured as unmanly, represented in almost sexual terms as passively allowing an outside power to "have its way" or fall upon them with its "crushing weight," while to "submit" was to bravely face and fight the adversity ahead. The *Gazette* further sought to motivate white men in Arkansas to register to vote by invoking families and property as what they would protect by such action: "If men value their lives, their property, and a peaceful home, they must endeavor to secure it by registering and voting for honest and sensible men for delegates to the convention."[212]

Combining political issues and domestic concerns was not a new practice. Nor was recourse to sexual metaphors for political conflict an unusual rhetorical device. The *Gazette's* discursive strategy reflected the long-standing association of a man's identity in private with his power in public. In the context of congressional Reconstruction, the *Gazette* employed this association to focus white men's political attentions not on class divisions but instead on race. The editors sought to rebuild a cross-class alliance of white men by convincing those seeking to oust Confederate leaders from power that the cost of their alliance with black male suffrage may well be their manhood.

After voters approved a constitutional convention for Arkansas at the election in November 1867, the *Gazette* turned its attention toward building a statewide organization that it hoped would mobilize enough voters to reject a new constitution when put to a popular vote. Though affiliated with the national Democratic Party, it sought to attract prewar Whigs and Unionists. Though organized by the planters and professionals dominating the state's conservative camp, it sought support from yeoman and poor whites who had turned against Confederate leaders. To unite the various splinters of the white male electorate, this movement foregrounded the components of identity that they all shared—race and gender—by calling their effort the White Man's Party.[213] The party's name and its platform, which called for "a white man's government" and opposed "negro rule," explicitly rejected the new liberal discourse of universal manhood suffrage and implicitly promoted race as the fundamental factor in political identification and interests. The *Gazette* publicized and promoted plans for a convention to initiate the party in Pulaski County, urged the "friends of a white man's government" throughout the state to begin "perfecting a complete and thorough organization of the conservative element within her borders,"[214] and applauded the organization of "white men's clubs" throughout the state.[215]

In the rhetoric surrounding this political effort, only race was declared relevant to white men's political interests. When the Democratic State Convention opened on January 27, 1868, in Little Rock's new City Hall, banners adorned the walls from states throughout the country declaring opposition to black male suffrage and support for a "white man's government" and the Democratic Party.[216] Behind the stage hung an emblem of the desired union of all white men across lines of previous party affiliation. "On the left there was the old whig coon and on the right the democratic rooster, with the motto reaching from one to the other: 'United in a just cause.' " Beneath this banner hung another, declaring "Arkansas all right for the white man's party."[217] W. W. Reynolds, temporary president of the convention, identified the gathering's constituency only by race, recognizing the delegates as "the representatives of the white citizens of the state." S. A. Saunders of Dallas County, appointed permanent president of the convention, declared the gathering "assembled not as whigs or democrats but as conservative men whose object was to defeat that radicalism which we believe is bringing the country to ruin."[218]

The front row of the audience observing the convention's proceedings was occupied by "a large number of ladies," who were responsible for having dressed the hall in "festoons of evergreen with artificial magnolias" and drapes in the colors of the national flag.[219] Saunders acknowledged their presence, declaring that "the handsome decoration of the hall by the fair hands and noble hearts testified that the true women of the country were with us to cheer us in our good work." These women were acknowledged again at the end of the convention, in a resolution offering "the thanks of this convention . . . [to] the ladies of Little Rock for the tasteful decorations of this city hall prepatory to their sitting" and declaring that "all good democrats cannot fail to be encouraged by this evidence of the good will of those who are as pure and patriotic as they are amiable and beautiful."[220] Conservative white women of Little Rock apparently contributed to initiating this new political organization. Yet the manner in which they were acknowledged offered them merely a dependent and ornamental role. Emphasizing feminine, delicate "ladies" "cheering on" the White Man's Party brought to the forefront the gender in the party's name. Although the presence of women at the convention and their efforts on its behalf suggest their interests in the political issues being discussed and their pursuit of ways to participate in those discussions, representations of them as observing but not participating in, as encouraging and decorating but not doing, "our good work" emphasized women's dependent roles and rearticulated political work as the work of men.[221]

The imagery of dependent women participating in the Democratic State Convention as "pure and amiable" "ladies" with "fair hearts and noble hands" also contrasted sharply with the *Gazette*'s portrayal of African American women's presence in political spaces. The paper's editors termed African American activities during the ratification election in March 1868 a "disgusting farce" and highlighted women's roles as the opposite of feminine or dependent.[222] For instance, recall the news coverage of the near "riot" at the polls in Helena that depicted black women urging black men to fight the police who attempted to arrest Lee Morrison, a freedman. The reporter insulted the women, labeling them "black strumpets," and depicted them as more aggressive and confrontational, as more masculine, than were the black men.[223] In the pages of the *Gazette*, white women's presence in politics confirmed white men's dominance, while black women's presence undermined the manhood of black men.

The most striking representation of gender reversal in political roles among African Americans was conservative charges that black women had actually cast ballots during the election. White conservatives observing polling places would make this claim along with accusations of other forms of fraud.[224] Although the charge was made that registrars overseeing the polling were knowingly permitting this violation of election law, reports also claimed that women were dressing in men's clothing in order to fool registrars. The *Gazette* reported that at the State House in Little Rock, where all "sexes" were allowed to vote "as often as they pleased," "it became a matter of common rumor that negro women arrayed in male apparel were voting."[225] A Union County newspaper made the unlikely charge that "the freedmen's bureau had been issuing a large quantity of clothing during the few days preceding the election" to facilitate "*female* negroes . . . at the polls, with trousers on *to swell the vote for the constitution."*[226] These representations of black women assuming the clothing and roles of men played with the image of even women's bodies somehow becoming male, or "swelling" inside their trousers. Overall, these reports represented black political participation as corrupting public life by blurring categories and turning power relations on their heads. Charges that black women were voting implied that removing racial boundaries from political participation meant introducing into public life not only men unworthy of citizenship but also the allegedly chaotic, undomesticated, and inappropriate gender roles and identities of former slaves.

These charges also contributed to an overall depiction of the ratification of the new constitution enfranchising black men as illegitimate. Once the military authorities determined that Arkansas's new constitution had been endorsed by a majority of the electorate, conservatives demanded an official inquiry into their charges of illegal electoral practices.[227] Colonel John E. Tourtelotte, working on behalf of General Alvan C. Gillem, then in command of the military district including Arkansas, came to the state to investigate these charges. His inquiry found minor irregularities too insignificant to have affected the outcome of the election.[228] Among these was convincing evidence that "in Jefferson County, a woman voted for the constitution, presenting the certificate of registration of her husband, who was in jail."[229] Given earlier reports of black women's presence at polling places, it is possible that more than one black woman attempted to vote for the new constitution. However, it seems more likely that the conservative reports of widespread cross-dressing and fraudulent voting were fabricated or exaggerated. One woman's actions, and maybe those of a few others, provided the raw material for rumors of a widespread practice that fit the conservatives' gendered critique of Reconstruction. Newspaper reporters and editors invoked the presence of black women in the spaces of politics as evidence of improper gender identities among former slaves as well as of the corruption of the political process promised by African American citizenship. Black men were not proper men, black women were not proper women, and thus their inclusion in the public sphere endangered the republic with corruption and disorder.[230]

In their discourse opposing black male suffrage during congressional Reconstruction, then, conservative newspaper editors and political leaders participated in a vast unmanning of African American men and misgendering of African American women. At the same time, white men who willingly admitted black men into the political community were represented in a variety of ways as not being "men" themselves. To rally support among white men across class lines, the press implied that the domestic and intimate realms of white men's power and identities—home, marriage, and sex—were at stake in the enfranchisement of black men. As these images circulated throughout Reconstruction-era Arkansas, they reinforced a construction of citizenship as only legitimately practiced by white men, all of whom were offered identities as honorable and worthy men in exchange for their opposition to black suffrage.

EMANCIPATION BROUGHT DRAMATIC changes in the practices and meanings of citizenship in Arkansas. African Americans seized the opportunity to "do our own talking" and organized collectively to support a new constitution that would be the basis for their citizenship. In the process they presented in the public spaces of politics a vision for political community very different from the exclusively white and male citizenship of antebellum southern society. Rejecting the challenge to prewar understandings of citizenship, white conservatives framed Reconstruction-era struggles over citizenship and race as contests over manhood. As conservatives struggled to preserve notions of a superior white manhood, they asserted new gendered meanings for race, representing black women and men as unworthy of citizenship because they were not properly women and men.

The Democratic State Convention that met in City Hall on January 27, 1868, to usher in the White Man's Party's campaign against a new constitution echoed the rhetoric of the conservative press. But the convention also introduced a trope new to Arkansas's Reconstruction-era debates when it coupled its opposition to black male suffrage with an opposition to "social equality." The convention's delegates resolved that black men were entitled to "all rights and guaranties except those of equal participation in making the laws, for which [they are] manifestly incompetent, and except the rights and privileges of a social equality."[231] At this time, the Arkansas constitutional convention was also in session. When debate recommenced at this convention the next day, a delegate would propose that the new constitution prohibit interracial marriage in the interest of preventing social equality. The movement of political rhetoric from one convention to the other throws into sharp relief how conservative political discourse shaped, and contorted, the process of enfranchising black men in the state of Arkansas. The debates over banning interracial marriage in the Arkansas constitutional convention of 1868 framed the struggle over the reorganization of Arkansas's government around issues of domestic and sexual relations. Conservative proponents of such a ban drew on constructions of virtuous manhood and womanhood to reproduce hierarchical meanings for race. The debates over such a ban, though, also ultimately opened up a space in which to protest the sexual coercion of black women by white men, right in the center of a political contest over the meaning of citizenship in a postemancipation world.

CHAPTER FOUR

A Constitutional Convention

The delegates to Arkansas's constitutional convention who met in Little Rock in January 1868 were charged with a momentous task. They were to design a new state constitution establishing for the first time in Arkansas a democracy without regard to race and thereby incorporate former slaves into the political community as equal citizens. This would be Arkansas's first postemancipation constitution, and it had to meet the requirements of the federal Reconstruction Acts. Above all, it had to establish universal male suffrage (excluding former government officials who gave aid to the Confederacy as specified under the Fourteenth Amendment) and thus extend previously denied voting rights to African American men. But on the eighteenth day of the gathering, John Bradley, a white southern delegate representing white-majority Bradley County, took the floor and argued that the revolutionary potential of Reconstruction—which he intended to resist—lay elsewhere. Bradley, who came to the convention a self-declared opponent of the planter elite that had ruled Arkansas before the Civil War and as a new ally of the Republican Party, claimed that "the great question that is agitating Arkansas from centre to circumference" was interracial marriage. He proposed that the new constitution, in addition to extending voting rights to black men, also contain a clause "forbidding any officer, either civil or ecclesiastical, to solemnize the rites of matrimony between a white person and a person of African descent."[1]

William Henry Grey, who attended the convention as a delegate from Phillips County and who had spearheaded the demand for African American

Engraving of William Henry Grey, n.d.
Courtesy of the Arkansas History Commission.

citizenship at the Convention of Colored Citizens in the same city just two years earlier, immediately mocked Bradley's seeming diversion from the more important task at hand: "I have no particular objection to the resolution. But I think that in order to make the law binding, there should be some penalty attached to its violation—kill them, quarter them, or something of that kind." Sarcasm aside, Grey quickly followed with a more serious response. He contended that the provision was "superfluous," as demonstrated by the fact that such prohibitions were not seen as necessary in the northern states, where interracial marriage was nonetheless rare. Furthermore, he challenged the proposal's exclusive focus on marriage rather than on cross-racial sexual relations outside marriage, where African American women, in particular, had suffered a long history of abuse and exploitation: "I know that such provisions have heretofore more or less obtained; but while the contract has been kept on our part, it has not been kept upon the part of our friends; and I propose, if such an enactment is to be inserted in the Constitution, to insist, also, that if any white man shall be found cohabitating with a negro woman, the penalty shall be death."[2] Grey's words were followed by laughter and applause from like-minded delegates and parties, many of whom were former slaves, observing the convention from the galleries above.[3]

Bradley, feigning surprise that there should be any opposition to his resolu-

House of Representatives Chamber, State House, Little Rock, Arkansas, where the debates of the constitutional convention of 1868 were held. Now in the Old State House Museum, restored to its antebellum appearance. Courtesy of the Old State House Museum, Little Rock, Arkansas.

tion, responded by implying that Grey's resistance to the measure raised questions about his own intentions toward white women: "If such a provision as I propose is not necessary, if you do not mean to rush into these practices, I ask, in all candor, why, in the name of God, do you object to having a line established, and to saying, to the white race and to the black,—'Thus far shalt thou go, and no farther?'" Bradley also offered his rationale for why an interracial marriage prohibition was indeed relevant to the task assigned to this convention: "As to the idea that no such difficulty exists in the Northern States, I am only able to use this argument in reply,—that there is no negro suffrage in the Northern States."[4]

Bradley was incorrect about this; there were places in the North where black men voted. Grey, too, had been mistaken, in that marriage across racial lines had been legally prohibited in various times and places in the North.[5] Yet accuracy did not, in fact, matter much in a debate whose significance would prove to be largely symbolic. Packed into this small exchange, the beginning of a debate over marriage and sexual relations that would occupy more than two days of Arkansas's constitutional convention, is evidence of an increasing recourse to discourses of gender and sexuality in battles over citizenship and the meaning of race following emancipation. Bradley's proposal and subsequent expressions of support for it—manifestations of the slippage between the political and the domestic, and between race and gender, that, as we saw in the last chapter, riddled debates over citizenship in Arkansas—were immediately recognizable as an outgrowth of an ever-widening discourse of "miscegenation" circulating throughout postemancipation political debates and conflicts. Rhetoric surrounding the Civil War–era neologism "miscegenation" and its companion terms "amalgamation" and "social equality" entailed the persistent conflation of the political empowerment of black men with "race mixing," particularly the idea that enfranchised black men would seek social interaction, marriage, and sex with white women.[6]

As we will see, though, measures such as Bradley's proposed constitutional ban were designed not so much to prevent white-black unions as to permanently identify them as illegitimate.[7] Despite the image of biological mixture invoked by the term "miscegenation," the issue driving this discourse was not, in fact, concern about the physical amalgamation of what were imagined to be two distinct races. Nor was it any immediate practical threat of widespread interracial marriage. Rather, Bradley's proposal and the regionwide discourse of which it was a part were driven by the question of what emancipation and the enfranchisement of black men would mean for the future significance of race as a social and political category. Close examination of miscegenation rhetoric reveals white southerners responding to the instability of race as a politically significant category in this moment just following emancipation by turning to domestic and social relationships to carve out a supposedly legitimate space for codifying racial difference and separation.[8]

This putatively legitimate sphere of difference, which would become widely identified in this discourse as the "social," would not, in the end, be distinguishable from the "political" and the "civil," where white men like Bradley claimed they were willing to grant equality to black men.[9] In white southern political culture, white men's exclusive claims to political authority had long been predicated on their social identities as responsible and honorable patriarchs.[10] The rhetoric of miscegenation, with its implications of an unrestrained and unruly sexuality among former slaves, was in the end a protest against representing African American men as similarly legitimate patriarchs and hence as honorable and independent men worthy of full citizenship and a voice in public affairs.[11] It was also a protest against depicting black women as "virtuous" and deserving state protection from sexual abuse. In its inscription of difference through gendered representations of race, the discourse of miscegenation would ultimately serve to rationalize the perpetuation of white men's political privileges even in a society of supposedly equal rights.

To investigate the politics of miscegenation during Reconstruction, this chapter closely examines the debate that followed Bradley's proposed inter-racial marriage prohibition, one that was similar to contests occurring in constitutional conventions, political meetings, and the press throughout the southern states at this time.[12] There have been few historical settings in which white southern politicians were obliged to explain, rather than simply assert, their alarm over the possibility of marriage and sex between black and white people or to reveal why they believed that political equality among men would impel these cross-racial sexual relations.[13] But post–Civil War political conditions and the constitutional conventions that resulted—in which African Americans as well as white supporters of a race-blind legal system had con-siderable influence over the requisites and content of political discourse—allowed opponents of an interracial marriage ban to directly challenge the measure. Thus its advocates were forced to articulate in its defense what would subsequently be accepted without explication, that is, the mechanisms connecting this supposed social taboo with political power. The debates over race, sex, and marriage that resulted highlight how gender and sexuality became instruments for constructing racial difference and inequality despite universal male suffrage. They also reveal how this gendered discourse of race shaped profound dilemmas and perilous political terrain for black leaders as they approached demands for equality.

The Rhetoric of Miscegenation and the Reconstruction of Race

Bradley's proposal that Arkansas's new constitution prohibit interracial mar-riage suggested his familiarity with a long-standing rhetorical tradition asso-ciating black empowerment and freedom with interracial marriage and sex. Since the onset of widespread activism demanding immediate abolition in the 1830s, supporters of slavery in the North and South had charged that those advocating an end to the institution were, in fact, promoting "amalgamation," a term invoking both social and biological interaction of black and white people and hence the obliteration of black and white as distinct social and physical groups.[14] Such accusations were hurled by Democrats at the new Republican Party in the 1850s, reached a fever pitch with the election of Abraham Lincoln as president in 1860, and continued to escalate during the Civil War.[15]

Democratic attacks often took the form of fabricated endorsements of cross-racial intimacy attributed to Republicans and abolitionists. For instance, in December 1863, northern Democrats printed what they called a "Black Republican Prayer," which counted among "the blessings of Emancipation" not only that "the illustrious, sweet-scented Sambo [may] nestle in the bosom of every Abolition woman, that she may be quickened by the pure blood of the majestic African," but also that "the distinction of color [may] be forever consigned to oblivion."[16] Most famously, the bogus political pamphlet penned by David Goodman Croly, the managing editor of the anti-abolitionist *New York World*, and George Wakeman, a reporter with that paper, that invented the term featured in its title, *Miscegenation: The Theory of the Blending of the Races, Applied to the American White Man and Negro*, claimed to be a pro-Republican tract declaring that "no race can long endure without commingling of its blood with that of other races" and advocating that "the white man should marry the black woman and the white woman the black man" in order to assure a "rich blending of blood." The pamphlet proposed "miscegenation" ("from the Latin *miscere*, to mix, and *genus*, race") as a new term for this process preferable to "amalgamation," whose actual definition referred to the mixing of metals, and advocated making the new term the central component of a Republican platform for "Political and Social Equality."[17] Although this pamphlet should be credited with coining the term "miscegenation" (which joined but never replaced "amalgamation"), its authors did not originate its themes. The pamphlet, which appeared during congressional debates over the Thirteenth Amendment in the spring of 1864, received immediate notoriety and was even believed by some to be the theory of a legitimate abolitionist thinker, because its authors merely refashioned a rhetoric already widely attributed to Republicans and abolitionists by their critics.

At the same time, abolitionists had long insisted that southern society and its slave system promoted interracial sex in its most licentious form.[18] In fact, John Bradley invoked this tradition as an insult upon the South when explaining why he proposed a constitutional prohibition on interracial marriage at Arkansas's constitutional convention. "I am here," he declared, "to enter my protest, with indignation, against the foul insinuations which have been thrown out, reflecting upon the integrity, the honor, and the nobility of the people of my country!"[19] Bradley's statements reflected a deep association of sex across racial lines with dishonor. This association was powerful in white southern society despite how common in practice cross-racial sex had been in the South, where white men in particular suffered few sanctions for such conduct—indeed, sex with black women was often understood to be white men's privilege.[20] Yet interracial sex was also considered inherently illicit and thus shameful if a man was not discreet. Few white men recognized their offspring with black women, and those who did risked being the objects of gossip and scorn.[21] Furthermore, in nineteenth-century white southern society, fathers were expected to maintain strict control over the courtship and marriage choices of their (legitimate) daughters, dictated more by economic and social considerations than by personal choice.[22] In this context, to accuse your political opponents of favoring circumstances that could lead to interracial sex was to accuse them both of private vice and of undermining white men's ability to fulfill their patriarchal responsibility to prevent the premarital seduction of, and to assure "proper" domestic matches for, their daughters. When it became public knowledge that a white woman or even a white man had engaged in cross-racial sex, it was understood within white political culture as shameful to a white man. Either gender's "indulgence" reflected a white man's failure as a "man": his failure to control his daughters—or worse his wife—or his failure to control his own passion and tendency toward sin. Sex across color lines, no matter how common, was represented as a mark of dishonor and a symbol of vice, and to engage in it or to allow it to occur within one's family was the opposite of virtuous manhood.[23] And a man's personal vice was a convenient means of calling into question his public virtue.

It seems that beyond its value as a means of discrediting one's political opponents, miscegenation was a common framework for political protest in these years because it offered a physical metaphor for a key social and political problem posed by emancipation: Without slavery, would race continue to be significant to the organization of southern society? Miscegenation and amalgamation conveyed the image of cross-racial reproduction obliterating separate biological categories of white and black. The future of race did not, in fact, rest in reproduction but, rather, in social relations and cultural representation. But this reality was obscured behind discourses of race that conflated "blood" and "civilization," so that miscegenation resonated with broad concerns about the political and social future of race. Would a republic that offered nominal equality to all men in civil and political realms nonetheless affirm racial difference and inequality in other areas? Were there realms outside the political and the civil, such as the social, where racial difference and inequality would continue to be legitimated and racial hierarchy reinscribed? Would white and black live in separate social worlds with separate collective identities, even while sharing political power and civil rights? Or would they integrate in all things and would race thereby lose its significance in social as well as political life? Would men of color who managed to gain property and schooling be able to move up in class status and join white society? Or would social hierarchies based on race regardless of wealth and education continue to prevail?

The fact that emancipation put in question the meaning that race would have in social as well as political and civil life sheds light upon a prevalent but ambiguous term in the vocabulary of miscegenation, and that is "social equality." Its specific referent opaque but nonetheless often employed in ways that presumed transparency, "social equality" referred broadly to forms of association between white and black people that did not convey a hierarchical meaning for race and that did not serve to mark racial difference. As historian Nell Irvin Painter has argued, " 'Social equality' meant people of two races, usually including black men, sitting down together at a table or on a train, sharing a smoke at a club, or belonging to the same organization on a footing of equality. When a servant sat with an employer, that was not 'social equality.' "[24] As used by white southern opponents of racial equality during Reconstruction, it referred both to integrated access to public spaces and facilities and to black access to the "private" spaces of white society and domestic life; in fact, the latter was presumed to follow from the former.[25] When used in the latter sense, the term intertwined race with class and invoked imagery of the forcible intrusion into white men's homes by their supposed social inferiors.[26] In theory, when backed by federal sanction of their "equality," black men, though uninvited, would be able to demand admittance into white society, and specifically into the "parlors" (spaces in nineteenth-century middle-class houses where women entertained in mixed-gender company) of white men's homes.[27] These demands were represented as a violation because the supposed intruders were men of inferior economic standing and cultural refinement. Yet, implicitly, rhetoric of social equality was also a protest against the possibility that black men who did obtain wealth and education might be allowed to enter white social spaces despite being of African descent.

Entering white men's homes, or parlors, in a society where premarital romance was closely chaperoned in at least middle-class families also implied courtship. Imagined intrusions of black men into white men's homes thus implicitly threatened that black men would seek marriage and legitimate sexual relationships with white women, who in a segregated social world would have been "protected" by their fathers or husbands from interaction with men of inferior racial and/or class status.[28] Thus when white southerners warned against "social equality," they were often understood to be referring to courtship, marriage, and sex.

Rhetoric of social equality and even miscegenation, though, was more than a euphemistic expression of a simple taboo against sexual relationships between white women and black men. This rhetoric was also more than pure ruse, propaganda meant to trigger indignation in masses of white voters (though it may often have been employed with this in mind). The debates over interracial marriage in Arkansas suggest that when white southern men spoke of social equality, they did, in fact, mean and deeply feel a threat of just that. Drawing on the general concept of "the social," which emerged in the mid-nineteenth century to delineate an imagined realm that was distinct from the political yet not entirely private,[29] the term seems to have invoked during Reconstruction not only equality in private space but also public manifestations of private relations, the spaces where the contours of legitimate private relationships were visible in public and where they, in turn, produced meanings of legitimacy. Who attended the theater or sat in a streetcar with whom and which women were escorted to public events by which men, as well as who was invited into whose home and who married whom, were important indicators of socially legitimate interactions. It was in this context that marriage came to matter so much. Courtship and marriage across racial lines, and thus public recognition and representation of legitimate private relations, could be powerful signs of a society organized without racial difference or hierarchy. Alternatively, requiring by law racial separation in personal relationships and thus the social sphere would help to consolidate a racially hierarchical society by making visible and meaningful distinct racial groups and by marking the manhood and womanhood of African Americans as inferior to that of whites. Rhetoric of social equality and miscegenation painted a picture of an integrated world in which equality for white and black men in civic life threatened white men's sense of power both in public realms and in other locations where white men experienced their identities as men, in their domestic space and relations. The visceral character of this discourse and its resonance, I will argue, stemmed not so much from white men's recoiling at the image of black men embracing their daughters but, rather, from the loss of supremacy for the white citizen/patriarch that this image suggested.[30]

In response to charges that black empowerment meant social equality, African American political spokesmen often asserted that it was only civil and political equality that they sought. For instance, when Bishop Campbell of the

African Methodist Episcopal Church addressed a crowd of some 400 freed-people and 50 whites outside the State House in Little Rock in early June 1867, he stressed that marriage with whites was not of interest to African Americans. The *Gazette* paraphrased his comments: "He did not want the government to elevate him. . . . Miscegenation was a bugbear. . . . All the negroes desired was freedom, citizenship, the right to vote without property qualifications, and under the same restrictions with whites, and an open road to all offices from constable to president."[31] Even though most black leaders opposed legal restrictions of any kind involving race, few would openly argue against the idea that cross-racial marriage was detrimental to society.[32] Instead, leaders mocked the hypocrisy of white southern men invoking cross-racial sex to depict black men as a threat. In the black press, editorials challenged conservative reasoning by pointing out white male responsibility for sex across racial lines and for black female victimization. In January 1866, the editors of the Augusta, Georgia, *Colored American* argued that "the black man" was not "so anxious" for "Social Equality" as white men charged, given that "*he has enough of that without his consent, God knows.*" Since "it is evident . . . that the white man is to blame for *forcing Social Equality* upon the *unwilling* colored man," the editors wondered why "the white man" pontificated so vehemently against a problem that he alone had created. They concluded, "He seems to be afraid that some of his daughters may do what a good many of his sons and himself has done time and again, and therefore he wants laws made to prevent *them* doing so."[33] A both humorous and angry retort was characteristic of the response of many African American men participating in formal politics during Reconstruction. When Ed Shaw, a saloon owner and politician in Memphis, addressed an African American benevolent society in that city, he responded to white Memphians' claims that the Civil Rights Act would lead to "social equality": "They say, 'Oh! You want to marry our daughters,'" Shaw mimicked for his audience, adding, "From the looks of this congregation it seems that one could hardly marry any other than their daughters!"[34] The history of white male sexual relationships with black women was recorded in the skin tones of Shaw's and many other audiences in postbellum black communities. This very fact indicates that biological mixture in itself was not a threat to racial distinctions if it occurred under conditions of social *in*equality.

Once the federal Reconstruction Acts mandated racial equality in the political realm, arguments invoking miscegenation and social equality began to appear with more frequency at the level of state politics, particularly as constitutional conventions met to form new state governments that would include black men as voters. Constitutional bans on interracial marriage similar to John Bradley's proposal in Arkansas were offered at the constitutional conventions of Alabama and Mississippi, where counterproposals to punish white men for illicit sexual relations with black women were also offered.[35] These southern states, along with Louisiana, Virginia, and South Carolina, also debated whether segregated or integrated public schools should be mandated by new constitutions.[36] And North Carolina's convention approved a resolution that addressed marriage, sex, and schools together, expressing the convention's "sense . . . that inter-marriage and illegal intercourse between the races should be discountenanced, and the interests and happiness of the two races would be best promoted by the establishment of separate schools." This pronouncement, which contained no legally binding stipulations, was proposed by an African American member of that assembly. One historian has argued that this delegate offered the resolution in order to counter charges that the convention intended social equality and to circumvent repeated proposals that segregation measures be incorporated into the constitution.[37] Although the issue of race and marriage consumed more of delegates' attention in Arkansas than perhaps anywhere else, participants in numerous state conventions where extension of suffrage to black men was practically inevitable promoted racial separation through a rhetoric of social equality.

As was the case in other southern states, black male enfranchisement was guaranteed by the makeup of delegates to Arkansas's convention. Due to federal restrictions on participation of the state's former political leadership, only twelve of a total of seventy men elected as delegates were conservatives who consistently opposed black male suffrage. These twelve faced a pro-Reconstruction alliance affiliated with the Republican Party that included eight African American delegates. These men, William Henry Grey, Monroe Hawkins, Thomas P. Johnson, James Mason, William Murphy, Henry Rector, Richard Samuels, and James T. White, came from divergent backgrounds. Six—excluding Grey and White—had been slaves prior to the Civil War, though Mason was the son of one of the wealthiest plantation owners and largest slaveholder in the state, Elisha Worthington, who provided for his son's education at Oberlin and in France. None of the other former slaves had had similar opportunities. Seven of the eight were native southerners; three, White, Johnson, and Grey, identified as ministers living in urban areas, while four, Hawkins, Murphy, Rector, and Samuels, identified as farmers. James Mason, who after the war became a leading Republican in Chicot County, was serving as Chicot's postmaster at the time of the convention, and he and White were the wealthiest of the black delegates.[38] Despite differences in experience and wealth, these men acted almost entirely in concert as a radical bloc opposing all efforts to limit citizenship rights for former slaves.[39] These eight were supported by seventeen white delegates who were of northern origin (having moved to Arkansas some time after 1860) and thirty-two white southern delegates, some of whom were veteran unionists and others of whom were simply making peace with Reconstruction for the sake of returning their state to the Union.[40] Together, these three groups easily overcame conservative opposition and produced a franchise article for the new constitution that established universal male suffrage and required electors to take an oath endorsing the "civil and political equality of all men."[41] Yet, the future of racial difference in spaces other than those defined as the "civil and political," such as one increasingly termed the "social," remained an open question. Indeed, the political chasm between these temporary pro-Reconstruction allies was brought to the surface by the issue of social equality and specifically interracial marriage.

Citizenship and Suffrage

Before the issue of interracial marriage was raised by John Bradley at the Arkansas state constitutional convention, conservative delegates to the meeting explicitly disputed black men's right and, indeed, capacity to be citizens. This position was first articulated by Jesse Cypert, a delegate from white-majority White County (black population, 12 percent) who was at one point labeled the "leader of the Opposition" by Republicans at the convention.[42] Cypert, a lawyer and migrant from Tennessee who arrived in Arkansas in 1851, was a property owner but not a slaveowner in 1860. He had at first opposed secession, a position he articulated as a member of Arkansas's secession convention in 1861. However, along with his constituents, he changed his position when shots were fired at Fort Sumter. He then joined the Confederate Army, where he served briefly as a captain.[43] During and after the 1868 convention, he would be a frequent speaker at Democratic and White Man's Party events.[44]

Cypert began practicing his arguments against Reconstruction on the sixth day of the convention, when he introduced an ordinance calling for the readoption of the Arkansas state constitution of 1864. Because this Civil War constitution explicitly enfranchised only white men, he revealed his intention to obstruct the task with which the convention was charged, enfranchising black men. "The highest judicial authority in the land has decided that the negro cannot be a citizen," Cypert told his fellow delegates, invoking the Dred Scott decision of the U.S. Supreme Court in defense of his opposition to extending suffrage to black men. Calling "the elective franchise . . . not a universal right, but a class right," Cypert continued, "It was only reasonable that the privilege of the ballot should be withheld, from negroes, or from any other class, not citizens of the United States, destitute of a knowledge of the principles and working of our government, and not by nature qualified to exercise with sufficient judgment the privilege of the ballot." Most importantly, Cypert claimed that black men were not in possession of an independent manhood comparable to that of white men that would qualify them for suffrage or citizenship. Black men, rather, were in a position of dependency: "Let us afford them the same protection that our wives and our daughters have,—the right of liberty, the right of property, and of the pursuit of happiness. Let us afford to them the same rights enjoyed by the white man under the age of twenty-one. Let them be as minors." Cypert concluded, "Let us not attempt to render homogeneous races essentially dissimilar and unequal. Our fathers made a government for the white man. Let us govern it."[45]

In an attempt to reclaim for white men the sole position of those worthy of political power and to repair the antebellum political alliance between white men, Cypert drew on notions of independent manhood to resignify race as a significant marker of inequality between men. But this was not the editorial room of the *Gazette* or a meeting of the White Man's Party. Appeals to the notion that white men were exclusively capable of exercising public authority did not sway an audience intent on, or at least intent on appearing to be intent on, enfranchising black men in order to reenter the Union. Ten southern white conservative delegates—all from overwhelmingly white-majority counties—supported the ordinance to adopt the 1864 constitution. But fifty-three other delegates voted against it, and the matter was rejected.[46] The coalition in support of Reconstruction had survived its first serious challenge. It was clear that the coalition had sufficient support to guarantee that the convention would fulfill the requirements of the Reconstruction Acts and craft a constitution that enfranchised black men. However, the impact of conservative efforts to distinguish between white and black manhood would continue to be felt as other white southern delegates would support black male suffrage but also seek different means of marking racial difference between men. They would turn to social equality, domestic relations, and constructs of gender and sexuality in order to question the virtue of black men. And on this conservatives would support them.

Sex and Marriage

It was John Bradley who mobilized the effort to stake out a compromise position between conservative opposition to the enfranchisement of black men and radical Republican visions for a liberal state that did not recognize race. Early in life Bradley had been a "humble mechanic" who—like Cypert—migrated to Arkansas from Tennessee. He subsequently became a minister and was successfully practicing law at the time of the convention. He had come to Little Rock an opponent of the planter and professional elite that had ruled Arkansas before the war—those whom he labeled "vile intrigning [sic] demagogues" for having led his state into a disastrous civil war.[47] Although he had served as a Confederate Army officer, in a speech made outside the State House in Little Rock on September 18, 1867, he claimed to have "opposed secession at its inception, . . . remark[ing] to a gentleman in Pine Bluff, when South Carolina seceded, that she deserved to be whipped back." Nonetheless, when Arkansas joined South Carolina, he "went with her." He claimed to have felt obliged to fight, given that "the lives, the honor and the property of his brothers were involved."[48] He made this speech in part to defend his own honor. He had been accused of cynically reversing his political position when, once defeat was clear and the government of Arkansas was reorganized under federal control in 1864, he took the oath of allegiance to the United States. He had then briefly served as an agent of the Freedmen's Bureau and now advocated Reconstruction under Congress's plan—"it was that or worse," he told his audience.[49] His defense—that he had always opposed secession, had done the only honorable thing then, and was doing the only practical thing now—did not make him many friends among the state's leading conservative opponents of Reconstruction. Particularly offensive to them was his position that congressional stipulations as to the manner of Arkansas's readmittance into the union were fair. "We dictated the terms on which we quit, and shall we now dictate the terms on which we will return? It is presumption to think of it," he said. Concerning Congress's refusal to seat the men elected by an unreconstructed Arkansas, he asserted, "Congress would be a fool to admit the men who lead us astray, into the councils of the nation."[50]

Like many white southern men from modest backgrounds, Bradley saw in the defeat of the Confederacy and the exclusion from office of the state's former political leadership an opportunity to take political control away from the antebellum slaveholding elite. Yet his distaste for this elite was matched only by his disdain for former slaves—"I believe that freedom is going to be a curse to the black race," Bradley at one point told the convention[51]—and, increasingly, his resentment of the new Republican "dynasty in Little Rock" that had recently repaid his offer of affiliation by denying him a nomination for a seat in Congress.[52] Soon thereafter, when it became clear that the radical wing of the Republican Party, dominated by northern-born whites and African Americans, would interfere with Bradley's political ambitions, he introduced his proposed ban.[53] In fact, the timing of Bradley's proposal for an interracial marriage prohibition suggests that he was responding to the political strategy of conservatives and perhaps attempting to build bridges between himself and their ranks. He offered his resolution as the first order of business the morning after the Democratic State Convention met in Little Rock. This convention of "conservative men" organizing "a white man's party" opposed extending to African Americans both suffrage and "the rights and privileges of a social equality."[54] Bradley seems to have discovered in this meeting's proceedings an issue that would guarantee his political prominence, distance him from accusations that Republicans were "miscegenationists," and demonstrate that a constitution enfranchising black men did not necessarily mean an end to racial hierarchy. When he introduced his resolution, he reminded his audience, "Declarations have been made . . . but recently, that social equality was the boon held in reservation for the citizens of Arkansas." Bradley's solution to the supposed threat of social equality was to propose writing social inequality, in the form of separation of domestic, social, and community life by race, into the constitution via a prohibition on interracial marriage.[55] Reflecting the complexity of the post–Civil War political landscape, it was this opponent of the Confederacy, former Freedmen's Bureau agent, and critic of conservative efforts to organize a White Man's Party[56] who first proposed the interracial marriage prohibition that threatened to stymie Reconstruction in Arkansas.

Despite Bradley's claim that marriage was "the great question . . . agitating Arkansas," emancipation had not yet presented any serious challenge to the state's 1838 statute declaring marriages between "whites" and "Negroes or mulattoes" to be "illegal and void."[57] When confronted with incidents of black and white people marrying in the years just following the Civil War, some white Arkansans pressed the Freedmen's Bureau to assess the continued validity of the 1838 statute. Although some lower-level officials expressed doubts that the antebellum law remained in force,[58] the assistant commissioner of the bureau for Arkansas, General John W. Sprague, issued a circular reprinting it, along with other marriage laws, "for the information of the Freedmen."[59] And when the Democrat-controlled state legislature passed a new prohibition on February 6, 1867, Sprague reprinted it in another circular "for the information of Officers of this Bureau and all concerned."[60] Arkansas was not the only southern state to impose such bans during presidential Reconstruction. South Carolina's black code instituted an interracial marriage prohibition for the first time in the state's history; Mississippi made more severe the punishment in its existing statute (imposing a life sentence); and Alabama added a similar provision to its 1865 constitution.[61] Once these states were under the control of Reconstruction governments, each of these measures would be overturned, and in Arkansas, the 1838 law would simply be omitted from the statute books.[62] Prior to that, however, many apparently concurred with Assistant Commissioner Sprague's reasoning that because "these laws apply to all white and black," they were not discriminatory and did not violate former slaves' civil rights.[63]

Arkansas's 1867 law had been proposed in a report by the Arkansas House Judiciary Committee on "extending to the former slave population additional rights and privileges, adapted to their changed conditions." This report recommended granting African Americans the rights of the "most favored citizen of the white race with some exceptions, considered essential to the safety of society, and rendered necessary by the past relations of the races." Lawmakers perceived it as "essential to the safety of society" that former slaves be prevented not only from marrying white people but also from voting, sitting on juries, and attending public schools with whites.[64] Thus despite arguments that an interracial marriage prohibition was not discriminatory, the initial post–Civil War state had resurrected the antebellum prohibitions on marriage of black and white people as part of a larger legislative agenda to limit African American citizenship rights.

Although this pairing of marriage with political and civil rights could have been used as evidence that Arkansas law was now in violation of the Civil Rights Act and the Fourteenth Amendment, no Republican in the state had publicly objected to prohibitions on cross-racial marriage until John Bradley's actions at the 1868 convention. His call for a constitutional clause prohibiting officials to marry "a white person and a person of African descent" made marriage a contentious political issue for the first time in the state. His proposal was strongly supported by many of his fellow white southerners—both moderate and conservative. But it was also vigorously opposed by black and northern white delegates. The first reaction to Bradley's resolution came from James Hodges, a white Union Army veteran from New York who had settled in Arkansas during the war: "If persons want to intermarry in this way, they ought certainly to have the privilege. . . . I, for one, am entirely opposed to legislation, or Constitutional enactment, upon any such subject."[65] Straightforward objection to legal interventions into domestic life and the assertion of the acceptability of cross-racial marriage, however, would prove politically unfeasible and were eschewed even by most who opposed the provision. Instead, many followed the approach introduced by William Henry Grey, who appeared willing to accept racial separation but pointed out the hypocritical character of a ban only on interracial marriage (implicitly relations between black men and white women) that ignored illicit sexual relations across racial lines (often exploitative ones between white men and black women).[66] In fact, at the end of two days of contentious debate, the convention approved a compromise resolution proposed by James Hinds, another white New York native who came to Arkansas with the Union Army, that was influenced by Grey's approach.[67] The compromise resolution approved by the convention read, "Resolved: That this Convention is utterly opposed to all amalgamation between the white and colored races, whether the same is legitimate or illegitimate. We would therefore recommend that the next General Assembly enact such laws as may effectually govern the same."[68] In place of a constitutional ban on marriage, the convention agreed to a general condemnation of "race mixing" and a nonbinding recommendation to future legislatures. Conservatives at the convention were joined by John Bradley and another white southern Republican, Ira Wilson, in opposition to this compromise. They argued that recommendations to the legislature carried no legal force and thus merely evaded the issue and continued to press for a constitutional prohibition of only marriage. Nonetheless, Hinds's resolution secured sufficient support, including the vote of every black delegate, to pass the convention.[69]

What did the original proposal and the final compromise mean to the various parties involved in Arkansas's constitutional convention? Why did Bradley and his supporters so vehemently endorse a constitutional ban on interracial marriage and then refuse to support an instruction to the legislature to prevent "amalgamation" of all kinds? And why were Grey and other black delegates willing to support the latter measure? Given that the state had reiterated its prohibition on cross-racial marriage and black leaders were neither opposing such proscriptions nor advocating marriage with whites, it seems that Bradley's, Hinds's, and other related proposals were largely symbolic, allowing their proponents to map out broader visions for postemancipation political community in terms of race. Underlying debates about interracial marriage and sex was a political struggle over the contours of African American citizenship and the meaning of race in this postemancipation world.

"Let Us Build a Wall"

The importance of the future meaning of race to John Bradley's proposal for a constitutional prohibition of interracial marriage was made evident in the arguments he offered in defense of the ban. When Grey first objected to Bradley's resolution as "superfluous," Bradley's response was telling. He began by affirming his commitment to what he understood to be the rights of African Americans: "[I intend] to give the negro every right that God in heaven . . . has assigned him. I am ready to recognize his civil and political rights." "But sir," he quickly added, "I am a white man."[70] Bradley thus coupled his endorsement of the civil and political rights of African Americans with an invocation of his own racial and gender identity. While ostensibly accepting political equality, he called for the preservation of race. Throughout the subsequent debates, more than any gesture toward preventing the "mixture" of "blood," Bradley and other supporters of his proposal would act to preserve the meaning, significance, and privilege of white manhood.

What exactly was the basis of distinction between "the white race" and "the black race" that Bradley sought to preserve? Bradley first articulated an essentialized notion of racial difference, representing his proposal as a principled stance against interracial sexual relations of all kinds and professing to offer it in the interests of maintaining what were supposedly two physically distinct races. Echoing common nineteenth-century understandings of race—as the characteristics and developments of a particular "civilization" carried from generation to generation through "blood"[71]—he called for a vote on his proposal in order to show where each delegate "stood . . . upon the idea of keeping his own blood and race pure and unadulterated from an inferior race." Though he clearly believed white "blood" to be superior, Bradley assured his audience that he was nonetheless equally concerned about preserving black uniqueness: "I do not mean to infringe upon the pure blood of the African race. . . . I do not want it adulterated with the blood of the white man." In fact, Bradley thought it an indication of his own honor that he himself had neither any history of nor desire for sex with black women. Regarding Grey's suggestion that "any white man . . . found cohabiting with a negro woman" be punished by death, Bradley proudly proclaimed, "I can say, sir, it will not circumscribe me in any of my social enjoyments or privileges. Thank God, I have no seed, to-day, that has germinated in human form, but is of my own color."[72]

Yet at other moments, Bradley revealed that he was far more concerned about marriage and legitimacy than sex and procreation and, thus, that the distinctions he sought to preserve were social and political, not physical. In frustration at objections to his resolution, Bradley at one point declared, "If men are so much alarmed about having a barrier in the way—why, if you want to, scratch under, and get to the other race; but for God's sake let us build a wall! Let it be understood as the organic law of the land that a white man shall be a white man, and a black man a black man, and that each shall have their rights in their respective spheres."[73] "Keeping . . . race pure," in Bradley's mind, was threatened more by a lack of racial distinction in social worlds and legitimate relationships than by sexual intercourse or reproduction by people of different races. Engaging in illicit forms of interracial sex, or "scratch[ing] under" in Bradley's phrase, did not portend for him the same disruption of racial difference and social order as long as legal norms kept this kind of crossing of racial boundaries illicit and the resultant relationships illegitimate. In other words, it was not the crossing but, rather, the representation of that crossing that concerned him most. The rhetoric of miscegenation, then, was first and foremost about marriage, not because marriage involved sex—which in the end was not of primary concern to Bradley—but because marriage was a means of organizing legitimate social life and relations.

Bradley further explained that his main motive for insisting that the constitution establish segregation in social relationships was to clarify the implications of racial equality in civil and political realms. "There is no limitation and distinction, there is no fixed determined meaning, to 'civil rights,' and 'equality before the law,'" he argued, "and so long as these terms stand undefined and uninterpreted, so long will this remain a vexed question for future generations to fight and war over." Bradley recognized emancipation as a critical juncture in racial meanings, and he feared that the establishment of political and civil equality in this moment held the potential to erase all racial boundaries and even possibly difference. He emphasized the responsibility the convention had "when we are launching out upon a new era" to "establish . . . a line between the races,—one that shall be recognized by all future generations"— that is, to assure that despite political equality, racial difference would be preserved. This responsibility he felt would be met through his proposed interracial marriage ban: "When the Constitution goes before [the people], let us not leave them in doubt whether that Constitution is susceptible of the interpretation of social equality and amalgamation. Let us plant it upon the ground that each race shall move in its own sphere. . . . There is no better time than now, to provide for this." On the final day of debate on the issue, Bradley expressed his dismay that, by rejecting his proposal, the convention had not preempted future confusion and contest but, rather, had shown itself to be "unwilling to fix the true status of the two races." Through his proposed interracial marriage ban and its establishment of a society without the pos- sibility of social integration and "social equality," Bradley sought to "fix" the "status" of white and black, that is, to permanently inscribe constructs of racial difference, and ensure distinct racial communities, despite the creation of formal political equality. By refusing to do this, he argued, the convention had neglected its most important task: "There is no earthly reason for our being here to-day, except to settle every part and particle, every word and syllable, of the negro question."[74]

One aspect of the challenge to racial distinctions that worried Bradley appears to have been the possibility that, in a world without slavery, white men might be more likely to recognize and legitimate their offspring with black women and thereby destabilize race through the social mobility of people of color. This is apparent in moments when he, perhaps unwittingly, indicated irritation at elite white men fathering children with black women— much as Grey's likely father, Governor Henry Wise of Virginia, had done, and as had James Mason's father, Elisha Worthington[75]—and then conferring so- cial status through education and inheritance on their mixed-race offspring. Certainly, Bradley had claimed that his proposal was aimed at defending the honor of white southern men maligned by northern critics for indulging in cross-racial sex. But it is difficult not to hear a similar maligning in some of Bradley's own words. When Bradley expressed his pride that he had "no seed . . . that has germinated in human form, but is of my own color," he added, "I have never belonged to a bleaching-machinery, and do not advocate the bleaching process. That is just what I want to put down."[76] Bradley thus chose a term that invoked lightening rather than darkening and thereby suggested that the threat at the back of his mind was not the pollution of whiteness but, rather, the potential social mobility through legitimacy and inheritance of those of mixed-race ancestry—the possibility of them "lightening" out of the ranks of a black lower class. He further suggested resentment against white men of privilege for liaisons with women of color when he encouraged the convention to ensure for the future that equal rights would not include the right to choose a sexual partner of another race: "I do not want a black man, in two years, coming to me and saying,—'That is a privilege granted to the white man; you must grant it to me;' and the white man saying,—'This is the privilege of the black man; I must have it too:' and off goes the white man to the cabin, and the black man, I suppose, somewhere else in a like manner." "To the cabin" effectively evoked an image of white men seeking sexual relations with their slaves, but Bradley apparently could not think of a comparable trope for black men seeking sex with white women. His verbal stumbling simultaneously confirmed that sex between white men and black women was far more common, accepted, and culturally recognizable than sex between black men and white women and that his proposal was designed at least in part with the actions of former slaveholding white men in mind. The plan on which he insisted—one that prohibited marriage but did not address sex—did nothing to prevent white men from running off "to the cabin," but it sought to ensure that any children born of such conduct would remain black and poor.[77]

When defending his proposal and its potential to preserve existing racial meanings, Bradley repeatedly deployed spatial metaphors, referring to the need to construct "partitions," "barriers," and autonomous "spheres."[78] Responding to James Hodges's position that if black and white people wanted to marry, they should be allowed, Bradley rejected an understanding of marriage as purely a matter of personal choice: "I am astonished that gentlemen get up and say,—'Let it be a matter of taste!' It shows me a man's taste, when he wants no distinction, no partition, but wants the two races mixed in one common amalgamation." Preventing such mixture, Bradley's choice of words suggested, was not simply a matter of protecting the supposed racial purity of "blood" but, rather, of social organization, and particularly the composition of households. Bradley's proposal made the domestic an inexorable line of racial demarcation, and thus the arena in which race would continue to reproduce its traditional social significance, even as it lost significance in politics, where black men now held power. Early in the debate, Bradley invoked the boundaries around landed property—the contours of a man's household in this highly agricultural society—as a metaphor for racial difference. In response to Grey's critique of the prohibition, Bradley stated, "I am well aware that there is a kind of vulgar idea abroad in the world, that we do not need land-lines between us. The presumption is that I and my neighbor are both honest—neither of us will cut timber on the other's land; and you say, when I desire to have the line established between us,—'Either one or the other is a thief.' Sir, that does not follow."[79] After likening women to men's property, in this case timber, Bradley equated interracial marriage with trespass: "If any man crosses the line and trespasses, let a statute be enacted, based upon this feature of our constitution, that shall fix the crime and the penalty."[80] Bradley thus imagined a society organized by boundaries around men's households that would spatially and socially constitute racial difference.[81]

Another white southerner, a yeoman farmer named Ira Wilson from Union County, who declared himself not in but, rather, "acting" with the Republican Party, endorsed Bradley's idea that a constitutional prohibition would "make . . . a line of demarcation." This was desirable, he added, because "I have promised the black people that I would give them suffrage, but never that I would give them my daughter."[82] Wilson thus implied that to him the issue hit close to home; specifically, it touched on his authority over who associated with the female members of his family. In an effort to appear evenhanded, he professed that he acted "for the protection, not only of my offspring, but of the offspring of the other race." Such statements, most likely disingenuous, did not take away from the overall effect of this discourse, that is, the circulation of images of black men, drunk with new powers and unrestrained by law and the state, intruding into the homes and imposing on the families of respectable white men.

Bradley and Wilson were not alone in demanding that the domestic realm remain an inviolable space of racial difference and separation or in justifying social segregation through a logic that conflated political empowerment of black men with their supposed pursuit of cross-racial social and romantic relations. One colleague at the convention, Gayle Kyle of Dallas County, a wealthy unionist before the war who claimed to have lost all of his property due to his opposition to the Confederacy, proclaimed, "I have said it was right to make [African Americans] equal in the courts of the country. I have said,— Give them their political rights. . . . But as for saying that they must be brought up upon an equality, socially, with the white race, I never will give my assent to it."[83] The law, though, would have to act to protect against the social leveling of racial groups, for he believed that freedpeople were clamoring for just such a change. Seeking to convince Republican critics that the fear of "social equality" was more than a political charade, Kyle insisted that "it is the highest climax of [former slaves'] aspiration, to come up socially, on an equal footing with the white race." As evidence, he recounted how "in my own neighborhood . . . a negro . . . misled an unfortunate step-daughter of his employer. . . . This negro started to run away with the unhappy girl, and did actually take her from her father's home." One white northern-born Republican had earlier charged that state intervention should be unnecessary to prevent respectable white women from choosing marriage with social inferiors. In response, Kyle prefaced his story by explaining that it was especially those whites who were poor and socially marginal—and thus his description of the woman in his story as an "unfortunate step-daughter"—who would be increasingly vulnerable to "social degradation" as former slaves gained wealth and status: "These colored people will acquire . . . money, they will acquire lands, after a while, and position in society . . . and they can insidiously make their advances to these unfortunate and helpless persons, and, by the use of their power, can mislead and misguide them, into error and folly."[84] Kyle employed common antebellum imagery disparaging the virtue of poor white women to help him out of a tight spot in a debate. But his discourse also revealed key dimensions to the logic impelling white men to support Bradley's proposal. Kyle argued that controlling the behavior of working-class white women as well as of black men was necessary in the interests of maintaining racial boundaries.[85] He simultaneously suggested that lurking behind his opposition to cross-racial sexual relations was the specter of black economic mobility and its consolidation, through racial integration, of a world in which race would no longer serve as a key marker of social groups and status. Finally, he presented this scenario as a threat to the peace and sanctity of the households of white men and a challenge to their patriarchal authority.

Yet despite the admission of concern about especially poor white women's complicity in cross-racial relationships, despite diplomatic declarations of concern with protecting the "offspring" of both white and black men, and despite a largely unstated interest in preventing white fathers from recognizing their mixed-race children, the rhetoric surrounding Bradley's proposal focused above all on the need to restrain black men. And it was the need to restrain black men in order to assure legally sanctioned racial separation more than the prevention of "amalgamation" or the "mixture" of "blood" that was endorsed by the white men supporting Bradley's proposal. By emphasizing the supposed danger of newly empowered black men "misleading" white women into social and sexual relationships, and the necessity of an outside force, the law, to prevent this, supporters of Bradley's proposal called into question the honor of black men, if honor was measured, as Bradley repeatedly contended, by concern with keeping one's race "pure."[86] The debate itself thus served to circulate images of black men as less willing and able than white men to restrain their passions for the good of their "race" and to exert the self-control necessary to a virtuous republic. This discourse not only disparaged the manhood and worthiness for citizenship of black men. It also imputed by contrast virtue and honor to an abstract white manhood now called on to protect its "race" by protecting white women and white homes from putative transgressions and intrusions by black men. As had Cypert's earlier critique of black male suffrage, this discourse ultimately depicted white men alone as capable of governing themselves and thus fit for a role in governing the republic. In this way, discourse opposing "social equality," with its implications of inferior black virtue and civility, would inevitably redound to white men's political power.

This can be seen in the ways that rhetoric favoring a constitutional ban on interracial marriage emerging from the convention was echoed in the conservative *Gazette*, as that newspaper's editors used Republican objections to Bradley's proposal to rally opposition to any constitution produced by the convention. The early defeat of Cypert's proposal to reinstate the 1864 constitution had made clear that there was sufficient support at the convention to pass a new constitution that extended suffrage to black men and disfranchised some white men, at least to the extent required by the Fourteenth Amendment. Conservatives still held out hope, though, that they would be able to defeat the new constitution when it was put to a popular vote, by drawing over to their side white male voters whom they had only recently failed to mobilize against a convention. This would require convincing many poorer white men, often unionist in sentiment and angry at Confederate elites for the devastation of the Civil War, that their best interests lay in a cross-class alliance based on race with those same elites. In this context, Bradley's proposal offered an opportunity. Through it, conservatives attempted to turn the attention of all white southern men, as those men contemplated the consequences of extending membership in the political community to black men, toward the putative collective interests and identities shared by white men.

For the most part, conservative delegates to the convention, such as Jesse Cypert and those who had joined in his open hostility to African American citizenship, said little during the debate over Bradley's and similar proposals.

However, they nonetheless contributed to prolonging discussion of the issue before the convention by opposing all efforts to stop the debate. All twelve conservative delegates voted as a bloc against the five efforts by Republicans to refer the issue to committees.[87] The conservative contingent at the convention thus acted to exacerbate dissension on this issue, doubtless hoping that it would cause the pro-Reconstruction coalition to self-destruct along racial and regional lines. Conservatives also hoped that Republican opposition to the prohibition would tarnish any white southern support for black male suffrage and thus the new constitution. And their efforts to prolong debate worked in conjunction with the conservative press. With each hour that the debate continued, the convention generated "news" that the conservative press reported and commented on as if Republicans were actively promoting interracial marriage. The first issue of the Weekly Gazette following the introduction of Bradley's proposal was a veritable campaign document for the White Man's Party framed around the issues of interracial marriage and social equality. Alongside a report on the proceedings of the convention containing the debates on Bradley's prohibition, one editorial titled "Showed Their Hands" opened, "When the piebald convention refused to allow a direct vote on the subject of miscegenation, evidence was furnished that negro social equality will follow close upon negro suffrage. In order to hold fast to the negro vote, vile white men refuse to declare themselves unalterably opposed to the amalgamation of races. They now sit side by side with them in convention, hug them in the league room, and when the negro expresses a wish to that effect, they will legislate him into private parlors."[88] Proximity between white and black in political spaces thus threatened proximity in domestic spaces. Another editorial on the same page, "Plain Facts for White Men," emphasized other spaces where social equality was threatened. It argued that newly enfranchised black men, "inflated with the notion of their own equality with the whites, will demand admittance on equal terms in theaters, steamboat cabins, rail roads cars, etc."[89] Both of these editorials that explicitly paired black male suffrage with social equality, and opposition to social equality with a prohibition on interracial marriage, concluded with calls to white men now supporting Reconstruction to identify and ally along racial lines: "White men of Arkansas! Can you longer affiliate with the advocates of miscegenation and mongrelism? . . . Come out from among the champions of mongrelism and join the great white man's party of Arkansas."[90]

Racial separation was bound up with honor, and both were tied to the White Man's Party in this rhetoric, while racial "mixing" of any kind was connected to shame and linked to Republicans. In the editions of the *Gazette* that followed the first report of the interracial marriage debate, editorials such as "Respectability Outlawed," "Radicalism the Patron of Miscegenation," and "Arkansas to Be Mexicanized" continued to call on the "White men of Arkansas" to oppose Reconstruction as a matter of honor. They emphasized that the "decent white men of the state" opposed interracial sex and intimacy and contrasted them with "the miscegen, negro suffrage party of Arkansas" that "recognize[s] no principles of honor or honesty."[91] Meanwhile, in a letter to the *Gazette*, the work of the convention had been labeled "the mongrel radical constitution" by a leader of the effort to organize the White Man's Party, and Republicans were called "miscegenationists" and "amalgamationists" throughout *Gazette* articles.[92] John Bradley himself used these terms to label his former political allies in two letters he wrote to the *Gazette* protesting opposition to his proposal.[93] At the end of the convention's work, the *Gazette* predicted that the authors of a similar constitution in Alabama would "live to receive the scorching, blasting contempt of honest men and virtuous women."[94] Thus despite the silence of conservatives on the convention floor, conservative discourse promoted Bradley's interracial marriage ban and employed it as a platform from which to attempt to bridge the political divide among white men through racialized constructions of honorable manhood. These constructions equated honor with collective racial identification and the building of a segregated society.

The transformation of slaves into citizens profoundly challenged constructions of racial difference and structures of racial hierarchy in southern society. In particular, black men's political rights threatened the erstwhile dominance and significance of white manhood. African American men now shared with white men at least the potential to obtain the most important traditional components of honorable masculinity: liberty, citizenship, property, marriage, independent households, public voice, and suffrage. In this context, white southern men of various political affiliations—both moderate and conservative—struggled to reaffirm a distinct, racially superior manhood for themselves. These men supported the prohibition as framed by Bradley because it replaced exclusive access to citizenship—now lost by white men—with a rhetoric of white men's honor and domestic authority to create at least a symbolic distinction between white and black men. It also envisaged a segregated social world that would give meaning to rigidly separated categories of "white" and "black" and seemed to assure that even in the context of enforced political equality, African Americans would never be "on an equal footing with the white race." Even though a constitutional ban on interracial marriage would ultimately fail to be enacted, the proposal represented an opportunity to elaborate a discourse of racial difference and hierarchy based on disparaging portrayals of African American men.

"A Place among Men"

African American delegates to the Arkansas constitutional convention recognized in the proposed ban on interracial marriage and in its broader discourse opposing social equality the potential for insidiously promoting racial inequality in political and civil realms. The two black delegates who spoke out extensively against the measure, William Henry Grey and his colleague from Helena, James T. White, denounced it as an effort to enshrine racial inequality in the very document intended to secure equality, the state's postemancipation constitution. They also identified the prohibition as an attack on the honor not only of black men but of black women as well.

Grey, the delegate who first rejected Bradley's proposal as "superfluous," led the way in formulating arguments in opposition, and he experimented with different approaches during the two days of debate. In his most impassioned appeal to the convention to reject the resolution, Grey—like Bradley—implored his audience to recognize the importance of the formative political moment in which they stood. Why was it, Grey asked rhetorically, that "men of proved valor, and patriotism, approved on many a well-contested field," who had lived in close proximity to black men for generations, were "now afraid of miscegenation from four million negro slaves?" "Because, in the progress of the nineteenth century, the negro has come up from the substratum, and claims, in the sentiment of the world, a place among men," Grey charged, "[you] propose to log off, little by little, here and there, those rights which they have at length obtained!"[95] Grey perceived that the impetus to regulate domestic relations by race reflected a desire to limit the meaning of emancipated black manhood and black men's equal place in public, their "place among men." Grey's primary objective was the opposite, to assure black men a voice in public on an equal footing with all other men, and this required precluding any representation of African American manhood and thus black men's worthiness for citizenship as subordinate to that of whites. Grey sought to establish in the constitution the basis for a society in which, "in the sentiments of the world," black men would have a place among—not beneath—

other men. The real question raised by the proposed constitutional ban for Grey and his supporters was how former slaves were to be represented as citizens, what model for race in a republic without slavery would the new constitution put forth, and what kind of freedom would this revolutionary constitution envisage. Grey advocated that instead of Cypert's depiction of black men not as "freemen" but, rather, as minors, or Bradley's depiction of black men as citizens but not "virtuous men," this constitution should represent black men as no different from white men. The constitution should recognize all as universal citizens. Seconding Grey's plea, James White would later implore the convention to free political rights from compromising and insidious proposals concerning domestic relationships: "There is one thing that I desire at the present time above all others, and that is that this honorable body may strip the question of negro suffrage of all outside issues, and present the subject of equal rights with all its bearings, to the people of Arkansas."[96]

The constitution was of particular importance to Grey, who emphasized the perils of legitimating illiberal distinctions between racial groups in what was to be the voice of authority for the principles of a new supposedly liberal republic. "When you place in your Constitution a provision of this nature," Grey told the convention, "you at once create an inequality." "Why is it necessary that the organic law of the land should contradict the very purpose for which we are assembled?" he asked. Grey refuted the notion that the social could be bracketed off as a space of inequality not touching upon the civil and political. Indeed, he dismissed the claim that this was his opponents' intention. He saw in any constitutional reference to social difference the production of inequality in a broader sense. He thus accused his opponents of promoting "a piece of prejudice" that would undermine the constitution, and he pleaded, "Do not touch that sacred instrument by inserting anything that indicates class legislation."[97]

Grey also criticized the notion that the law could "fix" race, a malleable social phenomenon, as if it were a transparent reflection of distinct types of "blood." He stated, "If we are to adopt this proposition, the Legislature will have to pass an act creating a board of scientific physicians, or professors of anatomy, to discover who is a negro. There is the trouble. The purity of blood, of which [Mr. Bradley] speaks, has already been somewhat interfered with." Even though Grey claimed that "if you can show where the line can be drawn, I am perfectly willing," in fact he was advising against drawing any lines in the law that would enshrine essentialized notions of race. Not only would a constitutional ban on cross-racial marriage harden and legitimate prejudicial racial constructs, but it would also be ineffective, simply forcing certain relationships underground. To Bradley's plea for building a "wall" even if some men would "scratch under," Grey responded with outrage, "I propose that we shall stop this crawling under the fence. I propose that if persons desire intermarriage with the other race, it shall be done honorably and above-board."[98]

Grey thus opposed reinscribing in the constitution racial difference and false notions of distinct physical races. He also favored measures granting legitimacy and security to black women involved in relationships with white men over laws that made these relationships and their offspring illegitimate. And yet he also revealed ambivalence about asserting this position as forcefully as had, say, James Hodges, who had objected to any state regulation of marriage choice immediately after Bradley offered his proposal. Instead, Grey repeatedly proclaimed that he shared white southern men's opposition to miscegenation, though he wished it to be recognized in all forms. "It does seem strange to me that gentlemen oppose [amalgamation] only when it takes place in a legitimate form," Grey told the convention. "They make no opposition to it when manifesting itself in an illegitimate form. They do not propose to punish anybody for illegitimate intercourse. Is that fair? . . . Surely the latter is just as vicious and harmful." He also sought, as in his initial retort to Bradley's plan, to place blame for "illegitimate intercourse" on white men and to establish for the record that his constituency was not responsible for "race mixing": "The census of the United States shows that forty per cent of us, already, have crossed the line. It is no fault of ours. No gentleman will lay it to our door. The intermixture has taken place illegitimately. Those gentlemen who so place themselves upon a pedestal of virtue, will not deny that this was wrong. Their own race has thus created the difficulty."[99]

The spirit of Grey's charge that it was white men who had historically shown a lack of restraint in relation to sex across racial lines was captured in a new resolution offered by John R. Montgomery, a white Ohio-born former Freedmen's Bureau agent representing Hempstead County.[100] Montgomery proposed as a substitute to Bradley's original proposal a resolution calling for "a clause in the Constitution, requiring the General Assembly to enact laws to more effectually prevent miscegenation, and thereby inaugurate a great reform in the State of Arkansas."[101] In explaining the intention of this substitute, Montgomery told the convention, "The resolution offered by myself covers the whole subject, both of marriage and of illicit intercourse."[102] Labeling the change a "great reform" further framed the measure as a means of righting a past and extant wrong, the rape of black women by white men, rather than addressing a current and future possibility of newly empowered black men courting white women. Montgomery declared that legislation resulting from his proposal would put a stop to "all the evils of this nature which have existed in Arkansas for the last two hundred and fifty years." Referring to the conservative Democrats who had met in convention the day before, he said, "The object of [my] resolution is to keep these gentlemen from rubbing out the mark [differentiating races]. They have been rubbing it out for the last two and a half centuries; and if you look at this crowd [turning to the galleries] you will not find a full-blooded African, nor will you find one in the State of Arkansas."[103] Though white men had been "rubbing out" racial difference in physical terms, social distinctions remained unaffected as long as interracial marriage remained illegal. Montgomery implied that the assurance of illegitimacy contained in interracial marriage bans contributed to white men's sexual exploitation of black women when he argued, "We do not desire the insertion of a clause which shall declare that no man shall marry a black woman, but which says, in effect, that a man may cohabit with a black woman, illegitimately, and at his will."[104] Montgomery's substitute proposal, seconding Grey's concern about the impact an interracial marriage ban would have on black women, emphasized white men's dishonorable and exploitative participation in "amalgamation." Thus, not surprisingly, Bradley strongly opposed it. He objected that its recommendation to future legislatures would not establish racial distinctions as permanently as a constitutional measure would.[105] It seems certain, though, that Bradley was also frustrated that Montgomery's proposal focused explicitly on white men's participation in cross-racial sexual relations outside marriage (as opposed to Bradley's own more implicit critiques), contributing to the "foul insinuations" against the integrity of white southern men Bradley himself had claimed to be protesting.

Another substitute proposal, offered by James Hodges on the final day of debate, also reflected Grey's contributions, but with far more radical implications than even Montgomery's resolution. Doubtless because of that, the resolution was ignored by the convention. Hodges's proposal prohibited only "illegitimate" or illicit sexual intercourse and sought to force all men to take responsibility for their sexual affairs. It would have legitimized as "marriage" all cohabitation and recognized as "heirs" all offspring regardless of race, thereby far better, he predicted, preventing "amalgamation." His proposal read,

Resolved: That the Committee on the Constitution, its Arrangement and Phraseology, be instructed to frame an organic Act, so as to effectually prevent amalgamation by all illicit intercourse. Also, that all persons [male] cohabiting with females without regard to color, shall be declared and considered in law as man and wife. . . .

And that all persons, without regard to color or previous condition . . . shall inherit estates of their ancestors, the same as though legitimately born. Also, that should it appear that, under such construction of law, citizens of this State are guilty of the crime of bigamy, they shall be punishable in accordance with the provisions of law.

Also: That there be an organic law preventing citizens of this State from disposing of their property by will, or otherwise, only to the heirs to such estates, as contemplated by the foregoing organic Act.

Hodges asked the convention, "If every man and woman cohabiting together should be declared man and wife, and the children of such illegitimate intercourse should inherit in like manner as if the parties had been regularly married," then "should [we] not have less cohabitation of the two races?" He predicted that all men at the convention who were "honest in their intention [to] prevent amalgamation" would support him.[106]

Although it seems likely that Grey and other black delegates might have supported aspects of Hodges's proposal, they did not do so openly. In fact, no interest was expressed in the resolution. It was never formally offered to the convention, and no vote was taken. Its radical character, though, may well have encouraged many moderates to support instead the compromise resolution proposed by James Hinds that same second day of debate, which declared the convention's opposition to "all amalgamation . . . legitimate or illegitimate" without putting any mention of such opposition in the constitution. This resolution did receive the endorsement of the convention, including Grey and the other seven black delegates. Certainly, the resolution's call for future legislation in place of a constitutional ban preserved the constitution as a race-blind document, thus heeding Grey's forceful plea. But why would such legislation not have been viewed by Grey and others as having pernicious effects in regard to reinscribing racial inequality similar to Bradley's original proposal?

That it would have the same effects was the position taken by a white member of the convention from Clark County, Miles Ledford Langley, who pointed to the patently illiberal character of efforts to restrict an individual's choice of marriage partner. An antebellum southern abolitionist who continued to associate with radical reform movements after the war, Langley objected to various proposals on the matter: "This is an age of improvement. Reform is the order of the day. I think we may get ourselves into a difficulty, by inserting in the organic law of the State something that will show to after ages that we acted in violation of the inalienable rights of man. . . . It is contrary to [that] doctrine . . . ; it is contrary to the doctrines of the Declaration of Independence. . . . I say that when we undertake to legislate upon such points, we act in violation of a principle that is, or should be, dear to us—we strike at the very fundamental principle of liberty itself."[107] When it came time to cast a ballot on Hinds's compromise resolution, Langley voted with the entire assembly for the first portion, declaring "that this Convention is utterly opposed to all amalgamation between the white and colored races, whether the same is legitimate or illegitimate."[108] But he asked to be excused from voting on the second half, which called for future legislation "as may effectually govern the same."[109] When the convention refused his request, he voted "nay" and explained, "I am opposed to amalgamation; but I am also opposed to prohibiting marriage between any persons, on account of color, as I consider it would be contrary to the doctrine of equal rights before the law, and not strictly republican."[110] Langley appealed to the African American men at the convention to join his opposition to any measure legally stipulating racial separation. "I hope the colored people will not be caught in a trap of this sort. I hope they will vote against any proposition of the kind."[111]

Yet, at the convention, the eight black delegates did just the opposite. How can we understand their choice? On one hand, African American support for Hinds's resolution seems to have been perceived as a necessary compromise. The resolution offered a measure acceptable to most southern white men at the convention that also avoided corrupting with inevitably invidious racial distinctions the document on which citizenship in a postemancipation republic would be based. At the same time, it protected black leaders and other Republicans from potentially damaging charges that they were promoting miscegenation. These charges threatened to split the pro-Reconstruction coalition at the convention. Approval of a constitution enfranchising all of the state's male citizens depended on the survival of this coalition.[112]

It also appears that clear acknowledgment of the history of rape of black women by white men was at stake for Grey and the other black men at the convention. Grey continued his critique of the proposed constitutional ban by insisting that such codes contributed to racially discriminatory rape law. He likened Bradley's proposal to a clause in Kentucky's constitution and predicted that it would lead to legislation also present in that state: "[In Kentucky] not only is a negro forbidden to marry into the Saxon race, but for the crime of rape, he is burned to death; yet that same law does not contemplate it as possible for a white man to commit a rape upon . . . a negro woman."[113] Kentucky was one of few postbellum southern states to keep in place the racial asymmetry that had characterized antebellum rape law—specifying white women as the only potential victims and singling out black assailants for harsher punishment.[114] Grey protested on the convention floor the exclusion of black women from rape laws as an unjust holdover from slavery and implicitly accused Bradley and his supporters of attempting to perpetuate this oppression in Arkansas by banning interracial marriage but not sex.

Narratives of black women as victims of rape did not sit well with the conservatives at the convention. One of their number, Robert S. Gantt of Prairie County, broke the conservative silence: "When the discussion commenced, I had not the most distant idea of participating in it. Some remarks, however, have been made, to which I conceive it due to myself at least, that I make some reply."[115] Gantt spoke in support of Bradley's proposal prohibiting marriage. However, given the course the debate had taken, he had to concede the issue of sexual relations outside marriage. "Now, so far as intercourse between the races is concerned, it is unfortunately true, that there has been illicit intercourse." But because sex outside marriage was far more difficult for the state to regulate, he contended that the only forces capable of preventing "illicit intercourse" were the racial pride and personal "virtue" of individual men and women: "If they love their race . . . they desire to preserve it pure; if they love virtue they will keep apart, and not engage in illicit intercourse." His subsequent comments then implicitly questioned the "love" of "race" and "virtue" of black women: "Whilst I sincerely and honestly believe that the virtuous and upright black woman should never consent to cohabit with a white man, such intercourse does take place," he said. "Affections may grow up between [black women and white men] . . . that would bring them together. But . . . I believe it would be better for both, and for the country at large, that the law should put its condemnation upon such marriages, even if it thus sacrifice an individual affection."[116] Gantt did not oppose the relationships themselves and, in fact, argued that the law could do nothing to prevent them; but he did oppose legitimating them with marriage as too detrimental to "the country at large." Rather than attributing such relationships to white male abuse or exploitation, Gantt implied that the "affection" of black women who were not "virtuous and upright" was at least equally responsible. Sex between white men and black women, in other words, was not coerced but, rather, was actively desired by the women involved.[117]

When James T. White subsequently took the floor, he claimed that he had been compelled to speak by such conservative insinuations: "I did not think that I would have anything to say upon this subject—that of amalgamation;—but the gentlemen on the other side of the house have forced me to say a few words." Responding to charges of dishonorable conduct by black men and women in matters of cross-racial sex, White declared, "Gentlemen, the shoe pinches on the other foot. The white men of the South have been for years indulging in illicit intercourse with colored women, and in the dark days of slavery this intercourse was in a great majority of cases forced upon the innocent victims; and I think the time has come when such a course should end."[118] White thus forcefully protested the long history of sexual exploitation of black women by white men, in essence calling it rape. And he echoed Montgomery's framing of the question of preventing amalgamation as righting a past wrong—the rape of black women by white men—rather than preventing a future problem.

Supporting Hinds's compromise condemning "all amalgamation" similarly allowed White, Grey, and their colleagues to protest a long-silenced history of sexual violence and the hypocrisy of white men on the issue of cross-racial sex. This, in turn, affirmed honorable gender identities for black men and women, which were important signifiers of their worthiness for citizenship. In this way black delegates to Arkansas's constitutional convention were ultimately drawn into endorsing measures that affirmed that all racial mixture was detrimental to society and thus into hardening racial boundaries in the law in ways to which Grey had originally indicated he was opposed. The ambivalence that Grey and White may have felt about Hinds's resolution was expressed indirectly by another black delegate to the convention. Henry Rector, a twenty-two-year-old former slave, asked to abstain from voting on the part of the resolution that opposed all amalgamation. When his request was denied, however, Rector joined the other black men in voting for the entire measure.[119] Working under extraordinary political constraints and facing multiple challenges, African American delegates to the Arkansas constitutional convention agreed to a compromise that achieved some of their aims while jeopardizing others.

On the other hand, the position ultimately endorsed on the issue of miscegenation may also reflect black delegates themselves experimenting with the future meaning of race, and with the possibility that a social separation could be established under conditions of, and even in the interest of, equality. In this moment, envisaging a thoroughly integrated domestic and social world was no doubt difficult for many of the black delegates at the convention, made all the more so by white delegates' degrading representations of African Americans and white disavowals of the history of the rape of black women. Provided that they were fairly and equitably imposed, restrictions on interracial sexual relationships might have offered some protection to black women and their communities from the inequities of what were likely to remain extramarital sexual relationships with white men and resultant "illegitimate" children. In that way, such restrictions may have been understood as problematic but nonetheless having the potential at least to work in the interests of equality. White explained his vote on Hinds's measure this way: "As I am in favor of the Legislature doing right to the colored people as well as to the white, I vote Aye."[120] More broadly, the idea of drawing boundaries around black communities in general likely held certain appeal, if it could be done in such a way as to avoid representing the manhood and womanhood of African Americans as somehow less than that of whites. The forceful protest Grey had offered against writing racial difference into the constitution suggests that he would have preferred that any separation in social life be voluntarily rather than legally established.[121] However, given the strategic utility of endorsing a legal—but not constitutional—prohibition, recommending future legislation was evidently not seen as too costly. Racial separatism in social and domestic life—but not public life—may not have been inherently objectionable to these black leaders or irreconcilable with their visions of freedom.[122]

Charged discourses of social equality and miscegenation possibly helped to shape other positions taken by black leaders at the convention. For instance, when white radical Miles Ledford Langley proposed that the convention endorse woman suffrage, no black delegates spoke up in support of the measure. Indeed, no one other than Langley himself spoke positively in its defense, and he was then openly derided and ridiculed by those in the conservative camp.[123] The only delegate who acted in any way that could be construed as supportive of Langley's effort was James Hodges of Pulaski County, who moved the adoption of Langley's clause in order to open debate on the issue. Making light of Langley's proposal, Robert Gantt moved "to refer the proposition . . . to Mrs. Lucy Stone." Jesse Cypert proposed as an amendment,

"That no man who has a wife shall be allowed to vote when the right is exercised by his wife," arguing that he was a "Union man" and did not wish to "give rise to secession in families."[124]

In South Carolina, Elsa Barkley Brown has found that "a significant proportion of . . . Reconstruction-era black elected officials favored woman suffrage or were at least open to a serious discussion of the issue." Similarly, Martha Jones concludes that it was "black political leaders [who] put women's suffrage on the agenda in the [Reconstruction] era's constitutional conventions and state legislatures."[125] It is possible that, despite their silence, some of the black delegates to Arkansas's convention were equally open to the issue. They may have been discouraged from voicing any support for debate on the controversial matter, however, by the fact that Langley presented his resolution after the new constitution had already been written and approved by the convention, and thus after it could have had any immediate, practical effect. Black delegates to Arkansas's convention might also have seen woman suffrage as simply a political impossibility at the time, while on the contrary, black male suffrage was riding the wave of a revolution created by the Civil War. They may have feared that negative publicity from debate on the issue would threaten victory in the pending ratification election for the constitution. In fact, during the debate over Cypert's proposal to reenact the 1864 constitution, Grey said as much. Opponents of black male suffrage had pointed out that it had recently been rejected in several northern states. To this Grey responded, "I think, sir, if the question of negro suffrage had been stripped of deserters' bills, woman suffrage, and everything that could be found that was unpopular, it would have been adopted; and even carrying this weight, we obtained the largest vote upon the subject, ever polled in Ohio."[126]

Lack of vocal support for woman suffrage at the convention by Grey and his colleagues may also reflect ways in which the rhetoric of miscegenation had itself furthered a gendered notion of citizenship incompatible with the image of women as voters among men like Grey, or at least a belief in the necessity of depicting black manhood and citizenship in ways that did not allow for simultaneous representation of black women as public actors. Having to maneuver through the minefield of charges of flawed and dishonorable black manhood and womanhood articulated around issues of sex and domestic relations, charges that threatened to undermine necessary white support for Reconstruction constitutions, appears to have promoted a gendered character to political discourse that would be contested within black communities over the decades to come. African American leaders taking on the role of black women's protectors and emphasizing "a place among men" in their struggle for suffrage bore a heightened patriarchal tone in comparison with what was apparent at the Colored Citizens Convention two years earlier, and this tone might have contributed to a construction of freedom and citizenship as "manhood rights" that did not allow for a clear position for black women in public life. Embracing such representations, though, would have placed these leaders in Arkansas in conflict with some of their constituents. Many black women in Arkansas at the time certainly perceived that they belonged in public life, as they attended political rallies, defended polling places from white interference, and perhaps even cast a ballot or two.[127] African American political cultures would continue to include spaces for women's political voice in ways unfamiliar to white southern public life. The next generation of black women took on roles in education and civic organizations unusual for white women and initiated reform and suffrage movements before white southern women did.[128] Nonetheless, gender and class conflicts among African Americans over the nature of citizenship for women and their appropriate role in the public sphere would emerge in the decades after emancipation.[129] The gendering of citizenship and the sexualized rhetoric of politics during Reconstruction no doubt helped to set the stage for those future struggles.

The Shadow Cast by Miscegenation

The impact of a discourse of miscegenation on the process of Reconstruction in Arkansas was evident as the convention completed its work and presented a new constitution to the public. In the days following the final vote on Hinds's compromise resolution, a constitution was finally drafted. Conservative delegates framed their objections to it in part by drawing on the rhetoric that appeared during the debates over interracial marriage. For instance, Jesse Cypert, a member of the Committee on the Elective Franchise, refused to sign that committee's majority proposal. He offered instead a minority report that paired his prior objection to enfranchising black men with opposition to social integration: "The investing of an inferior race with social and political equality, is the stepping stone to miscegenation, and the consequent utter deterioration and degeneration of the dominant race," Cypert wrote.[130] When the constitution itself was introduced a few days later for the convention's approval, W. D. Moore, another white conservative, opposed it because "that instrument surrenders manhood suffrage. It takes the right from us, and confers it upon an ignorant class." Echoing the charges of the supporters of an interracial marriage ban, he continued: "Nor do we stop there. In enfranchising the negro, you make him your political and social equal. It is to invite him into your house, and make him the companion of your social hours. In my opinion, if he should be enfranchised, he would be taken into the parlors of all that vote for him—to marry their daughters, and, if necessary, hug their wives!"[131]

Joining the conservatives, several white southern delegates to the convention who had originally supported black male suffrage—evinced by their opposition to reinstating the 1864 constitution—now opposed the constitution on grounds used earlier to support banning interracial marriage. Joseph Corbell of Sevier County opposed the constitution's franchise article "for the reason that I am unwilling to confer the right of suffrage on the colored population, coupled with, as I believe, the privilege and probability of its leading to amalgamation."[132] And John Bradley accompanied his vote against the constitution with the statement, "I ask no greater boon than to record my vote against that damnable instrument of ruin that proposes to crush my race."[133] Finally, during the popular election on the ratification of the constitution, many new white voters came to the polls hoping to reject it. The constitution was approved by an extremely close vote in which over 13,000 more voters turned out to oppose it than had opposed calling a convention the previous November. On the other hand, only 337 more voters endorsed the constitution than had voted "yes" in the previous election.[134]

The rhetoric of miscegenation had thus sutured some of the tears in the political hegemony of the white southern elite in Arkansas but was not enough to achieve conservative ends. The wounds from secession, violence against unionists, and a devastating Civil War dividing white men in Arkansas politics were also evident in the convention's final hours. Peter Misner, a white delegate from Independence County, objected only that the constitution did not deprive enough former Confederates of the vote: "I would have disfranchised every one of them. I have suffered too much at their hands."[135] And O. P. Snyder of the southeastern county of Jefferson, who called the constitution "the result of the combined labors of earnest, honest, and patriotic men," cast his vote for it "with this dark and bloody tyranny [of secession] yet fresh in my memory."[136] Thus despite the move to the conservative side by some white southern men at the convention, the constitution passed the assembly by a vote of 45 to 21.[137] One month later, by the small margin of 1,316 votes, the constitution produced by Arkansas's 1868 convention was ratified in a popular vote.[138]

Ultimately, charges of miscegenation and social equality did not undermine the process of political Reconstruction in Arkansas. But the debates in the convention did shape a segregationist discourse that circulated throughout the state in the subsequent ratification battles. The force driving the rhetoric was an energetic campaign by conservatives under the banner of the White Man's Party, aided by the editors of the *Gazette*, to secure votes against the new constitution. The *Gazette* announced conservative speaking events in thirty-eight of the state's counties in the weeks before the ratification election, as well as new local White Man's Clubs and contests similar to one in Ouachita County where "the ladies . . . offer[ed] a magnificent banner to the township of that county rolling up the largest majority 'against constitution.' "[139] Former convention members such as Jesse Cypert, Robert Gantt, and John Bradley addressed some of these meetings.[140] Reports such as the following from the *Gazette* suggest the issues discussed and the frameworks employed at these events: "We have news from all parts of the state that the decent white men are abandoning the party which favors negro suffrage and supremacy, negro juries, mixed schools, and looks upon the intermarriage of whites and blacks as a matter of taste."[141] Another claimed that those voting against the constitution were motivated by "respect for their own manhood, love of liberty, regard for their own lives and property, consideration as to the fate of their posterity and the feeling which prompts men to sacrifice even life rather than submit to dishonor."[142]

The impact of this conservative effort was evident in the words of one white man in Jacksonport, Arkansas, who was eager to join the campaign against black male suffrage. John Stayton wrote the following to his brother: "We are having excitement in regard to the election upon the new constitution. The past week we had three speeches from distinguished anti-constitution gentlemen, to wit—Garland, Gantt, and Hindman. . . . I never wanted to vote before. But being disfranchised, I can't do it (now). I hope you will go and give the negro-equality thing a Kick downhill—and if every *white* man will do the same we will defeat it in the state." Stayton, previously uninvolved in politics, was apparently motivated by the racialized rhetoric of the White Man's Party. He further suggested that this rhetoric had successfully framed for him the matters at stake in domestic and social terms. He continued, "I have tried to keep out of politics all my life and if this was no more than politics I should still try to keep aloof. But the bare idea of being ruled by the miserable whelps that prowl around your kitchen at night and tamper with your private affairs on every occasion presented, is too bad, too bad." The rhetoric of conservative spokesmen appears to have offered Stayton a framework in which to understand his own local conflicts with, and personal resentments toward, the black people amongst whom he lived. In this way, it brought calls to deny black men the franchise close to home for him and many white men.[143]

Despite the eagerness of many like Stayton to defeat "negro equality," they were often ineligible to vote. Thus conservatives were unable to defeat the constitution. Nonetheless, battles over African American citizenship and black male suffrage had been moved thoroughly onto social, domestic, and gendered ground. Furthermore, apparent in the debates over interracial marriage and in the rhetoric whose circulation the *Gazette* oversaw throughout Arkansas are racial ideologies that, though not politically victorious in this moment, contained the logic of segregation that would dominate politically by the 1890s.

A key component of segregationist logic was images of black men threatening white women with sexual violence. Such imagery would be used in subsequent decades to justify widespread lynchings of black men. Early hints of it, though, are apparent in the period of Reconstruction, including in the battle over a new constitution in Arkansas. Coincidental with debates over interracial marriage at the convention, in the *Gazette*'s reporting and in its juxtaposition of certain news items and editorials, the newspaper's editors began to blur the line between black men "aspir[ing] to win the affections of your youthful child with a view to matrimonial alliance" and rape.[144] They used rape metaphorically, for instance arguing that Congress's acceptance of Alabama's new constitution "will have the effect to fix upon Alabama, 'forcibly and against her will,' a constitution which, to the wishes of her people, and the people of the other southern states, would not be less repugnant than would be the enforced embraces of a thick lipped negro to his pure minded wife or daughter."[145] But the editors also paired reports on the convention, attacks on the constitution, and editorials about "negro suffrage and social equality" with news reports such as this: "Henry Wiley, who was indicted for administering chloroform to Nancy Barker, with intent to produce such stupor of mind, and weakness of body as to prevent effectual resistance, with intent to commit a rape, was convicted of the crime and sentenced to be hung on the 14th day of February next. . . . He . . . is a negro who is guilty of the attempt on a white girl."[146] This particular report appeared in the same edition of the paper as did the first reports and editorials on the interracial marriage prohibition proposal in the Arkansas constitutional convention. Two weeks later, after the campaign against the constitution had begun, another report of "the ravishing of a white woman by a negro man" referred to the crime as "one of those outrages that are becoming too frequent within the past few years."[147] Appearing on the same page and in the same column, another item, titled "We Are Making Progress," reported that one month earlier, a magistrate in Crawford County had married a black man and a white woman. The article concluded, "This consummation is but a part and parcel of the teachings of the radical party of Arkansas. Negro suffrage and negro equality go hand in hand—they are twin monstrosities."[148] This report and those of rape, which may or may not have been accurate, were pulled from other newspapers and reprinted in the *Gazette*'s "State News" columns. They were chosen by the editors from among numerous news reports, it would seem, for no other purpose than implicitly to associate politically empowered black men not only with a desire to marry white women but also with sexual danger.

The frequency of black men raping white women alleged by the *Gazette* had not been demonstrated in news reports either before, during, or after the convention, and these two particular reports did not represent hysteria around black male rape.[149] Yet they do appear to represent a calculated attempt to illustrate for white men the supposed consequences of the political issues being discussed in these same papers. A racialized threat to white men's sense of authority and responsibility as heads of families was offered as evidence of a shared interest among all white men in opposing a new constitution. And this threat was elaborated with suggestions not only that the federal government was metaphorically raping southern states by imposing black male suffrage and new governments upon them, but that these politically empowered black men themselves were likely to rape white women. This was not the same explicit rhetoric depicting black male "beasts" with uncontrollable sexual desires threatening white women that would characterize rape reports in the partisan southern press decades later. It does, though, suggest that the conservative editors, politicians, and spokesmen seeking to oppose black male political power were already experimenting with the strategy of posing the rape of white women as the consequence of the extension of suffrage to black men during Radical Reconstruction.[150]

DESPITE SOME SUCCESS in mobilizing white men to vote against the constitution, the conservatives did not win in 1868. In the early postemancipation years, opposition to social equality and interracial marriage—a response to political more than visceral concerns for white men—was still far from hegemonic, inevitable, or uncontested. Alternative visions for racial organization were possible and even held sway. And yet, simply by participating in debates over the constitutional ban on interracial marriage, white southern men helped establish a pernicious segregationist discourse that would gain ground in coming years, as political conditions shifted and federal support for full citizenship and suffrage for African American men waned. When the antebellum link between white manhood and an exclusive voice in the public sphere was severed by emancipation, some white southern men nonetheless fashioned a distinct, racially superior manhood for themselves through a rhetoric of miscegenation that drew on gender to signify race. This rhetoric helped to heal some of the Civil War wounds between white southern moderates (like Bradley) and conservatives (like Cypert) by promoting their shared political identities as "white men." It also obliged black leaders to endorse problematic legislative action that legitimated legally enforced racial separation and had dangerous implications for extending segregation beyond the realm of sex and marriage. This rhetoric both helped lay the ideological groundwork for the establishment of Jim Crow and set the stage for decades to come in which African Americans would be forced to maneuver around politicized gender discourses, identities, and violence as they struggled for equality.[151] In this rhetoric we can see efforts to consolidate a social and ultimately a political world divided rigidly between two racial groups, black and white, despite the complex reality and fluidity of actual racial identities and origins among members of southern society. This micro-history of political struggle over black male enfranchisement during Reconstruction suggests that the particular postemancipation trajectory, one of rigid and legally enforced separation and inequality within a white/black racial system, that would ultimately be taken in the United States, and that would distinguish the United States from other postemancipation societies in the Americas, may well rest on the gendered nature of racist rhetoric and practice in the years following the end of slavery.

More immediately, the intertwining of political, social, and domestic realms within the discourse of miscegenation gave shape to the ideologies of vigilante groups such as the Ku Klux Klan in the postemancipation South. Klan notices appeared for the first time in Arkansas days after the constitution was ratified. The organization was welcomed and encouraged by the *Gazette*. Its violence spread throughout the state over the next several months, terrorizing and sometimes assassinating conservatives' political enemies.[152] The most senior politician believed to have been killed by the Klan in the South during Reconstruction was Arkansas's James Hinds, the author of the political compromise over interracial marriage in Arkansas's convention who was subsequently elected to Congress. Hinds was shot in Monroe County on October 22, 1868.[153] However, most of the Klan's violence was directed toward ordinary freedmen and freedwomen and often aimed at preventing black men from exercising the franchise. At times as part of their terror campaign, in Arkansas and throughout the South, Klan members raped black women. As we will see in the next chapter, political rhetoric linking honor, patriarchy, and politics in opposition to black male suffrage and in favor of preserving "race," the discourse so prevalent during the struggle for a new constitution in Arkansas, constituted part of the symbolic world that gave this sexual violence its political meaning. In many ways, then, this rhetoric constituted a key part of the terror African Americans suffered during Reconstruction.

PART THREE

A Region of Terror

Violence in the South, 1865–1876

CHAPTER FIVE

Houses, Yards, and Other Domestic Domains

Late in May 1871, eleven disguised men rode up to a cabin on a plantation in Gwinnett County, Georgia. After tying up their horses about 100 yards away, they approached the house yelling, "Open the door." A former slave named Hampton Mitchell was inside with his wife, his son-in-law, and his wife's father. Before anyone inside the house was able to get to the door, the men outside had forced it open. Mitchell recognized three of the intruders, despite their masks, as white men from the area. After grabbing Mitchell's gun, these men ordered him to kneel beside the cabin's threshold. "Hampton, is this your house?" the intruders demanded. "Yes, sir," Mitchell replied. They repeated the question, "Is this your house?" and Mitchell repeated his reply. Then, with Mitchell remaining on his knees in the doorway, guarded and intermittently struck by two of the men, others forced members of his family to come out of the house one at a time. First, they called to his son-in-law and "gave him a severe whipping." Next, they beat Mitchell's wife with their guns. And last, they ordered his father-in-law to come outside, beat him, sent him back into the house, and then called him out and beat him again. Finally, they ordered Mitchell to go inside and close the door.[1]

Former slaves living throughout the South in the years following emancipation would have recognized this scene. The years of Reconstruction saw extensive campaigns of vigilante terror, making this one of the most violent eras in U.S. history. Bands of white men roamed the rural areas of the South, attacking African Americans in their homes. From groups known as "bush-

whackers" or "jayhawkers" during the war, to local vigilante gangs of returned
Confederate soldiers just after southern surrender, to men in costume claiming membership in the Ku Klux Klan during congressional Reconstruction,
intrusions in the night by companies of hostile white men were experienced
by many and feared by most former slaves. Although freedpeople made distinctions between these groups, they also labeled them all "night riders" and
perceived in all of them conspiracies of terror with similar overall practices,
objectives, and effects.[2] Former slaves understood attacks by any of these
vigilante gangs as violent efforts to crush their newly won rights and to limit
the meaning of their freedom.

Freedpeople went to great lengths to report night riders' actions to officials
and to seek redress, leaving extensive documentation of violence in the records of the Freedmen's Bureau, of state and federal prosecutions of Klan
members, and of an 1871 congressional investigation into Klan activity that
conducted hearings in Washington, D.C., North Carolina, South Carolina,
Georgia, Alabama, Mississippi, and Florida. These records reveal consistent
patterns of violence across the South as well as local and individual variations.
Forcing Hampton Mitchell to identify the site where he and his family were
attacked as his domain—and thereby mocking his power within it—may have
been unique. However, testimony suggests that night rider violence during
Reconstruction often operated through similar kinds of performance. These
attacks were not brief encounters. Assailants might have produced similar
states of terror simply by shooting at freedpeople from a distance. Instead,
akin to the practices of assailants during the Memphis Riot, intrusions in the
night lasted at times for hours and involved prolonged interaction and dialogue between assailants and victims. Through this interaction and dialogue,
through their words and actions, assailants staged meanings for race that
contested the rights and identities claimed by African Americans in freedom.
These scenes drew on gendered imagery to represent blackness as subordination and vice and whiteness as authority and power. In this way, assailants
invented and communicated a fantasy post–Civil War world wherein white
men's power approximated that before the war, thereby erasing military defeat
and reclaiming the political privileges of whiteness bestowed by the system of
slavery even on nonslaveholding white men. And the stage for acting out these
scenes charged with race and gender symbolism was most often the homes of
former slaves.

This chapter foregrounds these symbolic aspects of night rider violence.
Certainly, this violence had concrete political motives and material effects.

These motives were frequently explicit, and the effects were traumatic and often deadly. White gangs directed violence at agents of the radical social transformations that followed emancipation, particularly those people who most visibly exercised, promoted, or enabled the citizenship of former slaves. Common targets were black Union soldiers, black teachers, and black preachers. Freedpeople involved in labor disputes or able to purchase land coveted by local whites could also anticipate being the victims of a nighttime attack. Assailants undermined the independence of freedpeople by seizing their land or stealing their means of support and self-defense, such as weapons, food, cash, clothing, and other valuables. They interfered with collective action by preventing nighttime travel and assembly of African Americans. And when black men gained the right to vote in 1868, organized night riding moved directly onto the terrain of electoral politics, targeting Republican leaders, Union League members, black men suspected of voting Republican, and the families of these men. Night rider violence was, in fact, so seemingly instrumental and so explicitly targeted for political ends that it is difficult to resist reducing its meaning entirely to its apparent function.[3] Yet this violence also took striking forms seemingly unrelated to function that were consistent across a wide region and over several years. Most saliently, this politically targeted and instrumental violence was suffused with imagery of gender and sexuality beyond anything necessitated by the explicit political ends of its assailants.[4] The gendered nature of night riding, in turn, raises questions about understanding this violence as a mere instrument of force. It was also a complex rhetoric of power and a stage for the formation and contestation of racial and gender meanings, identities, and hierarchies.[5]

The symbolic dimensions of night riding are demonstrated in the accounts of violence recorded by freedpeople wherein assailants are represented as positioning themselves in and forcing victims to enact certain gendered roles and identities that disavowed the changes in social relations resulting from emancipation. Night rider violence can be read as a type of performance, a theatrical form of political expression that drew on gender to resignify race and to undermine African American citizenship.[6] The symbolism enacted through violence conveyed assailants' visions for a hierarchical racial order for southern society despite emancipation and formal legal equality. From the perspective of their creators, these brutal scenes righted a world turned upside down. In scenes such as the attack on Hampton Mitchell's house, white men acted out the impossibility of black men demonstrating the same kinds of mastery over their households, their property, and the security of their family members that white men claimed for themselves, a mastery powerfully linked to popular constructions of white manhood and of citizenship. In other scenes, particularly those involving sexual insult, assault, and rape, white men also rejected black women's potential identities as honorable wives and daughters, caring for and protected within their families. Instead, assailants' words and actions positioned black women and men outside proper domestic relationships and inside realms of the illicit, transgressive, and criminal.

This schema necessitated highly ironic patterns of displacement, wherein white men insisted on the criminal nature of black men and women while representing their own violent and criminal behavior as "justice," acting out the role of legitimate arbiters of an (extralegal) law governing the conduct of former slaves.[7] This was most obvious in scenes involving sexual violence or its threat. Although black men were often attacked by white men for alleged illicit or violent sexual conduct with white women, it was black women who faced the greatest threat of rape from these same white men. Part of what allowed such obvious contradiction was the representation of blackness upon which night riders' violence rested and which it helped to produce—representations of extreme otherness that positioned black homes as marginal spaces outside the community of respectable citizens. This allowed white men to behave within these spaces in ways they could not have in their own homes or under the gaze of their neighbors and families and still maintain the posture of honorable men. The theatrical nature of the night riding—wearing disguises and taking on identities different from those embodied during the day—further sustained white men's self-representation as honorable even as they participated in dishonorable acts.[8]

Though they rarely, if ever, communicated directly, throughout the South local vigilantes enacted similar scenes. What they did share was an antebellum culture that linked political and domestic authority in the idealized figure of a white citizen and patriarch whose exclusive claim to political power rested on fulfillment of his role and responsibilities in his household, as a supposedly benevolent lord providing for and protecting virtuous wives and chaste daughters. In other words, they shared assumptions about representing worthiness for public power through private roles.[9]

It was these shared assumptions that shaped the patterns evident in night rider violence. White men contested both the domestic and political identities achieved in freedom by former slaves by attacking freedpeople in their homes. Through violence in domestic spaces, assailants staged gendered forms of racial difference and inequality that had profound political implications.

Assailants throughout the South were also loosely connected through an informal public sphere built around the circulation of rumor. White southerners apologizing for night rider attacks spread rumors of black criminality and illicit sexual activity meant to explain the necessity and legitimacy of vigilante violence.[10] Fabrications traveling from assailants to their neighbors to local officials to state judges and then to other assailants, often then invoked in the midst of violent attacks, depicted a world of rampant black vice and violence. These rumors invested broad political significance in white men's local conflicts with their black neighbors, now evidence of the supposed widespread danger unleashed on southern society by emancipation, and authorized white men's violent reactions as part of a larger campaign to preserve order. These rumors also appear to have given shape to nighttime attacks, providing an overall script replicated and adapted to local conditions throughout the South. The shared script of night rider violence, passed from neighborhood to neighborhood, town to town, and county to county, helped establish an imagined community of white men and drew them into a world of vigilantism that restored meaning to and bestowed privilege on their whiteness.

This chapter examines the rumors and performances surrounding night riding during Reconstruction as integrally connected forms of racist political expression operating throughout the southern states. It lacks the local contextualization of previous chapters. Instead, it illuminates how phenomena already observed in more localized histories were in fact regionwide: gender and sexuality functioned in key ways within political violence throughout the South during Reconstruction; the rape black women suffered during the Memphis Riot was far from exceptional but, rather, part of a pattern of violence among conservative white southern men; and a white southern political culture linking public with private power helped to shape this gendered pattern of violent contests over race and citizenship in the postemancipation South.

The Domestic Stage of Political Violence

Night riding was not a new practice during Reconstruction. In most southern states during the antebellum years, governments authorized and conscripted groups of white men to enforce slave codes by patrolling roads and slave quarters after dark. These slave patrols were designed to prevent slaves' clandestine nighttime meetings, running away, and theft by limiting their mobility. Patrols also often intruded into slave cabins and inflicted physical punishment on their inhabitants, sometimes for specific infractions such as visiting with other slaves or holding a religious meeting on another plantation without a pass from an owner, at other times for no reason at all. The bands of white men attacking freedpeople in numerous regions of the Reconstruction-era South drew upon these practices of antebellum slave discipline and control.[11]

A form of night riding also emerged out of the conditions of war. Commonly called "bushwhackers" or "jayhawkers," groups of Confederate deserters formed armed guerrilla gangs that operated essentially as bandits in the rural outreaches of various southern states, requisitioning or stealing provisions from local residents and governing communities through fear or co-optation. After the war, these gangs continued to operate in some locales as alternative governments or "regulators" who resisted Union military authority and sought to restore antebellum social relations. They commonly disarmed black Union soldiers returning from battle and attacked former slaves who refused to continue working for their former owners. These men, too, were "night riders" who commonly represented their violence against freedpeople as punishment for some alleged infraction against a "law" they had established and sought to enforce.[12]

Events occurring in middle Tennessee, particularly Robertson and Sumner Counties, in 1866 offer a detailed glimpse into the world of one such gang of bandits in the years immediately following the war and into the role that gender played in their operations. Conditions in this previous stronghold of Confederate support became severe by summer of that year. Planters had no funds to provide wages to farm laborers or rations to those working on shares.[13] Freedpeople, facing starvation and working under conditions compared to slavery by federal officials, sought other means of subsistence.[14] But their increasing withdrawal from field labor for whites was bitterly resented by their former employers. Under these circumstances, a company of bandits, reported to be 150 strong and led by a Confederate guerrilla leader whom we know only as "Colonel Harper," essentially took over the region. Either in sympathy with the gang or terrified to oppose it, local officials deferred to its authority. "There is a perfect reign of terror existing in the several counties frequented by Harper and his gang," wrote the Freedmen's Bureau chief superintendent for the Nashville subdistrict, Captain Michael Walsh, after touring the area in the fall, "so much so that I cannot do justice to the subject. There is no doubt but that the will and law of . . . Harper, Guerilla Chief, is supreme in that section and the people both white and black are more subservient to it than to the laws of the General Government."[15]

Though local planters may have feared Harper's gang, they likely also patronized it in return for its efforts to regulate and coerce black farm laborers. Walsh observed that "there are many men who would be glad to see Harper and his gang cut off, if it were not for the freedmen, for the reason that the desperadoes are intensely proslavery and desire its restoration and these fellows are used really as tools by a certain class of citizens who assume airs of respectability in the hope that they will by the aid of these cut-throats get possession of their original slaves." The goal of compelling freedpeople to labor for their former owners was fairly well achieved, if Walsh's observations were accurate. He wrote, "All the col'd people have been obliged to go back to their former owners or loose [sic] their lives, and after serving their year out get nothing, unless a poor and bare subsistence." And labor conditions were harsh under the combined rule of former slave masters and bandits: "The negroes are kept at work all the time and the white men are not willing to pay them enough to live on and they have to work for what they can get. They have not money enough to leave and they are subjected to the tyranny of this band."[16]

Harper's gang effected this form of labor control using methods whose content, if not exact form, was similar to what a few years later would be widely practiced by gangs calling themselves "Ku-Klux." Harper's men promoted an image of themselves as a mysterious and all-knowing force ready to impose an extralegal code of conduct. In the fall of 1866 in Robertson and Sumner Counties, members of the gang made this code explicit, nailing copies of a printed notice detailing rules for laborers' behavior to freedpeople's front doors. The notice was titled "I Am Committee" and was also read aloud to groups of freedpeople by white men sympathetic to the aims of Harper's gang. It contained a list of laws that outlined what was essentially a slave code without slavery, stipulating that white men were to be employers and all black people—men, women, and children—were to be laborers. Means of subsistence for African Americans other than laboring on a white man's farm were forbidden. All freedpeople were ordered to be in the employ of a white person; black people were forbidden to hire other black people; and white men were prohibited from allowing freedpeople not in their employ to squat on their land. Freedpeople found stealing or bringing food and supplies from their employer to other freedpeople were warned that their punishment would be death. Also, "Running about late of nights shall be strictly dealt with"; thus, nighttime meetings that might allow organizing for better working conditions or sharing resources were prohibited. The list of rules ended with a claim to an omnipresence fitting the committee's lordlike appellation "I Am": "I am everywhere. I have friends in every place, do your duty and I will have but little to do."[17]

The "laws" printed on the "I Am Committee" notice made it clear that family labor arrangements, particularly women's labor, were an issue of special concern. Throughout the South after emancipation, white landowners complained that former slave women were unwilling to continue laboring in the fields. Such complaints were largely exaggerated, but historians have documented a decrease in the amount of labor done by black women for white landowners and a corresponding increase in their labor—tending garden plots, spinning cloth, and preparing food—for their families. Whether a practical allocation of family members' labor in ways that produced the greatest return or an effort to limit women's contact with white overseers and planters, this was apparently a decision on the part of freedpeople that was alarming to whites in Robertson and Sumner Counties in the summer of 1866.[18] The first two rules on the "I Am Committee" document essentially stipulated that freed families could not organize their labor along patriarchal lines, with men working for wages and women working at home. The requirements that "no man shall squat negroes on his place unless they are all under his employ male and female" and "Negro women shall be employed by white persons" left freedwomen no choice but to contract as laborers for white farmers or planters. Nor were black men and women to appear to be providing for their children, who were also expected to contribute their labor to whites: "All children shall be hired out for something" was the third rule on the document. Any appearance of a household economy organized around gendered and generational divisions of labor, or even a physical structure, a house, that might facilitate a private home life independent of white oversight, was forbidden. The fourth stipulation read, "Negroes found in cabins to themselves shall suffer the penalty."[19] That the I Am Committee employed violent methods to enforce these rules is suggested by reports made by Captain Walsh in the fall of 1866. For instance, he reported that Harper's gang had murdered freedman Ed Dye and his son and then compelled Dye's wife and daughter back to the plantation of their "old master."[20] Other cases implied that freedwomen who married and left their former owners might find their husbands dead and themselves, under threat of death, working again where and how they had as slaves.[21] Harper's men, then, insisted that black women subordinate themselves within and contribute their labor to white households only. At times the gang employed even murder to destroy any appearance of patriarchal social organization among freedpeople that might resemble the domestic arrangements and identities of "free white men" and the women and children in their families.

Similar resistance to an independent domestic life among former slaves shaped activities of later Reconstruction-era gangs, who would over time operate increasingly under the rubric of the Ku Klux Klan. In southern mythology, this organization is represented as having had innocuous beginnings in a secret club formed by six young white men in Pulaski, Tennessee, in the early summer of 1866 (just months before Harper's gang was first reported operating 100 miles to the north in the same state). These men were allegedly bored ex-Confederate soldiers seeking amusement. Amusement was supposedly found in, among other things, dressing as ghosts and setting out to frighten former slaves. This story is repeated in numerous historical accounts of the Klan, and the role of the six men in Pulaski in founding an entity they named the Klan seems certain.[22] However, it is doubtful that these men had no expectation that their amusement would be politically useful or would include violence.[23] Over the next year, numerous other "clubs" calling themselves the Ku Klux Klan appeared throughout middle and west Tennessee. The fact that the Klan spread here first may be connected to the fact that Tennessee was the first state to extend suffrage to black men (in a statute passed in February 1867) and the only southern state to do so before the Reconstruction Acts. Within less than a year of the founding of the infamous social club, leading Tennessee conservatives held meetings seeking a statewide organization to harness Klan tactics for electoral purposes, lending the Klan its first widespread legitimacy with elites.[24]

By 1868, after the Reconstruction Acts imposed black male suffrage on the other ten southern states, the order's secrecy and menacing rituals and reputation became useful to conservative leaders throughout the South as a means of resisting Republican political dominance. There is evidence of efforts by these leaders to coordinate organization across state boundaries and to establish governance and rules for the Klan.[25] It is almost certain, though, that these self-designated leaders had little contact with most white men calling themselves Klansmen and acting as regulators in their local communities. County-wide organization existed in some areas, with command hierarchies and coordination across different local "camps" that met to discuss targets, plan missions, and dispense and receive orders. Former members of local Klans in North Carolina testified to being called into neighboring areas to act on behalf of other camps in local conflicts.[26] But this sort of coordination was far from universal. Some local "Klans" operated on whim and placed few restraints on whom and how they attacked. Other groups of men with no connection or affiliation with a county, let alone regionwide, Klan used the name "KuKlux" when identification with a larger and foreboding power proved useful to them in local conflicts with freedpeople.[27] That various rituals and gimmicks associated with the Klan were widespread suggests some regionwide communication, but it is also likely that many men simply mimicked what they read in the newspaper or learned through rumor and word of mouth.[28]

The most useful innovation offered to would-be night riders by the emergence of the Klan was the element of disguise. Some of the more elaborate theatrics of the Klan intended to create an aura of mystery and superhuman power—posting cryptic notes using bizarre and apparently coded language at the offices of local newspapers, posing as ghosts of dead Confederate soldiers, or creating the illusion of an ability to drink enormous quantities of water by hiding tubes and buckets underneath the robes commonly used as Klan costumes—were prevalent in the early years but were dropped quickly, no doubt because they were both labor intensive and unconvincing. But disguises and the anonymity they provided continued to be useful. Not only did masking their faces, clothing, and even horses assist men in escaping identification and retribution under the law for their acts. The fact that it was anonymous "KuKlux" who patrolled the night, as opposed to the grocer, mechanic, hired hand, local sheriff, or plantation owner well known to the community, produced the sensation among assailants, at least, and perhaps the image for victims of something more ominous and powerful than local residents. Anonymity suggested an omnipotent and omnipresent force of white men whose numbers and specific identities were unknown and who had knowledge of black people's affairs, labor arrangements, and political activities.[29]

This aspect of Klan violence was recognized by freedpeople and incorporated into their modes of resistance. Freedpeople often scrutinized shoes, coats, stature, gait, or voice seeking ways to deny Klansmen the protection and power of anonymity, and victims even occasionally tore off disguises in the midst of attacks.[30] Identification of horses, too, could be used to undermine Klansmen's disguise. Two freedwomen whipped by Klansmen in their South Carolina home identified—and then reported—their assailants by searching town the next morning for the horses seen at their house the night before. The women reportedly followed the horses with their riders back to the men's residences and thereby learned who their attackers were.[31] Freedpeople also contested the Klan's self-fashioned image of omnipotence. A freedman in Madison, Georgia, stated boldly to a white neighbor that "they call themselves Ku-Klux, but they are just disguised white men."[32]

Another practice common to Klansmen was borrowed from earlier forms of night riding: during violent attacks assailants often articulated to victims rationales for why they or their family members were being hurt. In this way violence was represented as punishment or retribution for violation of a code of conduct that corresponded to antebellum racial hierarchy. Victims were told they were made to suffer for their or a relative's role in the Union Army, for refusing to labor for a particular planter, for insubordination to a white person, for membership in a Union League, or for voting for a Republican candidate. The actions for which freedpeople were allegedly punished represented the exercise of choice that accompanied freedom and citizenship. Expressing these rationales as integral parts of an act of violence allowed assailants to stage their own supposed governing authority and to produce and enforce a type of "law" in which the exercise of citizenship by former slaves was forbidden. This "law" governing social organization and particularly matters of race operated outside and against the existing state (though at times assailants were, in fact, local law enforcement officials). Often the supposed charges stemmed from a real event or conflict. At other times, rationales were pretexts, infuriating in their inaccuracy to the victims of violence. Specific charges were often forgotten in transit when relayed from one "camp" of Klansmen to another in a neighboring county, when the former asked the latter for assistance "punishing" a given freed family in the former camp's neighborhood. Thus accusations shouted at freedpeople as they were whipped were often fabricated or misrepresented.[33] Whether their content was accurate or false, rationales became part of the ritual of violence itself; they offered functional meaning to the acts committed and attributed to Klansmen extralegal governing power.[34]

The domestic setting of most night rider violence also echoed past practice. Although schools and churches were occasional targets for arson and political meetings were regularly broken up, the vast majority of violent encounters occurred in and around homes.[35] Rather than waylay victims on roads as they returned from church, meetings, or markets or confront them at work in a field, assailants preferred to catch freedpeople at home and most often in bed. Attacks almost always occurred after sundown and usually after midnight, when victims were asleep. White men in disguise surrounded houses and called for a particular resident to come out or banged on doors and forced their way inside. Assailants dragged victims outside in their bed-clothes, destroyed or stole their furnishings and clothing, and burned or tore down their houses. They whipped and beat freedpeople, sometimes in front of family members or at other times a distance away from their house and its other occupants. These practices imitated the conduct of slave patrols but also differed crucially as well. The houses in which attacks occurred were not slave cabins within the household of a white planter but, rather, the indepen-dent homes of free African Americans.

Catching victims off guard, in bed, and at night may have served practical ends, reducing avenues for escape and time to plan resistance.[36] But the consistent pattern of attacking freedpeople in, and by dragging them from, their homes also carried enormous symbolic significance. The practice speaks to the gendered political culture of assailants. A home was the space and symbol for white southern men of their identities and powers as men. It was the world in which they were constituted as patriarchs and masters, where they exercised domestic authority that, in turn, was widely represented as justifying their claim to citizenship and political power. It was the source of their economic self-sufficiency, where, in most cases, they and their family and, in some cases, their slaves produced their livelihood and thus their independence.[37] Important identities of southern white women also emerged from homes and the relations and activities contained within them, such as those of wife, mother, or daughter. Slaves, by contrast, had been forcibly incorporated into the households of white slaveowners and subjected to the constant interruption or severing of what domestic ties and arrangements they had been able to construct. Their lack of homes and of official recogni-tion of patriarchal or other domestic relationships distinguished slaves from "freemen" and "freewomen," as whites often identified themselves. By attack-ing African Americans' homes, night riders attacked not only African Ameri-can economic independence but also a key signifier of freedom and equal citizenship.

The meanings given to homes by former slaves most likely differed in important ways from those of white southerners, particularly in regard to the emphasis placed on male authority over the labor and property of women and children within the domestic realm as a justification for men's public power. Lines of authority within families and other gendered dimensions of African American family, community, and public life were in this moment evolving among freedpeople as they experimented and struggled in the new context of freedom.[38] Nonetheless, to former slaves, homes and the relations nurtured

"Visit of the Ku-Klux." Sketch by Frank Bellew, *Harper's Weekly*, February 24, 1872, 160. Courtesy of the Library of Congress.

within them were profound manifestations of personal liberty, as well as the means through which their economic subsistence was now secured.[39] Slavery had simultaneously destroyed families—as slaveholders had the power to separate families at will—and strengthened their cultural importance as institutions that sustained slaves through the difficulties of bondage. Historians have demonstrated how the centrality of family relationships to slaves was evident upon emancipation, as freedpeople went to great lengths to reunite with family members from whom they had been separated under slavery, to assert parental rights over their children in opposition to apprenticeship, and to legitimate their marriage vows.[40] The comments of an army chaplain for a regiment of black Union soldiers in Little Rock, Arkansas, in February 1865 were common: "Weddings, just now, are very popular, and abundant among the Colored People. They have just learned, of the Special Order No' 15. of Gen Thomas by which, they may not only be lawfully married, but have their Marriage Certificates, *Recorded*; in a *book furnished by the Government*. This is most desirable."[41] Officially recorded marriages meant state recognition and legitimation of former slaves' unions and, thus, of their rights and identities as wives, husbands, and parents. This chaplain added at the end of the letter on freedpeople's enthusiasm for marriage, "The Colord Peopl here, generally consider, this war not only their *exodus*, from bondage; but the road, to Responsibility; Competency; and an honorable Citizenship."[42] This represents the white chaplain's views more than those of former slaves, but it suggests a general understanding of marriage and secure domestic relationships as a right and practice of citizenship.[43]

Former slaves living in homes independent of white control and constituting domestic identities that had, from the perspective of white southerners, been signifiers of the distinction between freemen and slaves represented a powerful challenge to antebellum constructions of racial difference. The meanings assailants expressed through violence asserted not only white dominance and black subordination but also racial difference via asymmetric access to patriarchal rights and privileges. Night riders' intrusion into African American homes asserted that claims to a secure and autonomous domestic space, a man's authority over his home and his dependents, and a woman's protected status when in the company of her family were exclusively privileges of whiteness. When Klansmen asked Hampton Mitchell, "Is this your house?" they were, in fact, contesting his claim to it and asserting to him and his family that freedom did not mean that former slaves could now claim the right to privacy, autonomy, and authority within the boundaries of a home. Instead, the intruders enacted their own authority to rule over the members of the Mitchell household. Thus, rather than autonomous realms of black patriarchal power, freedpeople's homes were to continue to be penetrable at any and all moments by the power of white men. Neither were private black domains to constitute independence and the rights of citizenship. When white men attacked freedpeople's private identities as husbands and wives, they were also attacking their worthiness for public rights as citizens. The fact that white opposition to African American freedom and citizenship was expressed through attacks on gender identities embedded within domestic domains shaped the kind of violence that freedpeople suffered. Eli Barnes, a leading black Republican in his home county of Hancock, Georgia, told the congressional investigating committee, "It has got to be quite a common thing . . . to hear a man say, 'They rode around my house last night, and they played the mischief there; my wife was molested, my daughter badly treated, and they played the wild generally with my family.' "[44]

Ironically, some white southern men represented their membership in the Klan and other secret organizations as an effort to protect their own families from assault by former slaves. In October 1870, after his arrest in Alabama for participating in the Klan, John Humber confessed that "he had joined the company upon being told that the object was to protect the women and children in the country from the insults of the negroes."[45] Few men admitted to the congressional committee investigating Klan violence that they were members of something called the Ku Klux Klan (had they done so, they would have faced criminal prosecution under the federal Enforcement Acts and the Ku Klux Act).[46] Nonetheless, many white men, subpoenaed to appear because of suspected Klan involvement, acknowledged membership in secret societies. They also offered various rationales for these societies, from promoting the interests of the Democratic Party and counteracting the influence of Union Leagues to preparing for self-defense in the face of anticipated black violence.[47] Witnesses commonly conveyed the sense that the ability of white men to protect the women in their families had been challenged by emancipation. John B. Gordon, a white lawyer, Democratic candidate for governor of Georgia in 1868, and former Confederate officer living in Atlanta, explained to the committee his motives for helping to establish an organization of white men—described as a fraternity of sorts—designed "to keep the peace and preserve order in the State":

> Men were in many instances afraid to go away from their homes and leave their wives and children, for fear of outrage. Rapes were already being committed in the country. . . . It was therefore necessary, in order to protect our families from outrage and preserve our lives, to have something that we could regard as a brotherhood—a combination of the best men of the country, to act purely in self-defense, to repel the attack in case we should be attacked by these people. . . . We felt that we must at any cost protect ourselves, our homes, our wives and children from outrage. . . . We did not want to have in our State a war of races—to have our property and our lives destroyed. We feared the peril to our women and children.[48]

Repeatedly invoking an alleged danger posed to "our women and children," in his depiction of postemancipation conditions Gordon excluded African American men from the community of citizens concerned generally about their families and implied that they were instead the agents of this danger. He stressed the rights of white men—"our property and our lives"—and their capacity to fulfill their patriarchal duties, to "protect ourselves, our homes, our wives and children," as what was at stake for secret societies such as the Klan. Also invoking gendered roles and patriarchal ideologies of protection to defend vigilante violence, a white lawyer accused of being the "chief" of the Klan in Lincolnton, North Carolina, David Schenck, repeated to the committee the oath he had taken when he joined a secret organization in 1868. The fourth item to which he swore was that "females, friends, widows, and their households shall ever be special objects of our regard and protection."[49]

It could be argued that these representations had little relevance to the actual violence of night riders. John Gordon contended that his organization had not participated in any violence. David Schenck and John Humber insisted that they immediately ceased their association with the groups they had joined on learning that other members had committed acts of violence. (Denials of involvement in violence were, though, of course necessary to escape the immediate danger of criminal prosecution.) These men's testimony, particularly before the congressional committee, was also most likely carefully crafted to appeal to other men's sense of patriarchal responsibility in order to represent the organizations they had joined as both purely defensive and legitimate. (And the advice some white witnesses received from lawyers paid for through legal defense funds set up by wealthy conservatives in 1871 may have helped shape testimony in this way).[50] Nonetheless, by joining secret societies that adopted a Klanlike structure, these men appeared to endorse night riding as a practice, and their words suggest how the aims of that practice were perceived in explicitly patriarchal terms.

Night riding was also apparently being sold to Klan rank and file through the same patriarchal logic as expressed by elites. One Klan leader reportedly promoted the secret society to new members as "a good thing for . . . poor men," because it would allow them "to protect [their] families from the darkies."[51] Framing the need for vigilante societies in patriarchal terms argued to even those white men who had not been slaveholders that emancipation hit them where they lived and that racial identification and solidarity with a cross-class fraternity of white men were the only means to protect the domestic base of their mastery.

Rumors of Miscegenation and White Representations of Violence

The danger from which white men's families needed protection was often identified by conservative witnesses before the 1871 congressional investigating committee as a combination of allegedly corrupt Republican governance in the southern states and the criminality of black men. Witnesses claimed that by allowing black men to participate in politics, the Republican Party incited them to engage in violent acts. They argued that then Republican judges would not convict black criminals or that Republican governors would pardon them.[52] And the crimes supposedly enabled by an incompetent state included rape. Vague references similar to that made by John Gordon when he spoke before the congressional committee—that "rapes were already being committed in the country"—were offered frequently as rationales for the formation of secret societies such as the Ku Klux Klan. This is evident, for instance, in the testimony of Nathan Bedford Forrest, the former Confederate general from Memphis credited with leading efforts to coordinate the activities of local gangs of night riders into a statewide and then regionwide operation under the umbrella of the Ku Klux Klan. When Forrest was brought before the congressional committee, he denied any involvement with the Klan. But he nonetheless explained that the organization had formed in order to address "the great deal of insecurity felt by the southern people," and he added rape to a list of "alarming" behavior on the part of former slaves that included "holding night meetings; . . . going about; . . . [and] becoming very insolent." Forrest told the committee, "Ladies were ravished by some of these negroes, who were tried and put in the penitentiary, but were turned out in a few days afterward."[53] Southern conservative newspapers were full of similar charges, offering a visceral metaphor for threats to white dominance by linking assertive behavior on the part of freedpeople—or "insolence"—with rape. James Justice, a white Republican representative in North Carolina's legislature, explained to the committee that these papers "allege that [Klan] outrages were greatly exaggerated, if they existed at all; that incompetency upon the part of State officials, and insolence on the part of negroes in some parts of the State, their having committed rapes, &c., was the cause of it."[54]

The emergence of the Klan and the need to justify its atrocities and to maintain solidarity among its members seems to have led to an increase in the circulation among white southerners of a discourse representing black men as sexually dangerous.[55] The need to rationalize a regionwide vigilante organization that had political goals and used violent methods led white political spokesmen to reshape a critique of alleged state corruption—Republicans ignoring black criminality and corrupting the political process by allowing black men to vote—into a protest against rape as one of many threats to life and property resulting from emancipation and Republican political power. This image did not dominate white depictions of black criminality in these years; charges of stock stealing, larceny, or general unruliness, for instance, were equally as common.[56] But seeds had been planted for what would eventually become a full-blown rhetoric equating black masculinity with rape, and this rhetoric would prevail over other racist representations in the disfranchisement campaigns of the 1890s.[57]

During Reconstruction, this discourse of rape and criminality justifying the Klan's existence circulated in local communities in the form of rumor. H. W. Guion, a white conservative lawyer from Charlotte, North Carolina, told the committee that conditions in his community were overall "very good, with the exception of rapes and murders and thefts." Though he struggled to recall even one case of black men attacking white women, he insisted that "rapes are much more common than you have any idea of" and "Mecklenburgh [county] has always been famous for rapes." The committee's chair pressed Guion to be more precise and finally asked him in frustration, "Can you name a case at all?" Guion replied, "No, sir, I cannot; but I am pretty sure there has been more than one."[58] Most witnesses who made claims similar to Guion's could name few actual cases. Nathan Bedford Forrest admitted that "I merely heard of one or two cases, but I do not recollect them now."[59] Thus, through unsubstantiated claims, conservative white men produced and disseminated the general impression that black men threatened white women with rape, and that this was evidence of the bias and incompetence as well as dangerous nature of Republican rule, in order to legitimate Klan violence.

Rumors about the causes of specific acts of violence also circulated among whites. A U.S. district attorney prosecuting Klan members in northern Mississippi, G. Wiley Wells, explained to the congressional committee, "It makes no difference who the person was or what his character, or whether the party—woman or man—has been whipped, shot, or hung, [friends of the Klan] at once commence to assert and circulate charges; and they seem to have a method whereby they impregnate the community with the belief that the person so whipped or outraged was guilty of crimes, was a terrible enemy to society, and that, in fact, it was a justice to society that the party was killed or whipped; that it ought to have been done."[60] The rumors offered to justify a particular Klan attack at times alleged violent or criminal sexual conduct by a black man.[61] Caswell Holt, a freedman who was attacked twice by the Klan in Alamance County, North Carolina, was accused by his attackers of theft. However, after the attacks, Raleigh newspapers alleged he had "behaved indecently and exposed himself to white women."[62] Thomas Allen, a black Baptist preacher and politician who was run out of Marietta, Georgia, by the Klan, protested to the committee that whites in Madison had taken a black man from jail and murdered him. Asked what the man was charged with, Allen replied, "I heard that he had tried to commit a rape upon a white girl."[63] More often, though, rationales for vigilante attacks focused on illicit, presumably consensual cross-racial sexual relationships. Concerning a black man who was murdered by night riders in Tuscaloosa, Alabama, in 1871, a white circuit court judge told the congressional committee, "The report is, that this man . . . had lived in adultery with a white woman."[64] Similar pretexts—allegations that black men were crossing racial boundaries and violating social taboos— disseminated through newspaper reports, between local leaders, and among neighbors, circulated images that mystified the objectives of Klan violence and helped to legitimate the Klan among white southerners.

Rumors also alleged illicit sexual conduct or improper domestic arrangements on the part of black women and sometimes of white Republican men. In some cases, innocent circumstances were distorted to convey an image of impropriety. In 1868, George Ashburn, a white southern Republican noted for strong polemics, was murdered in his bed by thirty or forty men after he gave a political speech in Columbus, Georgia. This occurred just weeks after the end of Georgia's constitutional convention, when Nathan Bedford Forrest visited Columbus at the same time that Klan notices began to appear in the local papers. Because no white-owned hotels or boardinghouses in town would allow Ashburn to stay in their facilities, he had rented a room in the front of a black woman's home. One conservative white judge told the congressional committee that Ashburn was murdered because he "was said then to be living in a state of adultery with a negro woman in Columbus . . . and that he abandoned his family in defiance of public sentiment." Though the judge used what was essentially gossip to conclude that the murder was not politically motivated, he nonetheless qualified his statements, adding, "These are rumors or reports; I do not know anything about their truth."[65] In fact, Rev. Henry M. Turner, who had shared the stage with Ashburn during his speech on the night he was murdered, knew the woman with whom Ashburn boarded. When asked if they were living together in adultery by the chair of the Georgia subcommittee of the congressional investigation in 1871, Turner explained why he thought it unlikely: "I believe on the one hand that he was above such acts, and on the other hand, she is too religious a woman to be guilty of it."[66]

Another incident based on similar charges led to violence against black women rather than white men. Several women living with unmarried white farmers in Noxubee County, Mississippi, were whipped and run off to Macon in the spring of 1870. Alexander Davis, a black lawyer and member of a federal grand jury questioned one of the women, Betsy Lucas, seeking a reason for the attack. She could offer none.[67] But a white lawyer called before the congressional committee by the committee's conservative minority had heard a rationale: "The rumor was here that [Robert] Jackson [a farmer with whom Lucas lived] was living with her in open notorious adultery to the scandal of the community."[68] Another white lawyer from Macon, James Rives, who knew about the case "only from the report in the country at the time," explained how the initial story differed from what he now believed to be true: "The information I had at the time was they whipped the men and the women too, but I understood afterwards that they did not whip the men, and directed the women that they must leave."[69] The committee's Republican chairman asked Rives if relationships between black women and white men were so unusual that "it is thought worthy of a Ku-Klux visitation in order to correct such irregularity?" "Well, living together, as I understand they were living together, is a thing that is very uncommon," Rives replied. "I do not know any other instance within my knowledge either in this country or elsewhere. That white men and black women have frequent intercourse I have no doubt is true, but that they live together as these parties did, is a thing of rare occurrence." Although this assault was represented as retaliation for black women's "lewdness," Rives's response suggests the real infraction was that these women were being treated too much like wives. The representation of their relationships with white men bordered too closely on the legitimate, and thus their presence in the community blurred racial lines.[70]

Rumors circulating among whites to justify Klan violence described African American men and women as threatening the orderly arrangement of sexuality and domestic life along racial lines in southern society. The boundaries constituting appropriate spheres of social life imagined by men protesting black male suffrage (such as John Bradley in Arkansas) were depicted in white conversations about vigilante violence as imperiled by black sexuality. But representations of an unruly domestic world and illicit sexual practices among former slaves also portrayed black men as behaving improperly with black women in their own families. Henry Lowther, a successful merchant and leading black Republican in his Georgia village, was threatened by the Klan and then arrested after a party of black men gathered to protect him. Klansmen subsequently took him out of jail and castrated him. (The fact that he was asked by the alleged leader of the Klan in this region, Democrat and former confederate colonel Eli Cummins, if he was willing "to give up your stones to save your life" the day before he was taken from jail suggests that the castration was planned before the attack.) After his first nighttime visit from the Klan, Lowther learned from others that the assailants explained they were after him because he was "going to see a white lady." Lowther denied this charge to the congressional committee, adding, "I had a family."[71] Nonetheless, the charge stuck and became part of how the case was generally represented. And yet William F. Wright, a conservative Georgia superior court judge, told the congressional committee that he had heard that Lowther was castrated not by the Klan but by "the negroes themselves, because he violated the chastity of his wife's daughter."[72] An incident of torture and mutilation of a leading black Republican figure was thus twisted so as to circulate images of the inability of black men to serve as responsible patriarchs, evinced in this case by allegations not only of a black man's adulterous relations with a white woman but also of his violation of a young woman within his own household. The transgressions alleged in the form of rumor, then, evolved and were elaborated as some white southern men—Klansmen, judges, and their interlocutors—spun fantasies of black sexual violence, incest, and a generally unrestrained and uncivilized sexuality into politically useful falsehoods.

Similar (mis)representations of African American sexuality and domestic conduct were invoked in the midst of Klan attacks, suggesting that fantasies of black sexual transgression played important roles in shaping the specifics of violence itself. For instance, Elias Hill, a severely disabled black Baptist preacher and the Union League president in the Clay Hill precinct of York County, South Carolina, was beaten by the Klan in May 1871. As the assailants were hitting him, he later reported, they accused him of holding Union League meetings in his house, of giving political sermons, of ordering other freedpeople to burn farm buildings, and of "tell[ing] the black men to ravish all the white women."[73] The Klan also appears to have reveled in accusing black men and women of inappropriate conduct within their own families. Anderson Ferrell was shot in a dispute with Klansmen in Troup County, Georgia, when they were searching for another freedman who was charged with murdering his wife.[74] When the Klan beat the wife of a black preacher in Gwinnett County, Georgia, they told her she was being punished because "she had been knocking about with other men," something her uncle-in-law told the congressional committee could not have been true.[75] Punishing freedpeople for alleged dishonorable sex within their own communities had the same effect perhaps as forcing them to enact it, which was done in Rockingham County, North Carolina, in 1869. Here Klansmen whipped a black man while forcing him to feign sexual intercourse with a black girl. The assailants furthermore insisted that the girl's father be a witness to the scene.[76] By forcing freedpeople to perform transgressive and possibly violent sex, or by forcing them to passively allow it to occur within their families, vigilantes coerced black men and women into participating in white fantasies representing them as incapable of proper domestic relationships and virtuous gender identities, while assailants themselves performed the role of honorable men enforcing the norms of the community. Night riders and their white southern apologists employed patriarchal logic and even vivid pornographic imagination to construct gendered representations of racial difference.

At times apologists for Klan violence drew on the discourses of social equality that swirled around the politics of citizenship in these years.[77] When a white male teacher named Luke and four black male companions were killed in Cross Plains, Alabama, rumors were circulated not only that these men had threatened to burn the town but also that Luke was killed because he was a "miscegenationist." Peter Dox, a white planter and member of Congress from Huntsville, Alabama, who was called before the congressional committee by the conservative minority, testified that conditions in Alabama were overall peaceful and that the violence that had occurred was not political in nature. To explain the murder of Luke and the other four men, Dox shared the rumors he had collected with the committee: "I have in my pocket a letter from a man of character, General Burke, in which he says that Luke had made himself particularly obnoxious. He was a sort of miscegenationist. . . . Burke writes— and I have heard it from other sources—that this man affiliated or fraternized with the negroes socially."[78] Social interaction in public between white and black men in a fashion indicating equality was represented as immorality, "miscegenation" even, and justification for murder.

In other instances, discourses of social equality became part of the performance enacted in the violence itself. Clem Bowden, a sixty-one-year-old freedman, and his wife were taken from their home in Spartanburgh County, South Carolina, at night by Klansmen. They were chained and stripped as if they were slaves. The assailants marched them out into an "old field," beat them, and cut off part of Bowden's ear, again as if punishing a recalcitrant slave. Bowden was accused of having formed a militia company (which he denied), of being the election manager for the Republicans in his precinct (which he confirmed), and of having said that he was "going to commence on the white people at the cradle, and kill from that up" (which he denied).

Insulting Bowden by indicating that he was dominated by his wife, the assailants told her that she should have "taught [him] better than to be a radical."

Soon the assailants were joined by other Klansmen who had in their custody William H. Champion, a white teacher running a Sunday school for freedpeople. Champion told the congressional committee what happened next: "They made me kiss the negro man's posterior, and held it open and made me kiss it, and as well as I remember a negro woman's too, and also her private parts, and then told me to have sexual connection with her. I told them they knew, of course, I could not do that. . . . They asked me how I liked that for nigger equality. I told them it was pretty tough."[79] This elaborate performance represented social equality as white men degrading themselves before black people put on the social level of slaves. That degradation took the form of the violation of sexual taboos, violation which in this instance transgressed both race and gender norms. It also involved extreme humiliation for the three parties involved. The fact that Bowden himself recounted to congressional investigators the indignity he suffered in this scene, but not that suffered by his wife (other than to report that she too was beaten), suggests his unwillingness to have this insult and the denial of their relationship to each other as husband and wife reenacted in the hearing room.[80]

Thus gender and sexuality permeated night riders' violence and its representation in various ways, including through charges of miscegenation and social equality. Z. B. Hargrove, a former Georgia Confederate who had joined the Republican Party and now supported Reconstruction, attributed Klan violence entirely to the desire to prevent African American men from exercising the franchise and "to control the elections through intimidating the republicans." Yet he also observed that "a great many would-be decent fellows make a great fuss about republicans being in favor of negro equality. That is one thing they do not intend to have; no negro equality about it at all." Understanding "negro equality" to have sexual implications, the committee asked Hargrove if there was any reason for whites to "fear miscegenation with the colored race." Hargrove's reply, enlisting the same metaphor used by James T. White in Arkansas's constitutional convention, made it clear that he heard in "miscegenation" black men pursuing relationships with white women, but not the reverse: "No sir, it is all on the other foot." When asked to clarify, he replied with surprising honesty, "I mean that colored women have a great deal more to fear from white men."[81] Hargrove thus highlighted the irony of night riders and their apologists depicting and framing Reconstruction-era violence as a response to the sexual vice and danger allegedly promoted by African Americans. Despite assertions made by night riders during and through their attacks on freedpeople, despite the rumors that white southerners relied on to justify widespread political violence, and despite claims by night riders to be protecting the women in their families from assault, white men were far more likely than black men or women to engage in violent or threatening sexual conduct.

The Performance of Rape

Sexual violence was frequent enough during the postwar years for Essic Harris, a black man reporting the rape of a neighboring freedwoman by Klansmen in North Carolina, to say, "That has been very common . . . it has got to be an old saying by now." Harris also noted, though, "They say that if the women tell anything about it, they will kill them."[82] It is indeed safe to assume that many women who suffered sexual violence at the hands of night riders did not report it to officials for fear of retaliation.[83] (Rape has been a notoriously underreported crime under any circumstances, for this and other reasons.)[84] It is also likely that many rapes that victims and witnesses did wish to report nonetheless do not appear in the historical record. The documentation of rape in this period was conditioned by factors beyond freedpeople's readiness to testify. Whether or not a freedwoman or a friend or family member who decided to report a rape could do so depended on her or his access to a Freedmen's Bureau agent, federal prosecutor, or congressional hearing. Bureau offices and federal hearings were located in cities and towns, while the majority of night rider violence occurred in rural areas of the South.[85] Thus most victims had to have both time and means to travel in order to record their testimony. Whether or not testimony was preserved in federal records depended further on the competency of federal officials, especially if testimony was given to a local agent who, working in a makeshift office and without adequate staff or, in some cases, unsympathetic to freedpeople's concerns, might easily misplace or fail to file an affidavit.[86] These factors make it impossible to calculate how many women were raped by white men during Reconstruction-era political violence.[87]

Yet, despite threats of retaliation and obstacles to having one's words recorded and preserved, many women did manage to testify about these crimes before federal officials, as did family members who were present, neighbors who learned of rape after the fact, or even people who knew of it only as rumor, and their testimony can be found in federal archives. The research for this chapter and the next turned up stories concerning forty-five different women who suffered rape or other forms of sexual attack by white men between 1865 and 1871.[88] The testimony documenting each case varies greatly in degree of detail and in the proximity of the witness to the actual event. The form of sexual violence documented varies too, from rape or its attempt, threat, or simulation, to sexually charged humiliation, insulting solicitation, and beatings following refusals to have sex. In conjunction with comments such a Harris's, the stories discussed here—most likely only a small portion of the rapes that actually occurred during Reconstruction—reveal a pattern of violence of which freedpeople were acutely aware and which added to their trepidation, no doubt, whenever they entered into a conflict with white men.

Just such a pattern of violence was evident late in October 1866 in Robertson County, Tennessee. Here members of the band of regulators known as Colonel Harper's gang raped a fourteen-year-old former slave named Amanda Willis. The attack occurred when three men intruded into the Willis family's home, six miles from Springfield, at nine o'clock at night and commenced tearing through the family's belongings. They forced Amanda's father, Stanford, to stand facing the fireplace while one of the intruders held a gun at his back and demanded that he give them his money. They were infuriated when he insisted he had none and beat him as they continued to search the house, rummaging through the family's trunks and putting aside clothing and other items of value for themselves, all the while screaming at Stanford to tell them where he kept his cash. The men then gave the family five minutes to carry outside any remaining items before the men set the house on fire. As the house burned, they threw many of the belongings the family had rescued back into the flames.[89]

One of the men plundering the Willis family's home that night identified himself as Colonel Harper. Amanda Willis's older brother Henry told the chief superintendent of the Freedmen's Bureau for the Nashville subdistrict, Captain Michael Walsh, that when these men first entered the house, one demanded of a younger brother, "God damn you, do you know me?" When the boy replied, "No, sir," the man declared, "This is Colonel Harper." Although this may have been the infamous leader of the guerrilla gang, it is more likely that it was not. This intruder had confirmed that the family did not know him by another name before claiming Harper's identity. Members of Harper's gang most likely used their leader's name to hide their own identities while drawing on his reputation to instill fear; they also probably sought to feed that reputation by crediting all nighttime raids and acts of violence to Harper. Stanford Willis also told the bureau that this man called himself Harper but speculated that he was, in fact, someone else. Stanford knew one of the men as James Price and thought the other two, though strangers, were named Finch and Simpson.[90]

As the Willis house burned, the assailants told Stanford, as he later recalled, "The next time I built to build in some person's yard." This cryptic demand may have been intended to invoke one of the I Am Committee rules, "Negroes found in cabins to themselves shall suffer the penalty." The Willis family lived on the plantation of Thomas Willis, presumably their former owner and where, by the rules of the I Am Committee, they were supposed to remain. Perhaps, though, the family had reached an agreement with Thomas about where they would locate their house that displeased the gang. Or, more likely, these men did not know on whose land they stood but offered this nonetheless as a rationale for their intrusion that night. Barking this order at Stanford made theirs an attack on the independence of black households. In order to pose as more than opportunistic plunderers, then, perhaps they invoked as a pretext for their acts the general demand that freedpeople not live far from the oversight of whites.

Before raping Amanda, the men removed her from the oversight of her family. As they destroyed the structure constituting the protective space of her family life, they severed her from protective relationships with family members. Dramatizing this rupture of family ties and simultaneously rupturing Stanford's and Amanda's identities as father and daughter, they ordered Stanford to remain with the rest of his family on one side of the house while they took Amanda by the arm and, as Amanda later told the Freedmen's Bureau, "brought me down into the woods and had forcible connection with me."[91]

Amanda was not the only woman in the Willis family sexually threatened by Harper's gang. Henry Willis reported to the Freedmen's Bureau that on the same night that Amanda was raped, the men who attacked her also went to the house of his aunt, where "one of them was going to ravish [my aunt's] daughter Elizabeth, but one of the other men told him not, and he desisted." Furthermore, Henry reported, three white men had approached the Willis home a few days before this attack and called for his mother to come to the fence. Mrs. Willis went no farther than her door. The men then "used the most obscene language" in addressing Mrs. Willis and then threatened her with rape: "One of them asked her if she had connection with a man lately. She said she was not in the habit of doing it." Simply by asking, these men forced her to participate in an exchange in which she was removed from her role as a wife. And then they refused to accept her reassertion of that identity, that she was not "in the habit of doing" that, that she was not a loose or lewd woman. "He then said God damn you I will make you do it." This man drew his pistol, but instead of shooting, he jumped over the fence and propelled an object (a rock perhaps) from a slingshot, striking Mrs. Willis on the arm. She was badly injured, but the man did not follow through on his threat. The fact that this man failed to do as he threatened highlights again the importance of an almost scripted posturing to night riders' attacks. Much like the men's charge that Stanford build in someone else's yard, the solicitation and then threat against Mrs. Willis invested assailants' aggressive conduct with particular meaning, in this case signifying a crude but nonetheless unexceptional exchange with a lewd or immoral woman. Speaking a script that depicted black women's depravity, though, may not have been as effective or as satisfying to night riders as was compelling an actual performance of it. Henry Willis believed that these were the same men who attacked his family's home and raped his sister a few days later.[92]

These attacks on the Willis family were part of a larger campaign by Harper's gang in the Willises' neighborhood. In October, after learning that witnesses could connect members of the gang to the murder of several black Union soldiers in the area, Chief Superintendent Walsh advised the local bureau agent in Springfield, D. D. Holman, that "it is . . . stated that it is the intention of these men to drive out of the state or murder every Freedman who has been a soldier in the Union Army." His information was based on the report of a neighbor of the Willises, Simon Woodard, who had traveled to Captain Walsh's office in Nashville to report the murder of a black soldier named Irvin Powell. Woodard identified one of Powell's killers as James Price, one of the men whom Stanford Willis had recognized in the attack on his family.[93] When Price and the others who attacked the Willis family moved on to the home of Stanford's sister, there they demanded to know where Simon Woodard lived. When Stanford's sister told them, they responded, "That is what we want," and declared that they would go there to burn his house down.[94]

That the Willis family then clearly knew of the dangers of reporting violence to the Freedmen's Bureau makes it all the more striking that Amanda Willis testified before the chief superintendent of the bureau, Captain Walsh. Her affidavit, made one month after the attack, leaves us only a few of her words. The fact, though, that those words foreground the sexual assault and add information about the assailants' other actions only as an afterthought indicates that this aspect of the night rider campaign stood out most painfully in her memory. Her affidavit reads,

> On or about the 23rd day of October 1866, I saw three men at Mother's house, and after putting all of us out of the house and our clothes, one of the men got me by the arm and told me to follow him. he brought me down into the woods and had forcible connection with me.
>
> They all left immediately afterwards.
>
> They burned up father's house.

More detailed affidavits had already been taken from Amanda's father, Stanford (a few days earlier by a local justice of the peace in the presence of Springfield Bureau agent Holman), and her brother Henry (taken a month earlier by Walsh himself). Thus, before he spoke to Amanda, Walsh knew a great deal about the assailants' actions and had been told, by Henry, that Amanda had been raped. Did Walsh then seek out Amanda to give this testimony so that he could compile a complete and compelling record of the horrors being imposed in middle Tennessee by Harper's gang to pass on to a higher authority? Or did Amanda seek an opportunity to protest the assault herself? And was "forcible connection" her term for rape ("connection" was a term for sex commonly used among freedwomen, but that Amanda would choose "forcible" seems unlikely), or one offered to her by the bureau agent? ("Ravished" was the term used in Henry's affidavit.) And why did Stanford not mention that his daughter had been raped? Was he attempting to protect her from being questioned by the bureau? Did he not know, Amanda having told her brother but not her father? Was it too painful for him to represent to a group of white officials how other white men had hurt his daughter and to reveal his powerlessness to protect her from assault? Records left of the attacks suffered by freedpeople with officials of the bureau often leave as much uncertain and unknown as they reveal.[95]

The records do, though, demonstrate how the rape that Amanda Willis suffered—an attack surrounded by assaults on the symbols of black domestic autonomy and the capacity for both patriarchal protection and feminine virtue among former slaves—was embedded within larger postemancipation political contests. In a community struggling over the reorganization of labor after the end of slavery and over the symbols of masculine power following military defeat, assailants raped, threatened to rape, and propositioned former slaves as part of a larger performance of power resisting and disavowing the radical transformations in southern society brought by emancipation. Their actions forced freedpeople to manifest an apparent difference from whites through coerced performances of unchaste daughters and wives, incapable patriarchs, and a lack of moralizing and protective domestic domains.

Variations on the themes structuring the attack on the Willis family are evident in testimony describing violence enacted by other white men in the same region of Tennessee. In Sumner County, a night rider crudely propositioned and threatened with rape Patsy Duvall in ways that echoed the experience of Amanda Willis's mother. Patsy and her husband, Jim Duvall, reported to the Freedmen's Bureau that at the end of June 1866 they were visited in the night by two white men who were looking for their neighbor, Jim Warren. The men ordered Jim Duvall to direct them to Warren's home. Patsy recounted her hostile exchange with one of these men, whom she recognized as Richard Pentle: "I said to him that it would be a pity to kill Jim Warren from his children, when he answered back saying he would have his pistol and his God damned scalp after." The men did find Jim Warren, brought him back to just outside the Duvall house, and shot and killed him within earshot of Patsy. In his affidavit, Jim Duvall reported that after killing Jim Warren, "the one who shot him came in to my house and stayed some time; Both then left and when leaving, told me not to leave or have report made." Patsy's affidavit explained what Jim's did not: that while Pentle "stayed some time" in their house, he sought to coerce Patsy to submit to sexual intercourse with him. "Pentle came into the house and said he got Jim Warren's pistol and his scalp too," Patsy testified, "and that if he did not get connection with me he would also kill my husband." Patsy had invoked Jim Warren's responsibilities as a father to protest Pentle's intention to take his life. Pentle retaliated by forcing his way into her home and staging her incapacity to be a chaste and respectable wife. The fact that Jim Duvall omitted this aspect of Pentle's actions from his affidavit could indicate an attempt to avoid reliving before the Freedmen's Bureau the pain he felt at the indignity his wife suffered and the shame he felt at being positioned in a script in which he failed to act as his wife's protector. It was, in fact, Patsy who acted to protect her husband's life and her own. According to her report, she refused Pentle's demand and insisted that he would not hurt her husband either: "I said I would not do it, and that I thought he would not kill him, (my husband), for I thought he had done enough."[96]

In the same county in Tennessee, on the night of September 4, 1866, three white men came to the home of Ed Link and challenged him to protect his family while simultaneously making it impossible for him to do so. The white men demanded that Link tell them "how many girls I had in the family." Link informed the men that he had five daughters, the eldest eighteen years old. Link later told Captain Walsh of the choice with which these men then presented him: "They asked me which I would rather do, to go out to the woods myself, or let my girls go." It seems that Link ran out of the back of the house in search of a weapon but did not get far before he was shot and wounded by one of the intruders. This man apparently already had Link's daughter Elmira by the arm.[97] The silence in the affidavit on anything further happening to Elmira suggests two possibilities: that the man let her go when he ran after Link to shoot him, or that Link could not bring himself to testify to the fact that his daughter was raped.

In addition to creating situations that forced black men to fail as protectors, some white men appear to have structured interactions with black women that would force these women to demonstrate their own lack of virtue. For instance, assailants often sought submission, that is, a performance of consent, on the part of freedwomen more than they sought to force women to have sex. For instance, in September 1865, also in Tennessee, Sina, a nineteen-year-old former slave, rejected the proposition of Mr. May, a plantation overseer. Sina later told Bureau Superintendent John Seage that "Mr. May tied me up because I would not consent to him & tied my Clothes around my neck & beat me very badly then drove me off without pay or a morsel of bread." Seage observed in his recording of Sina's testimony that she was "whelted all over shamefully."[98] It would seem that if May was able to tie Sina up and beat her, he most likely would have been physically able to force sexual intercourse upon her as well. But he did not. Instead, he demanded her consent. She was punished for refusing to consent, but she was not forced to submit to sex. Perhaps May's wrath was brought on by Sina's refusal to participate in a performance of her own lewd character and thus by her rewriting of May's envisioned fantasy of racial difference.

Submission was similarly the desire of one among a large crowd of disguised night riders who surrounded the home of Rina Barry, her son George Moore, and his wife in the middle of the night in 1869 in Cherokee County, Alabama. Soon after this attack, George Moore recounted to a lieutenant at a nearby camp of federal troops that several of these men burst the door down and took him from the house. George then added, "Four men then guarded me while others went in and ravished a young girl who was visiting my wife." This young girl was seventeen-year-old Cynthia Bryant, who was sleeping in a bed with Rina Barry. Three days after the attack, Barry herself described what had happened to Bryant to a sympathetic white Republican named John Hamilton. Hamilton later wrote down Barry's story: "One came to the bed where she [Rina] and a neighbor woman were sleeping, and wanted to get in bed with them, and they refused him, but he said if the girl that was in bed with Reaner [Rina] did not submit to him, he would shoot her, and had a gun in his hand. The girl commenced crying, and said she did not want to die; and then he set his gun down by the bed and stripped off the cover and got on the girl in bed with Reaner." Barry also recounted how another assailant "tried to get George's wife out doors to some of the other men and let them have to do with her."⁹⁹ These intruders treated the Barry-Moore household not as a family's home but, rather, almost as if it were a house of ill repute, a place in which women were available to have sex with strange white men on demand. Rather than physically forcing sex, the man who raped Cynthia Bryant first asked for and then forced her submission. He rejected her refusal by threatening her with death and obtained her acquiescence, signaled to him when she said "she did not want to die," through terror. Compelling her to perform her consent allowed him to cloak his own brutality—he put his gun down—and to enact a scene of illicit but consensual sex.

Cynthia Bryant was raped during the era of night riding's distinctly political character. The Reconstruction Acts, enfranchisement of black men and political mobilization in freed communities, and the Republican state governments elected in most southern states created new obstacles for white men seeking to reclaim dominance of southern society and gave new impetus to violent secret societies. The Klan began to appear throughout the South, and victims were told more and more often that they were being punished for political activities and were ordered to cease voting or organizing for Republicans. The late night attack during which Bryant was raped occurred just before an election in Alabama, and the intruders first demanded to know for whom George had voted in the last presidential election. They cursed and beat him when he defiantly replied he had voted for Republican president Ulysses S. Grant. When George testified about the attack, he reported, "The cause of this treatment, they said, was that we voted the radical ticket."¹⁰⁰ Part of that "treatment," and part of constructing Moore as a man incapable of reasoned and legitimate political voice, was to construct his home as a space of vice, a place of indecency marginal to any community of upstanding citizens.

It was rumored that four women were raped during a riot in Meridian, Mississippi, in March 1871.¹⁰¹ This riot stemmed from a Klan-organized effort to unseat a municipal government dominated by Republicans. Klansmen from Sumter County, Alabama, just across the state line from Meridian, were apparently called on by some white Meridians to assist in putting pressure on many of the city's officials and black leaders. The presence of large numbers of Alabama Klan members in town over several days led to increasing tensions. Black residents held public meetings and demonstrations in protest, and in connection with these protests several black leaders were arrested. Their trial was disrupted by a gunshot from an unidentified source that triggered three days of rioting. During this rioting, gangs of white men—some of whom were Meridian residents, while others were from Alabama—searched black homes for guns and chased prominent black citizens out of the city. These gangs particularly targeted the homes of black men on the city's police force.[102]

Ellen Parton, a freedwoman who supported herself by "washing and ironing and scouring," lived in Meridian in the home of policeman Marshal Ware.[103] Parton described the actions of rioters in Ware's house over the three days of violence to members of Mississippi's legislature sent to Meridian to investigate: "On Monday night they said that they came to do us no harm; on Tuesday night they said they came for arms; I told them there was none, and they said they would take my word for it; on Wednesday night they came and broke open the wardrobe and trunks, and committed rape upon me."[104]

On the night that Parton was raped, eight intruders searched the house where she lived for Marshal Ware while he successfully hid in a back pantry. Parton believed that most of the intruders were not residents of Meridian. One of these strangers grabbed Parton. "He then took me in the dining room, and told me that I had to do just what he said; I told him I could do nothing of that sort; that was not my way, and he replied, 'by God, you have got to,' and then he threw me down." Like the attack on Cynthia Bryant, this assailant, a stranger to Parton, first informed her he wanted sex and then denied her right to refuse. This same man had also attempted to rape another woman in the house. "There is one other woman living with me named Alice Batt; this man had her in there first, and Alice Batt told me that he said to her to go away . . . and to call that other woman." This man thus approached the women in the house as if they were employees in a brothel, available for him to choose from for a sexual encounter. Parton added that "after he got through with me he came through the house, and said that he was after the Union Leagues."[105] This gratuitous comment was not particularly relevant to anyone to whom this man might have been speaking but, instead, appears to have been part of the overall fantasy he was enacting. In the midst of a riotous spree in a town in which he was not known, this man behaved in a variety of ways that allowed him to embody an identity of a powerful white man, an identity defined and experienced through political domination over black men—Union League members and police—and sexual domination over black women. And he faced no repercussion for his own dishonorable conduct. He posed not as a rapist but as a man visiting a house of ill fame.

Constructing black homes and communities as spaces for white men's pleasure framed other incidents of rape. In late December 1870, in Chatham County, North Carolina, a gang of white men intruded into a "settlement" of freedpeople living and working on the land of a white man named Mr. Finch. The intruders barged into several of the houses in the settlement and took weapons from the residents, activities suggesting that the invaders were on a political mission. But they were also dressed in a variety of disguises, and some were wearing women's clothing, indicating an impromptu dress-up and even the anticipation of a raucous "good time" violating proper social roles, much like carnival. This attitude was reflected in their actions. A freedman from the settlement told the congressional committee investigating Klan violence that in one house they "ate something there," and "some of them played a fiddle and danced awhile." They then moved on to a house where four freedwomen lived together with male relatives, called one of the women out of the house, and raped her.[106] Earlier that same month, in Madison County, Alabama, a gang calling themselves "Ku-Klux" found a dance going on in freedman Wiley Strong's house. Strong described what happened to a local Freedmen's Bureau agent, who in turn reported it to the congressional committee: "The negroes were having a little dance at the house, and these men rushed in on them. Some of the men, I understood, resisted them, and they drove them out, and then ravished . . . two women."[107] Both of these sexual attacks occurred in counties where numerous whippings and widespread gun theft by night riders had been reported.[108] Violent campaigns of this sort, then, also involved carnival-like revelry in which white men engaged in rowdy behavior and redefined black homes as dance halls, saloons, and brothels.

In other scenes possibly mimicking common practices in brothels, white men made spectacles of black women's naked bodies. One such scene surrounded a violent attack on Mary and Joe Brown in White County, Georgia, on May 21, 1871. The Browns lived with Mary's mother, Mary's younger sister, and another young woman named Mary Neal on land they had purchased in a community where some white residents were distilling whiskey. Two of the distillers had recently murdered an official seeking to prosecute them for their illegal trade, and one of those involved, Bailey Smith, believed that Mary Brown could identify him among the murderers. She apparently ran into him, his face blackened, as he headed toward where the official was subsequently killed. Smith tried to hide his identity, but Brown reportedly said, "I know you, Bailey Smith." After the murder, Smith fled to Texas but reportedly wrote back to his collaborators that he could return safely only if the Browns were run out of the area. In the middle of the night, a gang of men apparently appointed to accomplish this task came to the Browns' home.[109]

The intruders dragged Mary Brown, Joe Brown, and Mary Neal from their beds and into the yard, where they beat them severely. They demanded to know if Mary Brown planned to testify against Bailey Smith and yelled at Joe Brown, "God damn you, you shall not live here a bit. . . . We will burn your house down over you if you don't leave."[110] The aspect of this attack most striking and most difficult to read was the attention paid to removing women's clothing. Night riders commonly stripped women's clothing to their waists or pulled it up to their necks before beating them, as these same men may well have done in the past—as patrollers, overseers, or slaveowners—when beating slaves. In this case, though, assailants' disrobing of their victims seemed to be less about slaveowners or overseers punishing slaves than about men producing a spectacle—one that was titillating for the assailants and humiliating for the victims—of women's nakedness.[111] Testifying before the congressional committee, Mary Brown's mother noted that after the intruders carried her daughter from the house, "they then tore her clothes off; they did not pull them off, but just jibbeted them off, like paper."[112] Mary Brown herself told the congressional committee, "They had me there about the yard as naked as I was born."[113] That this may have had significance beyond practices common when night riders whipped women was suggested by what the assailants did to the other women in the Brown household. Asked if any of the other women were hurt that night, Mary Brown testified, "The rest they made show their nakedness; they did not strip them, but they made them show their nakedness."[114] That exposing women's genitals or buttocks was what Mary Brown meant by "show their nakedness" was clarified by Mary Neal, who was questioned about this event by the committee: "They made me pull off my drawers that I had on."[115] The fact that the assailants conducted this abuse as a performance for their own amusement was confirmed by Mary Brown's mother: "They had a show of us all there; they had us all lying in the road. . . . They had us all stripped there, and laughed and made great sport. Some of them just squealed the same as if they were stable horses just brought out."[116]

Mary Brown testified, "Well, it was the terriblest carrying on you ever saw; they had a powerful show; you never heard the like."[117]

Another case highlights how night riders' forcing black women to become spectacles of indecency might have been a direct response to freedpeople organizing their family lives in ways previously reserved for whites. Aury Jeter lived with her husband, Columbus, in Douglass County, Georgia, where he had contracted to work on the land of a white man named Morris. The Jeters' relationship with Morris was strained from the beginning. Morris objected to the fact that the couple, devout Baptists, attended a church that was twelve miles from his land, saying he did not want them away for long periods of time. He also opposed Aury teaching freedpeople to read in their house during the day and Columbus giving lessons at night. Morris confronted Columbus in a manner suggesting that the fact that Aury was not working as a field laborer also contributed to the contention between them. Columbus recounted their exchange: " 'Your wife, the damned bitch, is teaching a colored school.' I said, 'I work for her and maintain her; why should she not teach school? the laws of the country permit it.' " Morris then cursed Aury again, calling her "the damned nigger." Columbus objected to Morris's verbal abuse of his wife, responding, "Don't curse any," which led Morris to draw his knife. Columbus defended himself with a stick, and the fight that ensued ended with the Jeters leaving Morris's land.[118]

The family settled as laborers on another white man's land. One week later, they were awakened in the night by orders to open their door. Columbus scurried up their chimney before a group of white men burst into the house. These men beat Aury over the head, yanked her by the hair, and put a pistol to her chest as they demanded to know where her husband was. When she finally revealed his hiding place, the intruders fired shots up the chimney and pulled Columbus down. They then dragged both husband and wife from the house and whipped them. Aury reported that one of the men also "exposed me. . . . They turned my clothes up to my waist." That this gesture was intended to humiliate Aury by treating her indecently is suggested by the objection of one of the men. "One of them went up and said that I had told the truth and should be let alone; he said it was ridiculous to treat me in that way."[119] Another comment made to Columbus while the assailants were beating him is also suggestive: "Now Columbus, do you think a colored man is as good as a white man?" Columbus's efforts to support his wife while she engaged in something other than field labor and then to defend himself when assaulted by Morris were read by these assailants as challenges to their identities and superiority as white men. In retaliation, Aury, who represented herself as Columbus's wife, a Christian woman, and a teacher, was made to suffer the indignity of being made into a "show," as Mary Brown described it, a spectacle of sexual dishonor and humiliation.

Hannah Tutson's experience suggests a different framing of night rider violence, one in which coercion, rather than being cloaked in "shows" of lewdness or even prostitution, was explicit and represented as a form of punishment. Tutson and her husband, Samuel, had secured 160 acres of swampy Florida land in Clay County through the federal Homestead Act and moved there in 1868. Sam was in his fifties, Hannah was in her forties, and they had three small children living with them (three others were grown and lived on their own). The Tutsons' land sat at the edge of a pond around which all of the other landowners were white. In fact, Samuel supposed that there were no more than two or three black families in the entire county and none within four miles of their land. After settling here, the Tutsons paid a neighbor $150 worth of cotton for three adjacent acres in an elevated and wooded area above the swamp, land that was coveted by other area residents. After the Tutsons had fenced and cultivated these acres, another neighbor, Isaac Tire, announced that the land belonged to him and that the man who sold it to the Tutsons had had no right to do so. Though Tire may have had his heart set on these particular three acres, it seems that he and other whites in the area used this land dispute as a pretext to remove the Tutsons from their entire possession, knowing that they were still waiting for the title to their homestead to arrive from Washington and that if they vacated, others could occupy and claim the land. All the more reason Samuel and Hannah refused to move. Thus began six months of demands that the Tutsons give up their land, threats as to what would happen if they persisted in refusing, and defiant declarations —particularly from Hannah—in reply. "I am going to die on this land," she told one neighbor; "No law is going to move me from here except Tallahassee law," she told another. She also showed her determination to the congressional committee, telling them that, in regard to what she repeatedly referred to as her land, "I have paid too much, and I have worked too much to lose it."[120]

One Saturday in the early spring of 1871, several men from the area, including George McCrea, the local deputy sheriff, came to the Tutsons' house to insist they leave the land altogether. Hannah was there without Samuel, and after the men warned her that someone would hurt her if her family did not leave, she "spoke to them very rash," adding later, "I was sort of sorry I spoke to them in that way." She recalled before the 1871 congressional investigating committee what she had said: "In the red times, how many times have they took me and turned my clothes over my head, and whipped me? I do not care what they do to me now if I can only save my land."[121] Three weeks later McCrea and several other men returned in the middle of the night. Having been unable to convince the Tutsons to leave on their own, these men came this time in disguise and claiming the power of the Klan. Despite their faces being "all smutty" and their constant calling each other "True-Klux," they were easily recognized by Hannah and Samuel.[122]

When these poorly disguised and half drunk "Klansmen" arrived, the family was in bed. The men burst their door down and ran into the house. George McCrea grabbed Hannah first, while others held Samuel back as he tried to stop McCrea. Both Samuel and Hannah were dragged outdoors and taken to opposite sides of the land surrounding their house. Both were stripped naked, and their hands were tied around trees. Both were badly whipped: "They whipped me like the mischief," Samuel later recounted, and Hannah later said, "They whipped me from the crown of my head to the soles of my feet. I was just raw."[123] George McCrea was leading the men whipping Hannah, and he repeatedly orchestrated the other men's temporary departure, during which he would attempt to rape Hannah. "Every time they would go off, George McCrea would act scandalously and ridiculously toward me, and treat me shamefully," Hannah told the committee. "He would get his knees between my legs and say, 'God damn you, open your legs.' . . . He sat down there and said, 'Old lady, if you don't let me have to do with you, I will kill you.' "[124] It is not certain that he accomplished a rape; Hannah's testimony on this point is unclear. Perhaps fear that the other assailants would not cooperate with the form of punishment he wanted to inflict on Hannah, or perhaps his own drunkenness, interfered with his efforts.

As recounted by Hannah Tutson, this attack suggests the reenactment of a scene of the disciplining and domination of a slave. White men's physical coercion and violence were open and part of the scene being staged. Assailants sought to legitimate that violence by representing it as punishment for the victims' actions. As was common among night riders, the Tutsons' assailants claimed that Hannah deserved to be hurt because she had violated a "law" the men were empowered to enforce. While Hannah Tutson was being whipped, the assailants yelled at her, "You are living on another man's premises." One man also repeated her denial that she feared being whipped as she had been "in the red times" and demanded that she admit that these were, in fact, her words. Hannah believed that this attack was brought on by her defiance. She heard the assailants express surprise that Samuel was home when they arrived. And she later recounted that the men whipping her told her that her husband was suffering because of her: "You were a God damned old bitch to get the poor old man in this fix," she remembered them saying as they told her to listen to her husband's screams from the other side of the yard.[125]

Invoking the actions of a woman to justify an attack on a man was unusual. More often assailants told women that they were suffering due to the actions of their husbands. Rhoda Ann Childs, a freedwoman in Georgia who was pinned to the ground and whipped by eight white strangers in 1866, was also raped. After describing to the Freedmen's Bureau in excruciating detail the manner in which she was attacked, she added that one of the assailants "ran his pistol into me, and Said he had a hell of a mind to pull the trigger, and Swore they ought to Shoot me, as my husband had been in the 'God damned Yankee Army.' "[126]

When three Klansmen raped Harriet Simril in York County, South Carolina, they claimed she was being punished for her husband's political participation. This rape occurred in the midst of what was perhaps the most extensive Klan campaign against black men's voting during Reconstruction. After the Republicans carried the county in the 1870 state elections, freedpeople living in the countryside surrounding the town of Yorkville suffered almost nightly Klan violence for months.[127] When night riders first visited Simril's home, they whipped her husband, Sam, demanding that he "join the Democratic ticket." After this, Sam joined many black men in the area trying to evade further nighttime attacks by sleeping in the woods. Colonel Lewis Merrill, the commander of federal troops sent to York County to try to quell the violence, estimated that four-fifths of the county's black male residents did not feel safe sleeping at home.[128] Though some women, too, slept in the woods, Harriet chose at first to stay at home in the Clay Hill section of the county.[129] She subsequently described to a federal court prosecuting suspected Klan members what she suffered during a second Klan visit to her house: "They came after my old man and I told them he wasn't there. They searched about in the house a long time. They were spitting in my face and throwing dirt in my eyes. . . . After awhile, they took me out of doors and told me all they wanted was my old man to join the Democratic ticket. After they got me out of doors, they dragged me into the road and ravished me out there."[130] Assailants told Simril, as they had told Childs, that they raped her as a means of attacking her husband or of punishing her husband for challenging white men's dominance. This would be one way to interpret the comments of a woman in nearby Spartanburgh County who, along with her daughter, was whipped by Klansmen while her husband was "laying out." She explained to the congressional committee why both men and women in her area were fearful for their lives: "Because [when] men . . . voted the radical tickets they took the spite out on the women when they could get them."[131] One could read night riders raping black women as an attack on men through those who were supposedly "their" women and upon what were supposedly "their" households. Yet these women were also political actors, and these were their homes as well. In fact, women took on the political role of protecting their husbands and, in Simril's case, of protecting Republican votes by standing up to Klan members and refusing demands for information on their husbands' whereabouts. Their resistance was part of the collective political efforts that the Klan opposed. Perhaps "taking the spite out on the women" was not simply an effort to crush men's political participation but, moreover, a recognition of women's own political role. On the same night that Simril was raped, many other women in this area of York County were beaten for refusing to tell night riders where their husbands were hiding. And it was rumored that one of these other women, Julia Barron, was also raped.[132] When black men were forced to sleep in the woods, families were separated; this represented not only white men disrupting black family life, as they had before emancipation. It also created new political roles and dangers for black women.

Furthermore, patriarchal rationales for rape—in particular, the notion that men rape women to get at other men—are perhaps best treated as performative. Feminist historians have struggled with how to interpret indications that rape was primarily violence targeted at men through "their" women. Scholars have sought ways instead to place women at the center of any understanding of sexual violence.[133] However, rather than accepting or rejecting that punishing men was in fact the aim of rape, it may be useful to recognize that men enacting rapes seem to be telling themselves that this was the aim of rape. They also were telling Childs and Simril and the other African Americans in their communities that this was the case. If we do not approach an analysis of Klan violence as merely an instrument of force (and it may, in fact, in many cases have been ineffective as an instrument of force), then the articulation of patriarchal rationales in the moment of violence, much like the articulation of other rationales, becomes part of the ritual of Klan violence and part of the performance of rape itself. In other words, this patriarchal framing—that men can be punished and dominated through the rape and thereby dishonor of their women—seems to be part of the assailants' fantasy enacted through rape. It also posits black men's patriarchal possession of the women in their families only to defy it. The fantasy performed through rape, then, became one of white male domination of both black women and men through the articulation of this patriarchal framework.

Interactions between assailants suggest that at times they needed one another's participation to create desired illusions about their violence. In this way, too, night rider violence contributed to the building of solidarity among white men. Recall how when a man raped Cynthia Bryant in the bed where she lay with Rina Barry, other men sought to make this a collective experience by forcing George's wife to have sex with others of their gang.[134] Freedman Charles Smith overheard the men who attacked his family discussing the whipping of his sister. She had been stripped and beaten by one of the assailants, Sam Rich. He then encouraged his companion, William Felker, to take a turn. "This Sam Rich had sate down in the door, and Felker had sate down there. Rich spoke to Felker and said, 'Don't you want to use this hickory?' or something like that. He said, 'Yes, I want to taste of her meat.'"[135] This chilling glimpse into the minds of these two assailants suggests how the collective dynamics of night riding helped to produce an anticipation that violence would be pleasurable. It also suggests the need of some assailants to see themselves reflected in the actions of others in order to normalize their brutality and to reinforce their construction of it as a reflection of black women's dishonor as opposed to their own.

Not all assailants could normalize sexual violence. Most night riders did not rape the women they attacked. And as we have seen, sometimes one white man intervened to stop another from committing rape. At other times, one man told another not to whip a freedwoman any more, for she had given them the information they demanded. Recall that some of the men attacking Columbus and Aury Jeter objected to others exposing Aury's body.[136] Some night riders thus set limits on what kind of violence they felt justified in enacting. Perhaps to these men rape and sexual humiliation were dishonorable acts that contradicted the identities they sought to embody with their violence. And in the case of George McCrea, the deputy sheriff who tried to rape Hannah Tutson while she was tied to a tree, he seemed almost embarrassed that the others might catch him in an act of rape, sending the other men away to create the opportunity for rape and stopping as soon as they returned.[137] Apparently, rape was not part of the fantasy of power of all white men; it was outside the norms and limits accepted by some. And when one white man intervened in or protested the actions of another, he could interrupt a script that represented the act as legitimate and thereby stop a rape or other sexual abuse.

However, this was not the norm. Most assailants cooperated with one another's various innovations on the night rider script. Overall innovations fit within a larger framework of assertions of the power and authority of white men over the private spaces and identities of African Americans, indeed the power to interrupt or destroy those spaces and identities. In the case of rape, assailants most often removed women from their families before assaulting them: Cynthia Bryant was raped after George Moore was removed from the house; Amanda Willis and Hannah Tutson were taken a distance from their homes and other family members before they were assaulted; and Harriet Simril, Rhoda Ann Childs, and the women in Mary Brown's family were taken out of their houses and "into the road" before being attacked. This pattern was evident elsewhere. In the summer of 1871, in Fayette County, Alabama, a gang of thirty white men came to the plantation of an old white man named Mr. Cole who had in his employ several black farm laborers. The men in the gang "ran off the negro men and ravished the negro women."[138]

One could imagine a different scenario in which men were shown to be powerless when women in their families were raped in their presence. In fact, men were not always absent from the scene of a rape. In two other Klan raids on the workforce of a plantation, men reported witnessing white men rape black women. On December 26, 1870, in Floyd County, Georgia, a plantation owned by a former Union Army officer named Colonel Waltemire was visited by a gang of Klansmen who beat all the laborers and raped two of the women. "I have seen men who said they saw it," a witness before the congressional committee stated.[139] In this same county the next summer, when a band of white men were "going around through the country" assaulting freedpeople, three women were raped on another plantation. "They were violated by these same men, as testified to by parties who saw the act committed," another witness testified.[140] Finally, an older black woman told a Republican representative in North Carolina's legislature "that when the Ku-Klux had gone after a negro man in some places they had attempted, and in other places they had actually committed, rape upon colored women in the presence of their husbands."[141]

On the whole, though, women were removed from their families and often from their houses before being raped by white men. They were separated from the relationships and spaces from which they derived identities as wives, mothers, and daughters. The houses themselves were often destroyed: Hannah Tutson returned to her house to find it had been burned down; Harriet Simril's too went up in flames several nights after she was raped.[142] Gangs of disguised white men thus attacked a symbol of black family life as they denied black people public recognition of their identities as members of families. By representing their violence as legitimate, narrating it as either consensual though illicit sex or punishment, they claimed their own authority over freedpeople's homes.

THE CHAIRMAN OF the congressional investigating committee conducting hearings in Georgia was listening to the testimony of a white merchant and planter, John Shropshire. Shropshire was an opponent of the Klan, angered at the lawlessness and labor disruption that resulted from its campaigns. On hearing that local authorities had taken no action to prosecute Klan members, the chair at one point lost his composure and burst out in indignation, "Can you conceive of any greater outrage upon the rights of a citizen than to go to his house in the hours of the night, when he is asleep, with his family around him, and take him out of bed and whip and scourge him, and subject him to other brutalities?"[143] Although from a perspective sympathetic as opposed to hostile to African American citizenship, these words articulated perfectly the patriarchal reasoning of night riders that connected a man's authority in his house with his political power and with the rights of a citizen. This reasoning shaped the reign of terror to which night riders subjected black men and women struggling after emancipation to make themselves free. In efforts to suppress African American public power, white southern men attacked the spaces of private life. Rape and other acts of sexual violence interrupted the lines of authority and protection in black families that white men recognized in their own homes and allowed night riders to force their victims to embody roles and identities as noncitizens, not so different from slaves. Through sexual violence, white men compelled performances that equated blackness with depravity and undomesticated sexuality and thereby argued for the unworthiness of former slaves for membership in the polity. These assaults involved denying that black men and women had homes and the identities, relationships, and honor constituted therein, the source of white men's own sense of their rights to public power.

Night rider sexual violence during Reconstruction was in some ways, then, a brutal form of political expression. Violence served as a both verbal and corporeal language revealing the gendered political culture through which white southerners contested the changes in social relations resulting from emancipation and articulated their visions for the postemancipation meaning of race. But Reconstruction was also a rare historical moment when freedpeople had access to federal arenas in which to record black women's experiences of rape. By testifying to sexual assaults as violation and by constructing white men coercing sex with black women as rape, freedwomen and freedmen challenged the hierarchical meanings for race, and particularly the assertion of a denigrated blackness and virtuous whiteness, conveyed by assailants' actions. They therein fought to establish a meaningful citizenship. To be a potential victim of rape in the eyes of the law was also to be recognized as a citizen, and, we will see in the next chapter, freedwomen claimed this status and its attendant rights.

CHAPTER SIX

Testifying to Violence

In the summer of 1867, an unusual confrontation in a Freedmen's Bureau office in Murfreesboro, Tennessee, was brought on by the courage of a freedwoman. This woman and her young daughter left the plantation of Vincent Mullins, where both the woman and her husband, Moses King, were employed, to denounce Mullins before Freedmen's Bureau agent J. K. Nelson.[1] Mrs. King charged that Mullins had become abusive toward her and her children after the freedmen on his plantation voted for William Brownlow, the Republican candidate for governor in Tennessee. Just as Mrs. King was recounting this abuse to Nelson, Vincent Mullins himself entered the bureau agent's office. He and Mrs. King exchanged angry words. She then turned to Nelson and revealed a more personal dimension to the violence between herself and Mullins. She accused Mullins of being the father of three of her children. According to Nelson's report, Mrs. King further protested that "Mr. Mullins was angry with her because she would not permit him still to live in adultery with her." Mullins did not deny Mrs. King's charges. He offered only as an angry retort his claim that Mrs. King had already had three husbands and that Moses King, the man she now "had," was not, in fact, her husband at all.[2]

When King refused to have sex with her employer and probable former owner, she was exercising a freedom she had not had before emancipation. Mullins had coerced King into having sex with him probably for many years. When King left Mullins's plantation and went to the bureau office that day, she claimed the right to resist such coercion and to exercise control in her sexual relationships. By calling on state authority, she claimed the rights of a woman recognized by the law as worthy of protection against sexual abuse, a claim she made in the context of also asserting the right of men in her community to exercise the franchise. Calling on the state to recognize these newly won rights of citizenship, though, did not mean denying past sexual relations considered illicit or, in other words, attempting to craft her story to fit into a conservative vision of the "virtuous" woman who could be a legitimate victim of rape. When confronted by Mullins, King did not hesitate to reveal their past relationship. She placed any shame for this illicit sexual activity at Mullins's door, publicly naming it as unwelcome and abusive by enlisting the bureau's aid in her refusal to allow it to continue now that she was free. When Mullins found himself challenged by King in a public forum as a man who had acted dishonorably by fathering children with a slave and then seeking what the bureau agent euphemistically referred to as further "adulty" after emancipation, his retort did not address his own conduct. He did not deny his past and present aggression but only denied its criminal character. To defend himself, he represented his accuser as a woman who had had multiple sexual partners, including a current lover to whom, he alleged, she was not married. He represented her, then, as a woman without virtue, one who could not be raped, and thus one without the capacity to make a legitimate claim against him before the law. He thus represented her as a woman not worthy of citizenship.

Mullins's response to King's claiming the rights of citizenship was not simply the retort of one white man angered and embarrassed by his former slave's insubordination. It reflected dominant white ideology about black women's gender identity and sexuality and a common response—evident, for instance, in the actions of the Klan—to assertions of African American citizenship. At times this response included outright denials of black women's charges of sexual assault. This was the case when William F. Wright, a white conservative judge of the Tallapoosa circuit court in Georgia, a former Democratic Party candidate for Congress, and an apologist for Klan violence, spoke before the congressional committee investigating the Klan about Aury and Columbus Jeter's encounter with night riders. Aury's prior testimony before this same committee had described how the assailants in this attack had "exposed" her, that is, disrobed her from the waist down.[3] It was Wright who had, in his capacity as circuit court judge, first heard the evidence in the case brought by the Jeters against the men who attacked them. At that time, Wright accepted the alibis provided by the assailants and determined that there was not enough evidence to press charges. While he acknowledged that Columbus had been abused by night riders (though he believed that Columbus had misidentified the parties), Wright did not believe that "indignities had been offered to his wife." After repeating his conclusions to the congressional committee, the committee's chair pressed him on the matter. The chair's final question—"whether you [think] that lust was a moving passion [in the crimes alleged by Jeter]"—triggered this response from Wright: "Well, sir, you do not understand the character of our people or you would not ask that question. Of course it was not; I do not suppose they went there for any such purpose; I do not know that I have ever known of a body of men going in gangs in that way to perpetrate such crimes as that. . . . The conquest of such people is generally so easy that it does not require any resort to violence, for there is very little virtue in them."[4] Wright thus expressed to the committee his belief that black women were never raped. It was this construct of black women's sexuality around which all black women who testified about rape and other forms of sexual coercion and intimidation had to maneuver. And it was these gendered meanings for race—which impinged on the ability of African Americans to claim their rights as citizens—that black women resisted with their testimony about rape.

"WHO GETS TO tell the story and whose story counts as 'truth' determine the definition of what rape *is*," literary scholars Lynn Higgins and Brenda Silver have observed.[5] The period of Reconstruction was an exceptional moment in U.S. history when African American women's stories of sexual violence counted in official political arenas as "truth" and, temporarily, reshaped the meaning of rape, of black womanhood, and of citizenship. Despite the oppressive weight of extensive vigilante violence, African Americans, women and men, embraced the years after emancipation as a time of enormous possibility. Evincing their hope for and anticipation of a meaningful freedom, they went to great lengths and took enormous risks to seek out federal officials and to testify to, and to protest, racist political violence. Their desire to protest violence and to carve out new spaces for autonomy from white violation and control coincided with the desires of Republicans in Washington to document continued resistance among white southern men to federal dictates and to black freedom. These two sets of interests brought freedpeople and government officials together in spaces of federal power—Freedmen's Bureau offices or congressional hearings, for instance. Here they produced and recorded a narrative of black women as victims of white male brutality that federal officials granted the status of "truth" and that would support federal efforts to establish and protect African American citizenship rights. That narrative represented black women as citizens, worthy of equal protection under the law, of bodily integrity, and of voice.[6]

Women such as Mrs. King who told stories of sexual coercion to federal officials were engaged in a direct contest with conservative white southerners over the representation of violence. Their testimony countered white-generated imagery that blamed vigilante violence on black criminality; that positioned black men and women outside the norms of respectable society; that denied black people public recognition of their identities as husbands and wives, parents and children; and that thereby asserted racial difference and inequality by imputing to black women and men putatively inferior modes of gender. This imagery was articulated in conflicts such as that between Mrs. King and Vincent Mullins, in testimony such as that of William F. Wright, in myths surrounding the purpose of the Klan, and, most forcefully, in vigilante violence. In the moment of violence itself and in protests after the fact, black men and women offered alternative representations of criminal white men violating the rights of free and law-abiding black people. In doing so, they embodied alternative social and legal identities that gave meaning to the profound reordering of southern society against which vigilantes were reacting. Black women's testimony thus participated in a broader contest over the meaning of race in a society without slavery and over the contours of African American citizenship in a new, postemancipation republic. Their stories also challenged dominant understandings of what constituted rape and, in this way, contested patriarchal notions constraining women's citizenship more generally.[7]

We have seen how violence of the Reconstruction period not only reflected but also performed and produced certain meanings—how violence spoke, in a sense. This chapter explores how people spoke of violence and the ways this speaking contributed to the formation and contestation of racial meanings and citizenship rights after emancipation. It also explores how freedpeople's representations of violence invoked the authority of the new, postemancipation state, one imposed on defeated white southern elites through federal authority. By seeking out officials of this new, federally backed state in order to testify about sexual violence, freedwomen asserted the legitimacy of federal power over affairs in the southern states. The rights of freedwomen depended on the survival of this new state that rejected slavery and recognized African American citizenship, and by calling on its officials for assistance, they represented it as, and encouraged it to become, their protector. Ultimately, they would be disappointed, as the federal government would soon turn its back on African Americans in the South. But they did not anticipate this during the years of Reconstruction. Enormous hope for the future, not a sense of defeat, is evinced in freedpeople's testimony, and particularly in freedwomen's protests against rape.

Counternarratives of Rape

Freedwomen and freedmen used various means to resist the sexual violence of night riders. Though rare, some women were able to intimidate assailants sufficiently to prevent them from following through on their threats. When one of the Klansmen who came to the home Owen Gundy shared with his wife near Columbus, Tennessee, "called to Owen's wife in an indecent manner offering her five dollars for her person," an insulting demand for her "consent" that threatened sexual violence, "she ran for the fire shovel and he seeing her determination desisted from his attempt."[8] Most women, though, were overpowered by weaponry and turned instead to negotiation to resist violence in the moment of an attack. George Moore's wife, ordered out of her house in Cherokee County, Alabama, by night riders so that men outside could "have to do with her," successfully avoided their demand, telling them "she had just miscarried, and couldn't."[9] Another freedwoman told a North Carolina legislator that Klansmen had attempted to rape her daughter. However, the daughter and her husband had managed to stop the assailants by telling them that the daughter was in a condition "that ought to have deterred any man." Perhaps this referred to venereal disease or something similar to the miscarriage claimed by Mrs. Moore.[10] The man who raped Ellen Parton during the 1871 riot in Meridian, Mississippi, rejected the first woman he grabbed, Alice Batt, because, he told her, "she was rotten." Though he may simply have been insulting her, suggesting that her body carried disease, it seems possible at least that the assailant referred to Batt's behavior or attitude and that she, through her demeanor or words, somehow successfully disrupted his fantasy and thereby avoided being raped.[11]

Women also at times prevented, or at least attempted to prevent, violence by calling out to white men whom they recognized. This not only denied the men the anonymity they sought through disguise. By invoking a relationship under different circumstances between assailant and victim, this gesture also identified the assailant as someone other than a Klansman, drawing attention to the contradiction between his violence and his everyday posture as, say, a neighbor, a local shopkeeper, or an upstanding citizen. When the gang of men barged into Aury and Columbus Jeter's house, Aury recognized one man about to strike her as Doctor McClarty. "As he drew back to hit me, I said, 'O, doctor,' for I thought he would kill me. . . . When I said, 'O, doctor,' he let me go and went out of the house."[12] On the night when Ellen Parton was raped, she recognized one of the men in her house as a fellow Meridian resident, Michael Slamon, and she implored him to intervene when she was being attacked. "I called upon Mr. Slamon, who was one of the crowd, for protection; I said to him 'please protect me to-night, you have known me a long time;' this man covered up his head then. . . . Mr. Slamon had an oil-cloth and put it before his face, trying to conceal himself." Parton's appeal to Slamon based on an acquaintance of perhaps many years caused Slamon enormous discomfort. He responded to her with apparent shame, hiding his face and pretending he was not who she thought he was. He appeared at least momentarily confused by her words, as they tore him from the role he had taken on that night and placed him in another.[13]

In general, freedpeople had few means of preventing night riders from raping black women in the midst of a Klan attack, given the overwhelming imbalance in both numbers and weaponry, as well as the severe costs to other freedpeople of attempts at physical intervention. Freedpeople could, though, resist the meaning that night riders attributed to their acts by speaking about what had occurred. African Americans' narratives of rape reasserted identities of black women as family members and as citizens and represented the conduct of assailants not as illicit sex or legitimate punishment but, rather, as rape. Freedpeople most often first told one another about sexual violence. There is evidence in testimony before the congressional investigating committee that African Americans were sharing stories among themselves, parallel to and contradicting the widespread rumors about Klan violence spread by white southerners. Freedman Edward Carter, whose daughter was raped and whose family was run out of Tuscaloosa, Alabama, by Klansmen, was asked by the committee if he knew of other families who had been attacked by the Klan. Carter answered that, although he had not spoken directly to any other victims, "we could hear a good deal of it."[14] And freedman Essic Harris told the committee that a freedwoman working on the same plantation where he worked had told him that she had been raped.[15] Freedwomen seem particularly to have told one another news of rape. One freedwoman, when questioned about the Meridian Riot, stated, "I know of two women said to be outraged, . . . said to be four in all. . . . I understand from my sister that some of the parties undertook to outrage her." Another woman told the committee, "I know nothing further about the woman said to be outraged than what was told me by Parthenia Greene."[16]

Freedpeople, men and women, also boldly protested to whites when rapes occurred. Ellen Parton recounted her extensive efforts to make her experience of rape during the Meridian Riot known among whites in her community: "I complained to Capt. Early, who was acting constable. . . . I told a great many citizens about it, . . . I told Dr. Phillips and Mr. Rainey how they had done me, and I told some white ladies about it too."[17] A black man from Colonel Waltemire's plantation in Floyd County, Georgia, told a local white farmer and merchant about the two women who had been raped there.[18] This form of protest, though, often came at a high cost. Edward Carter testified before the congressional committee that after his daughter was raped, he and his family fled the area because "I had no protection there at all; they threatened to kill me, because I told in the neighborhood what they had done."[19]

In addition to telling "in the neighborhood," freedpeople sought out federal officials to whom they could report violence, seeking the power of the federal government to provide protection and redress. A military commander occupying the northern section of Alabama reported to the congressional committee that "I was constantly sought by persons who complained that outrages had been committed upon them, principally negroes . . . who were anxious to make statements."[20] Freedpeople also reported the stories they had heard about rape experienced by others. Another federal army commander told the congressional committee that he had heard that when a freedman named Rainey was beaten along with his wife just outside Yorkville, South Carolina, "it was charged that his daughter was raped at the same time."[21] And the U.S. district attorney for the northern district of Alabama shared with the congressional committee information about Klansmen who raped three women on a plantation in Fayette County, "as I had learned from various quarters, and I have not heard it contradicted by anyone."[22] Thus narratives of sexual violence circulated beyond the freedpeople who told them to either black or white neighbors and into the offices of federal officials.

Freedpeople told federal officials about violence they or their neighbors experienced because they understood the federal government to be their ally in local struggles with whites, or sought to make it so. When the congressional committee asked Thomas Allen, a black Baptist preacher and state representative from Jasper County, Georgia, about freedpeople's "hope and expectation for the future," Allen responded, "They expect to get protection from the Federal Government at Washington; that is all. You ask any one of my people out there, even the most ignorant of them, and they will tell you so."[23] Hannah and Samuel Tutson's extensive efforts to find officials who would hear and act on their story of being beaten and run off their land in Clay County, Florida, reveal how the necessity of a federal ally became evident to freedpeople. The night of the attack, Hannah walked twelve miles searching for neighbors to assist her. Her back was so sore and bloody she traveled the first five miles naked and then could put on but not "fasten" her dress. The next day, she and her husband made formal complaints before county officials. The cost of their efforts was high; the officials imprisoned the Tutsons for swearing to "false doctrine." In order to post bail, they were obliged to sell their ox and cart to a white neighbor. The local magistrate did eventually issue arrest warrants for the identified parties but allowed one of them to post bail for the others without anyone being taken into custody. Realizing the futility of seeking legal redress at the local or state level, the Tutsons then turned to the federal government. Samuel left for Green Cove Springs, Florida, after learning that a U.S. prosecutor was hearing cases there against the Klan. Though he arrived after the court had completed its session, he was not deterred. Samuel inquired around town about where he could find the prosecutor, whom he eventually encountered taking a bath at the springs. The prosecutor agreed to meet later in his office, where he recorded the names of the men who attacked the Tutsons. Although Samuel heard nothing further from him after making this report, it is likely that this meeting led to both Samuel and Hannah being subpoenaed to appear before a federal grand jury in Jacksonville. The family traveled to Jacksonville, where they remained for two weeks and testified twice in federal court before speaking before the congressional committee holding hearings in that city at the same time.[24] Sadly, it is unlikely that, for all their efforts, the Tutsons were ever able to safely return to Clay County and reclaim their land.

Despite the fact that testifying yielded few results, freedpeople placed their greatest hope and anticipation in the congressional investigation. Word of the arrival of the congressional committee in a given city or town spread quickly, and while some individuals were subpoenaed based on earlier reports of violence, others sought out the opportunity to tell their stories unsolicited by officials. When asked by the committee, "Who told you to come to the committee-room?" freedman Scipio Eager replied, "I heard it told around that here was the place that I could get my rights."[25] Eli Barnes, freedman and leading black Republican in Hancock County, Georgia, received a note from a friend in Atlanta telling him that the committee would soon be holding hearings there. The note asked him to "go forth with and fetch all the witnesses I could get" and bring them to Atlanta. Barnes attempted to recruit neighbors as witnesses but was unsuccessful. He arrived in Atlanta alone and told the committee, "I did not bring anyone, because they were afraid to come."[26] Fear of Klan retaliation for testifying was widespread. Republican leaders had to reassure and coax many witnesses before they would name assailants in the committee's hearing room. But others were less fearful and openly celebrated the committee's efforts. In Yorkville, South Carolina, on the night of the committee's arrival, Republican members were serenaded outside their hotel by a local black band.[27]

Naming one's assailants in a federal hearing challenged night riders' self-representation as an all-powerful but unidentifiable force. When Caroline Smith was beaten by night riders in Walton County, Georgia, they demanded several times to know if she recognized them. She suspected that she did know who two of them were, but she denied this to them out of fear for her life. Her husband, Charles, later recalled feeling triumphant when he obtained confirmation of the identity of one of the attackers. "They were in such a hurry to beat me that the mask of this man Felker dropped off on the ground. I thought to myself, 'I have got you;' but I did not say anything." Both he and Caroline would subsequently say something when they fled to Atlanta and, removed from any immediate threat to their lives, identified two of their attackers before the congressional committee.[28] Testifying in congressional hearings also defied night riders' power to suppress stories of their violence. Mary Brown's mother told the committee that the men who attacked her family in White County, Georgia, "said that if we came down here and swore against them they would kill us." Mary made a similar statement, recounting that "they got an old black lady to tell me that if I came down to Atlanta and told all their names they would kill me." And yet, when asked why she had come to Atlanta, where this particular congressional hearing was being held, Mary stated succinctly, "To give evidence against the Ku-Klux."[29]

When freedpeople testified to night riders' identities, they also represented them not as legitimate authority figures but as common criminals and dishonorable men. Witnesses to sexual attacks reported the behavior of assailants in particularly strong language. "You never saw such ill-behaved men," Mary Brown's mother asserted about the men who assaulted the women in her family.[30] Ellen Parton recounted how white neighbors whom she told she had been raped, "said it was scandalous."[31] After labeling also as "scandalous" the conduct of George McCrea, the man who raped her, Hannah Tutson added, "I tell you, men, that he did act ridiculously and shamefully, that same George McCrea." Tutson wanted to be certain that the committee understood that rape was what she meant to report. After once telling the story, she explained again to the committee, "Understand me, men, . . . George McCrea would make me sit down there, and try to have me do with him right there."[32] Tutson recounted her compliance with the assailants in the moment of the attack and how she advised her husband to do the same, hoping that submission would save their lives. As the assailants dragged the Tutsons in opposite directions from the house, Hannah called out, "Sam, give up; it is not worth while to try to do anything; they will try to kill us here." And she said to her assailants, "I will go with you" and "Yes, I am coming; I will come right along." She recounted her reply to McCrea when he said he would kill her if she would not have sex with him: "I said, 'No, just do what you are going to do.' "[33] But she also expressed her desire to resist her assailant now by telling her story fully and showed her satisfaction that she finally had the opportunity to do so before the committee. Referring to her earlier testimony before the federal prosecutor, she said, "I would have told this just the way you hear me tell it now before the others, but they stopped me." When she was asked, "Have you told us all you know about it?" she replied, "Yes, sir, and just as straight as I could tell it. I have told it straighter to-day than I did before, because when we had a trial here the other week they stopped me almost every word, and I missed some I told here to-day."[34]

Despite her compliance with her assailants, once Hannah Tutson had conveyed the circumstances under which she submitted to them—she was tied to a tree and beaten, her life was threatened, and her house was torn down—it is unlikely that she feared the committee would represent what happened to her as in accordance with her will. However, other women had a more difficult narrative task. Ellen Parton, raped in her house during the Meridian Riot, faced greater scrutiny of her depiction of what happened to her as "rape." The questions that the Mississippi legislators investigating this riot asked Parton were not recorded; only her answers were listed in the investigators' report. But the content and sequence of these answers suggest that the investigators asked why she submitted to her assailant when he did not appear to have used overwhelming physical force. Parton's answers were as follows: "I yielded to him because he had a pistol drawn; when he took me down he hurt me of course; I yielded to him on that account; he never injured me any ways, but hurt me with his pistol." It seems that investigators also asked about the location of the attack and if others had witnessed it. Parton's answers continue: "There was nobody in the room at the time he had me. . . . There was an old bed in the room, broken down and piled up; did not straighten out the bed; he just pressed me down."[35] The fact that the attack happened on a bed had apparently led an investigator to ask if the assailant had laid it out properly, a sign perhaps that he had taken his time to do this comfortably and thus that Parton had somehow indicated to him that she was willing.

The most damning evidence against Parton was the testimony of the white man to whom she had appealed for help. When Michael Slamon spoke to the investigators, he directly contradicted her account. He did not deny that he had been in Parton's house but only that she had been raped: "I know of no one committing rape upon Ellen," he told investigators. "[I] don't remember her appealing to me for protection; I saw her go off in company with no man; . . . I did not see any pistols while there." Perhaps recalling how Parton had shamed him in the midst of the attack by identifying him as a man who allowed her to be raped, he took the opportunity offered by his testimony before state legislators to reaffirm an honorable, patriarchal identity: "I did not go there to protect her, but would have protected her if she needed it." Slamon further undermined Parton's credibility as a witness by depicting her as having been overwrought and emotional that night: "Ellen was excited; I said, 'What is the use of being so much excited? no one is going to bother you.'" He concluded his testimony, "There was no rape committed to my knowledge."[36]

Parton responded to doubts that she had been assaulted by offering her own understanding of what constituted rape. She ignored clues from investigators as to how she might have represented herself as a more legitimate victim of rape. Near the end of her affidavit, she answered an apparent query about her marital status: "I am a married woman; have been parted from my husband since the surrender; I am not living with him." She was then living with Marshal Ware, a black Meridian police officer for whom the rioters who came to her house that night were searching. When the investigators inquired about Ware's marital status, she answered, "Marshal Ware's wife is dead; he is not married." Parton did not indicate the nature of her relationship with Ware. They may have been lovers, or she may have simply been renting space in his house, or he may have hired her to do domestic work for him. The investigators did not ask her to elaborate but, rather, merely implied that it did not reflect well on the character of a woman separated from her husband to be living in the home of another, unmarried man. Parton, however, refused to acknowledge that her living arrangements, or even a consensual sexual relationship, could be grounds for questioning her legitimacy as a witness and as a victim of rape. She followed her responses to questions about marital status immediately with "I never was treated that way before; I never was forced before." It was her experience of coercion—not her marital status, her living arrangements, her past sexual relationships, or even the appearance constructed by her assailant of consensual sex—that was significant, she insisted, to determining if this was an act of rape.[37]

It might seem striking that both Hannah Tutson and Ellen Parton were so insistent on telling their stories, so committed to speaking about an experience of sexual abuse, and in an official forum dominated by white men, who in Parton's case questioned her account. And yet that commitment was not unique. During Reconstruction, freedwomen testified about rape with remarkable frankness and, as suggested by Parton's words, even at times openly resisted white officials' efforts to shape their testimony or to cast doubt on their veracity. In their testimony in congressional hearings and other state forums, freedwomen claimed identities as honorable women, but not within the confines of conventional definitions of women's virtue. They did not represent themselves as women willing to die to prevent a sexual assault; they were, rather, women who understood the reality of having to submit to unwanted sexual intercourse in order to save one's life and to protect one's family. Nor did they represent themselves as women whose past and present experiences fit easily within conservative notions of proper sexual conduct for virtuous women. They represented themselves, instead, as witnesses who were truthful, as wives who sought to protect their husbands from assault and murder, and as mothers concerned with protecting their children from violence and with protesting their abuse. Their testimony called on the state to recognize them as citizens while also demanding a rejection of patriarchal definitions of a woman's virtue that could limit their access to their rights as citizens.

The lengths to which women went and the risks they took in order to testify about rape also reflect their belief in the importance of discourse and representation to the struggles for a meaningful freedom in which all freedpeople were engaged. Representations of black women as lacking virtue and as will-less subjects incapable of expressing consent or refusal had undergirded the system of slavery and reinforced notions of racial inequality. Telling stories of rape to their white neighbors and to officials allowed black women to challenge those representations and to claim identities as willful and entitled members of the political community within a new American republic.

Looking back on this history, we know that the state they called on to be their protector, the state whose authority they sought to legitimate by demanding that it defend their rights as citizens, the state that, for a time anyway, granted "truth" to their words, would ultimately turn its back on them.[38] In the years after the congressional investigation of Klan violence completed its work, support among northern white Republicans for federal intervention into the political and judicial affairs of southern states began to wane. Many Klan members were prosecuted under federal authority, and some served prison terms.[39] In the early 1870s, though violence continued, African Americans in the South exercised an impressive degree of electoral power. But this occurred simultaneously with the initial withering of the federal government's commitment to actively supporting the rights of citizenship of former slaves. The depression of 1873 and resultant labor conflict and class tensions in the North challenged the northern elite's support for expanding democracy, and subsequent party realignments and a Democratic victory in congressional elections in 1874 set the Republicans on a more conservative and cautious course. This course would lead initially to a decreased will to use federal power to suppress political violence in the South and ultimately to federal authorities turning a blind eye to turn-of-the-century policies of post-Reconstruction southern state governments—in the hands of conservative Democratic regimes since the late 1870s—designed to disfranchise African American men.[40] It would also lead to federal legitimation of racial inequality in the form of the decision in *Plessy v. Ferguson* in the U.S. Supreme Court in 1896. The ideological groundwork for this decision, which declared that legally enforced racial segregation was in accord with the Fourteenth Amendment, had been laid in part through the rhetoric of miscegenation during Reconstruction.[41]

Well before disfranchisement of African American men was achieved in the southern states and the *Plessy* decision was handed down, the postwar federal provision of official state arenas in which African Americans could protest violence would also come to an end. The Freedmen's Bureau ceased most of its activities on behalf of freedpeople at the end of 1868 and shut its doors entirely in 1872. And the 1877 compromise between northern and southern white political leaders that led to Republican candidate Rutherford B. Hayes's victory in a close and contested presidential election—one in which white southerners suppressed black votes with open violence and intimidation—

marked the demise of any kind of federal presence in local affairs in the South. Though African American political influence would survive in pockets scattered throughout the southern states, the federal government's role as an active protector of former slaves and their descendants from political violence would cease and would not be revived until the mid-twentieth century.[42]

However, before this occurred, during the years immediately following emancipation when the promise of federal backing of a new kind of republic was still real, African Americans, both women and men, embraced seemingly insurmountable challenges in order to realize the possibility of a meaningful freedom. By testifying to sexual assaults as violation and by depicting coerced sex between white men and black women as rape, freedwomen challenged the gendered representations of racial inequality that threatened to limit their citizenship and constrain their freedom. They sought, by speaking, to transform their experiences of violence from haunting memories of pain into means of social transformation and thereby to forge a new world.

Reconstruction's End and the Refutation of Freedwomen's Testimony

An unexpected postscript to the history of freedwomen's testimony about rape during Reconstruction serves as a sad allegory for the end of federal support for African American citizenship in the late 1870s and for what this withdrawal meant for one aspect of that citizenship, the public recognition of sexual violence against black women as rape. In 1876, ten years after she was raped during the riot in Memphis, Frances Thompson, one of five women who had testified before the congressional committee about sexual violence, would again appear in the historical record when she was arrested for "being a man and wearing women's clothing."[43] Thompson's arrest was allegedly triggered by a "well-known Memphis physician" who reported to local authorities his suspicions about her "true sex."[44] The charge was cross-dressing, a misdemeanor under a city ordinance prohibiting "offenses affecting good morals and decency."[45] Because Thompson's testimony before the congressional committee had occupied such a prominent place in the committee's final report, her arrest for cross-dressing—which might have received only passing mention in the local press under different circumstances—filled the city columns of Memphis's conservative newspapers for days and also appeared in papers in Arkansas, Illinois, Missouri, New York, Ohio, and Texas.[46] White conservatives had stumbled onto their chance to vindicate white men in

Memphis from the charges of brutality made against them in the congressional committee's report and to dismiss freedwomen's testimony about rape. Thompson's arrest also served the interests of conservatives in the 1876 presidential election campaign that would ultimately lead to the compromise of 1877 and the formal end of federal Reconstruction. In this context, the conservative newspapers contended that Thompson's cross-dressing proved her testimony about rape to have been a lie.[47]

The conservative newspapers in Memphis unleashed a campaign of vilification against Thompson that was designed to refute charges of white southern brutality against African Americans and to oppose the Republican Party. Drawing on the pre-riot discourse depicting black women as part of the illicit and dangerous criminal world of South Memphis, newspaper editors described Thompson as "lewd," associated her with prostitution, and portrayed her as the epitome of despicable sexual conduct. They attributed to her "vile habits and corruptions," decried her "utter depravity," and accused her of using her "guise" as a woman to facilitate her supposed role as a "wholesale debaucher" and "procuress" of numberless young women for prostitution.[48] For instance, the *Memphis Daily Appeal* wondered "how many women, both white and black, he has ruined."[49] The papers then used these charges to condemn their Republican opponents, reminding their readers that the Republican Party—now referred to as "the Frances Thompson Radical party"— had relied upon Thompson's "perjurious evidence" to condemn white men in Memphis for violence and brutality.[50]

The conservative press's charges that Thompson's testimony was merely a charade were used to discredit all the black women who testified that they had been raped during those violent days in Memphis. The *Memphis Daily Appeal* criticized Lucy Smith for her corroboration of Thompson's testimony, which was now dismissed as "utterly at variance with the truth." The paper also mocked Smith's claim that she herself had been "violated." The *Appeal* insinuated that Smith did not possess the "virtue" needed for a woman to protest rape, because—and this they asserted with no evidence—Smith had been "occupying the same bed with Thompson" prior to the reported rapes.[51] The other women who testified were not mentioned by name, but the conservative papers implied that Thompson's identity exposed the entire congressional report as "vile slander" manufactured by Republicans solely for political gain. With no new information other than Thompson's arrest for cross-dressing, one conservative paper denounced the report: "The evidence of the vilest wretches was received and worded in smooth phrase and published to the world to prove that the Southern people were a set of barbarians and as-sassins."[52] The *Appeal* went further, enlisting Thompson's image to vindicate all white southerners from accusations of racist violence during Reconstruc-tion: "Whenever you hear Radicals talking of the persecutions of the black race in the south, ask them what they think of Frances Thompson and the outrages committed on her . . . during the celebrated riots. These pretended outrages in the south are all of a piece with this Frances Thompson affair. It is out of such material as this that all their blood-and-thunder stories are manu-factured."[53] Critics of Reconstruction attempted to supplant recognition of African American women's experiences of sexual violence circulated nation-ally in the congressional committee's report—now mere "pretended outrages" —with the image of Thompson's allegedly "deviant" and "depraved" cross-dressing male body. As federal support for African Americans' rights as citi-zens was being withdrawn in these final years of Reconstruction, as black political leaders' ability to influence public discourse began to wane, and as the arenas in which black women had testified to being raped were dis-mantled, the conservative press in Memphis boldly declared that the black women who testified about rape had lied. The papers claimed that black women were not virtuous enough to be believed when they testified in a legal forum. They were not virtuous enough to be trusted with the rights of citizenship. The refusal to recognize the rape of black women common among white southerners during slavery was invoked to denounce African American citizenship at the end of Reconstruction.

In addition to being thus denigrated in the press, Thompson was forced to pay dearly for her alleged crime in more palpable ways as well. After her arrest, she was placed on the city's chain gang, where she was forced to wear men's clothing and suffered constant ridicule and harassment from crowds drawn by mocking press reports.[54] She had initially refused to cooperate with a medical examination intended to "prove" her "true sex" and only submitted after it was threatened that "force would be used."[55] While in jail, she protested to a reporter for the *Appeal* that the station-house keeper was treating her "very grossly whenever an opportunity presented," taking "evident delight in ex-hibiting [her] to the curious eye of the public." She alleged further abusive treatment that the paper reported only as "other acts which we cannot place in public print."[56] Thus in addition to an unwanted and intrusive medical exam, public humiliation, imprisonment, and hard labor, Thompson, it seems, was subjected to further sexual violence at the hands of those guarding her in jail. And as she had done a decade earlier, she protested this violence via the avenue available to her in the moment: in 1866, the Freedmen's Bureau and a congressional committee, and in 1876, a far less effective venue, a curious newspaper reporter. Thompson, still defiant, was nonetheless physically weakened by her prison ordeal. Soon after she completed her term of 100 days, she moved to a cabin in North Memphis, where she was soon discovered alone and seriously ill by members of the freed community. These people moved her to the city hospital, where she died of dysentery on November 1, 1876.[57]

The coroner's report of Thompson's death recorded that she was anatomically male.[58] This "finding" concurred with earlier reports of the medical examiners called in at the time of her arrest. These examiners, four white doctors, declared that Thompson "had none of the developments of a woman whatever, nor anything that could possibly be mistaken as any part of the identities of the female sex. The evidence shows that there is not part of a woman about him, the organs being entirely those of a male in every respect."[59] The insistence of both the doctors and the coroner that Thompson was clearly male is important but also, perhaps, not to be believed. It is likely that these men pronounced far greater clarity than existed. Thompson may have had an ambiguously sexed body. In fact, one newspaper report claimed that some in Memphis had understood that Thompson was intersexed or, in their words, "a hermaphrodite."[60] Another newspaper reported that Thompson had herself once insisted that she was "of double sex."[61] Perhaps responding to these claims, the official discourse insisted that she was unequivocally male.

After her arrest, Thompson protested the findings that she was "a man and not a woman in any respect."[62] She turned not to her body but, rather, to social practices and community recognition for evidence of her legitimate gender identity. A reporter from the Memphis Daily Appeal claimed that in an interview, Thompson insisted that her arrest and imprisonment were unjust because she "was regarded always as a woman," having worn female attire since she was a small child.[63] Newspaper reports further suggested that in Memphis Thompson had always been "supposed to be a woman"; one paper subtitled an article about her, "A Colored Man Who Has Successfully Passed as a Woman for Twenty-Seven Years."[64] Though we have to consider the possibility that she may have initially represented herself as female at the insistence of the man who owned her as a slave,[65] these reports suggest that once she was free, Thompson continued to identify and live her life as a woman.

However, those men examining her body sought to find a different "reality" behind the ambiguity Thompson represented. Insisting on fitting Thompson into a construct of gender that allowed for only one of two choices, into a gender-dimorphic world rooted firmly in imagined absolute distinctions in anatomy, they represented her claims to female identity as pure deception. By their declarations they refused to recognize the possible fluidity between maleness and femaleness that may have characterized Thompson's bodily experience.[66] Why was this denial so important to them? Intersexuality was not unknown in these years,[67] nor was cross-dressing in general seen as necessarily threatening. It had been a common part of carnival-like celebrations and occurred during the Memphis Riot itself as well as during night rides of the Klan. It was a practice even celebrated when women dressed as men so they could join the Confederate Army.[68] Frances Thompson, however, was a former slave who had enlisted federal power to challenge antebellum racial hierarchy and racist constructs of black womanhood, and whose testimony had been used to help establish African American citizenship rights. Allowing her to be "of double sex" for her social identity, and allowing social identities in general to be fluid and based on social practice and community recognition instead of biology or "blood," would, it seems, have thrown into question differences not only of gender but also of race. Such ambiguity might have suggested that the black men and women living as free people in the public spaces of Memphis and claiming the rights and privileges of citizenship in the city that had until emancipation been the sole property of whites, or that black men and women attending political conventions and marching to the polls and casting ballots on election day, could erase hierarchical meanings for race by living and acting equally with whites. Forcing Thompson to wear men's clothing and labor on a chain gang (punishment generally reserved for men)[69]—forcing her to perform a gender that these medical experts claimed was reflected in the essence of her body—reinscribed essential identities overall. It also allowed the conservative press to insist—not countenancing the possibility of male-on-male rape—that she and other black women had not suffered sexual violence. The challenge to racial hierarchy so evident in public life in the South after emancipation and in African Americans' protests against Reconstruction-era political violence was countered by conservative critics' insistence that Frances Thompson was male.

In 1866, Thompson herself had insisted before the congressional committee that the opposite was true, that she was a woman and, in fact, a particular "sort of woman," to use her words. The story of her subsequent arrest highlights what she was up against during her testimony. Thompson, along with the other women who testified that they had been raped, confronted the challenge of representing her experience of coerced sex as "rape" in the context of white discourse about black women's depravity. Beyond this, though, Thompson faced the added challenge of convincing the committee and the audience in the hearing room that she was a woman. She apparently did so. One can read her testimony that she was "not that sort of woman" as exemplifying the postemancipation contest between former slaves and white southerners over black women's claim to virtue, to being the sort of women who were not sexually available and who could thus claim that they had been raped. Alternatively, one could see Thompson's apparent adoption of conventional notions of different sorts of women to have been an added performative dimension, even a degree of excess, within her testimony. It is easy to understand how Thompson might have adopted this conventional framework for understanding womanhood and rape in order to tell her story. It was the framework endorsed by the men whom she sought to convince. As we have seen, though, other women operating under a different set of constraints, and perhaps less conscious about performing as "women," framed their testimony in different ways. Thompson's implicit representation of rape as something that can only happen to a particular sort of woman appears to have been the exception. And this exception was driven, it seems, by Thompson's vulnerable position within the discursive and cultural world of postemancipation Memphis, one even more vulnerable than that of the other women who testified to having been raped.

THE MEN WHO assaulted Frances Thompson during the Memphis Riot may well have known of Thompson's ambiguous and probable transgender identity and may have targeted her home for that reason. We will never know for sure. It is equally likely that who Thompson was, in fact, mattered little to her assailants; most important to them were the gendered scripts of racial domination they imposed on all of their victims. Though unusual, this story nonetheless confirms how both sexual violence and its representation functioned during Reconstruction as complex rhetorics of power, inscribing meanings for race through gendered roles and identities. The Civil War and Reconstruction were periods of extensive disruption and political upheaval. Southern society had been turned upside down, and social categories were thrown open to radical redefinition. In this moment of contest, flux, and uncertainty, white southern men employed gender—through violence and rhetoric—to fix hierarchical meanings for race despite the end of slavery and the establishment of formal legal equality. The conservative white response to Frances Thompson's arrest reveals this process in a microcosm. Conservatives sought to establish strict notions of what kind of gendered behavior was proper or virtuous for women and men and then represented African Americans as incapable of fulfilling those roles. One way conservatives excluded African Americans from representations of virtuous gender was to deny that black women had been, or could ever have been, raped. They could not do this publicly or forcefully until they were no longer under the military domination and legal scrutiny of the federal government for violation of civil and political rights, that is, until the federal government no longer supported freedwomen's stories of rape as "truth." The unique historical record black women created during Reconstruction reveals both the gendered nature of political struggles over race and, ultimately, how suppressing this record—how denying the rape of black women by white men in the United States—has ultimately served the solidification of new forms of racial inequality despite the abolition of slavery and the establishment, in principle, of equal citizenship.

Abbreviations

AMA   American Missionary Association Archives, Alderman Library, University of Virginia, Charlottesville

Appeal   *Memphis Daily Appeal*

Argus   *Memphis Daily Argus*

Arkansas BRFAL   Records of the Assistant Commissioner for the State of Arkansas, microfilm 979, Bureau of Refugees, Freedmen, and Abandoned Lands, RG105, U.S. National Archives and Records Administration, Washington, D.C.

Avalanche   *Memphis Daily Avalanche*

BM&A   Minutes of the Board of Mayor and Aldermen

BRFAL   Records of the Bureau of Refugees, Freedmen, and Abandoned Lands, RG105, U.S. National Archives and Records Administration, Washington, D.C.

CCC   *Proceedings of the Convention of Colored Citizens of the State of Arkansas, Held in Little Rock, Thursday, Friday, and Saturday, Nov. 30, Dec. 1&2.* Helena: Clarion Office Print, 1866.

Debates and Proceedings   *Debates and Proceedings of the Convention which Assembled at Little Rock, January 7th, 1868, Under the Provision of the Act of Congress of March 2d, 1867, and the Acts of March 23d and July 19th, 1867, supplement thereto, to Form a Constitution for the State of Arkansas.* Little Rock: J. G. Price, 1868.

FBC	Affidavits Taken before Commission Organized by the Freedmen's Bureau
KKK Testimony	U.S. Congress. Joint Select Committee to Inquire into the Condition of Affairs in the Late Insurrectionary States. *Testimony Taken by the Joint Select Committee to Inquire into the Condition of Affairs in the Late Insurrectionary States*, vols. 1–13. Washington, D.C.: Government Printing Office, 1872.
MC	Testimony Taken before Military Commission Organized by General George Stoneman
MDP	*Memphis Daily Post*
MR&M	U.S. Congress. House of Representatives. *Memphis Riots and Massacres*. 39th Congress, 1st session, 1865–66. House Report no. 101. Washington, D.C., 1866.
MSCA	Memphis and Shelby County Archives, Memphis, Tennessee
PL	*Public Ledger*
Tennessee BRFAL	Records of the Assistant Commissioner for the State of Tennessee, microfilm 999, Bureau of Refugees, Freedmen, and Abandoned Lands, RG105, U.S. National Archives and Records Administration, Washington, D.C.
UAF	Special Collections, University of Arkansas Libraries, Fayetteville
WAG	*Weekly Arkansas Gazette*

Introduction

1. Testimony of Mary Wardlaw, *MR&M*, 233. In fact, Tennessee voters ratified a state constitutional amendment outlawing slavery in March 1865, thus before the Thirteenth Amendment was ratified in December of that year. The Emancipation Proclamation had not applied to Tennessee, which was under Union control by the time it was issued, January 1, 1863. Nonetheless, many enslaved people in the state and certainly in Memphis had already secured their freedom in fact if not in name. On the dismantling of slavery in Memphis, see Cimprich, *Slavery's End in Tennessee*.

2. All from *MR&M*: testimony of Matthew Wardlaw, 233; Ann Patrick Ayr, 232; James E. Donahue, 198; Albert Harris, 62; and Cynthia Townsend, 162. See also testimony of Primus Lane, 96; Matilda Howley, 189; Mary Walker, 196; Lucy Smith, 197; Lucy Hunt, 200; and Emma Lane, 221.

3. See, for instance, Blackburn, *Overthrow of Colonial Slavery*; Holt, *Problem of Freedom*; Rebecca J. Scott, *Slave Emancipation in Cuba*; Laurent DuBois, *Colony of Citizens*; Cooper, Holt, and Scott, *Beyond Slavery*; Scully and Paton, *Gender and Slave Emancipation in the Atlantic World*, 9–10.

4. Holt, *Problem of Freedom*; Laurent DuBois, *Colony of Citizens*; Cooper, Holt, and Scott, *Beyond Slavery*.

5. Those escaping slavery were central actors in the production and circulation of discourses of universal freedom. See, e.g., Laurent DuBois, *Colony of Citizens*; Hahn, *Nation under Our Feet*, esp. 64.

6. Hunt, *Israel, Elihu, and Cadwallader Washburn*, 174, 183–206, 226–31, 235–38; Foner, *Free Soil, Free Labor, Free Men*, 105, 210, 288.

7. See, for instance, U.S. Congress, House of Representatives, *Report of the Joint Committee on Reconstruction*, esp. 13. Washburne was a member of the joint committee. See also, for instance, in the *New York Times*, "The State of Tennessee and the Reconstruction Committee," March 9, 1866, 5, and "Washington News," March 8, 1866, 1, which reported on Washburne's endorsement of the extension of suffrage for all African American men as an additional condition before the state of Tennessee be restored to the Union.

8. Testimony of Cynthia Townsend, *MR&M*, 164.

9. Ibid., 163.

10. Ibid., 162.

11. Ibid., 163. The woman to whom Townsend referred, Harriet Armour, testified herself about being sexually assaulted, as did four other women. See discussion of these rape attacks and these women's testimony in Chapter 2.

12. Testimony of Cynthia Townsend, *MR&M*, 162–64.

13. On exclusion as an inherent component of liberal political systems, see, e.g., Mehta, "Liberal Strategies of Exclusion." On representations of African Americans that rationalized their exclusion from suffrage at the end of Reconstruction, see Richardson, *Death of Reconstruction*. Most obviously, white women were excluded from political and many civil rights despite their nominal recognition as citizens in the nineteenth-century United States, a fact invoked at times in support of arguments for the legitimacy of excluding black men from suffrage during the postemancipation era (see below and Chapter 4). On gender exclusion as a central aspect of liberal discourse, see Pateman, *Sexual Contract*, and Wendy Brown, "Liberalism's Family Values."

14. I begin the period of Reconstruction at 1861 because the first Union occupation of Confederate territory late in this year, the occupation of the South Carolina Sea Islands, began the processes—emancipation, negotiation of a free labor system, establishment of schools and churches for former slaves, etc.—that make up Reconstruction. (See Rose, *Rehearsal for Reconstruction*.) Eric Foner uses 1863, the year of the Emancipation Proclamation, as his starting point; see Foner, *Reconstruction*, esp. xxvii. The end date is less clear; traditionally historians have ended Reconstruction at 1877, when the last federal troops left the South. And yet, despite the presence of some troops, there was little effective federal protection for freedpeople in the southern states by that point. On the other hand, many of the political gains of Reconstruction continued in different local areas for decades longer. On this point, see Edwards, *Gendered Strife and Confusion*, 218–21.

15. Similarly, David Blight identifies post–Civil War commemorations of emancipation by African Americans as embodying both joy at the progress made after slavery and horror at the realities of postemancipation racism; see *Race and Reunion*, chap. 9, esp. 304, 336.

16. Needless to say, in this study I approach race not as biological or physical difference but, rather, as a product of historical experience, including both material conditions and discursive representation, the "thousand details, anecdotes, stories" from which racial knowledge is produced (Franz Fanon, *Peau noire, masques blancs* [Paris, 1952], qtd. in Holt, "Marking," 2). Race is, then, a changing historical phenomenon the varied meanings of which can be traced, documented, and analyzed for their imbrication with and role in other historical changes. As Thomas Holt has written, " 'Race' inheres neither in biology nor in culture but must be summoned to consciousness by . . . encounters in social space and historical time" ("Marking," 1). For important discussions of race as a varied historical phenomenon and a subject of history that have, over the years, informed my thinking, see Holt, "Marking" and *Problem of Race*; Gilroy, *"There Ain't No Black in the Union Jack,"* chap. 1, esp. 38–40; Fields, "Race and Ideology in American History"; and Higginbotham, "African-American Women's History and the Metalanguage of Race."

17. For studies that approach race and racism as phenomena that were not given but which, rather, had to be reproduced in a postemancipation context, see, for instance, Holt, *Problem of Freedom* and " 'Empire over the Mind' "; Dailey, *Before Jim Crow*; Gaines, *Uplifting the Race*; Kantrowitz, *Ben Tillman*; Melish, *Disowning Slavery*; Mitchell, *Righteous Propagation*; and Hale, *Making Whiteness*. Historian Martha Hodes suggests the importance of analyzing race after emancipation when she writes that with the abolition of slavery, "categories of color bore the entire burden of upholding the racial hierarchy" (*White Women, Black Men*, 147). For a different approach to race in the postemancipation South, one that conceptualizes race as a matter of "mentality," see Williamson, *Crucible of Race*. On the making of race through everyday encounters in and discourses about slave markets in the antebellum South, see Johnson, *Soul by Soul*. On the reconfiguration of race in another crucial moment in U.S. history, see Ngai, *Impossible Subjects*.

18. On thinking about the articulation of race through and with other aspects of a social order and discursive context, such as gender, class, or nation, see Thomas Holt's work on race, esp. *Problem of Race*, 22, 27–28, and " 'Essence of the Contract' "; McClintock, *Imperial Leather*, esp. 4–9; and Higginbotham, "African-American Women's History and the Metalanguage of Race." Joan Wallach Scott's formulation that gender has been "a primary way of signifying relations of power" or "a primary field within which or by means of which power is articulated" has also influenced my thinking in this regard (see *Gender and the Politics of History*, 42, 44–45). Kathleen M. Brown explores "the uses of gender in constituting racial categories and legitimating political authority" in the origins of slavery in British North America, in *Good Wives, Nasty Wenches, and Anxious Patriarchs* (quotation from p. 2). For explorations of how race has been produced through gendered discourses and practices in the post-Reconstruction South, see esp. Kantrowitz, *Ben Tillman* and "One Man's Mob Is Another Man's Militia," and Dailey, *Before Jim Crow* and "Limits of Liberalism in the New South"; in other times and places,

see also Jennifer L. Morgan, *Laboring Women*, and Stoler, "Carnal Knowledge and Imperial Power."

Historian Nell Irvin Painter, reviewing Eric Foner's synthetic study, *Reconstruction*, drew attention to the need for a gendered history of this period; see "Prize Winning Book Revisited." Laura Edwards in particular has pioneered this path, drawing together in one analysis the gendered political culture of southern society and the social history of Reconstruction; see " 'Marriage Covenant' " and *Gendered Strife and Confusion*. See also Bercaw, *Gendered Freedoms*. For an analysis of Reconstruction in South Carolina that places white manhood at its center, see Kantrowitz, *Ben Tillman*, 40–79. Painter also noted the need to pay particular attention to how black women's experiences differed from black men's and to conflict within black families and communities. These charges have been taken up in different ways in Schwalm, *Hard Fight for We*; Hunter, *To 'Joy My Freedom*; Barkley Brown, "Uncle Ned's Children," "To Catch the Vision of Freedom," and "Negotiating and Transforming the Public Sphere"; Frankel, *Freedom's Women*; Bercaw, *Gendered Freedoms*; and most recently, O'Donovan, *Becoming Free in the Cotton South*. See also Jacqueline Jones, *Labor of Love, Labor of Sorrow*, chap. 2. Lee Ann Whites has addressed how the Civil War and emancipation undermined white male authority within their households and how conflict between white men and women was reflected in the politics of Reconstruction; see *Civil War as a Crisis in Gender* and "Civil War as a Crisis in Gender." On this point, see also Bercaw, *Gendered Freedoms*, esp. chaps. 2 and 3 and pp. 138–45.

19. This book in part, then, shifts the dominant focus of studies of race, sexuality, and violence in southern history away from accusations made against black men for allegedly raping white women and to the history of sexual violence against black women by white men. It thus responds to literary scholar Hazel Carby's critique that "the institutionalized rape of black women has never been as powerful a symbol of black oppression as the spectacle of lynching" (*Reconstructing Womanhood*, 39). Jacquelyn Dowd Hall has drawn attention to the rape of black women as a form of racial violence parallel to lynching in " 'Mind That Burns in Each Body,' " where she notes "most studies of racial violence have paid little attention to the particular suffering of women" (322), and in the second edition of her pioneering work *Revolt against Chivalry*, wherein she argues that "the racism that caused white men to lynch black men cannot be understood apart from the sexism that informed their policing of white women and their exploitation of black women." Here Hall notes her own surprise, rereading the original book, at "how little space I had actually devoted to the sexual exploitation of black women" (xxiv). For studies that trace change over time in representations of black men as rapists that were eventually used to justify lynching and the related social and legal sanctions against sexual relationships between black men and white women, see Hodes, *White Women, Black Men* and "Sexualization of Reconstruction Politics," and Sommerville, *Rape and Race* and "Rape Myth Reconsidered." Angela Y. Davis describes this same historical trajectory in *Women, Race, and Class*, chap. 11. Catherine Clinton has

criticized scholarship on rape during Reconstruction for focusing too much on white women as victims and black men as assailants, at the expense of exploring the history of the rape of black women by white men, as she does in her work. See Clinton, "Reconstructing Freedwomen," 319; "Bloody Terrain"; and "Caught in the Web of the Big House."

Some of the most eloquent critiques of the place of sexuality in racial oppression, which place the experiences of sexual violation of black women alongside those of lynchings of black men, come from the pens of the generation of black women intellectuals following Reconstruction (theorists and activists who incidentally connect these interrelated forms of racial oppression to U.S. imperialism emerging in that generation). See, for instance, Wells, *On Lynching*, and Hopkins, *Contending Forces*. See Hazel Carby's analysis of the writings of Ida B. Wells and Pauline Hopkins, as well as Anna Julia Cooper, in Carby, " 'On the Threshold of Woman's Era.' " Also on Wells and Hopkins, see Gunning, *Race, Rape, and Lynching*, chap. 3; on Ida B. Wells and Frederick Douglass, see Angela Y. Davis, *Women, Race, and Class*, chap. 11; and on Wells, see Valerie Smith, "Split Affinities," esp. 274. On both black women's protest against lynching and rape and on black women as victims of lynching, see Feimster, "Ladies and Lynching" and "Raped and Lynched," cited with permission of the author.

20. See also Steven Hahn's sweeping study of black political mobilization in the South during and after emancipation in *Nation under Our Feet*, esp. chaps. 3–5.

21. I have been influenced by critics of Jürgen Habermas, who have opened up his concept of a "public sphere"—which he imagined as a singular discursive space and uniquely bourgeois formation of the late seventeenth and eighteenth centuries wherein through rational discussion public opinion was formed and by which citizens exercised influence over the state—to incorporate multiple and conflicting public spheres, a model applicable to the time of Habermas's idealized public sphere and to times after. These critics have taken into account different degrees of power between speakers and between competing and oppositional publics, as well as the oppositional power marginalized groups exercise on dominant groups from counter publics. Some have also expanded the notion of discursive public arenas to include physical spaces, so that in addition to the words spoken, the events that occur within these spaces themselves can operate as texts of sorts, as visible and audible performances that observers and participants can read and that create and contest various ideological constructs, such as race, gender, and citizenship (see esp. Mary P. Ryan, *Women in Public*). See Habermas, "Public Sphere" and *Structural Transformation of the Public Sphere*. For critics and interpreters of Habermas, see Felski, *Beyond Feminist Aesthetics*, 164–65; Nancy Fraser, "What's Critical about Critical Theory?" and "Rethinking the Public Sphere." See the application of an expanded notion of public spheres in historical scholarship in Higginbotham, *Righteous Discontent*; Barkley Brown, "Negotiating and Transforming the Public Sphere"; and numerous essays in Calhoun, *Habermas and the Public Sphere*.

22. I use the term "conservative" as it was often used during Reconstruction, that is, to refer

to those who formerly supported the southern Democratic Party as well as those former Whigs who joined with former Democrats after the war in opposition to the federal program of Reconstruction and specifically African American citizenship. These politicians and their supporters were hesitant to label themselves "Democrats" during the early stages of Reconstruction, when federal officials were sensitive to and sought to suppress any sign of disloyalty among white southerners, for fear of associating too closely with the party thought to have brought on a disastrous and treasonous civil war. They also avoided the label "Democrats" in order to encourage white southerners who had once opposed the Democratic Party to join them in their campaign against Reconstruction. On the label "conservative" during Reconstruction, see Perman, *Road to Redemption*, 6, and Trelease, *White Terror*, xxv.

23. On the concept of "social equality," see Chapter 4 as well as, inter alia, Hodes, *White Women, Black Men*, esp. 166; Painter, " 'Social Equality' "; Richardson, *Death of Reconstruction*, esp. 123–24; Gaines, *Uplifting the Race*, chap. 2; and Dailey, *Before Jim Crow*, chap. 3, and "Limits of Liberalism in the New South."

24. I use the terms "public" and "private" to refer, respectively, to political and domestic realms of power relations, recognizing their separation to be imagined and ideological. My purpose is not to reify "separate spheres," a concept that emerged out of studies of northern white bourgeois society and which McCurry has argued is less applicable to the kinds of households—sites of production where labor was controlled through relations of class, race, and gender—that dominated nineteenth-century southern society (see *Masters of Small Worlds*, 21 n. 37). Rather, I intend to invoke the material and ideological connections and interdependence of white male political and patriarchal authority and the effects of this interdependence on the political discourse and struggles of Reconstruction. On the development of the concept of "separate spheres" by historians of women in the United States, and an argument for an understanding of the concept as a "trope, employed by people in the past to characterize power relations for which they had no other words and that they could not acknowledge because they could not name, and by historians in our own times as they groped for a device that might dispel the confusion of anecdote and impose narrative and analytical order on the anarchy of inherited evidence, the better to comprehend the world in which we live," see Kerber, "Separate Spheres, Female Worlds, Woman's Place," 39.

25. On the patriarchal political culture of the antebellum South, see esp. McCurry, *Masters of Small Worlds* and "Two Faces of Republicanism." For the influence of this culture on postbellum southern society and politics, see esp. Edwards, *Gendered Strife and Confusion* and " 'Marriage Covenant' "; Kantrowitz, *Ben Tillman* and "One Man's Mob Is Another Man's Militia"; and Bercaw, *Gendered Freedoms*.

26. On the persistence of racist imagery across time and place, and the need to "recognize that a new historical construct is never entirely new and the old is never entirely supplanted by the new. . . . Shards and fragments of [racism's] past incarnations are embedded in the new," see Holt, *Problem of Race*, 8, 20.

27. Stanley, *From Bondage to Contract*; Foner, *Free Soil, Free Labor, Free Men*, introduction; Holt, *Problem of Freedom*, " 'Essence of the Contract,' " and " 'Empire over the Mind' "; Hartman, *Scenes of Subjection*.

28. Seeking to explain "the inclusionary pretensions of liberal theory and the exclusionary effects of liberal practices," political theorist Uday Mehta has argued that implicit in liberal theory are certain "conventions and manners" necessary to realize the human capacity for rationality that makes legitimate an individual's participation in self-government ("Liberal Strategies of Exclusion"). I am suggesting here that those "conventions and manners" were highly gendered. See also Pateman, *Sexual Contract*, and Wendy Brown, "Liberalism's Family Values."

29. A concept central to the political vocabulary of the antebellum era, "virtue" was understood to be a personal characteristic crucial to a sound republic. It connoted citizens' ability to voluntarily subordinate their own individual—and more instinctive—interests and desires, through reasoned consideration and debate, to the overall public good. Since the early republic, dominant political discourses in the United States had justified restrictions on voting rights as allowing political authority only to those who were virtuous enough to exercise this power responsibly and in a way that would not threaten the political liberty of others. Revolutionary-era representations of this necessary civic virtue as inherently masculine were enhanced by the rhetoric of military valor emerging from the experience of the Revolutionary War. See Kerber, "May All Our Citizens Be Soldiers and All Our Soldiers Citizens" and " 'History Can Do It No Justice,' " 29. Given the common association of the term "virtue" with female chastity, it is worth noting that the root of the word is "vir," or man, which in Latin indicated manliness and valor. Linda Kerber notes this in *Women of the Republic*, 229, as does Ruth Bloch, quoting Hannah Fenichel Pitkin (*Fortune Is a Woman* [Berkeley: University of California Press, 1984], 25), in "Gendered Meanings of Virtue in Revolutionary America." For a discussion of how "virtue," "a word laden with assumptions about gender," came after the American Revolution to refer still to "male public spirit," but also increasingly to "female private morality," see Bloch, "Gendered Meanings of Virtue in Revolutionary America." See also Kerber, *Women of the Republic*, chap. 9, and " 'History Can Do It No Justice,' " 39. On the conflation of public and private virtue in manhood, of a lack of sexual discipline indicating a threat to political liberty, suggested in the writings of Montesquieu, see Kerber, *Women of the Republic*, 19–20.

30. McCurry, *Masters of Small Worlds*.

31. The common term in nineteenth-century political discourse, "freeman," often equivalent to "citizen," drew on the opposition between "liberty" and "slavery." Stephanie McCurry describes "freemen" as "the term privileged in legal discourse" in antebellum South Carolina; see ibid., 14. Amy Dru Stanley shows how, to Enlightenment thinkers developing classical contract theory, the ability to contract, a crucial right of citizenship, was what distinguished "freemen" from slaves; see *From Bondage to Contract*, chap. 1. Historians David Roediger and J. Mills Thornton have both argued that from the Revolutionary era through the antebellum period white men—for Roediger white northern

workers and for Thornton white southern farmers—defined themselves as "freemen" in opposition to the enslaved members of southern society. When defending their own "liberty," these scholars argue, white men were conscious of the real and present alternative of slavery that surrounded them, in addition to the abstract "tyranny" of monarchical government. See Roediger, *Wages of Whiteness*, 31–36, 55–56, and Thornton, *Politics and Power in a Slave Society*. Other historians have also argued that living amidst slavery made white men's notions of liberty and autonomy more than abstractions and their references to "tyranny" and "slavery" in opposition to various state actions more than mere metaphor. See also McCurry, *Masters of Small Worlds*; Edmund S. Morgan, *American Slavery, American Freedom*, 376; and Hahn, *Roots of Southern Populism*, esp. 89–90.

32. Renda, *Taking Haiti*, 15.
33. On sexual violence against black women by white men as central to the political violence of Reconstruction, see esp. Cardyn, "Sexual Terror" and "Sexualized Racism." (See also further discussion of Cardyn's work in Chapter 5, n. 4.) See also Clinton, "Bloody Terrain," 315, 317–18, 328–29, and "Reconstructing Freedwomen," 316; Edwards, *Gendered Strife and Confusion*, 208, and "Sexual Violence, Gender, Reconstruction," 248; Frankel, *Freedom's Women*, 110–13; Gutman, *Black Family in Slavery and Freedom*, 387, 393–96; Hodes, *White Women, Black Men*, 270 n. 32; Hunter, *To 'Joy My Freedom*, 33–34; Lerner, *Black Women in White America*, 180–88; Litwack, *Been in the Storm So Long*, 277, 280; Sommerville, *Rape and Race*, 147–57; Kidada Williams, "In the Space of Violence"; and Lou Falkner Williams, *Great South Carolina Ku Klux Klan Trials*, 35.
34. On the discursive dimensions of sexual violence, see, e.g., Marcus, "Fighting Bodies, Fighting Words." For a fascinating discussion of the violent potential of discourse more generally, see Berlant, *Queen of America Goes to Washington City*.
35. Sharon Marcus writes, "Masculine power and feminine powerlessness neither simply precede nor cause rape; rather, rape is one of culture's many modes of feminizing women. A rapist chooses his target because he recognizes her to be a woman, but a rapist also strives to imprint the gender identity of 'feminine victim' on his target. A rape act thus imposes as well as it presupposes misogynist inequalities; rape is not only scripted—it also scripts" ("Fighting Bodies, Fighting Words," 387, 388–89, 390, 391). See also Butler and Scott, *Feminists Theorize the Political*, xvi. For an early interpretation of acts of rape committed by white slaveowners against female slaves as efforts to produce, or one could say "script," a submissive gender for black women, in a landmark essay on sexual violence, gender, and racism, see Angela Y. Davis, "Reflections on the Black Woman's Role in the Community of Slaves." See also Walkowitz, *City of Dreadful Delight*, and Valerie Smith, "Split Affinities."

Sharon Marcus's essay was a direct intervention into debates in the late 1980s and early 1990s over the usefulness of poststructuralist theory to social history and feminism, debates that have shaped my own emphasis on exploring the meanings both enabling and produced through sexual violence. These debates emerged within historical scholarship around responses to "the linguistic turn," and particularly to Joan

Wallach Scott's arguing that historians do not have any direct, unmediated access to "real" experience of historical actors outside of discourse, and thus that social historical sources can illuminate not so much experience in the past but, rather, the discourses by which people represented and through which they came to understand their experience. (See Scott, *Gender and the Politics of History*; "On Language, Gender, and Working-Class History"; review of *Heroes of Their Own Lives*; "Response to Gordon"; " 'Tip of the Volcano' "; and "Evidence of Experience" and a shorter version of the same essay, "Experience.") While many historians shared Scott's embrace of a poststructuralist approach and its associated emphasis on the instability of categories such as gender, race, and class; on the impossibility of "truth"; on the multiplicity of perceptions; and on the political character of, and contest over, representation, others cautioned that emphasizing discourse could mean an end to politically engaged analysis, the loss of histories of women in favor of histories of gender, and an inability to analyze the "real" experiences of women in the past and today. Some of these critics invoked women's experiences with rape and other forms of violence as an example of something "real" that exists outside of or beyond discourse. (See, e.g., Downs, "If 'Woman' Is Just an Empty Category, Then Why Am I Afraid to Walk Alone at Night?," 414, and "Reply to Joan Scott"; Gordon, review of *Gender and the Politics of History* and "Response to Scott," 853; and Hawkesworth, "Knowers, Knowing, Known," 555. Christine Stansell also raised cautions about Scott's proposed approach to history in "Response to Joan Scott." For a different engagement with Scott's methodological proposals that also calls for a clarification of what she sees as the status or possibility of approaches to more material aspects of history, such as economic or political structures, see Holt, "Experience and the Politics of Intellectual Inquiry.")

This book began as an attempt to bridge these two positions, in that it seeks to show in a historically grounded, concrete fashion how rape, a "real," material, physical act of violence, happened through language, was intensely symbolic, and was a product of, manifestation of, and participant in political discourse. Specifically I find that one cannot understand rape and other forms of sexual violence, and their political force during Reconstruction, without considering the discourses that invested that violence with meaning for its assailants as well as its victims. Thus this work fuses the methods and themes of cultural analysis with the practice of social history in order to explore both the history of rape and the history of citizenship and their mutual imbrication with contests over racial meanings. For thoughts on the intersection of race and gender as a historical question that were formative in my thinking early on, see Barkley Brown, " 'What Has Happened Here?,' " and Hewitt, "Compounding Differences."

36. Darlene Clark Hine has suggested just how unique this record is in "Rape and the Inner Lives of Black Women in the Middle West." Hine notes that "one of the most remarked upon but least analyzed themes in Black women's history deals with Black women's sexual vulnerability and powerlessness as victims of rape and domestic violence" and concludes that one of the reasons for this is black women's own practices of self-protecting silence on issues relating to sexuality and abuse. She calls this a "culture of

dissemblance" and proposes that it was conditioned by "rape and the threat of rape" as well as "pervasive stereotypes and negative estimations of the sexuality of Black women." Though black women's testimony during Reconstruction does not give us access to their "inner lives," it does suggest that the "alarm, . . . fear, . . . [and] Victorian sense of modesty" that Hine finds inhibited speaking about rape among later generations of African American women (migrants from the South to midwestern cities) was not universal in the years of Reconstruction among southern black women who had been slaves. On Hine's interpretation, and on how "this culture of dissemblance functioned in tension and in tandem with a tradition of testimony," in a study of African American political mobilization in protest against the rape of black women by white men during the civil rights era, see McGuire, " 'It Was Like All of Us Had Been Raped.' " Similarly, see Green, *Battling the Plantation Mentality*, chap. 3.

Catherine Clinton has also examined freedwomen's testimony about rape before federal officials in "Bloody Terrain" and "Reconstructing Freedwomen." Lisa Cardyn uses similar sources in "Sexualized Racism" in conjunction with contemporary studies of the psychological impact of sexual violence in order to analyze the trauma suffered by women who were raped and their communities. Finally, Laura F. Edwards has used local court records from Granville County, North Carolina, to study rape during Reconstruction. Black women's testimony about interracial rape here, though, is more rare than in congressional hearings and Freedmen's Bureau records. During the two decades following emancipation, Edwards found one black woman pressing charges against a white man for rape in Granville County's local court. See Edwards, *Gendered Strife and Confusion*, 198–217, esp. 208. See also Edwards, "Sexual Violence, Gender, Reconstruction."

37. On sexual violence suffered by African American women under slavery, see Jennings, " 'Us Colored Women Had To Go Through A Plenty' "; Clinton, "Caught in the Web of the Big House"; McLaurin, *Celia, a Slave*; Stevenson, *Life in Black and White*, 137–38, 236–40; Jacqueline Jones, *Labor of Love, Labor of Sorrow*, 20, 38–39; and Block, *Rape and Sexual Power in Early America*, 65–74, 100–101. Thomas Cobb, a student of antebellum slave law, could write in 1858 that rape was "an offense not affecting the existence of the slave"; see *Inquiry into the Law of Negro Slavery*, 90, and see discussion of this text in Hartman, *Scenes of Subjection*, 60 and chap. 3 in general. On the rape of enslaved women and the law, see also Wriggins, "Rape, Racism, and the Law"; McLaurin, *Celia, a Slave*, esp. chap. 6; Bardaglio, *Reconstructing the Household*, 64–69; Block, *Rape and Sexual Power in Early America*, 246; Hartman, *Scenes of Subjection*, 79; Higginbotham, "African-American Women's History and the Metalanguage of Race," 262–64, and *Righteous Discontent*, 190; and Hunter, *To 'Joy My Freedom*, 34. See also Sommerville, *Rape and Race*, in which the author affirms this reading, even though she questions widespread agreement that "females of color, especially slaves, were left unprotected by sexual assault statutes" (esp. 64–68; quotation on 64). Sommerville's evidence shows only rare instances wherein black women's experiences of sexual assault were heard in court, let alone in which they were in fact protected by rape statutes in the antebellum South, and none where enslaved women received legal redress for rape by white men.

And Sommerville concurs that the dominant representation within legal culture was that any coerced sex black women may have suffered did not represent a crime. See also Sommerville, "Rape Myth in the Old South Reconsidered," 493 n. 34.

Historians have also noted the extent to which poor white women were denied legal recognition of sexual violence against them as rape during the antebellum era, even when the accused rapist was a black man. See Bynum, *Unruly Women*, 109–10, 117–18; Sommerville, *Rape and Race*, "Rape Myth of the Old South Reconsidered," and "Rape Myth Reconsidered," esp. chaps. 3 and 4; and Hodes, *White Women, Black Men*, esp. chap. 3. Yet, Hodes in particular also explores the ways that rape charges against black men were often false and how black men were still vulnerable to charges of rape by white women of any class. See also Edwards, "Disappearance of Susan Daniel and Henderson Cooper," 369–70, and *Gendered Strife and Confusion*, esp. 198–202. It is important to note (and Edwards in particular does) that even if in practice rape laws were not implemented in the interests of all white women, as written in most southern states until the last years of the antebellum era they *represented* all white women as worthy of protection against rape and excluded black women from equivalent rights. In this way the law produced an ideology distinguishing between women by race and conflating those hierarchical racial distinctions with those between citizens and slaves.

38. See Hartman, *Scenes of Subjection*, chap. 3.

39. Jordan, *White over Black*, 151; White, *Ar'n't I a Woman?*, 27–61; Bynum, *Unruly Women*, esp. chap. 2.

40. *George (a Slave) v. the State*, 37 Mississippi 317 (October 1859). This case, now well studied, is also discussed in, e.g., Bardaglio, *Reconstructing the Household*, 67–68; Hartman, *Scenes of Subjection*, 96; and Sommerville, *Rape and Race*, 65–66.

41. *Alfred v. the State*, 37 Mississippi 296 (October 1859), also discussed in Hartman, *Scenes of Subjection*, 84–85.

42. See Hartman, *Scenes of Subjection*, chap. 3, and, for instance, Block, "Lines of Color, Sex, and Service," 143, and *Rape and Sexual Power in Early America*, chap. 2.

43. See also Block, "Lines of Color, Sex, and Service," 154–55. In a similar vein, Stephen Kantrowitz writes, "Slaves had no authority to name the actions of white men"; see "One Man's Mob Is Another Man's Militia," 68.

44. Block, "Lines of Color, Sex, and Service," 143 (quotation), and *Rape and Sexual Power in Early America*, 65–74, and 130–33 for criteria used by the law to determine if a "rape" had occurred.

45. This was the case, for instance, for Celia, an enslaved woman who murdered her master after five years of sexual abuse; see McLaurin, *Celia, a Slave*. Note also the silences surrounding sexual abuse in many slave narratives written by women, Mary Prince and Harriet Jacobs being the most well-known among them. See Prince, *History of Mary Prince*, and Jacobs, *Incidents in the Life of a Slave Girl*, both in Gates, *Classic Slave Narratives*, as well as analysis of the latter text in Block, "Lines of Color, Sex, and Service," 140–57, and *Rape and Sexual Power in Early America*, 68–73, and Hartman, *Scenes of Subjection*, 102–12.

46. On how a broad conceptualization of citizenship as identity and practice as well as legal status is useful to capturing histories of struggle over rights and recognition of individuals as members of the nation, see Glenn, *Unequal Freedom*, esp. chap. 2; Canning and Rose, "Introduction"; Fraser and Gordon, "Contract versus Charity"; Rogers Smith, *Civic Ideals*, 30–31; Yuval-Davis and Werbner, *Women, Citizenship, and Difference*; special issue of *Feminist Review* 57 (Autumn 1997), and in that issue esp. Yuval-Davis, "Women, Citizenship, and Difference," and Lister, "Citizenship."

47. Rogers Smith has described Reconstruction as the era of "the most extensive restructuring of American citizenship laws in the nation's history, apart from the adoption of the Constitution itself"; see Rogers Smith, *Civic Ideals*, chap. 10, quotation on 286. Other works that focus on citizenship as an important area of contest and transformation following emancipation include Cooper, Holt, and Scott, *Beyond Slavery*; Laurent Du-Bois, *Colony of Citizens*; Masur, "Reconstructing the Nation's Capital"; and Rebecca J. Scott, *Degrees of Freedom*. The notion that Reconstruction was an era of revolutionary change rejects the emphasis of some scholars of the period on continuity between antebellum and postbellum life. As Eric Foner has written, this scholarship "questioned whether anything of enduring importance occurred at all" during Reconstruction, and in the words of C. Vann Woodward, concluded "how essentially nonrevolutionary and conservative Reconstruction really was" (Woodward qtd. in Foner, *Reconstruction*, xxiii). For an overview of this literature, see Foner, "Reconstruction Revisited." The radicalism of Reconstruction seems indisputable, especially when perceived from the perspective of the experience of African Americans. For the first work to argue this, see W. E. B. DuBois, *Black Reconstruction*. See also, inter alia, Foner, *Reconstruction*, and Hahn, *Nation under Our Feet*.

48. Foner, *Reconstruction*, xxv.

49. Citizenship also, of course, distinguished women from men. During the antebellum period, although white women, and in certain times and places women of color, were legally recognized as citizens, they held few of the rights associated with that status. Most importantly, in almost all instances women could not vote. Neither, once married, could they generally own property in their own right (and thus were not free to contract for the distribution of that property or even their labor), and neither did they sit on juries or serve in the military. See Kerber, *Women of the Republic*, 139–55, and "Paradox of Women's Citizenship in the Early Republic," and Glenn, *Unequal Freedom*, 40–48. On the political implications of the fact that women could not be soldiers, see Kerber, "May All Our Citizens Be Soldiers and All Our Soldiers Citizens" and *No Constitutional Right to Be Ladies*; see the latter also on women's exclusion from jury service. Not only were some citizens unable to vote; voters were not necessarily citizens. In the early nineteenth century, many states granted suffrage to white male immigrants as long as they intended to seek naturalization. See Cott, "Marriage and Women's Citizenship," 1445.

50. This act of racial exclusion passed in Congress without objection or debate. See Cott, "Marriage and Women's Citizenship," 1444; Jacobson, *Whiteness of a Different Color*, 22; Rogers Smith, *Civic Ideals*, 159–60. Other "racial" groups were also excluded from

citizenship at different times in U.S. history. On Native American Indians, see, for instance, Kettner, *Development of American Citizenship*, 288–300. On legal prohibitions against Asians obtaining American citizenship, see, inter alia, Cott, "Marriage and Women's Citizenship," 1458–70, and Kerber, "Meanings of Citizenship," 843.

51. The supreme courts of Tennessee and North Carolina recognized the citizenship status of free African Americans, the latter court arguing that if a person was not a slave, then he or she was necessarily either a citizen or an alien, depending on place of birth; the law allowed no other status. See Kettner, *Development of American Citizenship*, 316–17.

52. Berlin, *Slaves without Masters*, 8, 190–91.

53. On northern states, see, e.g., Horton and Horton, *In Hope of Liberty*, 167–68, and Roediger, *Wages of Whiteness*, 56–59. See also Glenn, *Unequal Freedom*, 27–31.

54. Berlin, *Slaves without Masters*, 190–91. Interestingly, though, these changes were not unanimously supported by white delegates to both Tennessee's and North Carolina's constitutional conventions.

55. State courts justified limits on the rights of free African Americans by constructing legal categories that, though not as unfree as "slave," were far less free than "citizen." Black people were termed "wards," "strangers to our constitution," "a degraded race," and "a third class." The term endorsed by a justice of the supreme court of Arkansas in 1846, first articulated by the Kentucky state supreme court in 1820, was "quasi citizens or at least denizens." See Kettner, *Development of American Citizenship*, 313–21 (quotations from 320–21).

56. On the Dred Scott case, see ibid., 324–32, and Fehrenbacher, *Dred Scott Case*.

57. See Foner, *Free Soil, Free Labor, Free Men*, on the emergence of the Republican Party, and 292–93 on Republican opposition to the decision in *Dred Scott v. Sandford*.

58. Bates, "Citizenship," 383. See also Lucie, "On Being a Free Person and a Citizen by Constitutional Amendment," 355; Cott, "Marriage and Women's Citizenship," 1445. In this opinion, Bates argued that Justice Taney's opposite conclusion about the capacity of men of color to be citizens was not binding, because in this regard he ruled on a matter that was not, in fact, before the court ("Citizenship," 412–13). See also *Diary of Edward Bates*, 424. Bates, a conservative Whig and then Republican from Missouri, appeared in this opinion to be eager to limit the rights that would necessarily accrue to former slaves when and if they became citizens. He wrote,

> In my opinion, the Constitution uses the word citizen only to express the political quality of the individual in his relations to the nation; to declare that he is a member of the body politic, and bound to it by the reciprocal obligation of allegiance on the one side and protection on the other. And I have no knowledge of any other kind of political citizenship, higher or lower, statal or national, or of any other sense in which the word has been used in the Constitution, or can be used properly in the laws of the United States. The phrase "a citizen of the United States," without addition or qualification, means neither more nor less than a member of the nation. ("Citizenship," 383)

Bates also mocked a resolution proposed in the Indiana state legislature to "confer full rights of citizenship upon negroes" (the resolution was rejected), writing, "Five cents reward for a definition of the phrase 'full rights of citizenship'" (*Diary of Edward Bates*, 517). On Bates as a conservative candidate for the Republican presidential nomination in 1860 and on his support for compulsory colonization of free African Americans, see Foner, *Free Soil, Free Labor, Free Men*, 212–13, 270, 277.

Nancy Cott has argued that American citizenship has always been an ambiguous legal status as well as a historically varied social and political identity, one "delivered in different degrees of permanence and strength," and never "a definitive either/or proposition" but, rather, "a compromisable one" ("Marriage and Women's Citizenship," 1440–42). Linda Kerber has also explored how citizenship, rather than a "permanent and fixed" status, has historically been "contested, variable, fluid," most obviously so in moments of change and instability; see "Meanings of Citizenship," 833.

59. Congressional leaders agreed that this was so because the Thirteenth Amendment had not been intended to interrupt, as a critic of the act posited, "the right the husband had to the service of his wife." See Stanley, *From Bondage to Contract*, 55–60 (quotation on 57). See also Rogers Smith, *Civic Ideals*, 305–8, 580 n. 44, and Foner, *Reconstruction*, 243–45.

60. Bates, "Citizenship," 383. Similarly, in congressional debates on the Civil Rights Act of 1866, Illinois senator Lyman Trumbull told his colleagues, "The granting of civil rights does not, and never did in this country, carry with it . . . political privileges." White women's disfranchised citizenship was held up as the model for what was being proposed for former slaves and all African Americans. See Cott, "Marriage and Women's Citizenship," 1449–51. On an understanding of citizenship as guaranteeing civil but not political rights as mainstream opinion within the Republican Party before 1860, see Foner, *Free Soil, Free Labor, Free Men*, 290–91. On more diverse opinion among white Republicans on this question expressed in the debates leading to the Fourteenth Amendment, see William E. Nelson, *Fourteenth Amendment*, 125–33.

61. *CCC*, 10. For a discussion of this gathering, the Convention of Colored Citizens of the State of Arkansas, see Chapter 3.

62. On widespread, though contested, support for woman suffrage among African Americans in the years just following the end of slavery, see Barkley Brown, "To Catch the Vision of Freedom" and "Negotiating and Transforming the Public Sphere." See also Terborg-Penn, *African American Women in the Struggle for the Vote*, 23–35, and Martha Jones, *All Bound Up Together*. Other scholars of the period have also noted the striking presence of black women at political events and their role in political mobilization. See, e.g., Holt, *Black over White*; Hahn, *Nation under Our Feet*, esp. 175–76, 185, 227–28; Hunter, *To 'Joy My Freedom*, 32; Saville, *Work of Reconstruction*, 169–70; and Finley, *From Slavery to Uncertain Freedom*, 42.

63. This is the argument made by Barkley Brown in "To Catch the Vision of Freedom" and "Negotiating and Transforming the Public Sphere."

64. Nor did Republican leaders' position reflect popular usage of the term "citizen" at the

time that often presumed it to be synonymous with "voter." Webster's dictionary from both 1828 and 1850 defined a citizen as "a person, native or naturalized, who has the privilege of exercising the elective franchise." Another dictionary from 1860 affirmed that the label applied to "an inhabitant of a republic who enjoys the rights of a citizen or a freeman, and who has a right to vote for public officers." (Dictionary definitions, from Webster's *American Dictionary of the English Language* [1850] and Worcester's *Dictionary of the English Language* [1860], cited in Cott, "Marriage and Women's Citizenship," 1447. Kerber quotes Webster's from 1828 in "May All Our Citizens Be Soldiers and All Our Soldiers Citizens," 93.) These definitions corresponded with the common use of the term "citizen" in the popular press to refer only to white men. See, for instance, "A Terrible Murder in Broad Daylight—The Victim Robbed," *Avalanche*, January 7, 1866, 3, which reports the murder of a "citizen" by a "negro"; "Dallas County Convention," *WAG*, December 31, 1867, 3, which reports that "the citizens of Dallas County are opposed to negro rule"; and "An Important Question," *WAG*, January 14, 1868, 2, which opposes federal reconstruction policy and asserts that "whether these states will reconstruct their governments is left to their citizens and the negroes to determine." From the perspective of protest, this definition was reflected in Frederick Douglass's 1853 depiction of free African Americans as "aliens . . . in our native land," because they were so often denied equal civil and political rights (qtd. in Blight, *Frederick Douglass' Civil War*, 13).

65. See, e.g., Rable, *But There Was No Peace*, 59; Foner, *Reconstruction*, 261–63. Steven Hahn places the beginning of the "great turning point of Reconstruction" earlier, in white northern concern about the violence against freedpeople and white Unionists during the Christmas insurrection scare of the fall and winter of 1865. He argues that it was thus the political action of rural freedpeople—in the form of the circulation of rumors of federal plans for land distribution to former slaves, a political practice borrowed from their experiences as slaves and to which white violence was a reaction—that made the shift of the Republican consensus toward black male suffrage possible. This shift had been sought by black urban leaders and Radical Republicans in Washington but was not something they could achieve on their own. See Hahn, *Nation under Our Feet*, chap. 3, esp. 157–59. The Memphis Riot was also a reaction to African American political action, in this case to urban freedpeople claiming access to public space under the same terms as other free people (see Chapters 1 and 2). This suggests that urban as well as rural freedpeople's mobilization and pursuit of a meaningful freedom led to the establishment of black male suffrage.

66. Foner, *Reconstruction*, 271–80. See also Rogers Smith, *Civic Ideals*, 312.

67. Both gendered rhetoric and violence have been shown in a recent historiography to have been central factors in the overthrow of Republican-dominated southern state governments at the end of Reconstruction, in the defeat of attempted biracial political coalitions at the state level in the post-Reconstruction period, and in the turn-of-the-century disfranchisement campaigns that ended black male suffrage and helped to solidify Jim Crow segregation. See, for instance, Kantrowitz, *Ben Tillman* and "One

Man's Mob Is Another Man's Militia"; Dailey, *Before Jim Crow* and "Limits of Liberalism in the New South"; Gilmore, *Gender and Jim Crow*; and Edwards, *Gendered Strife and Confusion*, chap. 6. Kantrowitz emphasizes that the violence of Reconstruction and post-Reconstruction politics was aimed not only at black political actors but also at southern whites who strayed from the program of "white supremacy" pursued by the region's elites, a form of violent coercion with a long history in the South that had also been key to sustaining a system of slavery.

68. Dailey, "Limits of Liberalism in the New South," 90. Dailey is speaking here specifically about the contention that the political, and thus public, empowerment of black men somehow threatened the patriarchal, and thus private, power of white men.

69. See Richardson, *Death of Reconstruction*.

70. On this process, see, for instance, Kousser, *Shaping of Southern Politics*; Kantrowitz, *Ben Tillman*; Gilmore, *Gender and Jim Crow*, esp. chaps. 4–5; and Dailey, *Before Jim Crow*. See also Rogers Smith, *Civic Ideals*, 346, and Foner, *Reconstruction*, 604.

71. Tennessee did not hold a convention, being the one former Confederate state not included in the provisions of the Reconstruction Acts. This was because by this point Tennessee's Republican state government had ratified the Fourteenth Amendment—the only former Confederate state to do so—and then quickly secured congressional approval of its readmission to the Union. Its state legislature also passed a bill enfranchising black men just weeks before the first Reconstruction Act became law. On the particulars of Tennessee's postwar history, see, e.g., Patton, *Unionism and Reconstruction in Tennessee*; Thomas Benjamin Alexander, *Political Reconstruction in Tennessee*; and Foner, *Reconstruction*, 261, 276. For other state convention proceedings, see, e.g., *Journal of the Proceedings of the Constitutional Convention of the State of Mississippi*.

72. On the transformations and tensions in white gender relations that resulted from the Civil War and Reconstruction, see, e.g., Faust, *Mothers of Invention*, " 'Trying to Do a Man's Business,' " and "Altars of Sacrifice"; Whites, *Civil War as a Crisis in Gender*; Edwards, *Gendered Strife and Confusion*, esp. chaps. 3 and 4; and Bercaw, *Gendered Freedoms*, esp. chap. 2. These studies do not point to contention among white men and women over racial politics and violence.

73. For a fascinating glimpse into the thoughts of an elite white southern woman, and specifically into her oscillation between criticizing the ideas and actions of her husband in regard to relationships first with slaves and then with freedpeople and then embracing similarly racist views and taking similarly oppressive action, see Burr, *Secret Eye*.

74. See Parsons, "Midnight Rangers," 824–27, 829–30; Hodes, *White Women, Black Men*, 159; Cardyn, "Sexualized Racism," 683 n. 21. See also Harcourt, "Who Were the Pale Faces?," on the appeal of the Klan to at least some white women, including one who wrote from Tennessee of it to her parents, "the good people here . . . think it a great institution, and say that they have been a great protection to the Country" (see 49, 50, 65). Unlike for the nineteenth century, white women have been shown in recent studies to have been central actors in white supremacist movements of the twentieth century. See MacLean, *Behind the Mask of Chivalry*, and Blee, *Women of the Klan*.

75. Hartman, *Scenes of Subjection*, 7.

76. Eric Foner makes a similar point in regard to literature that focuses on continuity of economic structure between the pre– and post–Civil War South. Those for whom "the drama of emancipation recedes into insignificance in the face of the survival of plantation agriculture and the continuing exploitation of the black laborer," Foner suggests, "would do well to recall that to blacks, emancipation appeared as the fundamental watershed in their lives" (*Nothing but Freedom*, 7). See also Foner, "Reconstruction Revisited." On this point, in a study of post-Reconstruction interracial political alliances, see Dailey, *Before Jim Crow*, esp. 2–10, and of white supremacist movements in South Carolina during and after Reconstruction, Kantrowitz, *Ben Tillman*, esp. 3. For a similar perspective on experimentation in matters of race from the end of slavery until the end of the nineteenth century, see Woodward, *Strange Career of Jim Crow* and *Thinking Back*, 82–83.

77. In his classic work on segregation, C. Vann Woodward argues that even in the 1890s, when the heady days of Reconstruction had long passed, such a rigid and transparently racist and illiberal outcome seemed unimaginable. See Woodward, *Strange Career of Jim Crow*.

Chapter 1

1. Louis Hughes, *Thirty Years a Slave*, 95, 131–34, 139–46, 172–76, 176–87; quotations from 131, 139, 134, 132, 172, 186. Louis and Matilda had good reason to be afraid. William McGee, a relative of their owner living with them in Mississippi during the war, shot and killed at least one and perhaps two slaves or former slaves who ran away and then returned to the plantation to retrieve family members. See ibid., 154, and *Memphis Morning Post*, January 18, 1866, 4. On Hughes, see also Ash, *Year in the South*.

2. Louis Hughes, *Thirty Years a Slave*, 176, 187. By "the citizens of Memphis," Hughes may have been referring simply to previous residents of Memphis from before the war, regardless of race, or he may have adopted the then-common usage of "citizens" to refer to whites. He would, however, later use the term to describe himself as an antebellum resident of Memphis to an agent of the Freedmen's Bureau: "We . . . told him that we were citizens of Memphis until the fall of Fort Pillow and Donelson, when our master had run us off, with a hundred other slaves, into Mississippi" (176–77).

3. Ibid., 176.

4. See Berlin, Fields, Glymph, Reidy, and Rowland, *Destruction of Slavery*, 1–56.

5. Louis Hughes, *Thirty Years a Slave*, 187.

6. Jane Dailey has found a similar phenomenon in the post-Reconstruction period in contests between black and white Virginians over street etiquette. On "how black men and women in the New South enunciated their claim to civic equality through their behavior in urban public spaces," see *Before Jim Crow*, 12, chap. 4, and "Deference and

Violence." On the role of activities in public space in the production of meaning, see also Mary P. Ryan, *Women in Public*.

7. For evidence of either the encouragement or tolerance of black people sharing public life with whites in Memphis, see, inter alia, testimony of Mary Grady, 186–88; Molly Hayes, 186; and Rev. Ewing O. Tade, 89–90, in *MR&M*.

8. For examples, see below. By conservative newspapers, I am referring to the papers, both Whig and Democrat before the Civil War, that opposed Reconstruction policies of the Republican Party after the war. In the early years of Reconstruction in Memphis, anti-Reconstruction, anti-Republican white southerners referred to themselves as "Conservatives" (see, for instance, Sigafoos, *Cotton Row to Beale Street*, 48, and letter from Unionist William H. Fitch Jr., September 23, 1865, to John Eaton, editor of the city's Republican newspaper, referring to the "so-called 'Conservatives,'" in subseries 1, series 1, Eaton Collection, University of Michigan). The papers used here representing the conservative position in Memphis are the *Memphis Daily Appeal*, the *Memphis Daily Argus*, and the *Memphis Daily Avalanche*. For a contemporary characterization of the different newspapers in Memphis, see testimony of Rev. Ewing O. Tade, *MR&M*, 91. For the use of newspaper titles to identify political positions, and different brands of conservatism in Memphis, see testimony of Dr. J. N. Sharp, *MR&M*, 158. The press in Memphis was highly partisan in ways that affected not just editorials but reporting of local, state, and national news as well. The conservative papers regularly attacked the Republican paper, the *Memphis Daily Post*, and vice versa. For a discussion of this style of journalism in the nineteenth-century South in general, see Osthaus, *Partisans of the Southern Press*.

9. For examples documenting this conduct, see below.

10. Parks, "Memphis under Military Rule," 56.

11. See Rable, *But There Was No Peace*, 59; Foner, *Reconstruction*, 261–63; *Harper's Weekly*, October 20, 1866; and *New York Tribune*, October 26, 1866. See also discussion of Hahn, *Nation under Our Feet*, in n. 65 of the Introduction, and Chapter 2.

12. Berkeley, *"Like a Plague of Locust,"* 8. Berkeley argues that Memphis developed from a "town" into a "city" between 1850 and 1860.

13. In 1860, 400,000 bales changed hands in Memphis's cotton markets; see Sigafoos, *Cotton Row to Beale Street*, 31.

14. The slave advertisements were counted by Frederic Bancroft for 1857; see Bancroft, *Slave Trading in the Old South*, 250–51.

15. Ibid., 264. Forrest was a prominent figure in Memphis history, becoming a Confederate general notorious for the murder of black Union soldiers at Fort Pillow and eventually a leader of the early Ku Klux Klan. See Chapter 5.

16. Quotations from a facsimile of several classified advertisements in the *Memphis Eagle and Enquirer*, from April 29, 1857, in Bancroft, *Slave Trading in the Old South*, photo between pp. 254 and 255.

17. See Robinson, "In the Aftermath of Slavery," 26–28. I owe special thanks to the late Professor Robinson for sharing this invaluable study of Reconstruction-era Memphis

with me. See also Berkeley, " 'Like a Plague of Locust,' " 47–48, and *"Like a Plague of Locust,"* 5 and 16, table 1; and Capers, *Biography of a River Town,* 110.

The African American population in Memphis was significantly smaller proportionally than that of other southern cities at the time. See Wade, *Slavery in the Cities,* 326–27. Although the black population in Memphis had increased somewhat over the ten years preceding the Civil War, the white population had increased at a greater rate, reducing the percentage of the city's population who were African American, from 28 percent of the total population in 1850 to 17 percent in 1860 (see Berkeley, *"Like a Plague of Locust,"* 16, table 1). The increase in white population was due largely to foreign immigration (see Capers, *Biography of a River Town,* 107; Berkeley, *"Like a Plague of Locust,"* 4, 14–17; and Tracy, "Immigrant Population of Memphis," 72). Slave populations decreased during the antebellum years in many southern cities, making 1860 a low for most. Memphis's decline from 28 to 17 percent shows the city even eleven years before the Civil War to have had a much smaller black community than others, due in part to the fact that Memphis was at that time a new city, young relative to the southern urban areas to its east. See Wade, *Slavery in the Cities,* 326–27, for population statistics from other cities. For the causes of decreasing urban slave populations, see Goldin, *Urban Slavery in the American South,* 1, 9–10, 123–24.

18. See Robinson, "In the Aftermath of Slavery," 26–28; Berkeley, " 'Like a Plague of Locust,' " 47–48, and *"Like a Plague of Locust,"* 16, table 1; and Capers, *Biography of a River Town,* 110. Charleston's free black population comprised 8 percent of the total African American population in that city in 1860; in Mobile, it was 10 percent; in Richmond, 18 percent; and in Savannah, 8 percent. See Wade, *Slavery in the Cities,* 326–27, for antebellum urban population statistics. One historian has suggested that the small size of Memphis's free black population (Nashville's free black population in 1860 was 719, over three and one-half times as large as that in Memphis) was due to the city's role as a major slave market, into which many free blacks may have been kidnaped. This practice, if it did occur, may have led others to keep their distance from the city. See Capers, *Biography of a River Town,* 110. See also, Berkeley, *"Like a Plague of Locust,"* 5 and 16, table 1. The following advertisement from March 1860 for Nathan Bedford Forrest's business suggests the possibility of slave trader complicity with such a practice: "500 NEGROES WANTED. I WILL PAY MORE THAN ANY OTHER PERSON, for No. 1 NEGROES, suited to the New Orleans market" (qtd. in Bancroft, *Slave Trading in the Old South,* 263 n). Bancroft refers to an instance where Washington Bolton, one of the proprietors of Bolton, Dickens & Co., sold as a slave a free black man who was apprenticed to him. The man thus sold managed to acquire a lawyer and secure his freedom. See Bancroft, *Slave Trading in the Old South,* 253.

19. Article III of the city charter, "Of the Board of Mayor and Aldermen—Their Powers, etc.," gave the city government the authority to "pass such laws as may be necessary to control and regulate free negroes and slaves"; see *Digest of the Charters and Ordinances of the City of Memphis, from 1826 to 1860,* 189.

20. See Robinson, "In the Aftermath of Slavery," 26–28; Berkeley, *"Like a Plague of Locust,"* 19–20; and England, "Free Negro in Antebellum Tennessee." See also *Digest of the Ordinances of the City Council of Memphis, from the Year 1826 to 1857*, 122–26, and *Digest of the Charters and Ordinances of the City of Memphis, from 1826 to 1860*, 85–91, 361–67.

21. "Free Negroes and Slaves," in *Digest of the Ordinances of the City Council of Memphis, from the Year 1826 to 1857*, 122–25; and in *Digest of the Charters and Ordinances of the City of Memphis, from 1826 to 1860*, "Markets," 269; "Misdemeanors and Nuisances," 272–73, 276; "Of Slaves, Free Negroes and Mulattoes," 362–64; and "Free Negroes and Mulattoes," 365–67.

22. For the various ordinances referred to in this paragraph, see "Free Negroes and Slaves," in *Digest of the Ordinances of the City Council of Memphis, from the Year 1826 to 1857*, 122–25; and in *Digest of the Charters and Ordinances of the City of Memphis, from 1826 to 1860*, see "Markets," 269; "Misdemeanors and Nuisances," 272–73, 276; "Of Slaves, Free Negroes and Mulattoes," 362–64; and "Free Negroes and Mulattoes," 365–67.

23. "Station House Register, Beginning the First Day of October, 1858," MSCA. Louis Hughes's biography demonstrates how much slaves could and did move about the city before the war. Yet, his account also shows the tight network slaveowners established to track slaves even in the hustle and bustle of urban and even interstate commerce, undermining some of the liberty and anonymity the city appeared to offer. See Louis Hughes, *Thirty Years a Slave*, 80–90, 101–5.

24. Kathleen Berkeley found that while slaves were dispersed throughout the city, 44.4 percent of free black people lived in Ward 7 (along with 25 percent of the city's white population) in 1860. (This ward was not part of the city in 1850, being one of two wards comprising South Memphis, a separate town that was incorporated into Memphis in 1857.) These conclusions led Berkeley to question the applicability of Richard Wade's thesis about urban slave life to Memphis. Wade in his early study of urban slavery found that slaves frequently hired out their own time and lived on their own, often among free blacks in segregated neighborhoods, where they found possibilities for creating their own public culture and social life. See Wade, *Slavery in the Cities*; Berkeley, " 'Like a Plague of Locust,' " 47–48, and *"Like a Plague of Locust,"* 27–28, table 5b; and Hooper, "Memphis, Tennessee," 155 n. 78.

25. Berkeley, *"Like a Plague of Locust,"* 19–20.

26. Quarles, *Negro in the Civil War*, 195; Hooper, "Memphis, Tennessee," 175.

27. Webb, "Black Soldiers of Civil War Left Impact on City." I am indebted to Mr. Webb, director of the Institute of African American History in Memphis, Tennessee, for sharing a copy of this article with me and for a copy of his unpublished manuscript "United States Colored Troops, 1863–1867." Fort Pickering was originally the name of a town established just south of Memphis along the Mississippi River, but this town was soon incorporated into South Memphis, another separate town, and then both were incorporated into the city of Memphis in 1857 (see Berkeley, *"Like a Plague of Locust,"* 40 n. 4, and Capers, *Biography of a River Town*, 124–26). When Union forces occupied the

city, they constructed a riverfront fort near the old Fort Pickering (maps from the period suggest the fort actually sat a bit north of the old town) and called it, too, Fort Pickering. See, e.g., Sherman, *Memoirs of General W. T. Sherman*, 314.

28. Population estimates for Memphis just after the war are inconsistent, but all demonstrate a dramatic growth in the proportion of African Americans in the city. In addition to 10,995 African Americans in Memphis, the city census found a decrease in Memphis's white population of more than 2,000 since the start of the war. See Robinson, "In the Aftermath of Slavery," 67–68; Berkeley, *"Like a Plague of Locust,"* 120–21; and "Census of the City of Memphis," Main Public Library, Memphis, Tennessee.

In his 1957 dissertation, Ernest Hooper estimated that "by the end of the war the number of Negroes, including those in freedmen's camps just outside the city, probably approached twenty thousand. . . . Many of these Negroes returned to plantations, and there were, perhaps, fewer than fourteen thousand Negroes and twenty-one thousand whites in the city in the summer of 1866." He also cites an August 24, 1865, article in the *Argus* reporting that there were 17,000 freedpeople in Memphis. See Hooper, "Memphis, Tennessee," 132.

29. Hooper, "Memphis, Tennessee," 135–36.

30. Ibid., 133; Cimprich, *Slavery's End in Tennessee*, 41.

31. Parks, "Memphis under Military Rule," 39; Cimprich, *Slavery's End in Tennessee*, 41–42; Hooper, "Memphis, Tennessee," 133.

32. Robinson, "In the Aftermath of Slavery," 57; Capers, *Biography of a River Town*, 166–67; Hooper, "Memphis, Tennessee," 133. According to Robinson, in Memphis only 879 voters, of an eligible electorate of 4,500, turned out to vote in the referendum on the constitutional amendment, and only 6 of these voters were opposed. From this low turnout the *Memphis Bulletin* concluded, "Clearly . . . a large majority of the people of Memphis are utterly opposed to the proceedings of the recent state convention" of unionists that drafted the amendment (February 24, 1865, cited in Robinson, "In the Aftermath of Slavery," 57; see also Foner, *Reconstruction*, 44).

33. On the Civil Rights Act, see, e.g., Foner, *Reconstruction*, 250–51, and Stanley, *From Bondage to Contract*, 55–59.

34. Robinson, "In the Aftermath of Slavery," 72–74, 93–94, 104–9; BM&A, book 11, pp. 133, 135–37, 140, 142–45, 150, 153, 155, 157, MSCA; Hooper, "Memphis, Tennessee," 136–38; Berkeley, " 'Like a Plague of Locust,' " 105–6, 121–24, 150 n. 23; Walker, "This Is White Man's Day," 34–35.

35. This is an extrapolation from the labor experiences recorded among the 535 freedmen and freedwomen in contraband camps on the outskirts of Memphis in March 1863 showing that 438, or 82 percent, had worked as field hands. See John Eaton to Professor Henry Cowles, March 13, 1863, document #H8832, microfilm reel 193, AMA. See also Berkeley, *"Like a Plague of Locust,"* 106, table 14.

36. Freedwomen testifying before the congressional committee investigating the Memphis Riot often stated their occupation. See testimony of Hannah Robinson, 193; Elvira Walker, 193; Frances Thompson, 196; Lucy Hunt, 201; Hannah George, 231; and Ann

George (Hayes), 258, in *MR&M*. See also testimony of Julia Yates, MC, 331, and statement of Rose Morris, FBC, 349, both in *MR&M*. Of freedwomen in contraband camps in Memphis in March 1863, nearly 23 percent had skills as cooks or seamstresses. Another 10 percent had experience as laundresses. See John Eaton to Prof. Henry Cowles, March 13, 1863, document #H8832, microfilm reel 193, AMA. See also Berkeley, *"Like a Plague of Locust,"* 106, table 14.

37. See, for instance, testimony of Taylor Hunt, 100; Austin Cotton, 101; William Coe, 102; George Jones, 103; Adam Lock, 115; Henry Alexander, 117; Frank Lee, 141; Joseph Walker, 143; Mary Walker, 196; James E. Donahue, 199; Henry Bond, 199; Celia Simmons, 220; Anthony Simmons, 221; Mat. Wardlaw, 233; Hannah Savage, 234; and George Williams, 259, all in *MR&M*. See also Lovett, "Memphis Riots," 12–13. Freedmen working as painters attempted to form an association in February 1866. See *Memphis Post*, March 1, 1866, cited in Hooper, "Memphis, Tennessee," 153.

38. See, for instance, statements of George and Sarah Armor, *MR&M*, 328–29; affidavits of Kit Temple, 336; Nelson Robinson, 337; Robert Bruster, 342; John Lane, 348; Richard Lane, 349; and Mose Harrison, 354, all in FBC, *MR&M*. See also testimony of Elvira Walker, *MR&M*, 194.

39. See testimony of Matilda Howley, 189, and Mary Black, 201, in *MR&M*.

40. See testimony of Cynthia Townsend, *MR&M*, 162; her husband and son were "seven miles in the country at work" while she lived in the city. See also statement of Elizabeth Burns, February 9, 1866, entry #3545, BRFAL.

41. See testimony of Mollie Davis, 200; Ellen Brown, 200; Lucy Smith, 196; and Frances Thompson, 196–96, in *MR&M*. See also statement of Elizabeth Burns, February 9, 1866, entry #3545, BRFAL.

42. See testimony of Celia Simmons, 220, and Anthony Simmons, 221, in *MR&M*, and statement of Amanda Olden, April 30, 1866, entry #3545, BRFAL.

43. Albert Harris had been raised in Virginia along with the woman he married in Memphis, after years of separation. See his testimony, *MR&M*, 62. For a report of forty freed couples marrying at the same time in one contraband camp and seventy-five in another on "Thanksgiving Day," see Report from Lucinda Humphrey, Camp Fiske, August 20, 1863, document #H8851, microfilm reel 193, AMA. See also Quarles, *Negro in the Civil War*, 289.

44. Affidavits of Andy Rawlins and Private Jacob Bell, both in entry #3545, BRFAL.

45. See, for instance, Aura R. Green vs. Spencer Page, August 7, 1865; Eliza Robinson vs. Wm Painter, May 18, 1866; and Leanna Douglass vs. Neville Douglass, December 28, 1865; and for other domestic disputes, Archer Thompson and Lizie Merick, August 16, 1865; Adeline Drivers vs. William Henry, January 30, 1866; and Almira Hollville vs. Bob Hollville, January 30, 1866, all from Docket of Freedmen's Court, Register of Complaints, entry #3544, BRFAL. See also Benjamin Woodward, U.S. Sanitary Commission, to Major Reeves, Provost Marshal of Freedmen, September 1865, entry #3545, BRFAL.

46. Quotation and other information from testimony of Tony Cherry, *MR&M*, 184. See also, from *MR&M*, testimony of A. N. Edmunds, 140; David T. Egbert, 122; Dr. S. J.

Quimby, 104–5; Mary Grady, 187–88; Captain A. W. Allyn, 245; and Exhibit No. 2, Report from Captain Arthur W. Allyn, 358.

47. Testimony of Tony Cherry, *MR&M*, 184. In 1862, military authorities had closed all saloons in Memphis, but in response to petitions from the city's Board of Mayor and Aldermen, saloons were later reopened under strict licensing requirements. These establishments, along with the grocery stores that also sold liquor, were prohibited from selling to "enlisted men." See BM&A, book 11, pp. 5, 91–92, 210, 249, 453–54, MSCA. See also "General Orders—No. 119" and "Selling Liquor to Soldiers," *Appeal*, December 22, 1865.

48. Testimony of Mary Grady, *MR&M*, 186–88.

49. Tucker, *Black Pastors and Leaders*, chap. 1, esp. 3–5; Berkeley, *"Like a Plague of Locust,"* 119–20.

50. Report of L. Humphrey, May 15, 1863, document #H8844; see also "Dear Missionary," from L. Humphrey Hay, February 10, 1864, document #H8861, microfilm reel 193, AMA. David Tucker writes, "A great many black Memphians worshiped in church far into the morning hours, frequently scandalizing whites by what appeared to be their wild heathenish dances as the brothers and sisters 'got happy' and 'got religion' " (*Black Pastors and Leaders*, 14).

51. Tucker, *Black Pastors and Leaders*, 8; Berkeley, " 'Colored Ladies Also Contributed,' " 182; Berkeley, *"Like a Plague of Locust,"* 127–30.

52. Tucker, *Black Pastors and Leaders*, 3, 6–8, 17–18; Berkeley, *"Like a Plague of Locust,"* 119–36.

53. See Ewing O. Tade to Corresponding Secretary, August 1, 1865, document #H8965, microfilm reel 193, AMA.

54. Berkeley, *"Like a Plague of Locust,"* 161–64; testimony of Orrin E. Waters, 259–60, and Rev. H. N. Rankin, MC, 313, in *MR&M*.

55. Testimony of Benjamin Runkle, *MR&M*, 277. On "John Brown's Body," see Nudelman, *John Brown's Body*, and Paul Finkelman, *His Soul Goes Marching On*.

56. Kathleen Berkeley argues that the small black elite in Memphis "took pains to avoid any activity or institution that would bring them into close proximity with the lower classes"; see Berkeley, " 'Like a Plague of Locust,' " 184–95, 174, 176.

57. Berkeley, *"Like a Plague of Locust,"* 130–36; Hooper, "Memphis, Tennessee," 154–55.

58. This picnic was postponed due to rain and was rescheduled for May 3, 1866. It is likely that it was never held, given that the Memphis Riot began on May 1. See "City News," *MDP*, May 1, 1866, 8. On Church's saloon and his $750 worth of property destroyed during the Memphis Riot, see testimony of Robert Church, *MR&M*, 226–27. On Joseph Caldwell founding the Young Men's Literary Society, see "Colored Literary Society," *MDP*, March 25, 1866, 8. Caldwell testified after the Memphis Riot that his hall and its contents of furniture and other items, burned by rioters, was worth $2,000; see affidavit of Joseph Colwell (Caldwell), FBC, *MR&M*, 346.

59. "Colored Literary Society," March 25, 1866, 8; "Young Men's Literary Society," April 8,

1866, 8; and "Meeting of Young Men's Literary Society," April 11, 1866, 8, all in *MDP*. See also Hooper, "Memphis, Tennessee," 170.

60. Testimony of Rev. Ewing O. Tade, *MR&M*, 93.

61. "Meeting of Colored People," *MDP*, April 10, 1866, 8.

62. Freedwomen and freedmen opened accounts for themselves and for black church, benevolent, and social organizations. See Bond, " 'Till Fair Aurora Rise,' " chap. 4, and Berkeley, " 'Colored Ladies Also Contributed,' " 191–92, and *"Like a Plague of Locust,"* 127–29.

63. Tucker, *Black Pastors and Leaders*, 26; *Memphis Bulletin*, June 7, 1864, and *Argus*, May 25, 1865, cited in Hooper, "Memphis, Tennessee," 171–72. On Emancipation Day and other commemorations of the end of slavery by African Americans into the early twentieth century, see Blight, *Race and Reunion*, 365–78.

64. Abbott, *For Free Press and Equal Rights*, 37, 120.

65. Eaton to Rev. George Whipple, December 2, 1864, document #H8914, microfilm reel 193, AMA.

66. For endorsement of Eaton's plans to create a "Unionist" paper in Memphis from leading white Republicans in the city, see letter from William H. Fitch Jr. et al., September 23, 1865, in subseries 1, series 1, Eaton Collection, University of Michigan.

67. Abbott, *For Free Press and Equal Rights*, 169, 215 n. 13; Frank B. Williams, "John Eaton, Jr.," 291–319; Walter J. Fraser Jr., "Lucien Bonaparte Eaton," 20–45.

68. See, for instance, Docket of Freedmen's Court, Register of Complaints, entry #3544, BRFAL, as well as numerous newspaper accounts.

69. Mary P. Ryan, *Civic Wars*, 49. Ryan argues that this customary right of access to the bustling street life of urban centers was crucial to the development of democratic practices and cultures in the nineteenth-century United States.

70. Berkeley, *"Like a Plague of Locust,"* 27–31, tables 5a–e; Waller, "Community, Class, and Race," 235.

71. Tracy, "Immigrant Population of Memphis," 72; Gleeson, *Irish in the South*, 35.

72. Berkeley, *"Like a Plague of Locust,"* 27–31, tables 5a–e; Waller, "Community, Class, and Race," 235. Both elites in Memphis at the time of the riot and scholars subsequently often mistakenly characterized residents of South Memphis as poor Irish immigrants and explained the Memphis Riot as the result of competition between these immigrants and newly arriving freedpeople over jobs. See discussion of this in Waller, "Community, Class, and Race," 234–35, 243 n. 7, and Walker, "This Is White Man's Day," 46–47.

73. A far smaller portion of neighborhood residents sat at the two ends of the class spectrum, with 10 percent reporting positions as lawyers and cotton merchants and another 10 percent as unskilled laborers. Information on the white residents of South Memphis comes from "Community, Class, and Race," 235, Waller's detailed demographic analysis of this neighborhood in her study of the Memphis Riot, and from "Census of the City of Memphis," Main Public Library, Memphis, Tennessee.

74. Waller, "Community, Class, and Race," 237. Waller argues that even policemen and

firemen, who earned only small salaries, were part of an upwardly mobile group. "Policemen most often came from the ranks of unskilled or semi-skilled laborers and their jobs
must have provided them with an increased sense of prestige and economic security, if
not prosperity" (ibid.). On one grocery owner in South Memphis named Callahan, an
Irishman whom a neighbor suspected of having lived in Memphis "a good while," see
testimony of Sophia Grey, *MR&M*, 114–15.

75. This is the term used by Barrington Walker to describe Irish immigrants who obtained
relatively high-status jobs as police ("This Is White Man's Day," 38).

76. Testimony before the congressional committee investigating the riot revealed the close
proximity between white and black homes. See, for instance, testimony of Cynthia
Townsend, 162; Molly Hayes, 186; Harriet Armour, 177; William Coe, 103; A. N. Edmunds, 140; Frank Lee, 141; and Sophia Grey, 114, all in *MR&M*. See also affidavits of
George Armour and Sarah Armour, both dated May 23, 1866, in entry #3545, BRFAL,
and from the *MDP*, "A fire broke out in the brick building, situated on the alley back of
Third street and between Gayoso and Main . . . which was entirely destroyed. The
building was occupied by Fritz Pfembert, as a saloon and residence, and by four other
families (one white and three colored) to whom he sublet different rooms" ("Fire,"
January 30, 1866, 4). Proximity did not necessarily mean familiarity. The congressional
committee asked one white woman to describe the appearance of a neighboring black
girl who was killed by the rioters, and the woman replied, "Indeed, I never took any
particular notice. I never knew one from the other" (testimony of Jennette Swells,
MR&M, 113).

77. See witnesses' reports of residence in *MR&M*.

78. Testimony of Lucy Tibbs, *MR&M*, 160.

79. See, e.g., Louis Hughes, *Thirty Years a Slave*; Meriwether, *Recollections of Ninety-Two
Years*.

80. Kathleen Berkeley has argued that in Memphis "the Civil War paved the way for a
middle class revolution in municipal politics; Reconstruction made that shift in leadership complete" ("'Like a Plague of Locust,'" 298–99). Although antebellum elites
returned to economic prominence in the city at the war's end, they did not regain
political control of the municipality until January 1879, when the state legislature re-
voked the city's charter and installed a governing commission (ibid., 302). That these
elites were strong critics of the new political officials is evident from their testimony
before the congressional committee investigating the Memphis Riot, which they blamed
in part on city officials' incompetence.

81. Waller, "Community, Class, and Race," esp. 240; Walker, "This Is White Man's Day," 37–
38; Gleeson, *Irish in the South*, 138, 167–68.

82. Testimony of B. G. Garrett, *MR&M*, 326–28. See also activities of the police committee
in BM&A, book 11, MSCA.

83. Parks, "Memphis under Military Rule," 39.

84. "A true and perfect list of the duly elected and regularly appointed officials of the City of

Memphis that were in the service of said City during the months of April and May, 1866" (attached inside the back cover of BM&A, book 11, MSCA; see also *MR&M*, 369); Gleeson, *Irish in the South*, 178; Holmes, "Underlying Causes of the Memphis Race Riot of 1866," 206–7.

85. For details, see below.

86. See BM&A, book 11, pp. 316, 405, 419–20, MSCA. Creighton also allegedly claimed to have substantial influence with the city's Board of Mayor and Aldermen and was once overheard saying that he "was able to wind the Council around his finger" ("City Council," *Appeal*, November 16, 1865, 3). This may have referred to failed efforts of the council to remove Creighton from his post when he himself was charged with murder. He was eventually acquitted of the charges when it was determined that it was a case of justifiable homicide. See, from the *Appeal*, "Recorder Creighton Shoots Ex-Policeman McCormack," November 11, 1865, 3; "Died" and "The Late Shooting Affray," November 12, 1865, 3; "The Examination of John C. Creighton" and "Recordership," November 14, 1865, 3; "Meeting of the Board of Aldermen" and "Recorder's Court," November 15, 1865, 3; "Trial of J. C. Creighton," November 29, 1865, 3; "Criminal Court," November 30, 1865, 3; "Criminal Court," December 1, 1865, 3; "Criminal Court," December 2, 1865, 3; "The Creighton-McCormack Case," December 3, 1865, 3; "Criminal Court," December 6, 1865, 3; and "Discharged," December 7, 1865, 3.

87. Testimony of Henry Porter, *MR&M*, 167.

88. Parks, "Memphis under Military Rule," 56. General Washburn was the brother of Elihu Washburne (though they spelled their last names differently), who would also come to Memphis in a capacity authorized by the federal government, in the latter's case as the chairman of the congressional committee investigating the Memphis Riot. See Introduction and Chapter 2.

89. BM&A, book 11, pp. 409, 422; Robinson, "In the Aftermath of Slavery," 56–57; Parks, "Memphis under Military Rule"; Berkeley, " 'Like a Plague of Locust,' " chaps. 3 and 6; Gleeson, *Irish in the South*, 167, 176, 235 n. 28.

90. See BM&A, book 11, pp. 695–97, MSCA, for the order from the superintendent of the Freedmen's Bureau in Memphis to the board establishing the power of the provost marshal.

91. Louis Hughes, *Thirty Years a Slave*, 176; Waller, "Community, Class, and Race," 235.

92. Michael Walsh to Judge Creighton, April 21, 23, 1866, entry #3541, BRFAL.

93. S. S. Garrett to Major William L. Porter, February 22, 1866, entry #3541, BRFAL. See also S. S. Garrett to Mr. M. H. Reilly, City Jailor, January 27, 1866, and S. S. Garrett to Captain John N. Slatey, February 2, 1866, both in entry #3541, BRFAL.

94. S. S. Garrett to Ben G. Garrett, February 10, 1866, entry #3541, BRFAL.

95. See, for instance, affidavit of Alex. McQuarters, FBC, *MR&M*, 343–44. McQuarters describes stopping at a "public house" to read the newspaper.

96. The conservative press also expressed open hostility to federal and military officials. Brig. Gen. Benjamin Runkle, superintendent of the Freedmen's Bureau for Memphis,

testified to the congressional committee investigating the Memphis Riot that he was "called a pimp in the public press" as well as insulted in the city's streets. See Runkle's testimony, *MR&M*, 278.

97. See, for instance, "The Veto: Its Reception and Excitement on the Subject," *Appeal*, April 1, 1866, 2, and the *Memphis Argus* qtd. in "A Specimen of Moderate Southern Sentiment," *Memphis Weekly Post*, April 28, 1866, 6. For indirect critiques of the Civil Rights Act, see, from the *Appeal*, "Colored Criminals," April 11, 1866, 3, and "Arrests," April 12, 1866, 3. This act was passed just weeks before the Memphis Riot. See Chapter 2.

98. See Foner, *Reconstruction*, 243.

99. Reprinted in "A Specimen of Moderate Southern Sentiment," *Memphis Weekly Post*, April 28, 1866, 6.

100. See Mary P. Ryan, *Women in Public*, 68–76, for a discussion of discourses of disorder and danger in other nineteenth-century cities.

101. "The Riot of Crime in Our Midst," *Appeal*, November 14, 1865, 3.

102. *Digest of the Charters and Ordinances of the City of Memphis, from 1826 to 1867*, 334–36. See, from the *Appeal*, "Meeting of the Board of Mayor and Aldermen," December 6, 1865, 3 (a petition from "a number of citizens" requesting that a "house of ill fame" in their neighborhood be closed); "An Excellent Step," January 5, 1866, 3 (applauding police raid on numerous houses of prostitution); and "Police Court," January 7, 1866, 3 (applauding police arrests of the keepers and inmates of several "houses of ill fame"). From BM&A, book 11, see August 19, 1862, 5 (ordinance passed making keeping house of ill fame a misdemeanor and setting fine); August 2, 1864, 446 (Provisional Council authorizes the mayor to act in conjunction with military authorities to "control and mitigate the evils of prostitution within the limits of the City"); and June 19, 1866, 944 (a petition from "sundry citizens" asking for the closing of a house of ill fame on Gayoso Street). For early actions by military authorities to close houses of prostitution and to restrict the actions of prostitutes on the streets, see Robinson, "In the Aftermath of Slavery," 55; Parks, "Memphis under Military Rule," 35; and Capers, *Biography of a River Town*, 160. While the city was under martial law in 1864 and 1865, prostitutes were required to obtain a license from authorities and to undergo weekly medical examinations. See James B. Jones Jr., "Municipal Vice," 35.

103. See "Concert Saloons," *Memphis Weekly Post*, April 28, 1866, 8, and from the *Appeal*, "The 'Free and Easy' Nuisance," November 8, 1865, 3; "An Increasing Evil," January 2, 1866, 3; "Concert Saloons Again" and "Meeting of the Board of Mayor and Aldermen," January 3, 1866, 3; and "Arrest of a Notorious Character," January 9, 1866, 3. On the history of concert saloons, see Long, *Great Southern Babylon*, chap. 2.

104. "The Riot of Crime in Our Midst," *Appeal*, November 14, 1865, 3. See also the "Local Matters" column of almost any issue of the *Appeal* from November 1865 through May 1866.

105. "Dangerous Vicinity," *Appeal*, December 1, 1865, 3, and "Riot of Crime in Our Midst," *Appeal*, November 14, 1865, 3. See also, from the *Appeal*, "Recorder's Court and City Jail," November 12, 1865, 3; "The Poor of Our City and the Approaching Winter,"

November 17, 1865, 3; "Noisy Characters," December 6, 1865, 3; and "Probable Fatal Injury," April 10, 1866, 3. From the *Argus*, see "Police Court," May 10, 1866, 3. In American, Latin American, and European cities in the nineteenth century, municipal governments often responded to visible shifts in gender norms and the racial or ethnic makeup of urban populations accompanying economic change by seeking to eliminate or regulate prostitution. See, for instance, Findlay, *Imposing Decency*, chap. 3; Long, *Great Southern Babylon*; Stansell, *City of Women*, chap. 9; and Walkowitz, *Prostitution and Victorian Society*.

106. Chapter XIV, Article 1, *Digest of the Charters and Ordinances of the City of Memphis, from 1826 to 1867*, 336. On the history of the legal concept of vagrancy, its racial and gender dynamics during Reconstruction, and its effects particularly for African American women, see Kerber, *No Constitutional Right to Be Ladies*, chap. 2; see also Stanley, *From Bondage to Contract*, chap. 3. The author of "The Riot of Crime in Our Midst" lamented the "straggling on street corners, and in and around saloons" of "thieves and vagrants" and wondered aloud why these problems were allowed to continue. "Is the vagrant law a dead letter?" he asked. See *Appeal*, November 14, 1865, 3. The association of people, particularly working-class people, using public space for pleasure as opposed to productive labor with "immoral" or criminal activity and even sexual "danger" was revealed in the Memphis city ordinance where vagrancy, gambling, selling liquor on Sundays, keeping or working in a house of prostitution, distribution of pornography, nudity, and cross-dressing were listed under one act as misdemeanors, termed "offenses affecting good morals and decency." See Chapter XIV, Article 1, *Digest of the Charters and Ordinances of the City of Memphis, from 1826 to 1867*, 334–36. This combination of vagrancy with other acts as "offenses affecting good morals and decency" began in May 1860 when sections concerning "Vagrants, Gamblers, Prostitutes, etc." were added to an ordinance so titled. See *Digest of the Charters and Ordinances of the City of Memphis, from 1826 to 1860*, 271, 274–76. The city ordinance compilation for 1857 had prohibited vagrancy under an act concerning "Beggars and Vagrants," without reference to other illegal activities. See *Digest of the Ordinances of the City Council of Memphis, from the Year 1826 to 1857*, 85.

107. "Our Chief of Police and Vagrancy," *Appeal*, November 17, 1865, 3.

108. *Argus*, February 3, 1866, 2.

109. When this would-be planter continued, "The shops are overflowing with them, squandering on themselves and each other what little money they have acquired, in everything that strikes their fancy," he unwittingly revealed that perhaps all freedpeople were not unemployed, given that they had cash to spend. See "The Labor Question in the Old South," *Appeal*, February 28, 1866, 1. This planter's interpretation of what he observed was most likely a misreading of the community support networks and perhaps gendered divisions of labor of the freed community.

110. Robinson, "In the Aftermath of Slavery," 98–99. See also numerous affidavits collected by the provost marshal of freedmen, esp. entry #3545, BRFAL.

111. Quotations are from "The Labor Question in the Old South," *Appeal*, February 28, 1866, 1.

112. "Obtaining Money Fraudulently," *Argus*, April 28, 1866, 3.

113. See, for instance, Foner, *Reconstruction*, 155–70; Nieman, *To Set the Law in Motion*, chap. 2; Schwalm, *Hard Fight for We*, esp. chap. 6; Stanley, *From Bondage to Contract*, esp. 122–30; and Powell, *New Masters*, 84–85.

114. See "Circular," reprinted in *Appeal*, November 8, 1865. About this action, Armstead Robinson writes, "The practical effect of such an order was to confine Freedmen to rural plantations where they were under the strict supervision of planters and to deny them the right to move about unless they explained their reasons to white men before leaving" ("In the Aftermath of Slavery," 112). On "freedom to travel" as an implicit right of free people openly violated by the application of vagrancy laws to freedpeople after the Civil War, see Kerber, *No Constitutional Right to Be Ladies*, 58.

115. Tillson to Clark, August 18, 1865, BRFAL, and *Argus*, August 23, 1865, as cited in Robinson, "In the Aftermath of Slavery," 104–5.

116. Major William Gray to Captain W. T. Clark, Memphis, Tennessee, September 13, 1865, qtd. in Hardwick, " 'Your Old Father Abe Lincoln Is Dead and Damned,' " 114; see 114–16 for a discussion of Freedmen's Bureau policies on vagrancy in Memphis.

117. Dudley to Clark, September 29, 1865, BRFAL, as cited in Robinson, "In the Aftermath of Slavery," 108–9. Such policies were the end result of many internal battles within the Freedmen's Bureau leadership, but ultimately the decision alienated freedpeople from the bureau, as it sent members of their community back to the labor exploitation and violence that they had just recently escaped. See Robinson for a detailed discussion of this process.

118. "The Freedmen's Bureau," *Appeal*, 3. On the need for black men and women to be engaged in "work that it was possible to *observe*" created by the application of vagrancy statutes after the Civil War, see Kerber, *No Constitutional Right to Be Ladies*, 56.

119. P. D. Beecher to General Runkle, Memphis, Tennessee, May 18, 1866, qtd. in Hardwick, " 'Your Old Father Abe Lincoln Is Dead and Damned,' " 114.

120. Brevet Brigadier General N. A. M. Dudley to Captain Clark, Memphis, Tennessee, September 30, 1865, qtd. in ibid.

121. "We Are Rejoiced," *Avalanche*, January 9, 1866, 2.

122. The Third U.S. Colored Heavy Artillery was often praised by the Republican press and military authorities for the talent of its band, which played frequently in the public square in the city. See BM&A, book 11, September 6, 1864, 482 (at this time the city was under military rule, and the board constituted the governing body of the provisional government). When this band gave one of its concerts in a downtown park just days before the Memphis Riot, "some [white] ladies who had been attracted by the music, on discovering the color and position of the players, uttered some derogatory remarks, elevated their noses and left in disgust" ("Music in the Park," *Memphis Weekly Post*, April 28, 1866, 8). On military processions in Memphis, see Cimprich, *Slavery's End in Tennessee*, 110.

123. See testimony of J. S. Chapin, 192, and Captain A. W. Allyn, 245, in *MR&M*.

124. Testimony of James Helm, 217; William J. Pearce, 218; and Captain A. W. Allyn, 248, in *MR&M*. It was the policy of the Union Army for officers to take away any pistols found in the possession of black soldiers; see testimony of William J. Pearce, 218, and Captain Allyn, 248, in *MR&M*.

125. "The fact is, when colored soldiers are about [the rebels] are afraid to kick colored women, and abuse colored people on the Streets, as they usually do," wrote Rev. Henry McNeal Turner to the secretary of war concerning violence between a soldier and a white civilian in Columbus, Georgia, much like the many incidents that occurred in Memphis (reprinted in Berlin, Reidy, and Rowland, *Black Military Experience*, 757). The *Appeal* revealed the empowering effect of having black troops nearby in one of their many editorials condemning the federal presence in Memphis:

> All our accounts establish the indisputable *fact*, that, in those parts of the country farthest removed from the operations of the Bureau—most remote from the influence of garrisons of negro troops, there the black labor of the country has settled itself down into habits of greatest industry, there is least of bickering and bad understanding between the whites and the blacks. . . . Wherever there is no Bureau, and no shiny-buttoned soldiers of his own color to make him, by contrast, discontented with his lot of unostentatious labor, the sensible good negro learns to look his situation fairly in the face, and settles down with some good white man that he knows will deal with him fairly and honestly, to patient industry for the support of his family. ("Why Any Bureau at All?," *Appeal*, March 3, 1866)

Private Isaac Warren was relieved from duty as an orderly in the offices of the provost marshal of freedmen on March 1, 1866, for having "been greatly careless in allowing a person to escape—a girl fined for dis[orderly] conduct." Perhaps soldiers not only assisted freedpeople in enforcement of the laws, but also aided them in avoiding the law's punishment; see letter to Captain Kaplan from S. S. Garrett, Provost Marshal of Freedmen, March 1, 1866, entry #3541, BRFAL.

126. See "Fifty-Fifth Regiment U.S.C.I.," *Memphis Morning Post*, January 20, 1866. Ira Berlin, Joseph Reidy, and Leslie S. Rowland write, "To the extent that black soldiers relished their role in the army of occupation, white Southerners loathed it. More than any other post-bellum figure, the black soldier represented the world turned upside down: the subversion of slavery, the destruction of the Confederacy, and the coming of a new social order that promised to differ profoundly from the old" (*Black Military Experience*, 735). See also Hardwick, " 'Your Old Father Abe Lincoln Is Dead and Damned.' "

127. *Avalanche*, January 4, 1866, 2.

128. Testimony of General George Stoneman, *MR&M*, 50. See also "Letter from Grenada, Mississippi," November 10, 1865; "Mississippi," November 28, 1865; "Conditions of Reconstruction," November 28, 1865; and "Letter from Mississippi," November 30, 1865, all in *Appeal*. See *Avalanche* of January 3, 1866, 2 (no title), for an objection to a bogus report in the *New York Herald* that "the editors of Memphis" had petitioned the presi-

dent to retain the black troops in the city. And see " 'Good Faith,' 'Conciliation,' and Premature Reconstruction. A Loyal Southern's View of the Times," in the *Weekly Republican*, March 22, 1866, 1, for a mocking description of former Confederates' newfound "loyalty" and their demands for "conciliation," imitated as "The army must be disbanded, military rule is past endurance, especially must the colored troops be withdrawn, they will not be reconciled so long as 'nigger' soldiers are kept among them."

A white doctor living in Memphis testified before the congressional committee that there were fewer problems with "the deportment . . . of these negro soldiers when on the street" since General Stoneman took command in Memphis, as "he broke up the practice of allowing negro soldiers to walk through the streets with their arms when not on duty" (testimony of Dr. Robert White, *MR&M*, 164). Frederick Hastings, a first lieutenant of the Third U.S. Colored Heavy Artillery stationed in Memphis, reported that only four soldiers from each of twelve companies were allowed out of Fort Pickering on any given day, suggesting efforts to restrict the number of off-duty black Union soldiers in the streets at one time (testimony of Hastings, *MR&M*, 207–8). Actions such as these on the part of military authorities to restrict the number of African American soldiers freely moving about the city and their appearance in public when armed suggest their efforts to respond to white objections to the visibility and presence of empowered and armed black men.

129. Bederman, " 'Civilization,' the Decline of Middle-Class Manliness, and Ida B. Wells's Antilynching Campaign," 6. Referring to the antebellum era, Stephen Kantrowitz writes, "Violence and restraint were the two faces of the Southern master class" ("Two Faces of Domination," 96). In his work on the role of cultural constructions of white manhood in southern politics and violence, Kantrowitz demonstrates how in the antebellum South in particular, white men lived surrounded by the extensive violence of their peers. Most perceived such violence as honorable, even manly, if and when unleashed under the proper circumstances. Conditions warranting the release of a man's violent impulses included a slight or insult to oneself or one's family or disobedience on the part of subordinates and dependents, the latter norm stemming directly from the collective aggression necessary on the part of white men to sustain a system of slavery. Within this white masculine logic, violence from those perceived to be subordinates was illegitimate by definition. See also "One Man's Mob Is Another Man's Militia" and *Ben Tillman*; Bercaw, *Gendered Freedoms*, 84–85; and Wyatt-Brown, *Southern Honor*, esp. 43, 352–61. On the complex working of these cultural norms regarding violence in the context of antebellum courts of law, see Edwards, "Law, Domestic Violence, and the Limits of Patriarchal Authority," esp. 742, 753–67. On nineteenth-century middle-class notions of masculinity in general, see Rotundo, *American Manhood*; Rosenberg, "Sexuality, Class, and Role in 19th-Century America," 221–54; and John Starrett Hughes, "Madness of Separate Spheres," 67–78 (esp. 57, 60). In this last article, the author suggests that the southern version of white masculinity discussed by Bertram Wyatt-Brown for the antebellum years began to take on characteristics of northern conceptions in the postwar years (see esp. 66). See also Horton and Horton, "Violence, Protest, and Identity," 80–

81, for a discussion of the prevalence of self-assertion and aggression in the variety of constructions of masculinity circulating in nineteenth-century America.

130. Testimony of James H. Swan, *MR&M*, 178.

131. Testimony of Rachel Dilts, *MR&M*, 67, 68. Dilts was describing a confrontation between a group of policemen and soldiers outside her front door the day before the Memphis Riot. See also testimony of P. G. Marsh, *MR&M*, 169. For another report of black soldiers being taunted in the streets, see testimony of Dr. D. P. Beecher, *MR&M*, 145. Other whites denied the frequency of the events thus reported; see testimony of Dr. J. N. Sharp, 157; J. S. Chapin, 192; and William H. Pearce, 218, in *MR&M*.

132. Testimony of Dr. Robert McGowan, *MR&M*, 127.

133. On police violence and false arrests of soldiers and other black men, see Brigadier General Benjamin P. Runkle, Superintendent, Freedmen's Bureau, "Report concerning the late riots at Memphis, Tenn.," in entry #3529, Reports relating to the Memphis Riot, BRFAL. See also "Report," 6, and testimony of Dr. J. N. Sharp, 156; Dr. D. P. Beecher, 145; James E. Donahue, 199; William H. Pearce, 218, all in *MR&M*.

134. Testimony of Brig. Gen. Benjamin Runkle, *MR&M*, 277.

135. Testimony of James E. Donahue, *MR&M*, 198.

136. "Negro Soldiers," *Appeal*, November 10, 1865, 4.

137. William Jericho, Clerk of Chief of Police, to Major A. T. Reeves, Provost Marshal of Freedmen, October 15, 1865, entry #3545, BRFAL.

138. William H. Pearce, captain of the Third U.S. Colored Heavy Artillery, the black regiment in Memphis thought to have the fiercest feud with the city police (see Brigadier General Benjamin P. Runkle, Superintendent, Freedmen's Bureau, "Report concerning the late riots at Memphis, Tenn.," in entry #3529, Reports relating to the Memphis Riot, BRFAL), described the behavior of black soldiers when outside Fort Pickering as "orderly and good." He also said, "Their conduct has been soldierly and, in general, excellent. I have never had any trouble with my men. I had over one hundred and fifty men under my command at a time, and they were obedient to orders, well disciplined and respectful" (testimony of William H. Pearce, *MR&M*, 218). See also testimony of J. S. Chapin, *MR&M*, 192, for a refutation of the claims that soldiers engaging in public drinking often harassed or abused white Memphians. Chapin, a white man from Wisconsin who moved to Memphis to sell insurance, described the "deportment of the negro soldiers on the street" as "as orderly and quiet as white soldiers." He said of one of the three instances in which he encountered drunk soldiers, "I saw perhaps a dozen . . . colored soldiers, under the influence of liquor; they were noisy, having sport, having 'a good time' generally, but entirely among themselves. They were troubling no one." He added, "I never saw colored soldiers so drunk but once that I could not go up to them and talk to them as a Christian man and stop their noise at once. That once I went up to a crowd and one of them was so drunk that he came up to me, and put his arms right round me to hug me." Minerva Hewitt, a white woman who claimed that she had not observed the conduct of many black soldiers because she lived north of South Memphis, nonetheless added in her relatively neutral testimony about the Memphis Riot that the

black soldiers she had seen were "more [quiet and orderly] than other soldiers. I've never been molested or seen any one molested by them at all. Every one I've seen has been respectful; always been so to myself and family" (*MR&M*, 135).

139. On white male drinking culture, see Ownby, *Subduing Satan*, 50–51. Ownby writes, "Drinking and drunkenness were the most popular recreations in Southern towns. Men drank while enjoying other recreations or drank as their sole recreation, drank at large gatherings or in small groups. But few drank in the home" (50).

140. "Cold Blooded Murder on South Street: A White Man Deliberately Shot Down by a Band of Lawless Negro Soldiers," *Appeal*, December 20, 1865, 3. See also "Selling Liquor to Soldiers," *Appeal*, December 22, 1865, 2, which suggests that a military order forbidding the sale of liquor to soldiers "strikes at the root of much of the disorder which has lately prevailed." On military authorities' efforts to restrict soldiers' access to liquor, see n. 47 above.

141. Testimony of Thomas J. Durnin, *MR&M*, 225.

142. Exhibit No. 2, Captain Allyn's Report, *MR&M*, 358.

143. "Another Outrage By Negroes," *Appeal*, February 15, 1866, 3.

144. See the following reports in the *Appeal* of alleged criminal activity of African American Union soldiers: "Negro Outrage," November 7, 1865, 3; "Negro Soldiers," November 10, 1865, 4; "Robbery," November 17, 1865, 3; "Garrotted," November 30, 1865, 3; "Attempted Robbery," December 1, 1865, 3; "Shot by a Negro," December 14, 1865, 3; "Robbery," December 17, 1865, 3; "Cold Blooded Murder on South Street," December 20, 1865; "Robbery by Negro Soldiers," December 21, 1865, 3; "Another Dastardly Outrage," January 7, 1866; "Outrages by Negro Soldiers," February 3, 1866; "Another Outrage by Negroes," February 15, 1866, 3; "Inquest" and "More Negro Outrages," April 17, 1866. See also Captain Walker to Captain W. W. Deane, July 21, 1865, entry #3545, BRFAL.

145. "Depredations on the Horn Lake Road—A Negro Beat to Death by a Gang of Negro Soldiers," *Appeal*, January 14, 1866, 3. See also "Interesting to the Citizens of South Memphis," *Appeal*, February 27, 1866, 3, which asserts that "for many months the citizens of South Memphis have been annoyed by depredations of negro troops."

146. "A Terrible Murder in Broad Daylight—The Victim Robbed," *Avalanche*, January 7, 1866, 3. The *Appeal* also reprinted reports of armed black soldiers being responsible for crime in other cities. On November 17, 1865, the *Appeal* reprinted a story from the *New Orleans Delta* claiming that "Negro soldiers, armed and insolent roam over the whole country, infest public roads and streets of the city by day and night, perpetrating robberies with impunity, and murder where resistance is offered" (2). See also concerning Louisville in the *Appeal*, "Policemen Attacked by Negroes," November 23, 1865, 1.

147. "Robbery," *Appeal*, December 17, 1865, 3.

148. Armstead Robinson found that during a two-month period in 1865, the percentage of those arrested in Memphis who were African American was lower than their representation in the overall population (27 versus 40 percent), from which he concludes that while some freedpeople were probably engaged in crime, they were in no way responsible for the alleged crime wave supposedly overtaking Memphis just after emancipa-

tion. Robinson also found that 40 percent of freedpeople arrested were charged with stealing, the most common offense, and that "a large number of the Blacks arrested for larceny were women caught stealing food and clothing." See Robinson, "In the Aftermath of Slavery," 77, and Recorder's Court Docket, January 1865 to February 1865, MSCA.

149. "The Murder of J. W. Hanks," *Appeal*, December 20, 1865, 3.

150. "Untrue," *Appeal*, December 21, 1865, 3. General Stoneman responded to the numerous accusations that soldiers were committing crimes with orders for an investigation and by expressing his suspicion that many freedmen were wearing the uniform of the Union Army while not actually being enlisted, as they either had no other clothes on discharge from the army or bought or stole the uniforms from actual soldiers. It was these men, not actual enlisted men, Stoneman speculated, who were casting dishonor on the military. See "A Good Order," February 27, 1866, 2; "Interesting to the Citizens of South Memphis," February 27, 1866, 2; and "Effects of General Stoneman's Order," March 2, 1866, 3, all in *Appeal*.

151. These reports appeared in the *Bulletin* and the *Argus*. An equally misleading story was carried in the *Commercial*, but this paper did not suggest that the murdered man had been a soldier. All three papers reported the man's name as Sam Evans, though the murder victim's name was, in fact, Tom Waller. See Captain T. A. Walker to Captain W. W. Deane, July 21, 1865, entry #3545, BRFAL. The editor of the *MDP* expressed his frustration at the constant fabrication or at least exaggeration of reports of crimes committed by freedpeople in the conservative press in this item:

> A BIT OF AN "OUTRAGE"—On Jefferson street, yesterday, a "white" man and a negro had an altercation about some matter or other, when the former, who was slightly intoxicated, struck the latter in the face. The negro, thus attacked, replied by calling the "white" man hard names, and the "white" man rejoined by shooting at the negro. Fortunately, he was so drunk as not to be able to fire straight, and his shot effected no injury.
>
> We expect to hear a "nigger outrage" manufactured out of this occurrence, The "niggers," of course, may be kicked, cuffed, bruised and beaten, but they must never reply. (*MDP*, January 20, 1866, 4)

The meaning of the quotation marks around "white" in this article is difficult to discern. Perhaps they were meant to critique the practice of the conservative press of asserting that anyone in conflict with a freedperson was a "white" man, either ignoring that they, too, might have been African American or, in attempting to emphasize race over class, ignoring that they may have been "rowdy" or from the "lower sorts."

152. In 1863, women made up over 40 percent of the 535 adults in the contraband camp in Memphis; see John Eaton to Prof. Henry Cowles, March 13, 1863, document #H8832, microfilm reel 193, AMA. Jacqueline Jones, *Labor of Love, Labor of Sorrow*, 74, found that single black women were generally unable to support themselves and their children in agriculture just after the war and thus were more likely than men or married women

to migrate to urban areas. See also Hunter, *To 'Joy My Freedom*, on African American women constituting the majority of migrants to Atlanta both during and after the war.

153. On negative portrayals of freedwomen in the press, see also Clinton, "Bloody Terrain," 325–26, and "Reconstructing Freedwomen," 313–14.

154. Statement of Lizzie Howard, July 26, 1865, entry #3545, BRFAL. A freedman fled from this same plantation after he, too, was beaten by Robert Bond. See statement of Burnell, July 26, 1865, entry #3545, BRFAL.

155. Eliza Jane House reported to the bureau that she feared returning to collect her clothing, as James House threatened to kill her if she ever came back; see statement of Eliza Jane House, August 15, 1865, entry #3545, BRFAL. Jane Coleman also fled to Memphis after her employer Benjamin Coleman repeatedly abused her; see statement of Jane Coleman, August 26, 1865, entry #3545, BRFAL.

156. Statement of Ellen Clifton, August 3, 1865, entry #3545, BRFAL. See also statement of Mary Rodgers, August 15, 1865, entry #3545, BRFAL.

157. For instance, Mary Ann asked the provost marshal's office for "protection [to] be sent with me after my effects"; see statement of Mary Ann, July 31, 1865, entry #3545, BRFAL. See also statement of Lizzie Howard, July 26, 1865, and statement of Elizabeth Jones, July 27, 1865, both in entry #3545, BRFAL.

158. That freedwomen's use of soldiers to assist them in claiming possessions from the plantations of former owners or employers, and the arming of black Union soldiers in general, had an impact on the consciousness of conservative whites in Memphis is suggested by a story recounted in the *Appeal*. The event described occurred in Mobile, Alabama. Nonetheless, the Memphis paper was "particularly desirous of calling attention" to it, "as it is only a fair sample of what we may expect to experience here during the present condition of affairs." In Mobile, a freedwoman had returned to the house of her former employer to collect her clothing, accompanied by "a party of negro soldiers." In a confrontation that followed between this company, the white residents of the house, and an army officer who interceded on their behalf, the soldiers were asked under whose authority they acted. The report alleged that "one of them slapped his gun and replied—'by this authority'" ("Outrageous," *Appeal*, November 8, 1865, 3). Given the style of reporting in Memphis's partisan press, it is as likely that the soldier did not utter these words as that he did. Nonetheless, that this story was circulating in the conservative public sphere suggests that freedwomen's use of black Union soldiers for protection was triggering a hostile response from whites in Memphis.

159. See numerous affidavits in entry #3545, BRFAL. The extensive record of conflict over wages at this time most likely reflects the turmoil of the first planting season following the end of the Civil War. It may also, though, merely mirror the opening of the Freedmen's Court in Memphis in July 1865. That many of the freedpeople making complaints shared last names with those accused of abuse or violation of contract reflects the fact that many owners attempted to keep their former slaves laboring for them on their lands throughout the process of emancipation by promising wages. It also reflects the tensions in these new labor relations between former masters and former slaves. A Freedmen's

Bureau agent reported as follows on labor conditions in the rural areas surrounding Memphis in the summer of 1865: "The general condition between the Freedmen and the employers is very bad. The owners of the large plantations have frequent meetings where they make resolutions to enslave the Freedmen in some future time by agreeing not to hire a colored man, only to their former slaves [sic] that if anybody hires Freedmen the employers as well as the employees are threatened with death" (C. W. Wedenstact (?) to Major A. T. Reeves, July 31, 1865, entry #3545, BRFAL).

160. Statement of Hannah Biby, August 2, 1865, entry #3545, BRFAL. See also statements of Sophia Morton, July 10, 1865, and Abraham Taylor, August 1, 1865, both in entry #3545, BRFAL.

161. Statement of Betsy Robinson, August 3, 1865, entry #3545, BRFAL.

162. Betsy Robinson vs. James A. Robinson, December 1, 1865, Docket of the Freedmen's Court, Records of the Provost Marshal of Freedmen, Register of Complaints, July 1865 to June 1866, entry #3544, BRFAL. Susan Brooks lost a similar charge against her employer, Doctor Easters: "The plaintiff having left defendant without cause whereby he was damaged in making his crop, it is not considered that she is entitled to compensation" (Susan Brooks vs. Doct. Easters, entry #3544, BRFAL).

163. See statement of Amy Covington, August 10, 1865, as well as statement of Abraham Taylor, August 1, 1865, in entry #3545, BRFAL. Mary Davis also sought the aid of the Freedmen's Bureau in the return of her children and in securing compensation for their labor. For the previous two years, planter Arthur Davis, presumably her former owner, had refused to let the children join their mother in Memphis. The provost marshal ordered that the children be delivered to Mary Davis, but there is no further mention of compensation in the record. See statement of Mary Davis, December 13, 1865, entry #3545, BRFAL.

164. Statement of Ellen Clifton, August 3, 1865, entry #3545, BRFAL. See also statement of Mary Rodgers, August 15, 1865, entry #3545, BRFAL, and the endorsement on statement of Elizabeth Jones, July 27, 1865, entry #3545, which names Thomas Jones of the Eleventh U.S. Colored Infantry, presumably family with whom she had settled in Memphis. That Eliza Jane House gave the bureau an address in Memphis where she could be found indicates that she made the freed community in Memphis her home for at least a while after fleeing abuse in the countryside. See statement of Eliza Jane House, August 15, 1865; see also statements of Sophia Morton, July 10, 1865, and Abraham Taylor, August 1, 1865, all in entry #3545, BRFAL.

165. Statement of Mary Ann, July 31, 1865, entry #3545, BRFAL.

166. Statement of Lucy Williams, August 9, 1865, entry #3545, BRFAL. See also Bercaw, *Gendered Freedoms*, 44, on the "extensive network" among freedpeople that assisted their migration to cities.

167. Tucker, *Black Pastors and Leaders*, 8.

168. Berkeley, " 'Like a Plague of Locust,' " 165.

169. Few freedpeople ever actually received rations from the bureau even when they were available. Only 3.1 percent of Memphis's black population relied on the Freedmen's

Bureau for support before funds were cut off in late 1865. Forty-four percent of relief given out by the bureau in Memphis went to whites. See Berkeley, " 'Like a Plague of Locust,' " 170, and " 'Colored Ladies Also Contributed,' " 189.

170. Berkeley, " 'Colored Ladies Also Contributed,' " 182. I do not know how many of these societies existed before the Memphis Riot in May 1866. Berkeley describes the time period from 1866 to 1874 and does not specify pre- and post-riot organization among freedwomen. She finds evidence of 220 African American organizations in Memphis in these years by examining records of deposits in the Freedmen's Savings and Trust Company Bank. Sixty-four of these organizations, or nearly 30 percent, were autonomous women's groups. While all sixty-four societies could not have been formed as early as 1866, certainly the spirit and energy of organization demonstrated by these numbers was beginning to take form.

171. The conclusion about the class makeup of freedwomen's organizational leadership is Kathleen Berkeley's; see Berkeley, " 'Colored Ladies Also Contributed,' " 193–94.

172. Statement of Catherine Martin, July 31, 1865, entry #3545, BRFAL.

173. Fisher was convicted and fined $30; see Salena Jones vs. Gustavis Fisher, August 1, 1865, Docket of Freedmen's Court, entry #3544, BRFAL. (Sentences by the Freedmen's Bureau Court, as well as the city's Police Court, were almost always fines. If a defendant was unable to pay a fine, he or she was then imprisoned and forced to labor long enough to work off the amount required. In the case of freedpeople, the bureau also often leased their labor to plantation owners in the surrounding countryside.) Miles, on the other hand, was acquitted. Apparently Mrs. Hill, Susan Hill's "employer," intervened with the Freedmen's Court on behalf of her employee's assailant, convincing the court that "there is no ground for action against Mr. Miles." See Susan Hill vs. H. B. C. Miles, December 1, 1865, Docket Freedmen's Court, entry #3544, BRFAL.

174. Michael Walsh to Ira Moore, June 11, 1866, Letters Sent, January 1866 to June 1866, entry #3541, BRFAL.

175. Letter to Lieutenant J. S. Turner, Assistant Provost Marshal of Freedmen, from Lieutenant S. S. Garrett, Provost Marshal of Freedmen, February 23, 1866, in entry #3545, BRFAL.

176. Statement of Betty Maywell, December 5, 1865, entry #3545, BRFAL. Perhaps facing similar recalcitrance, the provost marshal wrote to David Ingram and threatened the following: "If you do not pay Becky Pleasant in accordance with judgement rendered by this Bureau I shall forthwith seize what will pay her. I give you until 2 o'clock tomorrow to fulfill your portion of the matter" (Michael Walsh to David Ingram, June 5, 1866, Letters Sent, entry #3541, BRFAL). See also "The Negro Again," *Appeal*, March 3, 1866. There is no evidence for the outcome of many of the cases for which the original complaints to the Freedmen's Bureau have been preserved. Kathleen Berkeley has argued that few complaints actually ended in victory, though the evidence indicates Maywell's did; see " 'Like a Plague of Locust,' " 216 n. 24.

177. Statement of Elizabeth Burns, February 9, 1866, entry #3545, BRFAL.

178. Interestingly, when the *Appeal* reprinted Burns's testimony, it omitted the references

to the fact that Amanda Fuller was Archy Fuller's mistress and referred to her as "Amanda Howard, alias Fuller." Howard was not a name that Burns used in her testimony to identify Amanda Fuller. See statement of Elizabeth Burns, February 9, 1866, entry #3545, BRFAL, and from the *Appeal*, see "Cruel Treatment," February 15, 1866, 3, and "Cruel Treatment," February 23, 1866, 3.

179. From the *Appeal*, see "Cruel Treatment," February 15, 1866, 3, and "Cruel Treatment," February 23, 1866, 3.

180. From the *Appeal*, see "Cruel Treatment," February 15, 1866, 3, and "Cruel Treatment," February 23, 1866, 3.

181. One of the few references to African American women's civic activity in any paper other than the Republican daily was used to mock freedwomen's aspirations for respectability as well as political participation. Under the headline, "A Rather Rich Joke," the *Appeal* reprinted on its front page a story from a New Orleans paper about the following communication received by the Senate: "The undersigned, as a committee of ladies, acting in the name of a large number of loyal ladies of New Orleans, wish to present your honorable body with a United States flag." The Senate accepted the gift and planned a ceremony of acceptance. But later they allegedly ordered that all record of the communication be stricken from the Senate journal. "It is currently reported, and universally believed, that the 'ladies' of the aforesaid flag committee, and those they represent, are 'colored ladies.' . . . Well, it is a funny affair all around" ("A Rather Rich Joke," *Appeal*, December 6, 1865, 1).

182. Mary Ryan has shown such bifurcated representations of womanhood to have been a characteristic of the discursive mapping of nineteenth-century urban life in the United States. Ryan writes,

> Accounts of everyday life in the city streets fractured the false universalism of polite gender symbolism. The chaste, domesticated, altruistic feminine image displayed in public ceremonies could not accommodate the diverse manifestations of womanhood on the public streets, especially not those females who took their very identity from those social spaces—the streetwalkers, the public women. The cartographers of gender devised a dualistic classification of womanhood in order to account for the discrepancies between the feminine ideal and the untidy realities of gender on the streets in everyday city life. In so doing, the chroniclers of urban life implicitly acknowledged that gender was deeply divided by class. . . . The category of the dangerous woman encapsulated racial as well as class distinctions. The most dangerous female inhabitant of the public streets was singled out by her color. . . . The urban imagination encoded class and racial differences in the categories of the dangerous and the endangered and played out these social distinctions within the female sex. (*Women in Public*, 73)

See 76–92 for elaboration of her characterization of "dangerous" versus "endangered" women.

183. "The Negro Again," *Appeal*, March 3, 1866.

184. See letter to George R. Rutter, Esq., from Provost Marshal of Freedmen, March 3, 1866, entry #3541, BRFAL, and "The Negro Again," *Appeal*, March 3, 1866.

185. "Freedmen's Court," *Appeal*, November 26, 1865, 3.

186. This report also portrayed a feminized black Union soldier, allegedly deficient in mental shrewdness or physical force to control the "sharp wench": "A colored girl . . . was fined ten dollars in the Freedmen's Court yesterday, for being drunk and disorderly. Not having the money in her possession, she requested that a guard be sent with her to her residence to procure it. The Provost allowed a guard to wait on the wench, who, as soon as she found herself inside of her own door, locked it, and left the poor guard outside without the money. He returned to court without either the wench or fine" ("Sharp Wench," *Appeal*, March 2, 1866, 3).

187. According to the Oxford English Dictionary, the primary definition of "wench" is "girl, maid, young woman; female child"; the second meaning is "a wanton woman, a mistress"; the third meaning is "a female servant." According to various nineteenth-century dictionaries, "wench" had the particular meaning in the United States of "a black or colored female servant; a negress" and "a colored woman of any age; a negress or mulatress, especially one in service" (*Compact Oxford English Dictionary*, 2nd ed. [Oxford: Clarendon Press, 1991], 2295). It is telling that a term that meant female child would be used by white Americans in the nineteenth century for black women of all ages (much like "boy" was used for black men of all ages), and particularly a term that also had the combined implications of servitude and illicit sexual behavior.

188. "Female Roughs," *Appeal*, March 2, 1866.

189. "Robbery," *Appeal*, November 17, 1865. Elizabeth Meriwether, an elite white woman, wrote in her memoir of post–Civil War Memphis that she took offense at black women wearing finer clothing than white women. She described observing African American Union soldiers "playing the gallant to ugly, gaudily dressed negro women," while "the few white women whom I saw . . . were garbed in faded, rusty old black calico gowns." It is likely, of course, that the politics of the intervening fifty years before Meriwether recorded these observations—in 1916—affected her recollections. See Meriwether, *Recollections of Ninety-Two Years*, 167. Many reports of theft by freedmen and freedwomen included references to clothing. In December, the *Appeal* alleged that African American Union soldiers robbed four stores in South Memphis of "clothing, boots, etc." ("Robbery by Negro Soldiers," *Appeal*, December 21, 1865, 3). And the next April, the same paper reported "the arrest of a negro named David Dumbridge, who stole a calico dress and other articles of clothing from Simon Levy" ("Magistrate's Court," *Appeal*, April 11, 1866, 3). To the extent that any of these reports were founded, they suggest some of the needs and the desires of freedpeople. During the Memphis Riot, many rioters stole clothing from freedpeople. See Chapter 2.

190. He was concerned that these women were not earning their keep. It was not the city's policy to put women to work on the streets, as was done with male prisoners. See BM&A, book 11, p. 888, MSCA. (This position was not consistent in southern cities during these years. See Kerber, *No Constitutional Right to Be Ladies*, chap. 2, on Hous-

ton's policy of putting black women unable to pay fines for violation of city ordinances to work on the streets.) While the provost marshal had jurisdiction in all criminal cases involving freedpeople, the city police still often arrested freedpeople on their beats and housed them in the city jail. See "Weekly Returns of Fines Assessed by Provost Marshal of Freedmen in Cases of Arrest by City Authorities," entry #3546, BRFAL, for further evidence of the frequency with which freedwomen were arrested by city police.

191. "Freedmen's Bureau," *Appeal*, November 11, 1865, 3.

192. From the *Appeal*, "Freedmen's Court," November 29, 1865, 3, and "Police Arrests Friday Night," April 8, 1866, 3. *Nymph du pave* was a euphemism for prostitute, according to dictionaries of American slang from 1859 and 1902, qtd. in *Compact Oxford English Dictionary*, 1191.

193. The editor added with sarcasm, "What she was fined for calling for the watch when in distress, in addition to the personal abuse, we have not learned" ("Police Protection," *Memphis Morning Post*, June 7, 1866, 8).

194. Statement of Amanda Olden, April 30, 1866, entry #3545, BRFAL.

195. See testimony of Mollie Davis, *MR&M*, 200, and Bond for John Egan, April 17, 1866, entry #3545, BRFAL.

196. Michael Walsh to John Park, May 1, 1866, entry #3541, BRFAL.

197. See testimony of Mollie Davis, *MR&M*, 200, and Bond for John Egan, April 17, 1866, entry #3545, BRFAL.

198. See statement of C. C. Swears, Robert Church, and John Gains, February 17, 1866, entry #3545, BRFAL.

199. The mayor's apology offered this excuse for the officers' conduct: "From all I can learn the col'd people had a masked Ball. They had permission from me [required under city law] but the Police did not know it. . . . They acted under misinformation and are sorry for it." "Negro balls" and "masked balls" were prohibited in the city without permission from the mayor; his use of term "masked ball" is telling, given that practice's association with prostitution. See Gilfoyle, *City of Eros*, chap. 11, and Warren, *Thirty Years' Battle with Crime*, 125–32 (I thank Cynthia Blair for this reference). See statement of C. C. Swears, Robert Church, and John Gains; letter from S. S. Garrett to Major William L. Porter, February 17, 1866; its referral to Mayor John Park; and Mayor Park's response, entry #3545, BRFAL. See also letter from S. S. Garrett to Mayor John Park, February 22, 1866, entry #3541, BRFAL, in which Garrett inquired under what authority black people were required to obtain permits from the mayor for parties when whites apparently were not.

200. On Egan, see testimony of Mollie Davis, 200; Ellen Brown, 200; and Matt Wardlaw, 234, all in *MR&M*; "The Riot Continued," *MDP*, May 4, 1866, 8. For the role of a policeman named "Carroll" (slightly different spelling from the two options that appear in Olden's affidavit) during the Memphis Riot, see testimony of Margaret Gardner, 98; Adam Lock, 115–16; and Dr. Robert McGowan, 126, all in *MR&M*. Testimony of policeman James Finn, MC, *MR&M*, 332, suggests that this was David Carroll. Altina Waller also identifies this Carroll as David. See Waller, "Community, Class, and Race," 244. The conduct

described by Olden would be consistent with the activities of participants in the riot, and thus it is likely that David Carroll was the officer whom Olden reported. But I cannot be certain. "A true and perfect list of the duly elected and regularly appointed officials of the City of Memphis that were in the service of said City during the months of April and May, 1866" (attached inside the back cover of BM&A, book 11, MSCA; see also MR&M, 365–69) shows two officers named Carroll, a David and a William, on the force in April. Only David served in May. Thus it is possible that the "Carroll" who harassed Olden was William Carroll, that he was dropped from the force as a result of her charges, and that he was not the same Carroll identified among the rioters. Finally, affidavit of Lemuel (Samuel) Premier, FBC, MR&M, 338, identified Sweatt as one of the rioters.

Chapter 2

1. Testimony of Frances Thompson, MR&M, 196–97. For the history of Frances Thompson's arrest ten years later for "being a man and wearing women's clothing" ("A Mask Lifted," PL, July 11, 1876, 3), see Chapter 6. Though her body may have been either anatomically male or ambiguously sexed, I approach Thompson as a survivor of sexual violence aimed at black women. And I continue to use feminine pronouns to refer to her because that is how she identified herself.

2. Violence did occur in other areas of the city over the three-day period, but the vast majority of attacks occurred in South Memphis. Concerning violence in a neighborhood known as Chelsea, see testimony of Charles W. Anderson, 170–71, and John Martin, 136, in MR&M.

3. Historian Altina Waller has identified by name 68 men who were accused of perpetrating violence between May 1 and May 3, 1866, in Memphis, and she concludes that this number represents between half and three-quarters of the overall participants. Of those 68, she found addresses for 72 percent, 53 percent of whom lived in the city wards that comprised South Memphis. See Waller, "Community, Class, and Race," 235. The largest occupational category among those men identified by Waller as being among the participants in the violence, 28 percent, comprised small business owners, most of whom ran grocery-saloons. Police made up the next largest occupational grouping, 24 percent. Another 10 percent of those Waller identified were firemen; another 10 percent, clerks; 7 percent, artisans; and 4.5 percent, laborers.

4. "There is no doubt in the minds of your committee that many persons were killed whose killing has not been proved," concluded the committee's majority in their final report. "A vast number of colored people had come into Memphis and located in this neighborhood, who were but little known, and who, during the progress of the riot, fled in all directions. Nothing was ascertained from them what portion of their number was killed" ("Report," MR&M, 34).

5. Ibid., 34–36. The congressional committee's official count was forty-six African Ameri-

cans and two whites killed. But as Richard Banks has pointed out, although the killings of Ida Green and her baby were recounted in affidavits made before the Freedmen's Bureau and included with the committee's report, they were not included in the committee's final tally. See Banks, "In the Heat of the Night," and affidavits of Samuel Green and Emeline Wilson, FBC, *MR&M*, 353.

6. "Report," *MR&M*, 34–36.

7. In addition to Thompson, her roommate Lucy Smith, Harriet Armour, and Lucy Tibbs testified before the congressional committee that they were raped by white men during the riot. Rebecca Ann Bloom made a similar statement to the Freedmen's Bureau. See testimony of Lucy Smith, 197; Harriet Armour, 176–77; Lucy Tibbs, 160–62; and affidavit of Rebecca Ann Bloom, FBC, 351, all in *MR&M*. For further information on these rapes, see the testimony of Cynthia Townsend, 162–63; Henry Porter, 167–68; Molly Hayes, 186; Elvira Walker, 193–94; and affidavit of Peter Bloom, FBC, 348, all in *MR&M*. There is indication that rioters at least attempted to rape one other freedwoman, and one of the five women who did testify referred to having heard that an unnamed black woman was raped. This woman may or may not have been one of the other women who testified. See below and testimony of Lucy Tibbs, 161, and Mary Grady, 186–88, in *MR&M*.

8. See, for instance, on the United States, Richards, *"Gentlemen of Property and Standing"*; Gilje, *Rioting in America*; and Waller, "Community, Class, and Race." On Europe, see Natalie Davis, "Rites of Violence," 152–87; E. P. Thompson, "Moral Economy of the English Crowd in the Eighteenth Century," 76–136; and Desan, "Crowds, Community, and Ritual," 47–71.

9. Desan, "Crowds, Community, and Ritual," 48. In this regard, see, on the United States, Bernstein, *New York City Draft Riots*.

10. These are the arguments of, respectively, Kevin R. Hardwick, " 'Your Old Father Abe Lincoln Is Dead and Damned' "; Waller, "Community, Class, and Race"; and Walker, "This Is White Man's Day." On the riot being a planned attack, see esp. Waller, "Community, Class, and Race," 237–38, 245 n. 27, and Walker, "This Is White Man's Day." Further evidence is offered in a letter written by a northern white teacher living and working in Memphis describing how he was warned to leave by neighbors who knew what was being planned. See William Bailey to Elihu B. Washburne, May 30, 1866, in Washburne Papers, Library of Congress. Late historian Armstead Robinson also found the evidence that the riot was a planned attack convincing (personal communication, 1993), as did the congressional investigating committee (see "Report," *MR&M*, 6).

Earlier studies mis-characterized the riot as the manifestation of long-standing resentment between African Americans and Irish immigrants exacerbated by competition over low-skilled jobs. See Lovett, "Memphis Riots," esp. 12; James Gilbert Ryan, "Memphis Riot of 1866"; and Holmes, "Underlying Causes of the Memphis Race Riot of 1866," all of which accept contemporary observations from white Memphis elites that this labor/ethnic struggle caused the riot. Ryan, who also emphasizes racism overall and the responsibility of civilian and military officials for not stopping the violence sooner, is responding critically to Holmes's racist account that blames white "riff-raff," Radical Republican Reconstruction policy (disfranchisement, northern schoolteachers, the Freedmen's Bureau), and freedpeople, especially black Union soldiers. See also Holmes, "Effects of the Memphis Race Riot of 1866," 58–79.

Also on the Memphis Riot, see Rable, *But There Was No Peace*, 33–42; Riddleberger, *1866*, 177–201; Litwack, *Been in the Storm So Long*, 281; Foner, *Reconstruction*, 261–62; McFeely, *Yankee Stepfather*, 274–82; Gleeson, *Irish in the South*, 176–78; and Gilje, *Rioting in America*, 96.

11. One exception is Bond, " 'Till Fair Aurora Rise,' " 96–103.

12. Waller distinguishes rapes as "moments when the riot turned extremely brutal" from other kinds of violence that "reflected older traditions" of collective violence, such as "celebrations in the light of burning buildings, flag flying military formations and threats to anyone wearing the blue clothes symbolic of Union troops" ("Community, Class, and Race," 239). For reference to rape during the riot in other studies, see Hardwick, " 'Your Old Father Abe Lincoln Is Dead and Damned,' " 109, 122 (Hardwick uses the rapes as evidence of an indirect attack on black Union soldiers); Lovett, "Memphis Riots," 23; James Gilbert Ryan, "Memphis Riot of 1866," 243; Holmes, "Underlying Causes of the Memphis Race Riot of 1866," 195, 220; Foner, *Reconstruction*, 262; and McFeely, *Yankee Stepfather*, 277. Herbert Gutman discusses the testimony of the women raped during the Memphis Riot at length in *Black Family in Slavery and Freedom*, 25–28, as evidence of freedwomen's willingness to expose their suffering to the public and as an introduction to his discussion of black Union soldiers' thwarted efforts to protect the women in their families from the rioters.

13. Testimony of Dr. J. N. Sharp, 157; Margaret Gardner, 98; Ellen Dilts, 64; Rachel Dilts, 67; Andrew Reyyonco, 169; and "Report," 6, all in *MR&M*. See also Brigadier General Benjamin P. Runkle, Superintendent, Freedmen's Bureau, "Report concerning the late riots at Memphis, Tenn.," in entry #3529, Reports relating to the Memphis Riot, BRFAL.

14. Testimony of Dr. J. N. Sharp, *MR&M*, 157.

15. See *Appeal*, "Evening Dispatches," April 1, 1866, and "Negro Troops to Be Mustered Out," April 11, 1866. See also "Mustered Out," *Memphis Daily Tribune*, January 31, 1866, 4, and "General Orders No. 15," reprinted in the *Weekly Republican*, April 14, 1866, 5. On the mustering out of this regiment on April 30, 1866, see Report of Captain A. W. Allyn, exhibit #2, 358, and on their disarmament, see testimony of Thomas Durnin, 223, both in *MR&M*. For suggestions that the riot was planned ahead of time for this day by some of the rioters, see, in *MR&M*, testimony of John Moller, 87; Rev. Ewing O. Tade, 89–90; Hannah Robinson, 193; B. F. C. Brooks, 213; William Pearce, 218; Thomas Durnin, 223; and Captain Allyn, 248.

16. Quotation is from affidavit of Albert Butcher, FBC, *MR&M*, 346. On location of the crowd near several South Street saloons, see testimony of Tony Cherry, 182, and J. H. Johnson, MC, 315, in *MR&M*. It is noted in a report on the riot by General Benjamin P. Runkle, Chief Superintendent of the Freedmen's Bureau for Memphis, that there were many women and children in the crowd; see Brigadier General Ben P. Runkle to Major

General C. B. Fisk, Assistant Commissioner for Kentucky and Tennessee, May 23, 1866, entry #3529, BRFAL. Alex McQuarters testified before the military commission that there were more women on the street than men; see *MR&M*, 317. See also testimony of Adam Lock, 115–16; J. S. Chapin, 192; William W. Wheedon, MC, 320; J. Johnson, MC, 315; and James Finn, MC, 332, in *MR&M*.

17. Testimony of Tony Cherry, *MR&M*, 182.

18. For witnesses who observed Creighton ordering police to disperse the crowd of freed-people and soldiers, see testimony of Dr. Allen Sterling, 173; John Beatty, 115; and affidavit of Albert Butcher, FBC, 346, in *MR&M*. An early, and biased, conservative news report of the riot placed Creighton at the scene of the initial conflict, claiming he was one of the first who were "fired upon by the negroes." See "The Riot," *Argus*, May 3, 1866, 2.

19. Testimony of Tony Cherry, *MR&M*, 182.

20. Witnesses differed in their recollections of where soldiers aimed their shots. See testimony of Adam Lock, 116; William Wheedon, 320; Abram Means, 173; C. H. Bowman, 324; and affidavits of Albert Butcher, FBC, 346; and Patzy Tolliver, 351, all in *MR&M*.

21. See "Report," 7, and testimony of Tony Cherry, 182, in *MR&M*. Two of the three doctors who examined the wound of the police officer who fell on the bridge concluded that it came from his own gun, though one doctor disagreed. See *MR&M*, testimony of Dr. R. W. Creighton, 124–25; Dr. William F. Irwin, 131; and Dr. J. M. Keller, 133–34.

22. Testimony of Tony Cherry, *MR&M*, 182, 184.

23. See testimony of James Carroll Mitchell, 308–9, and "Report," 7–8, in *MR&M*.

24. Testimony of Dr. Robert McGowan, *MR&M*, 126. McGowan had been sitting in the drugstore he ran near where the fighting began, when he heard the shots. He was called on by the crowd to attend to the wound of one of the white men who was killed.

25. Testimony of Ellen Dilts, *MR&M*, 64.

26. See testimony of George Todd, 256, and Walter Clifford, 250, in *MR&M*.

27. On Pendergrast being well known, see testimony of Lucy Tibbs, *MR&M*, 160. Both Pendergrast and Roach were responsible for some of the most cold-blooded murders during the riot. Pendergrast ran a grocery store with the assistance of his mother and his two sons, Mike and Pat, near where the rioting began. The association of small business-men, such as Pendergrast, with artisans and skilled workingmen's culture in Memphis is suggested by the fact that one of the Pendergrast men addressed a meeting of the United Mechanic's Association at City Hall in Memphis about two weeks before the riot ("Mechanics' Meeting," *Appeal*, April 17, 1866, 3). John Pendergrast told Cynthia Town-send that "I am the man that fetched this mob out here, and they will do just what I tell them" (*MR&M*, 163), and he said to Henry Porter, "I am the ringleader of the mob out this morning" (*MR&M*, 167). He claimed to these freedpeople that it was his influence that protected them and their property from harm. On the Pendergrasts' role in the riot, see Waller, "Community, Class, and Race," 238, 244. For additional testimony about the Pendergrasts' role, see testimony of Mary Grady, 187; James Carroll Mitchell, 308; affidavit of David Smith, MC, 332; affidavit of Thomas Moseby, FBC, 342; affidavit of

Penny Le Muir, FBC, 343; affidavit of John Robinson, FBC, 344; and affidavit of Henrietta Cole, FBC, 347, all in *MR&M*.

On policeman David Roach's role in the riot, see testimony of Cynthia Townsend, 162; Henry Porter, 167; John Marshall, 181; Billy Johnson, 222; Robert R. Church, 226; affidavit of Coleman Default, FBC, 337; affidavit of Jordan Bufford, FBC, 338; affidavit of Eliza Groves, FBC, 342; and affidavit of Joseph Colwell (Caldwell), FBC, 346, all in *MR&M*. See also Waller, "Community, Class, and Race," 244.

28. See testimony of George Hogan, 149, and Captain A. W. Allyn, 247, in *MR&M*.

29. Officers who commanded Fort Pickering during the riot later described the discussions among black soldiers in the fort about what to do, knowing that their families were in danger in South Memphis, and their requests for their arms, their attempts to take them by force, and their efforts to leave the fort. They were prevented from accomplishing their aims by armed white officers under orders from the major general in command, George Stoneman, to keep the soldiers out of South Memphis until the disturbance had ended. See *MR&M*, testimony of Tony Cherry, 185–86; S. S. Garrett, 203–4; Frederick Hastings, 205–8; James Helm, 217; and Thomas Durnin, 223–25. See also W. H. Morgan to Elihu B. Washburne, May 11, 1866, in Washburne Papers, Library of Congress, in which Morgan describes how "it was not an easy task" to keep soldiers in the fort, "when these men were maddened at the sight of their Houses, Schools, and Churches being burned to the ground." On the morning of May 2, roll call in the fort revealed that 200 black soldiers were missing. Many of these 200 may have been injured or killed the day before; they may have been taken into police custody; they may have gone into hiding; or they may have managed to evade military officials and stay with their families and neighbors. See testimony of Frederick Hastings, *MR&M*, 206, 208.

30. Affidavits of Clary Johnson and Hannah Hersey, FBC, *MR&M*, 342–43, 349.

31. "The Riot—And Its Lessons," *Appeal*, May 4, 1866. For a discussion of the concept of "social equality," see Chapter 4.

32. For instance, see testimony of Samuel Dilts, 118, and Frances Thompson, 197, in *MR&M*.

33. *Appeal*, "The Riot in South Memphis," May 2, 1866, and "The Riot—And Its Lessons," May 4, 1866. See also, from the *Appeal*, "The Riot in South Memphis," "The City," and "Unfortunate Affair," May 3, 1866. From the *Argus*, see "Great Riot," May 2, 1866; "The Riot" and "The Riots," May 3, 1866; "The Memphis Riots—Facts to Be Remembered—The Radical Organ's Misrepresentation Exposed," May 4, 1866. In some reports, black people were represented as naive children irresponsibly inflamed and empowered by civil rights legislation, the Freedmen's Bureau, and white Republicans: "This time there can be no mistake about it, the whole blame of this most tragical and bloody riot lies, as usual, with the poor, ignorant, deluded blacks. . . . We cannot suffer the occasion to pass without again calling the attention of the authorities to the indispensable necessity of disarming these poor creatures, who have so often shown themselves utterly unfit to be trusted with fire-arms. On this occasion, the facts all go to show that but for this much abused privilege accorded to them by misguiding and misjudging friends, there would have been no riot" ("The Reign of Bloodshed," *Argus*, May 2, 1866).

34. *Avalanche*, May 5, 1866, reprinted in MC, *MR&M*, 334 (my emphasis). The editor of the *Avalanche* was present during, though not an active participant in, the riot. See testimony of M. C. Galloway, MC, *MR&M*, 325.

35. Statement of Ann Freeman, May 22, 1866, entry #3545, BRFAL.

36. When asked her age by the congressional committee on May 30, 1866, Tibbs responded, "I do not know exactly. I suppose about twenty-four." See testimony of Lucy Tibbs, *MR&M*, 160.

37. Ibid. The following details of Tibbs's experiences during the riot come from her testimony on 160–62.

38. Ibid., 161. On police and other rioters robbing soldiers who had just been paid, see "Another Record of Violence—Fire—Outrages Continued," *MDP*, May 5, 1866, 8.

39. Armour testified that Dunn lived on South Street; see *MR&M*, 177. On the same day that Armour was attacked, Dunn, accompanied by other men, broke into Sallie Hawkins's house, which was in this same neighborhood, and killed her husband, David. Hawkins reported to the Freedmen's Bureau that Dunn "keeps a grocery store on South street, near the bridge, across the bayou" (affidavit of Sallie Hawkins, FBC, *MR&M*, 339).

40. Testimony of Molly Hayes, *MR&M*, 186. I am guessing that Hayes was a widow, perhaps having lost her husband in the war, because she reported living in Memphis with only her two children and her mother-in-law. It is also possible that her husband was elsewhere looking for work, or that they had separated. The latter seems less likely only because she brought her husband's mother with her to Memphis.

41. Testimony of Harriet Armour, *MR&M*, 176–77.

42. Testimony of Frances Thompson and Lucy Smith, *MR&M*, 196–97. Based on where Thompson and Smith lived, it seems possible that one of these men may well have been Policeman David Roach. Brigadier General Benjamin Runkle suggested in his testimony before the congressional investigating committee that displaying pictures of Confederate military figures was a common form of conservative political expression in Memphis, perhaps one that Frances Thompson and Lucy Smith consciously responded to with their own pictures. When asked how the American flag was "regarded in Memphis generally," Runkle answered, "I have never seen it here except at United States headquarters. I have seen pictures of rebel generals in all shop windows and stores wherever I have been, but I have never seen those of such men as Lincoln, Grant, Sherman, Farragut, and such as them, displayed. . . . I never should have noticed the thing if I had not seen the pictures of Jeff. Davis, Lee, Beauregard, &c. displayed in such profusion" (*MR&M*, 278).

43. In a study of sexual violence in New York City at the turn of the eighteenth century, Marybeth Hamilton Arnold similarly finds most striking "the juxtaposition of the men's tone of calm, assured jocularity with their rough, brutal conduct" (" 'Life of a Citizen in the Hands of a Woman,' " 39).

44. Testimony of Lucy Smith, *MR&M*, 197.

45. Testimony of Frances Thompson, *MR&M*, 196.

46. Ibid., 196–97.

47. Testimony of Lucy Smith, *MR&M*, 197.

48. Testimony of Frances Thompson, *MR&M*, 196.

49. Testimony of Elvira Walker, *MR&M*, 194.

50. See Chapter 1.

51. This is how Walker recounted events. Rebecca Ann Bloom recalls her husband being taken out to find a candle, as the rioters had demanded that they light the room. (Often rioters' first demand was that freedpeople "get a light" so that they could see who and what was inside a given home.) Peter Bloom himself reported only that he was "taken into the other room," presumably Walker's room. See testimony of Elvira Walker, *MR&M*, 194, and affidavits of Rebecca Ann Bloom and Peter Bloom, FBC, *MR&M*, 351, 348.

52. Affidavit of Rebecca Ann Bloom, FBC, *MR&M*, 351.

53. For the use of this term also by black men to describe sexual intercourse, see Hodes, *White Women, Black Men*, 41, 127, and by a white woman in a Providence, Rhode Island, divorce petition in the mid-eighteenth century, see Block, *Rape and Sexual Power in Early America*, 66.

54. Affidavit of Peter Bloom, FBC, *MR&M*, 348.

55. See, for instance, Block, *Rape and Sexual Power in Early America*, 80–86; Stiglmayer, *Mass Rape*, 82–170, esp. 144–46, 157–59; and Barker, "Justice Delayed."

56. See Block, *Rape and Sexual Power in Early America*, esp. chap. 2.

57. Sharon Block's new study demonstrates that, while well-off white women were at times victims of sexual abuse (most often by someone known to them), women of color and other poor and marginal women were far more vulnerable to coerced sexual relations and violence; see *Rape and Sexual Power in Early America*, 4, chap. 2.

58. Testimony of Harriet Armour, *MR&M*, 176.

59. For an analysis of rape scenarios that intentionally foregrounded harm and humiliation, see Block, *Rape and Sexual Power in Early America*, 81–82; see also a scene of forced oral sex in the context of late-twentieth-century war that emphasized humiliation and harm, in Stiglmayer, *Mass Rape*, 145–46.

60. This man's objection went unheeded, and he did nothing else to interfere. Tibbs was raped in the presence of the other rioters who entered her room that night. See testimony of Lucy Tibbs, *MR&M*, 161.

61. Testimony of Lucy Smith, *MR&M*, 197.

62. Testimony of Mary Grady, *MR&M*, 186–89. "Secesh," colloquial term for secession, referred to those southerners who supported secession and the Confederacy.

63. Testimony of Dr. Charles S. Lloyd, *MR&M*, 150–51.

64. See affidavit of Henry Bankett, 352, and testimony of Mary Grady, 187, in *MR&M*. Guy Thomas, a fifteen-year-old former slave, reported that rioters burned down the house of a white woman married to a black sergeant in the Union Army and killed the husband. It is possible that this is an additional case, or that Thomas was mistaken about Henry Bankett's death. See testimony of Guy Thomas, *MR&M*, 236.

65. See testimony of David T. Egbert, 121–22, and of A. N. Edmunds, 139–40, in *MR&M*. For discussion of changing meanings of and attitudes toward "concubinage" relationships between European men and colonized women, see Stoler, "Carnal Knowledge and Imperial Power."

66. See Chapter 1.

67. Testimony of Mollie Davis, *MR&M*, 200.

68. In addition to Davis's testimony, see testimony of Ellen Brown, *MR&M*, 200, and Bond for John Egan, April 17, 1866, entry #3545, BRFAL. The neighbor was Mat. Wardlaw, a freedman who told the congressional committee that he heard Clark and Egan say that the "damned niggers ought to be hung"; see testimony of Mat. Wardlaw, *MR&M*, 234. See also "The Riot—Continued," *MDP*, May 4, 1866, 8. This article describes the burning of a building in which freedpeople were living but that was purchased by the Colored Methodist Society for eventual use as a church. "A policeman had been discharged through the influence of the Freedmen's Bureau, for extorting money from the occupants. It is reported that he warned some of them to leave, as the house would be fired on Thursday night, and, by a singular coincidence, the warning proved true." This appears to be where Mollie Davis lived.

69. See "Report," *MR&M*, 3.

70. For Stevens's motion in the House, see "Journal" of the investigating committee in *MR&M*, 45.

71. See Foner, *Reconstruction*, 243–61.

72. Washburne chaired the committee and signed its final report, along with Broomall. Shanklin was neither shown nor asked to sign this report, reflecting tensions and political disagreement between himself and the other members. He did, though, submit his own report, "Views of the Minority," to Congress. See Shanklin's Minority Report, in *MR&M*, 37–44. Thaddeus Stevens and Elihu B. Washburne had served on the Joint Committee on Reconstruction together.

73. Freedmen's Bureau agents were observed taking affidavits in the streets of South Memphis in the days just following the riot. See "Another Record of Violence—Fire—Outrages Continued," *MDP*, May 5, 1866, 8, and "Report of Casualties and property destroyed during the Memphis riots," entry #3529, BRFAL, clearly an early list identifying freedpeople and briefly naming the kind of violence they suffered and value of property lost, perhaps even written as the provost marshal walked through the streets. The *MDP* also referred to the collection of affidavits on which their reports were based, indicating that their own reporters were working with the bureau to gather accounts of violence. See "The Riot Continued," May 4, 1866, 8, and "Charge of Misrepresentation," May 6, 1866, 8, both in *MDP*. A surgeon who treated freedpeople wounded in the riot in the bureau's hospital told the congressional committee that "before I let any of them leave the hospital I reported them to General Runkle [superintendent of the bureau in Memphis], so that he could get their testimony" (testimony of Dr. D. P. Beecher, *MR&M*, 144). On General Stoneman calling a military commission to investigate and asking General Runkle to participate, see Brigadier General Benjamin P. Runkle, Super-

intendent, Freedmen's Bureau, "Report concerning the late riots at Memphis, Tenn.," in entry #3529, Reports relating to the Memphis Riot, BRFAL. See "Military Commission," *MDP*, May 8, 1866, 8, announcing the meeting of the military commission and calling on witnesses to present themselves.

74. Washburne to Stevens, May 24, 1866, container 3, May 1866 folder, in Stevens Papers, Library of Congress. See also General George Stoneman to Washburne, June 2, 1866, in Washburne Papers, Library of Congress, in which Stoneman recommends that the committee take testimony from certain witnesses.

75. Some witnesses referred to having been "summoned" by the committee, but most did not. Stoneman's military commission was given authority to "send for such persons and papers as may be thought necessary" ("Commission to Investigate the Riot," *MDP*, May 6, 1866, 8). Presumably the congressional committee had similar authority.

76. See *MR&M*, 50–313.

77. These are approximations because witnesses were not always identified by race. The congressional committee appended to their report submitted to Congress testimony from the previous investigations of witnesses who did not also appear before them. See *MR&M*, 313–58. There is evidence in records of the military commission that some witnesses testified before both the commission and the investigating committee. These witnesses' prior testimony was not included in the committee's report. See National Archives Microfilm Publications, M619, Letters Received by the Office of the Adjutant General, Main Series, 1861–1870, roll 520, National Archives.

Many of the freedpeople who made affidavits with the Freedmen's Bureau had already left town by the time the committee arrived. "They have scattered so much since the fuss," one freedwoman said of her many neighbors who left the city seeking safety in other areas; see testimony of Margaret Gardner, *MR&M*, 98. This was the response of many freedpeople to the violence of rioters. See "Report," *MR&M*, 2; *Avalanche*, May 5, 1866, reprinted in MC, *MR&M*, 334; "The Riot—Continued," *MDP*, May 4, 1866, 8. See also General Clinton B. Fisk, Assistant Commissioner, Bureau of Refugees, Freedmen, and Abandoned Lands, State of Tennessee, to Washburne, June 21, 1866, Washburne Papers, Library of Congress, in which Fisk sends Washburne affidavits of freedpeople who left Memphis after the riot and returned to the city only after the investigating committee had departed.

78. See "Civil Rights Test," *Argus*, May 11, 1866, 1. A bill that would grant African Americans the right to testify in courts in Tennessee was hotly debated in the state legislature in the months before the riot. See, from the *Appeal*, "The Nashville *Dispatch* of Tuesday, says . . ." November 25, 1865, 1; "We cannot comprehend the actions of the House of Representatives . . . ," December 10, 1865, 2; "Governor Brownlow Again," December 6, 1865, 1; and from the *Memphis Morning Post*, "News Summary," January 19, 1866, 1, and "Nashville Correspondence," January 23, 1866, 2. Some of the conservative papers in Memphis supported the testimony bill as a means of eliminating the presence and judicial powers of the Freedmen's Bureau, as well as a concession to Congress that might put off the imposition of black male suffrage. See, from the *Appeal*, "Conditions of

Reconstruction," November 28, 1865, 2; "The Mississippi *Clarion* says . . . ," November 29, 1865, 2; "The Issue," December 6, 1865, 2; "The Meeting Last Night," December 28, 1865, 3; "Negro Testimony," February 28, 1866, 2; and from the *Avalanche*, editorial beginning "We are rejoiced," January 9, 1866, 2. For opposition to the bill, see "Good Sign from the Radicals," *Argus*, February 4, 1866, 2.

79. I have been unable to determine exactly how each freedwoman came to testify before the committee. Frances Thompson reported the rape of Lucy Smith to the Freedmen's Bureau soon after the riot, and Rebecca Ann Bloom similarly reported that she had been attacked ("Report of Casualties and property destroyed during the Memphis riots," in Reports Relating to the Memphis Riot, Memphis, Tennessee, entry #3529, BRFAL), suggesting that they were eager to report the abuse. Cynthia Townsend in her testimony before the committee suggested that it was Molly Hayes, Harriet Armour's white neighbor, who first reported that Armour had been raped. Did this information in the hands of the bureau lead to these women being called by the committee as witnesses? Did they volunteer to testify again before the committee? Did those women not mentioned in any previous records, such as Lucy Tibbs, volunteer to testify?

80. Affidavit of Rebecca Ann Bloom, FBC, *MR&M*, 351. Bloom did not testify before the congressional committee, suggesting that perhaps she and her husband left the city after the riot.

81. Testimony of Frances Thompson, *MR&M*, 196.

82. Testimony of Lucy Smith, *MR&M*, 197.

83. Testimony of Lucy Tibbs, *MR&M*, 161.

84. Testimony of Harriet Armour, *MR&M*, 176.

85. Testimony of Lucy Smith, *MR&M*, 197.

86. Testimony of Lucy Tibbs, *MR&M*, 161.

87. Gail Bederman demonstrates a similar move in Ida B. Wells's writings intended to convince white northerners of the necessity that they act to stop lynching in the southern states. See Bederman, " 'Civilization,' the Decline of Middle-Class Manliness, and Ida B. Wells's Antilynching Campaign." See also Bederman, *Manliness and Civilization*, 45–76. Jacquelyn Dowd Hall makes a similar argument about the rhetorical strategy of Jessie Daniel Ames in *Revolt against Chivalry*, xxi.

88. Testimony of Lucy Tibbs, *MR&M*, 161.

89. Testimony of Harriet Armour, *MR&M*, 176. That her calculated move to avoid potentially deadly violence may well have saved her life is suggested by the fact that one of the men who attacked Armour, Mr. Dunn, and his companions killed David Hawkins in his home near where Armour lived. See affidavit of Sallie Hawkins, FBC, *MR&M*, 339.

90. On similar calculations by enslaved women, see Schwalm, *Hard Fight for We*, 44, 247.

91. Washburne at other moments framed questions in terms of women's "virtue." He asked both the superintendent of colored schools in Memphis and the superintendent of the Freedmen's Bureau, "Are the ladies who have been here as teachers of blameless life and conversation?" See testimony of Orrin Waters, 260, and Brig. Gen. Benjamin Runkle, 277, in *MR&M*.

92. Testimony of Cynthia Townsend, *MR&M*, 163.

93. Testimony of Harriet Armour, *MR&M*, 176.

94. Leslie Schwalm finds that slave communities rarely cast shame upon or ostracized women who were victims of sexual abuse. See *Hard Fight for We*, 247–48.

95. Testimony of Harriet Armour, *MR&M*, 177. Cynthia Townsend also testified that "I could have seen it if I had been a mind to. . . . There were white people right there who knew what was going on. One woman called me to go and look in and see what they were doing; that was when this thing was going on." Townsend clarified that the woman who called out to her, who presumably was Molly Hayes, did so in outrage and fear, by adding, "She is the woman who came and made a complaint . . . ; she is a very nice woman" (testimony of Cynthia Townsend, *MR&M*, 163). Hayes herself later testified to the committee that she saw nothing but heard some of what was going on. She said that she knew Armour had been raped only because Armour told her so after the fact. In her testimony, Hayes recounted observing much of the riot violence and of being threatened herself with having her house burned down. Yet she was hesitant. She was not forthcoming with the information about Armour's rape without being prodded by committee members' questions, possibly upset about the rioters' violence and her own inability to stop it, uncomfortable with having to discuss the event and her own knowledge of it in public, or fearful of retaliation from rioters. See testimony of Molly Hayes, *MR&M*, 186. It is possible that the "open shanty" in which Armour lived was not unusual and that many other attacks happened in view of others, the difference being perhaps that Armour was attacked in the morning. The other attacks occurred at night and thus would have been less visible.

96. Testimony of Henry Porter, *MR&M*, 168. Cynthia Townsend also made reference to this aspect of Armour's ordeal: "They all had connexion with her in turn around, and then one of them tried to use her mouth" (*MR&M*, 163).

97. Testimony of Henry Porter, *MR&M*, 168.

98. For a similar analysis that emphasizes resistance to denigration based on class rather than racial difference, see Edwards, "Sexual Violence, Gender, Reconstruction." Edwards argues that both freedwomen and poor white women "seized the issue of sexual violence to challenge the attitudes and patterns of power that justified the devaluation and exploitation of poor women of both races." See also Edwards, *Gendered Strife and Confusion*, chap. 5.

99. See, e.g., "Report of the Committee of Investigation on the Memphis Riots," *New York Times*, July 16, 1866, 1; "The Memphis Riots: Report of the Investigating Committee," *Daily Cleveland Herald*, August 1, 1866, 2; "The Memphis Massacre," *Chicago Tribune*, July 28, 1866, 2; and Rable, *But There Was No Peace*, 41.

100. "Report," *MR&M*, 5, 13. It is not clear whether the authors of this report in fact perceived a contradiction between rape and "vengeance," one that required a "conquer[ing] of prejudices," or, rather, if the quotation marks around this last phrase suggest they intended to be ironic.

101. Ibid., 5.

102. Ibid., 13–15. One of the first questions the committee often asked female witnesses was whether or not they were married.

103. The report also asserted that overall the testimony they drew on "is very full, and is believed . . . , as a general thing, to be entitled to the fullest confidence" (ibid., 5).

104. Laura Edwards argues that this discourse, rather than empowering all women to resist sexual violence, marked only those who remained subservient to patriarchal dictates for women's appropriate behavior as deserving of protection; see "Sexual Violence, Gender, Reconstruction." See also Edwards, *Gendered Strife and Confusion*, 210–13.

105. Stoneman to Washburne, June 2, 21, 1866, in Washburne Letters, Library of Congress. There is in the records of the Freedmen's Bureau a bond for Michael Pendergrast, son of John Pendergrast, for $5,000 assuring his appearance to answer charges for "his complicity in the recent riots in the city of Memphis" ("Bond, Michael Pendergrast, 1866," May 15, 1866, in entry #3545, BRFAL). However, I found no evidence of further action by the bureau.

106. See, in BM&A, book 11, petition of D. F. Slatting, June 7, 1866, 930, and petition of James Finn, June 19, 1866, 944, whose requests for $455.56 and $400, respectively, were granted. See also, in this same book of minutes, the resolution to reimburse the fire department for the funeral of Henry Dunn, who was "accidently killed in the late unfortunate riots" (June 7, 1866, 932). The minutes did not mention that he was killed by John Pendergrast, who mistook him for a black man (see above). A request for reimbursement for a house that was burned by rioters during the riot was rejected. See petition of B. Newman [?], June 19, 1866, 939. The *MDP* wrote critically, "We are anxious to see what disposition will be made of the little claim of $900 asked for by Policeman Malowney, late of the Nashville penitentiary, and also those for several hundred per month by policemen injured in the police riot for losses occasioned thereby. Go in, gentleman, on the past; the future is closed for your speculations" ("Meeting of the Board of Mayor and Aldermen," July 3, 1866, 8).

107. Two months after the riot, the *Avalanche*, Memphis's most sensationalist newspaper, did refer to Frances Thompson in an editorial as an "old hag" and "strumpet" and claimed that it was "absurd" to think that she could have been sexually violated (no title, *Avalanche*, August 7, 1866, 2). Other than this, I have found no mention in the conservative press, until a decade later, of women having been raped, or claiming they had been raped, during the riot. See Chapter 6.

108. This bill was modeled after New York State's police legislation. See "Metropolitan Police," *Appeal*, May 1, 1866, 2. From the *Argus*, see "The Metropolitan Police Bill," 2, and "Important Document," 3, both April 29, 1866; "The Memphis Riots. What Gen. Runkle of the Freedmen's Bureau Thinks About Them," May 12, 1866, 1; and "The Police 'Head Center,' " May 29, 1866, 2.

109. See Introduction, n. 65.

110. "Meeting of Colored Citizens at Helena," *MDP*, May 19, 1866, 8.

Chapter 3

1. "The Outside Show," *WAG*, April 9, 1867, 1.
2. Editorial "Friday's *Dispatch* contains . . . ," April 2, 1867, *WAG*, 2.
3. "The Outside Show," *WAG*, April 9, 1867, 1.
4. On the concept of the public sphere, see Habermas, "Public Sphere" and *Structural Transformation of the Public Sphere*. For critics of Habermas who have posited as more useful a model of multiple, and even competing, public spheres, see esp. Nancy Fraser, "What's Critical about Critical Theory?" and "Rethinking the Public Sphere." See also Introduction, n. 21.
5. See esp. Hahn, *Nation under Our Feet*, chap. 4; Saville, *Work of Reconstruction*, chap. 5; and Foner, *Reconstruction*, 281–91.
6. For an analysis of freedpeople embracing political rights as tools in economic struggles, see Saville, *Work of Reconstruction*, esp. chap. 5.
7. See Barkley Brown, "To Catch the Vision of Freedom" and "Negotiating and Transforming the Public Sphere." On black women's role in electoral politics during Reconstruction, see also Frankel, *Freedom's Women*, 174, 176–77; Hahn, *Nation under Our Feet*, 175, 185, 227–28; Holt, *Black over White*, 34–35; Hunter, *To 'Joy My Freedom*, 32–33; and Schwalm, *Hard Fight for We*, 187, 232.
8. On the destruction and class tensions caused by the Civil War in Arkansas, see Moneyhon, *Impact of the Civil War and Reconstruction*, esp. chaps. 6 and 9, and DeBlack, *With Fire and Sword*, esp. chaps. 2–4.
9. See also Kantrowitz, *Ben Tillman*, for a detailed analysis of the role of constructions of white manhood in conservative political mobilizations during and after Reconstruction.
10. See Linda Kerber, " 'History Can Do It No Justice,' " 30–31, and *Women of the Republic*. On southern republicanism and independence, see Edmund S. Morgan, *American Slavery, American Freedom*, 363–87, esp. 376–77; Ford, "Republics and Democracy," esp. 123, 128–29; and Ayers, *Vengeance and Justice*, 41–42. For critiques of the gendered character of notions of independence in southern republican thinking, see Edwards, " 'Marriage Covenant' " and *Gendered Strife and Confusion*, and McCurry, *Masters of Small Worlds* and "Two Faces of Republicanism." On the concept of republicanism as used by historians of the United States, see Rodgers, "Republicanism," and esp. 31 for a discussion of the concept as applied in southern history.
11. Stanley, *From Bondage to Contract*, 9–10.
12. Kerber, *Women of the Republic*, 139, and " 'History Can Do It No Justice,' " 31; Stanley, *From Bondage to Contract*, 10–11; Pateman, *Sexual Contract*.
13. Horton and Horton, *In Hope of Liberty*, 166–67; Berlin, *Slaves without Masters*, 187–88. The citizenship of native-born free African Americans was explicitly challenged in 1820 by white southern congressmen defending the proposed exclusion of free blacks and mulattoes from the new state of Missouri. These congressmen argued that citizenship status derived from, rather than preceded, civil and political rights. Because African Americans did not consistently possess the rights "of every other person in the commu-

nity, under like circumstances," they were not citizens at all. See Kettner, *Development of American Citizenship*, 312–14 (quotation is from Virginia representative Philip Barbour before Congress, p. 313). Racial identity itself could serve as a sign of dependence. As one South Carolina court of appeals argued in 1846, even free African Americans were excluded from citizenship because of "a strong repugnance . . . against a participation in the rights of citizenship by any who bear in their person the traces of their servile origin" (qtd. in Ford, "Republics and Democracy," 127). Laura Edwards similarly notes how "the residue of dependency clung" to single white women and free black women and men; see *Gendered Strife and Confusion*, 7.

14. Robert Steinfeld has argued that while property ownership remained an important indicator of independence, the ability to profit from one's own labor presented an alternative in the industrial economy of the early nineteenth century; see Steinfeld, "Property and Suffrage in the Early American Republic," *Stanford Law Review* 41, no. 2 (1989), 335–76, cited in Cott, "Marriage and Women's Citizenship," 1453. Amy Stanley has argued that the abolitionism of the 1830s remade the meaning of wage labor, transforming it from dependence and subordination into the demonstration of independence and freedom shown in the capacity to contract; see *From Bondage to Contract*, chap. 1, esp. 21.

15. See Cott, "Marriage and Women's Citizenship," 1451–57. Cott writes, "Having and supporting dependents was *evidence* of independence. Thus marriage as well as property empowered a man in civic status, showing his capacity for citizenship by making him a head of household. To be a husband was to command the personal and material resources of a household and therefore to deserve a voice in the polity" (1452). That marriage and heading a household alone could qualify men for citizenship and suffrage was suggested by a proposal made at the Maryland state constitutional convention in 1850 that "every married man above the age of 18 years, and having the qualifications of residence shall be entitled to the right of suffrage" (qtd. in ibid.). Thomas Jefferson expressed his support as early as 1776 for "extending the right of suffrage (or in other words the rights of a citizen) to all who had a permanent intention of living in the country. Take what circumstances you please as evidence of this, either the having resided a certain time, or having a family, of having property, any or all of them" (qtd. in Gundersen, "Independence, Citizenship, and the American Revolution," 64). In this article, Gundersen traces the increasing association of women with dependence in the Revolutionary era. Jefferson's quotation is also cited in Cott, "Marriage and Women's Citizenship," 1448. Jean-Jacques Rousseau presaged Jefferson's idea when he wrote in *Émile* that it is "the good son, the good father, the good husband, that constitute the good citizen" (qtd. in Kerber, *Women of the Republic*, 24).

16. Laura Edwards writes similarly that "in the decades before the Civil War, the gender, racial, and class dimensions of private and public power converged"; see " 'Marriage Covenant,' " 83, and *Gendered Strife and Confusion*, 7.

17. Ledbetter, "Constitution of 1836," 219–20. Ledbetter argues that statehood also appealed to white settlers in Arkansas because of the legitimacy it would confer, "lend[ing]

a certain polish to the wild, violent, and lawless image of frontier Arkansas" (220). An additional urgency to the drive for statehood at this time stemmed from Congress's preference that the admission to the Union of a slave state be accompanied by the admission of a nonslaveholding state. Michigan was seeking admission, and many feared that if Arkansas was not prepared at the same time, they would miss their chance for perhaps decades (221).

18. From an address to the territorial legislature in October 1835 by territorial governor William S. Fulton; Ledbetter, "Constitution of 1836," 223, quoting *Arkansas Advocate*, October 9, 1835. Those opposing statehood at this time, primarily for economic reasons, used the same language of independence and dependence to justify their position. See "Minority Report," House of Representatives, Arkansas Territory, October 14, 1835, 1, included in *Journal of the Proceedings of the Convention Met to Form a Constitution*. See also Ledbetter, "Constitution of 1836," 219, 224.

19. Report, House of Representatives, Territory of Arkansas, October 14, 1835, 4–5, included in *Journal of the Proceedings of the Convention Met to Form a Constitution* (my emphasis).

20. Carl H. Moneyhon reports that 90 percent of white Arkansans as late as 1860 were born in another southern state, with 30 percent coming from Tennessee, 16 percent from Mississippi, 11 percent from Alabama, 10 percent from Missouri, 9 percent from Georgia, 4 percent from Kentucky, and another 12 percent from other slave states. See Moneyhon, *Impact of the Civil War and Reconstruction*, 52.

21. John Meek to Dr. Rob't E. Campbell, in Mrs. Thomas Campbell, ed., "Two Letters of the Meek Family, Union County, 1842–1845," *Arkansas Historical Quarterly* 15 (1956): 260–66, reprinted in Williams, Bolton, Moneyhon, and Williams, *Documentary History of Arkansas*, 57–58.

22. Qtd. in Moneyhon, *Impact of the Civil War and Reconstruction*, 56. Moneyhon finds that most white men in Arkansas believed in widespread opportunity for economic mobility (56–58). Joan Cashin's study of antebellum migration to the Southwest argues that young white men were seeking in frontier settlement a "manly independence" that encompassed economic fortune as well as a less tangible social freedom far from established norms of family and community obligations on the eastern seaboard. Both economic and social independence was sought to free them from the control of older generations and allow them to thus be "men"; see Cashin, *Family Venture*, esp. 32–36, 102–8, 159 n. 7. Cashin does not consider sources from Arkansas for her study. She examines largely the first stage of migration, from the seaboard to Mississippi and Tennessee (as well as to Texas and Louisiana), while many settlers in Arkansas came from these states and were making perhaps a second move and were less likely to be from planter families and to have found the economic success they were seeking at their first destination.

23. See Ledbetter, "Constitution of 1836," 215–52; *Journal of the Proceedings of the Convention Met to Form a Constitution*; and Thorpe, *Federal and State Constitutions*, 264–86.

24. Moneyhon reports that even elites in early Arkansas warned against pretensions and

divisions that accompanied social organization in the East, valuing the belief that opportunities for advancement were available to all white men in Arkansas for the social stability it brought. See *Impact of the Civil War and Reconstruction*, 52–57.

25. Article IV, Sections 2, 4, and 5, "Constitution of Arkansas—1836," in Thorpe, *Federal and State Constitutions*, 271–72.

26. Article IV, Sections 4, 6, 31, 33, 34, in ibid., 271–72, 275–76. The compromise leading to this apportionment plan, seemingly cordially arrived at in the meetings of a select committee appointed to settle the issue, consisted primarily of assuring that each county would have at least one representative in the state's house of representatives, regardless of whether or not each county contained the 500 free white males otherwise required per representative. Hill country representatives had already fought with Delta leaders over the apportionment of delegates to the constitutional convention itself, when those from the Delta attempted to base representation on total population, not free white men. See Gatewood, "Arkansas Delta," 19; Ledbetter, "Constitution of 1836," 224–28, 235–40; and Turner, "Constitution of 1836."

27. Article IV, Section 2, "Constitution of Arkansas—1836," in Thorpe, *Federal and State Constitutions*, 271.

28. Article II, Section 21, in ibid., 270.

29. Berlin, *Slaves without Masters*, 187.

30. Article II, Preamble, and Section 1, "Constitution of Arkansas—1836," in Thorpe, *Federal and State Constitutions*, 269.

31. *Journal of the Proceedings of the Convention Met to Form a Constitution*, 15, and Ledbetter, "Constitution of 1836," 233.

32. Article II, Section 1, "Constitution of Arkansas—1836," in Thorpe, *Federal and State Constitutions*, 269.

33. In 1860, the only Arkansas communities with more than 1,000 residents were Little Rock, Camden, Fort Smith, and Pine Bluff. See Moneyhon, *Impact of the Civil War and Reconstruction*, 52.

34. For discussion of the centrality of "the household" and the interrelationship between political and domestic sources of white male mastery in antebellum South Carolina, see McCurry, *Masters of Small Worlds* and "Two Faces of Republicanism." See also Bardaglio, *Reconstructing the Household*, esp. chap. 1, and Fox-Genovese, *Within the Plantation Household*. For a discussion of similar issues in antebellum and Reconstruction-era North Carolina, see Edwards, " 'Marriage Covenant' " and *Gendered Strife and Confusion*. See also Bercaw, *Gendered Freedoms*. In a related argument, Thomas Holt has examined the impact on British emancipation policy in Jamaica of liberal policy makers' belief that a certain form of domestic relations was necessary to produce subjects appropriate for participation in the public sphere. See Holt, " 'Essence of the Contract.' "

35. This is part of Stephanie McCurry's argument in *Masters of Small Worlds*. She writes, "Because the question of 'independence' has assumed a pivotal interpretive role in virtually every study of the antebellum yeomanry, it is imperative, as I see it, to inquire into the relations of power and dependency out of which that vaunted yeoman indepen-

dence was produced and reproduced" (viii). Regarding the term "self-working farmers," she continues: "The very term expressed [the] successful appropriation of the labor of others: the women, children, and, sometimes, slaves who peopled their households and tilled their fields. The vitality of male independence that characterized the public sphere of marketplace and ballot box was tied intimately to the legal and customary dependencies of the household. Dependence was the stuff of which independence—and manhood—were made" (72). See also "Two Faces of Republicanism."

36. Moneyhon, *Impact of the Civil War and Reconstruction*, 38, table 5; 43, table 6; and 47, table 7.

37. Ibid., 49–51, including table 8.

38. Ibid., 16–24.

39. Ibid., 24–26.

40. Ibid., 14–16.

41. Elizabeth Anne Payne, " 'What Ain't I Been Doing?' " Payne writes, "All but the most privileged farm women expected to contribute to the cultivation and harvesting of the family's cash crop. Therefore, chopping cotton, gathering corn, and picking cotton were part of the farm woman's yearly routine. And the Arkansas Delta had its fair share of women who plowed" (141). White women also participated in stock raising and slaughtering. In 1832, Matilda Fulton, a "prosperous" white farm woman, described in a letter to her husband the labor she performed a few days before giving birth to their son: "I was in the midst of [slaughtering] my pork the day befor I was taken sick[. A servant] and myself cut up nine hogs[.] I spent the day in the smoke haus without seting down untill night" (qtd. in ibid., 139). The reference to a servant also suggests the likelihood that white women often worked alongside enslaved laborers, either owned or hired. For similar conclusions about white women's labor in yeoman households in South Carolina's Low Country in the antebellum years, see McCurry, *Masters of Small Worlds*, 78, 81–85.

42. Mrs. Thomas Campbell, ed., "Two Letters of the Meek Family, Union County, 1842–1845," *Arkansas Historical Quarterly* 15 (1956): 260–66, reprinted in Williams, Bolton, Moneyhon, and Williams, *Documentary History of Arkansas*, 57.

43. Taylor, *Negro Slavery in Arkansas*, 56.

44. There were 1,617 slaves in Arkansas in 1820 (11 percent of the population), 4,576 in 1830 (15 percent of the population), and 19,935 in 1840 (20 percent of the population). Although Arkansas ranked second to last in numbers of slaves held in southern states in these years, the territory became a state in the decade of the greatest growth in slave numbers, 335 percent. After statehood the slave population continued to grow until 1860, when Arkansas ranked fourth among slaveholding states in slave population. See ibid., 25–27, 48–49. On the average proportion of the white population belonging to slaveholding families across the antebellum South, see Watson, "Conflict and Collaboration," 273–74.

45. More wealth was produced in Arkansas in the 1850s, when cotton production expanded by 426 percent, than in any other decade in the state's history. See Holley, with Starlard

and Dougan, "Rural Delta," 51–52. See also Moneyhon, *Impact of the Civil War and Reconstruction*, 13–14, and Taylor, *Negro Slavery in Arkansas*, 128–29. Also, from 1820 to 1850, the slave population grew more quickly in Arkansas than in any other state, and from 1850 to 1860 only Texas showed a greater increase; see Fon Louise Gordon, "From Slavery to Uncertain Freedom," 101.

46. Taylor, *Negro Slavery in Arkansas*, 48–49, 59.

47. Ibid., 128.

48. This is based on Carl Moneyhon's classification of white Arkansans into four classes: an elite, an upper-middle class, a lower-middle class, and a lower class, with the upper- and lower-middle class comprising propertied men who were not wealthy enough to own twenty slaves. Moneyhon characterizes the upper-middle class as small planters and prosperous farmers, many of whom owned some slaves, and the lower-middle class as modest farmers, less likely to own slaves, though some did, and more likely to rent the land they farmed or to move in and out of ownership and renting. He finds that the lower-middle-class category, those I am calling small farmers, displayed the highest rate of upward mobility between class categories in the 1850s. See *Impact of the Civil War and Reconstruction*, 53–54.

49. Ibid., 52.

50. Holley, with Starlard and Dougan, "Rural Delta," 53.

51. Moneyhon, *Impact of the Civil War and Reconstruction*, 52–58.

52. Ibid., 75–83. On cross-class political cooperation among antebellum southern white men, see Watson, "Conflict and Collaboration," and, especially on the gender dynamics that helped shape their shared political ideology, McCurry, *Masters of Small Worlds*.

53. Act No. 151, "An Act to Remove the Free Negroes and Mulattoes from this State," February 15, 1859, in *Acts of the General Assembly of the State of Arkansas*, 175–78. For a description of the working-class movement that resulted in expulsion in Arkansas, see Lack, "Urban Slave Community," 283–86. See also Berlin, *Slaves without Masters*, 372–74.

54. McCurry, *Masters of Small Worlds*.

55. Steven Hahn has argued that these particular practices of citizenship were most common in urban areas, while the mass of freedpeople living in the countryside, at least immediately following the end of the war, engaged in forms of political mobilization that were more closely related to the particular forms of political action they had engaged in as slaves. One key aspect of this inheritance from slavery was the "grapevine telegraph," which Hahn investigates specifically in regard to circulating rumors about federal plans to confiscate the land of former Confederates and distribute it to former slaves during the fall and winter of 1865. It was through the interaction of rural freedpeople with urban representatives—returning urban migrants, black Union soldiers, and Freedmen's Bureau agents—he argues, that rural freedpeople learned to frame their most pressing demand—land—in the forms of citizenship noted here. See *Nation under Our Feet*, chap. 3, esp. 131–43.

56. See ibid., esp. chaps. 4 and 5; Saville, *Work of Reconstruction*, esp. chap. 5; and Barkley Brown, "Uncle Ned's Children," esp. chaps. 5 and 6.

57. *CCC*, quotations on 5 and 9–10. It is evident that those coming together in this convention intended to form an enduring institution. The *Proceedings* open with an announcement that "the Convention met to effect a Permanent Organization" (3). Included in the business of the first day was the formation of a committee for that purpose (4). On similar conventions held throughout the South in late 1865 and early 1866, see Foner, *Reconstruction*, 112–19; Litwack, *Been in the Storm So Long*, 503–24; and Hahn, *Nation under Our Feet*, 116–27.

58. In a biography of Wise, Craig Simpson explores this possibility. See *Good Southerner*, 34–36.

59. U.S. Bureau of the Census, *Eighth Census*, M653, roll 655, p. 14, and *Ninth Census*, M593, roll 60, p. 145; St. Hilaire, "Negro Delegates," 43, 60–61; Hume, "'Black and Tan' Constitutional Conventions," 321. On praise for Grey's skills as an orator, see "Public Meeting at Helena," *WAG*, June 4, 1867, 3. On his work against the Klan, see "Journal and Debates of the Senate and House of Representatives," *Morning Republican* (Little Rock), December 1, 1868, 2, and Letters #69 and 70, Correspondence Register, Governor Powell Clayton, 1869–1871, Governors Papers, General Governors Collection, Arkansas History Commission. Grey's political career ended when he was paralyzed in 1880. He died eight years later. His obituary in the *Arkansas Gazette* noted his "reputation of being Arkansas's colored orator." See "Death of a Colored Man," *Arkansas Gazette*, November 11, 1888, 6.

60. U.S. Bureau of the Census, *Ninth Census*, M593, roll 60, p. 136; St. Hilaire, "Negro Delegates," 46, 64–65; Hume, "'Black and Tan' Constitutional Conventions," 323.

61. In South Carolina, a state that unlike Arkansas had had a large free black population before the war, twenty-four of the forty-six delegates to a similar convention on November 25, 1865, were free-born African Americans. See Holt, *Black over White*, 15.

62. Rogers, *History of Arkansas Baptists*, 170; Lack, "Urban Slave Community," 269–70.

63. Before the Civil War, Rev. William Wallace Andrews had achieved an exceptional degree of autonomy for a slave. Andrews was literate, and in his church he held Sunday school classes in which he taught other slaves to read and write. In addition to being a minister of an important black church and openly violating laws against teaching slaves to read, he and his family lived not with his wealthy owner, Chester Ashley, but, rather, in a house in Little Rock that Andrews had built himself. Ashley apparently supported Andrews's activities, gave him access to the Ashley family library for study, and donated to him the land for both his house and his church. When the Union Army occupied Little Rock in 1863, Andrews set up the first full-time school for freedpeople in the city. Andrews's postemancipation political career ended abruptly when he died in 1866. For information on William Wallace Andrews, see Lack, "Urban Slave Community," 265, 270; John Eaton Jr., *Report of the General Superintendent of Freemen*, 69 (Eaton refers to Little Rock's first black teacher as Rev. Andrew Wallace, by which he must have meant William Wallace Andrews); and Kennan, "First Negro Teacher in Little Rock," 196–97. Kennan reports that Andrews's daughter, Charlotte Andrews Stephens, remembered, "Many of the Negroes who were able to participate in public affairs immediately upon

Emancipation used to bless 'Brother Wallace Andrews' for having taught them to read and write, even at the risk of punishment of himself and his pupils if the laws had been enforced against them" (197). It is Ross who reports that Andrews's antebellum church was named Mt. Warren Chapel, while Lack calls it Wesley Chapel.

64. Though there is no evidence that Warren worked as a minister before his ordination in the 1880s, CCC, 11, refers to the convention being led in prayer by "Rev. Nathan Warren." Warren appears in Jackson and Teeples, *Arkansas 1850 Census Index*, 91. See Ross, "Nathan Warren," and Taylor, *Negro Slavery in Arkansas*, 245–46.

65. CCC, 3–9, 11.

66. CCC, 3–4.

67. CCC, 5.

68. See Finley, *From Slavery to Uncertain Freedom*, 70–71. Widespread anti-unionist violence was also prevalent in Arkansas, beginning in the fall of 1865. When Home Guards organized by Unionist governor Isaac Murphy were unable to stop the attacks, Murphy requested federal troops to restore order in January 1866, though an adequate force was never supplied. See Moneyhon, *Impact of the Civil War and Reconstruction*, 192. The Arkansas convention was held at the height of the "Christmas Insurrection Scare of 1865," which Steven Hahn has argued became the justification for violent campaigns of intimidation by planters against any signs of independent political or economic action on the part of African Americans. See *Nation under Our Feet*, 146–52.

69. Qtd. in Foner, *Reconstruction*, 112.

70. Fourteen of the delegates were identified as coming from five different counties; no county identification was recorded for the other six. See CCC, 3–5.

71. One representative did come from west Arkansas, Sebastian County, where African American populations were far smaller (10.5 percent in Sebastian). Percentages are for 1870 and can be found in George H. Thompson, *Arkansas and Reconstruction*, 70, fig. 11. See also Finley, *From Slavery to Uncertain Freedom*, 25.

72. Three delegates represented Phillips County, where Helena had been permanently taken by federal forces in July 1862. One came from Sebastian County, where the Union Army had occupied Fort Smith in September 1863. The majority of delegates were from Pulaski County, where the federal army captured Little Rock also in September 1863. See Moneyhon, *Impact of the Civil War and Reconstruction*, 125–27. Phillips and Sebastian Counties also experienced decreases in white male populations of 52 and 88 percent, respectively, a demographic change that may have allowed freedpeople to organize and select leaders with less likelihood of violent interference (135). Because of Union Army occupation, all three counties were sites of large settlements of fleeing slaves during the war and thus were centers of the first organized freed communities in the state (137).

73. "Mass Meeting," *Western Clarion*, October 14, 1865.

74. About the hundreds of delegates attending similar gatherings throughout the South in 1865 and 1866, Eric Foner writes, "Some [were] selected by local meetings occasionally marked by 'animated debate,' others by churches, fraternal societies, Union Leagues,

and black army units, still others simply appointed by themselves" (*Reconstruction*, 112). Pulaski County was the location of many black institutions, and perhaps several different organizations selected delegates to attend. That many delegates already knew one another well and may have decided to attend together is suggested by the fact that Nathan Warren was the father-in-law of another delegate, A. L. Richmond. Warren had also been married to a woman who had worked as the cook for the Ashley family, wealthy slaveholders in Little Rock and owners of William Wallace Andrews, as well as many of Warren's own children. See Ross, "Nathan Warren," 58–59.

75. CCC, 3. Quotation is from the convention president, Rev. James T. White.

76. "Slavery republicanism" is Stephanie McCurry's term. See *Masters of Small Worlds*, viii.

77. Qtd. in Moneyhon, *Impact of the Civil War and Reconstruction*, 193. A few weeks after the Convention of Colored Citizens, Kyle explained what he thought were most white Arkansans' views on black male suffrage to the Joint Committee on Reconstruction, that is, that black men would have to prove that they were "worthy" of the privilege before exercising the franchise: "The question of suffrage is one that ought to be kept in abeyance for a while, and see what improvement the negro can make intellectually and morally, and see what can be done for him; and hereafter, if he shows a disposition to do something for himself to acquire property and make a good citizen, they would have no objection to giving him the right of suffrage" (testimony of G. H. Kyle, February 1, 1866, in U.S. Congress, House of Representatives, *Report of the Joint Committee on Reconstruction*, 53).

78. Moneyhon, *Impact of the Civil War and Reconstruction*, 195. Quotation is from J. R. Eakin, editor, *Washington Telegraph*, August 23, 1865.

79. "The President and Reconstruction," WAG, December 2, 1865, 4.

80. CCC, 10.

81. CCC, 5.

82. CCC, 6. Similarly, in the call for the meeting in Helena at which Grey was appointed a delegate to this convention, a call presumably written by Grey (he is listed as the chair of the committee issuing the call), readers were urged to "take the initiative step and respond cheerfully and promptly . . . and show to the world that we are not the inert, inanimate race that they look upon us to be, but we are fully alive to our position and have that same feeling . . . that gives us the right to possess all the immunities belonging to man. Life, liberty and the pursuit of happiness accompanied by our elective franchise" ("Mass Meeting," *Western Clarion*, October 14, 1865).

83. CCC, 10.

84. On courts being "more interested in disciplining the black population and forcing it to labor than in dispensing justice," as well as legislative efforts to control African Americans, see Foner, *Reconstruction*, 199–209.

85. Wilson, *Black Codes*, 114.

86. CCC, 10.

87. See testimony of George H. Kyle, February 1, 1866, and Charles A. Harper, February 17, 1866, in U.S. Congress, House of Representatives, *Report of the Joint Committee on*

Reconstruction, 53, 75, for aspects of this discourse in moderate white men's ideas about black suffrage. For conservative condemnations of black men's "unfitness" for political participation, see below. See also Barkley Brown, "To Catch the Vision of Freedom," 75. For a discussion of ideologies of fitness for political participation in British emancipation policy in Jamaica, see Holt, *Problem of Freedom* and " 'Essence of the Contract.' "

88. *CCC*, 7, 5.

89. Elsa Barkley Brown has argued that during Reconstruction, African Americans operated in two simultaneous public spheres, one internal to black communities and consisting of institutions and political norms shaped by African Americans, and one external and dominated by white institutions and official arenas of electoral politics. See Barkley Brown, "To Catch the Vision of Freedom," 74, and "Negotiating and Transforming the Public Sphere," 107–46. The Convention of Colored Citizens in Arkansas, although containing some elements of an internal political event, explicitly addressed the political world external to black communities.

90. The first motion at the convention was for the appointment of a Committee on Invitations and Arrangements. The second motion was to order that committee to "request Governor Murphy, General Reynolds, and General Sprague [assistant commissioner of the Freedmen's Bureau for Arkansas] to be present and address the convention" (*CCC*, 4). Murphy "made a few terse remarks of encouragement, &c., and distinctly and openly avowed that he, though he trespassed, advocated the rights of the entire colored race," at the end of the second day of the proceedings (*CCC*, 8). Reynolds and Secretary of State White attended the proceedings, at least for the fourth day. Oddly, Sprague of the Freedmen's Bureau did not attend (or at least was not noted in the proceedings).

91. *CCC*, 10.

92. *CCC*, 6.

93. Hahn, *Nation under Our Feet*, 128–42.

94. *CCC*, 11. Charles A. Harper, an Arkansas state supreme court justice, observed the convention's proceedings and later noted, "I was very much astonished listening to their proceedings. . . . There were two negroes in particular, from Helena, men of considerable education and intelligence. They addressed the congregation of their race, and their views were generally well expressed. . . . There were others of considerable intelligence; so that altogether they made a much better show than I supposed such a body of negroes in that State could do." Though this was the impression that one can imagine the convention wished to convey, it did not have the desired effect of convincing white officials of black men's capacity for political participation. Harper continued, "I think there is considerable intelligence among them in Arkansas at this time, but of course it is only now and then one of that kind; the most of them are rather of a low order." He did not support black male suffrage and speculated that it would be possible to extend suffrage in the future only under restrictions not faced by white voters: "only to those who had borne arms and could read and write, or perhaps a property qualification to show that the negro was thrifty." See testimony of Charles A. Harper, February 17, 1866,

in U.S. Congress, House of Representatives, *Report of the Joint Committee on Reconstruction*, 73–75.

95. *CCC*, 7.

96. Grey referred to citizenship and suffrage as "our inalienable right." *CCC*, 7.

97. *CCC*, title page, 5, 9.

98. *CCC*, 8. The fact that the secretary transcribing the proceedings of the convention put these words in capital letters suggests the crescendo in Grey's voice as he reached the end of his speech, and thus the importance of this issue to him. For similar sentiments expressed during the Convention of Freedmen of North Carolina, see Hahn, *Nation under Our Feet*, 124.

99. *CCC*, 5, 6.

100. Elsa Barkley Brown, "To Catch the Vision of Freedom," esp. 66–72, 82–85, and "Negotiating and Transforming the Public Sphere." On the autonomy sought in freedom as a collective condition, see also Holt, " 'Empire over the Mind,' " 283–314.

101. *CCC*, 11.

102. This rhetoric was particularly popularized by David Walker's *Appeal to the Coloured Citizens of the World*. See, for instance, Horton and Horton, *In Hope of Liberty*, 172–73.

103. It is this formulation that Barkley Brown's work has questioned. She has argued that only years after emancipation did gender-exclusive practices characterize African American political cultures, and that even then these exclusive practices were always contested across gender and class lines. She has cautioned against assuming that evidence from a later time indicates where freedpeople began when they first faced freedom. See "Negotiating and Transforming the Public Sphere" and "To Catch the Vision of Freedom." Cf. *Gendered Strife and Confusion*, in which Laura Edwards finds that freedpeople and their political leaders in North Carolina "relied on gender hierarchy to erase existing racial and class barriers—from political leaders who trumpeted the cause of manhood rights to ordinary men and women at the local level who tried to realize the promise of equal rights before the law." She argues further that by "using existing legal and political discourses to wedge their way into public space, . . . they also built their politics around a patriarchal structure that would later prove to be their undoing" (22). See also Bercaw, *Gendered Freedoms*, esp. chap. 4, and Jacqueline Jones, *Labor of Love, Labor of Sorrow*, 66. James Oliver Horton and Lois Horton consider that the phrase "manhood rights" might not necessarily have indicated to African Americans in the nineteenth century that only men were to participate in political affairs. They write, "The term 'manhood rights' was used during the nineteenth century to connote the rights of citizenship exercised by men in American society. Although the term carried obvious gender implications, it was used to refer to rights that could protect the race and that could be directly or indirectly exercised by men or women" (*In Hope of Liberty*, 317 n. 6). See also Martha Jones, *All Bound Up Together*, 184–85. On the degree to which patriarchal norms characterized African Americans' families after emancipation, see Chapter 5, n. 38.

104. That national debates on woman suffrage were heard and felt in Arkansas, and in Phillips County, where both James T. White and William Henry Grey were from, is

suggested by the 1864 entry in the diary of Susan Cook, a white woman living near Helena. Cook noted that "Mr. Higgings is passing the night with us; had quite a debate upon 'Woman's Rights,' that never ending theme" ("The Diary of Susan Cook," *Phillips County Historical Quarterly* 6 [March 1966], 35, qtd. in Payne, "'What Ain't I Been Doing?,'" 145). Grey, White, and the other black delegates to the Arkansas state constitutional convention of 1868 would at that gathering show a similar hesitancy to associate themselves with controversial positions such as support for woman suffrage. See Chapter 4.

105. CCC, 7–8.

106. Ibid., 3.

107. The "Colored Citizens of Nashville" submitted a petition to the Union Convention of Tennessee that stated, "But what higher order of citizen is there than the soldier? or who has a greater trust confided to his hands? If we are called on to do military duty against the rebel armies in the field, why should we be denied the privilege of voting against rebel citizens at the ballot-box? The latter is as necessary to save the Government as the former" (in Berlin, Reidy, and Rowland, *Black Military Experience*, 812; see also Berlin, Fields, Miller, Reidy, and Rowland, *Free at Last*, chap. 6). Most famously, Frederick Douglass declared that once a black man had "upon his person the brass letters U.S. . . . , an eagle on his button, and a musket on his shoulder, and bullets in his pocket, there is no power on earth . . . which can deny that he has earned the right of citizenship in the United States" (qtd. in Blight, *Frederick Douglass' Civil War*, 161). See also Martha Jones, *All Bound Up Together*, 124–25.

108. Barkley Brown, "To Catch the Vision of Freedom," 80. See also Stanley, *From Bondage to Contract*, 29–35, on black abolitionists' visions of citizenship in relation to gender.

109. Conservative victory over Unionists was facilitated by the state supreme court decision in *Rison et al. v. Fair* in December 1865 that invalidated a prohibition on voting by men who had voluntarily fought for the Confederacy. See Moneyhon, *Impact of the Civil War and Reconstruction*, 170, 194–205.

110. On this convention, see Moneyhon, *Impact of the Civil War and Reconstruction*, 242–44; Staples, *Reconstruction in Arkansas*, 162–67; "The Union State Convention," *WAG*, April 9, 1867, 1; and also in the *Gazette*, on conservative hopes of having some influence on the convention, "Appropos of the Union State Convention," April 2, 1867, 2, and on their disappointment with the radical outcome, "The Union State Convention (so called)," April 9, 1867, 2.

111. "The Outside Show," *WAG*, April 9, 1867, 1.

112. Quotations are paraphrases of the meeting's resolutions appearing in the *WAG*, April 2, 1867, 2.

113. CCC, 3, 11. Richmond was also married to the daughter of Rev. Nathan Warren's third wife. Warren, also a delegate to the Convention of Colored Citizens, helped to organize Rev. William Wallace Andrew's antebellum church into the Bethel AME and would ultimately take over as pastor. See Ross, "Nathan Warren," 58–59.

114. This observation draws on Saville's argument in *Work of Reconstruction*, chap. 5.

115. Editorial, *WAG*, April 2, 1867, 2.

116. Paraphrase of the meeting's resolutions appearing in ibid.

117. "The Outside Show," *WAG*, April 9, 1867, 1.

118. Saville, *Work of Reconstruction*, 172–73. See also Hahn, *Nation under Our Feet*, 175.

119. On different kinds of "rude insignia" used by freedpeople to "indicate that a [Union] league member was 'on duty,'" in South Carolina, see Saville, *Work of Reconstruction*, 181.

120. See Horton, "Freedom's Yoke," 53–55, 69–70, 73, for African American women's participation in but not dominance over political events in the antebellum North.

121. The writer, though, mocked this anticipation and represented freedpeople's demeanor as conveying a misguided approach to their civic roles, concluding that whether the "something" in which they were prepared to take part was to be "in the nature of a circus or a camp meeting, they were very much at a loss to determine" ("The Outside Show," *WAG*, April 9, 1867, 1). Black women continued to attend political events in Little Rock. Reporting on a speech made outside the State House by AME Church bishop Campbell in June 1867, the *Gazette* noted of the 400 people in the crowd, "nearly all were black, many being females" (no title, *WAG*, June 4, 1867, 2). At another political rally in July 1867, freedwomen constituted the majority of participants; see Finley, *From Slavery to Uncertain Freedom*, 42, citing E. G. Barker Report, December 9, 1867, Field Office Records for Arkansas, BRFAL.

122. "The Outside Show," *WAG*, April 9, 1867, 1. Among the three white Republicans addressing the crowd was James Hinds, one of the delegates to the Union State Convention selected by the meeting in Bethel Church. Hinds had been a lawyer and the U.S. district attorney in Minnesota before coming to Arkansas with the Union Army in 1865. He later served as a delegate to the 1868 constitutional convention (see Chapter 4) and soon thereafter as a congressman. On October 22, 1868, while holding this post, he was assassinated by the secretary of the Democratic Committee in Monroe County, who may have been connected to the Klan. See Hume, "'Black and Tan' Constitutional Conventions," 318; Moneyhon, *Impact of the Civil War and Reconstruction*, 244, 251; and Trelease, *White Terror*, 154. Also addressing the crowd was J. W. Demby, the white man who had served as a temporary secretary for the Convention of Colored Citizens in 1865. In his speech, Demby referred to himself as a regular at freedpeople's political meetings.

123. "The Outside Show," *WAG*, April 9, 1867, 1.

124. Lieutenant H. F. Willis, Agent, Rocky Comfort, Arkansas, Monthly Report, September 1, 1867, and W. S. McCullough, Agent, Devalls Bluff, Arkansas, Monthly Report, August 31, 1867, both in Reports of Bureau Operations, Operations Reports from Subordinate Officers, April–September 1867, Arkansas BRFAL, roll 25.

125. J. H. Carhart, Agent, Magnolia, Monthly Report, August 31, 1867, in Reports of Bureau Operations, Arkansas BRFAL, roll 25.

126. V. V. Smith, Agent, Lewisville, Monthly Report, September 1, 1867, in ibid.

127. Saville, *Work of Reconstruction*, 162–63.

128. Joseph L. Thorp, Agent, Camden, Monthly Report, August 31, 1867, in Reports of Bureau Operations, Arkansas BRFAL, roll 25.

129. Major J. T. Watson, Agent, Little Rock, Monthly Report, August 31, 1867, in ibid.

130. "The Outside Show," *WAG*, April 9, 1867, 1.

131. V. V. Smith, Agent, Lewisville, Monthly Report, September 1, 1867, in Reports of Bureau Operations, Arkansas BRFAL, roll 25.

132. Qtd. in Moneyhon, *Impact of the Civil War and Reconstruction*, 245.

133. Circular No. 2, April 8, 1867, in Circular, Arkansas BRFAL, roll 21. This circular was praised by the *WAG* in an editorial on April 16, 1867, 2. See also Finley, *From Slavery to Uncertain Freedom*, 59.

134. Circular No. 13, July 2, 1867, in Circular, Arkansas BRFAL, roll 21.

135. Lieutenant F. W. Thibant, Agent, Washington, Monthly Report, August 31, 1867, in Reports of Bureau Operations, Arkansas BRFAL, roll 25.

136. William A. Inman, Agent, Jonesboro, Monthly Report, August 31, 1867, in ibid. For black populations of various counties, see George H. Thompson, *Arkansas and Reconstruction*, 70, fig. 11.

137. Circular No. 13, July 2, 1867, in Circular, Arkansas BRFAL, roll 21.

138. J. H. Scroggins, Agent, Hampton, Monthly Report, August 25, 1867, in Reports of Bureau Operations, Arkansas BRFAL, roll 25.

139. J. H. Carhart, Agent, Magnolia, Monthly Report, August 31, 1867, in ibid.

140. See, for instance, Lieutenant H. F. Willis, Agent, Rocky Comfort, Monthly Report, September 1, 1867; W. S. McCullough, Agent, Devalls Bluff, Monthly Report, August 31, 1867; V. V. Smith, Agent, Lewisville, Monthly Report, September 1, 1867; Major J. T. Watson, Agent, Little Rock, Monthly Report, August 31, 1867; J. H. Carhart, Agent, Magnolia, Monthly Report, August 31, 1867; J. H. Scroggins, Agent, Hampton, Monthly Report, August 25, 1867; and Lieutenant J. C. Predmore, Agent, Napoleon, Monthly Report, August 31, 1867, all in ibid.

141. Moneyhon, *Impact of the Civil War and Reconstruction*, 226–38.

142. See, for instance, W. S. McCullough, Agent, Devalls Bluff, Monthly Report, August 31, 1867; E. W. Douglass, Acting Agent, South Bend, Monthly Report, August 31, 1867; Captain William Brian, Agent, Jacksonport, Monthly Report, August 31, 1867; and Major J. T. Watson, Agent, Little Rock, Monthly Report, August 31, 1867, all in Reports of Bureau Operations, Arkansas BRFAL, roll 25.

143. See, for instance, Lieutenant F. W. Thibant, Agent, Washington, Monthly Report, August 31, 1867, and J. L. Thorp, Agent, Camden, Monthly Report, August 31, 1867, both in ibid.

144. E.g., Lieutenant J. C. Predmore, Agent, Napoleon, Monthly Report, August 31, 1867, in ibid.

145. John W. Stayton to Joe Stayton, March 13, 1868, Jackson County Historical Society, reprinted in Luker, "Post Civil War Period."

146. Captain William Brian, Agent, Jacksonport, Monthly Report, August 31, 1867, in Reports

of Bureau Operations, Arkansas BRFAL, roll 25. See also Finley, *From Slavery to Uncertain Freedom*, 42. It appears that Captain Brian found this bold behavior on the part of freedwomen inappropriate and credited himself with having taught freedmen more proper conduct. He continued his report, saying that "little or no trouble" such as that coming from freedwomen had been "experienced from the men. . . . A proper estimate of manhood and of freedom I endeavor to instill in their minds, as well as a proper manner of exhibiting and maintaining it. I am clearly of the opinion that I can discern some improvement in this respect."

147. Counties with large numbers of black registrants turned out large majorities for the convention. See election and registration returns printed in *WAG*, December 10, 1867, 3. Large turnouts of black voters for similar elections in other states were noted in the *Gazette* as well. See, for instance, a report on Bolivar, Mississippi, noting that "the negroes turned out in great strength at the polls to exercise their cherished franchise." See "A Rich Illustration of Negro Suffrage," *Little Rock Daily Gazette*, November 28, 1867, supplement.

148. See, for instance, "Ratification Meeting" and "Union Meeting of Franklin County, Ark.," *Little Rock Evening Republican*, June 4, 1867, 3.

149. R. S. Gantt to Jesse Turner, September 15, 1867, Turner Correspondence, UAF.

150. Two reprints from the *Fort Smith Herald* in "State News," *WAG*, November 19, 1867, 1.

151. For information on the black delegates to the convention, see Hume, "Arkansas Constitutional Convention of 1868" and "'Black and Tan' Constitutional Conventions," esp. 321–24; St. Hilaire, "Negro Delegates"; *Debates and Proceedings*, 4–10; and Chapter 4.

152. Even Grey worked to represent the most important concerns of his rural constituents. At the constitutional convention he took up the question of land, perhaps feeling bolder than he had at the Convention of Colored Citizens now that congressional support for suffrage was already secured. Specifically, Grey introduced a resolution to the convention calling for a committee to investigate permanently settling freed families on tracts of government-owned land under the federal Homestead Act and using government loans to provide initial provisions. He thus proposed that this body go further than had the Convention of Colored Citizen's demand that Arkansas "deal justly and equitably for her laborers" (*Debates and Proceedings*, 251–52).

153. "Shadings of the Picture," *WAG*, January 14, 1868, 2. Applause and laughter coming from the galleries was noted by the convention's secretary at various points in the gathering's published proceedings. See *Debates and Proceedings*, esp. 363, 371, 373. Perhaps this vocal presence influenced the *Gazette* to editorialize that the convention held "its daily session in the capitol for the entertainment of the negroes in the gallery" ("Partizan Shamelessness," *WAG*, January 21, 1868, 2).

154. *Debates and Proceedings*, 630.

155. Ibid., 670.

156. Ibid., 684.

157. Ibid., 629–30.

158. Moses Jeffries, eighty-one years old, interviewed by Samuel Taylor in Little Rock, no

date given (based on Jeffries's reported age and birthdate, 1937 or 1938), *Arkansas Narratives*, pt. 4, in Rawick, *American Slave*, 9:42.

159. The emancipation celebration from January 1, 1864, is described by Charlotte Andrews Stephens, the daughter of William Wallace Andrews, in Kennan, "First Negro Teacher in Little Rock," 198–99. One of the churches involved in the planned processions was her father's AME chapel, and the other was Wilson Brown's Baptist Church.

160. Finley, *From Slavery to Uncertain Freedom*, 52. See also Hahn, *Nation under Our Feet*, 175, and, on similar processions in Mississippi, Frankel, *Freedom's Women*, 174.

161. "Incidents of the Election," *WAG*, March 31, 1868, 2.

162. The article also noted that "had it not been for the resolute energy, indomitable courage and unswerving loyalty of the freedmen, the constitution would have been defeated" (reprinted in "A Proper Tribute and a Frank Confession," *WAG*, April 7, 1868, 1).

163. "Incidents of the Election," *WAG*, March 31, 1868, 2.

164. Saville, *Work of Reconstruction*, 173–74.

165. Moneyhon, *Impact of the Civil War and Reconstruction*, 249; "We have of late . . . ," 2, and "Read and Remember," 2, both from *WAG*, March 3, 1868.

166. In Eagle township, close to Little Rock in Pulaski County, the *Gazette* reported that "there were a large number of negroes present from adjoining townships" who occupied the polling site even though they did not vote ("Election in Pulaski," *WAG*, April 7, 1868, 1).

167. "Incidents of the Election," *WAG*, March 31, 1868, 2.

168. "State News," *WAG*, March 31, 1868, 1, 2.

169. Elsa Barkley Brown writes of large numbers of freedpeople gathering at polling places in Virginia, "the principal reason for the group presence at the polls was protection. . . . But . . . the necessity for a group presence at the polls reinforced the sense of collective enfranchisement" ("To Catch the Vision of Freedom," 85).

170. "Incidents of the Election," *WAG*, March 31, 1868, 2.

171. *CCC*, 7.

172. Moneyhon, *Impact of the Civil War and Reconstruction*, 101–23, 179, and "Disloyalty and Class Consciousness in Southwestern Arkansas." For a similar phenomenon in Georgia, see Hahn, *Roots of Southern Populism*, 116–33.

173. For a similar argument about Reconstruction-era politics in South Carolina, see Kantrowitz, *Ben Tillman*, esp. introduction and chap. 2.

174. The *Gazette* was issued in both a daily and a weekly format, the latter released every Tuesday and consisting of a compilation of articles from the previous week's daily issues.

175. On the Reconstruction-era conservative press's partisan rhetoric and aims, see, for instance, Osthaus, *Partisans of the Southern Press*.

176. The *Gazette* had been sold in 1853 to Christopher Columbus Danley by its founder William E. Woodruff Sr. William E. Woodruff Jr. purchased back partial interest in the paper in July 1866. W. D. Blocher acquired the other half-interest in January 1867. For information on the history of the *Gazette*, see Ross, *Arkansas Gazette*, and Allsopp, *History of the Arkansas Press*, 324–25. For Woodruff Sr. as the owner of fourteen slaves in

Little Rock, see Taylor, *Negro Slavery in Arkansas*, 54. For his calls for the reenslavement or expulsion of all free African Americans in Arkansas, see Taylor, *Negro Slavery in Arkansas*, 248, 255, and Berlin, *Slaves without Masters*, 372.

177. Walker to William E. Woodruff Jr., September 24, 1868, in Walker Correspondence, folder 2, UAF.

178. Editorial "Upon the intelligence . . . ," *WAG*, March 12, 1867, 3.

179. Ibid.

180. See, for instance, editorial "The events of the past few months . . . ," April 9, 1867, 2; editorial "The enfranchisement of the negro . . . ," May 14, 1867, 2; and editorial "The recent acts of violence . . . ," June 4, 1867, 2, all in *WAG*. White conservatives echoed this interpretation of black political protest in their personal correspondence. Robert S. Gantt wrote to Jesse Turner on September 15, 1867, concerning his home county of Prairie: "As yet the negroes in this county have not been tampered with much. It will be done however. . . . They are ignorant and easily controlled particularly through the medium of such agencies and appliances [?] of Loyal leagues & other societies and no one in his senses doubts for one moment that these agencies will be industriously employed" (R. S. Gantt to Jesse Turner, September 15, 1867, Turner Correspondence, UAF).

181. This editorial was responding to a "misunderstanding" that led freedpeople in Little Rock to believe their homes were going to be attacked and thus to gather arms for self-defense. See editorial "The recent acts of violence . . . ," *WAG*, June 4, 1867, 2. Reports expressed increasing alarm over black men mixing politics and arms in Arkansas. See "A Disreputable Affair," September 3, 1867, 3; "State News," October 8, 1867, 2; "Editors Gazette," December 17, 1867, 2; and editorial "The issuance of a proclamation . . . ," December 24, 1867, 1, all in *WAG*. For "Telegraphic" reports from other states of alleged or feared black-initiated violence associated with politics, see the *WAG*'s "Telegraphic" and "State News" columns, April 2, 1867, 1; July 9, 1867, 2; July 16, 1867, 1; December 31, 1867, 2; May 14, 1867, 2; and no title, *WAG*, January 7, 1868, 1.

182. "It is announced from New Orleans that a trade in registration papers has sprung up in the city. White men who are refused the right to vote are buying the papers of colored men, who are willingly sell them [*sic*]" (*WAG*, May 28, 1867, 2). As registration proceeded in Pulaski County, the *Gazette* reported that "we have heard complaints that the board [of registration] is not strict enough in requiring proof of the ages of negroes where there is reason to believe that they have not yet reached their majority. The greater part of this class really have no knowledge of their precise age, and therefore are not aware of the character of the statement to which they make affidavit" ("Registration," *WAG*, July 30, 1867, 3). See also "A Scene at a Registering Office in Crawford County," *WAG*, August 6, 1867, 2.

Despite claims that the *Gazette* was concerned with assuring the "intelligence and virtue" of the voting citizenry, the paper's greater concern appears to have been the thousands of black men who were successfully registering to vote, in some parts of the state in greater numbers than white men. Numerous reports announced the numbers of white versus black voters registered in Arkansas townships and counties and in other southern states, and such statistics were used to warn white men that they would be outvoted if they did not take the necessary oaths and register. See, for instance, "When registration was progressing . . . ," May 28, 1867, 2; "Registration," June 4, 1867, 3; "We learn that in Pyeatte and Plant townships . . . ," June 11, 1867, 1; "It is stated that 180,000 voters . . . ," 2; Richmond item under "Telegraphic," July 2, 1867, 1; two Richmond items under "Telegraphic," July 16, 1867, 1; "State Items" and Charleston item under "Telegraphic," both from August 27, 1867, 1; and numerous items on registration totals in Arkansas counties and other states in September 3, 10, 17, 1867, all in *WAG*.

183. "A Poor Price for a Poor Article," *WAG*, January 21, 1868, 2. Another editorial explaining white conservatives' preference for continued military rule over black male suffrage argued, "There is infinitely more safety for life and property while the supreme power is in the hands of intelligent white men, than if it were lodged with a proletarian mass of illiterate negroes and their more unprincipled white allies" (editorial, *WAG*, December 31, 1867, 1).

184. "County Democratic Convention," *WAG*, December 17, 1867, 3.

185. Editorial "Now that the time has been indicated . . . ," *WAG*, October 8, 1867, 1.

186. See "Public Meeting at Pensacola, Florida—Views of Hon. S. R. Mallory," April 23, 1867, 1, and editorial "Every citizen who feels any solicitude . . . ," April 16, 1867, 2, both in *WAG*. On this rhetoric among federal military officials and the Freedmen's Bureau, see, e.g., Schwalm, *Hard Fight for We*, esp. chap. 5. For an analysis of the emphasis on "industry" and providing for one's (a man's) family as measuring "fitness" for political power in emancipation policy and discourse, see Holt, " 'Essence of the Contract' " and *Problem of Freedom*, and Barkley Brown, "To Catch the Vision of Freedom," 75.

187. "An Important Order," *WAG*, April 23, 1867, 2.

188. In *WAG*, see "Editors Gazette," December 17, 1867, 2, and no title, May 21, 1867, 1. Similarly, the paper reported, "There is a general complaint among planters that the negroes have done comparatively nothing in the way of work since the election" (editorial "According to the latest advices . . . ," *Daily Arkansas Gazette*, November 27, 1867, 2). See also "The Outside Show," *WAG*, April 9, 1867, 1.

189. "Editors Gazette," *WAG*, December 17, 1867, 2. See also editorial "We fear there will be great suffering . . . ," *WAG*, December 17, 1867, 1.

190. "Chicot County, Ark., Asking for Protection.—Deplorable Condition of Affairs," *WAG*, December 24, 1867, 2.

191. The editorial protested, "In the name of a suffering people, of innocent women and children, . . . we urge that no such cruelty and trouble be visited upon us as is inherent in the scheme to compel an impoverished, industrious white people, struggling against misfortunes, to support idle, lazy negroes" ("We published an order yesterday . . . ," *WAG*, December 24, 1867, 2).

192. "Tell Us of the Night!," *WAG*, January 7, 1868, 1.

193. For an interpretation of the political rhetoric advocating secession in South Carolina in the late antebellum years that has significantly influenced my reading here, see Mc-Curry, "Black Republicans and the Rape of the South." See also McCurry, *Master of Small Worlds*, chap. 8.

194. Editorial "The radical party has found . . . ," *WAG*, December 17, 1867, 2.

195. "Their Deeds Are Dark: The Gag-Law," *WAG*, January 14, 1868, 2.

196. See, for instance, editorial "The radical party has found . . . ," December 17, 1867, 2; editorial "Now that it is certain . . . ," December 24, 1867, 2; "So Very Honorable Indeed," January 14, 1868, 2; "The Galled Gade Winces," January 21, 1868, 1; "Partizan Shameless-ness," January 21, 1868, 2; "Usurpation by the Convention," January 28, 1868, 1; "The Mississippi Convention," February 4, 1868, 2; and, calling the document produced by Arkansas's convention a "bastard constitution," "Give Us a New Shuffle and a Fair Deal," February 18, 1868, 2, all in *WAG*.

197. McCurry finds that pro-secession rhetoric in South Carolina similarly used the trope "Black Republicans" to connect in one referent white Republicans and abolitionists with the slaves whom they were allegedly "inciting" to rebel. See McCurry, "Black Republi-cans and the Rape of the South," esp. 41–46.

198. "The Leavenworth (Kansas) *Commercial* . . . ," *WAG*, December 17, 1867, 4.

199. Editorial "Now that it is quite certain . . . ," *WAG*, December 24, 1867, 2.

200. On the incubus metaphor used more explicitly to represent black men as sexually threatening to white women at the turn of the century, see Gilmore, "Murder, Memory, and the Flight of the Incubus." See also Gilmore, *Gender and Jim Crow*, chap. 4, and Hodes, *White Women, Black Men*, chap. 8. On the historical variability of images of black men as a sexual threat to white women, see, along with Hodes, Sommerville, "Rape Myth in the Old South Reconsidered" and *Rape and Race*, and McCurry, "Black Re-publicans and the Rape of the South."

201. See McCurry, "Black Republicans and the Rape of the South," for a reading of the pro-secession rhetoric in South Carolina as working through intentional ambiguities in both the gender of an imagined rape victim (white southern men or white southern women?) and the race of an imagined assailant (white Republicans or black male slaves?) in imagery of politics as sexual violation.

202. "State News," *WAG*, December 17, 1867, 3.

203. "More Tinkering," *WAG*, January 14, 1868, 1.

204. Whether or not to cooperate with the congressional plan for calling a constitutional convention in hopes of controlling it and its outcome or, rather, to sit out of the entire process on the principle that the Reconstruction Acts were unconstitutional was an issue on which there was much disagreement among white elites. See, for instance, the views expressed in a letter from John R. Fellows to Jesse Turner (elected state senator in the conservative victory in state elections in 1866 and opponent of the constitution in 1868) on May 7, 1867 (in Turner Correspondence, UAF), versus those of Jonathan R. Eakin (a state legislator in 1866 and the editor of the Washington, Arkansas, *Telegraph*)

in his correspondence with his friend David Walker (president of Arkansas's secession convention in 1861 and chief justice of the state supreme court in 1866) in June 1867 (Eakin to Walker, August 27, 1867, Walker Correspondence, folder 2, UAF). (On Eakin, see Staples, *Reconstruction in Arkansas*, 49, 103.)

205. Editorial "It is not unusual . . . ," *WAG*, March 12, 1867, 1.

206. Editorial "The refusal of the United States Senate . . . ," *WAG*, April 2, 1867, 2.

207. "Movement in Georgia," *WAG*, March 19, 1867, 3.

208. The *Gazette* would continue to change its position on how its readers should vote if they successfully registered. For criticism of the *Gazette* for these reversals from Eakin of the *Washington Telegraph*, see editorial "We can properly appreciate the sentiments of the senior editor . . . ," *WAG*, May 21, 1867, 2, and for later criticism from David Walker, see Walker to Woodruff, September 24, 1868, in Walker Correspondence, folder 2, UAF. On various debates over political strategy among white Arkansas elites during Reconstruction, see George H. Thompson, *Arkansas and Reconstruction*.

209. Editorial "The events of the past few months . . . ," *WAG*, April 9, 1867, 2. This advice was repeated the next week in editorial "Every citizen who feels . . . ," *WAG*, April 16, 1867, 2.

210. "In a late number of the *White County Record* . . . ," *WAG*, April 23, 1867, 2.

211. Georgia governor Jenkins's address reprinted in "Gov. Jenkins . . ." and the *Gazette*'s rebuttal in editorial "If any acts were necessary . . . ," both in *WAG*, April 30, 1867, 2.

212. "In a late number of the *White County Record* . . . ," *WAG*, April 23, 1867, 2.

213. According to James Roark, "White Man's Parties" did not generally become the dominant strategy of conservatives until the 1870s, but the idea did appear in some places in the late 1860s. Arkansas was one such place; see *Masters without Slaves*, 191–92.

214. "County Convention," 3, and "The friends of a white man's government . . . ," 3, in *WAG*, December 10, 1867. The call for a "white man's government" drew presumably upon rhetoric used by northern Democrats in the election of 1864 and in opposition to the Thirteenth Amendment. See, for instance, Vorenberg, *Final Freedom*, 99.

215. For reports of the organization of white men's clubs, conservative clubs, and Democratic clubs, in support of a "white man's party" or a "white man's government," see "State News," December 31, 1867, 2; "State News" and "Large and Enthusiastic Democratic Meeting," January 7, 1868, 2; "Mass Meeting of the Conservatives of Washington County," 1, and "An Enthusiastic Meeting," 2, January 14, 1868; "Democratic Meeting," 1, "State News," 2, and "Proceedings of a Conservative Meeting," 3, January 21, 1868, all in *WAG*. The *Gazette* applauded efforts of J. S. Durham of the *Van Buren Press* to facilitate a white man's club in his county and reprinted the declaration form he had crafted, advocating that it be used in other locales for a similar organization; see editorial "The energetic manner in which our contemporary of the Van Buren *Press* . . . ," *WAG*, December 31, 1867, 1.

216. "Democratic State Convention," *WAG*, January 28, 1868, 3.

217. "An Immense Democratic Meeting—Big Rock Out in Force—White Men Aroused," *WAG*, February 4, 1868.

218. "Democratic State Convention," *WAG*, January 28, 1868, 3. Several men attending this convention, including Reynolds and Jesse Cypert, were conservative delegates to the Arkansas constitutional convention.

219. Ibid. This report did not make clear whether these ladies were also responsible for some or all of the political banners.

220. "Democratic State Convention," *WAG*, February 4, 1868, 1.

221. This point draws on analysis in McCurry, "Black Republicans and the Rape of the South."

222. "Incidents of the Election," *WAG*, March 31, 1868, 2.

223. "State News," *WAG*, March 31, 1868, 1, 2.

224. April 13, 1868, letter to General Gillem at Vicksburg, Mississippi, reprinted in *WAG*, April 21, 1868, 1. See also Gillem's message to Francis A. Terry, *WAG*, March 31, 1868, 2, and John J. Clendenin to David Walker, April 15, 1868, in Walker Correspondence, folder 2, UAF.

225. "Incidents of the Election," *WAG*, March 31, 1868, 2.

226. El Dorado *Democrat* report commented on in "State News: A New Dodge," *WAG*, March 31, 1868, 2 (emphasis in the original).

227. See letter sent to General Alvan C. Gillem, April 13, 1868, by white conservatives reprinted in *WAG*, April 21, 1868, 1. Conservatives compiled information for their charges by requesting affidavits from around the state attesting to violations of election law at the polls. See letter to Francis A. Terry from General Gillem, March 26, 1868, reprinted in *WAG*, March 31, 1868, 2, and John J. Clendenin to David Walker, April 15, 1868, in Walker Correspondence, folder 2, UAF.

228. Colonel Tourtelotte reported to General Gillem that the seemingly illegal practice in some precincts (particularly in Little Rock) of allowing men to vote who were registered in other counties—a practice helpful to freedmen seeking to vote together in cities rather than near their employers in rural areas—may have led to some fraud. However, he concluded that the resulting fraud was not extensive enough to have determined the outcome of the ratification election. For excerpts from General Gillem's final report on the subject, see *American Annual Cyclopedia and Register*, 8:38.

229. "Colonel Tourtelotte's Report," *WAG*, May 26, 1868, 1. See also editorial on Colonel Tourtelotte's investigation, *WAG*, April 21, 1868, 2. Barkley Brown writes that "others have suggested that, whenever black men were ill and unable to come to the polls to cast their ballot, their wives or other female relatives were allowed to vote in their place" ("To Catch the Vision of Freedom," 94 n. 36). She cites Benjamin Quarles, who found that in 1870 some black women cast ballots in elections in South Carolina. "By this act," Quarles adds, "the Negro became the first practical vindicator of woman's right to the ballot." If the reports from Arkansas were true, this vindication happened even earlier than Quarles imagined. See Quarles, "Frederick Douglass and the Woman's Rights Movement," 35. Quarles may have been referring to the testimony of E. W. Seibels, a South Carolina conservative, before a congressional committee in which he reported

that in his state, "women gave their votes for their husbands, or their brothers, who they said were sick" (qtd. in Saville, *Work of Reconstruction*, 172 n. 86).

230. See also Kantrowitz, "One Man's Mob Is Another Man's Militia," 69 and 84 n. 9.
231. "Democratic State Convention," *WAG*, February 4, 1868, 1.

Chapter 4

1. *Debates and Proceedings*, 363, 365.
2. Ibid., 363.
3. Ibid. See also 371, 373, for reference to African Americans observing the convention's proceedings from the galleries. See also "Shadings of the Picture," *WAG*, January 14, 1868, 2, and "Partizan Shamelessness," *WAG*, January 21, 1868, 2.
4. *Debates and Proceedings*, 364.
5. In 1860, black men voted equally with white men in five northern states, and by 1868, this was the case in eight states. Bradley was, though, no doubt referring to post–Civil War rejection of referenda calling for black male suffrage in other northern states. See Litwack, *North of Slavery*, 263, and Foner, *Reconstruction*, 223, 448. On interracial marriage prohibitions in northern states, see Fowler, *Northern Attitudes towards Interracial Marriage*; Cott, *Public Vows*, 40–41, 43; and Lemire, *"Miscegenation,"* 47, 57–58, 115.
6. On the origin of the term "miscegenation," see Kaplan, "Miscegenation Issue." On the conflation of black men's political power with desire for sex with white women, see Hodes, *White Women, Black Men*, esp. 143–48, 151–54, 165–69, 171–74; Painter, " 'Social Equality' "; Dailey, "Limits of Liberalism in the New South," esp. 90, and *Before Jim Crow*, 87; and Cott, *Public Vows*, 98.
7. Similarly, referring to miscegenation laws after the Civil War, Peggy Pascoe writes, "By defining all interracial relationships as illicit, miscegenation law did not so much prohibit or punish illicit sex as it did create and reproduce it" ("Race, Gender, and the Privileges of Property," 18). See also Pascoe, "Miscegenation Law, Court Cases, and Ideologies of 'Race,' " 49–50; Saks, "Representing Miscegenation Law"; Berry, "Judging Morality"; and Nash, "Hidden History of Mestizo America."
8. Both Peggy Pascoe and Eva Saks have emphasized how jurisprudence resulting from civil and criminal charges brought under miscegenation law reproduced "race" by articulating and enforcing racial hierarchy. See Pascoe, "Miscegenation Law, Court Cases, and Ideologies of 'Race,' " and Saks, "Representing Miscegenation Law."
9. In a history of the Readjuster movement in post-Reconstruction Virginia, Jane Dailey argues that white southerners supporting interracial political coalitions in the post-Reconstruction period adopted a similar division between a public world that could be integrated and a private, domestic, and social sphere in which discrimination and segregation were acceptable, as a way of harnessing black political power without obliterating social hierarchies based on race. This strategy may well have been learned

from Reconstruction-era political discourse. See "Limits of Liberalism in the New South" and *Before Jim Crow*. On the connection between civil/political rights and "social" rights, or what black political leaders in Louisiana termed "public rights," see Rebecca J. Scott, "Public Rights, Social Equality."

10. See, e.g., Edwards, *Gendered Strife and Confusion*, and McCurry, *Masters of Small Worlds*.

11. See also Cott, *Public Vows*, 45.

12. On these debates in Arkansas, see also Hume, "Arkansas Constitutional Convention of 1868," 191; Palmer, "Miscegenation as an Issue in the Arkansas Constitutional Convention of 1868"; Wallenstein, *Tell the Court I Love My Wife*, 62–63. For an overview of similar contests in other states, see Bardaglio, " 'Shameful Matches,' " 121–28. Arkansas's debate was unique, though, in how well it was documented in the convention's proceedings.

13. Laura Edwards writes about a different setting, an 1869 state supreme court decision in which Justice Edwin Reade defended North Carolina's right to prohibit interracial marriage: such marriages' "ill effects were so obvious to him that he did not even bother to explain them" (" 'Marriage Covenant,' " 89). Areas of the South with successful interracial political alliances in the post-Reconstruction, pre-disfranchisement period were also settings in which white politicians found themselves challenged by black leaders to explain their logic connecting political power and sex. See Dailey, *Before Jim Crow*, 89–93. Alarm over sex between black and white people was also expressed during southern state constitutional conventions that led to disfranchisement of African Americans in the late 1890s and beyond. However, in this setting, agents of this discourse faced only a few black political leaders and other supporters of black male suffrage rights (speaking now from embattled, minority positions) willing to challenge them to explain their reasoning. See, for instance, Kantrowitz, *Ben Tillman*, 238–41, and Perman, *Struggle for Mastery*, 111–13.

14. The *National Anti-Slavery Standard* of January 30, 1864, referred to this history: "Through the whole thirty-three years of anti-slavery discussion, no statement has been repeated with greater pertinacity, no accusation has been more effective in stirring up the rancor of editors and the brutality of mobs, than the charge against Abolitionists of advocating 'amalgamation' " (qtd. in Kaplan, "Miscegenation Issue," 58). See Harris, "From Abolitionist Amalgamators," 191–99, and Mary P. Ryan, *Women in Public*, 135. On both post-1830s imagery linking abolition with amalgamation and similar responses to abolition in the North before 1830, see Lemire, *"Miscegenation."*

15. See, e.g., Channing, *Crisis of Fear*, 287; Hodes, *White Women, Black Men*, 144; and Vorenberg, *Final Freedom*, 100–101, 160–67.

16. Qtd. in Kaplan, "Miscegenation Issue," 48–49, and reproduced in Wood, *Black Scare*, plate 4, after p. 92.

17. *Miscegenation*, as qtd. in Kaplan, "Miscegenation Issue," 50, 53, 49, 84 n. 6; see entire article (47–100) for overall history of the pamphlet, its production, and reception. It appeared on newsstands in New York City in December 1863. The authors, who at first remained anonymous, sent it to abolitionist leaders and advertised it in the abolitionist

press, and it quickly became notorious throughout the country. See also Wood, *Black Scare*, chap. 4; Hodes, *White Women, Black Men*, 144–45; Lemire, *"Miscegenation,"* chap. 5; Vorenberg, *Final Freedom*, 101; and Mitchell, *Righteous Propagation*, 200. See also "Miscegenation endorsed by Republicans," Campaign Document #11 in *Publications of the Central Executive Campaign Committee*, and Seaman, *What Miscegenation Is!*

18. See Walters, "Erotic South," esp. 185–86; Sánchez-Eppler, *Touching Liberty*, chap. 1; and, of related interest, Stanley, *From Bondage to Contract*, 25–27. As early as 1831, white abolitionist William Lloyd Garrison responded to a question from a slaveholder, "How should you like to have a black man marry your daughter?" with a similar deflection: "Slaveholders generally should be the last persons to affect fastidiousness on that point; for they seem to be enamoured with amalgamation" (qtd. in Walters, "Erotic South," 181). Some white southern women agreed, at least when confiding in their journals and diaries. See, for instance, Burr, *Secret Eye*, 167–69.

19. *Debates and Proceedings*, 364.

20. See, for instance, D'Emilio and Freedman, *Intimate Matters*, 95–96, and Hodes, *White Women, Black Men*, 3. As historian Martha Hodes has shown, before emancipation even relationships between white women and black men were met with a degree of "toleration" and remained "neighborhood dramas" rather than state or national political issues. Hodes is careful to define "toleration" not as tolerance but, rather, as "a measure of forbearance for that which is not approved." Whites nonetheless "judged harshly, gossiped viciously, and could completely ostracize the transgressing white woman." It is the fact that black men did not necessarily face violence as a result of such relationships before the Civil War that Hodes finds most noteworthy. See Hodes, *White Women, Black Men*, 3. See also Bynum, *Unruly Women*.

21. Gatewood, "Sunnyside"; see also Rothman, *Notorious in the Neighborhood*, and Adele Alexander, *Ambiguous Lives*.

22. See D'Emilio and Freedman, *Intimate Matters*, 94–95, for a contrast of this form of southern white patriarchy with what was developing in nineteenth-century northern society due to industrialization. See also Hodes, *White Women, Black Men*, 4.

23. Peter Bardaglio reports that southern conservative newspapers at times condemned white men for engaging in cross-racial sex. He offers an 1879 article from the South Carolina *Columbia Daily Register* that refers to such men as "adulterers" and insists that men "living unlawfully with negro women must be taught that virtuous society will not endure the evil which the law has especially condemned and provided punishment for" (Bardaglio, *Reconstructing the Household*, 180; quotation first appeared in Tindall, *South Carolina Negroes*, 298). On similar condemnations in a later period, see Gilmore, *Gender and Jim Crow*, 68–71.

24. Painter, " 'Social Equality,' " 53. See also Mitchell, *Righteous Propagation*, 200–201; Gaines, *Uplifting the Race*, 59; Hodes, *White Women, Black Men*, 166–67; Wood, *Black Scare*, chap. 7; and on the phrase's travel from "an expression of positive aspiration in 1848 France" to "a term of opprobrium in the nineteenth century United States," Rebecca J. Scott, "Public Rights, Social Equality," 786–87.

25. Hodes, *White Women, Black Men*, 166–67; Litwack, *Been in the Storm So Long*, 265; Painter, " 'Social Equality,' " 53; Rebecca J. Scott, "Public Rights, Social Equality," 781.

26. Painter observes, "The rhetoric of 'social equality' was couched in racial terms, but its deeper meaning was packed with class distinctions rooted in slavery. . . . [The] horror of the mixing of classes was an unacknowledged aspect of 'social equality,' and it was rooted in the unremunerated labor that masters extorted from slaves as well as in the masters' sensitivity to gradations in the social hierarchy" (" 'Social Equality,' " 54–55).

27. On the gendered spatial dynamics of nineteenth-century homes, see Spain, *Gendered Spaces*, pt. 2, and on parlors esp. see p. 123.

28. See also Painter, " 'Social Equality,' " 53, and Litwack, *Been in the Storm So Long*, 265. Martha Hodes finds that white southerners understood "social equality" to mean "fostering conditions that would lead to sex between black men and white women," and she argues that its threat thus applied only to racial integration in spaces occupied by both men and women; cross-racial interactions in homosocial spaces, she concludes, were not as threatening. See Hodes, *White Women, Black Men*, 166.

29. See Riley, *"Am I That Name?,"* chap. 3; Auslander, *Taste and Power*, 143–44, 185, 194, 212; Nancy Fraser, *Unruly Practices*, 156–58, 162 n. 32.

30. Although most historians who have analyzed discourses of miscegenation during Reconstruction conclude that white anxieties about interracial sex and fears of waning white supremacy were inextricable, many also posit in one way or another an inherent anxiety about cross-racial sex in and of itself as a driving force behind the rhetoric and resultant laws and practices. No such anxiety about sex as sex was evident in the debates over interracial marriage and social equality in Arkansas during Reconstruction. For one of the earliest investigations of the concept of social equality and its relationship to sexuality, see Wood, *Black Scare*, chap. 7, which emphasizes post–Civil War southern white men's desires to preserve the "purity" of white women in the face of what they imagined to be black men's superior sexual powers (143). Leon Litwack finds that fear of integration stemmed in part from a fear of black male sexuality and its potential proximity to white women: "Behind every discussion and skirmish involving racial separation lurked the specter of unrestrained black lust and sexuality, with the most feared of consequences—racial amalgamation, or as it was now popularly called, miscegenation. . . . Much of the furor over racial separation in public vehicles grew out of fears that white women and black men might otherwise find themselves seated next to each other" (Litwack, *Been in the Storm So Long*, 265). My analysis draws more from the approach taken by Martha Hodes in her work on the subject, in which she does not presume sexual anxiety as a driving force behind racism (*White Women, Black Men*, chap. 7, and "Sexualization of Reconstruction Politics"). Hodes argues that the taboo against sex between black men and white women stemmed from alarm about preserving racial difference after the end of slavery. Hodes, though, stresses the preservation of race as a matter of preventing physical mixture. She writes, "One of the most certain ways to sustain the racial categories of 'black' and 'white' was to make sure that people of African ancestry and people of European ancestry . . . not have children together" (174). I will

argue that it was having children under conditions of legitimacy that mattered most to white southerners during Reconstruction. In other words, it was the meaning given to mixed-race offspring, not their existence, that was at stake, and thus the greater emphasis on marriage than on sex in the policies emerging from debates over "miscegenation." Finally, see also Whites, "Civil War as a Crisis in Gender," esp. 10, and *Civil War as a Crisis in Gender*.

31. Campbell did, though, oppose state regulation of marriage in relation to race: "No general or state legislature has the right to interfere with social matters. These would regulate themselves" (no title, *WAG*, June 4, 1867, 2). (Campbell's speech was also paraphrased without any substantial differences in "Speech of Bishop Campbell," *Little Rock Evening Republican*, June 4, 1867, 2, suggesting the accuracy of the *Gazette* report.) Similar comments from other black leaders were noted in the *Gazette*, for instance, when it reported that "Fred. Douglass does not claim social equality for the negro. In a late letter he makes a broad and well-founded distinction between public and private rights of citizens" (no title, *WAG*, March 5, 1867, 3). For examples from South Carolina, see Williamson, *After Slavery*, 279. On appeals for "public rights" by black leaders in Reconstruction-era Louisiana as a way of claiming "status as honorable citizens" beyond the ballot box while also avoiding the political difficulties attached to a language of "social rights," see Rebecca J. Scott, "Public Rights, Social Equality," esp. 787.

32. Historian Martha Hodes writes, "Although many freedpeople looked down on marriage to whites, most emphatically did not wish to see it criminalized, knowing that statutes would be enforced largely against black men without protection for black women compelled into concubinage." And yet most Republican responses to efforts to criminalize cross-racial marriage did not include "defenses of marriage across the color line" (*White Women, Black Men*, 148–49, 271–72 n. 50). In contrast, the response of a freedman named Richard Hill, who asserted that marriage between white and black people "would not hurt the nation or trouble the nation," may indicate the attitudes of African Americans who were not in prominent political positions or most concerned about political strategy. See ibid., 150. See also Mitchell, *Righteous Propagation*, 198–99, on African American concerns about interracial marriage laws hurting black women in the post-Reconstruction period, and chap. 7 on African American responses to cross-racial sex in general in this later period. And finally, see Dailey, *Before Jim Crow*, 89–93, for black political leaders in post-Reconstruction Virginia opposing legal prohibitions on cross-racial marriage.

33. "Equality. Social and Political," *Colored American*, January 6, 1866, 2. (That social equality was forced upon the "colored man" rather than "women" or "women and men" reflected a notable patriarchal tone to this particular newspaper.) See also Henry McNeal Turner's sermon commemorating the "First Anniversary of Freedom," *Colored American*, January 13, 1866, 1, and Hodes, *White Women, Black Men*, 145, 167–68.

34. Qtd. in Tucker, *Black Pastors and Leaders*, 29–30. It is unclear in what year Shaw made this statement, though it appears to have been in 1872 and to have referred to Charles Sumner's Civil Rights Bill. Shaw was born in the Midwest and migrated to Memphis as a

free man in the 1850s. After emancipation, he owned a saloon and gambling house in the city and ran many times for political office. See ibid., 27–30.

35. Hume, " 'Black and Tan' Constitutional Conventions," 29–30; W. E. B. DuBois, *Black Reconstruction*, 492; Kolchin, *First Freedom*, 170–71; *Journal of the Proceedings of the Constitutional Convention of the State of Mississippi*, 199, 211–12.

36. Hume, " 'Black and Tan' Constitutional Conventions," 25–29, 92, 150–51, 340, 410; Holt, *Black over White*, 132.

37. Hume, " 'Black and Tan' Constitutional Conventions," 492, and for proposals for constitutional stipulations of racial separation in North Carolina's convention, see 489–91 and W. E. B. DuBois, *Black Reconstruction*, 529–30.

38. James T. White was married to a schoolteacher and employed one domestic servant in his home in 1870, suggesting his membership in an elite or aspiring class of African Americans during Reconstruction. See U.S. Bureau of the Census, *Ninth Census*, M593, roll 60, p. 136; on the term "aspiring class" for those African Americans with professional status and some means, see Mitchell, *Righteous Propagation*, 9–10. Mason also belonged to this class, being listed as a planter on the 1870 census with $10,000 in real estate and $2,000 in personal property; see U.S. Bureau of the Census, *Ninth Census*, M593, roll 49, p. 150. On Mason, see also record of him living as a student in Oberlin, Ohio, in 1860, U.S. Bureau of the Census, *Eighth Census*, M653, roll 1002, p. 216; Gatewood, "Sunnyside"; Whayne, "Labor Relations and the Evolving Plantation," 7–9, 30; and Finley, *From Slavery to Uncertain Freedom*, 63. Suggesting the tenuous quality of African Americans' upward mobility during Reconstruction in Arkansas, Hawkins, identified as a "minister-farmer" at the convention, would by 1880 appear in the census as a farm laborer owning no property; see U.S. Bureau of the Census, *Tenth Census*, T9, roll 51, p. 147.2000. On Grey's background, see Chapter 3. I was unable to identify Rector, Johnson, or Samuels with any certainty in the census. For more information on the black delegates to the convention, see Hume, " 'Black and Tan' Constitutional Conventions," esp. 321–24, and "Arkansas Constitutional Convention of 1868"; St. Hilaire, "Negro Delegates"; and *Debates and Proceedings*, 4–10.

Of all the southern state constitutional conventions called under the Reconstruction Acts, Arkansas's convention had the smallest number of black delegates (South Carolina, 73; Louisiana, 45; Georgia, 33; Virginia, 24; Alabama, 18; Florida, 18; Mississippi, 16; North Carolina, 13; Texas, 9; and Arkansas, 8), but their unity meant they contributed more to the outcome of the convention than larger numbers did in some other states. See Hume, " 'Black and Tan' Constitutional Conventions," 656.

39. Mason differed most in his views from the other black delegates, voting thirteen times in opposition to his colleagues, entertaining ideas about educational qualifications for suffrage, and opposing restrictions on the franchise for former Confederates. Nonetheless, in the end he voted with the other seven black men for a constitution that placed no educational restrictions on suffrage and did disfranchise white southerners to the extent mandated in the Fourteenth Amendment. See St. Hilaire, "Negro Delegates," 62–62, and *Debates and Proceedings*, 657, 671–72.

40. I base these political identifications on information and voting records detailed by Richard Hume in his studies of the Arkansas constitutional convention. My classification of some delegates, though, differs from Hume's. See Hume, "'Black and Tan' Constitutional Conventions," 269–324, and "Arkansas Constitutional Convention of 1868," 183–205, esp. 185 and 192–205. These numbers add up to 69, not 70, delegates because I have not included W. W. Adams. Due to a disputed election in Adams's home county of Izard, he was not seated until February 10, 1868, after all of the important votes I consider, other than the final vote on the constitution (on which Adams voted in the negative), had occurred. See *Debates and Proceedings*, 581.

41. Quotation is from the oath required for registration as an elector under the constitution produced by the convention. Grey was one of six members of the Committee on the Elective Franchise that crafted the franchise article of the constitution. See *Debates and Proceedings*, 14, 599.

42. Ibid., 106; George H. Thompson, *Arkansas and Reconstruction*, 70, fig. 11.

43. In 1860, Cypert owned $3,000 in real estate and $1,600 in personal property. No servants or slaves were listed as living in his household. See U.S. Bureau of the Census, *Eighth Census*, M653, roll 52, p. 829.

44. *Debates and Proceedings*, list of members. On Cypert, see also Hume, "'Black and Tan' Constitutional Conventions," 308–9, and in *WAG*, "Large and Enthusiastic Democratic Meeting," January 7, 1868, 2; "A Large Meeting," February 11, 1868, 2; and "State News," February 18, 1868, 3. He held subsequent offices in White County, for instance, as the commissioner of public buildings in 1872 and as a delegate to the constitutional convention of 1874.

45. *Debates and Proceedings*, 89, 91, 146, 152. On a similar argument made by conservatives to North Carolina's constitutional convention a month later, see Hume, "'Black and Tan' Constitutional Conventions," 485.

46. *Debates and Proceedings*, 157. Two of the twelve conservative delegates to the convention had not yet been seated, and thus only ten were present to vote for Cypert's resolution.

47. "According to announcement in the evening paper . . . ," *WAG*, September 24, 1867, 1; "Radical Congressional Nominating Convention," *WAG*, January 21, 1868, 2; *Debates and Proceedings*, 4, 122; Hume, "'Black and Tan' Constitutional Conventions," 307–8; Finley, *From Slavery to Uncertain Freedom*, 46; cf. Staples, *Reconstruction in Arkansas*. By 1870, Bradley was the father of seven children, owned $7,200 in real estate and $1,000 in personal property, and employed two white boys as farm laborers and a black woman as a domestic servant, suggesting that he had done well in life despite the modest beginnings he claimed. I was unable to locate Bradley in the 1860 census and thus do not know whether this wealth reflected postwar ambition and good fortune or prewar success after he migrated to Arkansas from Tennessee around 1848. See U.S. Bureau of the Census, *Ninth Census*, M593, roll 48, p. 551. Bradley continued to practice as a lawyer in 1880 and eventually served as a circuit court judge. See U.S. Bureau of the Census, *Tenth Census*, T9, roll 39, p. 3.2000, and Hume, "'Black and Tan' Constitutional Conventions," 307–8.

48. "According to announcement in the evening paper . . . ," *WAG*, September 24, 1867, 1. Six months after Bradley volunteered to the join the Confederate Army, "circumstances" caused him to resign and return to his home in Bradley County. The *Gazette*, mocking Bradley's claims to military valor and implying that he may have contracted venereal disease, added in brackets that these "circumstances" were "we presume, . . . too delicate to mention."

49. For Bradley as an agent of the bureau, see Staples, *Reconstruction in Arkansas*, 198; Hume, " 'Black and Tan' Constitutional Conventions," 307–8. Quotation and suggestion that he was responding to criticism for reversing his political stance from "According to announcement in the evening paper . . . ," *WAG*, September 24, 1867, 1.

50. For evidence of conservative contempt for Bradley, at least before his role in the constitutional convention, see quips by editors of the *Gazette* interjected into the article recounting Bradley's speech in "According to announcement in the evening paper . . . ," *WAG*, September 24, 1867, 1.

51. *Debates and Proceedings*, 121. Bradley's various comments on slavery simultaneously echoed antebellum arguments that reliance on slave labor hindered economic development and ingenuity in the South and postbellum predictions that African Americans would suffer more in freedom than they had in bondage. His ideas—that slavery was best for African Americans but a curse for whites—reflected a mixture of the "necessary evil" and "positive good" perspectives that Ira Berlin attributes to Upper South and Lower South antebellum society, respectively, in *Slaves without Masters*, 184–99.

52. "Radical Congressional Nominating Convention," *WAG*, January 21, 1868, 2. Bradley received only six of sixty-six votes cast.

53. Bradley's actions severed his tenuous ties to the Republicans, for the time being at least, and brought him into the conservative ranks. After introducing his proposal in the convention, Bradley would move closer and closer to the anti-Reconstruction conservatives in the convention. For instance, on February 1, 1868, he responded to criticism of his course that appeared in the *Evening Republican* by writing two letters to the *Gazette*, his former nemesis, defending himself and attacking the editors of the Republican journal as "amalgamationists" (see both letters titled "Editors Gazette," *WAG*, February 4, 1868, 2). He would subsequently vote with the conservatives supporting a final effort to adopt a franchise article that excluded black men from the electorate (*Debates and Proceedings*, 517), oppose the adoption of the final constitution, and, along with men such as Jesse Cypert, address the "regular Saturday night meeting of the democratic club of Big Rock township," where "the rapid progress of organization . . . and the flattering prospects of the conservatives" were discussed (see "A Large Meeting," *WAG*, February 11, 1868, 2). It is also possible that Bradley proposed the prohibition after consultation with, and maybe even promises from, the conservative members of the convention. During the debate over Cypert's ordinance to adopt the 1864 constitution, Bradley referred to a relationship "personal and social" with Jesse Cypert to explain why he sat with him, his supposed political opponent, during the debates; see *Debates and Proceedings*, 121.

Nearing the end of the convention, a white Radical delegate from Independence County, a farmer originally from Indiana who came to Arkansas during the war, would say about his one-time-Republican colleague Bradley, "The first time he made a speech, I said—'He has gone over, neck and heels, boots and spurs, to the Rebels.' 'O, no!' said some gentlemen who had more universal charity than I. . . . 'O, no! don't say anything— lets get him by the arm and pull him along.' I said,—'Kick him out! he is bound to go, any way.' Sure enough, over he went" (*Debates and Proceedings*, 720).

54. "Democratic State Convention," January 28, 1868, 3, and "Democratic State Convention," February 4, 1868, 1, both in *WAG*. See Chapter 3.

55. *Debates and Proceedings*, 364. Bradley's concern about these charges was echoed by another white southern delegate to the convention, Ira Wilson. See *Debates and Proceedings*, 375. On similar thinking among white "fusion" candidates in post-Reconstruction Virginia, see Dailey, "Limits of Liberalism in the New South" and *Before Jim Crow*.

56. "According to announcement in the evening paper . . . ," *WAG*, September 24, 1867, 1.

57. *Debates and Proceedings*, 365; *Revised Statutes*, 1838, p. 536, cited in Fowler, *Northern Attitudes towards Interracial Marriage*, 346.

58. When the mayor of Helena objected to a black man and a white woman married in Tennessee living in his city, the military commander in town, Colonel Bentzoni, commented to the Freedmen's Bureau agent, Captain Sweeney, "if the parties are legally married, I cannot see why they should not live together, or how their case would be improved by driving them away." Sweeney, though, seemed less certain. He referred the matter to General Sprague, assistant commissioner of the bureau for Arkansas, seeking "advice and instructions . . . to guide in all future cases of the kind" (Endorsements Sent, Volume 1[16], July 1865–December 1866, p. 34 of register, Arkansas BRFAL, roll 4). On marriages between white women and black men during these years, see Hodes, *White Women, Black Men*, 149, and Wallenstein, *Tell the Court I Love My Wife*, 61–62.

59. Circular Letter from J. W. Sprague, Assistant Commissioner, March 31, 1866, in Letters and Telegrams Received, Unbound Letters and Telegrams, Arkansas BRFAL, roll 12. Sprague was responding to orders from Freedmen's Bureau commissioner O. O. Howard, who in March 1866 instructed all assistant commissioners to "consult the State laws with regard to the marriage and divorce of white persons, and embody them for the benefit of freedmen," adding that "the greatest care must be taken to instruct all freed people what the law demands of them in regard to marriage." He also detailed particular issues in need of clarification, including "parties eligible to marriage [*sic*]," but did not specifically request pronouncements on the legality of interracial marriage. See Circular Letter from Major General O. O. Howard, March 2, 1866, attached to U.S. Congress, House of Representatives, "Report of the Commissioner of the Bureau of Refugees, Freedmen, and Abandoned Lands," 756–57. On efforts of the Freedmen's Bureau to encourage marriage among freedpeople as part of their efforts to promote a free labor system, see Schwalm, *Hard Fight for We*, 240–43.

60. *Acts of Arkansas*, 1866–1867, pp. 98–100, cited in Staples, *Reconstruction in Arkansas*, 83– 84; Circular No. 5, February 18, 1867, Circulars (22), p. 43, Arkansas BRFAL, roll 21.

61. See Williamson, *After Slavery*, 296, and *New People*, 91–92; Bardaglio, *Reconstructing the Household*, 179; and Wallenstein, *Tell the Court I Love My Wife*, 70, 82.

62. The Republican-dominated Alabama state supreme court rejected the state's constitutional ban on intermarriage in 1872 on the basis that the Civil Rights Act and the Fourteenth Amendment prohibited such restraint on any citizen's ability to contract with any other. Bans on cross-racial marriage were also rejected by courts in Texas and Louisiana; Republican-controlled legislatures in Mississippi and South Carolina repealed such laws; and both Arkansas (1874) and Florida (1872) omitted them from new compilations of statutes. In total, seven former Confederate states would, in one way or another, omit or reject bans on cross-racial marriage for some time during congressional Reconstruction. However, an interracial marriage prohibition was upheld in Georgia; the Alabama decision was overturned by a new court five years later; and similar bans were reinstated throughout the South after the 1870s. See Wallenstein, *Tell the Court I Love My Wife*, 8, and chaps. 4–8, esp. 80, 93; Bardaglio, *Reconstructing the Household*, 182–83; Pascoe, "Miscegenation Law, Court Cases, and Ideologies of 'Race,'" 50–51, and "Race, Gender, and the Privileges of Property," 22–23; and Cott, *Public Vows*, 99.

63. Circular Letter from J. W. Sprague, Assistant Commissioner, March 31, 1866, in Letters and Telegrams Received, Unbound Letters and Telegrams, Arkansas BRFAL, roll 12.

64. *House Journal*, 1866–1867, p. 200, cited in Staples, *Reconstruction in Arkansas*, 83 n. 6.

65. *Debates and Proceedings*, 363; on Hodges, see Hume, "'Black and Tan' Constitutional Conventions," 318.

66. Hodges himself quickly withdrew his initial objection to any action on the matter and endorsed Grey's counterproposal. See *Debates and Proceedings*, 363.

67. On Hinds, see Chapter 3, n. 122.

68. *Debates and Proceedings*, 489.

69. Ibid., 507.

70. Ibid., 364.

71. On the influence of Lamarckian theories on racial ideology in the United States, see, e.g., Bederman, *Manliness and Civilization*, 29, 92. Peggy Pascoe writes about nineteenth-century understandings of race, "The important point was not that biology determined culture (indeed, the split between the two was only dimly perceived), but that race, understood as an indivisible essence that included not only biology but also culture, morality, and intelligence, was a compellingly significant factor in history and society" ("Miscegenation Law, Court Cases, and Ideologies of 'Race,'" 47–48).

72. *Debates and Proceedings*, 371, 365. What form other than human that Bradley might have had in mind is not clear.

73. Ibid., 365.

74. Ibid., 370, 369, 490. On similar efforts by white southerners to solidify racial distinctions and hierarchy after emancipation by invoking cross-racial marriage and sex, see Hodes, *White Women, Black Men*, 147, 157–59, 173–74, 199–200, 202.

75. See Chapter 3.

76. *Debates and Proceedings*, 365.

77. Ibid. Peggy Pascoe in particular has emphasized how by regulating marriage, miscegenation laws aimed above all at granting social legitimacy and inheritance rights only to intraracial unions and offspring and thus at assuring the transmission of white property through marriage and inheritance solely to other white people. See "Race, Gender, and the Privileges of Property," and "Miscegenation Law, Court Cases, and Ideologies of 'Race.'"

78. Bradley's repeated use of the term "spheres" to describe the social segregation he envisioned drew perhaps on the presumed legitimacy of separation conveyed in the mid-nineteenth-century notion of "separate spheres" for men and women. See, for instance, Cott, *Bonds of Womanhood*, and Kerber, "Separate Spheres, Female Worlds, Woman's Place." Bradley's recourse to spatial metaphors presaged the arguments of white southerners leading the Readjuster movement in Virginia in the post-Reconstruction years, who, Jane Dailey shows, drew on the division between public and private spheres posited in liberal political theory to demarcate spaces of supposedly unthreatening integration versus legitimate separation and exclusion. See *Before Jim Crow*, 11–12, 84–87; on the rejection of this reasoning by black leaders within the Readjuster movement, see 89–93.

79. *Debates and Proceedings*, 364.

80. Ibid., 365.

81. See McCurry, *Masters of Small Worlds*, esp. chap. 1, and "Politics of Yeoman Households," for the location of the authority of southern white men within the spatial boundaries of their households, defined as a productive unit, the entirety of the land they owned and worked along with their dependents. See also Fox-Genovese, *Within the Plantation Household*.

82. *Debates and Proceedings*, 375. Wilson represented Union County, which sat along the southern border of Arkansas and had a 46 percent black population in 1870. The county just barely rejected the constitution once it was put to a popular vote (see George H. Thompson, *Arkansas and Reconstruction*, 70, fig. 11, and 74, fig. 12). Fifty-eight-year-old Wilson migrated to Arkansas from Georgia; in 1870 he owned a small farm worth $350. During the convention, he at first voted with the Republicans on important ballots, including in opposition to Cypert's proposal to reinstate the 1864 constitution. But after Bradley's proposal to prohibit interracial marriage, he voted consistently with the conservatives, joining the anti-Reconstructionists in opposition to the constitution framed by the convention. See U.S. Bureau of the Census, *Ninth Census*, M593, roll 65, p. 488, image 352; Hume, "Arkansas Constitutional Convention of 1868," 206; and *Debates and Proceedings*, 657, 681–82.

83. *Debates and Proceedings*, 494–95. Dallas County, in the central southern part of Arkansas, had nearly a 70 percent white population in 1870 and voted against the constitution by a small majority (George H. Thompson, *Arkansas and Reconstruction*, 70, fig. 11 and 74, fig. 12). Kyle, sixty-one years old, had been born in Tennessee but had lived in Arkansas for twelve years at the time of the convention. For his claim to have lost at least $10,000 worth of cotton, horses, mules, and household belongings during the war because of his loyalty to the Union, see *Debates and Proceedings*, 561. In 1860, Kyle's

personal property was worth almost $22,000, which he held in addition to the $10,000 worth of land; see U.S. Bureau of the Census, *Eighth Census*, M653, roll 40, p. 944, image 353. Like Bradley, he sought a Republican nomination for Congress. See "Radical Congressional Nominating Convention," *WAG*, January 21, 1868, 2. Kyle would generally vote with the Republicans at the convention but refused to join them in attempting to end debate on the divisive issue of interracial marriage. See *Debates and Proceedings*, 5, 367, 393, and Hume, "Arkansas Constitutional Convention of 1868," 205.

84. *Debates and Proceedings*, 494–95. The critique came from Joseph Brooks, a white Republican minister from Ohio representing Phillips County with William Henry Grey and James T. White. "I have no wish that there should be placed in the organic law of the State of Arkansas, anything to hinder me from giving my daughter to any one . . . that does not fit my bill. . . . I suppose I feel myself, and my daughters . . . perfectly competent to control and govern these matters for ourselves" (*Debates and Proceedings*, 380–81, 383).

85. See, e.g., Bynum, *Unruly Women*, 6–7; Hodes, *White Women, Black Men*, esp. 5; and Sommerville, *Rape and Race*. See also Hall, " 'Mind That Burns in Each Body,' " 336, for a similar analysis of lynching. An ideology that differentiated white womanhood by class would increasingly conflict with imperatives for preserving racial difference after emancipation. Hodes argues, "Just as white ideas about the dangers of black men intensified after emancipation, so, too, did white ideology about the purity of white women" (*White Women, Black Men*, 201). In 1877, a justice of Alabama's supreme court made an argument about the benefits of prohibiting cross-racial marriage similar to Kyle's. Upholding that state's new marriage ban, Judge Amos R. Manning argued, "It is . . . a fact not always sufficiently felt, that the more humble and helpless families are the more they need this sort of protection. Their spirits are crushed, or become rebellious, when other ills besides those of poverty are heaped upon them" (qtd. in Saks, "Representing Miscegenation Law," 50; also referred to in Berry, "Judging Morality," 839–40).

86. Bradley called for "a direct and manly vote" and for "every gentleman [to] come up . . . and record his vote; and let the record fly, like a blazing comet—let it fly through future generations, to show where he stood upon this great question" (*Debates and Proceedings*, 370–71). To vote against his proposal, Bradley warned, would leave a record of shame, because it "shows me a taste that makes Heaven frown, and stinks in the nostrils of man!" (ibid., 363, 365). (Ira Wilson similarly denounced those who would leave the issue of race and marriage to "taste": "They come here this morning and say they want no legislation upon the subject—it's all a matter of taste! I am astonished that any man will think such a thing, much less speak it!" He referred to the constitution already approved by the Alabama convention as an "illustrious example for neglecting" this issue, which he presumed would "suit the taste of some gentlemen, better than anything which will regulate the marriage relation" [ibid., 375].) In other words, it revealed his opponents' own dishonor because it suggested their intention or desire for sex with people of another race. Bradley depicted a vote for his proposal as a performance of

honorable and virtuous manhood, because it condemned interracial sexual relations and indicated a man's own personal restraint from sex that violated racial boundaries.

87. Ibid., 367, 378, 391–92, 394.

88. "Showed Their Hands," *WAG*, February 4, 1868, 2.

89. "Plain Facts for White Men," *WAG*, February 4, 1868, 2.

90. "Showed Their Hands," *WAG*, February 4, 1868, 2.

91. "Arkansas to Be Mexicanized," February 11, 1868, 2; "Respectability Outlawed," February 11, 1868, 2; "Radicalism the Patron of Miscegenation," February 18, 1868, 1; "Pure Scondrelism," February 18, 1868, 3, all in *WAG*. See also from *WAG*, "An Extract from the Sum of Villainies," February 18, 1868, 2; "Read and Remember This," February 18, 1868, 2; "How Goes the Work," February 25, 1868, 1; and "The White Men a Unit," February 25, 1868, 2.

92. "Editors Gazette," January 28, 1868, 1 (the letter was dated January 20, 1868); "Radical Congressional Nominating Convention," January 21, 1868, 2; "Nominating and Registration," February 11, 1868, 1, all in *WAG*.

93. Two letters titled "Editors Gazette," dated February 1, 1868, in *WAG*, February 4, 1868, 2.

94. "Heads I Win, Tails You Lose," *WAG*, February 25, 1868, 1.

95. *Debates and Proceedings*, 493. On similar arguments made by black political leaders in post-Reconstruction Virginia, see Dailey, *Before Jim Crow*, 89–93.

96. *Debates and Proceedings*, 502.

97. Ibid., 375, 492.

98. Ibid., 366. Miles Ledford Langley, a white minister who had been an abolitionist before the war and now represented Clark County, seconded Grey's argument: "I say, as a scientific man, you cannot draw a line between the races. In many cases there is not one drop of negro blood in ten. The blood of almost the entire negro race is intermixed with that of the white. Perhaps there are not five hundred full-blooded negroes in the state of Arkansas; and when you come to draw a line, you will have a very nice question to settle" (376).

99. Ibid., 498–99, 366. On similar responses among other black leaders to miscegenation rhetoric, see, e.g., Hodes, *White Women, Black Men*, 2, 145, 167–68.

100. Montgomery would soon become Arkansas's attorney general. See Hume, "'Black and Tan' Constitutional Conventions," 320.

101. James Hinds made a facetious recommendation that this proposal be referred to the Committee on Boundaries, which was followed by laughter. He withdrew that motion and moved instead that it be referred to the Committee on the Constitution, its Arrangement, and Phraseology. The motion was rejected. See *Debates and Proceedings*, 367.

102. Ibid., 368.

103. Ibid., 371.

104. Ibid., 372.

105. Ibid., 368.

106. Ibid., 503.

107. Ibid., 376–78. Langley's place of birth is not known. He made reference to his abolitionist past at the convention. Concerning his opposition to any action on the subject of race and sexual or domestic relationships, he said, "It may make me unpopular now, just as it made me unpopular, in '62 and '64, to say that all mankind ought to be free." By "'64" he presumably meant his role as a delegate from Clark County to Arkansas's constitutional convention of that year; see Hume, "'Black and Tan' Constitutional Conventions," 323–24.

108. Despite Langley's opposition to legal prohibitions on interracial marriage, he did feel it necessary to add, "I prefer to marry a white lady" (*Debates and Proceedings*, 376). But he also questioned the logic of members of the convention who "speak as if, if we fail to prohibit intermarriage between the races, we should compel it" (ibid., 377).

109. Ibid., 489.

110. Ibid., 509.

111. Ibid., 377.

112. Hume argues that Hinds "realized that the debate . . . had created serious divisions within the ranks of the assembly's 'reconstructionists'" and introduced his compromise resolution "to regain the support of the gathering's Southern whites" ("'Black and Tan' Constitutional Conventions," 285–87). Regarding how issues touching on "interracial contacts" were "gingerly handled" by African American delegates to South Carolina's constitutional convention, Thomas Holt concludes, "Such caution is understandable, given the rejection of black suffrage in many northern states just months before the convention" (*Black over White*, 132).

113. *Debates and Proceedings*, 374.

114. Though most southern states rewrote rape laws (and criminal codes overall) after emancipation, in 1867 Kentucky's statutes continued to characterize rape as "unlawfully and carnally know[ing] any white woman, against her will and consent." South Carolina rape law also continued to be racially discriminatory. See Sommerville, "Rape Myth Reconsidered," 379.

115. *Debates and Proceedings*, 385.

116. Ibid., 385, 388.

117. See White, *Ar'n't I a Woman?*, chap. 1, on the history of proslavery ideologues attributing sexual relationships between white men and black women to black women's desire and unchaste character.

118. *Debates and Proceedings*, 501.

119. Ibid., 507. The only other black delegate to comment in the debates over interracial marriage was Thomas Johnson, who suggested his feelings on the matter when he vehemently objected to one substitute proposal much like Bradley's original resolution: "I move to vote that question out of the house" (ibid., 504). James Mason of Chicot County showed his concern about the sexual exploitation of black women by white men through another issue before the convention. After Bradley offered his resolution on

January 29, but before the issue was voted on for the last time on February 5, the convention considered a petition to Congress asking for the continuation of the Freedmen's Bureau. Mason offered an amendment to this petition, asking that the Bureau be staffed by "more honest and efficient men" (ibid., 433). Mason declined to comment further on his amendment, but his motivation appears to have stemmed from a case in his home county where the local Freedmen's Bureau agent, Thomas Hunnicutt, was accused of sexually insulting and abusing black women who came to his office for assistance. Catherine Hanna, a freedwoman who reported Hunnicutt, angered him by insisting "she didn't do that," to which he reportedly replied that she would not be "the first damn yellow woman he had ever screwed." This case is recounted in Finley, *From Slavery to Uncertain Freedom*, 20. Finley also reports that Hunnicutt provided black laborers to plantation owners and received "large sums of money as blackmail" in return (ibid., 29), and that Mason's amendment was motivated by Hunnicutt's corruption (ibid., 165).

120. *Debates and Proceedings*, 510. For White, segregation in public life was another matter. White revealed his opposition to the insult, inconvenience, and inequality of segregated public transport at an earlier point in the convention, when he introduced the following resolution:

> *Resolved*: That whereas the public carriers and owners of public conveyances in the State of Arkansas, persistently refuse the ordinary accommodations to citizens of said State, *Therefore, be it resolved:* That the public carriers are the public servants, and that a refusal to perform their duties in carrying or transporting all citizens upon the same terms, and subject to the same rules and regulations, is an outrage upon the citizens of this State: *And be it resolved:* That this body recommend that the Legislature pass an act making such refusal to carry or transport citizens over the public highways of travel, subject only to the general rules governing all others on the various routes or modes of carrying, conveying, or transporting passengers, a penal offence. (ibid., 251)

For black leaders in Reconstruction-era Louisiana advocating similar "public rights," see Rebecca J. Scott, "Public Rights, Social Equality."

121. This sentiment was expressed by James W. Hood at North Carolina's constitutional convention when he endorsed racial separation "whenever it is possible, not by written law, but by mutual consent and the law of interest" (qtd. in Hume, "'Black and Tan' Constitutional Conventions," 491, 683; see also Bardaglio, *Reconstructing the Household*, 178).

122. See Hume, "'Black and Tan' Constitutional Conventions," 491, 683. Peter Bardaglio places black delegates' support for prohibitions on interracial sexual relationships of all kinds in the specific context of white male sexual abuse: "After generations of masters satisfying their sexual desires at the expense of female slaves, . . . many freedmen and freedwomen welcomed a certain degree of racial distance when it came to domestic

relationships" (*Reconstructing the Household*, 178). For thoughts on the willingness of some African Americans to accept other forms of segregation in the late nineteenth century, see Rabinowitz, "From Exclusion to Segregation."

123. *Debates and Proceedings*, 701–10. See also Lebsock, "Radical Reconstruction," 205.

124. *Debates and Proceedings*, 701, 702, 708.

125. Barkley Brown, "To Catch the Vision of Freedom," 79; Martha Jones, *All Bound Up Together*, 70–71, 146–48, 152–53 (quotation on 147).

126. *Debates and Proceedings*, 98.

127. See Chapter 3; Finley, *From Slavery to Uncertain Freedom*. On the noteworthy interest of ordinary African American women in politics and their frequent presence at political events during Reconstruction in places other than Arkansas, see also Frankel, *Freedom's Women*, 174, 176–77; Hahn, *Nation under Our Feet*, 175, 185, 227–28; Holt, *Black over White*, 34–35; Hunter, *To 'Joy My Freedom*, 32–33; Schwalm, *Hard Fight for We*, 187, 232; and Barkley Brown, "To Catch the Vision of Freedom" and "Negotiating and Transforming the Public Sphere."

128. See, for instance, Gilmore, *Gender and Jim Crow*, and Hahn, *Nation under Our Feet*, 339–41.

129. See Barkley Brown, "Negotiating and Transforming the Public Sphere," and Higginbotham, *Righteous Discontent*.

130. *Debates and Proceedings*, 515.

131. Ibid., 636–37. Robert Gantt offered his objections to the constitution in writing, which included, "It encourages the social equality of the white and black races" (ibid., 665–66). The other conservative delegates at the convention added their signatures to Gantt's document. One of them, Charles Walker, also announced that he voted against the constitution because "I consider it such a thing as no respectable white man could vote for" (ibid., 681).

132. Ibid., 517.

133. Ibid., 661. Bradley and Samuel Matthews, another supporter of a constitutional ban on interracial marriage, in their explanations of their votes against the constitution, both emphasized the document's provision for public schools that did not require that they be segregated. Less than a week earlier the Alabama constitution, it appeared, had been defeated by a popular vote in a campaign that had emphasized this issue. Perhaps Bradley and Matthews, having failed in their efforts to include a marriage ban, moved on to another signifier of social equality that appeared to have been successful at defeating a new constitution elsewhere. See Hume, "'Black and Tan' Constitutional Conventions," 27–29, 37–38. In its campaign against ratification of the new constitution, the *Gazette* also emphasized the issue of integrated schools. See, for instance, "The White Men a Unit," February 25, 1868, 2, and "How the Parties Stand," March 10, 1868, 2, both in *WAG*.

134. The constitution was ratified by a vote of 27,913 to 26,597 (Hume, "'Black and Tan' Constitutional Conventions," 296). Votes cast for (27,576) and against (13,558) the

calling of a convention listed in *Debates and Proceedings*, Appendix B, 770; slightly lower numbers (presumably incomplete) printed in "The Election," *WAG*, December 10, 1867, 3. Twenty-four counties that had turned out a majority vote favoring a convention also voted against the constitution, predominantly in the northwestern and southern portions of the state. See George H. Thompson, *Arkansas and Reconstruction*, 74, fig. 12, and compare with returns by county in *Debates and Proceedings*, 770.

135. *Debates and Proceedings*, 673. In the popular vote, Independence County, which had a 94 percent white population, opposed the constitution, suggesting that a majority of Misner's white southern constituents did not agree with him, at least not a month after the convention when the election took place. See George H. Thompson, *Arkansas and Reconstruction*, 70, fig. 11, and 74, fig. 12.

136. *Debates and Proceedings*, 679. Jefferson County had a majority-black population in 1870. See George H. Thompson, *Arkansas and Reconstruction*, 70, fig. 11.

137. *Debates and Proceedings*, 656.

138. Hume, " 'Black and Tan' Constitutional Conventions," 296.

139. For speaking events and Democratic or White Man's Party meetings, see, from *WAG*, "A Large Meeting," 2, and "Public Speaking," 3, both February 11, 1868; "State News" and "Public Speaking," both February 18, 1868, 3; "The Canvass," "State News," "Public Speaking," all February 25, 1868, 2; "From the West," March 3, 1868, 2; and "Good News from LaFayette" and "Public Speaking," both March 10, 1868, 3. On white women offering banners to reward the largest township votes against the constitution, see "State News," *WAG*, March 10, 1868, 3, and March 24, 1868, 3. Conservative speaking events spread through the north and then across the state from the northeast to the southwest. None were announced for the eastern counties along the Mississippi River, such as Phillips, Chicot, and Jefferson, with the largest black populations.

140. From *WAG*, "A Large Meeting," February 11, 1868, 2; "State News" and "Public Speaking," February 18, 1868, 3.

141. "The White Men a Unit," *WAG*, February 25, 1868, 2.

142. "How the Parties Stand," *WAG*, March 10, 1868, 2. One man offered to purchase a subscription to the *Gazette* for twenty-five others who could not afford it themselves, because he was interested in "the dissemination of conservative doctrines" ("Worthy of Imitation," *WAG*, February 25, 1868, 1).

143. John W. Stayton to Joe Stayton, March 13, 1868, Jackson County Historical Society, printed in Luker, "Post Civil War Period."

144. "Arkansas to Be Mexicanized," *WAG*, February 11, 1868, 2.

145. "Heads You Win, Tails I Lose," *WAG*, February 25, 1868, 1. Alabama's constitution had actually failed its ratification vote. The Reconstruction Acts called for approval of new constitutions in an election in which the majority of registered voters participated. Conservative strategy in Alabama had been to encourage white men to stay away from the polls so that a majority of electors would not cast votes. They were successful. Congress then passed an additional Reconstruction Act calling for ratification by a

majority only of those votes cast, undermining this conservative strategy in other states. Alabama was then admitted into Congress under the new constitution despite its never being legally ratified. See Foner, *Reconstruction*, 332–33.

146. "State News," *WAG*, February 4, 1868, 3.

147. "State News," *WAG*, February 18, 1868, 3. The *Gazette* also reprinted reports when the man accused of this rape was hung several months later. See "State News," *WAG*, April 14, 1868, 4, and "State News," *WAG*, May 5, 1868, 2. Martha Hodes notes, "Whites did not uniformly level rape accusations at black men in the early years of Reconstruction, though they began to put forth the idea that such a crime was becoming more frequent" (*White Women, Black Men*, 157). Her overall conclusion that white southerners focused more on interracial marriage than rape during Reconstruction (see, e.g., ibid., 146) is borne out by my findings in Arkansas.

148. Under "State News," *WAG*, February 18, 1868, 3. The next week, in the "State News" column, the *Gazette*'s editors reprinted two items from the *Arkadelphia Standard*. The first reported that conservative speakers would be addressing every township in Clark County; directly underneath, the second report read, "An old darkey living out on Antoine Creek, who was for many years the slave of one of our prominent planters, whipped his two grown up sons a few days since for advocating miscegenation" (*WAG*, February 25, 1868, 2).

149. In the years leading up to the Arkansas constitutional convention, I found three other scattered reports of black-male-on-white-female rape in the *Gazette*'s "State News" columns. See *WAG*, February 10, 1866, 1; September 8, 1866, 1; and June 11, 1867, 3.

150. See Angela Y. Davis, *Women, Race, and Class*, chap. 11, esp. 184–85, and Hodes, *White Women, Black Men*, esp. 157–58. Cf. Sommerville, *Rape and Race*, esp. 249–50.

151. See, e.g., Hall, "'Mind That Burns in Each Body'"; Gilmore, *Gender and Jim Crow*; Hodes, *White Women, Black Men*; Sommerville, *Rape and Race*; Dailey, *Before Jim Crow*; and Kantrowitz, *Ben Tillman*.

152. Trelease, *White Terror*, 99–103. For the *Weekly Arkansas Gazette* warning that a new constitution would bring "disorder" and require an organization such as the Klan, see "Secret Organization in Tennessee," *WAG*, March 24, 1868, 1, and for welcoming and justifying the Klan in Arkansas, see "The 'World' of the Ku Klux Klan," *WAG*, April 21, 1868, 4.

153. It was never proven that Hinds was murdered by Klansmen, but this was widely believed to be the case. See Trelease, *White Terror*, 154, and Moneyhon, *Impact of the Civil War and Reconstruction*, 251. See also Chapter 3, n. 122.

Chapter 5

1. Testimony of William Hampton Mitchell, *KKK Testimony*, 7:641–44. In citing testimony before this congressional committee, I will use volume numbers that correspond to a given volume's place in the entire set, not the volume numbers within each state's

series. For instance, testimony from Georgia covers two volumes, volumes 6 and 7 of the overall set, which are also identified on their title pages as "Georgia, Volume I (or II)." I will identify "Georgia, Volume I," as volume 6, because it is the sixth volume in the thirteen-volume series.

2. Fry, *Night Riders*, 3, 154–60. Fry emphasizes night riding precedents to the Klan in antebellum slave patrols and similarities and differences in African Americans' perceptions of these two groups. See also Litwack, *Been in the Storm So Long*, 278.

3. Traditionally, scholarship on white violence during Reconstruction, particularly that perpetrated by the Ku Klux Klan, has focused on its instrumental and functional aspects. Historians have argued about the political effectiveness of white violence, especially the Klan's, during Reconstruction, and about its responsibility for the demise of Republican state governments and the return to power of conservative elites. Historians have also debated the geography of violence and the class of the Klan's leadership versus its rank and file. For an overview of these debates, see Perman, "Counter Reconstruction." For historical overviews of the history of the Ku Klux Klan and the violence enacted under this banner during Reconstruction, see esp. Trelease, *White Terror*. See also Franklin, *Reconstruction*, chap. 9; Rable, *But There Was No Peace*; Foner, *Reconstruction*, esp. 425–44; W. E. B. DuBois, *Black Reconstruction*, esp. 674–84; and Lou Falkner Williams, *Great South Carolina Ku Klux Klan Trials*. For recent scholarship that in various ways analyzes the meaning revealed in the forms of violence employed by white southern men against former slaves after emancipation, see Hodes, *White Women, Black Men*, chap. 7, and "Sexualization of Reconstruction Politics"; Scott Nelson, "Livestock, Boundaries, and Public Space in Spartanburg" (which places Klan violence "in the context of the reshuffling of markets and masculinity" following the Civil War and emancipation) and *Iron Confederacies*, esp. chaps. 5 and 6; Parsons, "Midnight Rangers"; and Cardyn, "Sexualized Racism" and "Sexual Terror." See also Hahn, *Nation under Our Feet*, 265–88.

4. On the challenge that "the inexplicable excesses of racial phenomena, their seeming irrationality," pose to "purely materialist explanations," see Holt, "Marking," 5. For another perspective on the gendered nature of night rider violence, see Cardyn, "Sexualized Racism" and "Sexual Terror." Cardyn interprets night rider violence as "a calculated deployment of sexual violence" by the Klan to reestablish white male supremacy (Cardyn, "Sexualized Racism" and "Sexual Terror," esp. 677 and 154, respectively). Indeed, I read much of the sexual violence as a type of will to reestablish traditional visions of white rule in the very direct sense of reenactments of such rule within the terrible scenes of sexual violence themselves. It is not clear to me, though, how calculated and premeditated the sexual forms that Klan violence took were as a terroristic means to a political end. Nor is it obvious how such intentions translated into the ultimately unconscious realm of sexual arousal for the rapists. I am trying, in other words, to draw distinctions between function and consequence and origin and intention. There is a relationship but not a straight line between them.

5. For another exploration of the "expressive function" or "crucial discursive work" done

by Klan violence that focuses not on gender and sexual violence but, rather, on the costumes and popular cultural references within Klan activities, see Parsons, "Midnight Rangers" (quotation from 835). See also Harcourt, "Who Were the Pale Faces?," 49. Of related interest, see Hall, " 'Mind That Burns in Each Body,' " on lynching as "a dramatization of cultural themes," 330, 334; Hale, *Making Whiteness*, chap. 5; and Wiegman, *American Anatomies*, chap. 3.

6. Joseph Roach writes, "The social processes of memory and forgetting, familiarly known as culture, may be carried out by a variety of performance events, from stage plays to sacred rites, from carnivals to the invisible rituals of everyday life." To his list of types of "performance events" that invoke, communicate, produce, and transform cultural meaning I would add the ritualized and theatrical violence of night riding, to which Roach's definition of performance also applies: "To perform in this sense means to bring forth, to make manifest, and to transmit. To perform also means, though often more secretly, to reinvent" (*Cities of the Dead*, xi). On the constitution, reproduction, and reinvention of categories of identity, such as gender and race, through repetitive performances that both naturalize them and give them meaning, see Butler, *Gender Trouble*. See also Foster, "Choreographies of Gender," for an attempt to refocus Butler's analysis on bodily performances as opposed to primarily speech acts.

7. On the self-representation of Klansmen as an alternative law, see also Scott Nelson, *Iron Confederacies*, 111, and Cardyn, "Sexualized Racism," 799–812.

8. Cf. Parsons, "Midnight Rangers," esp. 829–31, which argues instead that "Klansmen were rejecting an honor culture" but which also finds similar significance in disguise as a means of adopting identities allowing violent behavior not possible for certain men in other guises. On this, see also Bercaw, *Gendered Freedoms*, 87–88; Cardyn, "Sexual Terror," 154; and Trelease, *White Terror*, xlviii.

9. See Chapters 3 and 4; Edwards, " 'Marriage Covenant' " and *Gendered Strife and Confusion*; McCurry, *Masters of Small Worlds*; and Kantrowitz, *Ben Tillman*. In "Midnight Rangers," Parsons argues that the disparate groups of white men calling themselves "Ku Klux" were connected not by "official channels of communication" but, rather, by shared popular culture references (815–16).

10. Hahn, *Nation under Our Feet*, 143–56, finds precedent for this use of rumor to legitimate violence in the Christmas insurrection scare of 1865.

11. Fry, *Night Riders*, esp. 3, 112–13, 146–47, 151, 154–56; Hadden, *Slave Patrols*, chap. 6; Hahn, *Nation under Our Feet*, 269–70; Lou Falkner Williams, *Great South Carolina Ku Klux Klan Trials*, 27–28. For descriptions of the Klan as a force controlling nighttime movement of African Americans, much like slave patrols, see also interviews with former slaves Chess Johnson, Primus Moore, Lawston Reed, Melinda Sutton, and Pete Newton, in Early Settlers' Personal History Questionnaires, Manuscript Records of the Arkansas Historical Records Survey, group A, box 96, file F, folder 1, and box 123, file F, folder 1, UAF. Hahn, *Nation under Our Feet*, 269–70, also emphasizes precedents to the Klan in local militias; Parsons, "Midnight Rangers," 818, argues Klan activities also drew on precedents in "carnivalesque" rituals such as folk serenading.

12. See Trelease, *White Terror*, xlv–xlvi, and Hahn, *Nation under Our Feet*, 267. The association of vigilante gangs with former Confederate soldiers is suggested by the military terms freedpeople sometimes used to identify them. Hampton Mitchell described to the congressional committee the man who beat his wife as "one of the privates, *as we call them*, not the captain" (my emphasis), meaning that this man was not the one who appeared to be in charge. See testimony of William Hampton Mitchell, *KKK Testimony*, 7:641.

13. Trelease, *White Terror*, 7–8. On the region as a stronghold of Confederate support, see Captain Michael Walsh, Chief Superintendent of Nashville Subdistrict, Report to Brig. General J. R. Lewis, Assistant Commissioner, November 29, 1866, Tennessee BRFAL, roll 34, "Reports of Outrages, Riots, and Murders." Walsh writes, "All the [white] inhabitants [of this section] were and are rebels, and traitors, heart and soul, with the exception of a half dozen men from the several counties." On similar labor conditions throughout the South in the summer of 1866, see Jaynes, *Branches without Roots*, 142. Jaynes reports that most planters had run out of funds just about the time that widespread reports of violence in Robertson and Sumner Counties began flooding the Freedmen's Bureau.

14. Referring to the affidavit of a freedwoman whose husband had been murdered, the Freedmen's Bureau superintendent for the region wrote, "You will see in a portion of her affidavit she gets nothing for her time and that she and her daughter are as much in slavery as before the war. There are hundreds like her in these counties" (Captain Michael Walsh, Superintendent, Nashville Subdistrict, to Bvt. Brig. General J. R. Lewis. Assistant Commissioner for Tennessee, December 13, 1866, Tennessee BRFAL, roll 34, "Reports of Outrages, Riots, and Murders").

15. Ibid., November 29, 1866. Harper's gang was apparently notorious and credited with inspiring other gangs of regulators or guerrillas challenging local governments in Tennessee. See "Lawlessness in Putnam County—Courts Set at Defiance," an article from the *Nashville Press and Times* reprinted in the *Memphis Weekly Post*, April 28, 1866, 3.

16. Information and quotations from Captain Michael Walsh, Chief Superintendent, Nashville Subdistrict, to Bvt. Brig. General J. R. Lewis, Assistant Commissioner for Tennessee, November 29, 1866, Tennessee BRFAL, roll 34, "Reports of Outrages, Riots, and Murders." Local Freedmen's Bureau agent D. D. Holman had reported just a few months earlier that "there is so much prejudice against the colored people that with all the means at his power, he has been unable to prevent abuses or forfeiture of contracts" (Letter/Report from J. R. Lewis, Chief Superintendent, Nashville Subdistrict, to Bvt. Major General C. B. Fisk, Assistant Commissioner for the State of Tennessee, August 28, 1866, Tennessee BRFAL, roll 34, "Reports of Outrages, Riots, and Murders").

17. "I Am Committee," enclosed in Lt. Chas B. Brady to Bvt. Lt. Col. A. L. Hough, January 29, 1867, Letters Received, series 4720, Dept. of the Tennessee, U.S. Army Continental Commands, in Berlin and Rowland, *Families and Freedom*, 189. According to Berlin and Rowland, this notice was nailed to doorways in January 1867. It had been circulated earlier as well. Captain Walsh reported in November 1866 that "Esquire Roury [Rowy?]

is one of the men distributing the tract or order of Harper called the '*I am Committee.*' He is a bad one. he read this document to Henderson Groves (col'd) and said he must attend to it" (Captain Michael Walsh, Chief Superintendent, Nashville Subdistrict, to Bvt. Brig. General J. R. Lewis, Assistant Commissioner for Tennessee, November 29, 1866, Tennessee BRFAL, roll 34, "Reports of Outrages, Riots, and Murders").

18. Jaynes, *Branches without Roots*, 228–32; Jacqueline Jones, *Labor of Love, Labor of Sorrow*, 58–59; Schwalm, *Hard Fight for We*, chap. 6; Frankel, *Freedom's Women*, 75–76; Clinton, "Bloody Terrain," 33, and "Reconstructing Freedwomen," 318; Foner, *Reconstruction*, 85–87; and Ransom and Sutch, *One Kind of Freedom*, 232–36. Cf. O'Donovan, *Becoming Free in the Cotton South*, 158–60, 178–79, on the role played by Georgia planters in the first planting season after the war in excluding especially single women from the plantation labor force, and chap. 4 on how women attached to men in families managed to negotiate their way back onto the plantations as workers.

19. "I Am Committee," enclosed in Lt. Chas B. Brady to Bvt. Lt. Col. A. L. Hough, January 29, 1867, Letters Received, series 4720, Dept. of the Tennessee, U.S. Army Continental Commands, in Berlin and Rowland, *Families and Freedom*, 189.

20. Captain Michael Walsh, Chief Superintendent, Nashville Subdistrict, to Bvt. Brig. General J. R. Lewis, Assistant Commissioner for Tennessee, November 29, 1866, Tennessee BRFAL, roll 34, "Reports of Outrages, Riots, and Murders."

21. One such case was referred to in two reports of outrages from Captain Walsh. Hudson Purdue, the husband of a freedwoman identified as both Rachel Purdue and Rachel Ray, was murdered near Mitchellville. Walsh sought an affidavit from Rachel but was not successful. "I spent nearly one whole day in hunting her up but was unable to obtain the necessary information for the reason of her being absent, which absence I am under the impression was caused by those by whom she is employed." When he finally did speak with her, she told him that she dared not recount the particulars of the killing of her husband, or she, too, would be murdered. It is about this woman that Walsh wrote, "You will see . . . she gets nothing for her time and that she and her daughter are as much in slavery as before the war." It is not necessarily the case that Rachel had left this employer to live with Hudson before he was killed; but the fact that her name was listed as both Ray and Purdue suggests that she married a man who had not been a slave on the plantation where she was before the war, and the fact that she was kept from Walsh by her employers and was terrified for her life would be consistent with that interpretation. See Captain Michael Walsh, Chief Superintendent, Nashville Subdistrict, to Bvt. Brig. General J. R. Lewis, Assistant Commissioner for Tennessee, November 29, 1866, and Walsh to Lewis, Additional Report of Outrages Committed in Sumner and Robertson Counties, December 13, 1866, Tennessee BRFAL, roll 34, "Reports of Outrages, Riots, and Murders."

22. See Trelease, *White Terror*, 3–6. One of these men, John C. Lester, who became a lawyer, co-authored a history of the Klan and recounted this story of its beginnings. See Lester and Wilson, *Ku Klux Klan*. Frank O. McCord was another of these men; in 1866 he was the local editor of the *Pulaski Citizen* and eventually became the paper's editor in chief. On these founders of the Klan, see also Parsons, "Midnight Rangers," 811–12. Parsons

investigates what might in fact have constituted "amusement" for the founders of the Pulaski Klan by linking the details of specific Klan rituals to popular musical and theatrical performances, including the figure common in mid-nineteenth-century minstrel shows who dressed as a ghost to frighten African American characters; see pp. 821–22.

23. John Hope Franklin suggests this in his discussion of the Klan in *Reconstruction*, chap. 9. See also Harcourt, "Who Were the Pale Faces?," 42 and 29–34, for a critique of how this story of the Klan's origins was used to apologize for terrorism and violence and to promote post-Reconstruction reconciliation between northern and southern whites.

24. Trelease, *White Terror*, 10–14, and Harcourt, "Who Were the Pale Faces?," 41–45.

25. See, for instance, various affidavits of previous Klan members in "Ku Klux Klan Papers, Depositions, etc., 1869–70," in Holden Papers, Duke University.

26. Ibid.

27. When asked by a member of the South Carolina subcommittee of the congressional investigation, "These were Ku-Klux that whipped you?" freedman Clem Bowden replied, "Yes, sir; *they called themselves such*" (my emphasis). See testimony of Clem Bowden, *KKK Testimony*, 3:382 (quotation), 385. See also testimony of Hannah Tutson, *KKK Testimony*, 13:59–64; Hahn, *Nation under Our Feet*, 267–68; and Parsons, "Midnight Rangers," 816.

28. Trelease, *White Terror*, 13–27, 51; Parsons, "Midnight Rangers," 815–16.

29. On the performative aspects of the disguises worn by Klansmen, see Parsons, "Midnight Rangers," esp. 818–22. See also Bercaw, *Gendered Freedoms*, 87–88, and Cardyn, "Sexual Terror," 154.

30. See, for instance, in *KKK Testimony*, testimony of Clem Bowden, 3:381, 382; the description of Martha Woods in Col. Lewis Merrill's testimony, 5:1474; and the description of Dean Reynolds in General Samuel W. Crawford's testimony, 9:1158. White victims of Klan violence also tried to identify assailants in the midst of attacks. For a description of a white woman who identified Klansmen who beat her husband by peering through the eye and mouth holes on their masks, see testimony of Walter Brock, 7:1007.

31. Descriptions of Creecy Adams and Phebe Smith in Col. Lewis Merrill's testimony, *KKK Testimony*, 5:1474.

32. George Flemister, *KKK Testimony*, 7:656.

33. See affidavits in "Ku Klux Klan Papers, Depositions, etc., 1869–70," Holden Papers, Duke University, and testimony of Aury Jeter, *KKK Testimony*, 6:566.

34. William Quackenbush told prosecutors in North Carolina that when he joined the Klan, he "understood the object of the organization to be to take the law in our own hands and to whip or hang any one we saw proper" ("Ku Klux Klan Papers, Depositions, etc., 1869–70," Holden Papers, Duke University). See also Scott Nelson, *Iron Confederacies*, 111, and Cardyn, "Sexualized Racism," 799–812.

35. On the significance of Klan attacks especially on freedpeople's schools, as sites of African American political empowerment, autonomy, and mobilization, see Hahn, *Nation under Our Feet*, 276–80.

36. On African Americans organizing to resist Klan attacks, and on the greater challenges of doing so in rural settings where freedpeople lived dispersed across plantations and farms, see ibid., 280–83.

37. See esp. McCurry, *Masters of Small Worlds*.

38. See testimony of Hannah Tutson, *KKK Testimony*, 13:59–64, for evidence of one freed-woman who understood the land that she and her husband had secured both through the Federal Homestead Act and through purchase to be *her* land.

Historians exploring African American families in the early years of freedom have found gender norms and expectations in regard to the organization of household economies and authority to have been varied and changing, as well as the subject of enormous contest between black women and men. Both norms and practices in this regard were influenced by freedpeople's experiences in slavery as well as postemancipation economic insecurity and thus continued necessity of women's labor outside their families. Most scholars have found a trend toward increasingly patriarchal family structures and norms among freedpeople over time, while offering different emphases and reaching different conclusions about when important shifts occurred. The evidence that is available to us of norms regarding gender and authority within families, though, is rarely unmitigated by the patriarchal bias of the discourse of white northern policy makers. See Penningroth, *Claims of Kinfolk*, 164, 176–86; Schwalm, *Hard Fight for We*, 236, 247, 260–63, 267; Bercaw, *Gendered Freedoms*, 5–6, 30, 99–116; Edwards, *Gendered Strife and Confusion*, 145–83, and " 'Marriage Covenant,' " 106; Foner, *Reconstruction*, 87–88; Frankel, *Freedom's Women*, 74–75, 80, 92–95, 105, 128–35; Hunter, *To 'Joy My Freedom*, 39–40; O'Donovan, *Becoming Free in the Cotton South*, 183–85, 192–204; and Regosin, *Freedom's Promise*, 153–57. On similar issues in the antebellum North, see Horton, "Freedom's Yoke," which explores how black middle-class pronouncements on proper gender roles that emphasized traditional patriarchal norms sat in tension with both the demands on working-class families that led most women to work for wages outside their homes and the public roles taken on by many black women. On the evolution and contestation of restrictions on public roles for African American women, see Barkley Brown, "To Catch the Vision of Freedom" and "Negotiating and Transforming the Public Sphere"; Martha Jones, *All Bound Up Together*, chaps. 4–6; and, on the post-Reconstruction era, Higginbotham, *Righteous Discontent*, and White, *Too Heavy a Load*.

39. See Penningroth, *Claims of Kinfolk*, chap. 6, for an exploration of evolving family and household economies among freedpeople after the Civil War.

40. See, for instance, Schwalm, *Hard Fight for We*, chap. 7; Berlin and Rowland, *Families and Freedom*; Edwards, *Gendered Strife and Confusion*, 45–47, and " 'Marriage Covenant,' " 99–106; Foner, *Reconstruction*, 84–86; Frankel, *Freedom's Women*, 42–43; Gutman, *Black Family in Slavery and Freedom*, 204–7; Hunter, *To 'Joy My Freedom*, 35–38; Litwack, *Been in the Storm So Long*, 229–47. See also Peggy Cooper Davis, "Marriage," and Franke, "Becoming a Citizen." Of course, other former slaves abandoned partners from before the war, either as circumstances of separation and hardship put strains on their

relationships or as freedom offered them an opportunity to leave a relationship with which they were not satisfied. And others saw little advantage in legalizing unions they and their communities had accepted as marriages for years. See, for instance, Berlin and Rowland, *Families and Freedom*, 140–45, 171–72; Edwards, *Gendered Strife and Confusion*, 54–60, and "'Marriage Covenant,'" 107–12; and Frankel, *Freedom's Women*, 80–84, 90–92, and 104–6.

41. Chaplain A. B. Randall to Brig. Gen. L. Thomas, February 28, 1865, in Berlin and Rowland, *Families and Freedom*, 163–64 (emphasis in the original).

42. Ibid.

43. Edwards, "'Marriage Covenant,'" 101, 118; Peggy Cooper Davis, "Marriage"; Franke, "Becoming a Citizen."

44. Testimony of Eli Barnes, *KKK Testimony*, 7:958. For a similar reading of white planters and overseers intruding into freedpeople's homes, see Schwalm, *Hard Fight for We*, 217–20.

45. As recounted in the testimony of John A. Minnis, U.S. District Attorney, who took his confession, *KKK Testimony*, 8:547.

46. See Trelease, *White Terror*, chap. 24.

47. Democratic members of the committee's minority often questioned such witnesses in ways that allowed them to defend and lend respectability to secret organizations by associating them with the "best men" of a given state and distancing them from violence.

48. Testimony of John B. Gordon, *KKK Testimony*, 6:308–9, 325.

49. Testimony of David Schenck, *KKK Testimony*, 2:363–64.

50. Eric Foner describes these funds, established to assist those facing prosecution in federal courts in 1871, in *Reconstruction*, 457.

51. *Trial of William W. Holden*, 1769–70, qtd. in Trelease, *White Terror*, 200.

52. See also Trelease, *White Terror*, 37–38; Scott Nelson, *Iron Confederacies*, 135–36; and Sommerville, *Rape and Race*, 162–64, 174–75.

53. Testimony of Nathan Bedford Forrest, *KKK Testimony*, 13:7. See also in *KKK Testimony*, testimony of Plato Durham, 2:310; Ambrose Wright, 6:274–75; W. M. Shropshire, 7:637; Carleton B. Cole, 7:1190–91; and Peter Dox, 8:446. And see Hodes, *White Women, Black Men*, 157.

54. Testimony of James Justice, *KKK Testimony*, 2:142.

55. See Hodes, *White Women, Black Men*, 148, 151–61, 157–58, and "Sexualization of Reconstruction Politics"; Cardyn, "Sexualized Racism," 695–97; and Sommerville, *Rape and Race*.

56. See testimony of Hampton L. Jarnagin, *KKK Testimony*, 11:513–14, for an emphasis on stock stealing and larceny rather than rape.

57. See also Hodes, *White Women, Black Men*, 157–58, 175, and chap. 8; Cardyn, "Sexualized Racism," 697; and Sommerville, *Rape and Race*, chap. 9. For a discussion of the evolution and circulation of this particular form of racist rhetoric in North Carolina's disfranchise-

ment campaign, see Gilmore, *Gender and Jim Crow*, chaps. 3–4. For an early analysis of the "myth of the black rapist" and its historical evolution, see Angela Y. Davis, *Women, Race, and Class*, chap. 11.

58. Testimony of H. W. Guion, *KKK Testimony*, 2:268–69.

59. Testimony of Nathan Bedford Forrest, *KKK Testimony*, 13:15.

60. Testimony of G. Wiley Wells, *KKK Testimony*, 13:1160.

61. See also Hodes, *White Women, Black Men*, 148, 151–65, 168; "Wartime Dialogues on Illicit Sex," 241; and "Sexualization of Reconstruction Politics." Jacquelyn Dowd Hall argues that stories of black-on-white sexual violence often told in excruciating detail "gripped the white imagination far out of proportion to their statistical significance" in the 1920s and 1930s and operated as a kind of "folk pornography." See " 'Mind That Burns in Each Body,' " 335.

62. Case cited in Trelease, *White Terror*, 193, 473 n. 17.

63. Testimony of Thomas Allen, *KKK Testimony*, 7:611.

64. Testimony of William S. Mudd, *KKK Testimony*, 10:1749.

65. Testimony of Hon. Augustus R. Wright, *KKK Testimony*, 6:136. A later witness believed that Ashburn had been living in "a house where some women of ill-repute were occupying rooms." Asked if they were all black women, the witness showed that he had only sketchy information to substantiate his belief: "I think one was a white woman; I do not know certainly about that. . . . I do not know that it was what would be called a house of ill-fame, where common prostitutes assembled." This witness, Rev. J. H. Caldwell, was sympathetic to Ashburn. He wrote an article for the *New York Tribune* about Ashburn's killing and the numerous rationales circulated after the fact, including allegations that he was murdered by Rev. Henry M. Turner, by federal soldiers, by other Republicans, and by freedpeople. The article concluded, "All of this is to cover up and confuse the whole affair, just as they did in the New Orleans, Memphis, and Mobile riots." Yet even he accepted and repeated the rumor that Ashburn was involved in some way in illicit sex. See testimony of Rev. J. H. Caldwell, *KKK Testimony*, 6:434, and *Tribune* article appended to Caldwell's testimony, pp. 451–53. On Ashburn's murder, see also Hunter, *To 'Joy My Freedom*, 33.

66. Testimony of Rev. Henry M. Turner, *KKK Testimony*, 7:1035–36.

67. Testimony of Alexander Davis, *KKK Testimony*, 11:469–70. Davis convinced one of the assailants to turn state's evidence. This assailant told the grand jury that Lucas was whipped because she was living with a white man. That the group of white men living with black women were "farmers" as opposed to "planters," meaning that they were men who owned and cultivated land but were of "moderate means," was explained to the committee by James H. Rives, *KKK Testimony*, 11:558.

68. Testimony of Hampton L. Jarnagin, *KKK Testimony*, 11:513–14.

69. Testimony of James H. Rives, *KKK Testimony*, 11:558. This witness could not answer the committee chair's question, "By what refinement of ethics were the women whipped and the men let to go free?" However, he did offer that "if I had been there I should have as certainly allowed it to the rascals as the women."

70. "Lewdness" was Rives's term; see testimony of James H. Rives, *KKK Testimony*, 11:558–59. See also Frankel, *Freedom's Women*, 114–15.

71. Testimony of Henry Lowther, *KKK Testimony*, 6:356–59. Rev. J. H. Caldwell told the committee that Lowther had admitted to him that he did, in fact, have sex with this woman, but only after he was first visited by the Klan and after she followed him into the woods and solicited him there. For these reasons, Lowther still felt that the charge of illicit sex was a pretext and that he was attacked because of his politics. See testimony of Rev. J. H. Caldwell, *KKK Testimony*, 6:426. See other discussions of this case in Hodes, *White Women, Black Men*, 154–58, and Cardyn, "Sexual Terror," 149, and "Sexualized Racism," 739–41. In these latter two works, Cardyn analyzes in detail what she terms "genital torture and mutilation" by the Klan, a form of sexual violence that she finds women were as likely to suffer as men. See "Sexual Terror," 147–51, and "Sexualized Racism," 736–44.

72. Testimony of William F. Wright, *KKK Testimony*, 7:973.

73. Testimony of Elias Hill, *KKK Testimony*, 5:1407.

74. Testimony of Anderson Ferrell, *KKK Testimony*, 7:618. See Frankel, *Freedom's Women*, 109, on an African American preacher killed by Klansmen allegedly for having beaten his wife. On Nathan Bedford Forrest beating to death a freedman employed on his plantation, who was at the time involved in a labor dispute with Forrest, supposedly to stop the man from beating his wife, see Bercaw, *Gendered Freedoms*, 117–18, 135–57.

75. Testimony of William Hampton Mitchell, *KKK Testimony*, 7:642.

76. Recounted in Trelease, *White Terror*, 195. See also Cardyn, "Sexual Terror," 144, and "Sexualized Racism," 706.

77. On the meaning of social equality, see Chapter 4.

78. Testimony of Hon. Peter M. Dox, *KKK Testimony*, 8:429. For more on this case, on charges that Dox interfered with black men voting in an election in which he was a candidate, and on Dox denying the charge, see testimony of General Samuel W. Crawford, *KKK Testimony*, 9:1161, and documents appended to his testimony, pp. 1191–92.

79. See testimony of Clem Bowden, 3:380, 382, and W. H. Champion, 3:366, in *KKK Testimony*. See also discussion of this incident in Fry, *Night Riders*, 111; Scott Nelson, *Iron Confederacies*, 131; Lou Falkner Williams, *Great South Carolina Ku Klux Klan Trials*, 30; Parsons, "Midnight Ranger," 828; and Cardyn, "Sexualized Racism," 734.

80. A similar scene of social equality as same-gender, cross-racial sex was staged in Monticello, Arkansas. The Reconstruction governor of that state, Powell Clayton, described the "well established facts" of this case in his memoirs: "Deputy Sheriff [William] Dollar was serving a writ and was killed by a gang of some fourteen Ku Klux. Then, in order to make an impressive tableau, they killed 'Fed' Reeves, an unoffending negro, and tied the white man and negro together in the attitude of kissing and embracing, and left them in the public road where they remained for about two days. During this time, to gratify their curiosity, many people visited them and left them as they found them" (Clayton, *Aftermath*, 117). After his murder, Sheriff Dollar was accused of living in adultery with a black woman. See John M. Harrell, *The Brooks and Baxter War: A History of the*

Reconstruction Period in Arkansas (St. Louis, 1893), 87, cited in Trelease, *White Terror,* 150, 462 n. 5.

81. Testimony of Z. B. Hargrove, *KKK Testimony,* 6:82–83.

82. Testimony of Essic Harris, *KKK Testimony,* 2:99–100. For similar statements indicating the frequency of white male sexual violence against black women during Reconstruction, see testimony of James Justice, *KKK Testimony,* 2:148, and testimony of Edward Carter, *KKK Testimony,* 12:1085. See also Cardyn, "Sexual Terror," 146.

83. See also Cardyn, "Sexual Terror," 140, and Sommerville, *Rape and Race,* 150.

84. See, for instance, Estrich, *Real Rape,* 10–15, and Temkin, "Women, Rape, and Law Reform," 20–24.

85. See, for instance, the locations of Freedmen's Bureau offices noted in Finley, *From Slavery to Uncertain Freedom,* map A, p. 11. On night rider violence occurring predominantly in small towns and rural areas, see Trelease, *White Terror,* 113.

86. See, for instance, Trelease, *White Terror,* xxiii, and Finley, *From Slavery to Uncertain Freedom,* 19–22.

87. Because in the case of rape "numbers are unprovable," Rhonda Copelon endorses standards such as "general frequency" and "patterns of abuse" rather than absolute numbers for determining whether rape has been committed as a war crime in instances brought before the International War Crimes Tribunal. See Copelon, "Surfacing Gender," 258.

88. All but four of these forty-five stories are referred to in this chapter and/or the next. For the additional four instances of sexual abuse, see Unity & Minerva vs. D. Beasley, Maria Posey vs. Andrew B. Payne, and Same Neal vs. Andrew B. Payne, all in John Seage, Report of Outrages, January 1866, Tennessee BRFAL, roll 34, "Reports of Outrages, Riots, and Murders"; and Testimony of G. Wiley Wells, *KKK Testimony,* 12:1165. Lisa Cardyn concludes from her research that sexual violence "was in retrospect, one of [the Klan's] most starkly defining features." See "Sexual Terror" (quotation on 143) and "Sexualized Racism," esp. 699, 704. In these two works, Cardyn treats many of the same stories that I do in this section. For her analysis, see "Sexual Terror," esp. 145–47, and "Sexualized Racism," 699–736. For additional examples of black women raped by white southern men during Reconstruction, as well as discussion of some of the assaults discussed here, see Clinton, "Bloody Terrain," 315, 317–18, 328–29, and "Reconstructing Freedwomen," 316; Edwards, *Gendered Strife and Confusion,* 208, and "Sexual Violence, Gender, Reconstruction," 248; Frankel, *Freedom's Women,* 110–13; Gutman, *Black Family in Slavery and Freedom,* 387, 393–96; Hodes, *White Women, Black Men,* 270 n. 32; Hunter, *To 'Joy My Freedom,* 33–34; Lerner, *Black Women in White America,* 180–88; Litwack, *Been in the Storm So Long,* 277, 280; Sommerville, *Rape and Race,* 147–57; and Lou Falkner Williams, *Great South Carolina Ku Klux Klan Trials,* 35. See also Kidada Williams, "In the Space of Violence."

The documentation of sexual violence in the southern states drops off after 1871 because of the end of the congressional investigation, but there is no reason to believe that the violence ceased. It may have lessened with the suppression of the Klan by federal authority in 1871 and 1872 (see, e.g., Lou Falkner Williams, *Great South Carolina Ku Klux Klan Trials*, chap. 6). Evidence in federal records of rape by organized gangs of white men reappears again in 1876, in, for instance, reports on election-related violence in Louisiana. See Steedman, "Gender and the Politics of the Household in Reconstruction Louisiana."

89. Based on information in affidavits of Henry Willis, Stanford Willis, and Amanda Willis, in Tennessee BRFAL, roll 34, "Affidavits Relating to Outrages." Throughout the rest of this chapter and the next, I will be inconsistent in the use of either first or last names to refer to historical actors. In some cases, such as this one, using first names will allow me to distinguish between members of the same family. In other cases, I have only first names for former slaves. I use last names when they are available and when their use does not risk readers' confusing one actor with another.

90. Affidavits of Henry Willis and Stanford Willis, Tennessee BRFAL, roll 34, "Affidavits Relating to Outrages." After establishing that Stanford's youngest son could not (or would not) identify at least one of the assailants, another ordered members of the family still in bed to pull their covers over their heads and not look at the intruders, an attempt presumably to avoid being identified.

91. Affidavits of Henry Willis, Stanford Willis, and Amanda Willis, Tennessee BRFAL, roll 34, "Affidavits Relating to Outrages."

92. Affidavit of Henry Willis, Tennessee BRFAL, roll 34, "Affidavits Relating to Outrages."

93. It seems likely that Henry Willis himself had been a soldier. Henry told Walsh that he knew of the murders of black soldiers in the area and had been warned by a local white man "that if I was a Union Soldier I had better leave." He never stated explicitly that he had been in the army, but it seems that he was not at home the night his family was attacked; perhaps he had reason to have been sleeping out in the woods. See ibid.

94. See affidavits of Stanford Willis and Henry Willis, Tennessee BRFAL, roll 34, "Affidavits Relating to Outrages," and Captain Michael Walsh, Chief Superintendent, Nashville Subdistrict, to D. D. Holman, Superintendent, Robertson County, Tennessee, October 6, 1866, entry #3602, BRFAL.

95. Affidavits of Amanda Willis, Henry Willis, and Stanford Willis, Tennessee BRFAL, roll 34, "Affidavits Relating to Outrages."

96. Affidavits of Patsy Duvall and Jim Duvall, Tennessee BRFAL, roll 34, "Affidavits Relating to Outrages." It is also possible that Jim Duvall remained outside during the exchange between Patsy Duvall and Richard Pentle, and even that Patsy never told him what had occurred. If this were the case, he was then forced to stand outside while an armed and hostile white man entered the house with his wife. In either case, Jim Duvall's role in these events was difficult to represent to the bureau as those of a properly protective patriarch.

97. Affidavit of Ed Link, November 27, 1866, Tennessee BRFAL, roll 34, "Affidavits Relating to Outrages."

98. Sina vs. Widow Brothers, in John Seage, Report of Outrages, January 1866, Tennessee BRFAL, roll 34, "Reports of Outrages, Riots, and Murders."

99. Affidavit of George Moore and letter from John Hamilton to Lieut. James Miller, August 29, 1869, appended to testimony of General Samuel W. Crawford, *KKK Testimony*, 9:1188, 1189–90. On efforts by assailants to "redefin[e] coercion into consensual sexual relations," see also Block, "Lines of Color, Sex, and Service," 147–48.

100. Events described in affidavits of George Moore, Cynthia Bryant, and Rina Barry, and letter from John Hamilton to Lieut. James Miller, August 29, 1869, all appended to testimony of General Samuel W. Crawford, *KKK Testimony*, 9:1187–90.

101. Affidavit of Peggy Johnson, appended to testimony of O. C. French, *KKK Testimony*, 11:36–37.

102. One recently resigned police officer, Granville Richards, who fled Meridian during the riot, explained to a Mississippi legislative committee investigating the violence, "I heard they were going to kill all of the nigger policemen" (affidavit of Granville Richards, appended to testimony of O. C. French, *KKK Testimony*, 11:53).

103. Parton never stated that Ware was black, but the circumstances of the attack on his house, in conjunction with Granville Richards's testimony, quoted in the preceding note, suggest that he was.

104. Affidavit of Ellen Parton, appended to testimony of O. C. French, *KKK Testimony*, 11:38–39.

105. Ibid.

106. Testimony of Essic Harris, *KKK Testimony*, 2:88. This woman told Essic, who lived in the same settlement, that she was raped. On Klan members drawing on popular music performances and carnival to stage their political violence, and on their use of women's clothing, see Parsons, "Midnight Rangers."

107. Testimony of John Wager, *KKK Testimony*, 9:930.

108. See, from *KKK Testimony*, testimony of Essic Harris, 2:86–102; John H. Wager, 9:930; and General Samuel W. Crawford, 9:1156–83.

109. Testimony of Joe Brown, *KKK Testimony*, 6:501–3; see also testimony of Mary Brown, 6:375–77; Mary Neal, 6:386; Caroline Benson, 6:386–88; and Rachel Arnold, 6:388–90.

110. Testimony of Caroline Benson, *KKK Testimony*, 6:388.

111. These assailants may have been imitating experiences in houses of prostitution. Nude dancing in the main rooms of brothels was reported as common, at least in post-emancipation establishments in New Orleans. See Roach, *Cities of the Dead*, 226–27. Lisa Cardyn argues that, rather than this case being distinct from past whippings of slaves, it was emblematic of the sexual meaning that permeated most whippings of enslaved and freedwomen. See "Sexual Terror," 143–45, and "Sexualized Racism," 710–11.

112. Testimony of Caroline Benson, *KKK Testimony*, 6:387.

113. Testimony of Mary Brown, *KKK Testimony*, 6:376.

114. Ibid., 377.

115. Testimony of Mary Neal, *KKK Testimony*, 6:386.

116. Testimony of Caroline Benson, *KKK Testimony*, 6:387.

117. Testimony of Mary Brown, *KKK Testimony*, 6:377. On similar forced performances and

on Klansmen imitating animal sounds as evocations of popular forms of theatrical performance at the time, see Parsons, "Midnight Rangers," 821.

118. Testimony of Columbus Jeter and Aury Jeter, *KKK Testimony*, 6:565–67, 560–65.

119. Testimony of Aury Jeter, *KKK Testimony*, 6:566.

120. This information drawn from testimony of Samuel Tutson and Hannah Tutson, *KKK Testimony*, 13:54–59, 59–64. Quotations from Hannah Tutson on pp. 61, 62, 64. After one of many times in which Hannah Tutson referred to the property in question as her land, saying that some of the night riders had earlier "told me it was not my land; that it was another man's," one member of the committee asked, "When you say your land, you mean you and your husband?" Hannah replied, "Yes, sir." She apparently had strong feelings of ownership in relation to this property, so much so that she often omitted mention of her husband when she articulated them.

121. Testimony of Hannah Tutson, *KKK Testimony*, 13:60.

122. Samuel Tutson told the congressional committee that the men who whipped him called themselves "Ku-Klux." "True-Klux" was the term repeated several times by Hannah Tutson in her testimony. This may have been a variation on the name crafted by the men who attacked the Tutsons; it may reflect their own misunderstanding of the more common term or Hannah's misunderstanding of their words. See testimony of Samuel Tutson and Hannah Tutson, *KKK Testimony*, 13:54, 59–60.

123. Ibid., 54, 60. Hannah later reported, though, that Samuel suffered more extensive injuries: "They did not begin to whip me as they did him" (*KKK Testimony*, 13:61).

124. Testimony of Hannah Tutson, *KKK Testimony*, 13:60.

125. Ibid.

126. Affidavit of Roda Ann Childs [*sic*—"Rhoda" on top of document, "Roda" at bottom], September 25, 1866, in Berlin, Reidy, and Rowland, *Black Military Experience*, 807–8.

127. In the months after the October 1870 election, 11 people were murdered and more than 600 were whipped, beaten, or otherwise assaulted by night riders in York County. South Carolina governor Robert K. Scott had responded to organized violence in 1868 by forming black militia companies. Subsequent Klan violence made special target of militia members. In retaliation, freedpeople began burning the barns and other buildings of suspected participants. White residents reacted with alarm, and Klan membership increased further, some estimating that 78 percent of the county's adult white male population were members of the organization in York County by the spring of 1871. These Klansmen focused on disarming black men (and were aided by the governor, who eventually sent officers to disarm and disband the militia he had formed). In widespread night rides, black men were commonly ordered to renounce Republicanism, and some leaders were compelled to promise to publish notices in the local paper declaring their opposition to the party. See Trelease, *White Terror*, 363–65, and 362–80, for overall conditions and Klan activity in York County. See also Lou Falkner Williams, *Great South Carolina Ku Klux Klan Trials*, 2, 17–19, 22–29, 38–40. The congressional committee conducted six days of hearings in Yorkville. See, from these hearings, esp. testimony of Elias Hill and Colonel Lewis Merrill, *KKK Testimony*, 5:1407–15, 1463–87.

128. Testimony of Colonel Lewis Merrill, *KKK Testimony*, 5:1485.

129. Merrill testified that the men stayed out at night and that "generally, the women did not." However, Elias Hill, a black political leader from outside Yorkville, reported that "sleeping out" was common for "men and women both. Some women would sleep out with their husbands. The women would be so excited when their husbands left that they would go too with the children, and one staid in the rain-storm while her husband was fleeing for his life, as they were about to kill him. There is June Moore; his wife went out with her little babe in the rain every night until late in the spring, and many, many of them did the same" (testimony of Colonel Lewis Merrill and Elias Hill, *KKK Testimony*, 5:1485, 1409). After she was raped, Simril "laid out" in the woods with her husband and children for four nights; see testimony of Harriet Simril, Proceedings of the United States Circuit Court, reprinted in *KKK Testimony*, 5:1861–62.

130. Testimony of Harriet Simril, Proceedings of the United States Circuit Court, reprinted in *KKK Testimony*, 5:1861–62. Simril's testimony is reprinted in Sterling, *Trouble They Seen*, 391–92. Her last name is spelled "Simrell" in Elias Hill's testimony (*KKK Testimony*, 5:1409) and "Simmrell" in Colonel Lewis Merrill's testimony (5:1475).

131. Testimony of Harriet Hernades, *KKK Testimony*, 3:586.

132. Testimony of Elias Hill and Colonel Lewis Merrill, *KKK Testimony*, 3:1409, 1478. Noralee Frankel makes a similar point in *Freedom's Women*, 128, as does Cardyn, "Sexualized Racism," 721, 729 n. 173.

133. Jacquelyn Dowd Hall writes about white men raping black women after emancipation, "Rape *was* in part a reaction to the effort of the freemen to assume the role of patriarch, able to provide for and protect his family. Nevertheless, . . . rape is first and foremost a crime against women. Rape sent a message to black men, but more centrally, it expressed male sexual attitudes in a culture both racist and patriarchal" ("'Mind That Burns in Each Body,'" 332). See also Clinton, "Bloody Terrain," 329, and "Reconstructing Freedwomen," 316. Cf. Lou Falkner Williams, *Great South Carolina Ku Klux Klan Trials*, 35–36.

134. Affidavit of George Moore and letter from John Hamilton to Lieut. James Miller, August 29, 1869, appended to testimony of General Samuel W. Crawford, *KKK Testimony*, 9:1188, 1189–90.

135. Testimony of Charles Smith, *KKK Testimony*, 7:597–601. See also testimony of Caroline Smith and Sarah Ann Sturtevant, *KKK Testimony*, 6:400–403, 462–65.

136. This was also the case in the beating and exposure of Mary Brown and the other women in her family. See testimony of Mary Brown and Aury Jeter, *KKK Testimony*, 6:387, 566.

137. Testimony of Hannah Tutson, *KKK Testimony*, 13:60.

138. Testimony of John A. Minnis, *KKK Testimony*, 8:547-48; he reported that three women were raped. Case confirmed by testimony of William S. Mudd, *KKK Testimony*, 10:1753.

139. Testimony of John W. Shropshire, *KKK Testimony*, 7:914, 921. Shropshire reported two women were raped, while a proclamation from Georgia governor Rufus Bullock offered a reward for information leading to arrest and conviction of perpetrators who among other things raped three women on Waltemire's plantation. See "A Proclamation,"

reprinted in testimony of B. F. Sawyer, *KKK Testimony*, 7:884. On this case, see also testimony of William M. Shropshire and G. B. Burnett, *KKK Testimony*, 7:628, 949–53. Burnett testified that the night riders also made the plantation owner "dance around some," which Burnett agreed would be a "great mortification to a high-minded man."

140. Testimony of Z. B. Hargrove, *KKK Testimony*, 6:75.

141. Testimony of James Justice, *KKK Testimony*, 2:148.

142. Testimony of Hannah Tutson, *KKK Testimony*, 13:60–61; testimony of Harriet Simril, Proceedings of the United States Circuit Court, reprinted in *KKK Testimony*, 5:1861–62.

143. Testimony of John Shropshire, *KKK Testimony*, 7:920. Echoing similar sentiments, Z. B. Hargrove, a white moderate Democrat who cooperated with Reconstruction and opposed the Klan, explained to the congressional investigating committee why he was not afraid when he observed large groups of Klansmen march past his house in Rome, Georgia, in the middle of the night: "I was not so uneasy about myself because . . . I did not think they would really attack me in my own house" (testimony of Z. B. Hargrove, *KKK Testimony*, 6:75).

Chapter 6

1. Unfortunately, this woman's name does not appear in the record of her charges. Therefore, I use her husband's name and identify her as Mrs. King.

2. J. K. Nelson, Agent, to Captain Michael Walsh, Sub-Assistant Commissioner for Tennessee, August 28, 1867, and Lieutenant S. W. Groesbeck, Acting Assistant Adjutant General, to Captain Michael Walsh, August 24, 1867, both in Letters Received, August 1866–June 1869, Rutherford County, Tennessee, entry #3562, BRFAL.

3. Testimony of Aury Jeter, *KKK Testimony*, 6:566.

4. Testimony of William F. Wright, *KKK Testimony*, 7:972. Wright's overall testimony appeared almost as a rehearsed rendition of the conservative position on the dangers of African American citizenship: "We thought we were friends to the colored people; but . . . we did not believe in making them socially our equals." From social equality, he moved to political rights: "The people of this country were exceedingly opposed to the negroes having political rights. . . . [They] believed that if you gave them the power to sit upon juries, the right to hold office, and the right to vote, it would result in the ruin of the country; they felt it would be injurious to society. Indeed they felt it would result in the loss of their own liberty; they did not believe it compatible with their ideas of liberty to incorporate into their system the negro as a citizen, and give him full political rights" (ibid., 971).

5. Higgins and Silver, "Introduction," 1.

6. See also Bercaw, *Gendered Freedoms*, 147, 150–52.

7. See also Edwards, *Gendered Strife and Confusion*, 200. Of related interest on an earlier period, see Block, "Lines of Color, Sex, and Service," esp. 148.

8. Affidavit of Owen Gundy, January 21, 1868, BRFAL, Tennessee, microfilm 999, roll 34, "Affidavits Relating to Outrages."

9. Affidavit of George Moore and letter from John Hamilton to Lieut. James Miller, August 29, 1869, appended to testimony of General Samuel W. Crawford, *KKK Testimony*, 9:1188, 1189–90.

10. Testimony of James Justice, *KKK Testimony*, 2:148.

11. Affidavit of Ellen Parton, appended to testimony of O. C. French, *KKK Testimony*, 11:38–39.

12. Testimony of Aury Jeter, *KKK Testimony*, 6:566.

13. Affidavit of Ellen Parton, appended to the testimony of O. C. French, *KKK Testimony*, 11:38–39. Anderson Ferrell told the congressional committee that he had demanded of one of the Klansmen who entered his home, "Is that not Mr. Hutchinson[?] He said nothing, and I asked again, and he shook his head" (*KKK Testimony*, 7:618).

14. Testimony of Edward Carter, *KKK Testimony*, 12:1085.

15. Testimony of Essic Harris, *KKK Testimony*, 2:99.

16. Affidavits of Peggy Johnson and Charlotte Fagan, appended to testimony of O. C. French, *KKK Testimony*, 11:36–37, 37–38.

17. Affidavit of Ellen Parton, appended to testimony of O. C. French, *KKK Testimony*, 11:38–39.

18. Testimony of John W. Shopshire, *KKK Testimony*, 7:914.

19. Testimony of Edward Carter, *KKK Testimony*, 12:1085.

20. Testimony of General Samuel W. Crawford, *KKK Testimony*, 9:1157. Freedpeople also often attempted to report attacks to local officials, but generally to no avail and at times at great cost. Few local law enforcement officials would act on freedpeople's charges, and several were Klan members themselves; thus a report might lead only to further abuse. See, for instance, Lou Falkner Williams, *Great South Carolina Ku Klux Klan Trials*, 37–38, and Bercaw, *Gendered Freedoms*, 145.

21. It is possible that Rainey or a member of his family made this report; but the commander does not say so, and the passive construction of "it was charged" sounds as if he had heard it from others. See testimony of Col. Lewis Merrill, *KKK Testimony*, 5:1481.

22. Testimony of John A. Minnis, *KKK Testimony*, 8:547–48.

23. Testimony of Thomas Allen, *KKK Testimony*, 7:611.

24. See testimony of Samuel Tutson and Hannah Tutson, *KKK Testimony*, 13:54–59, 59–64.

25. Testimony of Scipio Eager, *KKK Testimony*, 7:671.

26. Testimony of Eli Barnes, *KKK Testimony*, 7:956, 958.

27. Recounted in Trelease, *White Terror*, 375. One of the band members was shot by a local official, whom Trelease reports as also a Klan member. A near-riot was prevented by the intervention of Colonel Lewis Merrill.

28. Testimony of Caroline Smith and Charles Smith, *KKK Testimony*, 6:402, 7:597–98.

29. Testimony of Caroline Benson and Mary Brown, *KKK Testimony*, 6:386–88, 375–77.

30. Testimony of Caroline Benson, *KKK Testimony*, 6:386–88.

31. Affidavit of Ellen Parton, appended to testimony of O. C. French, *KKK Testimony*, 11:38–39.

32. Testimony of Hannah Tutson, *KKK Testimony*, 13:60.

33. This comment suggests that Hannah Tutson told McCrea that she would yield to save her life. Her subsequent testimony, though, seems to contradict this. The committee asked Tutson again about McCrea's "wanting to do with" her: "Did you give way to him?" "No, sir," she replied. She may not have seen submitting rather than being killed as "giving way" to him. She may also have told McCrea she would yield but did not in the end do so. It is also possible that McCrea himself was unable to enact the rape, and that is why she did not have to "give way." McCrea's elaborate efforts to make the other men leave and his apparent embarrassment about what he was doing might support this reading.

34. Ibid., 59–64.

35. Affidavit of Ellen Parton, appended to testimony of O. C. French, *KKK Testimony*, 11:38–39. A comment made by another woman questioned by these investigators—"I know of two women said to be outraged; do not know anything about their character"—implies that the committee was looking for corroboration or contradiction of Ellen Parton's account by asking witnesses about her "character." See affidavit of Peggy Johnson, appended to testimony of O. C. French, *KKK Testimony*, 11:36–37.

36. Affidavit of Michael Slamon, appended to testimony of O. C. French, *KKK Testimony*, 11:44–45.

37. Affidavit of Ellen Parton, appended to testimony of O. C. French, *KKK Testimony*, 11:39. For a contrary interpretation of Parton's testimony, see Cardyn, "Sexualized Racism," 725. Cardyn does not presume that Parton's sworn statement was shaped by questions being asked by interrogators, and thus concludes that Parton herself was attempting to represent her experience in ways that would appeal to legal understandings of rape.

38. It is perhaps this federal abandonment of African American citizenship that led to a public silence among black women about their experiences of sexual violence, which historian Darlene Clark Hine has suggested characterized the years following Reconstruction. See Hine, "Rape and the Inner Lives of Black Women in the Middle West."

39. Lou Falkner Williams, *Great South Carolina Ku Klux Klan Trials*, chaps. 3–6; Foner, *Reconstruction*, 457–59.

40. See Foner, *Reconstruction*, 460–582; Richardson, *Death of Reconstruction*; and Perman, *Road to Redemption* and *Struggle for Mastery*.

41. See U.S. Supreme Court, *Plessy v. Ferguson*. The decision in this case invoked the acceptance of legal prohibitions on interracial marriage as a legitimate use of state power as evidence that similar laws requiring racial segregation in public facilities did not violate the Fourteenth Amendment. The court reasoned that this amendment required political but not social equality. On this decision, Rebecca Scott writes, "The language of the majority decision thus incorporated a key tenet of white supremacist ideology—the sleight of hand through which *public rights* were re-characterized as importunate *social claims*. These in turn were associated with 'social equality,' with all the blurring of boundaries between public and private, the phantasms of 'miscegenation,' and the dangers of social transgression that phrase could evoke" ("Public Rights, Social Equality," 800). The reasoning of the *Plessy* decision thus indicates how crucial

the rhetoric of miscegenation (see Chapter 4) that evolved during Reconstruction was to the subsequent legitimation of Jim Crow segregation. See also an analysis of how the plaintiff's argument for equal access to public facilities in *Plessy* was similarly rooted in past struggles, in this case notions of equality that emerged in the Haitian Revolution and were carried through Reconstruction, in Rebecca J. Scott, "Atlantic World and the Road to *Plessy v. Ferguson*."

42. On continued political influence of African American men after Reconstruction, see esp. Dailey, *Before Jim Crow*. Dailey writes, "The votes of African Americans were not meaningless in the post-Reconstruction South, as some scholars continue to assert. Rather the very success of black men in politics contributed to their eventual exclusion from public authority at the turn of the twentieth century. Legal barriers to African American power and influence—the creation of the Jim Crow South—grew out of white southerners' specific and concrete encounters with black social, economic, and political power" (2). Steven Hahn argues that years of "paramilitary politics" and the political violence they entailed in the Reconstruction-era South set the stage for the "compromise of 1877," which, he also argues, was less a "compromise" than evidence of a "shared political sensibility in northern ruling circles that questioned the legitimacy of popular democracy." This northern questioning of the wisdom of popular participation in electoral politics stemmed in part from "exasperation with the 'annual autumnal outbreaks' in the Deep South and the consequent use of federal troops to maintain Republican regimes there." And this allowed white northern leaders to ignore the extensive violation of the political rights of African American citizens necessary to establish and maintain the new Democratic state governments in the South (Hahn, *Nation under Our Feet*, 310–13; quotations on 310 and 310–11).

43. See "A Mask Lifted," *PL*, July 11, 1876, 3, and "Local Paragraphs," *Appeal*, July 11, 1876, 4. See also Meriwether, *Recollections of Ninety-Two Years*, 180. Among other inaccuracies, Meriwether incorrectly reports Thompson's arrest as occurring in 1868. I thank Gerald Smith for directing me to this source and to Thompson's arrest for cross-dressing.

44. "The 'Bloody Shirt,'" *New York World*, July 16, 1876, 5. Meriwether remembered that Thompson was "discovered" as a result of the accusation by a "respectable negro woman" that her daughter, working as Thompson's housemaid, had become pregnant by Thompson; see Meriwether, *Recollections of Ninety-Two Years*, 180. I found no evidence to confirm this.

45. This same Memphis city ordinance also prohibited vagrancy, gambling, selling liquor on Sundays, keeping or working in a house of prostitution, distribution of pornography, and public nudity. See Chapter XIV, Article 1, *Digest of the Charters and Ordinances of the City of Memphis, from 1826 to 1867*, 334–36.

46. For newspaper accounts outside Memphis, see "Judge M'Clure's Open Letter," *Daily Arkansas Gazette*, October 18, 1876, 2; "Thompson's Joke," *Chicago Tribune*, July 12, 1876, 5; "Under False Colors," *St. Louis Daily Globe-Democrat*, July 15, 1876, 5; "The 'Bloody Shirt,'" *New York World*," July 16, 1876, 5; "A Man-Woman at Memphis," *Cincinnati*

Commercial, July 12, 1876, 1; " 'The Bloody Shirt,' " *Galveston Daily News*, July 27, 1876, 2; and "Notes and Opinions," *Galveston Daily News*, August 4, 1876, 2, and September 14, 1876, 2.

47. See, for instance, "Under False Colors," *Avalanche*, July 12, 1876, 4, and "Thompson," *Appeal*, July 13, 1876, 4.

48. See, in the *Appeal*, "Thompson," July 13, 1876, 4; "Frances Thompson," July 14, 1876, 4; and "Local Paragraphs," July 18, 1876, 4. In the *PL*, see "A Mask Lifted," July 11, 1876, 3, and "That Man-Woman," July 12, 1876, 3. In the *Weekly PL*, see "Frances Thompson Dead," November 7, 1876, 3.

49. "Thompson," *Appeal*, July 13, 1876, 4.

50. "Frances Thompson," *Appeal*, July 14, 1876, 4, and "Ledger Lines," *PL*, July 17, 1876, 3. See also "Ledger Lines," *PL*, July 14, 1876, 3.

51. "Thompson," *Appeal*, July 13, 1876, 4. Earlier the *Appeal* referred to Thompson and Smith as "Thomas and his paramour" (no title, *Appeal*, July 13, 1876, 1). (Newspaper articles attacking Thompson frequently misspelled her name.) Smith, who testified after Thompson, did not in fact corroborate the latter's testimony about having been raped but, rather, spoke only of her own experience. She did say that she and Thompson were "in bed" when intruders came to their house during the riot, though she did not specify whether they shared a bed or slept separately. Even if they were sleeping in the same bed, something that was not unusual in the nineteenth century, this would not necessarily have indicated that they were lovers. See Testimony of Lucy Smith, *MR&M*, 197.

52. "Time Makes All Things Even At Last," *PL*, July 19, 1876, 2.

53. *Appeal*, July 16, 1876, 2.

54. See "Local Paragraphs," *Appeal*, November 4, 1876, 4. From the *Avalanche*, see July 18, 1876, 4; July 19, 1876, 4; July 20, 1876, 4; and July 21, 1876, 4. From the *PL*, see "Ledger Lines," July 13, 1876, 3, and July 17, 1876, 3.

55. "Francis Thomas" [*sic*], *Appeal*, July 12, 1876, 4.

56. "Frances Thompson," *Appeal*, July 14, 1876, 4.

57. "Frances Thompson Dead," *Weekly PL*, November 7, 1876, 3. Her death was also noted outside Memphis. See "Telegraphic Notes," *Chicago Tribune*, November 4, 1876, 5, and "Death of a Notorious Negro," *Cincinnati Commercial*, November 4, 1876, 3.

58. Register of Deaths, Memphis and Shelby County Health Department, 1876–1884, p. 24, MSCA.

59. "Francis Thomas" [*sic*], *Appeal*, July 12, 1876, 4.

60. Ibid.

61. "A Mask Lifted," *PL*, July 11, 1876, 3. On the case of Thomas or Thomasine Hall, a person of ambiguous gender in Virginia in the seventeenth century who refused to choose a gender, claiming to be "both man and woeman," see Norton, *Founding Mothers and Fathers*, 183–97; Kathleen Brown, " 'Changed . . . Into the Fashion of a Man,' " 39–56, and *Good Wives, Nasty Wenches*, 75–80.

62. Quotation from "A Mask Lifted," *PL*, July 11, 1876, 3.

63. "Frances Thompson," *Appeal*, July 14, 1876, 4.
64. "Francis Thomas" [*sic*], *Appeal*, July 12, 1876, 4; "Under False Colors," *Avalanche*, July 12, 1876, 4.
65. "Frances Thompson," *Appeal*, July 14, 1876, 4.
66. See Butler, *Gender Trouble*, xxiii.
67. See Dreger, *Hermaphrodites and the Medical Invention of Sex*.
68. On the riot, see Testimony of Sophia Garey, *MR&M*, 114; on women dressing as men to fight in the Civil War, see Blanton and Cook, *They Fought Like Demons*.
69. See Kerber, *No Constitutional Right to Be Ladies*, and debates in occupied Memphis over using women on chain gangs, in BM&A, MSCA.

BIBLIOGRAPHY

Primary Sources

MANUSCRIPT COLLECTIONS

Arkansas
Arkansas History Commission, Little Rock
    Correspondence Register of Governor Powell Clayton
Special Collections, University of Arkansas Libraries, Fayetteville
    Historical Records Survey, Arkansas
    Jesse Turner Correspondence
    David Walker Correspondence

Michigan
Clements Library, University of Michigan, Ann Arbor
    John Eaton Jr. Collection

New York
New York Public Library, New York
    Walter L. Fleming Collection

North Carolina
Special Collections Library, Duke University, Durham
    William H. Brotherton Papers
    Walter Patterson Duke Papers
    Benjamin Sherwood Hedrick Papers

Hemphill Family Papers
William Woods Holden Papers
Ku Klux Klan Papers

Tennessee

Memphis and Shelby County Archives, Memphis
  Minutes of the Board of Mayor and Aldermen
  Shelby County Recorder's Court Docket, January 1865 to February 1865
  "Station House Register, Beginning the First Day of October, 1858"
Memphis and Shelby County Room, History Department, Memphis Main Public Library, Memphis
  "Census of the City of Memphis, Taken by Joe Bledsoe, Under a Resolution of the City Council, Passed April 25, 1865"

Virginia

Alderman Library, University of Virginia, Charlottesville
  Amos T. Akerman's Letterbooks
  American Missionary Association Archives (microfilm)

Washington, D.C.

Library of Congress, Manuscripts Division
  Thaddeus Stevens Papers
  Elihu B. Washburne Papers
U.S. National Archives and Records Administration
  Letters Received by the Office of the Adjutant General,
  National Archives Microfilm Publications, M619
  Records of the Bureau of Refugees, Freedmen, and Abandoned Lands, RG105
  U.S. Bureau of the Census, *Seventh Census of the United States, 1850*, M432, 1009 rolls
  U.S. Bureau of the Census, *Eighth Census of the United States, 1860*, M653, 1,438 rolls
  U.S. Bureau of the Census, *Ninth Census of the United States, 1870*, M593, 1,761 rolls
  U.S. Bureau of the Census, *Tenth Census of the United States, 1880*, T9

NEWSPAPERS

Arkansas Gazette (daily and weekly)
Chicago Daily Tribune
Cincinnati Commercial
Colored American
Colored Tennessean
Harper's Weekly
Little Rock Evening Republican
Memphis Daily Appeal
Memphis Daily Argus
Memphis Daily Avalanche
Memphis Post (morning, daily, and weekly)
Morning Republican (Little Rock, Arkansas)
New York Times
Public Ledger (Memphis, Tennessee) (daily and weekly)
Weekly Republican (Memphis, Tennessee)
Western Clarion (Helena, Arkansas)

Acts of the General Assembly of the State of Arkansas. Little Rock: General Assembly of the State of Arkansas, 1859.

Alfred v. the State, 37 Mississippi 296 (October 1859).

The American Annual Cyclopedia and Register of Important Events of the Year 1868, vol. 8. New York: D. Appleton and Company, 1869.

Bates, Edward. "Citizenship." In *Opinions of the Attorney Generals of the United States,* vol. 10. Washington, D.C.: W. H. & O. H. Morrison, 1868.

———. *The Diary of Edward Bates, 1859–1869.* Washington, D.C.: U.S. Government Printing Office, 1933.

Beale, Howard K., ed. *The Diary of Edward Bates, 1859–1866.* Washington, D.C.: U.S. Government Printing Office, 1933.

Burr, Virginia Ingraham, ed. *The Secret Eye: The Journal of Ella Gertrude Clanton Thomas, 1848–1889.* Chapel Hill: University of North Carolina Press, 1990.

Clayton, Powell. *The Aftermath of the Civil War in Arkansas.* New York: Negro Universities Press, 1969 (1915).

Cobb, Thomas. *An Inquiry into the Law of Negro Slavery.* Philadelphia, 1858.

Debates and Proceedings of the Convention which Assembled at Little Rock, January 7th, 1868, Under the Provision of the Act of Congress of March 2d, 1867, and the Acts of March 23d and July 19th, 1867, supplement thereto, to Form a Constitution for the State of Arkansas. Little Rock: J. G. Price, 1868.

Digest of the Charters and Ordinances of the City of Memphis, from 1826 to 1860, Inclusive, Together with the Acts of the Legislature Relating to the City, and Municipal Corporation Generally. Memphis: Saunders, Oberly, and Jones, 1860.

Digest of the Charters and Ordinances of the City of Memphis, from 1826 to 1867, Inclusive, Together with the Acts of the Legislature Relating to the City, and Municipal Corporation Generally. Memphis: Bulletin Pub. Co., 1867.

Digest of the Ordinances of the City Council of Memphis, from the Year 1826 to 1857: Together with all Acts of the Legislature of Tennessee which Relate Exclusively to the City of Memphis. Memphis: Memphis Bulletin Co., 1857.

Eaton, John, Jr. *Report of the General Superintendent of Freemen, Department of the Tennessee and State of Arkansas for 1864.* Memphis, 1865.

Gates, Henry Louis, Jr., ed. *The Classic Slave Narratives.* New York: New American Library, 1987.

George (a Slave) v. the State, 37 Mississippi 317 (October 1859).

Hopkins, Pauline E. *Contending Forces: A Romance Illustrative of Negro Life North and South.* New York: Oxford University Press, 1988 (1899).

Hughes, Louis. *Thirty Years a Slave: From Bondage to Freedom. The Institution of Slavery as Seen on the Plantation and In the Home of the Planter. Autobiography of Louis Hughes.* New York: Negro Universities Press, 1969 (1897).

Jackson, Ronald Vern, and G. Ronald Teeples, eds. *Arkansas 1850 Census Index*. Bountiful, Utah: Accelerated Indexing Systems, 1976.

Journal of the Proceedings of the Constitutional Convention of the State of Mississippi, 1868. Jackson, Miss.: E. Stafford, Printer, 1871.

Journal of the Proceedings of the Convention Met to Form a Constitution and System of Government for the People of Arkansas. At the Session of the Said Convention Held at Little Rock in the Territory of Arkansas, Which commenced on the Fourth Day of January, and Ended on the Thirteenth Day of January, One Thousand Eight Hundred and Thirty-Six. Little Rock: Albert Pike, 1836.

Meriwether, Elizabeth. *Recollections of Ninety-Two Years, 1824–1916*. Nashville: Tennessee Historical Commission, 1958.

Miscegenation: The Theory of the Blending of the Races, applied to the American White Man and Negro. New York: Dexter, Hamilton, & Co, 1864.

"Miscegenation endorsed by Republicans." Campaign document no. 11 in *Publications of the Central Executive Campaign Committee*. New York, 1864.

Proceedings of the Convention of Colored Citizens of the State of Arkansas, Held in Little Rock, Thursday, Friday, and Saturday, Nov. 30, Dec. 1&2. Helena: Clarion Office Print, 1866.

Rawick, George P., ed. *The American Slave: A Composite Biography*. Vol. 9, *Arkansas Narratives*, pts. 3 and 4. Westport, Conn.: Greenwood Pub. Co., 1941.

Seaman, L. *What Miscegenation Is! What We Are to Expect Now that Mr. Lincoln is Re-elected*. New York: Waller & Willetts, 1864.

Sherman, William Tecumseh. *Memoirs of General W. T. Sherman*, vol. 1. New York: Library of America, 1990.

Thorpe, Francis Newton, ed. *The Federal and State Constitutions, Colonial Charters, and Other Organic Laws of the States, Territories, and Colonies Now or Heretofore Forming the United States of American*, vol. 1. Washington, D.C., 1909.

U.S. Congress. House of Representatives. *Memphis Riots and Massacres*. 39th Congress, 1st session, 1865–66. House Report no. 101. Washington, D.C., 1866.

——. "Report of the Commissioner of the Bureau of Refugees, Freedmen, and Abandoned Lands," November 1, 1866. In *House Executive Documents*, no. 1, vol. 3. 39th Congress, 2nd session. Washington, D.C., 1866.

——. *Report of the Joint Committee on Reconstruction*. 39th Congress, 1st session, 1865–66. House Report no. 30. Washington, D.C., 1866.

U.S. Congress. Joint Select Committee to Inquire into the Condition of Affairs in the Late Insurrectionary States. *Testimony Taken by the Joint Select Committee to Inquire into the Condition of Affairs in the Late Insurrectionary States*, vols. 1–13. Washington, D.C.: Government Printing Office, 1872.

U.S. Supreme Court. *Plessy v. Ferguson*. 163 U.S. 537 (1896).

Warren, John H., Jr. *Thirty Years' Battle with Crime, or the Crying Shame of New York, as seen under the Broad Glare of an Old Detective's Lantern*. New York: Arno Press and the New York Times, 1970 (1875).

Wells, Ida B. *On Lynching: Southern Horrors, a Red Record, Mob Rule in New Orleans.* New York: Arno Press and the New York Times, 1969.

Secondary Sources

Abbott, Richard H. *For Free Press and Equal Rights: Republican Newspapers in the Reconstruction South.* Athens: University of Georgia Press, 2004.

Alexander, Adele Logan. *Ambiguous Lives: Free Women of Color in Rural Georgia, 1789–1879.* Fayetteville: University of Arkansas Press, 1991.

Alexander, Thomas Benjamin. *Political Reconstruction in Tennessee.* Nashville: Vanderbilt University Press, 1950.

Allsopp, Fred W. *History of the Arkansas Press for a Hundred Years and More.* Little Rock: Parke-Harper Pub. Co., 1922.

Arnold, Marybeth Hamilton. " 'The Life of a Citizen in the Hands of a Woman': Sexual Assault in New York City, 1790 to 1820." In *Passion and Power: Sexuality in History,* edited by Kathy Peiss and Christina Simmons, 35–57. Philadelphia: Temple University Press, 1989.

Ash, Stephen. *A Year in the South: Four Lives in 1865.* New York: Palgrave MacMillan, 2002.

Auslander, Leora. *Taste and Power: Furnishing Modern France.* Berkeley: University of California Press, 1996.

Ayers, Edward L. *Vengeance and Justice: Crime and Punishment in the 19th-Century American South.* New York: Oxford University Press, 1984.

Bancroft, Frederic. *Slave Trading in the Old South.* New York: Frederick Ungar Pub. Co., 1959 (1931).

Banks, Richard. "In the Heat of the Night." *Memphis,* June 1990, 71–72.

Bardaglio, Peter W. "Rape and the Law in the Old South: 'Calculated to Excite Indignation in Every Heart.' " *Journal of Southern History* 60 (November 1994): 749–72.

———. *Reconstructing the Household: Families, Sex, and the Law in the Nineteenth-Century South.* Chapel Hill: University of North Carolina Press, 1995.

———. " 'Shameful Matches': The Regulation of Interracial Sex and Marriage in the South before 1900." In *Sex, Love, Race: Crossing Boundaries in North American History,* edited by Martha Hodes, 112–40. New York: New York University Press, 1999.

Barker, Anne. "Justice Delayed." *Journal of International Law and Practice* 8 (1999): 453–85.

Barkley Brown, Elsa. "Negotiating and Transforming the Public Sphere: African American Political Life in the Transition from Slavery to Freedom." *Public Culture* 7 (Fall 1994): 107–46.

———. "To Catch the Vision of Freedom: Reconstructing Black Women's Political History, 1865–1880." In *African American Women and the Vote, 1837–1965,* edited by Ann D. Gordon with Bettye Collier-Thomas, John H. Bracey, Arlene Voski Avakian, and Joyce Avrech Berkman, 66–99. Amherst: University of Massachusetts Press, 1997.

———. "Uncle Ned's Children: Negotiating Community and Freedom in Postemancipation Richmond, Virginia." Ph.D. diss., Kent State University, 1994.

———. " 'What Has Happened Here': The Politics of Difference in Women's History and Feminist Politics." *Feminist Studies* 18 (Summer 1992): 295–312.

Bederman, Gail. " 'Civilization,' the Decline of Middle-Class Manliness, and Ida B. Wells's Antilynching Campaign (1892–94)." *Radical History Review* 52 (Winter 1992): 5–32.

———. *Manliness and Civilization: A Cultural History of Gender and Race in the United States, 1880–1917*. Chicago: University of Chicago Press, 1995.

Bercaw, Nancy Dunlap. *Gendered Freedoms: Race, Rights, and the Politics of Household in the Delta, 1861–1875*. Gainesville: University Press of Florida, 2003.

Berger, Iris. "Categories and Contexts: Reflections on the Politics of Identity in South Africa." *Feminist Studies* 18 (Summer 1992): 284–94.

Berkeley, Kathleen C. " 'Colored Ladies Also Contributed': Black Women's Activities from Benevolence to Social Welfare, 1866–1896." In *The Web of Southern Social Relations: Women, Family, and Education*, edited by Walter J. Fraser Jr., R. Frank Saunders Jr., and Jon L. Wakelyn, 181–204. Athens: University of Georgia Press, 1985.

———. *"Like a Plague of Locust": From an Antebellum Town to a New South City*. New York: Garland, 1991.

———. " 'Like a Plague of Locust': Immigration and Social Change in Memphis, Tennessee, 1850–1880." Ph.D. diss., University of California, Los Angeles, 1980.

Berlant, Lauren. *The Queen of America Goes to Washington City: Essays on Sex and Citizenship*. Durham: Duke University Press, 1997.

Berlin, Ira. *Slaves without Masters: The Free Negro in the Antebellum South*. New York: Vintage, 1976 (1974).

Berlin, Ira, and Leslie Rowland, eds. *Families and Freedom: A Documentary History of African American Kinship in the Civil War Era*. New York: New Press, 1997.

Berlin, Ira, Joseph P. Reidy, and Leslie S. Rowland, eds. *The Black Military Experience*. Series 2. *Freedom: A Documentary History of Emancipation, 1861–1867*. Cambridge: Cambridge University Press, 1982.

Berlin, Ira, Barbara J. Fields, Thavolia Glymph, Joseph P. Reidy, and Leslie S. Rowland, eds. *The Destruction of Slavery*. Series 1. Volume 1. *Freedom: A Documentary History of Emancipation, 1861–1867*. New York: Cambridge University Press, 1985.

Berlin, Ira, Barbara J. Fields, Steven F. Miller, Joseph P. Reidy, and Leslie S. Rowland, eds. *Free at Last: A Documentary History of Slavery, Freedom, and the Civil War*. New York: New Press, 1992.

Berlin, Ira, Thavolia Glymph, Steven F. Miller, Joseph P. Reidy, Leslie S. Rowland, and Julie Saville, eds. *The Wartime Genesis of Free Labor: The Lower South*. Series 1. Volume 3. *Freedom: A Documentary History of Emancipation, 1861–1867*. Cambridge: Cambridge University Press, 1990.

Bernstein, Iver. *The New York City Draft Riots: Their Significance for American Society and Politics in the Age of the Civil War*. New York: Oxford University Press, 1990.

Berry, Mary Frances. "Judging Morality: Sexual Behavior and Legal Consequences in the Late Nineteenth-Century South." *Journal of American History* 78 (December 1991): 835–56.

———. *The Pig Farmer's Daughter and Other Tales of American Justice: Episodes of Racism and Sexism in the Courts from 1865 to the Present*. New York: Knopf, 1999.

Blackburn, Robin. *The Overthrow of Colonial Slavery, 1776–1848*. London: Verso, 1988.

Blanton, De Anne, and Lauren M. Cook. *They Fought Like Demons: Women Soldiers in the Civil War*. New York: Vintage, 2003.

Blee, Kathleen M. *Women of the Klan: Racism and Gender in the 1920s*. Berkeley: University of California Press, 1992.

Blight, David W. *Frederick Douglass' Civil War: Keeping Faith in Jubilee*. Baton Rouge: Louisiana State University Press, 1989.

———. *Race and Reunion: The Civil War in American Memory*. Cambridge, Mass.: Belknap Press of Harvard University Press, 2001.

Bloch, Ruth. "The Gendered Meanings of Virtue in Revolutionary America." *Signs* 13 (Autumn 1987): 37–58.

Block, Sharon. "Lines of Color, Sex, and Service: Comparative Sexual Coercion in Early America." In *Sex, Love, Race: Crossing Boundaries in North American History*, edited by Martha Hodes, 141–63. New York: New York University Press, 1999.

———. *Rape and Sexual Power in Early America*. Chapel Hill: University of North Carolina Press, 2006.

Bond, Beverly Greene. " 'Till Fair Aurora Rise': African-American Women in Memphis, Tennessee, 1840–1915." Ph.D. diss., University of Memphis, 1996.

Brown, Kathleen M. " 'Changed . . . Into the Fashion of a Man': The Politics of Sexual Difference in a Seventeenth-Century Anglo-American Settlement." In *The Devil's Lane: Sex and Race in the Early South*, edited by Catherine Clinton and Michele Gillespie, 39–56. New York: Oxford University Press, 1997.

———. *Good Wives, Nasty Wenches, and Anxious Patriarchs: Gender, Race, and Power in Colonial Virginia*. Chapel Hill: University of North Carolina Press, 1996.

Brown, Wendy. "Liberalism's Family Values." In *States of Injury: Power and Freedom in Late Modernity*, 135–65. Princeton: Princeton University Press, 1995.

Brownmiller, Susan. *Against Our Will: Men, Women, and Rape*. New York: Simon and Schuster, 1975.

Butler, Judith. *Gender Trouble: Feminism and the Subversion of Identity*. New York: Routledge, 1999.

Butler, Judith, and Joan W. Scott, eds. *Feminists Theorize the Political*. New York: Routledge, 1992.

Bynum, Victoria E. *Unruly Women: The Politics of Social and Sexual Control in the Old South*. Chapel Hill: University of North Carolina Press, 1992.

Calhoun, Craig, ed. *Habermas and the Public Sphere*. Cambridge, Mass.: MIT Press, 1994.

Canning, Kathleen, and Sonya O. Rose. "Introduction: Gender, Citizenship, and Subjectivity: Some Historical and Theoretical Considerations." *Gender & History* 13 (November 2001): 427–43.

Capers, Gerald M., Jr. *The Biography of a River Town: Memphis, Its Heroic Age*. Chapel Hill: University of North Carolina Press, 1939.

Carby, Hazel. " 'On the Threshold of Woman's Era': Lynching, Empire, and Sexuality in Black Feminist Theory." In *"Race," Writing, and Difference*, edited by Henry Louis Gates Jr., 301–16. Chicago: University of Chicago Press, 1986 (1985).

———. *Reconstructing Womanhood: The Emergence of the Afro-American Woman Novelist*. New York: Oxford University Press, 1987.

Cardyn, Lisa. "Sexualized Racism/Gendered Violence: Outraging the Body Politic in the Reconstruction South." *Michigan Law Review* 100 (February 2002): 675–867.

———. "Sexual Terror in the Reconstruction South." In *Battle Scars: Gender and Sexuality in the American Civil War*, edited by Catherine Clinton and Nina Silber, 140–67. New York: Oxford University Press, 2006.

Cashin, Joan. *A Family Venture: Men and Women on the Southern Frontier*. New York: Oxford University Press, 1991.

Channing, Steven A. *Crisis of Fear: Secession in South Carolina*. New York: Norton, 1970.

Cimprich, John. *Slavery's End in Tennessee, 1861–1865*. University: University of Alabama Press, 1985.

Clinton, Catherine. "Bloody Terrain: Freedwomen, Sexuality, and Violence during Reconstruction." *Georgia Historical Quarterly* 76 (Summer 1992): 313–32.

———. "Caught in the Web of the Big House: Women and Slavery." In *The Web of Southern Social Relations: Women, Family, and Education*, edited by Walter J. Fraser Jr., R. Frank Saunders Jr., and Jon L. Wakelyn, 19–34. Athens: University of Georgia Press, 1985.

———. "Reconstructing Freedwomen." In *Divided Houses: Gender and the Civil War*, edited by Catherine Clinton and Nina Silber, 306–19. New York: Oxford University Press, 1992.

Cooper, Frederick, Thomas C. Holt, and Rebecca J. Scott. *Beyond Slavery: Explorations of Race, Labor, and Citizenship in Postemancipation Societies*. Chapel Hill: University of North Carolina Press, 2000.

Copelon, Rhonda. "Surfacing Gender: Re-Engraving Crimes against Women in Humanitarian Law." *Hastings Women's Law Journal* 5 (Summer 1994): 243–66.

Cott, Nancy F. *Bonds of Womanhood: "Woman's Sphere" in New England, 1780–1835*. New Haven: Yale University Press, 1977.

———. "Marriage and Women's Citizenship in the United States, 1830–1934." *American Historical Review* 103 (December 1998): 1440–74.

———. *Public Vows: A History of Marriage and the Nation*. Cambridge, Mass.: Harvard University Press, 2000.

Crenshaw, Kimberlé, Neil Gotanda, Gary Peller, and Kendall Thomas, eds. *Critical Race Theory: The Key Writings That Formed the Movement*. New York: New Press, 1995.

Dailey, Jane. *Before Jim Crow: The Politics of Race in Postemancipation Virginia*. Chapel Hill: University of North Carolina Press, 2000.

———. "Deference and Violence in the Postbellum Urban South: Manners and Massacres in Danville, Virginia." *Journal of Southern History* 63 (August 1997): 553–90.

——. "The Limits of Liberalism in the New South: The Politics of Race, Sex, and Patronage in Virginia, 1879–1883." In *Jumping Jim Crow: Southern Politics from Civil War to Civil Rights*, edited by Jane Dailey, Glenda Elizabeth Gilmore, and Bryant Simon, 88–114. Princeton: Princeton University Press, 2000.

Davis, Angela Y. "Reflections on the Black Woman's Role in the Community of Slaves." *Black Scholar* 3 (December 1971): 3–15.

——. *Women, Race, and Class*. New York: Random House, 1981.

Davis, Natalie Zemon. "The Rites of Violence: Religious Riot in Sixteenth-Century France." In *Society and Culture in Early Modern France*, 152–87. Stanford: Stanford University Press, 1975.

Davis, Peggy Cooper. "Marriage as a 'Badge and Incident' of Democratic Freedom." In *Marriage Proposals: Questioning a Legal Status*, 171–87. New York: New York University Press, 2006.

DeBlack, Thomas A. *With Fire and Sword: Arkansas, 1861–1874*. Fayetteville: University of Arkansas Press, 2003.

D'Emilio, John, and Estelle B. Freedman. *Intimate Matters: A History of Sexuality in America*. New York: Harper & Row, 1988.

Desan, Suzanne. "Crowds, Community, and Ritual in the Work of E. P. Thompson and Natalie Davis." In *The New Cultural History*, edited by Lynn Hunt, 47–71. Berkeley: University of California Press, 1989.

Downs, Laura Lee. "If 'Woman' Is Just an Empty Category, Then Why Am I Afraid to Walk Alone at Night? Identity Politics Meets the Postmodern Subject." *Comparative Studies in Society and History* 35 (April 1993): 414–37.

——. "Reply to Joan Scott." *Comparative Studies in Society and History* 35 (April 1993): 444–51.

Dreger, Alice Domurat. *Hermaphrodites and the Medical Invention of Sex*. Cambridge, Mass.: Harvard University Press, 1998.

DuBois, Laurent. *A Colony of Citizens: Revolution and Slave Emancipation in the French Caribbean, 1787–1804*. Chapel Hill: University of North Carolina Press, 2004.

DuBois, W. E. B. *Black Reconstruction in America: An Essay Toward the Part Which Black Folk Played in the Attempt to Reconstruct Democracy in American, 1860–1880*. New York: Meridian Books, World Pub. Co., 1962 (1935).

Eaton, Clemont. *The Growth of Southern Civilization, 1790–1860*. New York: Harper & Row, 1961.

Edwards, Laura F. "The Disappearance of Susan Daniel and Henderson Cooper: Gender and Narratives of Political Conflict in the Reconstruction-Era U.S. South." *Feminist Studies* 22 (Summer 1996): 363–85.

——. *Gendered Strife and Confusion: The Political Culture of Reconstruction*. Urbana: University of Illinois Press, 1997.

——. "Law, Domestic Violence, and the Limits of Patriarchal Authority in the Antebellum South." *Journal of Southern History* 65 (November 1999): 733–70.

———. " 'The Marriage Covenant Is at the Foundation of All Our Rights': The Politics of Slave Marriages in North Carolina after Emancipation." *Law and History Review* 14 (Spring 1996): 81–124.

———. "Sexual Violence, Gender, Reconstruction, and the Extension of Patriarchy in Granville County, North Carolina." *North Carolina Historical Review* 48 (1991): 237–60.

England, J. Merton. "The Free Negro in Antebellum Tennessee." *Journal of Southern History* 9 (February 1943): 37–58.

Epstein, Julia, and Kristina Straub, eds. *Body Guards: The Cultural Politics of Gender Ambiguity*. New York: Routledge, 1991.

Estrich, Susan. *Real Rape: How the Legal System Victimizes Women Who Say No*. Cambridge: Harvard University Press, 1987.

Faust, Drew Gilpin. "Altars of Sacrifice: Confederate Women and the Narratives of War." *Journal of American History* 76 (March 1990): 1200–1228.

———. *Mothers of Invention: Women of the Slaveholding South in the American Civil War*. Chapel Hill: University of North Carolina Press, 1996.

———. " 'Trying to Do a Man's Business': Slavery, Violence, and Gender in the American Civil War." *Gender & History* 4 (June 1992): 197–214.

Fehrenbacher, Don E. *The Dred Scott Case: Its Significance in American Law and Politics*. New York: Oxford University Press, 1978.

Feimster, Crystal N. "Ladies and Lynching: The Gendered Discourse of Mob Violence in the New South." Ph.D. diss., Princeton University, 2000.

———. "Raped and Lynched: Black Female Victims of Mob Violence in the New South, 1880–1930." Paper presented at the meeting of the Southern Historical Association, Fort Worth, Texas, November 4, 1999.

Felski, Rita. *Beyond Feminist Aesthetics: Feminist Literature and Social Change*. Cambridge, Mass.: Harvard University Press, 1989.

Fields, Barbara Jeanne. "Race and Ideology in American History." In *Region, Race, and Reconstruction: Essays in Honor of C. Vann Woodward*, edited by J. Morgan Kousser and James M. McPherson, 143–77. New York: Oxford University Press, 1982.

———. *Slavery and Freedom on the Middle Ground: Maryland in the Nineteenth Century*. New Haven: Yale University Press, 1987.

Findlay, Eileen J. Suárez. *Imposing Decency: The Politics of Sexuality and Race in Puerto Rico, 1870–1920*. Durham: Duke University Press, 1999.

Finkelman, Paul, ed. *His Soul Goes Marching On: Responses to John Brown and the Harper's Ferry Raid*. Charlottesville: University Press of Virginia, 1995.

Finley, Randy. *From Slavery to Uncertain Freedom: The Freedmen's Bureau in Arkansas, 1865–1869*. Fayetteville: University of Arkansas Press, 1996.

Fischer, Kirsten. *Suspect Relations: Sex, Race, and Resistance in Colonial North Carolina*. Ithaca: Cornell University Press, 2002.

Foner, Eric. *Free Soil, Free Labor, Free Men: The Ideology of the Republican Party before the Civil War*. New York: Oxford University Press, 1979 (1970).

——. *Nothing but Freedom: Emancipation and Its Legacy*. Baton Rouge: Louisiana State University Press, 1983.

——. *Reconstruction: America's Unfinished Revolution*. New York: Harper & Row, 1988.

——. "Reconstruction Revisited." *Reviews in American History* 10 (December 1982): 82–100.

Ford, Lacy K. "Republics and Democracy: The Parameters of Political Citizenship in Antebellum South Carolina." In *The Meaning of South Carolina History: Essays in Honor of George C. Rogers, Jr.*, edited by David R. Chesnutt and Clyde N. Wilson, 121–45. Columbia: University of South Carolina Press, 1991.

Foster, Susan Leigh. "Choreographies of Gender." *Signs* 24 (Autumn 1998): 1–33.

Foucault, Michel. *The History of Sexuality*. Vol. 1, *An Introduction*. New York: Random House, 1978.

Fowler, David H. *Northern Attitudes towards Interracial Marriage: Legislation and Public Opinion in the Middle Atlantic and the States of the Old Northwest, 1780–1930*. New York: Garland, 1987.

Fox-Genovese, Elizabeth. *Within the Plantation Household: Black and White Women of the Old South*. Chapel Hill: University of North Carolina Press, 1988.

Franke, Katherine M. "Becoming a Citizen: Reconstruction Era Regulation of African American Marriages." *Yale Journal of Law and the Humanities* 11, no. 2 (Summer 1999): 251–309.

Frankel, Noralee. *Freedom's Women: Black Women and Families in Civil War Era Mississippi*. Bloomington: Indiana University Press, 1999.

Franklin, John Hope. *Reconstruction: After the Civil War*. Chicago: University of Chicago Press, 1961.

Fraser, Nancy. "Rethinking the Public Sphere: A Contribution to the Critique of Actually Existing Democracy." In *Habermas and the Public Sphere*, edited by Craig Calhoun, 109–42. Cambridge, Mass.: MIT Press, 1994.

——. *Unruly Practices: Power, Discourse, and Gender in Contemporary Social Theory*. Minneapolis: University of Minnesota Press, 1989.

——. "What's Critical about Critical Theory? The Case of Habermas and Gender." In *Unruly Practices: Power, Discourse, and Gender in Contemporary Social Theory*, 113–43. Minneapolis: University of Minnesota Press, 1989.

Fraser, Nancy, and Linda Gordon. "Contract versus Charity: Why Is There No Social Citizenship in the United States?" *Socialist Review* 22 (July–September 1992): 45–67.

Fraser, Walter J., Jr. "Lucien Bonaparte Eaton: Politics and the Memphis Post, 1867–1869." *West Tennessee Historical Society Papers* 20 (1966): 20–45.

Fry, Gladys-Marie. *Night Riders in Black Folk History*. Athens: Brown Thrasher Books, University of Georgia Press, 1991 (1975).

Gaines, Kevin K. *Uplifting the Race: Black Leadership, Politics, and Culture in the Twentieth Century*. Chapel Hill: University of North Carolina Press, 1996.

Gatewood, Willard B. "The Arkansas Delta: The Deepest of the Deep South." In *The Arkansas Delta: Land of Paradox*, edited by Jeannie M. Whayne and Willard B. Gatewood, 3–25. Fayetteville: University of Arkansas Press, 1993.

——. "Sunnyside: The Evolution of an Arkansas Plantation, 1840–1945." In *Shadows over Sunnyside: An Arkansas Plantation in Transition, 1830–1945*, edited by Jeannie M. Whayne, 3–24. Fayetteville: University of Arkansas Press, 1993.

Gilfoyle, Timothy J. *City of Eros: New York City, Prostitution, and the Commercialization of Sex, 1790–1920*. New York: Norton, 1992.

Gilje, Paul A. *Rioting in America*. Bloomington: Indiana University Press, 1996.

Gilmore, Glenda Elizabeth. *Gender and Jim Crow: Women and the Politics of White Supremacy in North Carolina, 1896–1920*. Chapel Hill: University of North Carolina Press, 1996.

——. "Murder, Memory, and the Flight of the Incubus." In *Democracy Betrayed: The Wilmington Race Riot of 1898 and Its Legacy*, edited by David S. Cecelski and Timothy B. Tyson, 73–93. Chapel Hill: University of North Carolina Press, 1998.

Gilroy, Paul. *"There Ain't No Black in the Union Jack": The Cultural Politics of Race and Nation*. Chicago: University of Chicago Press, 1991 (1987).

Glatthaar, Joseph T. *Forged in Battle: The Civil War Alliance of Black Soldiers and White Officers*. Baton Rouge: Louisiana State University Press, 1990.

Gleeson, David T. *The Irish in the South, 1815–1877*. Chapel Hill: University of North Carolina Press, 2001.

Glenn, Evelyn Nakano. *Unequal Freedom: How Race and Citizenship Shaped American Citizenship and Labor*. Cambridge, Mass.: Harvard University Press, 2002.

Goldin, Claudia Dale. *Urban Slavery in the American South, 1820–1860: A Quantitative History*. Chicago: University of Chicago Press, 1976.

Gordon, Fon Louise. "From Slavery to Uncertain Freedom: Blacks in the Delta." In *The Arkansas Delta: Land of Paradox*, edited by Jeannie M. Whayne and Willard B. Gatewood, 98–121. Fayetteville: University of Arkansas Press, 1993.

Gordon, Linda. "Response to Scott." *Signs* 15 (Summer 1990): 852–53.

——. Review of *Gender and the Politics of History*. *Signs* 15 (Summer 1990): 853–59.

Green, Laurie B. *Battling the Plantation Mentality: Memphis and the Black Freedom Struggle*. Chapel Hill: University of North Carolina Press, 2007.

Gundersen, Joan R. "Independence, Citizenship, and the American Revolution." *Signs* 13 (Autumn 1987): 59–77.

Gunning, Sandra. *Race, Rape, and Lynching: The Red Record of American Literature, 1890–1912*. New York: Oxford University Press, 1996.

Gutiérrez, Ramón A. "What's Love Got to Do with It?" *Journal of American History* 88 (December 2001): 866–69.

Gutman, Herbert. *The Black Family in Slavery and Freedom, 1750–1925*. New York: Vintage, 1976.

Habermas, Jürgen. "The Public Sphere: An Encyclopedia Article (1964)." *New German Critique* 1 (Fall 1974): 49–55.

——. *The Structural Transformation of the Public Sphere: An Inquiry into a Category of Bourgeois Society*. Cambridge, Mass.: MIT Press, 1989.

Hadden, Sally E. *Slave Patrols: Law and Violence in Virginia and the Carolinas.* Cambridge, Mass.: Harvard University Press, 2001.

Hahn, Steven. *A Nation under Our Feet: Black Political Struggles in the Rural South from Slavery to the Great Migration.* Cambridge, Mass.: Harvard University Press, 2003.

———. *The Roots of Southern Populism: Yeoman Farmers and the Transformation of the Georgia Upcountry, 1850–1890.* New York: Oxford University Press, 1983.

Hale, Grace Elizabeth. *Making Whiteness: The Culture of Segregation in the South, 1890–1940.* New York: Pantheon, 1998.

Hall, Jacquelyn Dowd. " 'The Mind That Burns in Each Body': Women, Rape, and Racial Violence." In *Powers of Desire: The Politics of Sexuality,* edited by Ann Snitow, Christine Stansell, and Sharon Thompson, 328–49. New York: Monthly Review Press, 1983.

———. *Revolt against Chivalry: Jessie Daniel Ames and the Women's Campaign against Lynching.* Rev. ed. New York: Columbia University Press, 1993.

Harcourt, Edward John. "Who Were the Pale Faces? New Perspectives on the Tennessee Ku Klux." *Civil War History* 51, no. 1 (2005): 23–66.

Hardwick, Kevin R. " 'Your Old Father Abe Lincoln Is Dead and Damned': Black Soldiers and the Memphis Race Riot of 1866." *Journal of Social History* 27 (Fall 1993): 109–28.

Harris, Leslie M. "From Abolitionist Amalgamators to 'Rulers of the Five Points': The Discourse of Interracial Sex and Reform in Antebellum New York City." In *Sex, Love, Race: Crossing Boundaries in North American History,* edited by Martha Hodes, 191–212. New York: New York University Press, 1999.

Hartman, Saidiya V. *Scenes of Subjection: Terror, Slavery, and Self-Making in Nineteenth-Century America.* New York: Oxford University Press, 1997.

Hartog, Hendrik. "Lawyering, Husbands' Rights, and 'the Unwritten Law' in Nineteenth-Century America." *Journal of American History* 84 (June 1997): 67–96.

Hawkesworth, Mary E. "Knowers, Knowing, Known: Feminist Theory and Claims of Truth." *Signs* 14 (Spring 1989): 533–57.

Hewitt, Nancy A. "Compounding Differences." *Feminist Studies* 18 (Summer 1992): 313–26.

Higginbotham, Evelyn Brooks. "African-American Women's History and the Metalanguage of Race." *Signs* 17 (Winter 1992): 251–74.

———. *Righteous Discontent: The Women's Movement in the Black Baptist Church, 1880–1920.* Cambridge, Mass.: Harvard University Press, 1993.

Higgins, Lynn A., and Brenda R. Silver. "Introduction: Rereading Rape." In *Rape and Representation,* edited by Lynn A. Higgins and Brenda R. Silver, 1–14. New York: Columbia University Press, 1991.

Hine, Darlene Clark. "Rape and the Inner Lives of Black Women in the Middle West: Preliminary Thoughts on the Culture of Dissemblance." *Signs* 14 (Summer 1989): 912–20.

Hodes, Martha. "The Sexualization of Reconstruction Politics: White Women and Black Men in the South after the Civil War." In *American Sexual Politics: Sex, Gender, and Race since the Civil War,* edited by John C. Fout and Maura Shaw Tantillo, 59–74. Chicago: University of Chicago Press, 1993.

———. "Wartime Dialogues on Illicit Sex: White Women and Black Men." In *Divided Houses: Gender and the Civil War*, edited by Catherine Clinton and Nina Silber, 230–42. New York: Oxford University Press, 1992.

———. *White Women, Black Men: Illicit Sex in the Nineteenth-Century South*. New Haven: Yale University Press, 1997.

Holley, Donald, with Gwendolyn W. Starlard and Michael B. Dougan. "The Rural Delta. Part 1, Cotton Country." In *The Arkansas Delta: A Landscape of Change*, edited by Tom Baskett Jr., 51–60. Helena, Ark.: Delta Cultural Center, 1990.

Holmes, Jack D. L. "The Effects of the Memphis Race Riot of 1866." *West Tennessee Historical Society Papers* 12 (1958): 58–79.

———. "Underlying Causes of the Memphis Race Riot of 1866." *Tennessee Historical Quarterly* 17 (September 1958): 195–221.

Holt, Thomas. *Black over White: Negro Political Leadership in South Carolina during Reconstruction*. Urbana: University of Illinois Press, 1979.

———. " 'An Empire over the Mind': Emancipation, Race, and Ideology in the British West Indies and the American South." In *Region, Race, and Reconstruction: Essays in Honor of C. Vann Woodward*, edited by J. Morgan Kousser and James M. McPherson, 282–314. New York: Oxford University Press, 1982.

———. " 'The Essence of the Contract': The Articulation of Race, Gender, and Political Economy in British Emancipation Policy, 1838–1866." In *Beyond Slavery: Explorations of Race, Labor, and Citizenship in Postemancipation Societies*, by Frederick Cooper, Thomas C. Holt, and Rebecca J. Scott, 33–59. Chapel Hill: University of North Carolina Press, 2000.

———. "Experience and the Politics of Intellectual Inquiry." In *Questions of Evidence: Proof, Practice, and Persuasion across the Disciplines*, edited by James Chandler, Arnold I. Davidson, and Harry Harootunian, 388–96. Chicago: University of Chicago Press, 1994.

———. "Marking: Race, Race-Making, and the Writing of History." *American Historical Review* 100 (February 1995): 1–17.

———. *The Problem of Freedom: Race, Labor, and Politics in Jamaica and Britain, 1832–1938*. Baltimore: Johns Hopkins University Press, 1992.

———. *The Problem of Race in the Twenty-First Century*. Cambridge, Mass.: Harvard University Press, 2000.

Hooper, Ernest Walter. "Memphis, Tennessee: Federal Occupation and Reconstruction, 1862–1870." Ph.D. diss., University of North Carolina, Chapel Hill, 1957.

Horton, James Oliver. "Freedom's Yoke: Gender Conventions among Antebellum Free Blacks." *Feminist Studies* 12 (Spring 1986): 51–76.

Horton, James Oliver, and Lois Horton. *In Hope of Liberty: Culture, Community, and Protest among Northern Free Blacks, 1700–1860*. New York: Oxford University Press, 1997.

———. "Violence, Protest, and Identity: Black Manhood in Antebellum America." In *Free People of Color: Inside the African American Community*, 80–96. Washington, D.C.: Smithsonian Institution Press, 1993.

Hughes, John Starrett. "The Madness of Separate Spheres: Insanity and Masculinity in

Victorian Alabama." In *Meanings for Manhood: Constructions of Masculinity in Victorian America*, edited by Mark C. Carnes and Clyde Griffen, 67–78. Chicago: University of Chicago Press, 1990.

Hume, Richard L. "The Arkansas Constitutional Convention of 1868: A Case Study in the Politics of Reconstruction." *Journal of Southern History* 39 (May 1973): 183–206.

——. "The 'Black and Tan' Constitutional Conventions of 1867–1869 in Ten Former Confederate States: A Study of Their Membership." Ph.D. diss., University of Washington, 1969.

Hunt, Gaillard. *Israel, Elihu, and Cadwallader Washburn: A Chapter in American Biography.* New York: MacMillan, 1925.

Hunter, Tera. *To 'Joy My Freedom: Southern Black Women's Lives and Labors after the Civil War*. Cambridge, Mass: Harvard University Press, 1997.

Jacobson, Matthew Frye. *Whiteness of a Different Color: European Immigrants and the Alchemy of Race*. Cambridge, Mass.: Harvard University Press, 1998.

Jaynes, Gerald David. *Branches without Roots: Genesis of the Black Working Class in the American South, 1862–1882.* New York: Oxford University Press, 1986.

Jennings, Thelma. " 'Us Colored Women Had To Go Through A Plenty': Sexual Exploitation of African-American Slave Women." *Journal of Women's History* 1 (Winter 1990): 45–74.

Johnson, Walter. *Soul by Soul: Life inside the Antebellum Slave Market*. Cambridge, Mass.: Harvard University Press, 1999.

Jones, Jacqueline. *Labor of Love, Labor of Sorrow: Black Women, Work, and the Family from Slavery to the Present*. New York: Basic Books, 1985.

Jones, James B., Jr. "Municipal Vice: The Management of Prostitution in Tennessee's Urban Experience. Part 1, The Experience of Nashville and Memphis, 1854–1917." *Tennessee Historical Quarterly* 50 (Spring 1991): 33–41.

Jones, Martha S. *All Bound Up Together: The Woman Question in African American Public Culture, 1830–1900*. Chapel Hill: University of North Carolina Press, 2007.

Jordan, Winthrop. *White over Black: American Attitudes Toward the Negro, 1550–1812.* Baltimore: Penguin, 1969.

Kantrowitz, Stephen. *Ben Tillman and the Reconstruction of White Supremacy*. Chapel Hill: University of North Carolina Press, 2000.

——. "One Man's Mob Is Another Man's Militia: Violence, Manhood, and Authority in Reconstruction South Carolina." In *Jumping Jim Crow: Southern Politics from Civil War to Civil Rights*, edited by Jane Dailey, Glenda Elizabeth Gilmore, and Bryant Simon, 67–87. Princeton: Princeton University Press, 2000.

——. "The Two Faces of Domination in North Carolina, 1800–1898." In *Democracy Betrayed: The Wilmington Race Riot of 1898 and Its Legacy*, edited by David S. Cecelski and Timothy B. Tyson, 95–111. Chapel Hill: University of North Carolina Press, 1998.

Kaplan, Sidney. "The Miscegenation Issue in the Election of 1864." In *American Studies in Black and White: Selected Essays*, edited by Allan D. Austin, 47–100. Amherst: University of Massachusetts Press, 1991.

Kennan, Clara B. "The First Negro Teacher in Little Rock." *Arkansas Historical Quarterly* 9 (Autumn 1950): 194–204.

Kerber, Linda K. " 'History Can Do It No Justice': Women and the Reinterpretation of the American Revolution." In *Women in the Age of the American Revolution*, edited by Ronald E. Hoffman and Peter J. Albert, 3–42. Charlottesville: University Press of Virginia, 1989.

———. "May All Our Citizens Be Soldiers and All Our Soldiers Citizens: The Ambiguities of Female Citizenship in the New Nation." In *Women, Militarism, and War: Essays in History, Politics, and Social Theory*, edited by Jean Bethke Elshtain and Sheila Tobias, 89–104. Savage, Md.: Rowman & Littlefield, 1990.

———. "The Meanings of Citizenship." *Journal of American History* 84 (December 1997): 833–54.

———. *No Constitutional Right to Be Ladies: Women and the Obligations of Citizenship*. New York: Hill and Wang, 1998.

———. "The Paradox of Women's Citizenship in the Early Republic: The Case of *Martin vs. Massachusetts*, 1805." *American Historical Review* 97 (April 1992): 349–78.

———. "Separate Spheres, Female Worlds, Woman's Place: The Rhetoric of Women's History." *Journal of American History* 75 (June 1988): 9–39.

———. *Women of the Republic: Intellect and Ideology in Revolutionary America*. New York: Norton, 1986 (1980).

Kettner, James H. *The Development of American Citizenship, 1608–1870*. Chapel Hill: University of North Carolina Press, 1978.

Koenig, Dorean Marguerite. "Women and Rape in Ethnic Conflict and War." *Hastings Women's Law Journal* 5 (Summer 1994): 129–41.

Kolchin, Peter. *First Freedom: The Responses of Alabama's Blacks to Emancipation and Reconstruction*. Westport, Conn.: Greenwood Press, 1972.

Kousser, J. Morgan. *The Shaping of Southern Politics: Suffrage Restriction and the Establishment of the One-Party South, 1880–1910*. New Haven: Yale University Press, 1974.

Lack, Paul D. "An Urban Slave Community: Little Rock, 1831–1862." *Arkansas Historical Quarterly* 41 (Autumn 1982): 258–87.

Landes, Joan B. *Women and the Public Sphere in the Age of the French Revolution*. Ithaca: Cornell University Press, 1988.

Laqueur, Thomas. *Making Sex: Body and Gender from the Greeks to Freud*. Cambridge, Mass.: Harvard University Press, 1990.

Lebsock, Suzanne D. "Radical Reconstruction and the Property Rights of Southern Women." *Journal of Southern History* 43 (May 1977): 195–216.

Ledbetter, Cal, Jr. "The Constitution of 1836: A New Perspective." *Arkansas Historical Quarterly* 41 (Autumn 1982): 215–52.

———. "The Constitution of 1868: Conqueror's Constitution or Constitutional Continuity?" *Arkansas Historical Quarterly* 44 (Spring 1985): 16–41.

Lemire, Elise. *"Miscegenation": Making Race in America*. Philadelphia: University of Pennsylvania Press, 2002.

Lerner, Gerda. *Black Women in White America: A Documentary History*. New York: Pantheon, 1972.

Lester, J. C., and D. L. Wilson. *Ku Klux Klan, Its Origin, Growth, and Disbandment*. 2nd ed. Edited by Walter Lynwood Fleming. New York, 1905 (1884).

Lister, Ruth. "Citizenship: Toward a Feminist Synthesis." *Feminist Review* 57 (Autumn 1997): 28–48.

Litwack, Leon. *Been in the Storm So Long: The Aftermath of Slavery*. New York: Knopf, 1979.

——. *North of Slavery: The Negro in the Free States, 1790–1860*. Chicago: University of Chicago Press, 1961.

Long, Alecia P. *The Great Southern Babylon: Sex, Race, and Respectability in New Orleans*. Baton Rouge: Louisiana State University Press, 2004.

Lovell, Linda Jeanne. "African-American Narratives from Arkansas: A Study from the 1936–1938 Federal Writers' Project *A Folk History of Slavery in the United States*." Ph.D. diss., University of Arkansas, May 1991.

Lovett, Bobby L. "Memphis Riots: White Reaction to Blacks in Memphis, May 1865–July 1866." *Tennessee Historical Quarterly* 37 (Spring 1979): 9–33.

Lucie, Patricia. "On Being a Free Person and a Citizen by Constitutional Amendment." *Journal of American Studies* 12 (1978): 343–58.

Luker, Lady Elizabeth. "Post Civil War Period in Jackson County." *Stream of History* 4 (1966): 36–37.

MacLean, Nancy. *Behind the Mask of Chivalry: The Making of the Second Ku Klux Klan*. New York: Oxford University Press, 1994.

Marcus, Sharon. "Fighting Bodies, Fighting Words: A Theory and Politics of Rape Prevention." In *Feminists Theorize the Political*, edited by Judith Butler and Joan W. Scott, 385–403. New York: Routledge, 1992.

Masur, Katherine. "Reconstructing the Nation's Capitol: The Politics of Race and Citizenship in the District of Columbia." Ph.D. diss., University of Michigan, 2001.

McClintock, Anne. *Imperial Leather: Race, Gender, and Sexuality in the Colonial Contest*. New York: Routledge, 1995.

McCurry, Stephanie. "Black Republicans and the Rape of the South: Gender, Sexuality, and Civil War Politics." Unpublished paper presented to the Social History Workshop at the University of Chicago, 1996. Cited with permission of the author.

——. *Masters of Small Worlds: Yeoman Households, Gender Relations, and the Political Culture of the Antebellum South Carolina Low Country*. New York: Oxford University Press, 1995.

——. "The Politics of Yeoman Households in South Carolina." In *Divided Houses: Gender and the Civil War*, edited by Catherine Clinton and Nina Silber, 22–38. New York: Oxford University Press, 1992.

——. "The Two Faces of Republicanism: Gender and Proslavery Politics in Antebellum South Carolina." *Journal of American History* 78 (March 1992): 1245–64.

McFeely, William S. *Yankee Stepfather: General O. O. Howard and the Freedmen*. New York: Norton, 1994 (1968).

McGuire, Danielle L. " 'It Was Like All of Us Had Been Raped': Sexual Violence, Community Mobilization, and the African American Freedom Struggle." *Journal of American History* 91 (December 2004): 906–31.

McLaurin, Melton A. *Celia, a Slave: A True Story of Violence and Retribution in Antebellum Missouri*. Athens: University of Georgia Press, 1991.

Mehta, Uday S. "Liberal Strategies of Exclusion." In *Tensions of Empire: Colonial Cultures in a Bourgeois World*, edited by Frederick Cooper and Ann Laura Stoler, 59–86. Berkeley: University of California Press, 1997.

Melish, Joanne Pope. *Disowning Slavery: Gradual Emancipation and "Race" in New England*. Ithaca: Cornell University Press, 1998.

Mitchell, Michele. *Righteous Propagation: African Americans and the Politics of Racial Destiny after Reconstruction*. Chapel Hill: University of North Carolina Press, 2004.

Moneyhon, Carl H. "Disloyalty and Class Consciousness in Southwestern Arkansas, 1862–1865." *Arkansas Historical Quarterly* 52 (Autumn 1993): 223–43.

——. *The Impact of the Civil War and Reconstruction on Arkansas: Persistence in the Midst of Ruin*. Baton Rouge: Louisiana State University Press, 1994.

Moore, Sean T. " 'Justifiable Provocation': Violence against Women in Essex County, New York, 1799–1860." *Journal of Social History* 35 (Summer 2002): 896–918.

Morgan, Edmund S. *American Slavery, American Freedom: The Ordeal of Colonial Virginia*. New York: Norton, 1975.

Morgan, Jennifer L. *Laboring Women: Reproduction and Gender in New World Slavery*. Philadelphia: University of Pennsylvania Press, 2004.

Nash, Gary B. "The Hidden History of Mestizo America." In *Sex, Love, Race: Crossing Boundaries in North American History*, edited by Martha Hodes, 10–32. New York: New York University Press, 1999.

Nelson, Scott. *Iron Confederacies: Southern Railways, Klan Violence, and Reconstruction*. Chapel Hill: University of North Carolina Press, 1999.

——. "Livestock, Boundaries, and Public Space in Spartanburg: African American Men, Elite White Women, and the Spectacle of Conjugal Relations." In *Sex, Love, Race: Crossing Boundaries in North American History*, edited by Martha Hodes, 313–27. New York: New York University Press, 1999.

Nelson, William E. *The Fourteenth Amendment: From Political Principle to Judicial Doctrine*. Cambridge, Mass.: Harvard University Press, 1988.

Neuffer, Elizabeth. *The Key to My Neighbor's House: Seeking Justice in Bosnia and Rwanda*. New York: Picador, 2001.

Ngai, Mae M. *Impossible Subjects: Illegal Aliens and the Making of Modern America*. Princeton: Princeton University Press, 2004.

Nieman, Donald. *To Set the Law in Motion: The Freedmen's Bureau and the Legal Rights of Blacks, 1865–1868*. Millwood, N.Y.: KTO Press, 1979.

Norton, Mary Beth. *Founding Mothers and Fathers: Gendered Power and the Forming of American Society*. New York: Knopf, 1996.

Nudelman, Franny. *John Brown's Body: Slavery, Violence, and the Culture of War*. Chapel Hill: University of North Carolina Press, 2004.

O'Donovan, Susan Eva. *Becoming Free in the Cotton South*. Cambridge, Mass.: Harvard University Press, 2007.

Osthaus, Carl B. *Partisans of the Southern Press: Editorial Spokesmen of the Nineteenth Century*. Louisville: University of Kentucky Press, 1994.

Ownby, Ted. *Subduing Satan: Religion, Recreation, and Manhood in the Rural South, 1865– 1920*. Chapel Hill: University of North Carolina Press, 1990.

Painter, Nell Irvin. "A Prize Winning Book Revisited." *Journal of Women's History* 2 (Winter 1991): 126–34.

———. " 'Social Equality,' Miscegenation, Labor, and Power." In *The Evolution of Southern Culture*, edited by Numan V. Bartley, 47–67. Athens: University of Georgia Press, 1988.

———. "Three Southern Women and Freud: A Non-Exceptionalist Approach to Race, Class, and Gender in the Slave South." In *Feminists Revision History*, edited by Ann-Louise Shapiro, 195–216. New Brunswick: Rutgers University Press, 1994.

Palmer, Paul C. "Miscegenation as an Issue in the Arkansas Constitutional Convention of 1868." *Arkansas Historical Quarterly* 24 (Summer 1965): 99–119.

Parks, Joseph H. "Memphis under Military Rule, 1862 to 1865." *East Tennessee Historical Society Publications* 14 (1942): 31–58.

Parsons, Elaine Frantz. "Midnight Rangers: Costume and Performance in the Reconstruction-Era Ku Klux Klan." *Journal of Southern History* 92 (December 2005): 811–36.

Pascoe, Peggy. "Miscegenation Law, Court Cases, and Ideologies of 'Race' in Twentieth-Century America." *Journal of American History* 83 (June 1996): 44–69.

———. "Race, Gender, and the Privileges of Property: On the Significance of Miscegenation Law in United States History." Paper presented at the American Bar Foundation and Northwestern University Law School, February 24, 1995.

Pateman, Carole. *The Sexual Contract*. Stanford: Stanford University Press, 1988.

Patton, James Welch. *Unionism and Reconstruction in Tennessee, 1860–1869*. Chapel Hill: University of North Carolina Press, 1934.

Payne, Elizabeth Anne. " 'What Ain't I Been Doing?': Historical Reflections on Women and the Arkansas Delta." In *The Arkansas Delta: Land of Paradox*, edited by Jeannie M. Whayne and Willard B. Gatewood, 128–47. Fayetteville: University of Arkansas Press, 1993.

Penningroth, Dylan C. *The Claims of Kinfolk: African American Property and Community in the Nineteenth-Century South*. Chapel Hill: University of North Carolina Press, 2003.

Perman, Michael. "Counter Reconstruction: The Role of Violence in Southern Redemption." In *The Facts of Reconstruction: Essays in Honor of John Hope Franklin*, edited by Eric Anderson and Alfred A. Moss Jr., 121–40. Baton Rouge: Louisiana State University Press, 1991.

———. *The Road to Redemption: Southern Politics, 1869–1879*. Chapel Hill: University of North Carolina Press, 1984.

———. *Struggle for Mastery: Disfranchisement in the South, 1888–1908*. Chapel Hill: University of North Carolina Press, 2001.

Powell, Lawrence N. *New Masters: Northern Planters during the Civil War and Reconstruction*. New Haven: Yale University Press, 1980.

Quarles, Benjamin. "Frederick Douglass and the Woman's Rights Movement." *Journal of Negro History* 25 (January 1940): 35–44.

———. *The Negro in the Civil War*. New York: Da Capo Press, 1989 (1953).

Rabinowitz, Howard N. "From Exclusion to Segregation: Southern Race Relations, 1865 to 1890." *Journal of American History* 63 (September 1976): 325–50.

Rable, George C. *But There Was No Peace: The Role of Violence in the Politics of Reconstruction*. Athens: University of Georgia Press, 1984.

Ransom, Robert L., and Richard Sutch. *One Kind of Freedom: The Economic Consequences of Emancipation*. New York: Cambridge University Press, 1977.

Regosin, Elizabeth. *Freedom's Promise: Ex-Slave Families and Citizenship in the Age of Emancipation*. Charlottesville: University of Virginia Press, 2002.

Renda, Mary A. *Taking Haiti: Military Occupation and the Culture of U.S. Imperialism*. Chapel Hill: University of North Carolina Press, 2001.

Richards, Leonard L. *"Gentlemen of Property and Standing": Anti-Abolition Mobs in Jacksonian America*. New York: Oxford University Press, 1970.

Richardson, Heather Cox. *The Death of Reconstruction: Race, Labor, and Politics in the Post–Civil War North, 1865–1901*. Cambridge, Mass.: Harvard University Press, 2001.

Riddleberger, Patrick W. *1866: The Critical Year Revisited*. Carbondale: Southern Illinois University Press, 1979.

Riley, Denise. *"Am I That Name?" Feminism and the Category of "Women" in History*. Minneapolis: University of Minnesota Press, 1988.

Roach, Joseph. *Cities of the Dead: Circum-Atlantic Performance*. New York: Columbia University Press, 1996.

Roark, James L. *Masters without Slaves: Southern Planters in the Civil War and Reconstruction*. New York: Norton, 1977.

Robinson, Armstead. "In the Aftermath of Slavery: Blacks and Reconstruction in Memphis, 1865–1870." Thesis presented to the Scholars of the House Faculty of Yale College, May 1969.

Rodgers, Daniel T. "Republicanism: The Career of a Concept." *Journal of American History* 79 (June 1992): 11–38.

Roediger, David. *The Wages of Whiteness: Race and the Making of the American Working Class*. New York: Verso, 1991.

Rogers, J. S. *History of Arkansas Baptists*. Little Rock: Arkansas Baptist State Convention, 1948.

Rose, Willie Lee. *Rehearsal for Reconstruction: The Port Royal Experiment*. New York: Oxford University Press, 1964.

Rosenberg, Charles. "Sexuality, Class, and Role in 19th-Century America." In *The American Man*, edited by Elizabeth H. Pleck and Joseph H. Pleck, 221–54. Englewood Cliffs, N.J.: Prentice-Hall, 1980.

Ross, Margaret Smith. *Arkansas Gazette: The Early Years, 1819–1866*. Little Rock: Arkansas Gazette Foundation, 1969.

———. "Nathan Warren, a Free Negro for the Old South." *Arkansas Historical Quarterly* 15 (Spring 1956): 53–61.

Rothman, Joshua D. *Notorious in the Neighborhood: Sex and Families across the Color Line in Virginia, 1787–1861*. Chapel Hill: University of North Carolina Press, 2003.

Rotundo, E. Anthony. *American Manhood: Transformations in Masculinity from the Revolution to the Modern Era*. New York: Basic Books, 1993.

Ryan, James Gilbert. "The Memphis Riot of 1866: Terror in a Black Community during Reconstruction." *Journal of Negro History* 62 (July 1977): 243–57.

Ryan, Mary P. *Civic Wars: Democracy and Public Life in the American City during the Nineteenth Century*. Berkeley: University of California Press, 1997.

———. *Women in Public: Between Banners and Ballots, 1825–1880*. Baltimore: Johns Hopkins University Press, 1990.

St. Hilaire, Joseph M. "The Negro Delegates in the Arkansas Constitutional Convention of 1868: A Group Profile." *Arkansas Historical Quarterly* 33 (Spring 1974): 38–69.

Saks, Eva. "Representing Miscegenation Law." *Raritan* 8 (Fall 1988): 39–69.

Sánchez-Eppler, Karen. *Touching Liberty: Abolition, Feminism, and the Politics of the Body*. Berkeley: University of California Press, 1993.

Saville, Julie. *The Work of Reconstruction: From Slave to Wage Labor in South Carolina, 1860–1870*. New York: Cambridge University Press, 1994.

Schwalm, Leslie A. *A Hard Fight for We: Women's Transition from Slavery to Freedom in South Carolina*. Urbana: University of Illinois Press, 1997.

Scott, Joan Wallach. "The Evidence of Experience." In *Questions of Evidence: Proof, Practice, and Persuasion across the Disciplines*, edited by James Chandler, Arnold I. Davidson, and Harry Harootunian, 363–78. Chicago: University of Chicago Press, 1994.

———. "Experience." In *Feminists Theorize the Political*, edited by Judith Butler and Joan W. Scott, 22–40. New York: Routledge, 1992.

———. *Gender and the Politics of History*. New York: Columbia University Press, 1988.

———. "On Language, Gender, and Working-Class History." *International Labor and Working-Class History* 31 (Spring 1987): 1–13.

———. *Only Paradoxes to Offer: French Feminists and the Rights of Man*. Cambridge, Mass.: Harvard University Press, 1999.

———. "Response to Gordon." *Signs* 15 (Summer 1990): 859–60.

———. Review of *Heroes of Their Own Lives: The Politics and History of Family Violence* by Linda Gordon. *Signs* 15 (Summer 1990): 848–51.

———. " 'The Tip of the Volcano.' " *Comparative Studies in Society and History* 35 (April 1993): 438–43.

Scott, Rebecca J. "The Atlantic World and the Road to *Plessy v. Ferguson.*" *Journal of American History* 94 (December 2007): 726–33.

———. *Degrees of Freedom: Louisiana and Cuba after Slavery.* Cambridge: Harvard University Press, 2005.

———. "Public Rights, Social Equality, and the Conceptual Roots of the *Plessy* Challenge." *Michigan Law Review* 106 (March 2008): 777–804.

———. *Slave Emancipation in Cuba: The Transition to Free Labor, 1860–1899.* Princeton: Princeton University Press, 1985.

Scully, Pamela, and Diana Paton, eds. *Gender and Slave Emancipation in the Atlantic World.* Durham: Duke University Press, 2005.

Sigafoos, Robert A. *Cotton Row to Beale Street: A Business History of Memphis.* Memphis: Memphis State University Press, 1979.

Simpson, Craig M. *A Good Southerner: The Life of Henry A. Wise of Virginia.* Chapel Hill: University of North Carolina Press, 1995.

Smith, Rogers. *Civic Ideals: Conflicting Visions of Citizenship in U.S. History.* New Haven: Yale University Press, 1997.

Smith, Valerie. "Split Affinities: The Case of Interracial Rape." In *Conflicts in Feminism,* edited by Marianne Hirsch and Evelyn Fox Keller, 271–87. New York: Routledge, 1990.

Sommerville, Diane Miller. *Rape and Race in the Nineteenth-Century South.* Chapel Hill: University of North Carolina Press, 2004.

———. "The Rape Myth in the Old South Reconsidered." *Journal of Southern History* 61 (August 1995): 481–518.

———. "The Rape Myth Reconsidered: The Intersection of Race, Class, and Gender in the American South, 1800–1877." Ph.D. diss., Rutgers University, 1995.

Spain, Daphne. *Gendered Spaces.* Chapel Hill: University of North Carolina Press, 1992.

Stanley, Amy Dru. *From Bondage to Contract: Wage Labor, Marriage, and the Market in the Age of Slave Emancipation.* New York: Cambridge University Press, 1998.

Stansell, Christine. *City of Women: Sex and Class in New York, 1789–1860.* Urbana: University of Illinois Press, 1982.

———. "A Response to Joan Scott." *International Labor and Working-Class History* 31 (Spring 1987): 24–29.

Staples, Thomas S. *Reconstruction in Arkansas, 1862–1874.* Gloucester, Mass.: Peter Smith, 1964.

Steedman, Marek. "Gender and the Politics of the Household in Reconstruction Louisiana, 1865–1878." In *Gender and Slave Emancipation in the Atlantic World,* edited by Pamela Scully and Diana Paton, 310–27. Durham: Duke University Press, 2005.

Sterling, Dorothy, ed. *The Trouble They Seen: The Story of Reconstruction in the Words of African Americans.* New York: Da Capo Press, 1994.

Stevenson, Brenda E. *Life in Black and White: Family and Community in the Slave South.* New York: Oxford University Press, 1996.

Stiglmayer, Alexandra, ed. *Mass Rape: The War against Women in Bosnia-Herzegovina.* Lincoln: University of Nebraska Press, 1994.

Stoler, Ann Laura. "Carnal Knowledge and Imperial Power: Gender, Race, and Morality in Colonial Asia." In *Gender at the Crossroads of Knowledge: Feminist Anthropology in the Postmodern Era*, edited by Micaela di Leonardo, 51–101. Berkeley: University of California Press, 1991.

———. "Tense and Tender Ties: The Politics of Comparison in North American History and (Post) Colonial Studies." *Journal of American History* 88 (December 2001): 829–65.

Stolke, Verona. "Conquered Women." *NACLA Report on the Americas* 24 (February 1991): 23–28.

Taylor, Orville. *Negro Slavery in Arkansas*. Durham: Duke University Press, 1958.

Temkin, Jennifer. "Women, Rape, and Law Reform." In *Rape: An Historical and Social Enquiry*, edited by Syklvana Tomaselli and Roy Porter, 16–40. New York: Basil Blackwell, 1986.

Terborg-Penn, Rosalyn. *African American Women in the Struggle for the Vote, 1850–1920*. Bloomington: Indiana University Press, 1998.

Thompson, E. P. "The Moral Economy of the English Crowd in the Eighteenth Century." *Past and Present* 50 (1971): 76–136.

Thompson, George H. *Arkansas and Reconstruction: The Influence of Geography, Economics, and Personality*. Port Washington, N.Y.: National University Publications, 1976.

Thornton, J. Mills, III. *Politics and Power in a Slave Society: Alabama, 1800–1860*. Baton Rouge: Louisiana State University Press, 1978.

Tindall, George B. *South Carolina Negroes, 1877–1900*. Columbia: University of South Carolina Press, 1952.

Tracy, Sterling. "The Immigrant Population of Memphis." *West Tennessee Historical Society Papers* 4 (1950): 72–82.

Trelease, Allen W. *White Terror: The Ku Klux Klan Conspiracy and Southern Reconstruction*. Baton Rouge: Louisiana State University Press, 1971.

Tucker, David. *Black Pastors and Leaders: Memphis, 1819–1972*. Memphis: Memphis State University Press, 1975.

Turner, Jesse. "The Constitution of 1836." *Publications of the Arkansas Historical Association* 3 (1911): 116–17.

Vorenberg, Michael. *Final Freedom: The Civil War, the Abolition of Slavery, and the Thirteenth Amendment*. New York: Cambridge University Press, 2001.

Wade, Richard. *Slavery in the Cities: The South, 1820–1860*. New York: Oxford University Press, 1964.

Walker, Barrington. "This Is White Man's Day: The Irish, White Racial Identity, and the 1866 Memphis Riots." *Left History* 5 (Fall 1997): 31–55.

Walkowitz, Judith R. *City of Dreadful Delight: Narratives of Sexual Danger in Late-Victorian London*. Chicago: University of Chicago Press, 1992.

———. *Prostitution and Victorian Society: Women, Class, and the State*. New York: Cambridge University Press, 1980.

Wallenstein, Peter. *Tell the Court I Love My Wife: Race, Marriage, and the Law—An American History*. New York: Palgrave MacMillan, 2002.

Waller, Altina. "Community, Class, and Race in the Memphis Riot of 1866." *Journal of Social History* 18 (Winter 1984): 233–46.

Walters, Ronald G. "The Erotic South: Civilization and Sexuality in American Abolitionism." *American Quarterly* 25 (May 1973): 177–201.

Watson, Harry L. "Conflict and Collaboration: Yeomen, Slaveholders, and Politics in the Antebellum South." *Social History* 10 (October 1985): 273–98.

Webb, Arthur L. "Black Soldiers of Civil War Left Impact on City." *Commercial Appeal*, February (n.d.), 1989.

———. "United States Colored Troops, 1863–1867." Unpublished manuscript.

Whayne, Jeannie M. "Labor Relations and the Evolving Plantation: The Case of Sunnyside." In *Shadows over Sunnyside: An Arkansas Plantation in Transition, 1830–1945*, edited by Jeannie M. Whayne, 25–36. Fayetteville: University of Arkansas Press, 1993.

White, Deborah Gray. *Ar'n't I a Woman? Female Slaves in the Plantation South*. New York: Norton, 1985.

———. *Too Heavy a Load: Black Women in Defense of Themselves, 1894–1994*. New York: Norton, 1999.

Whites, Lee Ann. "The Civil War as a Crisis in Gender." In *Divided Houses: Gender and the Civil War*, edited by Catherine Clinton and Nina Silber, 3–21. New York: Oxford University Press, 1992.

———. *The Civil War as a Crisis in Gender: Augusta, Georgia, 1860–1890*. Athens: University of Georgia Press, 1995.

Wiegman, Robyn. *American Anatomies: Theorizing Race and Gender*. Durham: Duke University Press, 1995.

Williams, C. Fred, S. Charles Bolton, Carl H. Moneyhon, and LeRoy T. Williams, eds. *A Documentary History of Arkansas*. Fayetteville: University of Arkansas Press, 1984.

Williams, Frank B. "John Eaton, Jr., Editor, Politician, and School Administrator, 1865–1870." *Tennessee Historical Quarterly* 10 (1951): 291–319.

Williams, Kidada E. "In the Space of Violence: African Americans and the Dynamics of Racial Supremacy and Survival after Slavery." Ph.D. diss., University of Michigan, 2005.

Williams, Lou Falkner. *The Great South Carolina Ku Klux Klan Trials, 1871–1872*. Athens: University of Georgia Press, 1996.

Williamson, Joel. *After Slavery: The Negro in South Carolina during Reconstruction, 1861–1877*. Hanover, N.H.: University Press of New England, 1990 (1965).

———. *The Crucible of Race: Black-White Relations in the American South since Emancipation*. New York: Oxford University Press, 1984.

———. *New People: Miscegenation and Mulattoes in the United States*. New York: New York University Press, 1984 (1980).

Wilson, Theodore Brantner. *The Black Codes of the South*. University: University of Alabama Press, 1965.

Wood, Forrest G. *Black Scare: The Racist Response to Emancipation and Reconstruction*. Berkeley: University of California Press, 1968.

Woodward, C. Vann. *The Strange Career of Jim Crow*. New York: Oxford University Press, 1966 (1955).

———. *Thinking Back: The Perils of Writing History*. Baton Rouge: Louisiana State University Press, 1986.

Wriggins, Jennifer. "Rape, Racism, and the Law." *Harvard Women's Law Journal* 6 (Spring 1983): 103–41.

Wyatt-Brown, Bertram. *Southern Honor: Ethics and Behavior in the Old South*. New York: Oxford University Press, 1980.

Yuval-Davis, Nira. "Women, Citizenship, and Difference." *Feminist Review* 57 (Autumn 1997): 4–27.

Yuval-Davis, Nira, and Pnina Werbner, eds. *Women, Citizenship, and Difference*. London: Zed Books, 1999.

ACKNOWLEDGMENTS

One of the pleasures of having completed this book is that I now have the chance to express my gratitude to the many generous collaborators who made it possible. The work was born amidst the exciting intellectual community that I found at the University of Chicago. Thomas Holt, an exceptional mentor, galvanized my interest in postemancipation societies and encouraged me to pursue the topic of this book. He offered thoughtful responses to my writing that helped me to develop the book's fundamental questions and guiding themes. And his high standards as a researcher and writer have been a source of inspiration. I am similarly grateful to Leora Auslander for her extraordinary insights and perspectives on social history and feminist theory, which she kindly shared over many years and which helped to shape this book. George Chauncey also intervened in important ways, leading me to new frameworks and analysis. And Linda Kerber gave me expert advice on the writing of this book. It benefitted greatly from her close readings of early drafts and our ongoing conversations about citizenship.

I owe special thanks as well to James Grossman, whom I was lucky to have had as a teacher and who has always asked me those most demanding and thus most important questions. I am in Jim's debt too for his having introduced me to Laura Edwards, with whom long conversations at the Newberry Library about gender, sexual violence, and southern history helped me to formulate this project. I am also extremely fortunate that Julie Saville read the entire manuscript at a later stage and offered critical new ideas, including ones leading to the title of the work. Numerous other Chicago scholars contributed incisive suggestions and perspectives. I thank Lauren Berlant, Kathleen Conzen, Norma Fields, and Amy Dru Stanley for helpful and clarifying commentary, and Malathi de Alwis, Antoinette Burton, Laurie Green, and Pradeep Jeganathan for the insights they have shared over years of conversation about the ideas that are most important to this work. I also thank Deborah Cohen, Patricia Chu, Jill Dupont, Susan Gooding, and Nayan Shah for their comments and comradery as fellow graduate students. And finally, I thank Richard Turits, who carefully read and commented on the book's every word, and whose insights and probing queries helped to shape the project and subsequently pushed it to places far beyond where I ever thought it could go. Richard has accompanied me from the beginning to the end of this project and has been my most enthused, most creative, and most supportive interlocutor.

I had the good fortune to encounter wonderful colleagues at two research centers whom I would like to thank for their helpful suggestions: Arlene Diaz, Christopher Tomlins, and Victoria Woeste at the American Bar Foundation and Cindy Aron, Emilye Crosby, Rebecca Edwards, Ann Lane, John Mason, David Murray, Mary Osirim, Rebecca Popenoe, and Daryl Scott at the Carter G. Woodson Institute. During my time at the Woodson, I was privileged to have had the chance to learn from the late Armstead Robinson, who offered his expert knowledge of Reconstruction-era Memphis. Cynthia Blair was an indispensable research companion in Charlottesville and is a dear friend who continually offered critical suggestions for rewriting. And I wish to thank Patricia Sullivan for long conversations about race and racism in the United States and for her unique capacity to bring interesting people together.

This book also benefitted immeasurably from the engagement of my colleagues at the University of Michigan. Sueann Caulfield, Sandra Gunning, Tiya Miles, and Carroll Smith Rosenberg read the entire manuscript and offered wonderful insights that helped me shape especially the introduction to the work. I would also like to express my appreciation for the helpful feedback of Paul Anderson, John Carson, Matthew Countryman, Phil Deloria, Gregory Dowd, Laurent DuBois, Geoff Eley, Anne Hermann, Martha Jones, Mary Kelley, James McIntosh, Michele Mitchell, Maria Montoya, Gina Morantz-Sanchez, Damon Salesa, Rebecca Scott, Sarita See, Alexandra Stern, J. Mills Thornton, Penny Von Eschon, and Magdalena Zaborowska. I have incurred a special debt to Phil Deloria, Greg Dowd, Abigail Stewart, Valerie Traub, and Elizabeth Wingrove for crucial advice and support on the book and other professional matters. Afia Ofori-Mensa and Nicole Stanton provided expert research assistance, and Jinny Prais was a valued companion in Lane Hall, where I finished writing the book.

My academic travels have taken me far and wide, and along the way both I and the book profited from the contributions of many. Early conversations with Noralee Frankel and James Oliver Horton helped me get started. Beverly Greene Bond, Willard Gatewood, Carl Moneyhon, Leslie Rowland, Gerald Smith, Joseph Walk, Arthur Webb, and Jeannie Whayne shared materials and advice on sources. Jimmie and Golda Franklin, J. W. and Emily McAllister, and Sarah Rosen Wartell offered their hospitality when I was on research trips. I thank fellows and staff at the Newberry Library, including Sara Austin, Bruce Calder, John Horner, Mary Janzen Quinn, Jennifer Koflow, Stepanka Korytova, Sarah Long, Carla Mazzio, Carol Neel, Louis Nelson, Oona Paredes, Sarah Pearsall, Martha Pollack, and Frank Valadez, for lively engagement with my work. Beverley Greene Bond, Elsa Barkley Brown, Lisa Cardyn, Cori Field, Crystal Feimster, Alejandro de la Fuente, Mary Hamer, Evelyn Brooks Higginbotham, Darlene Clark Hine, Martha Hodes, Kate Masur, Steven Miller, Susan O'Donovan, Sherie Randolph, Pamela Scully, and Al Young also generously shared insights on chapters or versions thereof. Jacquelyn Dowd Hall, Tera Hunter, Leslie Rowland, and Christine Stansell read the entire manuscript at an early stage, and two anonymous readers for UNC Press read it at a later one. I thank them for their thorough and careful engagement that led to important changes in the overall framework of the book. Finally, this book has benefitted greatly from the guidance of Kate Torrey at UNC Press, and it would be far less readable without the expert copyediting of Stephanie Wenzel. I thank them both.

The book would not have been possible without the generous financial support of many institutions. The research and writing were funded by the University of Chicago, the Mellon Foundation, the American Historical Association, the Carter G. Woodson Institute for Afro-American and African Studies at the University of Virginia, the American Bar Foundation, and the Monticello College Foundation Fellowship at the Newberry Library. Crucial support was also provided by the Horace H. Rackham School of Graduate Studies, the Office of the Vice President, the Program in American Culture, and the Women's Studies Program at the University of Michigan. My research was facilitated by the knowledgeable staffs at many archives. I would like to thank especially the skilled archivists in the Military Reference Branch of the United States National Archives, Barbara Flanary at the Memphis and Shelby County Archives, Edward Frank at the Mississippi Valley Collection, and

Andrea Cantrell at the University of Arkansas for their efforts on my behalf. For help locating photographs, I thank Amy Peck at the Old State House Museum and Brian Robertson at the Butler Center for Arkansas Studies, both in Little Rock.

Finally, I thank my family. In the home in which I was raised by my parents, Barbara Behrens Rosen and Edward Arthur Rosen, knowledge for its own sake was the unquestioned norm, as was the integrity and compassion with which they move through the world. I would not have become a scholar had they not inspired and supported that goal in every way. I also want to thank my great aunt Trudy Rosen for her example of passion for creative work and for her frequent reminders to focus on those things that matter most. The rest of my family, especially Sarah and Ted Rosen Wartell, Amy Weinblatt, Jennifer Weinblatt McAndrews, Martha Rosen, Emily Frankelis, Judy Weinblatt, Nancy Morse, and Andrew Freund have been extraordinarily supportive of me through the difficult years of finishing this book. I thank them for respecting how important doing so was to me. Donna Hughes has facilitated my writing in ways that working parents with small children especially will understand. I wish to thank her and to say that I hope she finds the final product interesting. And last but never least, I do not have words to capture the depth of gratitude I feel for Richard Turits. His love has sustained me through this project and so much more. Though an inadequate token of my appreciation for all that he is and does, this book is for him.

Alcohol sale and consumption, 31–32, 47–
48, 57, 266 (n. 47), 275 (n. 138), 276
(nn. 139–40), 282 (n. 186), 352 (n. 45)

Alfred v. the State [Mississippi], 254 (n. 41)

Allen, Thomas, 196–97, 228–29

Amalgamation, 136–39, 149, 161–64, 166–
67, 170, 318 (n. 14), 319 (n. 18). *See also*
Miscegenation; Social equality

American Missionary Association, 34

Ames, Jessie Daniel, 293 (n. 87)

Andrews, William Wallace, 99, 109, 302–3
(n. 63), 304 (n. 74), 307 (n. 113)

Arkadelphia Standard, 334 (n. 148)

Arkansas: agriculture in, 94–96, 115, 122–23,
300 (nn. 41, 45); anti-unionist violence
in, 303 (n. 68); black population of, 329
(n. 98); boundaries of political community in antebellum period of, 89–97, 119;
charges of illegal electoral practices in,
129–30, 316–17 (nn. 227–29); churches
in, 99, 109, 302–3 (n. 63), 307 (n. 113);
citizenship for African Americans in, 87–
89, 98–119, 304 (nn. 77, 82); during Civil
War, 119; class differences among whites
in, 89, 97, 114, 119, 127–28, 301 (n. 48);
Colored Citizens Convention (1865) in,
98–109, 119, 133–34, 302 (n. 57), 305
(nn. 90, 94); Democratic Party in, 128–
29, 131, 144, 147; economy of, 91, 92, 94–
96, 114–15, 122–24; free blacks in, during
antebellum period, 96–97, 99, 108, 256
(n. 55); Freedmen's Bureau in, 108, 111–
14, 146, 147–48, 325 (n. 58), 331 (n. 119);
gendered language of conservative politics in, 119–31; impoverished freedpeople
in, 123–24; intimidation against black
voters in, 113–14, 118; Ku Klux Klan in,
99, 174–75, 308 (n. 122); legislative
apportionment in, 92, 299 (n. 26); property ownership in, 94–95; Republican
Party in, 104, 108, 111, 112–13, 115–17, 147;
secession convention in, 120, 144, 146;

slavery in, 92, 93–96, 300–301 (nn. 44–
45); statehood for, 89–93, 297–98
(nn. 17–18); State House in Little Rock,
110, 135; Union State Convention (1867)
in, 87–89, 108–13, 308 (n. 122); urban
areas in, 299 (n. 33); violence against
African Americans in, 115; voting rights
for African American men in, 87–89,
101–8, 112–19, 170–72, 304 (n. 77), 305
(n. 94), 312–13 (n. 182); voting rights for
white men in antebellum period of, 92–
97; White Man's Party in, 127–29, 131,
144, 147, 157, 171, 172, 315 (nn. 214–15);
white migration to, from other southern
states, 91, 298 (n. 20); whites' opposition
to black political activity in, 112–14, 119–
31, 145; white working class in Little
Rock, 96–97; women's labor in, 95, 300
(n. 41). *See also* Arkansas constitutional
convention (1868); Little Rock, Ark.

Arkansas Constitution (1836), 92–94

Arkansas Constitution (1864), 144–45, 156,
168, 170, 324 (n. 53), 327 (n. 82)

Arkansas Constitution (1868): and disfranchisement of former Confederates,
170; franchise article of, 170–72, 323
(n. 41); ratification of, 117–19, 129–
30, 170–71, 173, 311 (n. 162), 332–33
(nn. 134–35); vote against, at Arkansas
constitutional convention (1868), 170,
332 (nn. 131, 133). *See also* Arkansas constitutional convention (1868)

Arkansas constitutional convention (1868):
African American delegates to, 116–17,
143–44, 159–69, 322 (nn. 38–39); on
amalgamation and "race mixing," 149,
329 (n. 98); Bradley at, 133–38, 146–58,
162, 324–25 (n. 53), 328–29 (n. 86); on
citizenship and suffrage, 144–46, 159–
60; on cohabitation and inheritance
rights, 162–63; conservative delegates to,
143, 144–45, 149, 156–58, 162, 165–66,

Arkansas law against, in antebellum period, 147–48; ban on, and Arkansas constitutional convention (1868), 16, 17, 131–38, 146–67; Bradley for ban against, 133–38, 146–58, 161, 162, 328–29 (n. 86); and Freedmen's Bureau, 147–48, 325 (nn. 58–59); Garrison on, 319 (n. 18); Georgia ban on, 326 (n. 62); Grey on, 133–35, 149, 150, 154, 159–62; Hinds on, 149–50, 163, 164, 166–67, 169, 330 (n. 112); in Louisiana, 326 (n. 62); Mississippi ban on, 143, 148, 326 (n. 62); newspapers on, 157–58, 173; North Carolina ban on, 318 (n. 13); opposition to ban on, in Arkansas, 149, 153, 159–64, 328 (n. 84), 330 (n. 119); and social equality, 16, 17, 140–41, 170; South Carolina ban on, 148, 326 (n. 62); spatial metaphors referring to ban on, 153–54, 327 (n. 78); in Texas, 326 (n. 62); violence against interracial couple during Memphis Riot, 74. *See also* Miscegenation; Social equality

Interracial sexual relations. *See* Sexuality

Intersexuality. *See* Sexuality

Irish immigrants. *See* Immigrants

Jackson, Robert, 198

Jacobs, Harriet, 254 (n. 45)

Jamaica, 299 (n. 34)

"Jayhawkers," 180, 184. *See also* Night rider violence

Jaynes, Gerald David, 337 (n. 13)

Jefferson, Thomas, 297 (n. 15)

Jeffries, Moses, 117

Jeter, Aury, 213–14, 218, 223–24, 227

Jeter, Columbus, 213–14, 218, 223–24, 227

Jim Crow segregation. *See* Segregation

Johnson, Andrew, 39, 76, 82, 102

Johnson, Thomas P., 117, 143, 330 (n. 119)

Jones, Jacqueline, 277–78 (n. 152)

Jones, Martha, 168

Jones, Salena, 53

Justice, James, 195

Kantrowitz, Stephen, 258–59 (n. 67), 274 (n. 129)

Kentucky: free blacks in, during antebellum period, 16, 17; rape law in, 165, 330 (n. 114)

Kerber, Linda, 250 (n. 29), 257 (n. 58)

King, Moses, 222

King, Mrs., 222–23, 225

KKK. *See* Ku Klux Klan

Ku Klux Act, 193

Ku Klux Klan: African American women as victims of, 200–201, 215–16, 219; in Alabama, 193, 200, 227, 228; in Arkansas, 99, 174–75, 308 (n. 122); congressional investigation of, 180, 229–30, 234; disguise and anonymity of, 188–89, 226–27, 336 (n. 8), 339 (n. 22); domestic setting of violence by, 179, 189–90, 192, 215–17, 220; and fantasies of black sexual transgression, 199–202; in Florida, 229; founding of, 187, 338–39 (n. 22); genital torture and mutilation by, 198–99, 343 (n. 71); in Georgia, 192, 196–99, 219, 223–24; intimidation of black voters by, 201, 216; laws against, 193; murders by, 174–75, 196–97, 343 (nn. 74, 80); in North Carolina, 187, 194–96, 199–200, 202; organization and coordination of local groups of, 187–88, 336 (n. 9); rape by Klan members and other night riders, 8, 175, 201–20, 344–45 (n. 88); reasons for membership in, 192–202, 225; representation of, as alternative law, 189, 215–17, 339 (n. 34); resistance to, by freedpeople, 188–89, 190, 216–17, 347 (n. 127), 348 (n. 129); rituals of, 187, 188, 339 (n. 22); scholarship on, 335 (n. 3); and social equality, 200–201, 343 (n. 80); in South Carolina, 199, 200–201, 347 (n. 127); state and federal prosecu-

McDiarmid, George W., 108

McGee, William, 23, 260 (n. 1)

McGowan, Robert, 287 (n. 24)

McQuarters, Alex, 269 (n. 95), 287 (n. 16)

Meek, James, 95

Meek, John, 95

Mehta, Uday, 250 (n. 28)

Memphis: African American organizations and societies in, 33–34, 52, 280 (n. 170); African American women in public spaces of, 49–60; arrests of African Americans in, 25, 40–44, 57–58, 276–77 (n. 148), 282–83 (n. 190); assault and murder of freedpeople in, 35, 49, 52–55, 58, 277 (n. 151); band music in, 272 (n. 122); black population of, 28, 30, 262 (nn. 17–18), 263 (n. 24), 264 (n. 28), 277 (n. 152); businesses in, 31–32, 36, 38, 44, 47, 73–75, 266 (n. 47), 271 (n. 109), 321–22 (n. 34); challenges for freedpeople in, 35; churches in, 32, 33, 52, 62, 266 (n. 50); Confederate images versus American flag in, 289 (n. 42); crime in, 25, 35, 40–44, 47–49, 53–55, 57–58, 276–77 (n. 148), 282 (n. 189); economy of, 27–28; employment of freedpeople in, 31–32, 69; family relationships of freedpeople in, 31, 51–52, 265 (n. 43); former slaves as refugees in, 23–25, 29–30, 50–52, 60; Freedmen's Savings Bank in, 34; free people of color in, during antebellum period, 28–29; immigrants in, 36–37; map of, 26; municipal government of, 38–39, 268 (n. 80); "negro ball" in, 59, 283 (n. 199); newspapers in, 34–35, 39–44, 46–49, 55–57, 261 (n. 8), 269–70 (n. 96); parades in, 34, 44; professional and entrepreneurial African Americans in, 33–34; prostitution in, 25, 40–41, 43, 50, 55, 57–58, 270 (n. 102), 352 (n. 45); restrictions on free people of color and slaves in, during antebellum period, 28–

29; schools for freedpeople in, 32–33, 62; slave trade in, 27–28, 30, 262 (n. 18); South Memphis neighborhood, 35–40, 44, 47, 53–55, 61–66, 263 (n. 24), 267–68 (nn. 72–76); Union Army occupation of, during and after Civil War, 2, 16, 24, 25, 29–31, 37–39, 44–49; urban spaces, racial meanings, and contests over rule in, 27–40; vagrancy in, 25, 40–44, 57, 271 (n. 106), 352 (n. 45); white resistance to African Americans in, 25. *See also* African American soldiers; Freedmen's Bureau; Freedmen's Court; Memphis Riot; Police; Tennessee

Memphis Commercial, 277 (n. 151)

Memphis Daily Appeal: on African American women, 56, 57, 82, 236–37, 280–81 (nn. 178, 181); on black Union soldiers, 48, 273 (n. 125), 276 (n. 146), 278 (n. 158); conservative position of, 261 (n. 8); on falsehoods printed by newspapers, 49; on Memphis Riot, 65–66

Memphis Daily Argus, 39–42, 261 (n. 8)

Memphis Daily Avalanche: on black Union soldiers, 44, 48; conservative position of, 261 (n. 8); on Memphis Riot, 67, 289 (n. 34), 295 (n. 107)

Memphis Daily Post: on crimes committed by freedpeople, 277 (n. 151); editor of, 34; focus of, 34–35; founding of, 34; on Memphis Riot, 83, 295 (n. 106); offices of, during Memphis Riot, 62; subscribers of, 35

Memphis Riot: African Americans blamed for, 64, 66, 288 (n. 33); beginning of, 61, 63–65; and black Union soldiers, 61–64, 66–67, 286 (n. 12), 288 (n. 29); burning of buildings and other property damage during, 62, 65, 74, 75, 266 (n. 58), 268 (n. 76), 288 (n. 29), 290 (n. 64), 291 (nn. 68, 73); causes of, 61–62, 65–67, 285–86 (n. 10), 288 (n. 33); congressio-

Nelson, J. K., 222

New Jersey, 90

New Orleans: African American women in, 281 (n. 181); brothels in, 346 (n. 111); riot against African Americans in, 14; vagrancy in, 122; voter registration in, 312 (n. 182). *See also* Louisiana

New Orleans Delta, 276 (n. 146)

Newspapers: on African American women, 55–57, 236–38, 281 (n. 181), 295 (n. 107); on black Union soldiers, 46–49, 67; on Civil Rights Act (1866), 39–40; on crime, 40–44, 282 (n. 189); on Freedmen's Bureau, 43–44, 269–70 (n. 96), 273 (n. 125); on interracial marriage, 157–58; on interracial sex, 319 (n. 23); in Memphis generally, 34–35, 261 (n. 8), 269–70 (n. 96); on Memphis Riot, 25, 65–67, 76, 82, 295 (nn. 106–7); on rape, 295 (n. 107). *See also specific newspapers*

New York City, 289 (n. 43)

New York Herald, 273–74 (n. 128)

New York Tribune, 342 (n. 65)

New York World, 138

Night rider violence: against African American women, 179, 182, 197–98, 201–20; in Alabama, 193, 197, 200, 208–9, 211, 219, 227, 228; in antebellum period, 183–84; assumptions underlying, 182; by "bushwhackers" or "jayhawkers," 179–80, 184; and disguise and anonymity, 188, 211, 226–27; domestic setting of violence, 179, 183–94, 220; and fantasies of black sexual transgression, 199–202, 210–12; and gender, 181–82; in Georgia, 179, 189, 192, 196–99, 211–14, 219, 223–24, 230; by Harper's gang, 184–87, 203–7, 337 (n. 15), 337–38 (n. 17); in Mississippi, 196–98, 209–11; murder by night riders, 196–97, 205, 207, 338 (n. 21); in North Carolina, 187, 194–96, 199–200, 202, 211; patriarchal logic of, 191–94, 200, 220; as

performative, 180–83, 200, 205–20, 335–36 (nn. 5–6); political motives of, 180–81; rape by night riders, 182, 201–20, 335 (n. 4); reasons for participation in, 192–202, 225; by "regulators," 8, 184; reports and testimony on, by freedpeople generally, 180, 350 (n. 20); representation of, as alternative law, 189, 215–17, 339 (n. 34); and rumors of miscegenation, black criminality, and sexual activity, 183, 194–202; by slave patrols, 183–84, 190; and social equality discourses, 200–201; in South Carolina, 199, 200–201, 216–17, 228, 339 (n. 27); symbolic aspects of, 180–83; targets of, 181, 347 (n. 127); in Tennessee, 184–87, 203–8, 259 (n. 74), 261 (n. 15), 337 (n. 15); testimony of secret society members on, 193–94; white victims of, 197, 200–202, 339 (n. 30). *See also* Ku Klux Klan; Violence

Noland, William, 53

North Carolina: citizenship status of free blacks in, 256 (n. 51); constitutional convention in, 143, 322 (n. 38), 331 (n. 121); interracial marriage ban in, 318 (n. 13); Ku Klux Klan and other night rider violence in, 187, 194–96, 199–200, 202, 211, 226; rape and attempted rape of African American women in, 202, 211, 226, 253 (n. 36); segregated schools advocated in, 143

Olden, Amanda, 58, 59, 71, 284 (n. 283)

Otherness, 182

Ownby, Ted, 276 (n. 139)

Painter, Nell Irvin, 140, 247 (n. 18), 320 (n. 26)

Parades, 34, 44, 118, 119

Park, John, 37, 38

Parker, Sarah, 57

racial identity as sign of dependence, 90–94, 97, 103, 145, 297 (n. 14); and sexual anxiety of white men, 320 (n. 30). *See also* Amalgamation; Interracial marriage; Miscegenation; Slaves; *and* African American *headings*

Rainey, Mr. and Mrs., 228

Rankin, H. N., 33

Rape: African American men accused of rape of white women, 165, 172–73, 195–202, 254 (n. 37), 334 (n. 147), 342 (n. 61); of African American women by white men during Reconstruction generally, 3–4, 7–9; attempted rape charges in Memphis, 52–53; battery against black women in addition to, 73; and class, 294 (n. 98); congressional report on, during Memphis Riot, 81–82; in context of postemancipation struggles over meaning of race and freedom generally, 72, 73, 348 (n. 133); emotional distress of rape victims, 79–80; fear of rape victims, 77–78; forced oral sex, 72, 80, 290 (n. 59), 294 (n. 96); frequency estimates of, 344 (n. 87); Grey on, 164–65; justification of, by Ku Klux Klan, 194–202; justification of, during Memphis Riot, 68–70; by Ku Klux Klan members and other night riders, 8, 175, 182, 201–20, 335 (n. 4), 344–45 (n. 88); legal and customary definitions of, 9–11, 165, 224, 253–54 (n. 37), 330 (n. 114); lynching compared with, 247–48 (n. 19); during Memphis Riot, 4, 8, 27, 61–63, 68–73, 75–82, 285 (n. 7), 286 (n. 12), 294 (nn. 95–96); during Meridian Riot, 209–11, 227–28, 231–32, 346 (n. 102); "negro domination" portrayed as metaphorical rape by *Arkansas Gazette*, 124–26, 172–73, 195; newspapers on, 172–73, 295 (n. 107); in New York City, 289 (n. 43); older traditions of collective violence compared with, 286

(n. 12); as outside norms and limits accepted by some white men, 218–19; patriarchal definitions of and rationales for, 9, 217–18, 220; public silence among black women about, 351 (n. 38); questioning of rape victims, 77–79, 231–33, 351 (n. 37); racist language and gestures of assailants during, 7–8; refutation of African American women's testimony on, 235–41; removal of African American women from families before, 219–20; resistance to, by African American men and women, 8–9, 78–79, 226–29; scholarship on, 247–48 (n. 19), 251–54 (nn. 33, 35–37); of enslaved women by slaveowners, 9–11, 166, 251 (n. 35), 253–54 (nn. 37, 45), 294 (n. 94), 331–32 (n. 122); testimony by African American women on, 17–18, 61–62, 76–82, 202–7, 212–13, 216, 219, 221–41, 252–53 (n. 36), 293 (n. 79); underreporting of, 202; and virtue of rape victims, 78–79; white men's view of, as normal sexual exploitation of black women, 70–73, 224; of white women, 165, 254 (n. 37), 290 (n. 57), 330 (n. 114)

Ray, Rachel, 338 (n. 21)

Reade, Edwin, 318 (n. 13)

Readjuster movement, 317–18 (n. 9), 327 (n. 78)

Reconstruction: conservatives during, 89, 248–49 (n. 22); and Democratic Party, 89, 248–49 (n. 22); end of, 5, 234–41, 245 (n. 14); hope and terror during generally, 4–5; politics of citizenship and suffrage during, 11–16, 19, 255 (n. 47)

Reconstruction Acts: *Arkansas Gazette* on, 120–22, 124–27; and black political activity generally, 98; endorsed by African Americans in Arkansas, 108–9; passage of, as northern reaction to Memphis Riot, 14, 16, 25, 27, 75–76, 82, 83; on ratification of new southern constitutions, 333–34 (n. 145); and Tennessee, 259 (n. 71); violent secret societies as reaction to generally, 209; and voting rights, 14–15, 27, 87–89, 133, 145. *See also* Citizenship; Voting rights

Rector, Henry, 143, 166

Reeves, "Fed," 343 (n. 80)

Regulators (vigilante groups). *See* Night rider violence

Reidy, Joseph, 273 (n. 126)

Renda, Mary, 7

Republican Party: in Arkansas, 104, 108, 111, 112–13, 115–17, 147; and Arkansas Colored Citizens Convention (1865), 104; and Arkansas Union State Convention (1867), 108, 111; and "Black Republicans," 138, 314 (n. 197); and Bradley, 147; and congressional elections of 1874, 234; and Ku Klux Klan violence, 347 (n. 127); and miscegenation rhetoric, 137–38; and Reconstruction policy, 13, 14–15, 75–76, 82

Reynolds, W. W., 128, 305 (n. 90), 316 (n. 218)

Rich, Sam, 218

Richards, Granville, 346 (n. 102)

Richmond, A. L., 108, 109, 304 (n. 74), 307 (n. 113)

Riots. *See* Memphis Riot; Meridian Riot

Rives, James, 198

Roach, David, 65, 287–88 (n. 27)

Roach, Joseph, 336 (n. 6)

Roark, James, 315 (n. 213)

Robinson, Armstead, 264 (n. 32), 272 (n. 114), 276–77 (n. 148), 285 (n. 10)

Robinson, Betsy, 51

Robinson, James, 51

Roediger, David, 250–51 (n. 31)

Rousseau, Jean-Jacques, 297 (n. 15)

Rowland, Leslie S., 273 (n. 126)

Runkle, Benjamin, 43, 46, 269–70 (n. 96), 286 (n. 16), 289 (n. 42), 291 (n. 73)

Rural freedpeople: and citizenship, 301 (n. 55); field labor by black women, 186, 213, 338 (n. 18); labor conditions for, 184–87, 278–79 (n. 159); land for, 214–16, 258 (n. 65), 310 (n. 152), 347 (n. 120); night rider violence against, 179, 184–87; political action by, 258 (n. 65); restrictions on, 42–43

Rutherford, George J., 108

Rutter, Mrs., 56

Ryan, James Gilbert, 285–86 (n. 10)

Ryan, Mary P., 35, 267 (n. 69), 281 (n. 182)

Ryan, William, 49

Saint Domingue, 2

Saks, Eva, 317 (n. 8)

Sam (black Union soldier), 53–55

Samuels, Richard, 143

Saunders, S. A., 128

Saville, Julie, 109, 118

Schenck, David, 194

Schools: African American female teacher in, 213; integrated versus segregated schools debated in constitutional conventions in South, 143, 332 (n. 133); in Little Rock, Ark., 302–3 (n. 63); in Memphis, 32–33, 62

Schwalm, Leslie, 294 (n. 94)

Scott, Joan Wallach, 246 (n. 18), 251–52 (n. 35)

Scott, Rebecca, 351 (n. 41)

Scott, Robert K., 347 (n. 127)

Seage, John, 208

Secession, 120, 144, 146, 170, 314 (nn. 197, 201)

Segregation, 15, 19, 172, 174, 234, 258 (n. 67), 331 (n. 120), 351–52 (n. 41)

Separate spheres, 249 (n. 24); 327 (n. 78)

Sexual assault. *See* Rape

Sexuality: of African American men, 155–56, 195–96, 320 (n. 30); of African American women as dangerous, 6, 8, 10, 55–56,

73; fantasies of black sexual transgression and night rider violence, 199–202, 210–12; Grey on interracial sexual relations, 149, 151, 161; interracial sex as illicit and shameful, 138–40, 143, 165–66, 319 (n. 23); intersexuality, 235, 237–40, 284 (n. 1), 353 (n. 61); political conflict described in sexual metaphors, 124–27, 172–73, 195; poor white women and cross-racial sexual relationships, 155; sexual relationships and live-in arrangements between white men and black women, 74–75, 161–63, 165–67, 197–98, 342 (n. 67), 343 (n. 80); sexual relationships between black men and white women, 74, 153, 319 (n. 20); and social equality, 140–41, 320 (n. 28). *See also* Interracial marriage

Shanklin, George S., 76, 79

Shaw, Ed, 142, 321–22 (n. 34)

Sherman, William Tecumseh, 30

Shropshire, John W., 220, 348 (n. 139)

Silver, Brenda, 224

Simril, Harriet, 216–17, 219, 220, 348 (n. 129)

Simril, Sam, 216

Sina, 208

Slamon, Michael, 227, 232

Slatting, D. F., 295 (n. 106)

Slave narratives, 254 (n. 45)

Slave patrols, 183–84, 190

Slaves: in Arkansas, 92, 93–96, 300–301 (nn. 44–45); Bradley on, 324 (n. 51); families of, 191; and marriage, 10; Memphis restrictions on, 29; and Memphis slave trade, 27–28, 30, 262 (n. 18); rape of enslaved child by enslaved man, 10; rape of enslaved women by slaveowners, 9–11, 166, 251 (n. 35), 253–54 (nn. 37, 45), 294 (n. 94), 331–32 (n. 122); runaway slaves, 23, 260 (n. 1); severing of domestic ties of, 190; in Texas, 301 (n. 46); in

urban areas, 263 (n. 24); whippings and other violence against, 183–84, 346 (n. 111). *See also* Freedom for slaves

Smith, Bailey, 212

Smith, Caroline, 230

Smith, Charles, 218, 230

Smith, Lucy: battery against, in addition to rape, 73; biographical information on, 69; description of, as modest and respectable, 81; negative portrayal of, in newspapers, 236; political pictures in home of, 289 (n. 42); rape of, during Memphis Riot, 61, 69, 70, 71; relationship between Frances Thompson and, 236, 353 (n. 51); report of rape of, by Thompson, 293 (n. 79); testimony by, on rape, 77, 80, 285 (n. 7), 353 (n. 51)

Smith, Rogers, 255 (n. 47)

Snyder, O. P., 170

Social equality: African Americans' attitudes toward, 142, 321 (n. 31); *Arkansas Gazette* on, 142, 321 (n. 31); and black male suffrage, 131, 136, 169–70; and class, 320 (n. 26); definition of, 140; and integrated schools, 332 (n. 133); and interracial marriage, 16, 17, 140–41, 170; and Ku Klux Klan violence, 200–201, 343 (n. 80); and miscegenation rhetoric, 138, 140–43, 157–58; opposition to, at Arkansas constitutional convention (1868), 147, 154–55, 169–70, 332 (n. 131); and *Plessy v. Ferguson*, 351–52 (n. 41); as racial integration, 6, 140; and sexuality, 140–41, 320 (n. 28). *See also* Amalgamation; Interracial marriage

Soldiers. *See* African American soldiers

Sommerville, Diane Miller, 253–54 (n. 37)

South Carolina: and "Black Republicans," 314 (n. 197); Colored Citizens Convention (1865) in, 302 (n. 61); constitutional convention in, 143, 322 (n. 38), 330 (n. 112); election-day parades in, 118; free

Tire, Isaac, 214

Tourtelotte, John E., 130, 316 (n. 228)

Townsend, Cynthia, 1–5, 79, 245 (n. 11), 287 (n. 27), 293 (n. 79), 294 (n. 95)

Tracy, Sterling, 36

Trelease, Allen W., 350 (n. 27)

Trice, William, 51

Trumbull, Lyman, 257 (n. 60)

Tucker, David, 266 (n. 50)

Turner, Henry M., 197, 273 (n. 125), 342 (n. 65)

Turner, Jesse, 116, 314 (n. 204)

Tutson, Hannah, 214–16, 218–20, 229, 231, 347 (nn. 120, 122–23), 351 (n. 33)

Tutson, Samuel, 214–16, 229, 231, 347 (nn. 122–23)

Union League, 193, 199, 210, 211

Union occupation of Memphis. *See* African American soldiers; Memphis

Union State Convention (1867) in Arkansas, 87–89, 108–13, 308 (n. 122)

Vagrancy, 25, 40–44, 57, 103, 122, 271 (n. 106), 352 (n. 45)

Vigilante groups. *See* Night rider violence

Violence: anti-unionist violence in Arkansas, 303 (n. 68); in Arkansas against African Americans, 115; assault and murder of freedpeople in Memphis, 35, 49, 52–55, 58, 277 (n. 151); beatings and other physical abuse of African American women by employers, 50, 52, 278 (n. 155); and guns for black soldiers, 44, 48, 53, 63, 273 (n. 124), 274 (n. 128), 276 (n. 146), 278 (n. 158); and lynching, 172, 247 (n. 19), 293 (n. 87); and manhood of southern white men, 274 (n. 129); in New Orleans against African Americans, 14; older traditions of collective violence compared with rape, 286 (n. 12); police violence against African

Americans, 25, 37, 46, 63. *See also* Crime; Ku Klux Klan; Memphis Riot; Meridian Riot; Rape

Virginia: African American political practices in, 106, 311 (n. 169); case of Thomas/Thomasine Hall in, 353 (n. 61); constitutional convention in, 143, 322 (n. 38); free blacks in, 262 (n. 18); Readjuster movement in, 317–18 (n. 9), 327 (n. 78); segregated versus integrated schools debated in, 143; street etiquette of black and white Virginians, 260 (n. 6)

Virtue: and African American men, 121–22, 160; and African American women, 50, 77, 81, 136, 165–66, 208, 223, 233–34, 293 (n. 91); civic virtue in Revolutionary era, 250 (n. 29); and female sexual purity and impurity, 125–26, 328 (n. 85); gendered meanings of generally, 250 (n. 29); and independence, 103; of poor white women, 155; of rape victims, 78–79; and white men, 97, 124, 139, 250 (n. 29); and white women, 155, 250 (n. 29)

Voting rights: for African American men in northern states, 135, 317 (n. 5); and African American women, 14, 90, 169, 257 (n. 62), 316–17 (n. 229); and Arkansas Colored Citizens Convention (1865), 101–8; and Arkansas constitutional convention (1868), 144–46, 169–70; in Arkansas during Reconstruction, 87, 88, 101–8, 112–19, 170–72, 304 (n. 77), 305 (n. 94), 312–13 (nn. 182–83); and citizenship, 14–15; and disfranchisement of former Confederates, 133, 156, 170, 171, 234, 307 (n. 109), 322 (n. 39), 352 (n. 42); and election-related violence, 201, 209, 216, 222, 345 (n. 88), 347 (n. 127); for free black men during antebellum period, 12–13, 90; and independence, 90–93, 103, 145; for married men, 297 (n. 15); in Mississippi, 310 (n. 147); politics of, during